PSYCHOANALYTIC TECHNIQUES

PSYCHOANALYTIC TECHNIQUES

A Handbook for the Practicing Psychoanalyst

Edited by

BENJAMIN B. WOLMAN

BASIC BOOKS, INC., PUBLISHERS

New York London

© 1967 by Basic Books, Inc.
Library of Congress Catalog Card Number: 67–19469
Manufactured in the United States of America
Designed by Florence Schiller Silverman

THE AUTHORS

GERHARD ADLER, Ph.D., Founder Member, Society of Analytical Psychology, London; Vice President, International Association for Analytical Psychology; Fellow, British Psychological Society; Fellow, Royal Society of Medicine.

KURT A. ADLER, Ph.D., M.D., President, International Association of Individual Psychology Association, New York; Associate Dean and Medical Director, Alfred Adler Institute of New York; Medical Director, Jamaica Center for Psychotherapy, Jamaica, New York; Associate Psychiatrist, Lenox Hill Hospital, New York; Attending Psychiatrist, Gracie Square Hospital, New York.

MICHAEL BALINT, Ph.D., M.D., Clinical Assistant, Department of Psychological Medicine, University College Hospital, London.

HAROLD P. BLUM, M.D., Faculty, Division of Psychoanalytic Education, Clinical Assistant, and Professor of Psychiatry, State University of New York, Downstate Medical Center, Brooklyn, New York.

MEDARD BOSS, M.D., Professor of Psychotherapy, School of Medicine, and Head of the Training Institute of Medical Psychotherapy, University of Zurich, Switzerland; Member, International Psychoanalytical Association; President, International Federation for Medical Psychotherapy, Switzerland.

LEOPOLD CALIGOR, Ph.D., Faculty, Supervisor of Psychotherapy, Co-Director of Union Therapy Project, William Alanson White Institute; Associate Clinical Professor and Supervisor, Post Doctoral Program in Psychotherapy, Adelphi University.

JOSEPH T. COLTRERA, M.D., Clinical Assistant Professor, Division of Psychoanalytic Education, State University of New York, Downstate Medical Center, Brooklyn, New York.

GION CONDRAU, M.D., Ph.D., Privatdozent, School of Medicine, University of Zurich, Switzerland; Faculty of Philosophy, University of Fribourg, Switzerland.

MAX DAY, M.D., Instructor in Psychiatry, Harvard Medical School; Lecturer in Psychiatry, Boston University Medical School.

JOHN E. GEDO, M.D., Faculty, Institute of Psychoanalysis, Chicago; Department of Psychiatry, University of Illinois College of Medicine.

MARTIN GROTJAHN, M.D., Clinical Professor of Psychiatry, University of Southern California; Training Analyst, Southern California Psychoanalytic Institute.

MARK KANZER, M.D., Clinical Professor of Psychiatry, State University of New York, Downstate Medical Center, Brooklyn, New York; Visiting Psychiatrist, Kings County Medical Center, Brooklyn, New York.

HAROLD KELMAN, M.D., D.Md.Sc., Dean, American Institute for Psychoanalysis.

SAMUEL D. LIPTON, M.D., Training and Supervising Analyst, Chicago Institute.

GEORGE H. POLLOCK, M.D., Ph.D., Professor, University of Illinois College of Medicine; Director of Research and Assistant Dean, Institute for Psychoanalysis, Chicago.

NATHANIEL ROSS, A.B., M.D., Clinical Professor of Psychiatry, State University of New York, Downstate Medical Center, Brooklyn, New York; Co-Editor, *Annual Survey of Psychoanalysis;* Associate Editor, *Journal of the American Psychoanalytic Association.*

DAVID RUBINSTEIN, M.D., Clinical Assistant Professor of Psychiatry, Temple University Medical School; Medical Research Scientist, Eastern Pennsylvania Psychiatric Institute, Philadelphia.

HANNA SEGAL, M.B., Ch.B., Member of the British Psychoanalytic Society engaged in training.

SHELDON T. SELESNICK, M.D., Chief Psychosomatic Research, Coordinator, Psychiatric Research, Cedars-Sinai Medical Center, Los Angeles; Faculty, Southern California Psychoanalytic Institute; Assistant Clinical Professor of Psychiatry, University of Southern California; Secretary, Southern California Psychiatric Society, Los Angeles.

ELVIN B. SEMRAD, M.D., Director of Psychiatry, Massachusetts Mental Health Center, Boston; Clinical Professor of Psychiatry, Harvard Medical School, Boston.

HYMAN SPOTNITZ, M.D., D.Md.Sc., Fellow American Psychiatric Association, American Orthopsychiatric Association, American Group Psychotherapy Association, and New York Academy of Medicine.

AARON STEIN, M.D., Associate Professor of Psychiatry, Associate Attending Psychiatrist, Mt. Sinai Hospital, New York; Attending Psychiatrist, Hillside Hospital, Glen Cove, New York.

SIDNEY TARACHOW (deceased), M.D., D.Md.Sc., was Director, Division of Psychoanalytic Education, and Clinical Professor of Psychiatry, State University of New York, Downstate Medical Center, Brooklyn, New York.

JOSEPH W. VOLLMERHAUSEN, M.D., Assistant Dean, Training and Supervising Analyst, American Institute for Psychoanalysis, New York.

EARL G. WITENBERG, M.D., Director, Fellow, Training and Supervising Analyst, William Alanson White Institute, New York.

LEWIS R. WOLBERG, M.D., Dean and Medical Director, Postgraduate Center for Mental Health, New York.

BENJAMIN B. WOLMAN, Ph.D., Dean of Faculty and Director of Research, Institute of Applied Psychoanalysis; Professor of Psychology, Graduate Program, Long Island University; Clinical Professor in Psychotherapy, Adelphi University, New York.

PREFACE

Psychoanalytic treatment includes a variety of approaches and techniques. Although the mainstream of psychoanalytic thought remained faithful to Freud's conceptual framework, substantial and significant segments broke away and developed into independent schools with their own theoretical systems and treatment methods. At the present time the name "psychoanalysis" is applied to several quite different ideas and methods.

Despite the exasperating diversity in theory and practice, there are common elements that tie all of these distinct systems and techniques into one huge humanistic and therapeutic current. Freud started this journey into the hidden land of the human unconscious, penetrated into the realm of dreams and irrationality and paved the road to recovery for troubled human minds. A great many brilliant men followed in his footsteps and joined in the efforts toward understanding and healing.

Not all who learned from Freud have remained faithful to his teachings. Some have modified Freud's methods; some have outrightly refuted them. Some believe that they are following in the Master's footsteps; others, standing on his shoulders, believe that they are able to see further than he ever saw.

Certainly, there is no agreement between the various schools of psychoanalytic thought, and the issues of technique seem to be more controversial than anything else in psychoanalysis. However, it is precisely this diversity in unity, or this underlying unity despite the diversity, that bears witness to the vitality of psychoanalysis. Psychoanalysis is not a closed Confucian system. It is a live human thought and a never ending effort to understand in order to help, for help is what is so badly needed.

Upon my decision to incorporate in the present volume the diversified techniques of psychoanalysis, I was most fortunate to encounter so much understanding and cooperation among the leading representatives of the

vii

various psychoanalytic schools who wrote original chapters for the present collective volume.

This volume is collective in more than one sense. While planning a volume of such a broad scope I sought and received advice from several distinguished colleagues. Dr. Nathaniel Ross has been with me from the inception of this project as both a co-author and advisor. I relied upon his incisive insight and sound judgment to a great extent. The over-all planning and a great many of the assets of this volume should be credited to him. The mistakes are mine.

In addition to Dr. Ross, I consulted with Drs. Anna Freud, T. French, E. Glover, H. Hartmann, M. Kanzer, M. R. Khan, B. D. Lewin, S. Rado, M. H. Stein, and others. Through the untimely death of Dr. Sidney Tarachow, who co-authored a chapter with Dr. A. Stein, psychoanalysis has suffered a great loss. I had the opportunity of spending several hours with him and had the privilege of obtaining his wise guidance in planning the present volume.

Miss Barbara Gottlieb offered valuable assistance with the editorial work.

BENJAMIN B. WOLMAN

New York
May 1967

CONTENTS

Part I

THE
FREUDIAN
TECHNIQUE

1

THE COMMON RATIONALE OF THE DIVERSE PSYCHOANALYTIC TECHNIQUES

Benjamin B. Wolman

"Although our results at present are incomplete, it is only psychoanalysis that will reveal the hidden structure of this large group of mental diseases. And moreover, its first therapeutic results in this sphere justify us in the expectation that it may be reserved for psychoanalysis to lead psychiatry out of the *impasse* of therapeutic nihilism," wrote K. Abraham in 1911 (p. 156).

Therapeutic nihilism—that was the status of treatment of mental disorders prior to Freud. This nihilism was neither planned nor premeditated. It was the sad outcome of centuries of neglect, fear, escape, and cruelty.

3

For although mental disorders are as old as humanity, the treatment of them started with the French Revolution and Philippe Pinel's historic declaration: "These people are mentally sick, far from being guilty people deserving of punishment." These are "sick people whose miserable state deserves all the consideration that is due to suffering humanity" (quoted after Zilboorg and Henry, 1941, p. 323).

A lot has changed since Pinel, who related mental disorder to physical ailment, more specifically to the nervous system. At that time there was no other alternative. Pinel, Esquirol, Broca, Wernicke, and even Charcot insisted on the link between the nervous system and disorder behavior. Mental disorders were called "nervous diseases," and neuroanatomical and neurophysiological studies were believed the only path to follow.

Yet this path did not prove to be very encouraging. Despite the discoveries by Helmholtz, Hughlings Jackson, Ludwig, Brücke, and many other brilliant workers, there was no substantial progress in the treatment of neuroses and psychoses. Despite all the research no one really knew how to treat a mental patient.

That was undoubtedly the true situation in the field of treatment of mental disorders. Treatment consisted of unproven physico-chemical methods, a friendly pat on the back, and common-sense suggestions. A bundle of ill-described symptoms, a cluster of unrelated neurological data, an honest yet mostly futile effort to comprehend the incomprehensible behavior of mental patients—such was the content of the study of mental disorders. No wonder "treatment," if any, was a hopelessly futile task. Thus spoke Freud.

Freud did not accept the impasse in neurology as a death verdict for psychopathology. In the best tradition of empiricism, Freud believed that scientific inquiry had to go on in forming fresh hypotheses where the old ones could not discover or explain empirical data. Whenever observable data failed to form a continuum, science had to develop hypothetical constructs that would enable the scientist to view the universe in a causal chain.

Freud was faithful to empiricism, determinism, monism, and evolutionism all his life. Whenever empirical data contradicted his theory, the theory and not the data were changed. The psychological processes, wrote Freud in *An Outline of Psychoanalysis,*

> are in themselves just as unknowable as those dealt with by other sciences, by chemistry or physics, for example; but it is possible to establish the laws which those processes obey and follow over long and unbroken stretches their mutual relations and interdependences. . . . This cannot be effected

without framing fresh hypotheses and creating fresh concepts....We can claim for them the sense value as approximations as belongs to the corresponding intellectual scaffolding found in the other natural sciences, and we look forward to their being modified, corrected and more precisely determined as more experience is accumulated and sifted. So too it will be entirely in accordance with our expectations if the basic concepts and principles of the new science (instinct, nervous energy, etc.) remain for a considerable time no less indeterminate than those of the older sciences (force, mass attraction, etc.) (p. 36).

Freud's unswerving determinism made him search for causes where other research workers either gave up or allowed free rein to chance factors. Freud's discovery of unconscious motivation, dreams, and primary processes was the most cherished fruit of this staunch determinism. When other scientists dismissed the phenomena as irrational ripples on the waves of mental life, Freud's relentless search for truth brought the magnificent method of interpretation of dreams. Freud's insistence on causal continuity led to his search for hidden meaning beyond the apparent, manifest content of dreams. The same principle was instrumental in the discovery of the unconscious motivation of slips-of-tongue and daily-life errors.

The application of the causal principle to psychopathology led to the discovery of symptom formation. Freud did not admit chance factors; thus the fact that people acted in a strange, bizarre, and self-defeating manner could not remain unexplained. When organic factors failed to provide for a causal continuum, Freud had to form "fresh hypotheses" that explained pathogenesis of mental disorders in psychogenic terms. Methodologically speaking, this was the logical conclusion (cf. Wolman, 1964).

Yet Freud never abandoned the philosophical principles of monism. He believed in "the mysterious leap from mind to body"; his early theory of anxiety was indeed a theory of the transformation of physical into mental. Freud described his ideas as follows:

We know two things concerning what we call our psyche or mental life; firstly, its bodily organ and scene of action, the brain (or nervous system), and secondly, our acts of consciousness, which are immediate data and cannot be more fully explained by any kind of description. Everything that lies between these two terminal points is unknown to us and, so far as we are aware, there is no direct relation between them. If it existed, it would at the most afford an exact localization of the processes of consciousness and could give us no help toward understanding them. We assume, as the other natural sciences have taught us to expect, that in mental life some kind of energy is at work; but we have no data which enables us to come nearer to a knowledge of it by analogy with other forms of energy (1938, p. 44).

I have christened such an approach with the name "hoped-for-reductionism" (Wolman, 1965). Actually, Freud was, all his life, a monist who assumed the unity of the universe.

Karen Horney accused Freud of being biologically oriented. Certainly, Freud was always faithful to the biological point of view as espoused by Charles Darwin. The Judaeo-Christian theology has counterposed man to nature. Man was supposed to be the center of the universe, king of the world, a godlike creature. Western philosophy has perpetuated these ideas. Certainly, Kant's critical idealism, which has dominated German philosophers and a great many scientists, was conceived in the same tradition and brought the separation of man and nature to a pitch by counterposing the perceiving mind to the perceived objects.

Two men brought about a revolution in man's ideas concerning his place in the universe: Copernicus and Darwin. Copernicus dethroned man's earth and made it into a little speck circulating in space. Darwin destroyed the myth of creation, put man on the top of the evolutionary ladder, and made him part and parcel of organic nature. The two Darwinian principles, the principles of fight for survival and survival of the species, served as cornerstones of the house Freud built. Originally, Freud called them ego and libido instincts, respectively; later, he combined them into the over-all drive of life, Eros. Still later, Freud added, in Spencerian style, the concept of death.

The Rationale of Treatment

The above-mentioned four principles, namely, empiricism, determinism, monism, and evolutionary adjustment, are the underlying, fundamental rules of the therapeutic technique developed by Freud, for, according to Freud, mental disorder is governed by the same basic laws that control all other natural phenomena.

Therefore, Freud did not fight against symptoms; instead he sought the underlying causes of mental disorders. The causes are buried in the unconscious, and they must be brought up to the surface and resolved. One cannot fight an invisible enemy; the combination of insight into, and resolution of, the unconscious conflicts became a guiding principle of the psychoanalytic techniques and has been incorporated by disciples and dissidents alike.

At the beginning, Freud tried to force the unconscious into becoming conscious. He used hypnosis and later suggestive pressure to overcome amnesia and resistance. Some of the dissident schools still use these methods. Freud himself soon abandoned pressure; his keenly empirical approach to clinical data made him aware of the spontaneous help offered by the patient's unconscious. Freud discovered that whatever had been repressed tended to reoccur and reappear. Unhealed wounds called for help, and past traumas reappeared in dreams again and again. The principle of *repetition compulsion* was a logical inference from Freud's strict determinism and from the universal law of the preservation of energy, which Freud accepted. Undischarged energy called for a discharge, and there was no need for an external pressure.

Freud drew two conclusions at this point. The first was the rejection of the cathartic method; the second was the introduction of the method of free associations, which eventually became the fundamental rule of psychoanalytic treatment.

The cathartic method was based on an oversimplified interpretation of the law of the preservation of energy. Mental energy, according to Freud's monistic philosophy, is a derivative of physical energy. Moreover, whatever exists, exists in a certain quantity; mental processes are therefore *quantitative* processes of the accumulation and discharge of energy.

Yet, a momentary discharge of mental energy did not resolve inner conflicts. The belief in the therapeutic value of acting out was a childhood disease of psychoanalysis, but insight into the unconscious remained the cornerstone of the psychoanalytic method.

The technique of free association used as a gate to the unconscious became the "fundamental rule" in both Freudian and non-Freudian psychoanalytic treatment. All schools of psychoanalytic thought have learned from Freud to look for the hidden causes of symptom formation. A. Adler's teleologism and C. G. Jung's synchronicity cannot obviate the indisputable deterministic nature of mental disorders. One may deviate from Freud's nosology or reject the Freud-Abraham timetable of etiology or introduce new stages and concepts concerning personality development, yet no one can deny the fact that mental disorders are an inevitable consequence of a cluster of unconscious causes.

Freud introduced the principle of overdetermination and included the hereditary factors in the id; he stressed the biologically determined developmental stages that are dependent upon interaction with the environment; he spread a broad net of phylogenetic and ontogenetic factors that interact with environmental forces shaping the human personality. It is small wonder that faithful disciples and ardent dissidents went further in their studies, stressing one aspect of Freud's work against other factors.

Freud's work is not a catechism to be recited, but a pioneer work that broke through the barriers of ignorance and opened new vistas in the treatment of mental disorders. Several innovations and modifications have been developed, and there is room for more to come, but the basic approach to human nature in its normal and pathological behavior is the one set by Freud. Man is part and parcel of nature and is as such subject to biological laws. Man is a product of evolution, both phylogenetically and ontogenetically. Mental disorder is regression. Mental disorders (except for organic cases) are caused by unconscious motivation, as determined by inherited instinctual forces and early childhood experiences. Notwithstanding explicit or implicit modifications, these are the ingredients that form the common rationale underlying all psychoanalytic techniques.

Transference and Resistance

Most of the chapters in this volume stress the specificity of the diverse psychoanalytic techniques. The aim of the present introductory chapter is to point out the common elements, not so much in detailed tactical moves, as in the over-all therapeutic strategy.

The crucial issue in the treatment of mental disorders is transference. One cannot help anyone without that magic power of the emotional bond that develops between patient and analyst. Transference is the melting pot of human feelings. When the patient re-experiences his past emotional involvements, using the analyst as his target, he enables the analyst to help him to grow up.

Some neoanalysts have accused Freud of reducing the totality of analyst-patient relationship to the phenomenon of transference. This accusation is unjustified. In the paper "Analysis Terminable and Interminable" (1937, p. 217), Freud wrote: "Every happy relation between an analyst and the subject of his analysis, during and after analysis, was not to be regarded as transference; there were friendly relations with a real basis, which were capable of persisting."

The impersonal doctor-patient relationship of the prepsychoanalytic era was transformed by Freud into a meaningful interindividual relationship. Transference is the cornerstone of any analytic technique, whether classic Freudian, neo-Freudian, or non-Freudian. It is the main tool, common for all techniques, even when they prefer to substitute Freud's term by the term "interpersonal relations."

Transference becomes resistance or, at least, includes resistance. The same unconscious forces that repress undesirable feelings and impulses prevent their unraveling. Thus, no matter what technique is used, it always has to account for, and to cope with, the unconscious forces that resist cure. Primary and secondary gains, even that of the "escape into illness," have been envisaged in the technique of treatment developed by Freud.

Certainly Freud's followers deviated from Freud's technique. The present volume bears witness to a multitude of modifications, though it does not cover all of them. Some psychoanalysts follow Freud's principles with little change; others prefer to be more or less active in the interpretation of unconscious phenomena, in merely accepting or actively manipulating transferences, in struggling with resistances, or in offering or withholding approval, guidance, and instinctual gratification. There is no use denying or belittling these differences. In some instances the deviations have gone very far, and one can doubt whether certain psychotherapeutic methods merit the name "psychoanalysis" as coined by Freud. Undoubtedly, all analytic methods have *common roots,* and it is advantageous to group them together under a common roof, for their common roots aid in understanding their diverse tactics yet common rationale.

Ego Therapy

Over a period of years Freud shifted emphasis from the topographic elements toward the structural aspects of personality (1919). To put it in a somewhat simplified way, the treatment of the ego and its defense mechanisms became more prominent than the handling of repressions. The emphasis on ego therapy is quite general in current theory and practice. Fenichel (1941), Glover (1955), and especially Hartmann, Kris, and Loewenstein (1946) have explained the therapeutic necessity of strengthening the ego. The ego, as Freud put it in a pictorial way, is the servant of three "masters," the id, the superego, and reality. But when the ego is strong enough, this alleged servant holds the keys to the household and, in alliance with reality, controls the id and the superego.

Freudian technique has encompassed all aspects of personality, stressing ego strength in the last phase of treatment. A realistic outlook on life, a rational control of impulses and actions, and self-esteem are the basic ingredients of a strong ego and a healthy personality structure.

There is no psychoanalytic technique, Freudian or non-Freudian, that can omit this aspect of treatment of mental disorder. Of course, there are great variations in regard to approach, timing, degree of directiveness, and emphasis. But, notwithstanding factual and semantic differences, the essence of any psychoanalytic treatment is to strengthen the individual's control apparatus, enabling him to conduct his life in a rational way. Resolution of irrational conflicts and strengthening of the patient's self-controlling forces is the essence of psychoanalytic techniques. It is always directed toward a better adjustment to life in the Darwinian sense of the word, with minor or major deviations from Freud's staunch Darwinism.

The Concept of Cure

Any therapist, Freudian or not, must keep in mind the end product, as it were, the expected result of treatment. The concept of cure, coated in psychoanalytic terms, means first of all a rational balance of the inter- and intraindividual cathexes of libido and destrudo. A "cured" individual is reasonably narcissistic and reasonably object-directed; while his libido is properly divided and partly sublimated, his destrudo must be partly sublimated and partly kept in check for object-directed and reasonable self-defense and self-cathexis.

This concept of cure was defined in terms of a balance of cathexes of libidinal and destructive energies. A proper balance in mental topography is an additional prerequisite of good mental health.

According to Freud, unconscious conflicts must be brought to the surface. "The patients are aware in thought," wrote Freud (1913, p. 142), "of the repressed experience, but the connection between the thought and the point where the repressed recollection is in some way imprisoned is lacking. No change is possible until the conscious thought-process has penetrated to this point and has overcome the resistances of the repression there."

How much of the unconscious has to be made conscious to insure a "cure" of a mental disorder? Neither Freud nor anyone else could answer this question in a categorical manner. The supremacy of secondary processes over primary processes was a necessary element in Freud's concept of cure. Perhaps A. Adler overstressed the role of the conscious, whereas C. G. Jung underestimated it. In either case Freud's homeostatic model of a healthy personality stands out as a prototype for disciples and dissidents alike.

The structural theory plays a crucial role in Freud's concept of cure. As mentioned earlier, an ego-controlled personality structure became the core concept in Freud's theory of mental health. When the ego struggles against the onslaughts of the id and/or the superego, a neurosis results. When the ego accepts the symptoms, as it were, and the symptoms become a defensive, neurotic armor, a character neurosis develops. A collapse of the ego indicates the onset of psychosis. The strength of the ego is the most important determinant of mental health (Wolman, 1966). The strong ego resists regression and organizes all the parts of personality into a harmonious entity.

Not all schools of psychoanalytic thought use Freud's personality model and his terminology, but no school of psychoanalytic thought ever broke completely away from Freud's concept of structural balance and rational control.

There have been a great many papers and books analyzing the results of treatment (Feifel and Eels, 1963; Ford and Urban, 1963; Goldstein, 1962; Wolman, 1964; and many others). There is apparently no agreement on who is most successful in treatment of mental disorder—or when or why. At the present time it is rather difficult to evaluate the results of treatment objectively. The lack of objective diagnostic methods and the lack of agreement in regard to the theory and classification of mental disorders prevent such an evaluation. All research in this area is, at best, an approximation or an estimate, and a final judgment must wait till more precise research tools become available. However, there cannot be any doubt that whatever makes treatment successful is rooted in the basic principles of Freud's teachings.

REFERENCES

[Note: S.E. refers to *The Standard Edition of the complete psychological works of Sigmund Freud* (London: Hogarth Press).]

ABRAHAM, K. Notes on the psychoanalytical investigation and treatment of manic-depressive insanity and allied conditions. *Selected papers.* London: Hogarth Press, 1927. (Also published by Basic Books, New York, 1953.)

FEIFEL, H., and EELS, J. Patients and therapists assess the same psychotherapy. *Journal of Consulting Psychology,* 1963, 27, 310–318.

FENICHEL, O. *Problems of psychoanalytic technique.* Albany, N.Y.: *Psychoanalytic Quarterly,* 1941.

FORD, D. H., and URBAN, H. B. *Systems of psychotherapy: a comparative study.* New York: Wiley, 1963.

FREUD, S. Further recommendations in the technique of psychoanalysis. On beginning the treatment (1913). S.E., Vol. 12, pp. 121–144.

FREUD, S. Lines of advance in psychoanalytic therapy (1919). S.E., Vol. 17, pp. 157–168.

FREUD, S. Analysis terminable and interminable (1937). S.E., Vol. 23, pp. 209–254.

FREUD, S. *An outline of psychoanalysis* (1938). S.E., Vol. 23, pp. 144–208.

GLOVER, E. *The technique of psychoanalysis.* New York: International Universities Press, 1955.

GOLDSTEIN, A. P. *Therapist-patient expectancies in psychotherapy.* New York: Macmillan, 1962.

HARTMANN, H., KRIS, E., and LOEWENSTEIN, R. *Comments on the formation of psychic structure. The psychoanalytic study of the child.* Vol. 2. New York: International Universities Press, 1946. Pp. 11–39.

WOLMAN, B. B. Evidence in psychoanalytic research. *Journal of the American Psychoanalytic Association,* 1964, 12, 717–733.

WOLMAN, B. B. Principles of monistic transitionism. In B. B. Wolman and E. Nagel (Eds.), *Scientific psychology: principles and approaches.* New York: Basic Books, 1965.

WOLMAN, B. B. Classification of mental disorders. *Acta Psychotherapeutica,* 1966, 14, 50–65.

ZILBOORG, G., and HENRY, G. W. *A history of medical psychology.* New York: Norton, 1941.

2

FREUD'S PSYCHOANALYTIC TECHNIQUE—FROM THE BEGINNINGS TO 1923

Joseph T. Coltrera
Nathaniel Ross

From the beginning, in the monograph on aphasia (1891), Freud enunciated the basic principle that the measure of understanding in the clinical psychoanalytic process is the analyst himself, writing that it gave him an uncanny feeling when he was *unable* to gauge someone's emotions through his own. From this point on in the history of the idea of a psychoanalytic technique, the elaboration of understanding in the psychoanalytic situation was in large part determined by the instrumental

13

limitations imposed by the operations of the psychic apparatus of the analyst himself. It is a mark of Freud's genius that, even before he appreciated the full significance of the transference, he made a nuclear statement about the crucial role of countertransference in the processes and techniques of the clinical psychoanalytic situation.

An understanding of the historical development of technique is necessary for a grasp of the course of psychoanalytic theory, for, with Freud, considerations of technique always preceded theoretical formulations and their reconsiderations. Disagreeing with Breuer's belief in hypnoid states as causative in hysteria, Freud made the critical decision in favor of a nosogenic frame of reference. This permitted him a basic insight into the defensive character of symptoms and their overdetermination and into the function of resistance. Freud's technical papers in the second decade of the twentieth century laid the groundwork for his conceptualization of the psychic apparatus, containing not only a beginning appreciation of the structural point of view but also much of what later became ego psychology.

As with the body of Freud's thought, very little was systematically developed into a formal synthesis of technique. In the spirit of Freud's great image of analytic technique being analogous to chess in that, in each, we can systematically describe only the opening moves and the end game, we can approach understanding of the vast and subtle ambiguities of the art and style of the middle game only through a historical approach to the development of technique in Freud's thought.

On Easter Sunday, April 25, 1886, in the Viennese *Neue Freie Presse,* a notice was printed that psychoanalysis was about to be born: "Dr. Sigmund Freud, lecturer in neurology at the University of Vienna, has returned from a six months' stay in Paris and now resides at No. 7 Rathaustrasse." A private mailing of this notice was sent to two hundred doctors in Vienna. Dr. Sigmund Freud, thirty years of age and newly married, had entered into private practice, a private practice whose history over the next two decades would formalize itself into the practice of clinical psychoanalysis.

These two decades of psychoanalytic beginnings could be characterized according to several high-water marks: the relation with Josef Breuer and the publication of the *Studies on Hysteria* (Breuer and Freud, 1895); the rise and decline of the friendship and correspondence with Wilhelm Fliess, and the self-analysis; the case of Dora; the onset of psychoanalysis proper upon the publication of *The Interpretation of Dreams* (Freud, 1900); and the essential definition of psychoanalytic psychology as we know it in the latter's quintessential Chapter 7. Six hundred copies of *The Interpretation of Dreams* were printed as a first edition; by 1902 some two hundred and twenty-eight copies had been sold. It took six years to exhaust that first edition, whose sale rewarded its author with the munificent sum of two hundred dollars. Yet, during these twenty years were enunciated the three basic ideas that would define the interests and goals of psychoanalysis, as a theory and a technique, in a time of id psychology, to persevere until the formal beginning of an ego psychology in 1923. These ideas were: the dynamic unconscious, the libido theory, and the conjoined nature of transference and resistance.

We now know, as a result of the publication in 1950 of the correspondence with Wilhelm Fliess (Freud, 1887–1902), that this prepsychoanalytic period was not the conceptual wasteland it had been thought to be in the historical development of the psychoanalytic idea. A measure of the extraordinary sophistication of Freud's psychological thinking can be gained from his letter of October 20, 1895 (Freud, 1887–1902, pp. 129–130), to Wilhelm Fliess, in which Freud, discussing his "Psychology for Neurologists," writes:

> . . . Everything fell into place . . . the three systems of neurones, the "free" and "bound" states of quantity, the primary and secondary processes, the main trend and the compromise trend of the nervous system, the two biological rules of attention and defence, the indications of quality, reality, and thought, the state of the psycho-sexual group, the sexual determination of repression, and finally the factors determining consciousness as a perceptual function—the whole thing held together. I can naturally hardly contain myself with delight (Freud, 1887–1902, p. 129).

Therefore, in the 1890's, although his techniques were still not truly psychoanalytic in the formal sense, his theoretical premises were necessary to, and compatible with, the direction of psychoanalysis as a clinical theory and its techniques; neurosis was already defined as inner conflict, involving a defense against unbearable ideas. Here are implied the bare bones of the conflictual model that would concern the classical therapeutic approaches of the next three decades: an inner conflict, its repression, and the return of the repressed.

This prepsychoanalytic period was dominated by Freud's relationship with two men, Josef Breuer and Wilhelm Fliess, and by his self-analysis. The origin of psychoanalysis as a clinical discipline must be dated back to Freud's close relationship to Josef Breuer (1892–1925). Like Charcot, Breuer used hypnosis in treating hysterical patients. Whereas the former sought to influence such patients by direct suggestion, Breuer preferred to let them describe their own symptoms and to enable them to find relief by re-enacting, as far as possible, while under deep hypnosis, the original traumatic situation. He called this new approach the "cathartic method."

Between December 1880 and June 1882, for some sixteen months, Breuer treated a twenty-one-year-old girl with a severe paralysis, hallucinations, and other nervous symptoms; this was the famous *ur*-case of psychoanalysis, Fräulein Anna O. Her severe symptoms disappeared, to Breuer's surprise, after she had spoken freely of them under hypnosis. It was her spontaneous utterances under hypnosis that gave Breuer the idea that patients should be allowed to talk freely. In 1882, her intense sexual transference, manifesting itself as a false pregnancy, caused Breuer to break off the treatment precipitously.

Breuer often discussed this case with his younger colleague when Freud was at Brücke's laboratory. It was not until three years later, while Freud was in Paris at the Salpêtrière, that he related the case to Charcot (Freud, 1925). But, although Charcot could speak in general of certain hysterical disorders with aphoristic clarity—*"C'est toujours la chose génitale, toujours, toujours"*—he showed no interest in Fräulein Anna O., for he failed to see the basic truth inherent in his aphorism as an operational principle and as a clue to the central dynamics of hysteria. Where Charcot saw an aphorism, Freud apprehended nosogenesis.

Following his return from Paris to Vienna, Freud soon became disillusioned with the current methods of treating the hysteric. He quickly became disillusioned with the inadequate premises and purposelessness of such techniques as hydrotherapy, electrotherapy, massage, and the Weir-Mitchell rest cure. In his second letter to Fliess, on December 28, 1889 (Freud, 1887–1902, p. 53), he spoke of the fateful step he had taken, one that was necessary for a psychoanalytic psychology, its processes and techniques, away from the concept of brain as a Helmholtzian closed system of determinate physicochemical processes, and directed toward the concept of a mind filled with psychic contents—ideas. With this critical shift in commitment from an idea of brain to one of mind, the semantic nature of the clinical psychoanalytic process became possible, for if mind is defined by a psychic content of ideas, then psychopathology and its resolution must too be defined by processes that are also ideas.

In Letter 2, on December 28, 1887, he wrote Wilhelm Fliess (Freud, 1887–1902, p. 53), "During the last few weeks I have plunged into hypnosis and have had all sorts of small but peculiar successes." A detailed account has been given of one of these successes (Freud, 1892). During his short commitment to hypnosis and his increasing dissatisfaction with the permanency of its results—especially through the summer of 1889 in Nancy with Liébault and Bernheim—Freud came to a growing certainty about the existence of powerful processes "hidden from the consciousness of man." He began where Charcot did not see, with the case of Anna O., and where Liébault and Bernheim could not follow: "From the first, I made use of hypnosis in *another* manner, apart from hypnotic suggestion" (Freud, 1925d). This "another manner apart from hypnotic suggestion" was the cathartic method.

The *Studies on Hysteria* (Breuer and Freud, 1895) must be considered the textbook of the cathartic method. The case of Frau Emmy von N. (Breuer and Freud, 1895) was the first to be treated by the cathartic method or by use of hypnosis beyond Charcot's usage of hypnotic suggestion. However, a measure of Freud's ambivalence about his allegiance to the cathartic method can be assumed from his translation of separate works on hypnotic suggestion by Bernheim in 1888 and 1892, and a visit to the clinics of Liébault and Bernheim at Nancy in the summer of 1889—this last *after* beginning the treatment of Frau Emmy N. on May 1, 1889, using hypnosis as the cathartic method. The case was published in 1895 and is spoken of as an "analysis" (Breuer and Freud, 1895, p. 48). Freud had used the terms "analysis," "psychical analysis," and "hypnotic analysis" in "The Neuro-Psychoses of Defence" (Freud, 1894) in the previous year, and he formalized the word "psychoanalysis" in a paper on the etiology of neuroses written in French in 1896 (Freud, 1896a).

Fräulein Elizabeth von R. (Breuer and Freud, 1895, pp. 135–181) came to treatment in the autumn of 1892, and her case was described by Freud as his "first full-length analysis of a hysteria." There had been other cases between 1889 and 1892, especially that of Frau Cäcilie M. (Breuer and Freud, 1895, 69–70 ff.), who because she could be recognized was not reported in depth (a tradition, which is adhered to until this day, of not publishing case material on those who could be recognized or who might recognize themselves). Apart from the prime consideration of the discretion, which is the patient's right, to publish case material even with the patient's permission, such publication could seriously complicate a final resolution of the transference and so compromise the termination of the analysis after its formal cessation. It was the joint study of the case of Frau Cäcilie M. with Breuer that led directly to their "Preliminary Communication." Miss Lucy R. (Breuer and Freud, 1895, pp. 106–124) follows Fräulein Elizabeth R. and Katherina (pp. 125–134).

The cathartic method described in the *Studies on Hysteria* (Breuer and Freud, 1895) was the first statement of a psychoanalytic instrumentality directed to a scientific understanding of the human mind. With the lifting of the hysterical amnesia in Fräulein Anna O., we must accept empirically that, from here on, an immediate consciousness has no operational meaning apart from consideration of the existence of a dynamic unconscious. In the case of Fräulein Anna O., the instrument of investigation was the hypnotic suggestion used to persuade the patient to plumb the unconscious regions beyond the conscious processes and their amnesiac gaps. With Frau Emmy von N., Freud came to appreciate the fact that some patients were less amenable to the cathartic method than others, as represented by Fräulein Anna O.

Whether it was because Freud, as he confessed, was not adept at hypnosis (Breuer and Freud, 1895, pp. 107 ff.) or because of the patients' resistiveness, he gave up hypnosis, shifting the therapy situation forever into a situation of the waking state and its varieties of awarenesses, especially those of reflective awarenesses. In 1892 Freud developed a "concentration technique." At first he pressed his hand upon the patient's head, enjoining him to dwell upon some aspect of his illness, in the hope that the patient might recall events of his past life, which would bring some light to bear on the origins of his illness. However, he soon became convinced that physical contact with the patient was unnecessary, and on the direct request of a patient, he realized the importance of granting the latter an absolute freedom to say whatever came to mind. From its beginnings, in the case of Frau Emmy von N. in 1889 (Breuer and Freud, 1895, p. 56), and through its more explicit development between 1892 and 1896, there evolved the concept of free association, which has been the "basic rule" of psychoanalytic technique ever since.

The pressure-concentration technique was first used with Fräulein Elizabeth R. (Breuer and Freud, 1895, p. 110); she was told that she would see something or have some ideas when Freud released his pressure (p. 145) or that the ideational awareness would persist while the pressure was maintained on her forehead (p. 270). Freud had given up his pressure technique before he wrote the chapter on the state of his technique in the Loewenfeld book in 1904 (Freud, 1904)—probably before 1900—for he made no mention of it in his brief account of his procedure in the beginning of Chapter 2 in *The Interpretation of Dreams* (Freud, 1900, p. 101). In this passage Freud recommends that the patient keep his eyes closed during the analytic period, representing a last remnant, along with the ritual of lying down, of the original hypnotic method. The latter will be specifically disavowed in the Loewenfeld chapter (Freud, 1904, p. 250).

In the years following the *Studies on Hysteria,* a subtle though critical shift occurred in Freud's technique as regards the traditionally dominant role of the doctor to the patient. Giving up the cathartic techniques of concentration and deliberate suggestion, Freud became increasingly committed to the "basic rule" of free association, whose principles were discernible as early as 1889 in his treatment of Frau Emmy von N. (Breuer and Freud, 1895, p. 56). No longer was the patient to be dominated by imperatives of word and act. Instead, the doctor was enjoined to assume a ritualized neutral and nonintrusive position of relaxed attention, to listen not to an ordered sequence of discursive thoughts but to what often would seem like the senseless maunderings of an irrational being. And, above all, analysts were admonished to do their work with "tact, seriousness and discretion." Jones (1953, pp. 246–247) believed that the essential shape of the "basic rule" was known to Freud since he was fourteen, at which age he had been given the works of Ludwig Börne. In an essay guilelessly entitled "The Art of Becoming an Original Writer in Three Days," Börne advises writers to free-associate ideas for three days running and then to begin to write.

The shift from deliberate suggestion and concentration to free association represents more than a simple progression in technique. For the device of free association facilitates the thinning out of the quantitative and qualitative distributions of attention cathexes necessary for the "widening of attention" previously effected by hypnotic suggestion and the technique of concentration in the cathartic method. Therefore, the "basic rule" of free association is implemented by the stimulus-deprived situation of the nonintrusive analyst, the use of the couch, and the radical restriction of reality cues, each of which is directed to the end of inducing a topographic regression, represented phenomenologically as a "widening of attention." For, with the "widening of attention," the ever topographic regressive direction of the states of consciousness of the analytic situation—and its correlate, topographically regressed states of reflective awarenesses—facilitates the appearance of the least-hypercathected unconscious derivatives able to escape the work of repression into the preconscious. Although this is presented in the context of the topographic point of view, within which it developed historically toward the end of the prepsychoanalytic period (1887–1900), it might not be amiss to hypothesize in a later structural framework that the hypercathectic energic regression, both quantitively and in modality, facilitated by the relative stimulus deprivation fostered by the psychoanalytic situation, must of necessity compromise the countercathectic systems, which are in themselves an expression of quasi-stable deployments of attention cathexes. Any regression in the structural conditions of the ego's defenses will facilitate the appearance of unconscious derivatives heretofore repressed into one of the more marginal states of consciousness, now available to the hypercathectic work of the analysis. This will raise the derivatives to reflective awareness. The hypercathectic device may consist of an interpretation or confrontation by the analyst, or, more ideally, it could be the synthetic and integrative ego work of reflective judgment on the part of the patient.

Through his own self-analysis and in his daily practice, Freud was forced empirically to acknowledge that the first principle of a psychoanalytic technique must be an overriding consideration for the structural conditions that allow for topographic regression and that any technical maneuver that compromises the topographic regression is to be considered a break in technique. Once this principle is understood, it is patent that the silence of the analyst, far from being an expression of passivity, is in reality the most "active" of techniques. Patients who dread the unconscious id confrontations at the end of a topographic regression become marvelously adept at causing the analyst to break his silence so as to compromise the feared topographic regression. By the same token, the silence of the analyst must be carefully weighed against the greater danger of compromising the tenuous autonomies of psychic structure in severely depressed patients and the "as if" personality. These may respond to extended silences as situations of critical stimulus deprivation by a subsequent decompensation of psychic structure, expressed clinically as profound narcissistic withdrawal and/or a runaway topographic regression. Clinically, a situation of runaway topographic regression and decompensation of psychic structure may manifest itself by complaints of difficulty in recovering spatiotemporal contexts on getting off the couch, or, in some cases, a feeling of depersonalization and self-confusion when getting off the couch or when waking from sleep. These are more properly the problems of the "widening application of psychoanalysis" in our present time of ego psychology, but they are more easily understood if the purpose of the topographic regression in the analytic situation, as meant by Freud from the beginning, is understood. Implied in these considerations is the question of the timing of interpretations and, clearly, an interdiction against intervention by the analyst simply to break a silence that he finds onerous. An interpretive rationale must be based on the psychodynamic constellations of the psychoanalytic process.

According to the topographic model, which Freud assumed of the psychic apparatus at the close of the prepsychoanalytic period, just before the publication of *The Interpretation of Dreams* in 1900, the interpretation discharges a very necessary hypercathectic function by providing the additional quantum of attention cathexes above and incidental to the attention-directing function of a semantic explanatory proposition whose content is one of elucidation and synthesis. Thus, although an interpretation is usually equated with the synthetic function of its explanatory contents, it cannot be separated from its form elements. These fix attention and cause the unconscious derivatives, which have passed beyond the repressive barrier into the preconscious, to be raised to full consciousness. At this level the synthetic and integrative functions of the ego can be brought to bear on the content elements of the interpretations. To assign a hypercathectic function to the formal elements of an interpretation—its timing, syntax and imagery, and cognitive style—may explain why the same interpretation in the hands of two analysts, fully agreed on the dynamics of a case, will have diverse effects. It may also explain why in deeply depressed patients, with their narcissistic hypercathexes and depletion of cathexes for the work of attention and reflective judgment, interpretations must be directly simple to be effective.

It should not be forgotten that the concept of interpretation developed in a historical context of the need to maintain the advantage of the cathartic method in psychoanalysis proper. The technical device of a "widening of consciousness" facilitated the topographic regressive pathway into the unconscious. Freud's researches into dream analysis had been given impetus by his own self-analysis, to be formalized in *The Interpretation of Dreams* (Freud, 1900) a few years later. Here he declared the primary process to be the mechanism of the unconscious and conceptualized the metapsychology of topographic regression in the famous seventh chapter of that work. While Freud had used the German word *Deutung* ("interpretation") before *The Interpretation of Dreams, Die Traumdeutung* (Freud, 1900), in his paper on screen memories (Freud, 1890) in the sense of an elucidation, it was popularized in the second chapter of *The Interpretation of Dreams* to show that dreams not only were physiological processes but that they had meaning as well.

Quite explicitly, then, Freud developed his idea of interpretation (*Deutung*) as an explanatory proposition about the derivatives closest to the unconscious in the historical context of his inquiries into the dream. In 1904 he defined the interpretative role of the analyst as demonstrating to the patient that which is hidden, *that which is unconscious* (Freud, 1904, p. 252). Although Freud explicitly restricted the interpretation to things unconscious, he clearly used the concept to mean unconscious derivatives heretofore repressed and now resident in the system-Pcs. We have already commented on the hypercathectic function of the interpretation in raising these preconscious derivatives of the unconscious to reflective awareness, so that the synthetic and integrative tasks of working through may be accomplished. An interpretation is directed to derivatives in the system-Pcs. in Freud's topographic model. To do otherwise and interpret "directly" to the system-Ucs. is to fall into the error of "wild analysis."

Even in the present time of ego psychology, we have not meaningfully directed ourselves to the significant roles of language and imagery in interpretation. To consider but one aspect, language bears a cognitive relationship of a kind to reality, and in our own Indo-European language system, what we call logic is more properly a description of the grammar and syntax of the Aristotelian structure of our language. Therefore, the very discursive nature of the interpretation, as a linguistic device of explanation and exposition, will of itself implement the synthetic work of the ego. More conjecturally, the language determinants of an interpretation probably supplement the ego work of neutralization. The very syntax and grammatical structuring of language offer additional supplies of (neutralized) nonmotivational cathexes used in psychic structure-building. In itself this contributes to the structural shifts, which do not in themselves compromise the over-all integrity of psychic structure. Such processes lead to an "alteration in the ego."

Plainly, the nuances of interpretation, as a "timed" explanatory proposition about the unconscious to the patient, fall more within the ambiguities of an art form than the synthetic expositions of a science. Freud always looked upon technique as being closer to art than science, and in his 1922 paper "Psychoanalysis" (Freud, 1923a) defined psychoanalysis as an art of interpretation, speaking of the evenly suspended attention of the analyst and his ability to listen simultaneously to different levels of mental functioning immediate to the psychic event.

Essentially, then, from about 1900 onward, a valid psychoanalytic interpretation consisted of a dynamic and genetic explanatory proposition about unconscious determinants, which leads eventually to "alterations in the ego," expressed as a personality change. This was brought about by means of reconstruction of past infantile conflicts by a lifting of repression and by their resolution in the treatment situation proper. A valid interpretation must be both a genetic and dynamic proposition. As a genetic proposition it must reconstruct a correct hypothesis about a past infantile conflict that continues to be maintained in the present. And as a dynamic proposition it must be able to cause reconstructive personality changes aphoristically expressed as "alterations in the ego." Because the psychic apparatus as a psychological system represents the most open of all the open biological systems, an interpretation can never be "exact," but it can be "correct." As a scientific proposition in an open system, that is, as against a closed physical system, scientific verifiability is more properly a question of confirmability of a prediction about an order of probability, and not of certainty. In point of fact, certainty as a measure of scientific verifiability has in itself been seriously questioned by Heisenberg (1958) even in a closed physical system. Freud took a similar position in the *Introductory Lectures on Psycho-Analysis* (1916–1917), explaining that interpretation cannot be judged in the context of certainty, but should be considered according to varying degrees of probability with the trustworthiness of the results depending on the skill, the experience, and the art of the analyst.

Before leaving the problem of interpretation, we might touch on the related device of confrontation, although it later became the special technique of resistance analysis during the era of ego psychology. Quite simply, confrontation can be defined as a technique of direct intervention that calls attention to behavior, which is not ego syntonic and as such represents the major device by which the paradoxical nature of neurosis is presented for the work of the analysis. It is particularly suited to point up the more subtle suspensions of reality-testing and reflective judgment in character resistances.

Almost as soon as Freud enunciated the "basic rule," he saw how it could be used as resistance. In the *Studies on Hysteria* (Breuer and Freud, 1895, pp. 67 ff.) he described the resistance of "false connections." The compulsion to associate and the tendency of obsessive personalities to use free association in the service of resistance are called to our attention in the beginning of Section II in "The Neuro-Psychoses of Defence" (Freud, 1894).

A misunderstanding has grown up about the nature of free association. Since it was meant to continue into psychoanalysis the instrumentality of "the widening of consciousness" inherent to the cathartic method, it was thought to be an end in itself and not just the device of technique that Freud conceived it to be. Considering free association to be restricted to the historical context of the cathartic method gave rise to the misapprehension that psychoanalysis is a "talking cure," a nonspecific form of catharsis, which resembles the extralogical "speaking with tongues" common to certain mystical sects. This misunderstanding has even been "legitimized" as the rationale of several neocathartic intuitive psychotherapies down into our own time. In itself, this neocathartic distortion of the analytic process represents the most enduring heritage of the prepsychoanalytic cathartic method, deriving from the "Preliminary Communication" (Breuer and Freud, 1895, pp. 1–15). The myth has persisted that the essential work of psychotherapy is to bring about a discharge of a blocked affect. The therapeutic rationale of the cathartic method was based upon the effects of bringing into consciousness the original traumatic experience, together with its affect. With the affect, previously held in thrall to the repressed original experience, now discharged as an "abreaction," the force that had maintained the symptom was dissipated, and the symptom disappeared. Therapy came to be thought of as a firing in the crucible of serial affective experiences, which were in themselves the discharge of previously blocked affects.

Since that time, the idea of therapy as an affective purgation has persisted as a recurrent belief in the efficacy of considerations of form over those of content. From the neocathartic experiments of Sándor Ferenczi down through the Paracelsian belief of the Reichian in the blocked orgonal flux locked within the neuromuscular elaborations of character-armoring, and into the intuitive affective immediacies of existential analysis, a darker and lesser therapeutic tradition continues to hold that analytic work is defined as an affective abreaction. Curiously, it is a return to the Romantic belief that affect is a form of cognition (Coltrera, 1965). Regarding free associations simply as the agent of a cathartic experience is among the most critical errors of technique. Such an approach necessarily compromises understanding of the function of the interpretation as an intervention directed toward the bridging of the unconscious. It especially overlooks the critical role of the timing of interpretations and confrontations in the analyzing of resistances in their conjoined id- and ego-meanings.

The role of abreaction and the entire neocathartic attitude (Ferenczi and Rank, 1924) toward free association demand careful metapsychological scrutiny, for these historical misunderstandings of the psychoanalytic idea seriously compromise the rationale of psychoanalytic technique.

The limits of a cognitive experience—its contexts and meanings—are defined by the structural characteristics of the state of consciousness in which it occurs. These structural characteristics are a function of the distribution and patterning of the deployment of attention cathexes and their modalities and, as such, constitute distinctive modes or qualities of experience, the different ways in which we can be aware. Thus, different cathectic organizations endow an idea with its qualitative cognitive order as percept, image, or memory. For example, the affective storms of the hysterical character form a major resistance in analytic work. They specifically disrupt the quasi-stable hypercathectic equilibrium of the cognitive organizations attached to the "widened" states of consciousness, which arise during the associative flow of the patient. They are especially disturbing to the cognitive organizations of reflective awareness. Too often these affective storms pass through the analysis untouched, for all appearances like so many microcosmic fugue equivalents. They are isolated from any sense of reflective awareness and remain unaffected by the synthetic and integrative ego work of an ongoing psychoanalytic process. Needless to say, the transference in these patients is markedly in the service of resistance.

Insofar as the ends of technique are concerned, we must ask why an affect should be discharged and why the consequences of its not being discharged should be of concern. Any technique whose prime purpose is such an end— and it is a device of attitude in many of the so-called corrective experiences manipulated within the transference—subscribes to the homeostatic needs of the "principle of constancy," first alluded to at the end of "The Neuro-Psychoses of Defence" (Freud, 1894) and given its name by Breuer in *Studies on Hysteria* (Breuer and Freud, 1895, pp. 192 ff.). Although Freud mentions the "principle of constancy" in the early pages of "Instincts and Their Vicissitudes" (Freud, 1915b) and then a last time in *Beyond the Pleasure Principle* (Freud, 1920c), this in no way indicates a continuing commitment to abreactive technique to assure cathectic constancy, and it is, more properly, another example of Freud's well-known reluctance to completely let go of an idea. In Freud the operational validity of an idea is indicated more by his conceptual usages than by any passing acknowledgment in the text.

Even toward the end, in an attempt to reify some of his thinking on technique and the goals of analysis according to the newer ego psychology, Freud (1937a) specifically stated that the criteria for termination have less to do with an ability to abreact than with the ego's ability to transmute the modality of motivational cathexes into the nonmotivational cathexes necessary for continuing psychic structure-building. Termination has more to do with the ability to effect new sublimations than to abreact.

The second major early modification of technique, which is also antithetical to the first neocathartic modification already discussed, was that of an intellectual reconstruction of the causative infantile conflict. Directly opposed to the emphasis of the form elements in the psychoanalytic process fostered by a neocathartic technique, the modification of intellectual reconstruction and insight therapy concentrated on precise interpretations of content and on the reconstruction of the infantile conflict in order to lift the infantile amnesia. As affective abreaction without intellectual insight is ineffective, so must the converse apply. Emotional abreaction and intellectual insight must be conjoined to have psychological validity. When these are separated in an analysis, resistance must be assumed; when separated as modifications of technique, a technical compromising of the psychoanalytic process can be assumed.

Compared to interpretation, a lesser contrapuntal role is assigned by Freud to reconstruction in his many discussions of technique. Two extensive reconstructions are central to the analysis of the "Rat Man" (Freud, 1909b, pp. 182, 205), and the case of the "Wolf Man" (Freud, 918, pp. 50 ff.) devolves upon a reconstruction of his infantile conflict. The reconstruction of the infantile neurosis of the "Wolf Man" (Freud, 1918)—more specifically, his psychosexual stage development and its determinant infantile conflicts —represented a critical part of Freud's answer to the generalizing vitiation of the libido theory by C. G. Jung. Reconstruction played a most important role in the case history of the homosexual girl (Freud, 1920a, pp. 50 ff.). And, to the end, Freud was committed to reconstruction as a proper analytic technique; in 1937 Freud (1937b) likened the reconstructive work of the analyst to that of the archaeologist:

His work of construction, or if it is preferred, of reconstruction, resembles to a great extent an archaeologist's excavation of some dwelling-place that has been destroyed and buried or of some ancient edifice. The two processes are in fact identical, except that the analyst works under better conditions and has more material at his command to assist him, since what he is dealing with is not something destroyed but something that is still alive—and perhaps for another reason as well. But just as the archaeologist builds up the walls of the building from the foundations that have remained standing, determines the number and position of the columns from depressions in the floor and reconstructs the mural decorations and paintings from the remains found in the debris, so does the analyst proceed when he draws his inferences from the fragments of memories, from the associations and from the behaviour of the subject of the analysis. Both of them have an undisputed right to reconstruct by means of supplementing and combining the surviving remains. Both of them, moreover, are subject to many of the same difficulties and sources of error. One of the most ticklish problems that confronts the archaeologist is notoriously the determination of the relative age of his finds; and if an object makes its appearance in some particular level, it often remains to be decided whether it belongs to that level or whether it was carried down to that level owing to some subsequent disturbance. It is easy to imagine the corresponding doubts that arise in the case of analytic contructions (Freud, 1937b, p. 259).

To understand the role of genetic reconstruction in the history of psychoanalytic technique, we must examine the critical difference between the analysis of Frau Emmy von N. done in 1889 (Breuer and Freud, 1895, pp. 48–105) with that of Dora from 1900 to 1901 (Freud, 1905d): between those two analyses fell Freud's own self-analysis. The self-analysis, as a recurrent theme in the letters to Fliess (Freud, 1887–1902) and as the autobiographical shadow of *The Interpretation of Dreams* (Freud, 1900), has several implications for theory and technique. The most important implication was that the analyst of Frau Emmy von N. and of Dora differed; in the latter case the analyst had undergone a personal analysis. The analyst of Dora was aware of countertransference and criticized himself for not properly handling the resolution of Dora's transference neurosis. Freud's self-analysis must be considered the first training analysis. From this point on in the history of the psychoanalytic idea, the principle was clear—although it would not be formalized until 1910 (Freud, 1910c)—that the first requirement of an analyst, overriding all considerations of the conceptual grasp of theory and technique, must be his personal analysis. From this point in history the course of any analysis would be a reciprocal function of two possible neuroses, the presence of a transference neurosis and the absence of a countertransference neurosis; in the presence of the latter, the success of the analysis would depend on the successful resolution of both neuroses by the same analyst in both cases.

The extensive correspondence with Wilhelm Fliess between 1887 and 1902 must be considered as a necessary adjunct of Freud's self-analysis. It may be conjectured that the correspondence served to "write through," as a more distant variety of "working through," Freud's transference relationship to Fliess, thus apprising him in some part of the importance of the continuous ongoing nature of the transference as process. The relationship between the two men contributed directly to certain critical psychoanalytic concepts of theory and technique. Freud considered Fliess's idea of bisexuality as important as the concept of defense; he wrote, "I am accustoming myself to the idea of regarding every sexual act as a process in which four people are involved" (Freud, 1887–1902, p. 289). The concepts of sublimation and of the latency period more properly belong to Fliess than to Freud according to Jones (1953, p. 318), who believed that the idea of a "repetition compulsion" arose from Fliess's idea of periodicity.

Freud's self-analysis, apart from its importance as the first training analysis, initiated the researches into dream analysis and into the genetic role of infantile psychosexual conflict. Until his self-analysis, Freud's views on sexuality and childhood could be viewed as a belief in childhood innocence, too often traumatized by sexual stimulation by an adult, with the effect delayed till puberty, at which time the memory of the trauma became exciting. Here is the theoretical premise of the cathartic method of the *Studies on Hysteria* (Breuer and Freud, 1895). Therefore, even before coming to a realization of ubiquity of the Oedipal conflict in his own self-analysis, Freud was committed to a genetic point of view in his technique. First, he reconstructed the infantile psychosexual conflict as an actual seductive trauma experienced in childhood; then, upon learning that the "memories" of his patients had been fantasies, it dawned on him that it did not matter if they were, for the fantasies represented the unconscious psychosexual conflicts of the child in the developing Oedipal configuration (Freud, 1887–1902, pp. 215–218).

Between 1896 and 1897 Freud returned to an organic basis for these infantile excitations, localizing them in the region of the anus and the mouth. He first spoke of an "erotogenic zone" in the letter of December 6, 1896 (Freud, 1887–1902, pp. 173–181), calling the mouth an "oral sexual organ" in his letter of January 3, 1897 (pp. 182–184). From May 1893 to September 1897, Freud believed the essential cause of hysteria was a seduction of an innocent child by an adult, most often the father. For four years he believed that these incestuous assaults were common and that the father perversely used the child's mouth or anus. He even indicted his own father in the letter of February 11, 1897 (Jones, 1953, p. 322). In the letter of May 13, 1897, he wrote of his growing acceptance of the universality of the Oedipal configuration in recounting his own dream of his American niece Hella as concealing his own incestuous wishes for his older daughter. On April 13, 1897, he wrote Fliess (Jones, 1953, p. 322) of an awareness of matricidal wishes on the part of the daughter, which corresponds to the son's parricidal wishes. An interesting example of resistance to a final acceptance of infantile sexuality appeared to be operating in Freud himself, for while he seemed to have accepted it as an empirical fact as early as his self-analysis (Freud, 1887–1902, pp. 218–221, 221–225), he described the Oedipus complex in the first edition of The Interpretation of Dreams (Freud, 1900) according to an early bias that children are free of sexual desires (Freud, 1900, pp. 130, 262–263). The corrective footnote did not appear until the third edition, in 1911 (Freud, 1900, p. 130 n.). It is evident, however, that by the time he formulated the case history of Dora (Freud, 1905d), at the beginning of 1901, the basic premises of his theory of sexuality had been put down.

In his self-analysis Freud was able to validate certain genetic reconstructions he had made through a dream—the famous dream of the Leipzig station (Freud, 1887–1902, pp. 235–237; 1900)—by the simple expedient of asking his mother, who was still alive, about the events that had taken place at the time.

By 1900, Freud knew that the intellectual reconstruction of an infantile conflict and its expected concomitant abreaction of an associated affect was not enough to produce a therapeutic effect. He was committed in substance to two of the three ideas that occupy a central position during the heyday of the id psychology. This period began with the publication of *The Interpretation of Dreams* (1900) and ended with the appearance of *The Ego and the Id* (1923b). To the two theories set forth in these works—the unconscious and the libido theory—he was forced, by the empirical evidence that intellectual reconstruction and abreaction did not cure his patients, to add a third, the conjoined clinical relationship between transference and resistance. From this point on in psychoanalysis, transference and resistance defined a valid and ongoing psychoanalytic process. Any considerations of technique had now to be considered within the clinical contexts of the transference and resistance.

In 1890 Freud (Breuer and Freud, 1895, pp. 154, 268) had referred to the patient's difficulty in recalling his past as "resistance." "One gets the impression of a demon striving not to come to the light of day because he knows that will be his end." The concepts of "repression" and "conversion" derived from that of "resistance." The historical development of the idea of resistance for a clinical psychoanalysis and its technique became clear in 1894 when Freud (Freud, 1894) became committed to the idea that the central task of psychoanalysis was to lift "repression," invariably a "repression" of sexual experiences in childhood. When Freud gave up the theory of infantile seduction in favor of a construct in which an interdicted unconscious wish is denied access to consciousness by repression, with a subsequent "return of the repressed" in the form of a symptom or a dream, he arrived at the essential model of an inner conflict, a model that has determined in major part the task of technique down into our own time.

About 1892 Freud (1925) came to the second defining criterion of a clinical psychoanalysis, that of "transference." Transference is the process by which during the course of the analysis the patient projects his infantile feelings onto the person of the analyst, with psychic relief coming from admitting such feelings to consciousness, resolving their unrealistic determinants, and re-experiencing them with the nonambivalent analyst as the new love-object. The working through of the transference, with its recapitulation of archaic relationships, is the major device of the genetic work of the analysis, avoiding the resistive insights of an intellectual reconstruction isolated from emotional dimension, by the inherent nature of the transference, which quintessentially develops in an overdetermined context of a range of affective meanings.

The idea of transference was first used in the narrow sense in *Studies on Hysteria* (Breuer and Freud, 1895, p. 302), although Freud realized even then the double meaning of the transference as a major tool for the work of the analysis and as a resistance in itself (pp. 301 ff.). Its unsettling effect on Breuer in the case of Anna O. (pp. 21–47)—her florid transference manifestation of a false pregnancy—certainly impressed Freud as to the resistance every transference can and does serve. Transference was used in its critical sense for the first time in Section C of Chapter 7 (Freud, 1900, pp. 562 f.) and again toward the close of the case of Dora (Freud, 1905d, pp. 116 ff.).

Between the introduction of the "basic rule" of free association and the first systematic elaboration, around 1913, of the principles of psychoanalytic technique as we use it today, Freud came to believe that a complete synthesis of technique was not truly possible, nor desirable.

A hint is given of why Freud chose a course closer to a functionalist theory construction than to a more strictly synthetic hypothetico-deductive construction of theory, in the fact that his technical papers always historically precede his papers on theory. His theoretical statements about clinical psychoanalysis and its technique are functionalist propositions, and it will be characteristic of Freud's cognitive style to tend to an understated utilization of organized conceptualizations. These theoretical propositions emphasize their tool character, reflecting their heuristic elaboration over a historical progression of technical papers, which empirically precede the more theoretical ones. The two high-water marks of metapsychology, Chapter 7 (Freud, 1900) and the "Metapsychological Papers" (Freud, 1915–1917), will be separated by some two decades of clinical practice.

Freud's propositions, more those of technique than the purely theoretical ones, can also be considered to be positivist-inductive in that they are essentially often summary statements of empirical relationships that end in constructions minimal in their inferential commitment and recourse to deductive progressions. For these epistemological reasons, Freud (1916–1917) was correct when he insisted that his interpretations—as with all his other propositions about technique—should be judged in the order of a series of probabilities and not in the order of certainty. Only those who do not understand the kinds of theoretical construction involved in his propositions about technique will continue to insist that the verification of the validity of psychoanalytic technique be done within the reductive hypothetical fiction of a laboratory situation. The first two decades of this century were spent by Freud in understanding that the kind of theory construction that goes into propositions about technique excludes any formal synthetic elaboration of psychoanalytic technique as such.

After a long discussion of the technique of psychotherapy—the cathartic method—in the *Studies on Hysteria* (Breuer and Freud, 1895), Freud wrote nothing on the subject till 1904, and then only at the behest of his friend Loewenfeld did he contribute a chapter on psychoanalytic technique for Loewenfeld's book on the obsessional neuroses.

Speaking of himself in the third person in this contribution, "Freud's Psycho-Analytic Procedure" (1904), he related that new findings had caused him to abandon the cathartic method for a different, though not contradictory, concept of the therapeutic process. This is a statement that has more to do with Freud's well-known reluctance to give up on an old concept, for we have but to read his account of the new psychoanalytic therapy to realize how radical the break had been.

A great deal had transpired in little over a decade, and the Freud who treated Frau Emmy von N. in 1889 was not the analyst of Dora in 1900. The friendship with Josef Breuer culminating in *Studies on Hysteria* and their break; the death of his father and the self-analysis that began soon after; the rise and decline of his relationship with Wilhelm Fliess as reflected in their correspondence; and, finally, there was an end to beginnings with the publication of the autobiography of his self-analysis in *The Interpretation of Dreams* (Freud, 1900) and the onset of psychoanalysis proper. The case of Dora (Freud, 1905d), extending into technique the researches into dream analysis of the period of self-analysis, was formulated about two critical dreams and thus must be considered as the connecting link of a series that began with *The Interpretation of Dreams* (Freud, 1900) and ended with the *Three Essays on the Theory of Sexuality* (Freud, 1905c). This linked series of three papers critically defined the contextual limiting ideas—the unconscious, the libido theory, and the transference resistance—which structured the conditions of instrumentality for a psychoanalytic technique in a beginning age of the id psychology. Many of the abuses of proper technique done in the name of the ego psychology began in a defective historical understanding that psychoanalytic technique started in a time of id psychology and, as such, was restricted historically to an instrumentality valid to functionalist propositions—of theory and technique —about the unconscious, the libido theory, and transference resistance. Any transposition of the principles of psychoanalytic technique must have respect for, and be constructed in accordance with, historical principles. As a valid development *within* the psychoanalytic idea, the idea of an ego psychology must syncretically assume within its structure all that had been valid to an id psychology.

Three valuable papers on technique, which must be regarded as the proselytizing tracts of the new method, were published between 1904 and 1905: the chapter on technique in Loewenfeld's book (Freud, 1904), the case of Dora (Freud, 1905d), and *On Psychotherapy* (Freud, 1905a).

"Freud's Psycho-Analytic Procedure" (Freud, 1904), written in 1903 and published in 1904, was the first and last comprehensive title on technique. Beginning with an account of the early cathartic method of the 1890's, Freud described the fundamental changes he had made, primarily the replacement of hypnosis with an investigation by "free association." "The cathartic method of treatment presupposed that the patient could be hypnotized, and was *based on the widening of consciousness*" (Freud, 1904, p. 249). Comment has already been made that the topographic regression that effects "the widening of consciousness" is carried forward into psychoanalysis by a specific group of techniques: the "basic rule" of free association and the strict conditions of a topographic regressive psychoanalytic situation of stimulus deprivation—the neutrality of an unseen analyst; the use of the couch; and a critical restriction of reality cues. The psychoanalytic process is a function in time, to be expressed in the formal time period of the "psychoanalytic hour" and the spacing of the sessions to cover a major part of the week. The first rule of technique from this point on was that any intervention on the part of the analyst—verbal or nonverbal—intrudes upon and compromises the topographic regression represented by a "widening of consciousness." For it is the topographic regression that provides the regressive cathectic organization necessary for the increased appearance of unconscious derivatives into one of the marginal "widened" states of consciousness, from whence it can be brought to full reflective awareness by the hypercathectic effects of the interpretation.

We have seen that the technique of the construction of infantile psychosexual conflict represented, in part, the vagaries of Freud's lingering loyalty to the theory of actual infantile seduction by a parent. And, although Freud acknowledged that these memories of infantile conflict were really unconscious fantasies best understood within the framework of the developing Oedipal conflict and had even accepted the explicit evidence of Oedipal conflict from the materials of his self-analysis as early as 1897, he did not completely accept the idea of an infantile psychosexual conflict repressed as an infantile amnesia, to be lifted by technique. He gave up the last vestige of loyalty to the cathartic theory of an actual infantile seduction in the third edition of *The Interpretation of Dreams* (Freud, 1900, p. 130 n.) and did not fully commit himself to the idea of infantile sexuality until he began to write the "Formulations on the Two Principles of Mental Functioning" (Freud, 1911a) and the "Metapsychological Papers" (Freud, 1915–1917). It was only then that the notion that unconscious psychosexual stage fixations to be recapitulated in the tides of the transference neurosis was fully accepted. And in 1912 he could then write that

". . . finally every conflict has to be fought out in the sphere of the transference" (Freud, 1912a).

But in 1904 the method of reconstruction had special meaning for technique with regard to the new interest in the dynamic unconscious. One of the negative proofs of unconscious determinants is derived from the more obvious elisions within the presentational façade of the associations, in the same manner that we assume a continuity where there is discontinuity in a Japanese inkbrush painting. Technique was then conceived as an interpretive linking-up of these elisions in the associative flow, so that the unconscious determinants, heretofore exerting their dynamic presence by the negative fact of a purposive elision in the associative façade, were now raised to reflective awareness. The concern for the reconstruction of these elisions in the material caused interpretation to grant an equal role to the dynamic aspect of the interpretation, whereas heretofore its genetic aspect had been emphasized. From then on the interpretation could be considered both a dynamic and genetic proposition about the unconscious of the patient. In terms of technique, a correct interpretation was now considered to exert its effect on both the dynamic and genetic determinants of the transference, for the transference at any given moment in the analysis was an expression of both past and present.

The process of filling in elisions of the patient lent itself, as we have seen, to an intellectual reconstruction of a simplistic and naïve order. Apart from its exclusion of the affective meaning, original to the reconstruction, it could in no way encompass the vast complexities constituting the psychic event. The problem would not simply reduce itself to one of repression and distortion; for how to explain the old problem of "screen memories," first mentioned in a letter to Fliess (Freud, 1887–1902, p. 271) and in *The Interpretation of Dreams* (Freud, 1900)? In his 1913 paper, "On Beginning the Treatment" (Freud, 1913b), Freud remarked that in the early days of intellectual reconstruction no distinction was made between the patient's knowledge of what was forgotten and the analyst's comprehension of that fact. The difference lay in that the patient recovered in the transference, while the analyst reconstructed. An ironic commentary can be read in this observation, that it was the analyst who was committed to the virtues of reconstruction in technique, while the patient "knew" all along that the true genetic work of the analysis must come out of the transference.

The ideal of reconstructing the infantile amnesia within the psychoanalytic process led to a new concept, that of *analyzability* as distinguished from help in psychotherapy. What was developing out of the early researches in the reconstruction of the infantile conflict was the evolving idea that there is an eddying process of regressive work crucial to the course of the analysis, ultimately to be realized in the development of true transference neurosis on the part of the patient, wherein the entire affective constellation of the infantile psychosexual (and aggressive) conflict, and its contingent archaic relationships to the original libidinal and aggressive objects, is recapitulated toward the analyst. Analyzability could now be defined as a prime function of the ability to form a true transference neurosis and to possess the basic ego integrity necessary to resolve it.

In 1904, the first *descriptive* criteria of analyzability were put down.

. . . To begin with, he [the patient] must be capable of a psychically normal condition; during periods of confusion or melancholic depression nothing can be accomplished even in cases of hysteria. Furthermore, a certain measure of natural intelligence and ethical development are to be required of him; if the physician has to deal with a worthless character, he soon loses the interest which makes it possible for him to enter profoundly into the patient's mental life. Deep-rooted malformations of character, traits of an actually degenerate constitution, show themselves during treatment as sources of a resistance that scarcely can be overcome. In this respect the constitution of the patient sets a general limit to the curative effect of psychotherapy. If the patient's age is in the neighborhood of the fifties the conditions for psychoanalysis become unfavorable. The mass of psychical material is then no longer manageable; the time required for recovery is too long; and the ability to undo psychical processes begins to grow weaker (Freud, 1904, p. 254).

The rationale of a technique of reconstruction was summed up in the didactic statements that "the task of treatment is to remove the amnesias" and that "all repressions must be undone." However, it soon became apparent that the removing of the memory did not lead to the resolution of neurosis. The expected abreaction to the recovery of these repressed memories was not always forthcoming, and when it did happen it was not enough. No amount of reconstruction alone seemed to lead to the expected resolution of the neurosis. Freud was faced with the fact that the "expected success was not forthcoming" out of an intellectual reconstruction of the infantile amnesia and that analysis appeared to devolve more upon the phenomenological recapitulation of the continuing affective residue of an infantile conflict in the immediacy of the transference neurosis. Therefore, long before there arose the neo-Freudian and existential critique of psychoanalysis as an isolated intellectual reconstruction of no present existential contingency for the patient, Freud had given up the resolution of neurosis as an isolated synthesis of what transpired in the past (Coltrera, 1962). It would be difficult to imagine a more existential affective experience than the many dialogue constellations of the true transference neurosis; in direct point of technique, Freud continually warned against intruding any synthetic intervention that would compromise the white affective heat of the unfolding transference neurosis. But, by the same token, to exclude the genetic meaning of a transference neurosis in favor of the view that it is simply an affective immediacy, a phenomenon of simple process awareness, is to overlook the conjoined genetic *and* dynamic content derivatives by simply considering them as vaguely assumed to exist in affective forms.

On December 12, 1904, Freud gave an address, *On Psychotherapy* (Freud, 1905a), to the College of Physicians in Vienna. At that time he countered the argument that psychoanalysis was a form of suggestion, emphasizing "the greatest possible antithesis" between the two. Utilizing the famous image of Leonardo's painting and sculpture, he declared that suggestion worked as did painting—*per via di porre*—by adding successive layers of paint on a blank canvas, as did suggestion by additions of imperatives that offset the morbid idea. Sculpture and psychoanalysis work *per via di levare,* by taking away from the rough stone. This analogy is reminiscent of the metaphor of Plotinus in the *Enneads*—the sculptor finds beauty within the stone and then must extract it from its encasement. For the first time, Freud advanced in this lecture the opinion that with advances in technique it would be possible to influence certain psychoses by psychoanalytic approaches. The statement can also be understood to contain intimations of his belief that the theory of the ego would develop out of the study of the narcissistic neuroses or psychoses. As 1904 drew to its close, he sadly related that no colleague had as yet asked him how to carry out a psychoanalysis. He had a few pupils, but no inquiries from his peers.

In many ways the most significant contribution to technique in the years between *The Interpretation of Dreams* in 1900 and the *Three Essays on the Theory of Sexuality* in 1905 was the case of Dora (Freud, 1905d). For the first time we are permitted to observe Freud at work, to see how he deals with various situations in the analysis, the rationale and timing of his interpretations, and the central and early position of dream interpretation in his technique. Lewin (1952) believes that it is this early historical development of dream analysis within id psychology that causes the dream to be usually understood according to a topographic point of view, when all else in a case might be interpreted in terms of the structural point of view. This contributes in great part to the relative demise of dream analysis in this time of ego psychology.

In 1909, the "Notes upon a Case of Obsessional Neuroses" (Freud, 1909b)—the case of "The Man with the Rats"—was published. It was the first case in which Freud's day-to-day notes are available (in Strachey's excellent translation [Freud, 1909c, pp. 251–318]). Freud's technical style is interesting to observe not only for the timing of his interpretations but for his characteristic use of analogies, as an index of the role played by cognitive style—as a device of language and metaphor—in the unique form qualities of technique as a style. Freud always believed that the analyst's style should be constant and true to his autonomous ego gifts, in what seem to be spheres of cognitive style and language giftedness, specifically saying: ". . . this technique is the only one suited to my individuality; I do not venture to deny that a physician quite differently constituted might find himself driven to adopt a different attitude to his patients and to the task before him" (Freud, 1912b, p. 111). Analytic style must be autonomous and, as such, exist in the nonconflictual ego sphere, and it must not compromise transference by any idiosyncratic intrusiveness. The question of the analyst's style as a unique vicissitude of inherent ego gifts has special meaning in the question of choosing candidates for psychoanalytic training. Certainly, gifts of ambiguous appreciation and language abilities—which are preponderantly ego gifts—would bear meaningfully on a hypothetical pre-adaptability to become an analyst.

The case of "The Man with the Rats" (Freud, 1909b) also demonstrates Freud's continuing tendency to work according to tentative hypotheses, to their confirmation and disapproval according to the associations, dreams, forms of behavior, and personality changes in the patient.

We might summarize some features of Freud's technique at this time. He gave his patients fuller expositions of psychoanalytic theory than he would later, not so much to convince the patient as to provoke relevant material; he permitted a more familiar attitude toward his patients than he did later. Therefore, any change from these practices he began with had to be derived from empirical considerations and not from any intrinsic personality needs, as popular legend would have it. Indeed, in the 1890's he went so far as to invite patients to meals with his family and, as late as the case of "The Man with the Rats" in 1909, he would have refreshments brought in for both himself and his patients. And, even into World War I he would go so far as to collect funds to help the now almost destitute "Wolf Man" cut off from his estates in Russia. Therefore, the "newer" and more flexible familiar relationships between patient and therapist, advocated by the non-

Freudian schools, can be seen as historical phases in Freud's evolving technique.

The Salzburg Congress of 1908 represented a turning of the tide. With the growing acceptance and interest in his work Freud was encouraged to give a further account of his methods. This was an important decision, for it led Freud to a final realization about the nondiscursive nature of technique and the difficulty of a formal synthesis.

In the six months that followed the congress Freud began a systematic exposition of technique, to be called "A General Account of the Psychoanalytic Technique." He wrote to Karl Abraham that he had thought of publishing it in the second series of the *Sammlung,* which was to appear the next year. In a month's time he had written thirty-six pages but found himself too tired at the day's end to make more progress. He told Sándor Ferenczi in a letter that it would be some fifty pages and hoped to have it ready by Christmas. A series of postponements ensued: first Freud put it off to work on the case of "The Man with the Rats"; then he postponed it during vacation; then he had to prepare for his trip to America; and then, in the next year, he resorted to a final stratagem by saying it would be better to let it lie in the drawer. At the end Freud decided to abandon the systematic approach and develop the proposed "Account" as a group of six essays.

Freud took up the problem again in his address to the Nuremberg Congress in 1910, "The future prospects of psycho-analytic therapy" (Freud, 1910b). He related that the method had been much more strenuous in its beginnings to both analyst and patient, with the analyst pressuring the patient to express his thoughts freely. Gradually the sophistication of the technique, especially its more precise timing of interpretations and the growing understanding of the transference, had made its practice easier.

Since the days of his critical disagreement with Breuer, the aim of the therapy was directed to elucidating the defensive nature of the symptoms, and from the understanding of the symptoms to that of the neuroses in general. With the increased appreciation of the meaning of common and recurring symbols, a semantic interpretation became possible. As always in the history of technique, symbol interpretation very often became a synthetic and reductionist intellectual technique, often correct in general but contributing little in particular. A symbol is an overdetermined psychic event, granted an entire series of contexts and meaning by the unique elaboration of an inner conflict and representative of a cognitive style of a particular person. Symbol formation is a unique gift in the service of conflictual elaboration (Coltrera, 1965).

Symbols have little meaning in themselves apart from the context of associations and, although symbolic elaboration is a mechanism of the unconscious, it can only be interpreted meaningfully according to the context of associations in which it is placed by the patient.

Attention was also drawn in the above paper to countertransferences, which the practicing analyst was obliged to take into account in an ongoing process of self-analysis.

With the increasing acceptance of psychoanalysis, the task of psychoanalysis was being eased. Freud concluded his 1910 Nuremberg address with some remarks on the attitude of society to neurotic difficulties and the prophylactic advantages that might derive from a more honest understanding of their meaning; a warning was directed against therapeutic fanaticism, pointing out that some patients deprived of the secondary gains of their illness would be much worse off. Freud here introduced a psychodynamic rationale for the support of neurotic defenses in some patients whose overall psychic economy would be little served by the loss of a necessary neurotic defense. For example, it might be better to support denial in some hypomanic processes rather than resolve the defense, leaving the patient with a profound depressive process now no longer denied.

A few months later, in 1910, Freud published his significant paper on " 'Wild' Psychoanalysis" (Freud, 1910c). Here he warned against the indiscriminate applications of his theories without understanding them. Again he took a strong stand against psychoanalytic technique as pedagogy, stating that technique cannot be learned didactically from books, but in a preceptorship with those who have mastered it. Freud (1904) had already touched on "wild" analysis in his chapter on psychotherapy in Loewenfeld's book in 1904. This paper has a subsidiary interest for technique, in that in it Freud still alluded to an actual neurosis, the lingering loyalty to a concept of an infantile neurosis born of a seductive trauma. He coupled this allusion with an emphasis on the need to distinguish between anxiety neurosis and anxiety hysteria (Freud, 1910c, pp. 224 ff.). Anxiety hysteria had been introduced not long before in connection with the case of "Little Hans" in 1909 (Freud, 1909a, pp. 115 ff.).

Some eighteen months after his statement of intent, Freud began to write the six critical papers on technique. The first four were written quickly, over a period of fifteen months, between December 1911 and March 1913. These four papers mark the beginning of the general body of technique as we know it today, and for this reason the general principles of psychoanalytic techniques as now practiced are usually dated to around 1913. As such they must be considered against the historical elaboration of *On Narcissism* (Freud, 1914b) and, particularly, the "Metapsychological

Papers" (Freud, 1915–1917). Another pause and the last two papers of the project six appeared in November 1914 and in January 1915. The last four of the six papers shared a common title and were published in 1918 under the heading of "On the Techniques of Psychoanalysis." Freud regarded these six papers as forming a series (Freud, 1913b, pp. 123 ff.). Although they cover a range of important topics, they cannot be considered a systematic exposition of psychoanalytic technique. They were as close as Freud would get—or cared to get—to a systematic elaboration of technique.

The first of the six came out in December 1911 and was entitled "The Handling of Dream-Interpretation in Psycho-analysis" (Freud, 1911b). Ever the clinical analyst, Freud was concerned with the two opposite ways in which dreams could be used for resistance. In the first instance, the patient, believing the dream to be critical for the ongoing work of analysis, may bring none at all, so that the analysis would not proceed. The patient must be shown that the analysis will go on without them, and only then will such a patient produce some dreams. Or, he may overwhelm the analyst with many dreams or produce a single dream of convoluted length, neither of which can be analyzed in any given session. Freud underscores the need not to permit the interest of the analyst in the dream as a psychic phenomenon to intrude upon the associative immediacy of the thoughts and affects of the patient. An obvious research interest on the part of the analyst toward the dream would most certainly compromise the transference. Technically, any dream material so lost would be sure to recur in associations closer to the mainstream of the transference.

Freud made four contributions to the practical use of dreams in treatment. Earlier in the same year in which he published the aforementioned paper, Freud had written a paper on the elucidation of various symbols, called "Additions to the *Interpretation of Dreams*," which has been incorporated in the main text in the Standard Edition of "A Metapsychological Supplement to the Theory of Dreams" (Freud, 1917a). A third small paper (Jones, 1955, p. 240) was written on a dream that bore testimony to an actual event the dreamer had denied. A patient had told Freud the dream of someone else, and it was offered to compare the interpretations they both gave. The last of the four contributions to the use of the dream in practice is an important one. "Remarks on the Theory and Practice of Dream Interpretation" (Freud, 1923c) consisted of ten sections with separate themes. Freud distinguished several methods of beginning the interpretation of a dream according to circumstances, enumerating the various ways in which different types of dream make their appearance during analysis and how their interpretation could be utilized in the working through. Freud returned in this paper to the suggestive influence of the analyst on the dream and its possible role in resistance.

A month later, in January 1912, Freud published the important paper "The Dynamics of Transference" (Freud, 1912a). It might be well to place this paper in the historical context of the development of the idea of the transference from his first awarenesses of it as a resistance during the days he practiced hypnotic therapy (Freud, 1925). However, the first insight into the role of transference in psychoanalytic therapy dates from the letter of April 16, 1900, in which he wrote Fliess: "I am beginning to see that the apparent endlessness of the treatment is something of an inherent feature and is connected with the transference" (Freud, 1887–1902, p. 317). The historical context in which transference developed began with Freud's self-analysis and the investigation into the unconscious, just as the publication of *The Interpretation of Dreams* in 1900 ushered in the period of id psychology. The case of Dora (Freud, 1905d), characterized by Freud's technical difficulties with the resistance features of her transference neurosis, must be considered as the paradigmatic case history of the development of the transference as a clinical concept.

The paper under discussion, "The Dynamics of Transference" (Freud, 1912a), has a subsidiary historical meaning for technique, in that it marks the final and irrevocable break with Freud's last loyalty to the disguised infantile seduction trauma of the cathartic period. Here he finally understood that infantile sexual conflicts can be meaningfully recovered and worked through by the patient only in the transference and not out of any memorial reconstruction of the original infantile psychosexual conflict. Striking his colors and last loyalties to a technique of intellectual reconstruction, Freud unequivocally set the arena for every analysis, in which finally every conflict is "played out in the phenomena of the transference" (Freud, 1912a, p. 108).

After comparing the manifestations of transference in psychoanalysis with those in ordinary medical situations, Freud dealt with the technical paradox that transference is both indispensable to progress in the analysis and at the same time the greatest of its resistances. Transference was particularly shown to be in the service of resistance when the analysis came to deal with the more conflictual contexts of the unconscious derivatives of sexuality and aggression.

Two statements of far-ranging importance and application were made in the paper. The first was the controversial idea that all positive feelings—of sympathy, friendship, confidence, and trust—are derived from sexual drives, no matter to what degree their aims might be deflected or altered:

"Originally we knew only sexual objects" (Freud, 1912a, p. 105). Freud was returning to the idea of sublimation—an idea he credited to Fliess—and which would be more fully dealt with in the "Metapsychological Papers" (Freud, 1915–1917). Here, sublimation was equated with aim inhibition and not with a change in the modality of conflictual energies. As such, his statement is often read out of historical context in the direct techniques of a variety of "wild" psychoanalysis, for not to assume the fact of autonomous ego nuclei in the formation of character, and a nonconflictual hierarchy of ego (and self) interests,[1] is to bring about interminable analyses in which the transference becomes an impassable resistance in the face of an infinite series of interpretations.

Freud noted that the emerging unconscious materials during treatment often shared features with the primary process he had described in *The Interpretation of Dreams* (Freud, 1900) and later in "Formulations on the Two Principles of Mental Functioning" (Freud, 1911a). Instead of simply recalling the repressed memories and their intrinsic conflictual drive wishes, the patient tries to repeat them in action, with thought and behavior being as one at that level. Although Freud does not say it explicitly, this transference resistance can take two forms. It can be "acted out" with an auxiliary transference figure away from the analysis, in which the transference often becomes split with negative and positive aspects becoming distributed extramurally, with their subsequent loss to the working through; in the second form, the transference resistance may become "acted in" the analytic situation proper, a circumstance that seriously challenges not only technique but also the analyst's ability to analyze in himself the demands such "acting in" may make upon countertransference and counterfeeling. Ferenczi, in particular, did not appreciate this variety of transference resistance, for he did not see that his "active" techniques caused the transference to be realized nondiscursively and nonconceptually by a fostering of an "acting in" of the transference, in the mistaken belief that the transference was essentially an extralogical affective experience, to be recovered in an act rather than a reflective insight in the process of working through. In the end, Ferenczi's neocathartic experiments would lead to the straining of his ties with Freud. Ferenczi has left a heritage of a burgeoning host of neoromantic intuitive psychotherapies whose techniques are based on faith in affect as a form of cognition (Coltrera, 1962, 1965).

[1] The characteristic narcissistic devices used in any object relationship, by which we assure a persisting source of "nutriment stimulus" necessary for the maintenance of the integrity of psychic structure, would be such an ego interest.

The dissensions in the movement in 1912—those with Jung, Adler, Stekel, and their followers—strengthened Freud's resolution to give extensive and formal training in his methods, feeling strongly that the dissensions were largely due to the failure to adhere to the current theories of technique. Yet, he still felt that a systematic and definitive exposition of technique was neither possible nor desirable. Only general principles could be put down; their applications had to be left to practice and experience.

Freud essayed to approximate these principles in a special series of four papers of the projected six, published between 1912 and 1915 under the general title of "Recommendations to Physicians Practicing Psychoanalysis."

The first paper in the series took the title of the series, "Recommendations to Physicians Practicing Psychoanalysis" (Freud, 1912b); it dealt with the fundamental question of the mental state of the analyst during his work. Jones (1955, p. 234) tells us that Ferenczi had suggested the theme to Freud. As with the patient, the analyst's attention too must be "widened," in a passive-receptive manner, to effect the "evenly hovering attention" necessary for the work done by the analyst.

In our present-day ego psychology, in which consciousness is considered a function of the ego, the ability of the analyst to effect and accept the role of hovering attention might be determined in a large part by a primary ego autonomy in the cognitive control of scanning and, more broadly, in terms of the autonomies of a cognitive style, which enter into a talent for tolerating ambiguity. In the male analyst, the ability will also be a genetic function of a successful aim-reversal at the close of the phallic period, which results in a full working through of the passive aims of his drives in analysis. In some analysts, activity may represent a countertransference difficulty to be passive rather than a commitment of technique.

Freud warned that no more attention should be paid to one piece of the material than to another; the material must be allowed to develop and prejudgment must be avoided. For the same reason the analyst should take no notes during the analysis either for therapeutic or scientific purposes, nor should the patient be allowed to make notes nor to prepare material beforehand. Freud's extraordinary autonomous gift in memory ability no doubt played a role in the rule prohibiting note-taking. Freud himself was able to recall all the separate analytic hours of the day and write them down at the end of the day. Spontaneity, a complement of the patient's free associations, was to be the keynote of the analyst's attitude.

Again Freud stressed the personal analysis, continuing to equate the act of analyzing with the ability of the analyst to recognize his countertransference and counterfeelings and to be able to work them through.

Freud listed some of the mistakes an analyst can make, warning against the following. The analyst should not encourage the patient by describing part of his own inner life, for this would compromise the development and working through of the transference neurosis; the analyst should be a mirror to his patients. Using a famous image, Freud advised the analyst to imitate the surgeon's attitude during an operation by keeping his personal feelings in abeyance and by directing himself simply to the analytic material at hand. It was an unfortunate image, for surgery and the psychological processes of psychoanalysis are not of the same order, and its use has led to much confusion about the nature of the empathic ties between the analyst and his patient in which so much of the art of psychoanalysis lies. It has also resulted in creating a picture of a most compassionate man—reflect on his going so far as to collect funds for the destitute "Wolf Man" and his invalid wife during World War I—as one whose personality was actually one of cold and unfeeling scientific detachment. Freud warned against the danger of an excessive ambition for the patient, whether therapeutic or cultural. One cannot ask more of the patient than his capacity. This last mistake is a most common and pernicious one. It may be played out particularly in the countertransference "acting out" of the analyst's unresolved narcissistic object relationship, so that the patient may be treated literally as an extension of the analyst's unconscious sexual and aggressive drives. It is not uncommonly seen in the analysis of creative people and, patently, would be a problem specific for the training analysis.

The next paper, "On Beginning the Treatment" (Freud, 1913b), published in January and March 1913, dealt with the various problems that arise at the inception of therapy, such as what to say during the first interview, the arrangements about time and money, and the suitability of various cases. Employing his great metaphor of a game of chess, Freud apologized for not being able to be more specific about the whole course of analysis:

> Anyone who hopes to learn the noble game of chess from books will soon discover that only the opening and end-games admit of an exhaustive systematic presentation and that the infinite variety of moves which develop after the opening defy any description. This gap in instruction can only be filled by a diligent study of games fought out by masters. The rules which can be laid down for the practice of psychoanalytic treatment are subject to similar limitations (Freud, 1913b, p. 123).

Therefore, it is of the essence that all rules be unequally applied.

It was Freud's custom to accept a new patient for a trial period of several weeks, during which the patient followed the analytic rules and the analyst made no interpretations. This was done not only to test suitability but to force out into the open any psychotic process masked as a neurosis. Freud applied rigorous standards to his work, for although as a psychiatrist he could make mistakes, as an analyst mistakes would bring discredit on the method. He advised against lengthy discussion before beginning treatment, as it would jeopardize the development of a true transference neurosis. He warned against the patient who postpones beginning and pointed out that if an analyst ventured to treat the children or wife of a friend he would have to reconcile himself to the loss of that friendship. Several comments were made on the length of psychoanalysis and the question of the fee. He had seen a few patients for over ten years daily for no fee, and he enumerated the difficulties entailed in this practice. Psychoanalysis is a long affair, not only because of the inherent difficulty of the neurotic process itself, but also because of the timelessness of the unconscious and the slowness of deep changes. Further, it is unreasonable to ask for a selective analysis of certain symptoms while leaving others alone. Taking up the question of the ritual of the couch as against sitting up, he related that in the early days it was especially humiliating to American patients, dating the ceremony to the days of hypnosis and to his own personal dislike for being stared at for long periods of time. However, these are extrinsic sides to the fact that lying on the couch facilitates free rein of thought. The reclining position prevents the patient from "reading" the face of the analyst and from thus impairing the development of the transference. Great stress was laid on adherence to the "basic rule" of free association, with the patient free to choose the starting material. Freud closed with the complaint to be handed down in time, that he was helpless with the patient's relatives and that their hostility and dissatisfaction were to be expected and dealt with in the analysis.

"Recollecting, Repeating and Working Through" (Freud, 1914d), published in December 1914, is the most difficult and sophisticated paper of the series, portending more of what was to come in the rationale of technique. Freud directed himself to the struggle of keeping the recapitulation and resolution of the regressive conflicts of the transference neurosis within the continuing work of the analysis—a "working through"—to be defined within an entire range of metapsychological contexts of repetitive recollections of the original infantile psychosexual (and aggressive) conflicts *recovered* within the transference and turned over to the synthetic and integrative ego work of resolution of the heretofore repressed conflicts. Technically, he advised that the serious resistance of "acting out" the transference in extramural behavior to the working through of the analysis proper would best be handled by referring it back by direct interpretation into the conflictual context of the transference proper, where a measure of control could be exercised. Technically, then, Freud regarded the transference "acting out" behavior as a species of negative transference to be kept on a tight tether for the sake of the ongoing work of the analysis, a resistance to be given short shrift by a prompt interpretation—and/or confrontation—which would bring it back within the confines of the transference proper. Apart from the obstacles produced by resistance, the "working through," insofar as it represents the synthetic and integrative work of the ego done upon the numerous metapsychological levels, subsumed in the overdetermined immediacy of the psychic event, must develop over a period in time. In effect, it was the extension in time of the phenomenon of catharsis. A partial explanation is here offered for the length of psychoanalysis, abetted by the very "timelessness" implicit in the nature of the unconscious. Here is the essential paradox of the psychoanalytic process and the crux of the modern existential critique of classical psychoanalysis, that the "working through" of the multiple levels of the psychic event occurs as an extended sequence in time, being of a qualitatively differing order from the actuality of the psychic event, which is of the order of an over-determined ambiguous immediacy in time (Coltrera, 1962). The rationale of Freud's technique, especially as represented in the necessary process of working through, is based on an ontological wager Freud made in giving up the cathartic method for psychoanalysis proper, namely, that man is the only animal who is capable of a reflective consciousness made up of moieties of overdetermined psychic immediacies, which he binds in time by granting them meaning as a psychological continuum of contexts and meanings. The genetic point of view is based on the phenomenological continuity of time as a series of before-and-after events. If man is then a time-binding and symbol-making animal capable of a reflective act of consciousness, then "working through" is phenomenologically more representative of man's psychological nature than an existential "acting in," which is "known" as an extralogical affective cognition apart from the reflective work of the ego. Further, to restrict man's psychological nature to a sum of separate existential psychic immediacies leaves us, in the end, with an associationist view of man as a simple sum of his parts—his psychic events and processes. Any associationist assumption about the psychic event must founder on the intrinsic conjoined nature of the psychobiological system whose effect is always greater than the sum of its parts (Coltrera, 1965).

Freud believed that the last paper of the series, "Observations on Transference-Love" (Freud, 1915a), published in January 1915, was his best.

As early as Breuer's occasion of retreat engendered by the false pregnancy of Anna O., Freud recognized that the analysis must utilize the intense processes of transference love as a naturalistic phenomenon of a humanistic value. He viewed it as a kind of falling in love and avowed that the reality of the patient's feeling cannot be denied. Transference love must be worked through for its infantile magical determinants, allowed to run its course in the service of the analysis, and at the end be resolved as respect and/or affection for the analyst as a real person. Needless to say, reluctance to resolve the transference love would constitute a resistance to terminating the analysis and, it might be pointed out, not always only on the part of the patient, for the termination is also a leave-taking for the analyst. The latter works through in himself a counterfeeling that may impinge upon a countertransference neurosis activated, in some cases, by the termination.

Upset by the outbreak of World War I, Freud wrote Karl Abraham that he had completed the two last papers of the group concerned with technique.

On September 28, 1918, Freud spoke before the psychoanalytic congress at Budapest, the first since the one at Nuremberg in 1910. Entitled "Lines of Advance in Psychoanalytic Therapy" (Freud, 1919), the paper begins with a justification of the use of the word "analysis" as analogous with chemical analysis. Freud's old pre-1895 associationist bias—to Herbart, not to the English associationists—is evidenced in his lingering inclination to consider highly complicated psychic productions as a simple sum of their component "elements." However, Freud's intent must always be read in the context of his usage, and it is clear that he is in the mainstream of biological thought in always considering the synthesis of such elements as constituting a totality of effect greater than any sum of its parts.

It is crucial for an understanding of the development of technique in Freud's thought to understand that his analogical uses of analysis cannot be extrapolated into a simple mechanistic model. If this were so, then "analysis" should simply reduce itself to a reconstructive recapitulation of the component elements of a behavior apart from any considerations of resistance and transference. However, the history of the psychoanalytic idea and its techniques shows that Freud was forced empirically to give up any hope for a reconstructive "analyzing" of behavior as a sum of its present and past component parts. Freud's passage through a phase of intellectual reconstruction led him to his insights into transference and resistance as being the definitive components of the clinical psychoanalytic process. "Analysis" is an analogy, not a reductionist program for technique.

Freud then turned, in "Lines of Advance in Psychoanalytic Therapy" (Freud, 1919), to Ferenczi's suggestion that it was time to go beyond the more passive techniques of psychoanalysis, which had replaced hypnotic suggestion, toward various forms of activity. Asserting that privation, which generated neuroses, had to be continued in the analysis as a stimulus to a motivation for recovery, Freud issued warnings against the "active" analysis. Privation was not necessary in the sphere of sexuality, but specific privations might be chosen according to the individual's needs and the particular features of the analysis at each stage. Great improvements were often followed by a search for a gratification, which in itself would become a resistance by doing away with the goad privation supplies. Freud observed pessimistically that an unhappy marriage and physical disease were the commonest ways of keeping a neurosis alive, for both have satisfied the need to suffer and the self-punishment demanded by the repressions. Contained in this technical paradox is a partial explanation of why a successful beginning to an analysis may cause the patient to get "sicker," with the appearance of symptoms from the basic neurosis heretofore defended against by a neurotic life-situation or attitude, now to be seen, and given up, in the first workings through of the analysis. Freud also warned against the many ways by which a patient may be indulged within the transference situation.

A very special technical critique was directed against the tendency of the Swiss analysts to guide their patients' lives in particular directions, to instruct them in the aims of life, and induce them to adopt the analyst's personality as a model. In the same vein, Freud objected to Putnam's attempt to foist a particular philosophy on his patients.

Freud suggested several other forms of activity. At a certain point in the analysis phobic patients were urged to endure the anxiety evoked by the dreaded situation rather than wait until the final resolution of the symptom appeared in the analysis. In certain severe obsessional neuroses a change of technique is called for, in which the analyst allows himself to become part of the obsessive tendency and then actively interprets the expanded transference situation.

"Fausse Reconnaissance (Déjà Raconté) in Psychoanalytic Treatment" (Freud, 1914a) is a short paper in which clinical examples of *déjà raconté* analogous to *déjà vu* are described. In such instances the patient falsely believes he has already related something to the analyst. What the patient is really referring to is that an intention to do so has been strong, but has been resisted, whereupon he confuses the intention with having actually related it to the analyst. When the patient says about some unconscious material that he has known it all along, the analysis is complete; some part of the patient's mind had indeed known it all along.

It may be said that beyond the deliberately unsystematized elaborations contained in the six papers on technique between 1912 and 1918—which in themselves approximate the body of technique as we know it today—Freud would only make a few more explicit contributions in the next twenty years, such as a discussion of the "active" methods of analysis at the Budapest Congress in 1918, a few practical elaborations on dream analysis in 1923, several references in the case histories, particularly to the case of the "Wolf Man" (Freud, 1918), which is contemporary with six papers on technique, and an extensive statement on principles set down in Lectures XXVII and XXVIII in the *Introductory Lectures on Psycho-Analysis* (Freud, 1916–1917, pp. 257–285) in 1916 and 1917. Freud did not return to problems of technique until 1937, in "Analysis Terminable and Interminable" (Freud, 1937a) and "Constructions in Analysis" (Freud, 1937b). And these are not, in truth, reconsiderations of his basic technique, but are more in the nature of a "last hurrah" in the voice of the new ego psychology upon which the "master" had closed out his life.

The essential principles of psychoanalytic technique had thus been laid down in substance before 1920. Freud had advanced from hypnosis and the cathartic method to an increasing awareness of the necessity of allowing free rein to the processes in human beings, which would most facilitate a widening of the field of consciousness ultimately necessary to self-mastery and a liberation of the capacity to enjoy life within the framework of sound object relationships. From a literal emphasis upon the revival of memories of traumatic events, he had arrived at the realization that a recapitulation of the personal history of his patients could be achieved only through the instrumentality of the transference by means of the resolution of resistances. Beyond that point, developments in ego psychology were to open up possibilities for "the widening scope of psychoanalysis."

REFERENCES

[Note: S.E. refers to *The Standard Edition of the complete psychological works of Sigmund Freud* (London: Hogarth Press).]

BREUER, J., and FREUD, S. *Studies on hysteria* (1895). S.E., Vol. 2. (Also published by Basic Books, New York, 1957.)

COLTRERA, J. T. Psychoanalysis and existentialism. *Journal of the American Psychoanalytic Association,* 1962, 10, 166–215.

COLTRERA, J. T. On the creation of beauty and thought: the unique as vicissitude. *Journal of the American Psychoanalytic Association,* 1965, 13, 634–703.

FERENCZI, S., and RANK, O. *The development of psychoanalysis* (1924). New York and Washington: Nervous and Mental Disease Publishing Co., 1925.

FREUD, S. *The origins of psycho-analysis: letters to Wilhelm Fliess, drafts and notes: 1887–1902.* Marie Bonaparte, Anna Freud, and E. Kris (Eds.) Trans. by E. Mosbacher and J. Strachey. New York: Basic Books, 1954.

FREUD, S. *On aphasia, a critical study* (1891). New York: International Universities Press, 1953.

FREUD, S. The neuro-psychoses of defence (1894). S.E., Vol. 3, pp. 45–61.

FREUD, S. Heredity and the aetiology of the neuroses (1896). S.E., Vol. 3, pp. 141–156.

FREUD, S. Sexuality in the aetiology of the neuroses (1898). S.E., Vol. 3, pp. 263–268.

FREUD, S. Screen memories (1899). S.E., Vol. 3, pp. 303–322.

FREUD, S. *The interpretation of dreams* (1900). S.E., Vols. 4–5. (Also published by Basic Books, New York, 1955.)

FREUD, S. Freud's psycho-analytic procedure (1904). S.E., Vol. 7, pp. 249–256.

FREUD, S. *On psychotherapy* (1905). S.E., Vol. 7, pp. 257–270. (a)

FREUD, S. Psychical treatment (1905). S.E., Vol. 7, pp. 283–304. (b)

FREUD, S. *Three essays on the theory of sexuality* (1905). S.E., Vol. 7, pp. 130–245. (c) (Also published by Basic Books, New York, 1962.)

FREUD, S. Fragment of an analysis of a case of hysteria (1905). S.E., Vol. 7, pp. 3–124. (d)

FREUD, S. Analysis of a phobia in a five-year-old boy (1909). S.E., Vol. 10, pp. 5–149. (a)

FREUD, S. Notes upon a case of obsessional neurosis (1909). S.E., Vol. 10, pp. 153–220. (b)

FREUD, S. Five lectures on psychoanalysis (1910). S.E., Vol. 11, pp. 3–58. (a)

FREUD, S. The future prospects of psycho-analytic therapy (1910). S.E., Vol. 11, pp. 139–152. (b)

FREUD, S. "Wild" psychoanalysis (1910). S.E., Vol. 11, pp. 219–230. (c)

FREUD, S. Formulations on the two principles of mental functioning (1911). S.E., Vol. 12, pp. 218–226. (a)

FREUD, S. The handling of dream-interpretation in psycho-analysis (1911). S.E., Vol. 12, pp. 89–96. (b)

FREUD, S. The dynamics of transference (1912). S.E., Vol. 12, pp. 97–108. (a)

FREUD, S. Recommendations to physicians practicing psychoanalysis (1912). S.E., Vol. 12, pp. 109–120. (b)

FREUD, S. An evidential dream (1913). S.E., Vol. 12, pp. 267–277. (a)

FREUD, S. On beginning the treatment (1913). S.E., Vol. 12, pp. 121–144. (b)

FREUD, S. The occurrence in dreams of material from fairy tales (1913). S.E., Vol. 12, pp. 279–287. (c)

FREUD, S. On psychoanalysis (1913). S.E., Vol. 12, pp. 205–211. (d)

FREUD, S. Fausse reconnaissance (déjà raconté) in psychoanalytic treatment (1914). S.E., Vol. 13, pp. 201–207. (a)

FREUD, S. On narcissism: an introduction (1914). S.E., Vol. 14, pp. 73–102. (b)

FREUD, S. *On the history of the psycho-analytic movement* (1914). S.E., Vol. 14, pp. 7–66. (c)

FREUD, S Recollecting, repeating and working through (1914). S.E., Vol. 12, pp. 145–156. (d)

FREUD, S. Observations on transference-love (1915). S.E., Vol. 12, pp. 157–171. (a)

FREUD, S. Instincts and their vicissitudes (1915). S.E., Vol. 14, pp. 117–140. (b)

FREUD, S. Repression (1915). S.E., Vol. 14, pp. 146–158. (c)

FREUD, S. The unconscious (1915). S.E., Vol. 14, pp. 166–215. (d)

FREUD, S. *Introductory lectures on psycho-analysis* (1916–1917). S.E., Vols. 15–16.

FREUD, S. A metapsychological supplement to the theory of dreams (1917). S.E., Vol. 14, pp. 222–235. (a)

FREUD, S. Mourning and melancholia (1917). S.E., Vol. 14, pp. 243–258. (b)

FREUD, S. From the history of an infantile neurosis (1918). S.E., Vol. 17, pp. 7–122.

FREUD, S. Lines of advance in psychoanalytic therapy (1919). S.E., Vol. 17, pp. 157–168.

FREUD, S. The psychogenesis of a case of homosexuality in a woman (1920). S.E., Vol. 18, pp. 147–172. (a)

FREUD, S. A note on the prehistory of the technique of analysis (1920). S.E., Vol. 18, pp. 263–265. (b)

FREUD, S. *Beyond the pleasure principle* (1920). S.E., Vol. 18, pp. 1–64. (c)

FREUD, S. Psycho-analysis (1923). S.E., Vol. 19, pp. 235–254. (a)

FREUD, S. *The ego and the id* (1923). S.E., Vol. 19, pp. 12–66. (b)

FREUD, S. Remarks on the theory and practice of dream interpretation (1923). S.E., Vol. 19, pp. 109–124. (c)

FREUD, S. An autobiographical study (1925). S.E., Vol. 20, pp. 3–74.

FREUD, S. Analysis terminable and interminable (1937). S.E., Vol. 23, pp. 216–253. (a)

FREUD, S. Constructions in analysis (1937). S.E., Vol. 23, pp. 257–269. (b)

HEISENBERG, W. *Physics and philosophy*. New York: Harper, 1958.

JONES, E. *The life and works of Sigmund Freud*. Vol. 1. New York: Basic Books, 1953.

JONES, E. *The life and works of Sigmund Freud*. Vol. 2. New York: Basic Books, 1955.

LEWIN, B. D. Phobic symptoms and dream interpretation. *Psychoanalytic Quarterly*, 1952, **21**, 295–322.

3

LATER DEVELOPMENTS IN FREUD'S TECHNIQUE (1920–1939)

Samuel D. Lipton

Certain difficulties arise in describing analytic technique. To begin with, it has an expedient quality because the difficulties encountered in each case are unique and unpredictable, except in general terms. Although one can be certain that resistance will be encountered, one cannot predict its precise form, and therefore it must be dealt with on the basis of principle rather than by resorting to predetermined technical expedients. It is as if one set out to describe the technique of an appendectomy and described the preoperative preparation, the surgical approach, the possible anatomical anomalies, and the closure, and then added an entirely new dimension. The patient, hypothetically conscious, now changes his mind, objects to the procedure, insists on shaking hands, or concludes that his judgment about the cost of the procedure was deficient and that he will have to stop. Returning to analysis, once the analytic situation is established the analyst is guided by its purpose, the reconstruction of the past or the expansion of the ego, and cannot expect that any technical guide will serve in every contingency.

In addition to this expedient quality, the technique also has a spontaneous quality. Again, once the analytic situation is established, there is a natural quality to the analytic dialogue, which can be jeopardized by preoccupation with correct technique. What Freud sometimes referred to as the positive transference, which is now more often referred to as the realistic relationship, demands a stable but spontaneous response from the analyst. Granting that the analytic dialogue is not a conversation or a discussion but rather a unique combination of free association on the patient's part and free-floating attention and interpretation on the analyst's part, along with an increment of discussion, it still follows that the analyst's attitude is both natural and dependable. A critique of the technique necessarily has a retrospective quality, for it is often only after the fact that the analyst can correctly evaluate his technique.

A third difficulty lies in the relation of theory to technique. It is a relatively simple matter to describe technique in explicit terms, but it is very difficult to evaluate the technical repercussion of a theoretical increment. For example, does the analyst who believes that aggression is one of the two fundamental instincts deal with the clinical aspects of aggression differently than the one who does not? Would Freud have dealt with Dora's vengeful wishes, reported in 1901, in different words three decades later, after he had conceptualized the death instinct? There are no self-evident answers to such questions. To some extent the application of theory to technique is determined by individual factors and one's point of view. All that one can be certain of is that mastery of theory has connections with, and reflections in, technique. A familiarity with unconscious processes particularly leads to approaches and insights that cannot be reduced to technical rules.

This essay is based on a review of Freud's publications from 1920 until the end of his life, and this introduces an additional difficulty. The comprehension of Freud's writing is linked with one's own analytic experience. All that can be done is to make this factor explicit in the manner I have already done when I referred to my understanding of Freud's use of the term positive transference. Ideally I would also have wished to take explicitly into account not only what Freud wrote but also what many other analysts wrote about his work, but that has not been practicable. On the positive side I have had the advantage of using the Standard Edition, a true masterpiece of scholarship as well as an adequate translation. Freud was never pedantic, never a precisionist. He used metaphors and analogies freely, and the context in which they are used is of great import.

In his suggestions to contributors the editor of the present volume wrote that this is "not a book on theory." I have followed the spirit of this suggestion as well as I could. The plan of this chapter is a review of Freud's published works, with a running commentary, followed by a summary. In the review I have sharply, perhaps even ruthlessly, curtailed theoretical references and focused my attention on technique and particularly on explicit references that are scattered through theoretical essays and are often tangential to the purpose of the essays. The reader should be fully aware that this focus of interest precludes an adequate review of theoretical developments in themselves and that these are referred to only insofar as their technical applications seem evident.

Beyond the Pleasure Principle (1920a) is essentially a theoretical treatise devoted to metapsychological description, particularly the repetition compulsion and the death instinct. Freud early (pp. 19–20) makes a statement that explicitly adumbrates the later structural model. I think it is most interesting and significant that he introduces these ideas as concerning a shortcoming in *terminology.* He writes that we know from experience that the motives of the resistances, indeed the resistances themselves, are unconscious at first during the treatment. He has already stated that resistance arises from the higher strata of the mind that originally carried out repression. He now states we shall "*avoid a lack of clarity*" if we make our contrast not between the conscious and the unconscious but between the coherent ego and the repressed, adding that much of the ego is unconscious. He now states that when we replace a purely descriptive terminology with one that is systematic or dynamic, we can say that resistance arises from the ego and that the compulsion to repeat comes from the repressed.

I have stressed this passage because it lucidly indicates that Freud did not construe the introduction of the idea that resistances came from the unconscious ego as necessitating a technical revision. The technical management of resistance hinged on the recognition that it was unconscious, not which system it belonged to. Descriptively, the work of the analyst consists of making the unconscious conscious in any case.

In the third chapter of this work, Freud turns his attention to technical problems directly. He states that, at first, in the development of analysis, the analyst could do no more than discover the unconscious material that was concealed from the patient, put it together, and communicate it to him at the right moment. Incidentally, Freud's phrase, "at the right moment," indicates a recognition of resistance, even in the early phase he refers to. He also states that since this communication in itself did not solve the therapeutic problem, a further aim became evident: to oblige the patient to confirm the analyst's construction from his own memory. In that effort the chief emphasis lay on identifying the patient's resistances as quickly as possible to induce him, by suggestion operating as transference, to abandon them. Freud places the term transference in half-quotation marks, implying that he means the actual relationship to the analyst, and implies, I think, that persuasion had a place at this point.

However, Freud continues, it became clear that the aim of making the unconscious conscious was not completely attainable by that method. The patient could not remember all that was repressed and indeed might not be able to remember precisely the essential part. He therefore could not acquire a sense of conviction of the correctness of a construction that had been communicated to him. Freud implies that the necessity of the sense of conviction. In order to reach and acquire conviction about repressed material, it is necessary to use that part that the patient had to repeat as if it were a contemporary experience. These reproductions of past experience have some element of infantile sexual life as their subject and are acted out in the sphere of transference, that is, in the patient's relationship to the analyst. At this stage the earlier neurosis has been replaced by a transference neurosis. Here, Freud refers to the concept of transference as it relates to the irrational element of the relationship.

The analyst tries to keep the transference neurosis within the narrowest possible limits by forcing as much as possible into the channel of memory and by allowing as little as possible to emerge as repetition. I would add that an important connotation is that the method of limiting the intensity of the transference neurosis is interpretation and construction, facilitating recollection. This connotation is supported by his following assertion that the ratio of what is remembered to what is reproduced varies from case to case and that the analyst cannot spare the patient this portion of the treatment. If, with the inevitable increment of re-experiencing, the patient can retain sufficient detachment to recognize, ultimately, that what appears at the moment to be reality, is in fact a reflection of the past, the patient's sense of conviction is won together with the therapeutic success that is dependent on it.

I have already cited Freud's statement that resistances arise from the ego. In maintaining its resistance the ego follows the pleasure principle. The analyst tries to secure the tolerance of unpleasure by appealing to the reality principle.

Freud's purpose in interpolating the technical section was to lead to his point that the tendency toward repetition led beyond the repetition of experiences that could ever have been pleasurable. My own purpose was to demonstrate from his writing that, at the outset of this period, the principles of his technique were the same as they had been, once he had discovered what we now conceptualize as the analytic situation as a method of investigating and reconstructing those pathogenic experiences of the past that had remained operative in the disguise of neurosis. I do not think any subsequent work impeaches this proposition, but this idea will be defended in detail in the present review.

Freud states that patients contrive to feel scorned, to be treated coldly, to feel jealousy, or to produce a grand plan or gift in the place of the once-wished-for baby. A compulsion to repeat transcends the pleasure principle. We rarely see the compulsion to repeat in pure form, and the best examples of this compulsion are traumatic dreams. Particularly in the transference the compulsion to repeat is "drawn over by the ego to *its* side" in the interest of resistance. I think it follows that only the actual resistances, not the repetition compulsion, can become the subject of interpretation.

Developing his theoretical premise, Freud states that the repetition of dreams in the traumatic neurosis is not in the service of the pleasure principle but "is helping to carry out another task, which must be accomplished before the dominance of the pleasure principle can even begin." That task is to master the stimulus retrospectively by developing the anxiety whose omission was the cause of the traumatic neurosis. He had already explained how anxiety, by hypercathecting the receptive systems, protects against fright, which signifies a breach in the protective barrier against stimuli and results in trauma.

Now Freud introduces an idea of considerable technical importance. He states that, in addition to the dreams of the traumatic neurosis, the dreams during psychoanalysis that bring to memory the psychical traumas of childhood are also not so much in the service of the pleasure principle as they are in obedience to the repetition compulsion. Freud adds that the compulsion is supported by the wish to remember, which is encouraged by analysis. I would interpolate that Freud had already demonstrated in his case histories how the analyst can use dreams to reconstruct traumas. In such work the repetition compulsion is taken for granted, and the actual analytic work is concerned with the interpretation of events or motives of psychological importance and with filling in gaps in memory.

It is the task of the higher psychical systems, Freud writes, to bind the freely mobile energy of the system-Ucs. If this binding fails, a condition analogous to a traumatic neurosis arises. Until this energy is bound, the task of mastery takes precedence over the pleasure principle. Because the manifestations of the repetition compulsion have an urgent quality and because they can act in opposition to the pleasure principle, they give the appearance of a "demonic" force. Thus, a patient may insistently act in an infantile manner or may be disinclined to detach himself completely from the analyst at the conclusion of the analysis. The technical implication (I interpolate) is that the analyst must consistently relate himself to the hidden historical repetition, when confronted by these situations.

As far as I can understand it, Freud's concept of the death instinct as he develops it here is without direct technical implication.

In his introduction to *Group Psychology and the Analysis of the Ego* (1921) Freud makes some comments that are pertinent to the occasional misconception that psychoanalysis is concerned only with the individual in isolation and not with the reality he lives in. He points out that, from the very first, analysis was necessarily concerned with the relationship of the individual to persons important to him and, in that sense, analysis is a social as well as an individual psychology. From the standpoint of technique, I would add that this aspect of analysis does not imply direct interventions into the area of adaptation but essentially the recognition that the various object representations that emerge in the course of analysis have some degree of correspondence with reality.

In a footnote (p. 75) on Le Bon's conception of the unconscious, Freud makes the interesting comment that Le Bon's unconscious contains the most deeply buried features of the racial mind, "which as a matter of fact lie outside the scope of psychoanalysis." Then he adds that we "recognize . . . that the ego's nucleus, which comprises the 'archaic heritage' of the human mind, is unconscious, but in addition to this we distinguish the 'unconscious repressed,' which arose from a portion of that heritage." To recognize the existence of an unconscious part of the ego, which is not repressed, on the one hand, and to distinguish it from the repressed unconscious and to state, on the other hand, that this very recognized area is outside the scope of analysis seems paradoxical. Perhaps Freud meant that this area lay outside the scope of clinical technique, specifically that the sense of conviction essential to the therapeutic work would not be extended to the concept of the racial unconscious.

In his discussion of hypnosis Freud makes a comparison between some elements of the hypnotic situation and the analytic situation; the similarity is of minor but explicitly technical relevance. The hypnotic subject focuses his attention on boring stimuli while unconsciously he is preoccupied with the analyst. In analysis the patient sometimes becomes silent and then states that his only thoughts concern objects of no importance in the room. His unconscious thoughts are of the analyst himself and can be unearthed by explanation. In this note presumably Freud is using the term unconscious in the descriptive sense and, topographically, these ideas would be preconscious.

The theoretical exposition of this essay involves no changes in analytic technique, but there are further explanations of his advancing concepts of the structural model, which are of importance clinically. A distinction is made between identification in the ego and the replacement of the ego ideal by an object. (In this essay Freud is designating as the ego ideal what he was later to call the superego.) With the aid of the concept of the replacement of the ego ideal by an object, it became possible to understand extreme developments that sometimes occur in states of being in love in which the subject appears to be in bondage. In these states all the functions of the ego ideal are surrendered, so to speak, and left to the person who is the object of love. The subject remains intensely tied to and submissive to the other person. In identification within the ego, on the other hand, the actual object is given up to the extent to which the identification in the ego is effective.

When the individual ego ideal has been replaced by the representation of an object, it becomes possible to recognize the functions of the individual ego ideal, since they are notable by their absence. From the different conditions under which this replacement occurred, Freud found that there might occur excessive compliance, dominance of affects over judgment, regression in intellectual functioning, loss of initiative, and other similar characteristics. On this basis he attributed reality-testing to the ego ideal. In 1923 he was to retract his formulation and attribute it to the ego. However, it may be that whereas the recognition of reality can better be attributed to the ego, the validation of reality and a sense of conviction about it may be construed as being superego functions.

In "The Psychogenesis of a Case of Homosexuality in a Woman" (1920b), Freud states early in his discussion that "the ideal situation for analysis is when someone who is otherwise his own master is suffering from an inner conflict which he is unable to resolve alone, so that he brings his trouble to the analyst and begs for his help. The physician then works hand in hand with one portion of the pathologically divided personality, against the other party in the conflict." He goes on to discuss how regularly the wishes of relatives turn out to be in conflict with those of the patient as the analysis develops. In the case presented it was the parents who wanted analysis for the patient, who was not complaining of her homosexual attachment.

Another obstacle was that the girl "was not in any way ill," that is, she did not suffer or complain. Thus, the task did not consist of resolving a neurotic conflict but in converting one variety of genital conflict into another. This, Freud states, is difficult, and adds that what success he has had with homosexuals is in making access to the opposite sex possible. "After that it lay with him to choose whether he wished to abandon the path that is banned by society, and in some cases he has done so." He states that, in general it is no more promising a prospect to convert a fully developed homosexual into a heterosexual than would be the reverse, and that a favorable prognosis is to be envisioned only when the homosexual fixation is not strong or when there are considerable rudiments of a heterosexual object choice.

These comments of Freud are of basic importance in conceptualizing his technique, though they are by no means new developments. He clearly has the ultimate aim of promoting insight and as clearly views direct influence as outside the sphere of analysis. He remains neutral in regard to adaptation and considers his task finished when the maximum insight has been reached.

Freud writes that in a number of cases the analysis falls into two phases. In the first phase the analyst procures information, acquaints the patient with the premises and postulates of analysis, and unfolds to him the reconstruction of the genesis of his disorder as deduced from the material. In the second phase the patient works on the material, recollects what he can, and tries to repeat the rest. In this way he can confirm, supplement, and correct the analyst's inferences. Only during this second period does the patient acquire the convictions that make him independent of the authority of the analyst. Whereas the general idea is confirmatory rather than new in relation to technique, it is of interest in the light it throws on the place of intellectual work in Freud's technique.

In regard to prognosis Freud considered it favorable that the girl had not obtained genital satisfaction. He also thought it a favorable sign when initially she said frankly that she would cooperate in the treatment for the sake of her parents. With all his misgivings, Freud did undertake the analysis and continued it until he became convinced that the patient's powerful wish for revenge against the father would destroy the analysis with him. His conclusion finally was grounded on developments within the analytic situation itself and not on the preliminary doubts, which he had formulated on a theoretical basis. This is important in connection with the selection of patients.

On page 154, Freud writes a remarkable sentence: "The psychoanalyst customarily forgoes a thorough physical examination of his patients in certain cases." If the word "thorough" and the phrase "in certain cases" were to be eliminated, the unequivocal statement would be only expected. As it stands, it implies that in some cases a physical examination is done or that in many cases a cursory examination is carried out. I would construe it to refer to the psychoanalyst acting only as a diagnostician and, in the context, attempting to evaluate the degree of physical hermaphroditism, an unimportant point actually.

In the dynamics of the case Freud placed a great emphasis on defiance and revenge. The patient's initial resentment was crystallized by the birth of a brother when she was sixteen. With the revival of the Oedipus complex at puberty, this came as a bitter disappointment, and she then unconsciously identified with her father and took a mother-substitute as a love-object. When she realized how much this change could hurt her father, "she remained homosexual out of defiance against" him. She wanted her father to know of the homosexual relationship that horrified him because "of her keenest desire—namely, revenge."

Concerning the patient's serious suicide attempt, it is noteworthy that Freud's discussion makes no reference to the death instinct he had recently hypothesized. He cites the patient's explanation that she was in despair because the woman she loved had said she never wanted to see her again. To this, he adds, from the manner of the attempt, an unconscious wish to bear the child of her father, and, second, the unconscious wish to kill her father—and possibly also her mother—with whom she had identified. "For analysis has explained the enigma of suicide in the following way: probably no one finds the mental energy to kill himself unless, in the first place, in doing so he is at the same time killing an objeect with whom he has identified himself, and, in the second place, is turning against himself a death-wish which has been directed against someone else."

Turning to the recognition of the particular resistance that led Freud to terminate the analysis, he describes how, for example, a single powerful conviction like doubt can render all the analytic work useless. In this case he became convinced that the transference was dominated by revenge, displaced from her father. He decided that this would not be accessible to interpretation, since it would manifest itself in the detachment and aloofness that would nullify any intervention he could make. He therefore recommended that she be treated by a woman analyst. He considers the reason "obvious." I assume that he meant that the overwhelming negative transference might be attenuated if the analyst were female. I do not think he intended to convey any generalization about the sex of the analyst. This patient was not neurotic, and, in my opinion, the neurotic patient with a more stable ego is prone to establish transferences with greater independence of the sex of the analyst.

Freud detected that the intention to mislead him, conscious or preconscious, had entered into dreams that seemed to indicate that the patient hoped to be cured and looked forward to heterosexual life. He calls the dreams false or hypocritical. The intention to mislead had become connected with the unconscious wish to please the father and in this way created the "lying" dream.

Another point of technical interest is Freud's observation that moments of profound importance in erotic life can pass almost unnoticed. This patient had been unaware of significant precursors of her consuming attachment. Adults sometimes conclude what they thought was a casual love affair or passing attachment and only later recognize its intensity. Severe results may follow an abortion decided on without hesitation.

Freud notes that, whereas the retrospective analysis of a case may provide a convincing causal explanation, the reverse is not true. Prediction is not possible because we know only the quality and not the strength of etiological forces.

In the understanding of homosexuality it is important to distinguish object choice, the element that is usually given primary importance, from the sexual attitude of the subject. A man with characterologically feminine attributes, for example, may have no disturbance at all in object choice.

In two papers on telepathy (1922a, 1941a) there are few points of technical interest. Freud pointedly divorces telepathy from analytic work. "The analyst has his own province of work which he must not abandon: the unconscious element in mental life. If in the course of his work he were to be on watch for occult phenomena, he would be in danger of overlooking everything that more nearly concerned him" (1941a, p. 179). He remains open-minded about occult phenomena that may "force themselves on him." In the course of his discussion he makes the point that every psychic event that occurs during sleep should not be designated as a dream. Certain so-called dreams are nothing but night fantasies devoid of the hallmark of the dream, the dreamwork.

At another point Freud notes that recurrent dreams often turn out to be not identical. Details are changed or additions are made with the recurrences. In a further discussion of dreams and screen memories he refutes the importance of Silberer's "anagogic" interpretations. A comment about a delusion merits note: that it derives its strength and unassailable character from having a source in unconscious psychical reality.

In "Certain Neurotic Mechanisms in Jealousy, Paranoia, and Homosexuality" (1922b) Freud points out that it is insufficient to describe the behavior of paranoiacs by simply stating that they project on others what they do not want to recognize in themselves. It is true they do this, but there is more to it. They let themselves be guided by their knowledge of the unconscious and displace to the unconscious mind of others the attention they have withdrawn from their own. They thus become aware of clues, which they utilize to provide themselves with perceptual confirmation of the correctness of their ideas. I think it is most important to realize this in working with these patients. Freud writes they are not usually amenable to analytic investigation but that he was "nevertheless, by an intensive study of two paranoiacs," to discover something new to him. Evidently, the intensive study was in fact an attempt at treatment, despite his misgivings.

After reporting his finding that classical persecutory ideas can be present without finding belief or acceptance on the part of the patient and suggesting that it may be true that what we regard as new delusions in the outbreak of paranoia may have been in existence much earlier, he states that this fact may be an "important discovery," that is, that the qualitative factor, the mere presence of certain "neurotic formations," has less practical significance than the quantitative factor, which is the degree of cathexis these structures attract. This appears to be a point of central importance in diagnosis and selection of cases, since it implies that the mere presence of psychotic mechanisms cannot be taken as conclusive evidence of psychosis in an operational sense.

Freud's encyclopedia articles (1923a) offer valuable reformulations of analytic theory and technique and are especially noteworthy because they were written subsequent to the introduction of the death-instinct theory and just before the introduction of the structural model in its final form.

He designates the abandonment of hypnosis and the introduction of free association as the beginning of psychoanalysis, after pointing out that two discoveries made while practicing the earlier so-called cathartic procedure "have not been shaken by subsequent experience." These two discoveries were that hysterical symptoms have sense and meaning and that uncovering this unknown meaning is accompanied by the removal of the symptoms.

He states that "a strong belief in the strict determination of mental events" played a part in the choice of free association to replace hypnosis.

From that time on the fundamental technical rule, the requirement that the patient report his associations, has been maintained. The most advantageous complementary attitude of the analyst he designated as evenly suspended attention. His elaboration of these points does not diverge from earlier descriptions.

He maintains a distinction between the actual neuroses and the psychoneuroses. The former are caused by contemporary abuses in the patient's sexual life and could be removed if these were brought to an end. The psychoneuroses were caused by past traumas.

Explicitly writing on the development of technique, Freud stated that after the analyst's "curiosity" had been gratified by the elaboration of the technique of interpretation, interest turned to the most effective way of influencing the patient. He here evidently distinguishes knowledge gained to the satisfaction of the analyst from information that is of use to the patient. He states that it soon became clear that the task of the analyst was to acquaint the patient with the resistances (of which the patient was unaware) that emerged in the treatment, and to help him overcome them. The essential part of the process of cure lay in overcoming these resistances, and unless this was achieved no permanent mental change could be brought about. He adds that, with the recognition that the analyst's efforts should be directed upon the patient's resistance, analytic technique has attained a certainty and delicacy rivaling surgery. It is noteworthy that this emphasis on the analysis of resistances preceded the introduction of the structural model.

As a therapeutic procedure he considers the province of analysis above all to be the transference neuroses, hysteria, and the obsessional neuroses. Beyond these he includes all kinds of phobias, inhibitions, deformities of character, sexual perversions, and difficulties in erotic life. He considers "some kind of age-limit" necessary but does not specify it. He adds with a typically Freudian independence of traditional nosology that, since analysis requires the devotion of long and intense attention to the individual patient, "it would be uneconomical to squander such expenditure upon completely worthless persons who happen to be neurotic."

In contrasting analysis with suggestive psychotherapy, Freud states that in analysis the suggestive influence inevitably exercised by the physician is diverted to the task of overcoming the resistances. The aim of the treatment is to remove the patient's resistances and to pass his repressions in review, and thus to bring about the most far-reaching unification and strengthening of his ego, to enable him to save the mental energy he is expending upon internal conflicts, to make the best of him that his inherited capacities will allow, and so to make him as efficient and as capable of enjoyment as possible. He adds a negative comment, which I think is one of the most cogent statements on technique conceivable: *"The removal of the symptoms of the illness is not specifically aimed at, but is achieved, as it were, as a by-product if the analysis is properly carried through"* (italics mine—SDL). He concludes that the analyst respects the patient's individuality and is glad to avoid giving advice and instead arouse the patient's power of initiative.

Strachey designates *The Ego and the Id* (1923b) as the last of Freud's major theoretical works. He traces its origins all the way back to the "Project," as well as citing an unpublished paper in which Freud refers to the unconscious part of the ego. In his own preface Freud designates the monograph as a further development of lines of thought begun in *Beyond the Pleasure Principle*.

Freud writes that the distinctions between conscious, preconscious, and unconscious have proved inadequate and introduces the concept of a coherent organization of mental processes, the ego. Consciousness is attached to the ego, and the ego controls the discharge of excitation into the outer world. The ego is the source of the censorship of dreams, repression, and, in analysis, resistance. He therefore would derive neuroses no longer from a conflict between the conscious and unconscious but from a conflict between the ego and the repressed. The change is necessary once it is understood that the unconscious does not correspond to the repressed but that a part of the ego is unconscious. I interpolate the point made in *Beyond the Pleasure Principle* that this conception does not involve any fundamental change in technique, since the work of analysis is to make the unconscious conscious in any case. The broadening of the concept of unconscious can enhance the effectiveness of analytic work, but cannot alter its basic character.

Freud cautioned that, with these new concepts, we must beware of ignoring the central characteristic of consciousness, "for the property of being conscious or not is in the last resort our one beacon light in the darkness of depth-psychology." All our knowledge is invariably bound up with it, and we can know about the unconscious only by making it conscious. We must start from the perceiving surface, with sensations or feelings that are conscious from the start, or with thoughts that first became preconscious by becoming connected with word presentations and then becoming conscious. Here, as consistently subsequently, Freud continued to use the earlier description of mental qualities. Word presentations are residues of memories, he wrote. They were once perceptions, and any idea arising from within must once have been a perception if it is to become conscious. We make the repressed conscious by supplying the Pcs. intermediate links through the work of analysis. The interposition of word presentations allows the ego to convert internal thought processes into perceptions. The ego starts from the perceptual system, and for the ego, perception plays the part that in the id falls to instinct. Prior to this statement Freud introduced the concept of the id for what was previously the unconscious. He characterizes the ego in relation to the id as a man on horseback. In his subsequent writing, however, Freud on many occasions still used his original term, the unconscious.

Connected with his retention of the concept of the preconscious, now a part of the ego, Freud noted that subtle and difficult intellectual operations can be carried out preconsciously, as for example in sleep. (He had already pointed this out in *The Interpretation of Dreams*.)

Freud now discusses a differentiating grade in the ego, the ego ideal or superego, as he puts it here, and retracts his idea of two years before in "Group Psychology" that it be given the function of reality testing, stating that this belongs to the ego.

In discussing identification as the source of the ego, Freud points out that when a sexual object is given up identification results and that this may indeed be the only condition under which the ego gives up its objects. Of central and technical importance, I interpolate, is that an object relation is hidden behind an identification. The maintenance of an identification can serve as a resistance against the recovery in memory of an object relation of importance, and the analysis of such an identification can be a most important part of analytic work.

Freud writes that the first identifications are of lasting importance and that identifications with the parents are the basis of the superego. It represents not only the residue of object choices but reaction formations against them. Since much of the superego is unconscious, I think that the main technical expansion that results from its formulation is again a broadening of the concept of what is unconscious and a further opportunity to perfect interpretation. Integrated with this is a recognition of the function of the superego as the carrier of the conscience and moral demands as well as the often accentuated antagonism to impulses.

Continuing, Freud states that the ego is influenced by the instincts, Eros and the destructive instinct. The regular fusion of these instincts is indispensible. "Both kinds are active in every particle of living substance," he states, though defusion occurs. Among other comments Freud writes that for purposes of discharge the instinct of destruction is habitually brought into the service of Eros (p. 41), that when we trace instinctual derivatives they prove to come from Eros, and that the death instincts are mute. These comments and others have led me to conclude that Freud conceptualized the death instinct and its fusion and defusion with Eros as a theoretical addition, but he continued to adhere to the idea that the actual analytic work was mainly with the derivatives of the erotic instinct. I interpolate here a comment Freud made ten years after this work in the *New Introductory Lectures on Psycho-Analysis.* There, after a discussion of fusion and defusion and a statement that these concepts might lead to important investigations in the future, he wrote: "But these conceptions are still too new; no one has yet tried to apply them in our work" (p. 105).

Freud writes that the most powerful impediment to recovery, stronger than narcissistic inaccessibility, is an unconscious sense of guilt, which leads to a negative therapeutic reaction. One can attempt only to make it conscious. If it is the product of an identification, an old object relation can be uncovered. He states there may be a temptation to play the part of a savior but that this is opposed to the rules of analysis.

Concerning a mechanism that was to maintain his interest, and to which the name, disavowal, was to be given, Freud wrote, "The hysterical ego fends off a distressing perception with which criticisms of its superego threaten it, in the same way in which it is in the habit of fending off an unendurable object-cathexis—by an act of repression" (p. 51). He later differentiated the mechanism used against instinctual derivatives from that used against perceptions.

In "A Seventeenth Century Demonological Neurosis" (1923c) Freud makes some interesting technical points in his conclusion. He states that Haizmann, the subject, wanted simply to make his life secure. He tried to achieve this with his delusional or fantasied pact with the Devil at the cost of his salvation; and when this failed, he tried to achieve it by becoming a monk and giving up the possibilities of enjoyment in life. His neurosis appears to be a masquerade overlaying a serious, if commonplace, struggle for existence. This occurs not infrequently. A businessman threatened by financial catastrophe may develop a neurosis as a by-product and may conceal his worries about real life behind his symptoms. Treatment is unprofitable. Apart from this, the neurosis serves no useful purpose, since it uses up forces that would have been more profitably employed in dealing rationally with the dangerous situation. More often neurosis is more autonomous and more independent of the interests of self-preservation, and libidinal interests are more involved. In any case a dammed-up libido, which cannot be satisfied in reality, succeeds, with the help of a regression to old fixations, in finding discharge through the repressed unconscious. Of special technical importance is the ineffectiveness of treatment when the secondary gains of the neurosis are too great.

A pair of essays on the theory and practice of dream interpretation (1923d and 1925a) are of great technical value. Freud states that in interpretation one may elicit associations chronologically, start with some clear element or with spoken words, try to elicit the day residue, or let the dreamer proceed in his own way, particularly if he is experienced.

The *majority* of dreams in a difficult analysis are under a high pressure of resistance and are impossible to interpret adequately. Associations broaden rather than converge. When the resistance is not too high, the dream thoughts become clear as the associations converge. Clearly, Freud expects a certain intelligent expectancy in regard to their recognition. Even without high resistance a number of dreams are untranslatable. They represent free renderings of the latent dream thoughts and are like successful creative writing in which basic themes are extensively revised. They serve in treatment as an introduction to thoughts and memories without their own actual content coming into account.

Dreams from above and from below are distinguished. Those from below are provoked by a repressed wish, which has found a representation in the day residues. Those from above correspond to thoughts or intentions of waking life, which have been reinforced during the night by repressed material. Analysis disregards the unconscious ally and inserts the latent thoughts into the texture of waking thought.

Sometimes dream life and waking life become separated in analysis, and one dream takes off from another. More often they are interpolated into successive portions of waking thought.

Two phases of interpretation, translation and evaluation, should be kept separate. The value of a dream should not be overestimated. It is a thought like any other, granting the fact of the dreamwork. Analytic practice has sometimes placed too much importance on it. For example, dreams of recovery may mean nothing more than a wish to be well in order to avoid some unpleasant work of analysis. It is difficult to draw conclusions from a correctly translated dream. The meaning may have been reversed in a forgotten dream of the same night or a remembered one of the next. "The true state of the conflict can only be determined by taking into account all the indications, including those of waking life."

Both the manifest content and the latent thoughts may be influenced by suggestion, but the dreamwork is not. Sometimes confirmatory dreams occur subsequent to a reconstruction, and the question of suggestion arises there. Remembering is helpful, but it may not be available for a fantasy that was always unconscious. The answer lies ultimately in the internal consistency of the entire complex situation.

The only function of the dream is to preserve sleep. It is not meant to be a communication. If we can undo the dream's distortions we can overhear preconscious thought taking place in states of internal reflection, which could not have attracted consciousness to themselves in daytime.

Dream interpretation is part of the work of analysis and cannot be done in isolation. Outside of analysis, associations are still necessary. Without associations interpretation is unscientific virtuosity. In analysis we direct our attention to either the preconscious or unconscious content according to necessity.

It is not easy to decide if an interpretation is complete, that is, "whether further preconscious thoughts may have also found expression in the same dream" (p. 129). It seems clear that Freud considers the practical work of interpretation to be the recovery of latent thoughts. He adds that the latent thoughts may themselves be uncertain.

One is, of course, responsible for one's dreams just as one is responsible for one's id. It is up to the jurist to construct, for social purposes, a responsibility that is artificially limited to the metapsychological ego.

In his paper, "The Infantile Genital Organization of the Libido" (1923e), Freud wrote that a difficulty in the work of research in psychoanalysis is that despite decades of observation, features of general occurrence and situations that are characteristic can be overlooked. He had previously stated that the choice of an object characteristic of pubertal development had already been effected in childhood, but that the combination of component instincts and their subordination under the primacy of the genitals had been effected only very incompletely or not at all. Now he stated that he would not be satisfied with that statement, for even if a proper combination of component instincts under genital primacy had not been effected, interest in the genitals had acquired a dominating significance, which fell little short of that attained in maturity. However, this infantile genital organization differs from the genital organization of the adult in that for both sexes only one genital, the male one, comes into account. What is present, therefore, is a primacy not of the genital but of the phallus.

Freud goes on to describe the fact that the boy first disavows his impression of the absence of the penis in girls. From this point on, Freud refers repeatedly to disavowal in other papers. It is important to note that in other translations the same German word is translated as denial. The editors of the Standard Edition chose disavowal for Freud's *Verleugnung* and negation for *Verneinung*. He points out that the significance of the castration complex can only be rightly appreciated if its origin in the phase of phallic primacy is also taken into account.

For a long time the child thinks that women he respects, including his mother, have a penis. Not until he understands that only women give birth to babies does he realize they do not have penises. These and other ideas have indirect importance in technique, since they lead to the understanding of otherwise puzzling material. It is also the type of information that can be confirmed in analytic work but is difficult or impossible to become convinced of otherwise.

Soon after publishing *The Ego and the Id* Freud published, in "Neurosis and Psychosis" (1924a), a brief application of the structural model to the differentiation between neurosis and psychosis. He suggested that the most important genetic distinction between a neurosis and a psychosis is that neurosis is the result of a conflict between the ego and its id, whereas psychosis is the analogous outcome of a similar disturbance in the relations between the ego and the external world.

In regard to the genesis of delusions he states that "a fair number of analyses" have taught us that a "delusion is found applied like a patch over the place where originally a rent had appeared in the ego's relation to the external world" and adds that this precondition of a conflict is not much more noticeable to us because of the attempts at self-healing or reconstruction. I quote the statement of the "fair number of analyses" because it is one of the clues that indicates Freud's acceptance of analytic work with psychotic patients despite his consistent pessimism. The other quotation is of interest in connection with his later statement in "Constructions in Analysis" (1937b) in which he indicates that this "patch" itself is by no means determined at random but has its own specific genesis, which includes an element of truth.

Freud states that the etiology of neurosis and psychosis is always the same, the frustration of a childhood wish, one of those which remains "forever undefeated" and which are deeply rooted in "our phylogenetically determined organization." This frustration is external, granting that in the individual case what was originally external may have been taken over by the superego.

He suggests that transference neuroses correspond to a conflict between the ego and the id; narcissistic neuroses to a conflict between the ego and superego; and psychosis to a conflict between the ego and the external world. Thus, neuroses and psychoses originate in the ego's conflicts with its various ruling agencies.

Furthermore, there are two factors that will determine whether such ubiquitous conflicts will result in illness. One is the economic factor, that is, the magnitudes of the trends involved. The other is the possibility that the ego can avoid a rupture in any direction by deforming itself or by effecting a cleavage or division within itself. Later on Freud expanded this view in his papers on "Splitting of the Ego in the Process of Defence" (1940b) and the *Outline* (1940a). Freud wrote, "In this way the inconsistencies, eccentricities and follies of men would appear in a similar light to their sexual perversions, through the acceptance of which they spare themselves repressions." It seems to me that he thus classifies these peculiarities as the minute vestiges of a break with reality and thus genetically related to the psychoses; that they might be conceptualized as psychotic character traits. I see no objection to such a view except the traditional ominous connotation of the term, psychosis, and the corresponding reluctance to consider the possibility that psychotic disorders, albeit minor ones, are as common as neurotic ones.

In conclusion, Freud states that the mechanism analogous to repression by which the ego detaches itself from the external world must, like repression, constitute a wihthdrawal of cathexis by the ego. He does not actually use the term, disavowal, though he seems to have it in mind.

Soon after this paper was published, Freud expanded his description to take into account the disturbance in the relation to reality that occurs in neurosis as well as in psychosis (1924b). He points out that the sharp contrast between neurosis and psychosis exists only at the beginning of the neurosis. It is only then that the ego in the service of reality sets about the repression of the instinctual impulse. This is not yet the neurosis that consists not of this initial repression, which may be entirely successful although at some expense to the ego, but is the failure of repression and the return of the repressed. The loosening of the relation to reality occurs as a consequence of this *second* step, and the loss of reality affects precisely that piece of reality as a result of whose demands the instinctual repression had occurred.

In psychosis also there might be two steps, though different agencies are involved. The first step would drag the ego away, not from the id, but from reality; the second step would try to re-establish the ego's relations to reality at the expense of the id, rather than to the id at the cost of sacrificing an element of reality. In fact, there is a second step in the psychosis, which is intended to make good the loss of reality, but it does not occur at the expense of a restriction of the id—as happens in neurosis at the expense of the relation to reality—but by the creation of a new reality, which no longer raises the objections of the old one that had been given us. The second step in the psychoses is supported by the power of the id and in that way is similar to the second step in neuroses; their difference is far greater in their introductory reaction than in the steps that follow.

Returning to the issue of disavowal, Freud confined here this mechanism to the psychoses, but later on when he came to describe more fully the split in the ego, he did not continue to confine it so. Here he states that neurosis does not disavow reality but merely ignores it, whereas psychosis disavows it and tries to replace it. This statement refers to the initial step in which the activity of the ego in neurosis is against the id, whereas in psychosis it is against reality. Freud wrote that normality combines features of both reactions in that it disavows reality as little as does neurosis and then attempts to remodel reality as does psychosis. However, normal remodeling is carried out on the external world; psychotic remodeling is carried out on the internal representation of the external world.

The psychotic internal remodeling is carried out on the psychical traces of former relations to the external world and on fresh perceptions, which may take the form of hallucinations. The fact that the various new perceptions are distressing indicates that the whole process is carried out against forces that oppose it. Just as anxiety results when a repressed instinct forces its way to consciousness in neurosis, probably in psychosis the rejected piece of reality constantly forces itself on the mind. Here again, rather than mentioning disavowal explicitly, Freud writes that the elucidation of the various mechanisms, which in the psychoses turn the subject away from reality and then reconstruct reality require specialized "psychiatric" study. For what it is worth, he selected the term that tends to take the study into the broader field, perhaps in connecion with his conviction about the analytic inaccessibility of the psychoses.

Freud continues with a final resemblance between neurosis and psychosis. In both, the inner world of fantasy is used to remodel distressing reality. However, in neurosis the replacement is circumscribed, like the play of children; in psychosis external reality is replaced.

Although these two papers present no specific technical recommendations, they point out lines of approach to the analytic treatment of the psychoses and to ideas for further study. Particularly, they indicate similarities as well as distinctions and speak against the artificial separation of the two disorders from each other and from normality.

In a short account of psychoanalysis (1924d) written for a book, Freud makes no new statements, but a few of his comments have a special clarity. In addition, the article is of interest because it was published in 1924 after the structural model had been formulated.

Concerning free association, Freud wrote that a plentiful store of ideas is produced, which puts one on the track of what had been forgotten. The material *did not bring up* what had actually been forgotten but brought up clues and hints which, with supplementation and intepretation, could lead to reconstruction. Thus free association *with the addition of interpretation* took the place of hypnosis, that is, the recovery of memories.

Despite his recent formulations he stated (p. 197) that repression stemmed from the "conscious personality" rather than from the unconscious ego. He also described psychoanalysis (p. 209) as a psychology of the id and its effects on the ego and mentioned the psychology of the ego as if it were a separate field. Strachey refers to these restrictions as unusual.

In the "The Economic Problem of Masochism" (1924c) Freud takes up the application of the death instinct to certain clinical phenomena. He had previously written that any excitation, even a painful one, would initially cause some degree of sexual excitation. He had become dissatisfied with this idea as an explanation of masochism because the regular link between masochism and sadism was not explained. He now states that libido has the task of diverting the death instinct outward with the help of the muscular apparatus. It then becomes the destructive instinct, the instinct for mastery, or the will to power. Part of this instinct is placed in the service of the sexual function, where it becomes sadism proper. Another portion remains libidinally bound within the organism as the original erotogenic masochism.

He states we are without "*physiological*" understanding of how the death instinct is tamed by libido and that, so far as psychoanalysis is concerned, we can only assume that there is extensive fusion and defusion, so that we never deal with pure life instincts nor pure death instincts. Freud traces the original erotogenic masochism through various phases of libidinal development.

In connection with moral masochism, Freud points out that the sexual bond is broken. The suffering itself is what matters: ". . . the true masochist always turns his cheek whenever he has a chance of receiving a blow." He suggests that speaking to the patient of a need for punishment is both more accurate and more believable than referring to an unconscious sense of guilt. He traces moral masochism to regressive sexualization of morality that had originally been desexualized when the Oedipus complex was resolved. He considers moral masochism a classic piece of evidence for the fusion of instinct. The logic of his argument can be passed over here, except for the point that has technical implications, which is that the cultural suppression of instincts leads to demands on oneself for still greater suppression. Paradoxically, it is not true that an ethical sense demands instinctual renunciation to begin with but rather that the first externally enforced renunciation creates an ethical sense. A repetition of the demand for instinctual renunciation will re-evoke the demand for still further renunciation.

In "A Note upon the 'Mystic Writing Pad'" (1925b), Freud gives an ingenious account of the operation of the perceptual and memory systems by exploiting the analogy that struck him between these systems and this particular pad, the type in which one writes with a stylus and in which the writing disappears when the celluloid strip is raised. He states the system Pcpt-Cs. is periodically cathected as the unconscious stretches out feelers to the external world and hastily withdraws them as soon as it has sampled the excitations. As a corollary the system Pcpt-Cs. is periodically unexcitable.

While Freud does not say so, it seems most likely that this mechanism is at the basis of disavowal to which he refers in other papers. It is also of interest that the whole description is written without the explicit utilization of the terminology of the structural model though it is, of course, a contribution to ego psychology.

In "Negation" (1925b) Freud draws attention to his old observation that an association that is a negation can nevertheless be a confirmation, since the content of the association has reached consciousness. He states that a convenient method of reaching repressed material is to ask the patient, "What would you consider the most unlikely imaginable thing in that situation?" If the patient falls into the trap and says what he thinks is most incredible, he almost always makes the right admission.

I suspect that some analysts might consider Freud's illustration to be merely figurative or to be an intrusion on free association and perhaps an error. I believe that in this illustration Freud meant exactly what he said and would, in fact, make use of such questions.

Continuing, he points out that negation allows the content of repressed material to reach consciousness, though it is not accepted. Thus, the intellectual function is separated from the affective process. With the help of negation, the ideational content of the repressed reaches consciousness.

With the help of negation, thinking frees itself from the restriction of repression and enriches itself with material that is indispensable for its proper functioning. Freud states that even the negation can be conquered and a full intellectual acceptance of the repressed can be gained without removing the repressive process. I presume he means the intellectual conviction about analytic constructions, which can have the same therapeutic effect as the recovery of memories themselves.

Judgment is concerned with two types of decision. The earlier one genetically is whether something is good or bad, whether it should be incorporated or ejected by the pleasure ego. The second decision, by the reality ego, is whether it is external or internal, that is, whether a presentation in the ego can be rediscovered in perception. Since all presentations originate with perceptions, originally the mere existence of a perception was a guarantee of its reality. The antithesis between objective and subjective does not exist at first. It comes from the fact that thinking can bring before the mind something that was once perceived by reproducing it as a presentation without the external object having still to be there. Then the first aim of reality-testing is not to find an object but to refind it, to demonstrate that it is indeed external. Reality-testing also checks on the differences that develop between a presentation and the external perception. A precondition for the establishment of reality-testing is that objects which once brought real satisfaction shall have been lost.

Judging is the intellectual action that decides on the course of motor action and concludes the postponement due to thought. Thought is experimental action and is learned from the experimental periodic cathexis of the perceptual system that preceded it. Judgment is ultimately derived from the interplay of primary instinctual forces, with affirmation belonging to Eros and negation to the instinct of destruction. This view of negation fits with the fact that we do not find a "No" in "the unconscious."

I put the last words in quotations because Freud was using the term "unconscious" here, as he did so often, in the sense of a system for which he had already proposed to substitute the term, the id. In general terms, the technical clues in the paper are minor, but the theoretical implications and the indirect effect on techniques are important.

In the first of two important papers on female sexuality (1925c) Freud refers to disavowal. Referring to the female genital, Freud states that the boy disavows what he has seen; he softens it down or looks about for expedients to bring it into line with his expectation. In contrast, when a girl sees the male genital, she makes her decision in a flash. She has seen it and knows that she is without it and wants to have it.

However, a process like disavowal may set in. He states here that this process is neither very uncommon nor dangerous in children, though in an adult it would mean the beginning of a psychosis. (Other statements about the loss of reality in neurosis would seem opposed to this view.) Penis envy can have far-reaching implications. The girl may remain convinced that she has a penis and may insist on being like a man. Penis envy may be displaced into jealousy and also tends to loosen the girl's relation with her mother. Additionally, a repercussion of penis envy is a powerful struggle against masturbation, a forerunner of the repression of clitoral sexuality. Humiliation over clitoral masturbation is bound up with penis envy. At this point child and penis are equated, and with the purpose of getting a child she takes her father as a love-object. Thus the Oedipus complex is a secondary formation made possible by the castration complex.

In boys, normally, the Oedipus complex is demolished by the shock of castration, and the superego becomes its heir. In girls this motive for the demolition of the Oedipus complex is lacking, since castration has already had its effect. It may be slowly abandoned or repressed, or its effects may persist. For this reason the superego of women is not so impersonal or so independent as that of men.

In "Female Sexuality" (1931b) Freud returns to the importance of the pre-Oedipal attachment to the mother in the little girl, pointing out that she reaches the positive Oedipus situation only after she has surmounted a period that has been governed by a negative Oedipus complex and that this insight comes as a surprise, comparable to Europe's discovery of the Minoan-Mycenaean civilization behind the civilization of Greece. He states that women analysts could perceive these facts more easily because of the transference to a suitable mother-substitute. This is one of Freud's rare statements about the possible advantage or disadvantage in analysis of the sex of the analyst.

The facts that struck him as new were that a woman's strong dependence on her father merely took over the heritage of an equally strong dependence on her mother and that this earlier phase had lasted for an unexpectedly long time. He stated that the vagina is practically nonexistent until puberty and that the main genital occurrences of childhood are related to the clitoris. Ultimately there must be a shift from clitoris to vagina and also a shift in the main object, from mother to father.

The castration complex can lead to a revulsion from sexuality, to a defiant self-assertive attempt at masculinity, or to a normal feminine attitude. The Oedipus complex is not destroyed but created by the influence of castration.

A prohibition against masturbation becomes an incentive for giving it up but also becomes a motive for rebelling against the person who prohibits it. Another reason for rebelling against the mother is that she did not give the girl a proper penis. Other reasons include the child's resentment against not being given boundless love and boundless milk.

Now Freud arrives at the concluding phase that began with his early error, when he believed that his women patients had been literally seduced by their fathers. He soon recognized that in most instances the seduction was a fantasy. Now he adds that inevitably with toilet-training and being cleaned, the mother came to represent the first seducer and in later fantasies she was replaced by the father. He also emphasizes the girl's phallic activity toward her mother.

Although there is no direct technical development in these two papers on female sexuality, they illustrate the implication of theoretical advances of technique. I think the fact that Freud states that this material was not discovered earlier has individual applicability, since, as he states, the transference to the mother is not so evident to the male analyst as the transference to the father. This theoretical formulation enables the analyst to become aware of it more easily. There is a certain similarity between the recognition of unconscious mechanisms and learning to use a microscope. (I have the uneasy feeling that I read this and am not originating the observation.) Only after one has learned what to expect, to some extent, does recognition become most adequate. This trained expectation is exploited as a criticism that analysts therefore fit all patients into preconceived molds. This is not true except as an individual error, any more than it would be true that the pathologist who has learned to identify cirrhosis will then "find" it when it is not there. On the contrary, adequate knowledge of unconscious mechanisms carries with it more secure vigilance against misconception.

In the Preface to Aichhorn's *Wayward Youth* (1925d) Freud wrote that one should not be misled by the statement, although true, that the psychoanalysis of an adult neurotic is equivalent to an aftereducation. A child, even a wayward and delinquent child, is still not a neurotic, and aftereducation is something quite different from the education of the immature. "The possibility of analytic influence rests on quite definite preconditions which can be summed up under the term 'analytic situation'; it requires the development of certain psychical structures and a particular attitude to the analyst. Where these are lacking—as in the case of children, of juvenile delinquents, and, as a rule, of impulsive criminals—something other than analysis must be employed, though something which will be at one with analysis in its purpose." What Freud refers to can be designated as attributes of a relatively intact ego. It is noteworthy that he simply excludes analysis as a possibility and thus gives a clear indication of what he considered the limits of analysis, though at the same time not the limits of the efforts of analysts themselves.

In Freud's "An Autobiograhical Study" (1925e) there are points of technical interest. He maintained here his viewpoint on the so-called actual neuroses. He thought that the symptoms of these disorders, regardless of concurrent mental conflicts, were the direct toxic consequences of such sexual abnormalities as *coitus interruptus,* unconsummated sexual excitation, and excessive masturbation, and could be corrected directly by ending these practices.

He also stated (p. 40) that the theories of resistance and repression, of the unconscious, of the etiological significance of sexual life, and of the importance of infantile experiences were the principal constituents of the theoretical structure of psychoanalysis. Notable by their absence in this statement are the death instinct and the structural model.

Concerning the advantages of free association, Freud stated that it exposes the patient to the least possible amount of compulsion and that it never allows loss of contact with the current situation. The course of the analysis is left to the patient and "any systematic handling of particular symptoms or complexes thus becomes impossible." He emphasized that repressed material does not occur to the patient, but is only alluded to, and that the art of interpretation is required to both interpret the resistance and the repressed material. He later adds a description of the transference, which is not different from his standing views. In this essay he took the position that analysis was the starting point for a new science of the mind and implied it had broad applicability.

He stated (p. 60) that the analysis of the psychoses was impracticable because of its lack of therapeutic results. The reason is the incapacity of these patients to form a positive transference. I believe that the term is used here to mean, not irrational reactions, but what corresponds to rapport or the realistic part of the relationship with the analyst. However, he adds that nevertheless a number of approaches are available. Transference may be present to some extent, and with cyclical depressions, light paranoiac modifications, and partial schizophrenias, analysis has achieved successes. Furthermore, he adds, the diagnosis may be uncertain for a long time and thus justify continued therapeutic effort, at least long enough to make valuable discoveries, if not effect cures.

These statements do not imply any change in technique and again confirm its stability in view of theoretical advances. Although not polemical, several of Freud's comments give me the impression that they might have been formulated in response to some of the endless series of misconceptions that kept (and keep) arising about psychoanalysis. For example, it is a common misconception that the analyst does not interpret and construct the significant past experiences from the patient's current associations, but simply waits until the patient literally reports memories.

Inhibitions, Symptoms and Anxiety (1926a) is a complex theoretical work with relatively less importance from the standpoint of technique. Here again the technical repercussions are largely indirect. Freud here abandoned his former view that the cathected energy of a repressed impulse was automatically converted into anxiety. He maintained instead that the ego is the actual seat of anxiety, which he described as an affective state reproduced in accordance with an already existing memory. He explains, however, that his earlier observation was phenomenologically correct and that there was indeed a correspondence between the strength of the impulse that had to be repressed and the intensity of the resultant anxiety. Granting this, I do not think that the metapsychological correction necessitated a direct technical change. Under both the old and the revised view, the technical task would still be to maintain an optimum level of anxiety.

Concerning defenses Freud returned to the view that repression was only one of the defenses. To it he added reaction formation, regression, isolation, and undoing, all recognizable in his earlier case material.

He states (p. 124) that in neurosis it is against the demands of the libido and not against any other instinct that the ego defends itself, granting that there is always an element of fusion with aggression. His comments illustrate the greater importance that he considered the vicissitudes of libido, rather than aggression, played in clinical work with neuroses.

He defined the situation of danger, to which the ego responds with anxiety, as the nonsatisfaction of a need, and traced it genetically to birth and progressively from the economic situation of need-frustration through separation from the mother, from the genital, and from the approval of the superego.

The defensive process was described as an attempt at flight from instinctual danger. When in analysis the ego recovers its power over the repressed, instinctual impulses can run their course as if the old danger no longer existed. Thus we bring about in analysis more quickly, more reliably, and with less expenditure of energy something that would otherwise have occurred itself.

Concerning his continuing interest in disavowal, though the term is not used here, Freud states that in hysteria there is a special type of vigilance which, by means of restrictions in the ego, causes situations that would entail dangerous perceptions to be avoided or, if they do occur, manages to withdraw the subject's attention from them. He adds that the task of defense against a dangerous perception is common to all neuroses.

Resistance proceeds from the ego, which finds it difficult to direct its attention to perceptions and ideas it has been avoiding. He stated we first have to make the resistance conscious and then bring "logical arguments" against it and that we promise the ego "rewards and advantages" if it will give up its resistance. (This point comes up again in "Analysis Terminable and Interminable.")

Freud's classification of resistances is important technically. He stated there were three from the ego and two others.

1. Repression resistance
2. Transference resistance—a repression is reanimated, which should have been recollected
3. The gain from illness
4. Id resistance—the compulsion to repeat
5. Superego resistance—the need for punishment

The delightful and charming *The Question of Lay Analysis* (1926b), written as a dialogue with Freud's "Impartial Person," with interpolated comments to the presumably more sophisticated reader, is a masterpiece of lucidity. For years I have recommended it as a desirable initiation to the reading of Freud's works. For the present purpose, it is most cogent to observe that Freud relied heavily on his old technical papers and introduced no substantial technical revisions.

He defends his use of the terms the "I" and the "It" (*Ich* and *Es*) and states that "our theories must be understood by our patients." (I do not know why no translator, to my knowledge, rendered the terms that way.) He states, "However much philosophy may ignore the gulf between the physical and the mental, it still exists for our immediate experience and still more for our practical endeavors." Since the work is written for the layman, one must be cautious about the significance of the utilization of his old and stable views alone. Yet granting this reservation, I think it is a piece of evidence that points to the stability of the technique.

Perhaps a comparable reservation might be maintained, but the evidence is similar in a short encyclopedia article (1926c). He writes that "theoretical speculation" leads to the "suspicion" that there are two fundamental instincts but, without observing such precautions, goes on to state that neurotic symptoms are the substitutive satisfactions of repressed sexuality.

In *The Future of an Illusion* (1927a) Freud has become more positive about the existence of destructive trends. He makes the point that men are not spontaneously fond of work and that the necessity to restrain instincts provokes opposition.

An illusion need not necessarily be false. We call a belief an illusion when wish fulfillment is a prominent factor in its motivation, and in doing so we disregard its relation to reality (p. 31). This point is, I think, not regularly appreciated. It is in accord with this that Freud writes that we cannot evaluate the reality value of religious illusions, and to assess the truth value of religious doctrines does not lie within the scope of his inquiry. In more general terms the analytic situation, I would add, is designed to establish internal psychic reality, not to deal with or authenticate external reality.

In *Civilization and Its Discontents* (1930) Freud adds to his description of the ego. Originally it subjectively includes everything. Later it separates an external world from itself. Work is of great importance psychologically (p. 80). No other technique for the conduct of life attaches the individual so firmly to reality as laying emphasis on work. His work gives him a secure piece of reality in the human community. He now writes (p. 120) that he can no longer understand how he could have overlooked the ubiquity of nonerotic aggressivity and destructiveness. However, he later adds (p. 121) that the energy of the death instinct is very difficult to grasp. It escapes detection unless its presence is betrayed by its being alloyed with Eros. Its existence is "mainly based on theoretical grounds." Only when authority is internalized is it correct to speak of conscience or a sense of guilt (p. 125). Later, internalized authority enters into the superego and gains all the aggression the child would have liked to have used against the authority. The sense of guilt is the most important problem in the development of civilization (p. 134). Education conceals both the importance of sexuality and the aggressiveness the subject will be exposed to (p. 134).

Guilt is a topographical variety of anxiety; it coincides with a fear of the superego. The need for punishment is an instinctual manifestation on the part of the ego that has become masochistic under the influence of a sadistic superego. A portion of the destructive instinct present in the ego is employed for forming an erotic attachment to the superego. Owing to the omniscience of the superego, the distinction between an intended aggression and one carried out loses its force.

Neurotic symptoms are essentially substitutive satisfactions for unfulfilled sexual wishes. In the course of analytic work we find that perhaps every neurosis conceals a quota of unconscious sense of guilt, which in turn fortifies the symptoms by making use of them for punishment. It seems plausible that when an instinctual trend undergoes repression, its libidinal elements are turned into symptoms and its aggressive components into a sense of guilt.

In "Fetishism" (1927b) Freud returns to the question of disavowal and states that the boy "refused to take cognizance" of his observation that women did not have a penis. Here he suggests that a distinction be made between an idea and its affect, and that repression be applied to the affect and disavowal to the idea. Later, in the *Outline,* he was to suggest a different categorization, that is, that repression apply to defense against internal instinctual demands and disavowal to defense against the claims of the external world.

He maintains here that the perception persists and that a very energetic action is undertaken to maintain the disavowal. The idea that the woman has a phallus is not maintained unaltered. The belief is both retained and given up. He maintains that the woman does have a penis, but it is changed. A substitute is formed (the fetish), which inherits the interest of its predecessor. The last impression before the uncanny one (of the genital) is retained as a fetish.

Turning to the distinction between neurosis and psychosis in regard to the break with reality, Freud states that it has now become clear that the disavowal of a piece of reality did not necessarily lead to psychosis. Two men who "had failed to take cognizance" of the deaths of their fathers in their childhoods had not developed psychoses. Like the fetishist only "one current" in their mental lives had not recognized the death. Another "current" took full account of the fact. I quote the word "current" because it seems to me so typical of Freud's style of writing. He was not restricted in his descriptions to the terminology of the metapsychology he had formulated.

In a short paper on "Humour" (1927c) Freud makes an interesting comment on paranoia. He found that ideas of persecution can be formed early and exist for a long time without any perceptible effect until, as the result of some precipitating event, they receive sufficient amounts of cathexis to become dominant. The cure of such paranoiac attacks would lie not so much in the resolution and correction of the delusional ideas as in a withdrawal from them of the cathexis that had been lent to them. How is this to be done? For what it's worth, the context of the essay is concerned with the benign aspect of the superego particularly as it is expressed in humor.

In his essay on Dostoevsky (1928) Freud utilizes the new dual-instinct theory when he states, for example, that Dostoevsky had a very strong destructive instinct, which found its main expression in masochism and a sense of guilt (p. 178). He considered the epileptic reaction as one that could be put at the disposal of a neurosis, regardless of its organic basis. He points out that deathlike attacks represent an identification with a dead person. He describes the bisexual conflict of the boy with special lucidity. Castration is the threat either for hating the father, as external punishment, or for loving the father, as an internal prerequisite. The former is normal, and the latter results in its pathological intensification. As he so often does, Freud takes into account the possible resistance of the reader by stating that he is "sorry," though he cannot alter the facts, if the account of the influence of the threat of castration is unsavory or incredible.

His explanation of Dostoevsky's deathlike attacks is particularly clear. He identified with his father in his ego and thus became his father, but dead. Further, he was being killed *by* his father, with whom he had also identified in his superego. Thus for the ego the death symptom was at the same time the satisfaction of a masculine wish and a masochistic wish. It is dangerous, Freud writes, if reality fulfills repressed wishes. All defensive measures are reinforced when fantasy is reinforced by reality.

In a brilliant analysis of a story by Stefan Zweig, Freud shows the existence of a fantasy of puberty that the mother should initiate the boy into sexual activity to save him from masturbation. Strachey notes that already in 1897, in a letter to Fliess, Freud had suggested that masturbation was the primal addiction from which all later ones stemmed. He concluded that the addiction to gambling was a disguised repetition of the compulsion to masturbate. Here is still another illustration of the potential integration of theory and technique.

In a letter to Leroy (1929) Freud comments on the difficulty of working on dreams when there is no way to find their attachment to the external world. Certain dreams are "from above," that is, they are formulations of ideas that could just as well have been created in a waking state, and only certain parts derive their contents from deeper levels. The part of the dream that stems from above is readily and easily explained by the dreamer.

The short essay on "Libidinal Types" (1931a) is of particular interest in its correlation of character structure with the structural model and in its emphasis on the importance of libido in this connection. Freud describes the erotic, the narcissistic, and the libidinal types.

The erotic type has the main interest of loving and being loved and represents the demands of the id; varying amounts of aggressiveness may be blended in. The obsessional type is distinguished by the predominance of the superego. Such people fear their conscience instead of loss of love and exhibit an internal rather than external dependence. They develop a high degree of self-reliance. The third type is narcissistic. These subjects are independent and interested in self-preservation; their ego has large amounts of aggressiveness at its disposal; there is little tension between the ego and superego. The types can be combined, and a combination of all three would be the ideal normal.

I think the relatively secondary role of the vicissitudes of aggression is an interesting reflection on Freud's utilization of this instinct in his clinical descriptions.

In the *New Introductory Lectures on Psycho-Analysis* (1933a) Freud reviews dream interpretation and designates it as his sheet anchor when he doubted the correctness of his analytic findings. In this connection he describes the analyst as listening passively to the material and avoiding reflection, like the patient who is reporting his ideas without critically evaluating them. I think it is clear that Freud meant that the analyst's relatively passive, evenly hovering, uncritical attention had the aim of making perception maximal, of avoiding premature conclusions, and of allowing the fullest range to associative connections. I would add also that it is a difficulty of analysis that the analyst cannot bring effort to bear directly on his work. To use an analogy from physical competitive sport, the analyst cannot exert effort or he will "choke up."

The Forsyth incident (pp. 47–56) is brought up to illustrate the possibility of telepathy.[1]

Concerning the difference between the analysis of children and of adults, he states that some of our patients have retained so many infantile characteristics that the analyst cannot avoid making use of certain of the techniques of child analysis with adults (p. 148). Freud never lost sight of the vicissitudes of actual practice and was always flexible in his technical recommendations.

Regarding therapy, Freud states, "I discussed the theoretical side of this question fifteen years ago (in the *Introductory Lectures*), and I cannot formulate it in any other manner today" (p. 151). Thus, he explicitly disclaims any technical revision on the basis of the structural model, the new instinct theory, and the new concept of anxiety. He then proceeds to discuss a problem that was to occupy his attention periodically for the rest of his life: the achievements and limitations of psychoanalysis as a therapy.

It is often said that Freud was a therapeutic pessimist, but I do not think

---

[1] Incidentally, in the course of documenting his material, Freud has the occasion which he rarely bothered with, to reveal what was clearly the warm, friendly, respectful, candid attitude that I am convinced was his natural one with his patients. Although the case was unusual in that Freud had already given up the hope of therapeutic success and had so informed the patient, and even more unusual in that the patient knew that Freud was going to stop the analysis when he got a patient with money (this patient had none), I believe that it still reflects Freud's realistic attitude. For anyone who has been deceived by the myth that Freud was a stern, forbidding, austere figure, I know of no better antidote in his published works than this description.

that the idea is supported in his writings. He states here that psychoanalysis is the most powerful of the psychotherapeutic procedures, that it has its triumphs and defeats, its indications and its limitations like any other. However, what seems to have been a source of serious concern to him was the possibility that the endless efforts made to gain therapeutic success would have the effect of undermining analytic principles. He writes that there is a danger of being forced away from analysis into endless experimentation. He states that the expectation that every neurotic symptom can be cured stems from a lack of appreciation of the fact that the neuroses are severe, constitutionally fixed illnesses, which rarely restrict themselves to only a few attacks but persist as a rule through long periods or throughout life.

He calls the psychoses inaccessible and warns that their close relation to the neuroses should restrict our pretensions in regard to the latter. Further, not everything psychical can be revived, and some changes are definitive. There can be a general "stiffening" of mental life and an inability to find new paths.

The field of application of analytic therapy lies in the transference neuroses—phobias, hysteria, and obsessional neurosis—and character abnormalities. Everything else is unsuitable, more or less, but it is impossible to exclude psychoses from treatment because often it is only in the course of analysis that the diagnosis can be made. With his usual freedom from nosological stereotypes he states that there are "severely handicapped" people (p. 156) who are kept under analytic supervision all their lives and are taken back into analysis from time to time.

In "The Acquisition and Control of Fire" (1932) Freud supports his hypothesis that men had to renounce the homosexually tinged desire to put out fire with a stream of urine with an analysis of the Greek myth of Prometheus and related myths. He is able to integrate historical reconstruction, symbolic fantasy, and physiology, ultimately linking his hypothesis with clinical evidence. The child originally believes the two functions of the penis, urination and ejaculation, are one and holds the theory for a time that babies are made by a man urinating into a woman's body. The technical repercussions are indirect in the manner mentioned of expanding the knowledge of the unconscious.

A short article "Why War?" (1933b) again leads Freud to refer to our "mythological theory" of instincts. His obituary of Ferenczi (1933c) includes the danger of therapeutic ambition. An analysis of an error he made (1935) is both convincing and clear and, I think, might have been written the same way three decades earlier.

"A Disturbance of Memory on the Acropolis" (1936) was written when

Freud was eighty and referred to an event that had occurred thirty-two years before, describing it with precision and masterful insight of its genesis as well as the reason for its recollection. He describes derealization as a defense that aims at "keeping something away from the ego, at disavowing it." He states that the occasion for defensive measures arises from both the real world and the internal world. The most primitive and thoroughgoing defense is repression. Between repression and the normal method of fending off what is distressing or unbearable by means of recognizing it, considering it, making a judgment on it, and taking appropriate action lie a whole series of more or less clearly pathological methods of behavior on the part of the ego. As a "marginal" case of this type of defense he cites a king who, on learning of the loss of a city, burned the letters and killed the messenger. He points out how reactions of derealization are linked with the past. I think these concepts are important in shifting the mechanism of the disavowal of reality away from psychosis.

Concerning the work of analysis, Freud states in *Moses and Monotheism* (1939), (p. 74) it alone "can bring about a knowledge of the forgotten experiences, or, to put it more vividly but also more incorrectly, bring them back to memory." This is a confirmation of the importance of analytic reconstruction accompanied by a sense of conviction even when remembering is absent.

A discussion of the clinical problems of neurosis (pp. 75 ff.) is again noteworthy because of its reliance on the vicissitudes of libido. In a later description of the structural model, which Freud refers to as topographical, he again retains the qualities of conscious, preconscious, and unconscious. Referring to his Lamarckian concept of the inheritance of acquired characteristics, Freud writes (p. 100) that, although he is cognizant of the repudiation of this idea by modern biological science, he nevertheless considers it correct and cannot do without it. How he used his belief, or if he used it, technically, is not clear to me. What I find difficult to grasp is how a patient can develop a sense of conviction about such ideas. My tentative assumption is that Freud utilized it in a corroborative manner and not alone. This idea is supported by his comment, cited earlier, that the racial heritage is outside the scope of psychoanalysis (1921).

The lucid, terse, unfinished *Outline* (1940a) contains a chapter on technique. At the outset Freud writes that the ego of the psychotic is unable to adhere to the analytic pact, and it is for that reason we cannot cure psychotics by analysis. This statement, in my opinion, confirms what I stated earlier, that when Freud in other places stated the psychotic could not develop a transference, he meant transference in its rational, realistic sense of participating in the analytic contract. A bit later Freud includes in the positive transference the fact that it becomes the true motive force of the patient's collaboration. Freud also mentions that the patient also attributes to the analyst the power his superego has over his ego and that this authority must not be abused by the analyst in any attempt to become a teacher, model, or ideal. Again he acknowledges that some neurotics are so infantile they must be treated like children.

Ideally the patient should act as normally as possible outside the analytic situation and confine his abnormal reactions to the transference. Describing the severe unconscious need for punishment that leads to a negative therapeutic reaction, Freud states it may be assumed that there has been an extensive defusion of instinct with liberated aggression turned inward but implies no technical application as far as I can tell.

Concerning the instinctual element in neuroses, Freud states (p. 186) that experience shows that the pathogenic instinct is always some component of sexual life. The central importance of the Oedipus conflict is re-emphasized.

Again turning to the relationship to reality, Freud writes that the ego has to defend itself against the demands of both the internal and the external world and adapts the same method of defense against both. He states that the child's ego gets rid of undesirable instinctual demands by repressions and fends off a demand of the external world by means of the disavowal of perceptions. Disavowal is always incomplete and is supplemented by acknowledgment, so that it involves a split in the ego. This split in the ego is a universal characteristic of the neuroses. Finally, Freud states, as I understand it (p. 204), that it is not always easy to recognize in a particular instance whether one is dealing with a repression or a disavowal. In either case the success of the ego is incomplete.

In "Analysis Terminable and Interminable" (1937a) Freud again placed great weight on the limitations of analysis. As I have stated, I think he was concerned with the preservation of psychoanalysis against the understandable pressures for faster treatment and greater therapeutic results.

One point that becomes clear is that, although Freud made every possible attempt to preserve the analytic method, he clearly advocated great flexibility both in what the analyst himself might be called on to do and also in what he was willing to call analysis from the standpoint of duration. Thus, in one of his case examples the analysis was evidently only six weeks long— according to Strachey, citing Jones—and a second was nine months long.

Freud warns that we cannot activate an inactive conflict in analysis and, from the opposite standpoint, cautions that analysis is not suitable in crises.

The analytic situation "requires" the collaboration of the normal ego, but this normal state is an ideal fiction. Actually, the normal ego approaches that of the psychotic in some part or other and to a greater or lesser extent (p. 235). As far as I know this statement, and other similar ones, which link not just neurotic but also psychotic phenomena with the normal has been insufficiently appreciated.

Concerning the relation to reality, Freud again refers to defenses against unpleasant perceptions. Like defenses against internal perception, the truth of external perceptions must be sacrificed. The defense mechanisms are repeated in the analysis and form half of the analytic work, which swings like a pendulum between id analysis and ego analysis.

"The therapeutic effect depends on making conscious what is repressed, in the widest sense of the word, in the id." Interpretations and constructions prepare the way, but the unconscious resistances in the ego must be overcome. Now Freud states, "One might suppose that it would be sufficient to treat them like portions of the id and, by making them conscious, bring them into connection with the rest of the ego" (p. 239). But this would not reckon on the resistance against the uncovering of the resistances. What happens is that the ego withdraws more or less seriously from the analytic agreement. The patient becomes inaccessible to sound argument and behaves like a child with a stranger he distrusts. The outcome of the treatment then depends on the degree of the alteration of the ego and the strength of these resistances. Economic issues are the answer. Here again Freud emphasizes the limits of analytic influence.

Freud is not explicit about the boundaries of resistance that dictate the vitiation of analysis. I suspect that these boundaries might be defined as the consistent or repetitive disruption of the analytic situation. He states that certain resistances, such as unduly mobile libido or undue adhesiveness of libido, cannot be localized. Fusion and defusion of the instincts he again places in the sphere of research in the future.

A discussion of the psychology of the analyst and the necessity for analytic work on himself is included. The well-known recommendation that the analyst should submit to analysis periodically, perhaps every five years, is made here. The context makes it clear that Freud had in mind quite short periods of time, not the protracted period that we now associate with analysis.

"Constructions in Analysis" (1937b) conveys more important points in technique. Freud emphasizes that the work of the analyst is to *construct* from the patient's material, from the associations, dreams, and symptomatic behavior, the forgotten or, more precisely, repressed past ideas and affects.

He defines an interpretation as relating to a single element of the material, whereas a construction is more complex. For example, one might say, "Up to your n^{th} year you regarded yourself as the sole and unlimited possessor of your mother; then came another baby and brought you grave disillusionment. Your mother left you for some time, and even after her reappearance she was never again devoted to you exclusively. Your feelings toward your mother became ambivalent, your father gained a new importance for you and so on." This example is in my opinion an impressive demonstration of the complexity of organization of which Freud was capable and illustrates that construction is a far more difficult process than interpretation.

Furthermore, Freud emphasizes, the confirmation of the correctness of the constructions comes from the following associations, not from a simple agreement or disagreement, which for many reasons may be ambiguous. As an example Freud cites an interchange that occurred in an extra-analytic consultation. Although not related to analytic technique, the scene itself allows one a glimpse of Freud as a person of charm, empathy, and humor, lecturing—perhaps slightly tongue in cheek—a young wife in the presence of her husband on the advisability of having sexual relations with her husband and of the detrimental repercussions that might ensue if she continued to refuse.

Freud points out that whereas the result of construction may be recollection, this may not be possible, and an assured conviction may have the same therapeutic effect. Sometimes following a construction there is a recollection not of the subject of the construction but of related details. Apparently the upward drive of the repressed has been displaced onto adjacent memories of minor significance. Freud then hypothesizes that delusions may have a similar structure, also dependent on the emergence of repressed material, which exploits the break with reality to erupt into consciousness. The resistances stirred up by this process and the tendency toward wish fulfillment would account for the distortion of this material. From this hypothesis it follows that delusions have a kernel of truth, and the recognition of this truth might be of use in dealing with psychotic patients. At least knowledge might be advanced "even if it led to no therapeutic success." Delusions, then, can be considered like constructions in analysis, attempts at explanation and cure, even though under the conditions of psychosis they can do no more than replace a fragment of currently disavowed reality by another fragment already disavowed in the past. The task of the investigator would be to reveal the connection between the present disavowal and the original repression. (The substitution of the term, repression, for disavowal in the previous sentence is Freud's.) Just as a construction is effective only because it recovers a fragment of lost experience, so the delusion owes its convincing power to the element of historical truth it inserts in the place of rejected reality. Thus, those suffering from delusions would be like hysterics suffering from their own reminiscences.

In the essay "Splitting of the Ego in the Process of Defence" (1940b) Freud yet again describes disavowal. He describes how the child's ego confronted with a threatening experience, which shows that the continued gratification of a powerful instinctual derivative will lead to intolerable danger, reacts in a paradoxical manner by means of a split in the ego. On the one hand "with the help of certain mechanisms he rejects reality and refuses to accept any prohibition; on the other hand, in the same breath he recognizes the danger of reality, takes over the fear of that danger as a pathological symptom and tries subsequently to divest himself of that fear." The cost of this arrangement is a rift in the ego that never heals but that increases as time goes on.

Describing the disavowal of the sight of the female genital in the genesis of fetishism, he states that there is a turning away from reality that we prefer to reserve for the psychoses. In fact, it is not very different. The distinction is that the boy did not simply contradict his perception and hallucinate a penis where there was none to be seen. He effected no more than a displacement of value, transferring the importance of the penis to another part of the body with the aid of regression.

A short note jotted down by Freud and preserved (1941b) states that the ultimate cause of work inhibition is the inhibition of masturbation in childhood. Possibly not the actual inhibition but the actual lack of orgastic satisfaction is important. This missing satisfaction may manifest itself in equivalents such as absence (brief lapses in attention, I presume), outbreaks of laughing or weeping, and in other ways. This short note seems to me a typical example of the interaction of theory and technique. No technical alteration is required as the result of this hypothesis. Yet it can lead to more effective, more knowledgeable interpretations and constructions, which then become subject to confirmation.

Summary

I have reviewed Freud's published papers from 1920 until his death to determine from them what could be learned about the development of his technical views. Practical necessity has precluded the explicit consideration of the massive literature that is connected with this subject. I can only acknowledge this deficiency and, in defense of my conclusions, maintain that they are documented and supported by direct reference to Freud's work.

During this period Freud wrote a good deal about broad theoretical issues and matters of social importance that did not have technical repercussions. However, I think that three developments are found in his writing that impinge on technique.

The first, and the broadest and most difficult to define, is the general application of theoretical development. I have given many illustrations in my review: the new insight into female sexuality, into various unconscious mechanisms, and so on. This is an area that can be brought into the framework of technique only indirectly, and indeed it would be an error to try to attempt it any other way.

Putting this issue in other words, it is the obligation of the analyst to master basic theoretical developments and allow their integration in his work, or justify their exclusion, and there can be no substitute for this theoretical knowledge in the form of direct technical applications advised by someone else. The analyst can carry out legitimate analytic work only on the basis of his own personal conviction of its theoretical correctness, and this conviction can be based on nothing but his personal knowledge of the relevant theory and, also, his personal conviction about *irrelevant* theory, which he cannot apply. I have indicated at a number of points what I could understand of Freud's position on the applicability of theory to clinical work. In addition, I have referred to the evidence in his writing that indicates to me that the second instinct theory, the fusion-defusion concept, and even the second anxiety theory—as significant as they were theoretically—did not necessitate any technical revision.

The second major technical development was a more exact, more refined recognition of resistance and of certain defense mechanisms. I say more exact and more refined advisedly, because it is clear that the technical *principle* of the analysis of resistance was already known. The conceptualization of the ego, which Freud at one point called a terminological correction, nevertheless allowed for the more complete recognition of resistances and led Freud ultimately to characterize analytic work as veering from ego analysis to id analysis and back, allowing equal importance to both. The various types of identification particularly could be better conceptualized with the utilization of the concepts of the ego and the superego.

More specifically in regard to defense, Freud's development of the function of the ego led him to describe its relation to external reality and particularly the defense of disavowal. Initially, he thought this mechanism was confined to children and psychotics. Later, after conceptualizing the split in the ego, he brought it into closer relationship with the neuroses and normality. Thus, more precisely, the relationship to external reality as well as to the id and superego was incorporated into technique.

Finally, the third development might better be designated as a tendency or a goal in Freud's writing. Actually, it seems to me that his central preoccupation was not so much the development of psychoanalytic technique as its *preservation*. As was cited, Freud at one point stated that a former work had been "forgotten," and, whether with this idea in mind or not, he reiterated the principles of technique established before 1920 on many occasions: the central importance of the psychoanalytic situation; the juxtaposition of free association by the patient and evenly hovering attention and interpretation and construction by the analyst; the interpretation of resistances; the development and resolution of the transference; the aim of genetic reconstruction of pathogenic experiences; the impossibility of directly attacking symptoms; the necessity of consistently starting from the current surface of the material; and the proper place of dream interpretation were all repeatedly stressed.

Without engaging in polemics, Freud seemed to be concerned with misconceptions that arose. Particularly he thought of unreasonable therapeutic ambition, which might stem in part from a denigration of the severity and significance of neurotic illness, as a threat to technique. He therefore tried to delimit the legitimate applicability of analysis. At the same time Freud was aware of the fact that the efforts of the analysts, themselves, necessitated flexibility and acknowledged that some patients had to be treated like children, that some needed endless analytic supervision, and that in others various modifications were necessary. Although he was consistently pessimistic about the therapeutic results in psychoses, he recognized that the mere existence of a psychotic mechanism did not make analysis impossible, recognized that protracted analytic work might be necessary before the diagnosis was established, recognized the potential scientific value of analytic work with psychotic patients, and made a number of suggestions regarding approaches.

In addition to these developments there are two personal characteristics, which, though neither technical in themselves nor a new development, have their place in the conceptualization of Freud's method and can be gleaned from his writing. The first is intellectual brilliance. To me this seems most evident in the scintillating complexity of his constructions. The second is the warmth, empathy, candor, and benign humor that shine through his clinical descriptions. The stubborn misunderstanding that in using the screen analogy Freud was recommending that the analyst actually be detached or impassive is regularly refuted in his case reports. In fact, he meant only that the analyst should confine his personal attributes to establishing and maintaining a working alliance, or positive transference in a realistic sense, and devote all his efforts to expanding the patient's understanding rather than attempting to influence him directly.

In the period subsequent to Freud's death there have been many important developments based on his work, which must be judged on their merits. From the work itself, as I have attempted to demonstrate, I think that Freud considered that by 1920 the fundamental premises of psychoanalytic technique were established and that he devoted his efforts to theoretical expansion, to technical refinement, and to the stabilization and preservation of the basic premises against the numerous forces that jeopardized them.

REFERENCES

[Note: S.E. refers to *The Standard Edition of the complete psychological works of Sigmund Freud* (London: Hogarth Press).]

FREUD, S. *Beyond the pleasure principle* (1920). S.E., Vol. 18, pp. 1–64. (a)

FREUD, S. The psychogenesis of a case of homosexuality in a woman (1920). (1922). S.E., Vol. 18, pp. 223–232. (b)

FREUD, S. A note on the prehistory of the technique of analysis (1920). S.E., Vol. 18, pp. 263–265. (c)

FREUD, S. Group psychology and the analysis of the ego (1921). S.E., Vol. 18, pp. 69–143.

FREUD, S. Dreams and telepathy (1922). S.E., Vol. 18, pp. 197–220. (a)

FREUD, S. Certain neurotic mechanisms in jealousy, homosexuality, and paranoia (1922). S.E., Vol. 18, pp. 223–232. (b)

FREUD, S. Two encyclopedia articles (1923). S.E., Vol. 18, pp. 235–239. (a)

FREUD, S. *The ego and the id* (1923). S.E., Vol. 19, pp. 12–66. (b)

FREUD, S. A seventeenth century demonological neurosis (1923). S.E., Vol. 19, pp. 72–105. (c)

FREUD, S. Remarks on the theory and practice of dream interpretation (1923). S.E., Vol. 19, pp. 109–121. (d)

FREUD, S. The infantile genital organization (1923). S.E., Vol. 19, pp. 141–145. (e)

FREUD, S. Neurosis and psychosis (1924). S.E., Vol. 19, pp. 149–153. (a)

FREUD, S. The loss of reality in neurosis and psychosis (1924). S.E., Vol. 19, pp. 183–187. (b)

FREUD, S. The economic problems of masochism (1924). S.E., Vol. 19, pp. 154–170. (c)

FREUD, S. A short account of psycho-analysis (1924). S.E., Vol. 19, pp. 191–209. (d)

FREUD, S. Some additional remarks on dream interpretation (1925). S.E., Vol. 19, pp. 127–138. (a)

FREUD, S. Negation (1925). S.E., Vol. 19, pp. 235–239. (b)

FREUD, S. Some psychological consequences of the anatomical distinction between the sexes. (1925). S.E., Vol. 19, pp. 248–258. (c)

FREUD, S. Preface to Aichhorn's *Wayward youth* (1925). S.E., Vol. 19, pp. 273–275. (d)

FREUD, S. An autobiographical study (1925). S.E., Vol. 20, pp. 7–74. (e)

FREUD, S. A note upon the "mystic writing pad" (1925). S.E., Vol. 19, pp. 227–232. (f)

FREUD, S. Inhibitions, symptoms and anxiety (1926). S.E., Vol. 20, pp. 87–174. (a)

FREUD, S. The question of lay analysis. (1926). S.E., Vol. 20, pp. 183–258. (b)

FREUD, S. Psychoanalysis (1926). S.E., Vol. 20, pp. 263–270. (c)

FREUD, S. *The future of an illusion* (1927). S.E., Vol. 21, pp. 5–56. (a)

FREUD, S. Fetishism (1927) S.E., Vol. 21, pp. 152–157. (b)

FREUD, S. Humour (1927). S.E., Vol. 21, pp. 161–166. (c)

FREUD, S. Dostoevsky and parricide (1928). S.E., Vol. 21, pp. 177–196.

FREUD, S. A letter to Maxime Leroy on a dream of Descartes (1929). S.E., Vol. 21, pp. 203–204.

FREUD, S. *Civilization and its discontents* (1930). S.E., Vol. 21, pp. 64–145.

FREUD, S. Libidinal types (1931). S.E., Vol. 21, pp. 217–220. (a)

FREUD, S. Female sexuality (1931). S.E., Vol. 21, pp. 225–243. (b)

FREUD, S. The acquisition and control of fire (1932). S.E., Vol. 22, pp. 187–193.

FREUD, S. *New introductory lectures on psycho-analysis* (1933). S.E., Vol. 22, pp. 5–182. (a)

FREUD, S. Why war? (1933). S.E., Vol. 22, pp. 203–215. (b)

FREUD, S. Sándor Ferenczi (1933). S.E., Vol. 22, pp. 227–229. (c)

FREUD, S. The subtleties of a faulty action (1935). S.E., Vol. 22, pp. 233–235.

FREUD, S. A disturbance of memory on the acropolis (1936). S.E., Vol. 22, pp. 239–248.

FREUD, S. Analysis terminable and interminable (1937). S.E., Vol. 23, pp. 216–253. (a)

FREUD, S. Constructions in analysis (1937). S.E., Vol. 23, pp. 257–269. (b)

FREUD, S. *Moses and monotheism* (1937–39). S.E., Vol. 23, pp. 7–132.

FREUD, S. *An outline of psychoanalysis* (1940). S.E., Vol. 23, pp. 144–208. (a)

FREUD, S. Splitting of the ego in the process of defence (1940). S.E., Vol. 23, pp. 275–278. (b)

FREUD, S. Psychoanalysis and telepathy (1941). S.E., Vol. 18, pp. 177–193. (a)

FREUD, S. Findings, ideas and problems (1941). S.E., Vol. 23, pp. 299–300. (b)

4

CLASSICAL PSYCHOANALYSIS SINCE 1939

Mark Kanzer
Harold P. Blum

Historical Survey

Three closely interwoven aspects of psychoanalysis should be differentiated: (1) its therapeutic applications; (2) its use as a scientific method of investigation; (3) its development as a system of psychology (Freud, 1922). The evolution of these three areas since 1893 has shown shifting balances and interactions among them. "Classical Psychoanalysis" refers inherently to the progressively changing methods of therapy that have as their connecting link the analytic setting, which Freud devised, and the aim of fundamentally revising the personality through the resolution of the transference neurosis that develops in this setting. As early as 1920, when Freud introduced the second instinct theory, he listed three major

93

phases in the history of analytic technique (Freud, 1920). Ahead of him, however, lay structural psychology (Freud, 1923) and the unending impetus it has given to further developments in all three areas of psychoanalysis.

The prestructural orientation (before 1923) has become known as depth psychology and was based on the "topographic hypothesis," which explored the relationship between the unconscious and the conscious portions of the mind. The former was regarded especially as the source of the sexual impulses, the latter of self-preservative tendencies (the libido theory). Conflicts between them gave rise to repression of the sex impulses and to neurosis. Therapy was designed to undo the repression and find healthier solutions for the conflicts—a goal that was virtually synonymous with the revival of the infantile sex life and its reintegration into the mature personality. Structural psychology examines the total personality (id, ego, superego), of which the unconscious and conscious are aspects, establishes its patterns of maturation in typical (phase-specific) environmental settings, and uses this data as a basis for its concepts of mental health, illness, and therapy. The clinical goals and methods of psychoanalysis have accordingly gained in complexity.

Freud's own clinical contributions were limited after 1926 when he delineated in *Inhibitions, Symptoms and Anxiety* (Freud, 1926) essential reformulations in line with structural concepts. These involved especially a shift in emphasis from the libidinal to the ego aspects of personality growth and functioning, from the unconscious search for satisfactions to the defenses against inner and outer dangers which this shift entails. Inevitably, new consideration was given to object relationships and to the environmental conditions associated with both satisfaction and danger. In the last years of Freud's life, two works appeared, which were to establish fundamentally the lines of development that were still largely latent in structural psychology: Anna Freud's *The Ego and the Mechanisms of Defence* (1937) and Heinz Hartmann's "Ego Psychology and the Problem of Adaptation" (1937). Both were interrelated approaches to the total personality, not only in its defenses against danger, but in its adaptive activities as well. Significantly, the background of these emerging leaders of the post-Freudian generation introduced viewpoints from outside of the classical analytic situation: Anna Freud from child analysis and Heinz Hartmann from a broad orientation in the natural and social sciences and the humanities.

Anna Freud's pioneering work with the analysis of children and adolescents enabled her to place psychoanalytic hypothesis concerning early development on a sound empirical basis. Analysts had previously formed their perspectives through inferences derived from the neuroses of their adult patients. Now, such experiences in childhood could be directly confirmed. Moreover, Anna Freud and other child analysts did not confine themselves to the treatment of the disturbed, but employed direct observation to assess the behavior of normal as well as abnormal children in varied family settings, in school, during physical illness, and so on. The psychology of parents and their influence upon childhood development became better understood.

These observations were used to provide new insights into metapsychological processes and their relationship to actual behavior. Anna Freud introduced and made familiar such constellations as the "identification with the aggressor," the asceticism and altruistic surrender of the adolescent, and phase-specific aspects of denial through fantasy, word, and action. The relationship of these processes to the situations in which they were developed advanced the analyst's knowledge of defenses directed against dangers from without, thus counterbalancing the disposition of depth psychology to emphasize the dangers from within.

Anna Freud further correlated particular neuroses with the tendency to use phase-specific defenses and also combinations of defense mechanisms with inner drives, on the one hand, and external objects on the other, a viewpoint that made analysts more aware of adaptive problems of the total personality at successive states of maturation. The real world of the child—not only his sex fantasies in later years—thus became the basis for concepts of mental health and illness.

Heinz Hartmann reinforced the shift of the analyst from a view of the ego as a defensive or inhibitory organization to a recognition of its functions as an adaptive agency that impressed positive aims on all behavior. Seeking to bring depth psychology into a framework that reconciled it with a hitherto rather neglected general (or surface) psychology, he drew upon some of Sigmund Freud's last formulations to depict the ego as equipped with an inborn (primary autonomous) apparatus possessing functions of perception, motility, and thought, which form a basis for the "non-conflictual sphere" of psychic activity. Personality development normally occurs through interactions of the conflictual and the nonconflictual: Thus, intelligence may be stimulated or inhibited by conflict and may itself be a determinant of the outcome of a conflict. Mental health, or successful psychic adaptation, depends on a proper balance among the structures of the personality (id, ego, superego), which makes pathogenic conflicts and a distorted use of defenses unnecessary.

From this standpoint, ego strength is not to be measured (as previously) in terms of the ability of the ego to defend itself from the instincts or the external world, but rather through its synthesizing function in uniting all components of the personality harmoniously. The mature ego displays a high degree of resistance to regression (secondary autonomy); for example, it does not resort to fantasy in a situation that can be solved by appropriate action.

This thesis required a review of oversimplified theories of genetic development. It was not sufficient to suggest that the artist "sublimated" infantile smearing impulses in his applications of paint to the canvas; the complexity of interactions in both development and regression would have to be traced. (The demonstrations of this principle by Ernst Kris in the field of aesthetics have been of special significance; 1952.) The concept of "change of function," introduced by Hartmann from the field of biology, lent new sophistication to genetic constructions: A child's interest in painting might be initiated during a smearing period and serve temporarily or permanently as an outlet for smearing impulses (a possible pathogenic fixation point), but painting might also become an independent ability that was only partly, if at all, connected in mature years with the impulses and situation in which it originated.

The potentialities inherent in the work of Anna Freud and Heinz Hartmann took many years to develop and transform the long-established theoretical and clinical formulations of depth psychology. The immediate period after Freud's death (1939) found psychoanalysis subjected to tremendous outer and inner stresses. Hitlerism transported the bulk of the analysts of the European continent to the United States, making it the new center of gravity of the analytic movement. World War II scattered the younger American analysts and brought them into contact with the exigencies of military psychiatry. Postwar training needs expanded to unprecedented proportions, so that there were endless demands for analysts and analytic orientation in therapeutic and educational endeavors that included pioneering applications to medicine (such as in the development of the psychosomatic field), to psychiatry (brief therapy, group therapy, hypnotherapy, child psychiatry, the treatment of the psychoses) and to community mental health (education, child guidance, social work, pastoral counseling, etc.). In Freud's last years, "culturalist" trends in the United States and the Kleinian school in England periodically initiated various degrees of outright and partial splitting; local tone was added by the affiliation of analytic groups with universities and hospitals and by the increasingly widespread geographic distribution of the analysts. Differences emerged between adherents of the depth and structural schools as well as between the older generation of analysts and the younger generation, which was more oriented to the sciences than to the humanities and had come to psychoanalysis not only for a fulfillment of inner needs but as an accepted part of professional training.

The time was ripe for the systematizing contributions of Otto Fenichel. In 1941, a course of lectures that he had given to students in Vienna in 1936 was published in English under the title, "Problems of Psychoanalytic Technique." This was supplemented by a chapter on therapy in "The Psychoanalytic Theory of Neurosis" four years later. As he noted in the first work,

> Questions of technique are approached in only a small proportion of psycho-analytic writings. In the first place, because the young science of psycho-analysis has as its object of study the totality of human mental phe-nomena, it must set itself so many questions that the problem of therapeutic technique becomes just one subject among many others. Second, analysts doubtless have a particular aversion to a detailed discussion of this subject, based in part on subjective uncertainty or restraint, but to a greater extent based upon the objective difficulties of the matter itself. A third reason is, however, the decisive one; the infinite multiplicity of situations arising in analysis does not permit the formulation of general rules about how the analyst should act in every situation, because each situation is essentially unique.

He found it necessary to plead with his colleagues that an organized pres-entation of their own written views was not necessarily unjust to the intuitive element or to the creative aspects of the analytic relationship.

Certainly, the misconceptions of many analysts about goals and means emerged from the confrontations implicit in unified and comparative ex-aminations of data among themselves. Actually, it was in analytic as well as scientific tradition to examine, not to gloss over, difficulties and differences. This Fenichel could illustrate by references to Freud's then recent article, "Analysis Terminable and Interminable" (1937). It was apparent, however, that part of the diversity of views prevalent among analysts called for more than frank discussions, mutual tolerance, and further research in a science that some among them felt was an art and others almost a religion: It was also necessary to provide adequate and supervised training for younger analysts—a course of action that was already well under way (Lewin and Ross, 1960).

Fenichel's 1945 chapter takes the position: "There are many ways to treat neuroses, but there is only one way to understand them." He provides a conscientious review of various forms of nonanalytically and analytically oriented therapies, extending from mental hygiene and counseling to shock and drug therapy, with a discussion of the psychodynamic indications for, and effects of, each. With respect to psychoanalytic therapy, his presentation follows the traditional line that it is the only method that fundamentally revises the personality and the processes that are at the root of neuroses; that its applicability lies especially in the treatment of the transference neuroses; and that in individual instances, and with special variations, it may benefit character neuroses, perversions, addictions, and impulse disorders.

The second half of the 1940's saw great progress in analytic metapsychology, in child analysis and its interrelations with developmental psychology, and in analytic education and organization. Analytic influence on psychosomatic medicine and various forms of community psychiatry flourished. Classical analysis showed the least change but received a stimulating challenge from a reinterpretation of its goals and practices as put forward by Franz Alexander and a group of co-workers (1946).[1] Probably the crux of Alexander's teachings, which he considered a legitimate evolution of Freudian theory, was his concept that the essential therapeutic factor consisted in the "corrective emotional experience." He further believed that the transference neurosis contains within it elements of a regressive evasion, which can be avoided by such measures as planning the course of therapy, role-playing (especially "opposite" to that assumed by an original traumatizing figure), and varying the frequency of sessions so as to correct imbalances between therapeutic dependency and the demands for adjustment in the real-life situation.

To most analysts this seemed to offer a possible program for analytically oriented psychotherapy. In relationship to concepts of the goals and therapeutic methods of psychoanalysis, however, it suggested not a progression but a regression to earlier stages of catharsis, specific traumas, and suggestion, from which their therapy had emerged. Nevertheless, Alexander's views were given careful and formal consideration in several articles and panels during the early 1950's that provided not so much the occasion for rejecting his contentions as an opportunity to restate and expand traditional analytic doctrines in terms of modern structural psychology.

A brief survey of this "identity crisis" will serve to introduce a systematic study of contemporary "classical analysis." For this purpose, we find it useful to consider papers by Leo Stone on "The Widening Scope of Indications for Psychoanalysis" (1954); K. R. Eissler on "The Effect of the Structure of the Ego on Psychoanalytic Technique" (1953); and selected reports from

[1] For a detailed discussion of their views see Chapter 7 (Ed.).

two panels of the American Psychoanalytic Association, "The Traditional Psychoanalytic Techniques and Its Variations" (Zetzel, 1953) and "Psychoanalysis and the Dynamic Psychotherapies: Similarities and Differences" (Rangell, 1954).

The position of Dr. Stone as director of the Treatment Center of the New York Psychoanalytic Institute was itself a part of the significant changes that had been taking place. Originating as a voluntary project by members of the New York Psychoanalytic Society in 1946 to provide clinical services for veterans, it became an integral part of the New York Psychoanalytic Institute and its training system, requiring each student analyst to gain experience outside the classical setting and become conversant with various modifications of analytically oriented therapy. This type of supplementary experience is now widely employed throughout the institutes and clinics of the American Psychoanalytic Association (Lewin and Ross, 1960).

Taking into account the expanding applications of classical analysis and its modifications to a great variety of disorders, Stone listed as essential for this form of treatment: (1) a setting and routines conducive to the mobilization of a transference neurosis (usually the couch technique, free association by the patient and the analyst's attitude and interventions); and (2) the resolution of this neurosis by interpretation and working through of the resistances. The use and progression of the treatment necessarily involve the conceptual framework of psychodynamics with which the analyst operates, that is, the unconscious, the theory of infantile sexuality, the genetic viewpoint, and so on. Those forms of treatment in which interpretation is the main therapeutic tool, but in which reliance must be placed on other technical devices (see Eissler below on "parameters"), may be regarded as "modified psychoanalysis."

With such criteria, Stone felt that the admixture of psychotic and psychosomatic elements in the patient's personality makeup ordinarily diminished the prospects for classical analysis. Addictions and perversions might prove accessible if a sense of illness provided a continued incentive for therapy. Preliminary supportive and other special measures, such as strengthening the hold on reality, can prepare a borderline group for ultimate analysis. Valuable in this connection would be more detailed case histories than classical analysts often take, stress on the ability to relate to people in the past and at present, psychological studies, and positive personality resources (talents, capacity to sublimate, courage, patience, etc.). The reactions of the prospective patient and the analyst to each other are of fundamental importance; these are not limited to factors of transference and countertransference but include the impact of two real personalities upon each other.

In conclusion, Stone averred that "the scope of psychoanalytic therapy has widened from the transference psychoneurosis, to include practically all psychogenic nosologic categories. The transference neuroses and character disorders of equivalent degree of psychopathology remain the optimum general indications for the classical method. While the difficulties increase and the expectations of success diminish in a general way as the nosological periphery is reached, there is no absolute barrier; and it is to be borne in mind that both extranosological factors and the therapist's personal tendencies may profoundly influence the indications and prognosis." In discussing this paper, Anna Freud, who found herself in agreement with Stone's other points, differed only where he expressed doubt as to whether classical analysis should be used for "trivial" or incipient or reactive illnesses. She felt it was indeed a worth-while procedure for young persons with good prospects in life who were disturbed in their enjoyment and efficiency by even comparatively mild neuroses (1954b).

K. R. Eissler approached much the same problems from the standpoint of a detailed discussion of the analytic technique itself, introducing perhaps the most widely used term in this field since Freud's own work, namely the "parameter" (1953). In general, he noted, psychoanalytic technique depends on three variables: (1) the patient's disorder and personality; (2) the present circumstances; and (3) the personality of the analyst. Consideration in his article would be given to the first of these factors alone. For this purpose, he suggested that the basic model for psychoanalytic technique had been developed in relation to hysteria, in which ego strength is such that the patient can adhere fundamentally to the basic rule, whereas interpretation, as the essential tool of the analyst, provides the insight that is needed for the achievement of therapeutic goals. Therapeutic factors are not limited to interpretation and insight; the others nevertheless are adjuncts to these as the specific agencies of analytic technique.

Where, as in phobias, a point in treatment is reached when it becomes evident that interpretation does not suffice as a therapeutic tool and the pathogenic material cannot be attained, a new technical device becomes necessary, such as the advice or command to confront the dreaded situation in real life. This accessory maneuver is termed by Eissler a parameter, a deviation from the basic model technique. For such a variant to be compatible with the classical procedure, four conditions should be fulfilled: (1) It must be introduced only when it is evident that the basic model does not suffice. (2) It must never transgress the unavoidable minimum. (3) It must be self-eliminating; the results should prove conducive to the restoration of the basic model. (4) The transference relationship must never be permanently disrupted.

The ego has sustained a greater lesion in phobia than in hysteria and thus requires the parameter. Nevertheless, symptomatic differences are uncertain indicators of the operation and pathology of the ego organization. A more reliable guide is provided by the hypothetical "normal ego," which, in the analytic situation, would "guarantee unswerving loyalty to the analytic compact." The deviant ego has sustained modifications, owing to defense mechanisms that have exacted their price for protection by leaving permanent deformities. In delinquents and schizophrenics, these modifications usually make the preliminary employment of the basic technique inexpedient.

Despite these schematizations and some criticisms as to certain of the assumptions involved, the notion of a model technique, with recognized variants within the framework of analytic conceptions, had great appeal and a clarifying effect for most analysts. These efforts of Eissler and Stone to define and clarify issues may be brought into relation to the two panels mentioned above, which sought, respectively, to resolve differences on the subjects of "The Traditional Psychoanalytic Technique and Its Variations" and "Psychoanalysis and Dynamic Psychotherapy."

The ensuing review of the analytic position proved among the most comprehensive and valuable in this field. In the first panel, Robert Waelder and Heinz Hartmann were among those who emphasized the inherent balancing of regressive with reintegrative tendencies in the course of analysis. There is a need, however, to attain sufficient controlled regression for transferences to aid recall and permit the acquisition of insight. In this connection, Phyllis Greenacre saw the transference interpretation as the decisive core of all analytic technique. An ultimate focal point of difference was found to lie in the conception of neurosis as a fault in interpersonal adaptation in childhood (Alexander) as contrasted with a fault within the personality that is only partly caused by environmental conditions. From the latter standpoint, the substitution of "opposite" behavior by the analyst in place of "faulty" behavior by the parent (even if the precise nature of this latter were determinable) could not be the sole motivator of change.

The relationship between classical psychoanalysis and dynamic forms of psychotherapy, those that are entirely or partly inspired by analytic psychology, received equally definitive discussion in the second panel. Edward Bibring offered a frame of reference for the categorization of all therapeutic techniques so that meaningful comparative studies might be made for this purpose. Techniques involve, he suggested, "any purposive, more or less typified, verbal or nonverbal behavior on the part of the therapist which intends to affect the patient in the direction of the (intermediary or final) goals of the treatment" (Bibring, 1954). He then distinguished five basic therapeutic techniques, each with its curative agency: (1) suggestion, acting through resultant beliefs, impulses or actions; (2) abreaction, producing relief from acute tension; (3) manipulation, favoring the progress of treatment or producing changes in adjustment; (4) clarification (Carl Rogers), providing insight into phenomena that operate on the conscious and preconscious level; and (5) insight through interpretation of unconscious material, producing deep-seated changes within the personality. (George Devereux's concept of "confrontation" has much in common with "clarification" [1951].)

Bibring saw different forms of psychotherapy as depending on one or another of these techniques, or on various combinations. Classical analysis utilizes all therapeutic techniques, but the dominant reliance is on interpretation. The latter is based on hypotheses derived from prolonged observations on the total verbal and nonverbal behavior of the patient, occurs not as a single act but as part of a prolonged process, and produces both an intensification of and insightful reorientation toward infantile conflicts, which are surmounted in the working-through phase that follows the interpretation.

Leo Rangell and Leo Stone were among the other panel discussants. The former felt that the achievement of classical therapeutic goals required the analyst, for technical purposes, to assume a peripheral role as an observer whose activity was directed toward the establishment of conditions favorable for the development of a transference neurosis and for its resolution through the systematic use of interpretations or supplementary interventions as needed. In keeping with this principle, the recognition of a patient's dependency would call for an interpretative approach to its origins, control, and resolution (not role-playing or discontinuance of intense treatment!). Rangell also expressed the opinion that certain qualitative differences between psychoanalysis and other forms of therapy would militate against attempts to establish a common framework for purposes of comparison.

Dr. Stone suggested the following points of differentiation: In psychoanalysis, progress in treatment makes for radical new discoveries by both patient and analyst, which in themselves prove to be incentives for further therapy; in nonanalytic procedures, limited goals are set up and sought. The former method is conducive to exploration of the past, the latter to exploration of the present. In the classical situation, the patient automatically creates a difference between the real analyst and an image that he conjures up from his childhood. In directive therapies, the therapist actually assumes parental functions and advises the patient about contemporary problems. Even with directive techniques, however, analytic insight can be helpful to the therapist in seeking to achieve adjustments that do justice to the true complexities of the personality.

The Analytic Setting

The classic psychoanalytic setting and procedure have undergone little change among analysts who seek a fundamental revision of the personality through: (1) the establishment of conditions that favor the development of a transference neurosis; (2) the resolution of the neurosis through interpretation and working through. Nevertheless, "the most profitable view to adopt toward the analytic technique seems to consider the use of the couch, free association, the handling of the transference, the handling of the transitional forms of acting out, etc., as mere tools of treatment"; and, as Anna Freud has pointed out, "tools of any trade are periodically inspected, reviewed, sharpened, perfected, and, if necessary, altered. As in all other cases, alterations should not be carried out arbitrarily and without sufficient cause" (1954a).

The time-tested procedures undergo variants in specific cases, in modified situations, and in the hands of different analysts. The degree of variation is likely to increase in proportion to the deviation of the case from the "standard model," which is the adult from twenty to forty years of age with a psychoneurosis and a stable environment that makes devotion to a lengthy period of treatment (two or three years or more) feasible. The favored number of sessions is four or five times weekly. Child and adolescent analyses have developed their own goals and techniques, which will not be reviewed in this chapter.

The analytic setting—the environment and arrangements that form the background for the therapeutic procedure—may be distinguished from the intrinsic nucleus of this process, the analytic situation, which, as Freud defined it, consists of a pact between two partners, patient and physician (1938). The former commits himself to reveal all his thoughts without reservation; the latter commits himself to the therapeutic use of these confidences. The patient's commitment is called the "fundamental rule"; ideally it results in an untrammeled flow of mental contents ("free association"), which are expressed in words ("verbalization"). The voluntary, and particularly the involuntary, failure to adhere to the fundamental rule is termed "resistance." As used in its broadest sense, resistance includes any motivated departure from the commitment to therapy, such as lateness or failure to arrive for a session. The preservation of an external situation favorable for analysis usually includes an admonition to the patient not to undertake major new decisions without adequate consideration of the meaning from the standpoint of treatment (principle of abstinence).

Adherence to the fundamental rule in the analytic setting has as its complement a basically self-effacing position of the analyst that is designed to eliminate, as far as possible, the conventional personal relationships that deter the individual from freely developing and expressing his innermost thoughts. The ideal approached by free association is a relaxed mental state, close to the boundaries between the ego and the id, which favors the appearance of fantasies and the entrance into consciousness of somatic awareness (instinctual drives). Against the appearance of certain of these fantasies and drives, a mobilization of defensive tendencies can be noted; conflicts then occur, and detours of the thinking process may be observed. The analyst assumes that the core of the neurosis is gradually approached through the decipherment of these phenomena (interpretations) and the changes effected as a result (the working-through process, which involves fundamental changes in the personality).

The inner scene of these mental events, as visualized by Freud, is close to the semihypnotic state in which dream and symptom formation take place. It is by no means uncommon for a patient's dreams to develop more deeply the line of thought that occurs on the couch and for symptoms to come to the fore during the process of free association. The conflicts between the ideas that seek to penetrate into consciousness and the defenses (censorship) against them tend to involve the analyst increasingly: On the one hand, demands are made upon him; on the other hand, there are great efforts (under the impetus of shame and guilt) to control these demands.

Both the permissive attitude of the analyst and his interpretations are conducive to a fuller expression of the hidden ideas. The latter, linked by an inexorable psychic determinism, are traced to deeper and deeper levels and invariably lead back into traumatic experiences of childhood that are intimately associated with the formation of the neurosis. The substitution of the analyst for the original figures in these traumatic episodes and the current revival of old conflicts, which now center about his person, constitute the transference neurosis. Insight, control, and integration succeed infantile defensive maneuvers, splitting of the personality and symptom formation, as the formerly traumatic experience is mastered with the aid of analytic procedure.

This course of events still provides the basic model for the analyst. However, the conceptualization of the personality and its functioning, of trauma and neurosis, of the interactions between the fundamental rule, free association, the interpretation, the recall of the past, and so on, have all undergone substantial changes, which will be discussed in detail in the course of this chapter.

The ever widening view of the personality, which has developed with the structural approach in psychoanalysis (since 1923), now requires detailed knowledge of each stage of the patient's history. It is no longer sufficient to postulate an Oedipus complex or a primal scene; the exact relations between the individual and the persons in his environment, their behavior as well as his own, the identifications he made, and his handling of aggression, anxiety, and object relationships must and can be reconstituted with the key provided by the transference neurosis. It is not enough to discover a memory and dispose of a neurosis as though it were an extraneous body embedded in an otherwise healthy one; the interrelations between disease and health must be explored, understood, and changed in their balance as part of the reorganization effected through treatment. The reliving of a trauma is not a sufficient goal. The patient must be made to understand why the experience occurred, how it affected him, and what part it played in his subsequent development up to the present time. It is important to reconstruct all the phases of maturation, not merely the Oedipal period, for this purpose.

The "normal ego" and its healthy cooperation in the "therapeutic alliance" (Sterba, 1934) share attention with the neurotic ego and its "resistances" to the fundamental rule. The therapeutic alliance is an agreement between patient and physician to establish a working partnership to treat the illness. The analytic pact (or compact) is an instrument of the therapeutic alliance. In the analytic setting, the analyst uses passive neutrality as a technique; he is not passively neutral to the illness, which he has undertaken to treat, nor is he a detached scientific observer except insofar as science contributes to the therapeutic tasks at hand. Freud long ago made this clear when he advised the analyst to forego the study of dreams during treatment unless these promoted the progress of the analysis (1911). His warnings against "therapeutic ambition" have been as subject to distortion as many of his other comments. It is clear that he was referring to an overambition on the part of the therapist, which might lead him to stamp his own image on the patient and impel him to assume an identity of purpose that was not in the analysand's interest. The warning applies, in effect, to the analyst's countertransference.

The entire problem of the analyst's role and the extent to which he should support and further maturational processes during subsequential reliving has been subject to much discussion in relation to modern concepts of personality formation. Freud did not hesitate to suggest the appropriateness of advice, support, and parental guidance, subordinated, however, to the attainment of ultimate analytic goals. A more prominent position for these forms of directive management has been urged by analysts who believe that the early child-mother unity can be approached in this way and that faults in development, otherwise inaccessible, can be corrected by utilizing parental tendencies already inherent in the analytic relationship. Others doubt that early pre-Oedipal character formations can be revised through such techniques and warn against the promotion of regressive evasions. Many contemporary analysts are inclined to the view that free association is not a withdrawn soliloquy but a two-person interaction at all times, a concept that, as usual, can be traced to Freud ("purposive ideas," 1900).

The effects of the analytic setting and routine on the mental state of the patient and the progress of treatment have also been the subject of considerable discussion. The restrictions on the motility and will of both patient and analyst, the limitations on the analysand's vision, and the enforced discharges of tension through speech provide frustrations, gratifications, and special channels for the mastery of drives and object relations, which must be evaluated, along with the transference neurosis and the therapeutic alliance, in following the course of treatment (Spitz, 1956; Stone, 1961).

Transference and the Transference Neurosis

The transference is the underlying system of fantasies and associated affects, attitudes, and motor dispositions, which tend to cluster about current figures and situations and utilize them to revive the past. As such, transference is an aspect of memory. The pernicious effects of transference arise from the fact that it is essentially unconscious, rooted (like dreams and symptoms) in infantile wishes and fears and does not prove accessible to reality-testing. Memory is not used as an aid in adapting to present needs; rather, the present must be fitted into the past and appear as a repetition of it. Semidelusional and sometimes frankly delusional elements adhere to such confusion between present and past, and the dangers of these cognitive equations become even greater when it is the remote past that must be relived. The adult mother is, in her unconscious really a child, from this viewpoint, and she will treat her children as her mother treated her—or, in permanent protest, in a different fashion. The junior executive adopts a filial attitude toward his elders, which curbs his initiative or leads to senseless and harmful defiance. In these instances, the individual is really not living in the present or acting as other than a disguised child.

Transference is deeply embedded in all personalities and constitutes an element in character. Where it is under the control of the rational ego, it may lend warmth and empathy in relationships to other people; its influence on the imagination may reveal itself in creativity or in hobbies; it plays its part in intuitive judgments, which may be an asset. Where it dominates the rational ego, the scene is set for a neurosis, which represents, in its symptoms, a last-ditch effort to contain the transference within reasonable boundaries. The arm that is impelled to act out the transference may become painful, paralyzed, or contracted; the rest of the personality remains as best it can in the world of present reality.

The analytic setting and procedure are especially designed to draw into the open, and in sheltered surroundings, the underlying fantasy. The cathartic method of treatment, from which psychoanalysis evolved, sought to recapture a specific memory associated with the transference use of the arm that had to be inhibited through symptom formation. If the individual were to recall with emotion the occasion when he wished to throw something at his father and curbed this dangerous impulse, the injured arm would be restored to use. Perhaps father had caught him using the arm in a masturbatory act. Controlled by consciousness and reason, such a situation no longer threatened the security of the individual and he could deal (in later years) in a more constructive manner with sexual excitement or dangerous aggression. Even in reviewing the past in his mind, memories assumed a different meaning and he would see the painful episode between himself and his father in a new light.

The direct recall of memories ceased to be the goal of psychoanalysis in 1894. What evolved was more and more purposefully an examination of the painful episode as a nucleus (screen memory) with an infinity of ramifications, which involved the entire relationship of the patient with his father over many years. His experiences with his mother and other members of the family and his attitudes and character formation before and after the episode would also have to be taken into account in order to understand the events and the reasons for the aftereffects. Even after the arm symptom has seemingly subsided, a recurrence may direct attention to some contemporary situation in which the patient is afraid to "punch the boss in the nose." (The impulse to do so must be made conscious; health need not be a matter of accommodating the impulse.) Symptoms have present as well as past contributaries.

The neurotic transference is found to be based on a stereotyped fantasy that has become an unshakable myth. Over and over again, this fiction (usually a "family romance") seeks to superimpose itself upon reality and demands to be treated as the only reality. Its effect is like that of a traumatic experience—as though a moment of shipwreck were being relived and nothing else could possibly command attention except the question of immediate life and death.

Yet it would be misleading to assume that the patient had ever been involved in a shipwreck or even been to sea. Perhaps an episode of bed-wetting will have become fused with a television viewing of a shipwreck. A symbolic equation is formed; eventually, analysis must disentangle the latent content of inglorious bed-wetting from behind the preoccupation with a more glamorous but equally frightening shipwreck.

The discovery of the role of sex in such hidden fantasies long provided the key used for research and treatment by depth psychology. This aspect is still indispensable; no theory of the neuroses that fails to explain the role of infantile sexuality in symptom formation can be considered seriously by analysts. Therapeutic results that bypass the sexual factors are, of course, possible. However, long before Freud's death, transference interpretations had to reconstruct in symptoms and underlying fantasies the relevant aspects of aggression, of ego and superego functions, and of environmental factors in both the past and present.

Thus, the bed-wetting of our "shipwrecked sailor" will probably be brought into conjunction with the phallic phase of maturation as it represented all the forces acting on the child during the period when his Oedipus complex was most pronounced. The libido theory construct—that the bed-wetting was a masturbatory equivalent and the tall masts of the sinking ship presumably a phallic symbol—will probably prove to be correct. Nevertheless, details of the fantasy reveal other important facts about the Oedipal situation and its resolution. The shipwreck scene may well feature a fight at sea (aggression against the competitive father) and the rescue of an aged couple by the hero (a reaction formation against sex and aggression, which betokens superego formation and the establishment of ego controls over the drives). The awarding of a medal at the happy ending conveys approval and may conclude the identity crisis of the adolescent's psychosocial phase (Erikson, 1959).

There are many clusters of "transferences" operating in, and emerging from, such a fantasy. The unraveling of the intricacies becomes more and more associated with the art of inducing, translating, and resolving the transference neurosis. The present-day explorations of the roots of neurosis go back far beyond the Oedipal period and postulate pre-Oedipal experiences of separation and reunion of the infant with the mother at successive stages of development. The cycle between sleeping and waking probably contains in least-altered form rudiments of the early relationships to the mother, a hypothesis that Bertram D. Lewin has used most instructively in tracing the psychopathology of elations and depressions (1950). Under debate today is the extent to which the analyst is justified in making pre-Oedipal constructions and even adapting his technique to the concept of assisting in the revival and resolution of difficulties of the pre-Oedipal period. These problems will receive more detailed consideration in subsequent sections.

The healthy aspects of integrated transference dispositions have been stressed both in the patient (Loewald, 1961) and the analyst (Spitz, 1956). The structural viewpoint, which assumes that many early features of personality formation cannot be "dissolved" by treatment, differentiates between the dissolution of the transference neurosis and the dissolution of the transference. The outcome of the analytic process should place the latter, entrenched at the genetic and functional core of the personality, in a mutually beneficial relatedness to the more highly evolved activities of the ego and superego.

The therapeutic alliance becomes the organizing focus for the healthy transference as opposed to the resistant aspects that perpetuate the transference neurosis. Freud always emphasized the helpful role of the positive transference, yet agreed that it was also a source of resistance. The distinction within the "positive transference" of an element, which is actually the realistic therapeutic alliance, should clarify a source of theoretical and practical confusion. Similarly, the "negative transference" may include protests on the part of the normal ego for failure to accord due recognition to the mature portion of the personality. Transference manifestations can be recognized and tested only in the context of total behavior.

Defense and Resistance

Although the terms "defense," "defense mechanism," and "resistance" are sometimes used interchangeably, this article makes the following distinctions: (1) A defense is a protective action or attitude directed against a danger. (2) A defense mechanism is a specific technique used by the ego to ward off inner or external dangers (identification, projection, reaction formation, isolation, denial, repression, etc.). (3) A resistance is a departure from the fundamental rule or, more broadly, the therapeutic alliance through which the patient pledges his cooperation in the analytic procedure. The failure to verbalize during free association is the most traditional illustration of all these forms of defense. It is most truly a resistance when nothing really comes to mind; more frequently, there is, however, a conscious content the patient finds difficult to verbalize. This may relate, for example, to a hostile feeling against the analyst, which is "dangerous" because a breach may ensue. Such a feeling, even in an incipient stage, can be subjected to repression and instead a thought may come to mind about a friend whose faults the patient pities (displacement and reaction formation). (4) At this point, the associations may cease entirely—the substitute formation has not achieved its purpose, and a deeper repression has been initiated. Really, "nothing comes to mind," yet in his silence and withdrawal from the analyst, the hostility actually finds expression.

Although such behavior is still an essential aspect of the analytic process and a basis for interpretations, structural psychology places it in more complex perspectives. These pertain to: (1) the role of consciousness; (2) the relations of the drives to the inhibiting agency; (3) the choice of defense; and (4) the interplay between the defensive and the adaptive functioning of the ego.

With respect to consciousness, it is no longer sufficient to know that an unconscious idea or impulse is being excluded; the analyst must ascertain the means and the reason for this exclusion (choice of defense, manner of expressing resistance, etc.). The topographic (conscious-unconscious) element in the conflict is only one aspect, though an important one, of a complexity of interactions that the analyst must illuminate. Today, the latter emphasizes the need to provide "insight" rather than to make conscious, that is, to relate meaningfully the totality of the behavior involved in the resistance.

The impulse warded off by a defense mechanism is no longer seen as a simple libidinal or aggressive drive. The structural interpretation is likely to postulate a mature, as confronted with an archaic, organization of the personality, which includes both drive representations and dissociated portions of the ego itself. The task is not merely to find a discharge for the drive but, by reintegration of the ego, to provide new and appropriate forms for activities that once proved dangerous. The original as well as the present danger situations must be reconstructed: For example, a disposition to bed-wetting can no longer be conceptualized only in terms of urethral erotism but must be brought into connection with the precipitating circumstances, such as regressive imitation of a newborn sibling as a means of regaining the mother's attention. In the transference neurosis, a hostile flow of words on the couch can present a contemporary equivalent, which the patient unconsciously seeks to avert by urinating before the session. The resulting compliance with the fundamental rule must be brought into conjunction with the hidden defense measure.

Freud's systematic description of defense mechanisms and resistances in their structural framework gave special emphasis to anxiety and the danger situation that provoked it (1926). The choice of defenses in different neuroses was found to be related to typical dangers encountered at phase-specific stages of development. Thus, "identification" is particularly associated with the hysterical repression of sexual impulses; "avoidance," with the phobic projection of hostility during the phallic period of development. In their translation into resistances during treatment the hysterical female may fall silent, whereas the phobic patient will associate freely but find such a disposition to incur accidents while driving his car that he may have to give up its use temporarily (an avoidance of dangers impelled by uncontrolled and unrecognized hostility). In the latter instance, the analyst may himself have to introduce a "parameter"—the advice or command to discontinue driving until the underlying impulses can be controlled by interpretations.

In all these instances—the patient who ritually urinates before the session, the silent woman, the phobic and accident-prone driver—the libidinal gratifications of "urethral erotism" may be a factor. However, the individual forms of defense, characteristic of the specific neurosis, constitute the more immediate problems that must be unraveled through management of the resistances to treatment. The defenses in turn must be traced to the danger situations in which they arose, the influence of the persons who figured in these danger situations, and the adaptive as well as defensive aspects of the total behavior pattern.

Thus, the ritual urinator may be protecting his penis and privacy from an all-too-inquisitive and possessive mother; under the circumstances, there are elements of healthy individuation both in experiments with masturbatory equivalents and in separation from the mother. The silent patient, unconsciously guarding her fantasies, may identify with and obey the mother who told her that she should not speak to strange men—a measure not without prudence. The danger-inviting driver may in turn identify with an omnipotent father whose driving once impressed him as an acme of daring and ambition, which he must not imitate. Nevertheless, this identification may have developed in him useful initiatives. Unless and until such details have been carefully worked out and the hierarchical structure of experience, as organized in the personality, has been established, the management of a case must be tentative and calculated to promote gradual acquisitions of insight through fostering the development of the transference neurosis.

Rudolph M. Loewenstein's term "reconstruction upwards" (1951) recognizes the need of the analyst to proceed not merely from the surface to the depths and from the present to the past, but also in reverse directions. For example, the emergence of oral-sadistic hostility during treatment may call at the moment, not for a detailed exploration of the pre-Oedipal phase, but rather for an investigation of some regressively depicted episode from a later period (the discovery of the primal scene or an adolescent disappointment in love), which may also find its counterpart in current problems.

Robert Waelder's concept of "multiple function" (1936) also takes cognizance of the complicated interrelationship between components of behavior as viewed from their structural aspect. In a similar sense, he speaks of the "isomorphism of symptoms and defense" (1951) as a clue to the events implicated in the formation of the personality and the corresponding explanation of a resistance. The fetishist, in the very insistence with which his symptoms requires him to look at and touch a phallic object, reveals the need to "deny" the horror with which he discovered that the female genital possessed no penis like his own that could be seen and touched. Where denial, in such instances, was the defense mechanism employed, the symptom is based on a compensating claim: "I did indeed see and touch something." Earlier analytic descriptions would have emphasized the libidinal desires of the fetishist; the structural approach also recognizes and gives priority to the dangers incurred in connection with the libidinal strivings.

A contemporary desire to look at and touch the analyst during free association may produce the same defensive and adaptive functioning of the ego that contributed to the formation of the symptoms. The analytic setting then serves as an inherent protection against these dangerous impulses, which will be "acted out" elsewhere unless they can be drawn into relation to the hidden processes of transference and resistance involved. This larger view makes possible a corresponding insightfulness in the management of the course of treatment.

Interpretations and Other Interventions

"Interpretation," in its classical sense, refers to a verbal intervention by the analyst into the process of free association in order to demonstrate and remove a resistance. The patient may have been describing a stern, silent man who is devoid of human feelings; there is then a period of silence, which the patient finally terminates with the statement: "Nothing comes to my mind." On the basis of inferences he has been making, the analyst interprets: "This man reminds you of myself" (displacement). The response from the patient is confirmatory: "I do not really think so, but I wondered if you were thinking that yourself." Here, of course, the patient reveals that her mind was not in fact a blank and that there had been a deliberate violation of the fundamental rule. The analyst's intervention had elicited nothing that the patient had been unaware of, so that it may be categorized as a "confrontation" that deals with the surface (conscious and preconscious) rather than the depths (unconscious) of the patient's mind.

The image of the stern, inhuman analyst, as brought into the foreground, may now be explored from different viewpoints. It is a multidetermined symbol with ramifications that extend into wide areas of the mind. The mental processes themselves fail at this juncture in their function of discriminating among possible meanings; the analyst must come to the patient's assistance by an interpretation that will discover the source of the confusion and point to a path that can be followed for the continuance of relaxed free association.

Least controversial as to meaning and most important for treatment are the suggested implications that the analyst is really a frightening person for the patient and that a therapeutic relationship is difficult to sustain. The course of the analysis and the context of the present resistance having indicated that this is not a genuine problem, that the patient has "basic trust" and every intention of continuing treatment, other aspects of the resistance may now be examined in a stratified and systematic "approach from the surface."

Clearly, there has been a violation of the fundamental rule, which is the main instrument of the therapeutic alliance and the guide to the labyrinthine interconnections of the "image of the analyst" that has become the focal point of transference conflicts. The resistance, in effect, deprives the analyst of access to the patient's mind; instead, she seeks to penetrate the analyst's. Has she guessed correctly the inferences he has been making as she speaks?

(This happens to be the case.) There is both a defensive and an intelligently inquisitive aspect to this reversal of the analytic task. From the standpoint of therapy this attitude cannot be allowed to serve as a resistance, diverting a secret current of associations that isolates her true thoughts from the façade she presents to the analyst. It is perfectly permissible to wonder about the analyst, but not to withhold her ideas on the subject. The surrender of privacy on this point will bring therapeutic rewards.

The dichotomy of thought behind the present resistance has genetic antecedents in games of outwitting her father during childhood and in identifications with the mother who, in similar fashion, deceived him. There are also "deeper" sexual connotations; the "refusal to be penetrated" and the "reverse penetration" of the partner, constitute important factors in the patient's frigidity with her husband and a refusal to accept the female role. The path from the "surface" to the "depths" of these stratified meanings is apparent to the analyst but cannot be revealed to the analysand until she is prepared to understand and accept such interpretations.

As a first step, the "confrontation" of the patient with her consciously resistant attitude produces immediate gains in depriving the image of the "stern" analyst of puzzling aspects that have temporarily impeded the progress of treatment. The silence has been filled in by the revelation of associations that had been withheld. An attitude that contributed to alienation between analysand and analyst has been converted into a new instrument of understanding and mutual acceptance between them.

The patient's curiosity about the analyst's methodology actually portends a useful aspect of the treatment. It reflects the need for insight that becomes a powerful factor in the therapeutic process. In conjunction with the analyst's interpretations, it will serve to initiate revisions in the patient's personality by setting the "observing ego" in opposition to the "experiencing ego" (Sterba, 1934), a major step in establishing intellectual control over behavior.

However, free association initially requires the patient to suspend critical functions, which he delegates to the analyst as a precondition for expanding the inner boundaries of consciousness. Earlier sexual curiosity with respect to the father now emerges but is blocked by the censor, which produces the image of a stern and punitive father. The therapeutic alliance is broken off at this point, and associations cease.

Now the analyst's interpretation invites the patient to resume temporarily the exercise of critical functions to become aware of and combat the censorship. He demonstrates the seductiveness of the game of "outguessing" and teasing the analyst. The focus changes from the anxiety to the underlying wish. It will also be demonstrated that the mixed feelings to the analyst are incompatible with the therapy the patient needs and with the realistic attitude that the patient actually experiences toward him. There will be no occasion for self-approach or shame on the part of the patient. The infantile origins soon become apparent and promote an understanding of similar behavior toward the father during the Oedipal stage. Alternations between free association and interpretation and between transference formations and their renewed dissolutions into therapeutic alliances will gradually extend the conquest of the mature ego over the residues of infantilism.

The interventions of the analyst are not limited to interpretations. The revival of infantile tendencies may lead to inexpedient forms of behavior in everyday life that become the objects of the analyst's concern, especially where they imperil the continuance of treatment. Thus, the patient may "act out" by threatening to leave her husband, a multidetermined intention, which, to the extent that it is dominated by unconscious fantasies, calls for analysis rather than action. The preliminary rules of the treatment may be invoked, such as the admonition to avoid important decisions while motivations and values are undergoing change. The refusal of the patient during moments of emotional turmoil to be bound by such rules constitutes a nonverbal form of resistance and may confront the analyst with the need to establish a prohibition: the statement, for example, that a divorce is incompatible with the continuance of treatment. Here he invokes the "principle of abstinence," which, like the fundamental rule, is an "indispensable" instrument of analytic therapy.

The variations of character structure and the changes in external circumstances, with respect to each patient, bring unique factors and experimental conditions into every analysis and usually require, at one time or another, the use of different agents of psychotherapy, as delineated by Edward Bibring (see above). Interpretations and other interventions unleash and seek to control all the complex and formidable forces of the personality in its efforts to adjust to life. The analytic setting and its rules, however, can only set up a harbor for temporary protection and repair work. External and internal storms must be met with understanding and helpfulness, which require the analyst to utilize the routines as an aid, not as an artificial restriction, in achieving ultimate goals. There must be a balance, which each analyst in each case finds for himself, between flexibility and firmness, between inventiveness and tradition, in coping with the demands made upon his therapeutic equipment. The base lines of the analytic procedure—

the fundamental rule and the verbal bridge—are as valuable as guides for the analyst as they are for the patient in finding his bearings while coping with the unpredictable adventures of life that they have agreed to share.

The "Construction"

The construction is the analyst's ever widening basis of operation from which he makes his interpretations. It is the analyst's hypothesis about the total personality organization revealed by the transference neurosis. From the initial resistance to the communication of a thought, the motive for which the analyst can scarcely judge, the resistance becomes in time a carefully defined surface of interaction in which each nuance of feeling and behavior in the patient's life bears discernibly and, to a great extent predictably, on the flow of ideas in the analytic situation. The slight hesitation at the beginning of the session may find its contemporary prototype in the insertion of a diaphragm and its past model in the restrictions on the anal impulses imposed by toilet-training. Constructions are the jointly composed charts that analyst and patient alike have formed from data about behavior that increasingly demand one hypothesis and no other—charts that have been chosen among possible alternatives, and have delicately organized the inner as well as the external experiences of the analysand. The interpretation becomes more and more the precise instrument for the refashioning of the biography that is being lived out once again in relation to the analyst. The reaction of the patient is, in turn, the experimental validation that widens the basis for the next construction and narrows the point of contact for the next interpretation.

Our above-mentioned patient will have come for treatment because her adolescent daughter is insolent and impossible to manage at home. The school record shows steady deterioration and the guidance counselor suggests that the child, and perhaps the mother as well, undergo some form of treatment. Previous therapy of the girl had produced little benefit, and she is most averse to a resumption. The father and family physician, as well as friends of the patient, urge her to undertake psychoanalysis herself. The mother is reluctant, but agrees that something must be done for her daughter. On this altruistic note she consults the analyst. A routine anamnesis quickly brings the acknowledgment of great unhappiness: frigidity, doubts as to the future of her marriage, a plethora of mild but unmistakably neurotic symptoms, and a quick shift in the presenting "resistance"; from pretending to be a healthy woman who seeks aid for her child, she now describes such distress that she wonders if treatment can help. Reality-testing has begun as the patient confronts her illness. Time and sacrifice must be devoted to it; a physician must be asked to assist. All conditions, including prognosis, having been found favorable, a therapeutic alliance is formed and the analytic setting is provided.

The initial alternation between a pseudo identity (the conscientious, helpful mother) and the real identity (the unhappy, misunderstood child in search of a conscientious, helpful mother) proved to be no ordinary or adventitious state of affairs but a fundamental principle of the patient's personality structure, the understanding of which was to deepen progressively as the analysis proceeded. It was also the polarizing force in the relationship to the analyst, both in its positive and negative aspects—the alliances and the resistances. The first resistances came predictably in the form of altruistic demands on behalf of her child—she wished the schedule reduced so that she could spend more time with the girl at home (the scene of their constant clashes).

When the analyst pointed out the incompatibility of this request with the analytic program to which she had so recently agreed, another request soon took its place. An exhibitionist had recently been seen in the neighborhood; could the schedule be rearranged so that she might escort her daughter home from school? This likewise could not be arranged—a situation that caused the patient to turn upon the analyst as insensitive, inhuman, and selfish. The treatment nevertheless continued.

Neither confrontations nor interpretations had been offered; the necessities of the analytic procedure were merely counterpoised against the necessities for interfering with the analytic procedure. The patient had sought in a preliminary way to test and control the analyst (compare the excerpt of the case history in the preceding section). Deep anxieties were unleashed by the failure to do so; it was really her neurosis with which she could not effect a compromise. At night she became sleepless and dreamed that men were breaking into her house; in her associations she recalled in detail several anxiety states during childhood and adolescence, which had been glossed over in the initial history. These anamnestic data filled in the outlines and confirmed the diagnosis of a hysterical personality disorder. Analytic formulations about hysteria in themselves provide a valuable guide to expected experiences of the patient and the presumptive course of treatment.

With analysis under way, the first moves toward interpretation were in the nature of "confrontations," which in effect extended the personality study. Why did she have so many clearly sexual dreams about men in her past and present in whom she professed not the slightest interest? Why did she demand love from her husband when he was clearly not in the mood and reject him when he was? Why was she so submissive, though a grown woman, to her mother's outrageous demands? And why did difficulties with her own daughter arise so regularly and predictably after a visit from the mother? A disposition to repress her true feelings and to project these into a myriad of other characters literally spelled itself out in her dreams: Wherever she went (more and more clearly to the analyst's office) her mother, her daughter, her friends accompanied her, so that she was never alone for a moment with the analyst—any more than, in similar fantasies, she was alone with her husband when they were in bed.

As she was thus deprived of her surface identities through such initial insights (which she usually consciously rejected), resistances in the form of violations of the fundamental rule began to succeed the resistances through the acting out of false identities. She would begin sessions with the remark, "I have nothing to say today." Interpretations took the place of confrontations, drawing support from the growing awareness of each detail of the patient's experiences and fantasies and undermining her defense mechanisms by tracing them to their origins. Her silent states at the beginning of a session could definitely be related to a defiant element in her frigidity. Her more overt rebelliousness could be compared to that in her daughter, which she unconsciously instigated, and which expressed through projection the concealed hostility to her own mother. Characteristically, while voicing skepticism of the analyst's interpretations, the behavior of the patient changed, and she reported clashes with her mother while the difficulties with the daughter and husband subsided. The overt transference was hostile; the underlying therapeutic alliance was strong. The Oedipal relation to her father was found to provide a model for this dichotomy, which was stormy and critical on the surface to cover the deep bond that mother would not tolerate.

Such a "construction," a proposition about a pattern of behavior that defines its details in the present and past as well as in the links between them, can only be established by the gradual coordination of much information and the experimental testing of the proposition itself. The interpretation deals with an immediate resistance, an idea that is not verbalized. The construction clarifies the history of the patient and the functioning of his personality as manifest in the resistance, in the neurosis, and in total behavior.

The formation of such an integrative hypothesis involves the correlation of data, empirically obtained in a controlled setting by means of a standardized technique, with theoretical formulations as to the psychodynamics, psychopathology, and psychotherapy involved. It is for this reason that psychoanalysis has had to develop its interrelated aspects as a method of treatment, a tool of investigation, and a system of concepts about normal and abnormal mental processes. Its intricate metapsychology involves genetic, topographic, structural, dynamic, economic, and adaptive viewpoints. The genetic viewpoint is both the first and still the most practical available to the analytic therapist. It has inevitably passed through different phases and is differently conceived of by different analysts. As Leo Rangell (1961) points out: "Psychoanalysis has always been predicated upon a genetic exploration toward the early years of life, a principle which [is] considered one of the primary 'points of view' in psychoanalytic metapsychology" (1961). Although concepts about personality formation and development and their influence upon present psychopathology may change or be a cause of dissension, the importance of the childhood period is always confirmed.

Actually, as Rangell indicates, the differing outlooks on child development "approach the field from opposite directions, the findings of which complement each other." The most traditional approach is that of the analyst of the adult patient, who has to infer childhood experiences from the reports available to him from his patients. Evidence of infantile imprints on the present personality was also to be found in preverbal residues such as affective expressions, gestures, posture, dreams, and psychosomatic disorders. Later, child analysis became a field that permitted more direct observation. Today, developmental studies at many centers bring with them valuable information about personality formation, which have considerably influenced the analyst's constructions about the origins of his patient's difficulties.

A panel on the subject of infantile neurosis chaired by Ernst Kris in 1954, that year of outstanding activity and clarification in psychoanalysis, afforded an opportunity to examine transitional aspects of the change from an older to a more modern frame of reference as it was affecting classical analysis, more immediately perhaps in the area of construction formation than in any other aspect of technique. Emphasizing the broad scope of the analyst's task, Anna Freud suggested that the "emergence of neurotic conflicts has to be regarded as the price paid for the complexity of the human personality." Reconstructions of the past could no longer be limited to the libidinal phases of development.

We have of course long left behind that earliest stage when masturbation was regarded as a pathological factor, something between a breeding ground and a forerunner of later neurotic symptom formation. We have discarded also a conception held in earlier years, that all other autoerotic activities (thumb-sucking excepted) are masturbation substitutes. They merely assumed that aspect for us when we reconstructed events backward from the study of the phallic phase. When working upwards from the beginning of life, we see them fall into place as distinct expressions in their own right, reaching their respective peaks at the maturational peak of the libidinal phase by which they are determined. Thumb-sucking in the first year of life, anal play and interest in excrement in the second and third, phallic masturbation and exhibitionism between the ages of three and five, have assumed the settled status of normal and legitimate pregenital activities (in contrast to the "polymorphous perverse" evaluations placed upon them from the older standpoint).

The consequence of the more recent orientation is an absorption in the establishment of developmental norms and variants that still respect the concept of "constitution" but have found more detailed and ontogenetic explanations for phenomena, which in the past were ascribed to inherited memories. The actual personalities of the parents and other figures in the child's life and his experiences with the group's ideals and institutions must be "reconstructed," along with the drive vicissitudes, in evaluating not only the resistances but the adaptive behavior of the patient during treatment.

Heinz Hartmann, at the 1954 panel, raised pertinent questions as to the bearing of newer knowledge of personality development on concepts of child and adult neurosis and their relatedness to each other: "When Freud first approached this problem, he found that what he actually considered a neurosis was frequently considered naughtiness and bad upbringing by the parents and by the teachers; today we are confronted with the reverse situations; that is, in rather broad circles, every naughtiness, actually every behavior of the child that does not conform to the textbook model, every developmental step that is not according to plan, is considered 'neurotic.' " What does this mean? It means that the broad range of normal variations of behavior is not recognized and that the specific features of what analysts call a neurosis are lost (Kris, 1954). Genetic concepts must use referents of normal behavior in order to postulate a neurosis.

Dr. Hartmann then raised questions as to the relationship between childhood neurosis and adult neurosis likely to emerge from such a perspective. He did not think that a later neurosis must always be modeled on an earlier one. Each arises in its own context as an adaptive interaction between the personality dispositions of the moment and the satisfactions and demands presented by the environment. A childhood neurosis may actually prove to be a more favorable reaction than apparently normal behavior (for example, nightmares after a tonsillectomy in contrast to placid withdrawal). Correspondingly, not all ego distortions and fixations of childhood need be detrimental to the adult. Maturation has both modifying and disturbing effects on earlier dispositions; each period of development brings with it phase-specific capacities as well as inadequacies. Simple genetic continuities and repetition compulsions should not be postulated; the genetic construction must include a functional appraisal of each stage of development in its own context.

The rapid growth of analytic knowledge, which has both contributed to, and been stimulated by, the field of child observation, has included such outstanding work as that of René Spitz on hospitalism and anaclitic depression (1945), Margaret Mahler on the autistic and symbiotic psychoses of children (1958), the observations of Greta Bibring and her associates on the psychological processes in pregnancy and the formation of the earliest mother-child relationships (1961), and the fruitful work at Yale University (Jackson and Klatskin, 1950; Ritvo and Solnit, 1957), to name but a few of the outstanding persons and projects that have ushered in for psychoanalysis an age of statistical study and group collaboration. (The research of Anna Freud and the Hampstead Clinic group will receive consideration in a later section.)

Hartmann's concept of the "self" (1950) has been ably taken up in Edith Jacobson's *The Self and the Object World* to establish a longitudinal picture of the self-concept as developing out of earliest phases of differentiation from the primal mother-child unity and operative both in normal and abnormal mental conditions at successive stages of maturation. The "defense mechanism" of identification has been brought into line with structural and adaptive viewpoints that examine its multiple and phase-specific functions in relation to objects (such as the mother's personality and influence on the child). The Oedipal reactions to the primal scene thus acquire a long history of earlier determinants, which reduce the need to invoke "constitutional" factors or "racial memories" as explanations.

Constructions based on the mutual organization of the individual personality with its environment are envisioned in multidimensional perspectives by Erik H. Erikson's concepts of "epigenesis" and the "life cycle" (1959). He postulates an evolution of the personality through a succession of identities that enable the individual to experience and integrate a hierarchically organized succession of roles as he passes through "psychosocial phases" of his development. At the end of adolescence, if circumstances have been favorable, the "ego identity" will successfully incorporate past roles and prepare the individual for his adult functions.

Erikson compares and contrasts identifications and identity. The former are mental mechanisms for relating to objects; the latter "arises from the selective repudiation and mutual assimilation of childhood identifications, and their absorption in a new configuration, which, in turn, is dependent on the process by which a society (often through subsocieties) identifies the young individual, recognizing him as somebody who had to become the way he is." The process through which the adolescent finally unifies the discordant forces exerted by the diffusion of identities within himself is termed by Erikson the "identity crisis." Identity itself "appears as only one concept within a wider concept of the human life cycle which envisages childhood as a gradual unfolding of the personality through phase-specific psychosocial crises: the epigenetic principle."

Erikson proceeds to apply this viewpoint to the disorders that the analyst encounters and the therapeutic tasks involved. "Diffusion of identity" may mark the reactions of the adolescent to demands made upon him for physical intimacy, occupational choice, energetic competition, and self-definition. Regressive efforts to avoid the integration of roles may result in "loss of identity" or the choice of a "negative identity." In therapy, these abnormalities are especially prone to appear in borderline cases with a disposition to malignant acting out. Mockery and self-destructiveness characterize "identity resistance," a phenomenon that is not limited to adolescents (compare Freud's concept of the negative therapeutic reaction!). Erikson comments on this problem in the training of analytic candidates. He further maintains that analysts should systematically relate the integrative tasks of the ego to the organized values and institutions of society and in this sense reviews the famous Dora case (1962) to demonstrate the enhancement of the analytic instrument through the epigenetic viewpoint. Basic trust, not merely basic anxiety or basic sexual needs, should be included in the analysis of the transference neurosis.

Recall and Insight

The course of analysis shows the powerful influence of the past in maintaining neuroses as strongholds of infantilism in contemporary life. This influence must be reduced. The recall of the past, however, was never an end in itself for the analyst. Even in the Breuer-Freud period, the uncovering of the traumatic memory was regarded as a condition for the reintegration of the personality, which had been split by repression. It was not sufficient to recall an event; it had to be "abreacted," that is, fitted emotionally and intellectually into the psychic organization of the patient.

The topographic viewpoint and the use of hysteria as a model favored the disposition of the analyst to see the lifting of the infantile amnesia as virtually synonymous with the achievement of integrated mental functioning. The structural viewpoint replaced the therapeutic goal, "make the unconscious [memory] conscious" with the formula, "where id was, there shall ego be." The function of memory was still a guide to the organization of the personality, but the transference neurosis had come to be understood and treated in terms of a broader spectrum of strivings, defenses, and mastery techniques for reconciling inner needs with external conditions.

The fixation on the past was now understood as a multidetermined set of attitudes in which particular memories possessed crystallizing and signal functions. The relationship of experience to character and symptom formation could no longer be established merely by recall but had to be inferred by "insight," which placed particular memories in their causal contexts and thus indicated the corrective measures that were necessary. It was not a single glimpse of the parental genitals that established penis envy or castration anxiety; the entire psychological climate of a family would have to be reconstructed as the background for an understanding of the maturational tendencies that were revived and guided in new directions through the analysis.

It may not be a particular event that is forgotten, but rather the affective and behavioral associations, which have to be restored by insight. Thus, the patient recalls without emotion the death of his mother but has an implacable hostility to the father, whom he unconsciously and unjustly blames for depriving him of his mother. Or he may develop a subway phobia in reaction to the same event: He does not wish to repeat the last visit to the hospital, which was followed by a permanent separation. Insight replaces such magical methods of inner and external adaptation with conscious controls that develop the capacity of the personality to meet problems realistically.

The relationship between memory and insight is partly a result of the analytic process itself. Ernst Kris describes the "imperceptible transition from reporting to remembering, from repetition to recall," which develops in the course of free association (1956c). The analytic setting, as well as the therapeutic needs of the patient, predispose him to introspection and reconsideration of his past. This tendency is increased by the development of the transference and the genetic reconstructions of the analyst. There is the danger of "regressive evasion," of a flight into the past, with an avoidance of its relationship to later stages of maturity and to contemporary problems. Kris describes, for example, the "personal myth" (1956b), the perpetuation of certain past memories at the expense of others, which may mislead the analyst into sharing a misconception of the patient's true history.

Analytic theorists have taken different views as to the meaningfulness of insights to be gleaned from the past. This has already been pointed out with reference to transference and constructions. The role of early memories in shaping the experience of insight itself has become of considerable interest to analysts. Thus Bertram D. Lewin (1950) finds in insight a derivative of the tactile grasp and the narcissistic omniscience of the infant; Ernst Kris speaks in a similar sense of "id" as compared to "ego" aspects of insight (1956a).

The Kleinian analyst usually places greater weight than the Freudian on the earliest childhood memories and their direct perpetuation in the current neurosis (1955). Freud himself was quite skeptical about the extent to which the earliest memories could be directly awakened except in the context of present needs stimulated by the relationship to the environment (1937). There is also a question about the modifiability of pre-Oedipal, and especially preverbal, experiences. The Hartmann view of maturation, with its emphasis on evolutionary changes of function and shifting relationships between defense and adaptation, does not favor the assumption that multi-determined and ever evolving interactions between present needs and past dispositions will find solution through an isolated reconstruction and re-capitulation of early infantile experiences.

However, all analysts agree that the genetic viewpoint, in a structural context, should be fully utilized. Anna Freud probably expresses the opinion of most classical analysts when she suggests that "where an individual has not developed towards the oedipus complex but has been arrested in his development in the pre-verbal phase or soon after, we lack in analysis the background against which these early phases can be analysed. I would end even with a more sweeping statement. I believe where the phase of dependence has never been overcome and independence has not first been reached and then lost again, it becomes impossible to cure in analysis the state of dependency" (1962). The therapeutic alliance itself, as she points out, "is based on ego attitudes that go with later states [of development] namely, on self-observation, insight, give-and-take in object relationship, the willingness to make sacrifices." Thus, the analyst cannot find leverage for modifying the earliest infantile reactions.

Maxwell Gitelson argues, however, that the transference alliance will not even be established without arousing and including strong residues of infantile object relationships (1962). "We are dependent on the reoccurrence in the analytic situation of those 'primitive mechanisms' of introjection-projection which phenomenologically we call 'rapport,' and which eventuate in transference," he declares. The anaclitic (dependent) attitude with which the patient presents himself for treatment finds a complementary disposition in the diatrophic function of the analyst (Spitz, 1956), that is, his healing intentions, which reproduce "fostering influences of the kind which emanate from the effective mother during the child's early development." Against this background Gitelson sees therapeutic agencies such as suggestion, manipulation, and confrontation as potential expressions of the diatrophic attitude, which may be "directed towards increasing the patient's autonomy and preparing the way for analysis proper."

Elizabeth Zetzel (1965) agrees that "the analytic situation demands from the outset maximal mobilization of those ego attributes which remain for the most part contingent on the success achieved at a relatively early stage of psychic development. Such mobilization will be fostered by intuitive adaptive responses on the part of the analyst which may well be compared to those of the successful parent." The problem raised by Gitelson and Zetzel in this connection concerns the need of the analyst, in taking into account and utilizing with insight early stages of psychic development, to modify his traditional neutrality. Gitelson believes the diatrophic function is sufficiently inherent in flexibly used classical technique to make specific modifications unnecessary. Zetzel, who takes a similar position, also urges the analyst to consider the mature portion of the personality and "respond at all times to affect which indicates the patient's need to feel respected and acknowledged as a real person." Although the analyst must retain an objective and dispassionate role, which insures against uncontrollable regression, his areas of sympathetic alliance with the patient in his sufferings and reliving activities inherently expand his functions beyond that of the object and interpreter of the transference neurosis and makes him a participant in reliving experiences that revise the personality.

Verbalization

The relationships between recall and insight, as well as between infantile and mature dispositions of the personality, achieve an ultimate focus in the analytic setting through the verbalized contacts between patient and analyst. The aim of the patient's verbalization, as originally delineated by Freud, was essentially to express his thoughts automatically. The ideal process was supposed to coincide with complete exclusion of self-consciousness and of the analyst as a shaping force—attitudes to be fostered by the neutrality and self-obliteration of the latter as principles and methods of technique.

Transference, regarded as a form of resistance, was considered to begin with the dawning of awareness of the analyst's presence and soon manifested itself through interruptions of verbalization. The analyst could infer at such times that the patient's flow of thought had encountered an inner obstacle (a defense against impulses to verbalize) and that this obstacle was then projected to the person of the analyst. An idea (rooted in a forgotten memory) would evoke initial reactions of anxiety and shame, which the patient experienced through a preoccupation with the analyst's opinion about him. This concern would be registered in his verbalizations either directly or through their interruption.

The classical interpretation was presumed to break down the resistance to verbalization and to replace it with the idea that was being warded off. The patient could then return to his narcissistic state, which was conceived of as close to sleep and conducive to the entrance into consciousness of unconscious and preconscious material. The neurosis came to an end when conflicts between the conscious and the unconscious failed to arise and when permanent inner harmony was achieved. At that time, no further preoccupation with the analyst took place, and his function would be eliminated.

In early Freudian descriptions, the analyst's verbalizations (interpretations) were regarded especially from the standpoint of lending conscious qualities to unconscious ideas (1915). Repression, in contrast, deprived the ideas of this quality. Verbalization was supposed ultimately to complete the endopsychic process by which ideas normally progressed from the unconscious to consciousness. Dreams, symptoms, and acting out provided symbolic equivalents, a hidden code of language for ideas deprived of verbal expression; conversely, the interpretative interventions of the analyst translated the code and thereby deprived it of its value for the concealment of the true ideas. The useless code (namely, the symptom) was abandoned; the patient was not necessarily free of conflict nor happy, but would have to face his problems consciously and work them out realistically.

The views propagated by ego psychology modify this thesis in a number of ways: (1) Free association is not necessarily a withdrawal into a dreamlike state but rather a freely flexible flow of attention through various areas of consciousness. The integrity of the personality is not regulated merely by the border between the ego and the id but by its total organization. (Freud, for example, came to recommend that the present must be brought into the patient's range of associations if he himself failed to do so.)

(2) The mental state of the patient is no longer considered to alternate between narcissism and object relatedness (that is, awareness of the analyst). Even in the most deeply regressed state, remnants of the original mother-child unity may be presumed to operate and, with them, a transference disposition to the analyst. Correlatedly, the relationship between the analyst and the patient is not limited to words but includes feelings, attitudes, and actions, both of a spontaneous nature and as instilled by the analytic arrangements and developments themselves. The surface of contact extends beyond moments of resistance, followed by interpretations that produce a self-elimination of the analyst, and includes the therapeutic alliance as it exists at all times. The incorporated image of the analyst after the interpretation remains as a permanent new structure within the ego—a representative of reason and benevolence as guiding forces in personality formation.

(3) The relationship between the unconscious and consciousness—now placed in the perspectives of a structural model—no longer revolves about the endowment of an idea with words. Silence may be a mode of self-expression or relatedness that is not necessarily resistant (Waldhorn, 1959), whereas verbalization can conceal resistances, for example, through affectless reporting or acting out. More generally, the relation between consciousness and the unconscious, as mirrored in words, becomes merely one facet of resistance as viewed in a structural framework. Freud's older concept of unconscious thought, for example, would now be considered as evidence of ego, rather than instinctual, activity.

The structural psychologist is now more aware of the function and genesis of language in its relationship to external objects, especially during the primordial stages in which it served as a means for differentiation of the self from the mother. Analysts, therefore, follow verbalization as a clue to changing states of mental organization, which reflect the history of internal as well as external adaptive tendencies pertaining to neurosis and health. The role of the superego in post-Oedipal phases also contributes important elements to verbalization.

Genetically, the observations of René Spitz on the evolution of "verbal dialogue" from "action dialogue" in the infant show in detail the relationship between the acquisition of speech and the organization of the personality (Crocker, 1961). Spitz compares the analytic setting, with the induced regression, passivity, and dependence of the patient, to phases in which the child acquires and utilizes speech through mutual interactions with the mother (1956). He further suggests in this connection that the dependent (anaclitic) attitude of the analysand should be complemented by a supportive (diatrophic) attitude on the part of the analyst.

The analytic setting and the verbalized relationship are examined in a similar sense by Leo Stone (1961), who finds that they reproduce a succession of separation experiences from the mother. Analytic neutrality should not be conceived of as analytic indifference; the base line of the analyst's relationship to the patient should include the physician's benevolence, which in turn establishes connections with the warmer and object-forming side of the human experiences of the child. This latter aspect is approached from the standpoint of the therapeutic alliance by Elizabeth Zetzel (1965).

Rudolph Loewenstein, referring to the inherent distribution of language between the "expressive" functions of the analysand and the "cognitive" functions of the analyst, points to the interpretation as a union of two functionally dissociated portions of a single personality (1956)—a standpoint especially emphasized from the genetic and therapeutic aspects by Hans Loewald (1960) as reproducing formative two-person relationships with the mother; (see also M. Balint, 1950). The linguistic bridge between patient and analyst is widened to include the dream as well as affects and motor behavior by Mark Kanzer (1955, 1958, 1961), so that these are seen not as alternatives but as related parts of a total range of intrapsychic and interpersonal communicative activities.

The structural viewpoint has emphasized and added detail to the concept of the analyst as an actor and creative participant in every phase of the therapeutic proceedings. This is scarcely a departure from Freud's description of him as a substitute parent and an educator who not only interprets but guides old conflicts to new solutions. He even spoke of patients so infantile that "in analysis too they can only be treated as children" (1937). However, ego psychology and pre-Oedipal observations have clarified these tasks of the analyst in revising the personality. The verbal bridge remains an indispensable but not exclusive organizer, within the analytic setting, of the multiple aspects of the patient-physician relationship.

These concepts acquire practical and specific features in the treatment of different forms of neurosis. In the analytic setting, the hysterical patient, especially, misses the behavioral cues on which he is usually dependent for his identifications and object controls; it is these nonverbal aspects of speech that—formed through the peculiarities of his own upbringing—predispose him to rely upon intuitive judgments, acting out, and repressive techniques for communicative purposes. The obsessive individual, drawing upon his own formative experiences, finds it easier to fit his ordinary intellectualizing defenses into the model required in the analytic setting. To a considerable extent, he must learn through analysis to replace verbalized associations with hitherto excluded affective and motor bridges to the analyst, to other persons, and especially to himself. He must become acquainted with his true feelings and admit their influence into his actions.

Whereas the verbalizations of the analyst have meanings for the patient that revive and echo early mother-child experiences, they also span and draw upon intermediate phases of maturity, which should not be lost from view at any time. Speech is an adjunct to, but not a substitute for, adaptive problems and functions, which culminate not in verbal interchanges but in the ability to love and work, activities that may occur in complete silence.

Working Through and Termination

"Working through" is essentially the inner process by which the interpretations of the analyst achieve their effects in leading to the abandonment of resistances and defenses, so that the barriers within the personality can be reorganized in the direction of health rather than mental disorder. Insights are partly the result of interpretation and working through and partly the instrument of interpretation in securing further working through. Recognition of a hysterical patient's defensive identification with her mother is an insight that follows slowly from preparatory interpretations and requires their working through, perhaps by a combination of acting-out behavior and negative-transference manifestions, which yield at last to further interpretations. The insight gradually broadens into an understanding of many phases of past development, which are relived with a different outcome: It may be more permissible now, for example, to recall warm feelings toward the father, which were repressed through reinforcement of memories of his sterner moments. At last a full and integrated view of the father is attained, and his influence can take its place in a perspective governed by present needs rather than by the perpetuation of childish overdependency on identification with the mother as a means of adaptation.

The empirical limits of insight and working through in achieving effective change must be brought into relation to the theories of analytic goals and their attainment. Freud's 1937 paper on "Analysis Terminable and Interminable," carrying to new horizons the viewpoint of structural psychology, listed such ultimate barriers to the working-through process as: (1) the inaccessibility of early memories to recall under conditions that prevail in real life and the analytic setting; (2) limitations to the modifiability of basic components of the personality, such as the repetition compulsion, the psychic apparatus, and the influence of the environment; and (3) limitations of the analytic apparatus of therapy itself. (For a modern reappraisal of Freud's paper, see Pfeffer, 1963.)

The need to relinquish attachments to the early objects of drives and ego-mastery techniques has long been regarded as the special task of working through. Topographic theories emphasized the adhesiveness of the libido; structural descriptions view the same clinical phenomena from such vantage points as early mother-child relationships, the choice of defenses by the ego, and the formation of automatisms of behavior, which serve as pathological adaptive instruments of the personality. The resolution of the transference neurosis provides the essential means for replacing the entrenched infantile and neurotic formations with more flexible, mature, and conflict-free patterns.

The capacity of the personality to operate successfully in the present is the ultimate test of the therapeutic process. The aging spinster cannot utilize newly released potentialities to achieve the same ends as might have been available to her twenty years earlier. The middle-aged man whose educational opportunities were impaired by neurosis cannot realistically fit himself into society and its opportunities for satisfaction in the same way at forty as he might have at twenty. Individual talents and handicaps, as well as economic and social position, inevitably influence both the course and the outcome of personality regeneration through analytic methods. Sickness, disaster, and human inadequacy will always limit the capacity of the mental apparatus to function healthfully in resolving the problems of life. Full recognition of these factors sometimes earned Freud the reputation of a pessimist; the analyst is an optimist to the extent that he favors maximum recourse to the therapeutic opportunities afforded by his method for enabling the individual to surmount neurotic difficulties and to avoid the creation of new ones. This is perhaps the ultimate structural framework in which to view the working-through process, as described in Freud's practical and metapsychologically meaningful statement: "The business of analysis is to secure the best possible conditions for the functioning of the ego; when this has been done, analysis has accomplished its task" (1937).

The criteria for the end of treatment include such an attainment of health as will be manifested clinically by the cessation of symptoms; such adaptive potentialities as the capacity for love and work; such metapsychological standards as a stable and mature balance between the components of the personality; and such signs in the analytic setting as attest to the dissolution of the transference neurosis. Thus, the cessation of infantile demands and fears in relation to the analyst, the overcoming of dependency, the withdrawal of interest from treatment and a concomitant increase in object relatedness to the external world and in subject relatedness to the inner world, are signals that the terminal phase is in prospect.

Clinical experience must be utilized, of course, to determine whether there are elements of a flight into health or a temporary adjustment, which under less favorable circumstances may lead to further bouts of neurosis. Presumably there is no ultimate certainty in such matters; like the analyst, the patient must accept the fact that there cannot be such certainties in real life; and that for the present, a haven has been reached and that a further, if presumably more limited, exposure to the analytic process may ultimately be necessary (Gray, 1965).

The impetus to termination may come from either the patient or the analyst; ideally, both will be in accord on the setting of a date, usually after a preliminary period in which the prospect of termination has had a chance to exert its effect. Frequently, there are exacerbations of symptoms during the terminal period as the prospect of the analyst's support is withdrawn and as anxiety, guilt, and resentment take its place. Much important material for further insight and working through is obtained in this way. One must, in fact, be prepared for the possibility that the "termination" may end in a new phase of treatment. In other instances, the supportive but not self-eliminating features of the analysis will be apparent only some time after termination, in which case the residua of the transference neurosis can then be seen in better perspective and subjected to therapy.

The real relationship to the analyst, not merely the unresolved transference, constitutes an obstacle to the end of treatment. There is a realistic need for a detached, informed, and trusted observer to provide insight at the critical moments of life. The discovery that such persons exist may be one of the most valuable products of treatment. To a certain degree, these functions of the observing ego are acquired by the patient for himself in the course of treatment. Complete autonomy of self-analytic abilities, however, can never be attained even by the analyst himself, and the extent to which the former patient can find others in his environment to assume a needed supplementary role may be a determinant of the success with which he masters that phase of the working-through process, which always follows the completion of treatment in the actual analytic setting. It is therefore common for the analyzed person to insist on analysis for a husband or wife, as a precondition for true sympathy of outlook, or to develop new sublimations after treatment, which in essence permit substitutions for the analytic relationship. An interest in art, for example, may provide an outlet for propensities to apply insightful understanding to other persons and thus perpetuate mature identifications with the analyst as well as an objectivated and more or less conscious continuance of the process of self-exploration.

Validation

The validation of psychoanalytic therapy is an inherent aspect of its use. The empirical test—the appeal that it possesses not only for patients but for practitioners—is evidenced by its growth over a seventy-year period. This, of course, can serve only as a limited testimonial; other methods of treatment also claim success. A more explicit guide for the analyst himself lies in each interpretation and in the responses evoked in the patient—a constant and inexorable submission of his theories and skills in an experimental setting to the invariably critical judgment of the analysand. The effects of the interpretation can be traced by means of many criteria, not least of which is the progressive development in the direction of therapeutic aims. In no other science is the self-esteem of the experimental object so prejudiced against cooperation and a desire for the success of the experiment; in no other field of medical practice are miscalculations so likely to be registered immediately in terms of emotional and social upheaval. In no other specialty is the preliminary training of the experimenter so stringent, with every opportunity (and requirement) calculated to require a lifetime of review not only of one's own results but of his colleagues'.

The inherent difficulties in subjecting the analytic process and its results to more precise scientific evaluations have been well known since the days of "Dora" (1905). Briefly, these difficulties include: (1) the confidential nature of medical communication; (2) the intimacy of the patient-physician relationship (which most practitioners feel would be disturbed by any recordings, including note-taking by the analyst—an opinion that nevertheless should be submitted to experimental verification); (3) the lengthiness of therapy and the meandering aspects which would make description and elucidation tremendously difficult and time-consuming tasks; (4) the multi-determinants of each disorder and the unique elements of each cure that give every analysis a special character; (5) the fact that an analyst can see relatively few cases in the course of his entire professional life, during which time his techniques are constantly maturing; (6) the fact that most analyses involve private arrangements between individual patients and practitioners, and which therefore emphasize the immediate therapeutic, rather than the ultimate scientific, goals; and (7) the difficulties in evaluating analytic methods and results by criteria other than the analyst's own evidence, such as have been well described by Benjamin B. Wolman (1964).

The standardization of an analytic case history must involve endless intricacies. How is "incentive for treatment" to be measured? Health and illness do not necessarily coincide with the structure of a particular disorder. Uncontrollable external circumstances are likely to occur at one state or another of a prolonged analysis, exerting their complicating influence on the course of treatment. How shall the ability to love and work be charted? Or are these capacities insufficiently scientific? What arrangements can be made by the individual practitioner for suitable follow-up studies? The analyst himself has his own formidable metapsychological criteria—ego strength, the capacity for controlled regression, the dissolution of the transference neurosis—which likewise do not lend themselves readily to qualitative descriptions, much less to quantitative demonstrations.

Yet psychoanalysts are exceptionally well-trained physicians and scientists, with no less a hunger for professional certainty or acceptable publications than their colleagues in other fields. Freud offered follow-ups of his own cases, which have also been treated and discussed by other analysts over the years. More modern and systematic reanalyses (McLaughlin, 1959), and follow-up studies of recent cases are being undertaken (Pfeffer, 1963b). The role of dreams; the meaning of symptoms, of transference, of resistance, and so on; the effects of treatment on all types of cases are under constant survey and have been the subject of countless panels and publications.

Recent developments in psychoanalysis, particularly in clinical settings, which make possible the quantitative and systematic recording of data and comparative studies of the methods of different analysts, suggest that the era of "scientific validation" is drawing closer. Thus, at a panel to examine "Criteria for Analyzability," Herbert F. Waldhorn presented a paper on "Some Technical and Theoretical Observations Concerning Assessment of Analyzability," using material that grew out of discussions of a Kris Study Group at the New York Psychoanalytic Institute in 1957–1958.

"The study was undertaken because of the growing awareness of the need for a precise approach to the problem of estimating analyzability," noted Samuel A. Guttman, the panel reporter (1960).

> There usually exists little agreement on the meaning and use of such frequently employed terms as ego strength, motivation for cure, dependable transference potentialities, etc. making it difficult even to discuss analyza-

bility. Certain diagnostic indices have been recommended by Fenichel and Glover, among others, but no really meaningful gradations could be made due to complex, overlapping, clinical features.

Waldhorn, whose detailed presentation has been published elsewhere (1960), provided the panel with a historical survey of concepts and methods of determining analyzability and showed the increasing sophistication that had developed with the maturation of analytic theory and technique. Nevertheless, many limitations still persist in defining personality traits on the basis of structural concepts (ego strength, etc.), in relating these to the behavior of the patient in the analytic setting ("dependable transference potentialities"), and in establishing a uniformity of approach, methodology, and mode of investigation among large groups of analysts.

Waldhorn further stressed the importance, in any consideration of analyzability, of assessing

what demands analysis will make on the patient, and what will be the probable vicissitudes of his illness and life situation in the course of his analysis. Next we must know what functions and resources of his mental and physical makeup will be called upon to meet these demands. The significance of the structural hypothesis and the principle of multiple functioning for all analytic therapy requires evaluation not only of those ego functions which seem appropriate to study, but also of the significant operations of the id and superego structures and the impact of external reality as they relate to the psychic experience of being analyzed.

Among personality features to be assessed in terms of the demands placed upon the patient by the analyst, Waldhorn cited "a reasonable tolerance of frustration." The need imposed by analytic treatment to assume a passive role places special strains on certain homosexual, mildly paranoid, and sadomasochistic individuals. Ego functions involved in speech, introspection, and insight are also deserving of careful attention in evaluating the prospects of patients in their potential responses to analytic therapy. So, too, do the special motivations and backgrounds of workers in the field of mental health themselves, psychiatrists, physicians, social workers, and the like, who constitute the largest category of patients in analysis.

Aaron Karush and Sidney Levin, as other panel speakers, showed how different groups of analysts were working, each in its own way, on the problem of selecting proper cases. Karush, representing a Columbia group, sought criteria of ego strength in terms of functions of the ego such as intelligence, learning capacity, introspective dispositions, and identifications conducive to the formation of a successful analytic relationship. Sidney Levin, participating in a Boston project, discussed the limitations of inferences to be drawn from the case history, the psychiatric interview, and metapsychological assessments of personality traits, which cannot entirely replace trial analysis itself as an ultimate test of analyzability. Peter Knapp and co-workers, reporting later on additional findings of the same Boston group, cited the need to "standardize" the analyst himself as a judge of analyzability (1960). On an empirical basis, impressive similarities of assessments of analyzability by different analysts could be demonstrated, but their conclusions were attained by different methods.

The emergence of psychoanalysis, from the individual, private, and empirical, to the group enterprise with records, statistics, and a methodology for comparative research and experiment (a course of evolution not too dissimilar from contemporary trends in general medicine), was considerably facilitated by the growth of child analysis and observation, which developed in close symbiotic interchanges with adult analysis. The new phase was nowhere more in evidence than at the Hampstead Child-Therapy Clinic under the guidance of Anna Freud. In a discussion of the work in process there, she commented: "Analysts have been reproached often for taking no interest in planned research and the methods serving it; of making their discoveries haphazardly and incidentally; of not choosing their material according to plan; of working as individuals and not in teams; and of allowing their case material to drift out of sight without follow-up. All these failings exist, or have existed, but have to be attributed to the conditions of the past when psychoanalysis was wholly a matter of private practice and hedged in by the difficulties and restrictions imposed by the circumstances of the latter (1959).

> Conditions changed in this respect when psychoanalysis began to make contacts with established research centers and when the first psychoanalytic clinics were established. . . . New research activities . . . did not confine themselves to the field of psychoanalysis proper but explored the borderlines, on the one hand between psychoanalysis and organized medicine, on the other hand between psychoanalysis and academic, genetic psychology. In both instances, extraneous research techniques were either added to the analytic method or substituted for it for purposes of exactness. It remained an open and debated question whether research could be planned to take place without analysis itself, on topics of purely analytic interest, carried out by analysts who employ the analytic method only, without sacrificing any part of it.

In anticipation of an affirmative answer to this question, a number of research projects have been undertaken at the Hampstead Clinic, including the pooling of clinical material among a group of analytic workers and the planned selection of cases. Cases of similar type are distributed among different analysts who discuss developments at regular conferences. Although analytic technique precludes experiments, this "can be compensated by the selection for treatment of cases in which either nature, or fate, has caused the elimination or the exaggeration of one specific either innate or environmental factor" (Anna Freud, 1959). Thus, one group selected for study consisted of blind children; another, of institutional children orphaned in early life. The interrelationships of the maternal personality with that of the child were explored through the simultaneous treatment of both partners.

An indexing project was also begun, with the aim of categorizing and classifying on index cards the abundant clinical material in the weekly and bimonthly reports of cases in analytic treatment. Joseph Sandler and co-workers (1962) explored the relationship between the superego as a hypothetical area of the personality and its manifestations as they could be traced in this clinical material. This included, for example, the responses of the ego to authority figures. A list of headings was adopted, which showed promise of resolving the difficulties apparent from the reports of the panel on analyzability. Conferences within the group undertook to link "superego functions" with specific clinical material; thus the "need for self-punishment" was illustrated by actual observations of a boy who, after having been discovered in a theft, chopped off bits of his hair and cut pieces out of a ruler. While playing cards during the following session, he did not cheat as usual, but lost every game.

By 1963 Anna Freud was able to delineate the outlines of a diagnostic profile in use at the Hampstead Clinic, along with a concept of developmental lines, "which trace the child's gradual outgrowing of dependent, irrational, id—and object-determined attitudes to an increasing mastery of his internal and external world. Such lines—always contributed to from the side of both id and ego development—lead, for example, from the infant's suckling and weaning experiences to the adult's rational rather than emotional attitude to food intake; from cleanliness training enforced on the child by environmental pressure to the adult's more or less unshakeable bladder and bowel control" (Anna Freud, 1963). Thus, the loosely genetic description of personality development in terms of libidinal phases has been incorporated into, and replaced by, "the picture of any given child against the background of a developmental norm into which the state of his inner agencies, his various functions, conflicts, attitudes and achievements have to be fitted." Her 1965 book, *Normality and Pathology in Childhood,* implements these concepts in a work that spans and completes the initial statement of such goals as contained in *The Ego and the Mechanisms of Defence* nearly thirty years earlier.

Similar active work has been taking place in child development and treatment in the United States (Schafer, 1965). In adult analysis, the possibilities of validation have centered to a considerable extent on predictions with respect to patients' responses to interpretations, which are regarded as an inherent unit of the analytic process. Peter H. Knapp, who carried out a survey of the problems and literature in this field (1963), found that the tasks to be solved are as complex as those that confront the clinician in the gathering of anamnestic data and the evaluation of details pertaining to analyzability, progress, and the results of treatment.

In summary, patience and persistence continue to be the indispensable qualities that must characterize the psychoanalyst as scientific investigator, just as they characterize him as therapist, and as they must characterize others who deal with the multidimensional medical and social problems of the human race. The framework of analytic therapy today is the pattern of individual biographical data that must be fitted into a definable scheme of healthful adaptation. Judgment in such matters is ultimately arrived at through congruence between the opinions of the patient and the analyst— or through lack of congruence. The ultimate yardstick of therapeutic progress is the indefinable welfare of the patient; the ultimate instrument of therapeutic progress is the analyst himself, with his human, as well as scientific, limitations.

Van Buren O. Hammett, expressing wonder at the willingness of the analyst to invest the time, effort, and financial sacrifice in a specialty whose results cannot be made to appear statistically more impressive than other methods of therapy, which make less demands both on patient and physician, nevertheless has some relevant statistical data to offer: "In the Philadelphia area, which is fairly typical of the eighteen or twenty major centers of psychiatric training in the United States, there are currently 125 residents in training for the specialty. Concurrently, the number of active students in the two psychoanalytic institutes in Philadelphia is 106. The analogous figures for the entire nation, according to the most reliable information available, are: 3,617 residents in psychiatric training, 1,009 students enrolled in psychoanalytic institutes (1963–1964 figures)" (1965).

Pondering the causes for the appeal of psychoanalysis to the young psychiatrist, Hammett suggests:

> It is a truism that psychoanalytic theory and its application in therapy continue to exert a profound influence upon psychiatry generally . . . [in historical perspective], it swung the emphasis in psychiatry away from description toward deeper phenomena, and in so doing, lifted psychiatry out of the doldrums of taxonomy . . . revised the specialty and made it attractive to men with active minds. . . . There is no way of knowing how many physicians have been recruited for psychiatry by the appeal of psychodynamic [analytic] theory, or how many residents it has saved from quitting their training.

Perhaps much the same thing can be said for the analyst's patients, even if this means of validation cannot yet be registered in the statistics. Whereas the minds of therapists and patients alike are baffled by enigmas, analytic insights continue to open doors and provide pathways that lead more deeply into the mind than any others.

Summary

The evolution of classical psychoanalytic therapy has continued consistently along structural lines since the death of Freud in 1939. The theoretical contributions of Heinz Hartmann have greatly influenced the clinical viewpoint, leading to emphasis on the externally adaptive as well as the inwardly self-regulatory functions of the mental apparatus. Child analysis and its ally, child observation, have strengthened this disposition and made the analyst better acquainted with the experiences and techniques of object relatedness that characterize the patient at successive stages of development. Panoramic surveys of personality differentiation (A. Freud, E. H. Erikson, E. Jacobson) become the points of departure for contemporary assessments of mental health and illness that guide the analyst through the complexities of selection and treatment of his cases. This trend toward widened longitudinal and cross-sectional frames of reference has been matched by the expansion of the analyst's own contacts with his community in therapeutic, educational, and scientific enterprises outside the analytic setting.

Nevertheless, classical analysis, as the innermost core of analytic theorizing and therapy, has undergone relatively little change—one that is to be measured more in the analyst's outlook and use of his techniques than in their formal aspects. The applicability of the classical methods beyond the traditional sphere of the psychoneuroses has not been notably extended except in the hands of individual practitioners with special interests and aptitudes, who frequently introduce variants into the procedure. It should not be forgotten that modified forms of analysis are as legitimate descendants of psychoanalytic insights as is the classical model.

The stabilization in the status of classical analysis has found its counterpart in the diminution in force and frequency of deviant movements, which now tend to show wide areas of agreement with the established school, differentiate at later stages of development, sometimes consider themselves to be the correct interpreters of Freud, and may find representation and mutual tolerance in official psychoanalytic organizations.

Such disputes as now occur have prompted the efforts of classical analysts to define the essential features of their specialty through distinctions made between "basic techniques" and "parameters" (Eissler, 1953). The former are usually considered to involve: (1) the induction and resolution of a transference neurosis in the analytic setting; (2) the organization of the patient-physician relationship by means of a verbal bridge, which makes interpretation the specific tool of the analyst and insight the effective force that initiates and guides therapeutic revisions in the personality.

The adaptive viewpoint, as developed since 1939, has amplified the genetic element in the analyst's constructions. The Oedipal phase now takes its place in a libidinal sequence that extends from infancy to maturity (and involution) and is interrelated from the beginning with other essential components of the personality in their adaptive strivings. The ego and its functions, as organizers of these strivings, receive a pivotal role in the analyst's therapeutic considerations and techniques; only the ego can be influenced directly through the analytic process.

From this standpoint, the adaptive emphasis has brought to the fore the therapeutic alliance as the representative of the healthy and reality-oriented aspects of the patient's personality, which cooperate in treatment and expose the resistances stemming from the morbid components active in the transference neurosis. With the resolution of the latter, the operations of the personality are gradually regrouped, undergo maturation and integration, and are enabled to insure a maximum potential for the procurement of enjoyment and efficiency on the part of the individual.

Such therapeutic transformations are made with the assistance of increasing knowledge of child development. There is less need to invoke such hypothetical motivators as racial memories; vague formulations with respect to constitution are being replaced by more specific postulates about the inherited equipment of the personality and typical problem-solving patterns at various stages of maturation. The post-Oedipal phases of development are likewise placed in the sequence of events with which the analyst must deal.

The specific influence of the analytic setting itself has become a subject of careful study. Sensory deprivation, motor deprivation, sexual deprivation, and the relaxation of critical intellectual functions create artificial attitudes and behavior, for which there is no precise analogy in normal life. The role of speech as the special vehicle of object relatedness and personality revision has been illuminated both by genetic observations on the mother-child relationship and by structural correlations of verbal with nonverbal behavior. The analytic technique of neutrality has become increasingly differentiated from the underlying attitude of medical helpfulness, which characterizes the analyst as physician (Stone, 1961), and has roots in the anaclitic-diatrophic symbiosis from which the individual personality differentiates (Spitz, 1954).

The current developmental tendencies in psychoanalysis, as in other fields of medicine, presage the arrival of an era of group collaboration, comparative studies of cases with the aid of statistics and research, and standardization of the training of that ultimate instrument of psychoanalytic therapy, the analyst himself. New evolutionary activity in classical psychoanalysis may well be expected under these circumstances.

REFERENCES

[Note: S.E. refers to *The Standard Edition of the complete psychological works of Sigmund Freud* (London: Hogarth Press).]

ALEXANDER, F., and FRENCH, T. M. *Psychoanalytic therapy: principles and applications.* New York: Ronald Press, 1946.

BALINT, M. Changing therapeutical aims and techniques in psychoanalysis. *International Journal of Psychoanalysis,* 1950, 31, 117–124.

BIBRING, E. Psychoanalysis and the dynamic psychotherapies. *Journal of the American Psychoanalytic Association,* 1954, 2, 745–770.

BIBRING, GRETA L., DWYER, T. F., HUNTINGTON, DOROTHY S., and VALEN-STEIN, A. F. A study of the psychological processes in pregnancy and of the earliest mother-child relationship. In *Psychoanalytic Study of the Child,* 1961, 16, 9–72.

CROCKER, D. Psychoanalytic considerations concerning the development of language in early childhood. Panel report. *Journal of the American Psychoanalytic Association,* 1963, 11, 143–150.

DEVEREUX, G. Some criteria for the timing of confrontations and interpretations. *International Journal of Psychoanalysis,* 1951, 32, 19–24.

EISSLER, K. R. The effect of the structure of the ego on psychoanalytic technique. *Journal of the American Psychoanalytic Association,* 1953, 1, 104–143.

ERIKSON, E. H. *Identity and the life cycle. Psychological Issues,* 1959, No. 1. New York: International Universities Press.

ERIKSON, E. H. Reality and actuality. *Journal of the American Psychoanalytic Association,* 1962, 10, 451–475.

FENICHEL, O. Problems of psychoanalytic technique. Albany, N. Y.: *Psychoanalytic Quarterly,* 1941.

FENICHEL, O. *The psychoanalytic theory of neurosis.* New York: Norton, 1945.

FREUD, ANNA. *The ego and the mechanisms of defence.* London: Hogarth Press, 1937.

FREUD, ANNA. Problems of technique in adult analysis. *Bulletin of the Philadelphia Association for Psychoanalysis,* 1954, 4, 44–70. (a)

FREUD, ANNA. The widening scope of psychoanalysis. Discussion. *Journal of the American Psychoanalytic Association,* 1954, 2, 607–620. (b)

FREUD, ANNA. Clinical studies in psychoanalysis. *Psychoanalytic Study of the Child,* 1959, 14, 122–134.

FREUD, ANNA. The theory of the parent-child relationship. *International Journal of Psychoanalysis,* 1962, 42, 240–242.

FREUD, ANNA. The concept of developmental lines. *Psychoanalytic Study of the Child,* 1963, 18, 245–265.

FREUD, ANNA. *Normality and pathology in childhood.* New York: International Universities Press, 1965.

FREUD, S. *The interpretation of dreams* (1900). S.E., Vol 5. (Also published by Basic Books, New York, 1955.)

FREUD, S. Fragment of an analysis of a case of hysteria (1905). S.E., Vol. 7, pp. 7–122.

FREUD, S. The handling of dream-interpretation in psycho-analysis (1911). S.E., Vol. 12, pp. 89–96.

FREUD, S. Recollecting, repeating and working through (1914). S.E., Vol. 12, pp. 145–156.

FREUD, S. The unconscious (1915). S.E., Vol. 14, pp. 159–216.

FREUD, S. *Beyond the pleasure principle* (1920). S.E., Vol. 18.

FREUD, S. Psychoanalysis (1922). S.E., Vol. 18, pp. 235–254.

FREUD, S. The ego and the id (1923). S.E., Vol 19, pp. 3–68.

FREUD, S. Inhibitions, symptoms and anxiety (1926). S.E., Vol. 20, pp. 77–178.

FREUD, S. Analysis terminable and interminable (1937). S.E., Vol. 23, pp. 209–254.

FREUD, S. An outline of psychoanalysis (1938). S.E., Vol. 23, pp. 141–208.

GITELSON, M. The curative factors in psychoanalysis. *International Journal of Psychoanalysis,* 1962, **43**, 194–205.

GRAY, P. Limitations of psychoanalysis. Panel report. *Journal of the American Psychoanalytic Association,* 1965, **13**, 181–190.

GREENACRE, PHYLLIS. The role of transference. *Journal of the American Psychoanalytic Association,* 1954, **2**, 671–684.

GUTTMAN, S. A. Criteria for analyzability. Panel report. *Journal of the American Psychoanalytic Association,* 1960, **8**, 145–151.

HAMMETT, VAN BUREN O. A consideration of psychoanalysis in relation to psychiatry generally. *American Journal of Psychiatry,* 1965, **122**, 42–54.

HARTMANN, H. Ego psychology and the problem of adaptation (1937). *Journal of the American Psychoanalytic Association, Monograph Series,* 1958, No. 1.

HARTMANN, H. On rational and irrational action (1947). *In Essays on ego psychology.* New York: International Universities Press, 1964. Pp. 37–68. (a)

HARTMANN, H. Comment on the psychoanalytic theory of the ego (1950). In *Essays on ego psychology.* New York: International Universities Press, 1964. Pp. 113–141. (b)

JACKSON, EDITH B., and KLATSKIN, ETHELYN H. Rooming-in research project. *Psychoanalytic Study of the Child,* 1950, **5**, 236–274.

JACOBSON, EDITH. *The self and the object world.* New York: International Universities Press, 1964.

KANZER, M. The communicative function of the dream. *International Journal of Psychoanalysis.* 1955, **36**, 260–266.

KANZER, M. Acting out, sublimation and reality testing. *Journal of the American Psychoanalytic Association,* 1957, **5**, 633–644.

KANZER, M. Image formation during free association. *Psychoanalytic Quarterly,* 1958, **27**, 465–484.

KANZER, M. Verbal and non-verbal aspects of free association. *Psychoanalytic Quarterly,* 1961, **30**, 427–450.

KLEIN, MELANIE. *New directions in psychoanalysis.* London: Tavistock, 1955.

KNAPP, P. H., LEVIN, S., McCARTER, R. H., WERMER, H., and ZETZEL, ELIZABETH. Suitability for psychoanalysis. *Psychoanalytic Quarterly,* 1960, **29**, 459–477.

KNAPP, P. H. Short-term psychoanalytic and psychosomatic predictions. *Journal of the American Psychoanalytic Association,* 1963, **11**, 245–281.

KRIS, E. *Psychoanalytic explorations in art.* New York: International Universities Press, 1952.

KRIS, E. Problems of infantile neurosis. *Psychoanalytic Study of the Child.* New York: International Universities Press, 1954, **9**, 16–74.

KRIS, E. On some vicissitudes of insight in psychoanalysis. *International Journal of Psychoanalysis,* 1956, **37**, 445–455. (a)

KRIS, E. The personal myth. *Journal of the American Psychoanalytic Association,* 1956, **4**, 654–681. (b)

KRIS, E. The recovery of childhood memories in psychoanalysis. *Psychoanalytic Study of the Child*, 1956, 11, 54–88. (c)

LEWIN, B. D. *The psychoanalysis of elation*. New York: Norton, 1950.

LEWIN, B. D., and ROSS, HELEN. *Psychoanalytic education in the United States*. New York: Norton, 1960.

LOEWALD, H. W. On the therapeutic action of psychoanalysis. *International Journal of Psychoanalysis*, 1960, 41, 16–33.

LOEWENSTEIN, R. M. The problem of interpretation. *Psychoanalytic Quarterly*, 1951, 20, 1–14.

LOEWENSTEIN, R. M. Some remarks on the role of speech in psychoanalytic technique. *International Journal of Psychoanalysis*, 1956, 37, 460–468.

MAHLER, MARGARET S. Autism and symbiosis. *International Journal of Psychoanalysis*, 1958, 39, 77–83.

McLAUGHLIN, F. Problems of reanalysis. Panel report. *Journal of the American Psychoanalytic Association*, 1959, 7, 537–547.

MENNINGER, K. *Theory of psychoanalytic technique*. New York: Basic Books, 1958.

PFEFFER, A. Z. Analysis terminable and interminable—twenty-five years later. Panel report. *Journal of the American Psychoanalytic Association*, 1963, 11, 131–143. (a)

PFEFFER, A. Z. The meaning of the analyst after analysis. *Journal of the American Psychoanalytic Association*, 1963, 11, 229–244. (b)

RANGELL, L. Psychoanalysis and the dynamic psychotherapies. Panel report. *Journal of the American Psychoanalytic Association*, 1954, 2, 152–165.

RANGELL, L. The role of early psychic functioning in psychoanalysis. *Journal of the American Psychoanalytic Association*, 1961, 9, 585–609.

RITVO, S., and SOLNIT, A. J. Influences of early mother-child interaction on identification processes. *Psychoanalytic Study of the Child*, 1958, 13, 64–85.

SANDLER, J. On the concept of the superego. *Psychoanalytic Study of the Child*, 1960, 15, 128–162.

SCHAFER, R. Contributions of longitudinal studies to psychoanalytic theory. Panel report. *Journal of the American Psychoanalytic Association*, 1965, 13, 605–618.

SPITZ, R. A. Hospitalism. *Psychoanalytic Study of the Child*, 1945, 1, 53–74.

SPITZ, R. A. Countertransference. *Journal of the American Psychoanalytic Association*, 1956, 4, 256–265.

STERBA, R. The fate of the ego in psychoanalytic therapy. *International Journal of Psychoanalysis*, 1934, 15, 117–126.

STONE, L. The widening scope of indications for psychoanalysis. *Journal of the American Psychoanalytic Association*, 1954, 2, 567–594.

STONE, L. *The psychoanalytic situation*. New York: International Universities Press, 1961.

144 CLASSICAL PSYCHOANALYSIS SINCE 1939

WAELDER, R. The principle of multiple function. *Psychoanalytic Quarterly,* 1936, **5**, 45–62.

WAELDER, R. The structure of paranoid ideas. *International Journal of Psychoanalysis,* 1951, **32**, 166–177.

WALDHORN, H. F. The silent patient. Panel report. *Journal of the American Psychoanalytic Association,* 1959, **7**, 548–560.

WALDHORN, H. F. Some technical and theoretical observations concerning assessment of analyzability. *Psychoanalytic Quarterly,* 1960, **29**, 478–506.

WOLMAN, B. B. Evidence in psychoanalytic research. *Journal of the American Psychoanalytic Association,* 1964, **12**, 717, 731.

ZETZEL, ELIZABETH R. The traditional psychoanalytic technique and its variations. Panel report. *Journal of the American Psychoanalytic Association,* 1953, **1**, 526–538.

ZETZEL, ELIZABETH R. The theory of therapy. *International Journal of Psychoanalysis,* 1965, **46**, 39–52.

Part II

FREUDIANS
AND
NEO-FREUDIANS

5

SANDOR FERENCZI'S TECHNICAL EXPERIMENTS

Michael Balint

Introduction

It proved difficult to find the right place in this volume for the chapter dealing with Ferenczi's technical experiments. The first reason for this is that Ferenczi, unlike Jung, Adler, Melanie Klein, Sullivan, Alexander, and others, did not have "a technique." These writers, and many others besides them, had ideas on technique originating either from their clinical experiences or from theoretical considerations, stuck to them, and developed them into a kind of system. In some cases these ideas could even be given a name—to mention only one, Alexander's "corrective emotional experience"—which enabled one to refer to or to identify the technical system in a few words. Although the technique of psychoanalytic treatment was perhaps Ferenczi's favorite topic and occupied his creative mind most

147

of the time during his analytical career, it was always the treatment itself that mattered to him and never the working out of a tidy system.

Moreover, there can be no question that a very large part of his technical experiments, about which he reported largely but not exclusively in the early years of his analytical career, have become so much part and parcel of what is called the classical technique, that they are used nowadays as a matter of course, perhaps without one realizing that they originated with Ferenczi. On account of this, the correct place for this chapter would be in the part on classical Freudian technique.

However, at another period, which partly coincided with and partly followed the previous one, Ferenczi developed what is called the "active technique." This unfortunate name has led to all sorts of misapprehensions and misunderstandings, but it must be admitted that this "active technique" was in many respects a departure from the classical technique—a fact that Ferenczi never failed to emphasize *in the later stages of this period.* On account of this, this chapter ought to have been placed in the part of the volume dealing with the deviationist non-Freudian techniques. We would then have had the unpleasant task of explaining the historical fact that for quite some years Freud wholeheartedly supported Ferenczi's experiments in this direction and went even so far as to claim that the original idea which suggested these experiments to Ferenczi was his (Freud, 1918).

In the last phase of his technical experiments which developed in an unbroken line from the "active technique" and with which he continued practically to his death, Ferenczi discovered a fair number of clinical phenomena and technical procedures that are still in the center of our interest today. Among them I would like to mention the following: the immense therapeutic value of regression in the analytic situation, provided it is properly handled; and overriding importance of transference interpretations as compared with anything else that the analyst may do; the influence of the analyst's "professional hypocrisy" on the developing transference relationship and, with it, the need for absolute sincerity to the extent of the use of, what is nowadays called countertransference interpretations; the dangers of driving the patient by consistently adhering to the classical objective passivity into a repetition of the original pathogenic trauma whose effects may be as deleterious as that of the original one. If we concentrate our examination on these technical experiments, then the right place for this chapter would be in a nonexisting part of this volume, which should have a title like: "Pointers to Future Developments."

This was Ferenczi's fate: He could not be easily fitted into any preconceived pattern. He was too alive, too sensitive, and much too ready to respond. He was always willing to experiment with new responses until one of them led him to a new idea or to a new insight. True, the new idea in some cases had to be modified or qualified by further experience, but much more often than not it was revealing, stimulating, and—this was also part of Ferenczi's fate—it very often upset something in which other people still firmly believed, bestowing upon him the doubtful reputation of an iconoclast, the *enfant terrible* of psychoanalysis.

In what follows I shall try to describe Ferenczi's contributions to the technique of psychoanalysis under these three headings: (1) Contributions to Classical Technique; (2) The "Active Technique"; (3) Pointers to Future Development.

Contributions to Classical Technique

If one disregards Ferenczi's classical paper on "Introjection and Transference" (1909) because of its mainly theoretical implications, the beginning of this period is marked by his paper on "Obscene Words" (1911); the last papers belonging to this group, "Washing-Compulsion and Masturbation" and "The Dreams of the 'Clever Baby'" were published in 1923, but possibly even "The Problem of Acceptance of Unpleasant Ideas" (*Das Problem der Unlustbejahung*) (1926) can be considered as belonging to this group.

All these papers start with an everyday clinical observation, well known to every analyst, which, however, just because of this familiarity, had hitherto escaped proper notice and evaluation. This ability was one ingredient of Ferenczi's individual gift—for him everything that happened in the analytical situation remained alive forever; nothing was finally dealt with and filed away as fully understood. He retained this gift of fresh perception until the end of his life; he truly remained a child whose perceptions and apperceptions could never be pressed into conventional petrified patterns. Thus, all the papers belonging to this group have something surprising and refreshing in them.

Another important feature is that they extend the field of phenomena that the psychoanalyst should include in his observations. There is a very old tendency in psychoanalysis to concentrate the analyst's attention too much on the verbal contents of the patient's associations. For Ferenczi this concentration was too narrow, and in addition to the verbal contents, he watched constantly for the *formal elements,* as well as for what presently would be called the *pervading mood* of the associations. His short paper "Dirigible Dreams" (1912) is a good illustration of how he uses these two aspects. In a half-sleepy state like that just before awakening, the dreamer who is not satisfied with the outcome of his dream rejects it and causes an alternative ending to be dreamed. At times several endings are produced till one is eventually accepted, it even happens that the dreamer must wake up dissatisfied. In this example, the influence of both the pervading mood of irritation and the formal element of the successively produced alternatives is clearly observable.

The first impetus to this way of thinking originated with Freud and his theory of "symptomatic acts," many examples of which were described in his *Psychopathology of Everyday Life* (1901), chapters 8 and 9. Freud indicates here that many people perform, either occasionally or habitually, certain insignificant, that is, "unobtrusive" and "meaningless," acts, which, if properly examined, show a meaning and a structure similar to those of a neurotic symptom. All the symptomatic acts and parapraxes examined and described by Freud were due to the actions of voluntary muscles, such as habitual gestures, "bungled" actions, motor habits—for instance, playing with money or keys in one's pocket, and so forth.

Ferenczi, who was famous among the early analysts for his proneness to "bungled" actions and who was often called the king of parapraxes, found it easy to extend the boundaries respected by Freud. Not only the actions performed by the voluntary muscles, but all actions of any part or system of the whole person, or as expressed in modern usage, any piece of behavior became for him a challenge asking for examination and understanding. The result of his investigation was published in a paper, "Transitory Symptom-Constructions during the Analysis" (1912), which, though hardly quoted today, in fact started a new chapter in analytic technique.

The subtitle of this important paper runs as follows: "Transitory Conversion, Substitution, Illusion, Hallucination, 'Character-Regression,' and 'Expression-Displacement.'" This enumeration, which is not complete, indicates clearly at what points Ferenczi went beyond Freud's theory of the symptomatic acts. It is demonstrated in this paper that, in addition to the action of voluntary muscles, changes in other functions of the body or parts of the body may show a psychological structure that can be observed, understood, and interpreted in the same manner as a neurotic symptom. To cite a few: alteration of the breathing rhythm, of the pitch of the patient's voice, a suddenly appearing urge to urinate or to defecate, a feeling of giddiness either during or after a psychoanalytic session, toothache, the onset of profuse salivation, a bitter taste in the mouth, a sudden feeling of cold in the body, drowsiness, and so on. To explain these phenomena Ferenczi assumed that the analytic process may have stirred up some repressed but quiescent feelings, conflicts, or thought representations and brought them to the threshold of consciousness. In the last moment, however, because of the amount of unpleasure caused by them for the consciousness, they were met with a renewed repression, but their libido cathexis became so strong by that time that it managed to break into consciousness in the form of a transitory symptom.

An important quality of all these observations is that they belong without any exception to the sphere of transference. In other words, although these transitory symptoms represent only new, and sometimes somewhat distorted, editions of old conflicts, they have been brought to light by the force of transference, which, in turn, was prompted by the analyst's individual technique. Doubtless most, if not all, transitory symptoms belong to the category of what Freud described two years later, in 1914, as "acting out," but apparently, if properly understood and handled, these symptoms form an important step toward adjustment, that is, they also have a therapeutic function. Further, in these favorable cases, the patient acquires, as described by Ferenczi in this paper, an unshakable conviction of the truth of analytical interpretations because he has been helped to feel their effects literally in his own body.

From the point of view of technique this conclusion meant that every analyst had to learn to extend his field of observations so as to include these phenomena, to watch for the appearance of these symptoms and, instead of treating them as an undesirable nuisance, to welcome them as if they were free associations. For quite some time this extension of the technique was thought to be the privilege of a few talented people like Ferenczi, and it took quite some time before this sort of work was accepted as an integral part of the analyst's everyday routine.

As will be shown in the next section, well before this integration was achieved, Ferenczi was already engaged in the next stage of his technical experiments, following logically from this discovery of the importance of symptomatic acts. If the appearance of a transitory symptom, provided it is understood and properly interpreted, can lead to important therapeutic developments, then perhaps it is the analyst's duty to *facilitate* its emergence. This idea led to the theory of the "break-through of an instinctual drive" and, on the technical side, in the first instance, to his experiments with active technique.

There is yet another important aspect of these phenomena. Whereas Freud, in his theoretical elucidation of symptomatic acts, restricted himself to pointing out the dynamic structure between the wishful gratification, that is, the instinctual drive, on one hand, and the repressive forces on the other, Ferenczi investigated the changes in this dynamism brought about by the analytic process, chiefly by transference. This study was one of the sources from which his later theory of object relationships developed. Several papers written during the period reviewed in this section show how alive his interest remained in this aspect. Some of these are: "To Whom Does One Relate One's Dreams?" (1913); "A Transitory Symptom: The Position during Treatment" (1913); "Sensation of Giddiness at the End of the Psycho-Analytic Session" (1914); "Embarrassed Hands" (1914); "Psychogenic Anomalies of Voice Production" (1915); "Talkativeness" (1915); and "Dreams of the Unsuspecting" (1917).

Before closing this section, I have to review one more important paper, "On the Technique of Psycho-Analysis," which was given as a lecture to the Hungarian Psychoanalytical Society in 1918 and was published in 1919. Whereas the "Transitory Symptom-Constructions" shows Ferenczi already making important discoveries in the very early stages of his analytical career, barely four years after he met Freud and started his analytic practice, this paper presents him as an accomplished master of the classical analytical technique. It must be added that in the same volume of the *Internationale Zeitschrift,* in which this paper appeared, and only a few months prior to it, Ferenczi published "Technical Difficulties in an Analysis of Hysteria" (1919), which heralded the beginning of his active technique, the second period of his technical experiments.

"On the Technique of Psycho-Analysis" is a typical Ferenczi paper. It consists of four apparently independent sections, which, however, are intimately linked by a few main ideas that served him as beacons during this whole period. In addition to the verbal contents of the free association, the analyst must be aware all the time of the significance of the *formal elements* in the analytical situation, the importance of the *pervading mood* of the associations, and the *interplay between the patient's transference and the analyst's technique,* that is, his *countertransference.*

The first section of this paper deals with the abuse of free associations. What Ferenczi tries to show here are the ways in which patients, prompted by their resistance, abuse their right, or duty, of associating freely. These ways, the formal elements of how the patient associates and not what he produces, if properly understood, tell a most important tale. The tale is about the patient's prevailing mood of the day toward analysis in general and the treatment that he has been receiving from his analyst in particular. Thus, the study of the ways used by patients for free associations is tantamount to the study of the interaction between transference and counter-transference.

The same general topic is treated in sections 2 and 3 of Ferenczi's paper, which deal with the patient's questions and decisions during the treatment and with the use of the phrase "for example" by the patient during his analysis.

The title of the last section, "The Control of the Counter-Transference," is a topic that grew increasingly important for Ferenczi in the next period and became the focal point of his interest in the third and last period of his technical experiments. First, he refers briefly to his discovery—described first in "Introjection and Transference" (1909), to which he returned time and again in his later writings—that in the last analysis every transference in the treatment situation is directed either toward the *indulgent mother* or the *stern father*. Conversely, this means that in principle every patient is a kind of child and that one of his most important wishes is to be treated as such by his analyst. In consequence, every analyst must learn how to *graduate* his sternness, indulgence, or sympathy, as the case may be. Expressed in different words, the analyst has a double task. On one hand, he must listen sympathetically and accept everything that the patient offers to him, so as to be able to infer or reconstruct the patient's unconscious from the verbal material produced and from the patient's actual behavior; on the other hand, he must be in full control of his countertransference. In the 1919 paper Ferenczi remarked that quite a number of analytic treatments ended in an impasse because of faulty control of the analyst's countertransference, which allowed the patient to become aware of his analyst's unconscious sentiments.

This remark is followed by a warning against a too-rigid control, which might force the analyst to adopt a much too distant and too unapproachable attitude, which would, in turn, certainly thwart the development of any natural transference. This was Ferenczi's first recorded encounter with the great problem that occupied the remaining fifteen years of his active life: What is the right, that is, the most therapeutic, form of countertransference? On this occasion he contented himself with stating his guiding principle: The analyst shall try to keep to a happy medium between responding too readily to the patient's emotions and controlling in a frightened, over-cautious, and rigid way his own emotional responses. He ended this paper by describing what, in his opinion, the analyst's right attitude should be. First, he should let himself go, following the patient's associations and fantasies in a way reminiscent of the free associations; then, at some signal from his preconscious, the analyst should stop himself and subject both the material produced by the patient and his own responses to it to a searching scrutiny, a sort of reality-testing, in order to see whether any and, if so, what interpretation should be given at this point.

The "Active Technique"

The technical experiments summed up under this label are certainly the best known of the many undertaken by Ferenczi, and on almost every occasion when Ferenczi's technique is mentioned, his "active technique" is what is referred to. In view of this, it is remarkable that much more often than not his ideas are misunderstood, misquoted, and misrepresented. A good part of this confusion is caused by the convenient but misleading label of "active technique"; the usual misunderstanding is that, in contrast to the classical analytical passivity, the analyst should be more active. However, it is not the analyst, but the patient, who is induced to be more active, that is, to do something or to avoid doing something. Since the other factors contributing to these confusions are largely historical, I shall give a brief résumé of the facts leading to Ferenczi's experiments with "activity."

At the outbreak of World War I in 1914 both Freud and Ferenczi found themselves abandoned by their patients. Ferenczi used the few months before his call up for military service to start his training analysis with Freud. Afterward, since he was stationed in Pápa, a small provincial town in western Hungary not very far from Vienna, his analysis was continued during his leaves and, on occasions, during Freud's visits to Pápa. There can be no doubt that Ferenczi's analysis made a very great impression on him. Although he knew the importance of transference from the analyst's point of view, he now experienced at first hand what it meant from the patient's side. The first reaction to it, as far as his technical experiments are concerned, was revision and readjustment. This can be easily demonstrated by the rate of his publications. Whereas he published a great number of papers in 1914/15, he published few papers in 1916, 1917, and 1918, and none of them has any connection with technique.

In 1916 Ferenczi was transferred from Pápa to Budapest and, because of his age, forty-three, was allowed to engage in part-time private practice. This enabled him to start his technical experiments again, after almost two years of enforced inactivity. As we have seen in the previous section, he arrived at this point of new departure with four important results. These were: (1) The importance of the formal elements of the patient's behavior in the analytical situation, in particular the expressive behavior of his body and his bodily functions. (2) These formal elements, and especially the expressive behavior, always represent an unconscious conflict, stirred up by the analytic process, between a particular drive and the repressive forces. (3) It has always proved an important step forward in the treatment if the drive could be freed from the repression. (4) To achieve this, the analyst has to have a proper analytic technique, which means a proper control of his countertransference.

Another historical fact is that it was in the summer of 1914 that Freud finished his treatment of the "Wolf Man" by an unorthodox method, that is, by the analyst fixing the date by which the treatment had to be terminated. The date fixed was July 1914, and we know that Freud wrote his epoch-making monograph, "From the History of an Infantile Neurosis," in October and November 1914, about the time of Ferenczi's analysis. Knowing the intimate relationship between the two men, it is nearly certain that Ferenczi heard about this technical innovation and its spectacular consequences. A further fact is that in Freud's Budapest Congress paper, "Lines of Advance in Psychoanalytic Therapy," delivered in 1918 and published in 1919, when referring to Ferenczi's new experiments with "active technique," Freud claimed that the original idea that stimulated them was, in fact, his and quoted his two technical devices: (1) That severely phobic patients should, at the proper moment of their treatment, be induced to expose themselves to the dreaded situation. (2) That in certain cases, such as that of the "Wolf Man," the analyst should fix a date for the termination of the treatment. Freud then mentioned Ferenczi's paper, "Technical Difficulties in an Analysis of Hysteria" (1919), as showing the way along which psychoanalytic therapy should develop. This is another important factor of the prevailing confusion; "active technique," in its early phases, was both claimed and fully supported by Freud; in its later stages it could almost be considered as a deviationism.

The first paper belonging to this period was the one just mentioned, while the last, "Contra-Indications to the 'Active' Psycho-Analytic Technique," was read before the Congress at Bad Homburg in 1925 and published in 1926. In fact, it is remarkable that Ferenczi wrote only five essays on his "active technique," which are, in addition to the two mentioned, "The Further Development of the Active Therapy in Psycho-Analysis" (1921), "On Forced Fantasies" (1924), and "Psychoanalysis of Sexual Habits" (1925). This is an incomparably smaller number than that of his technical papers in the classical period or that in the period to follow after the "active technique"; and still, surprisingly, it is for his experiments with "activity" that he is usually remembered.

The underlying idea was that in many cases in which the flow of free association had become stagnant and unproductive; this was caused by the disappearance of libido from the actual analytical work into unconscious fantasies and unconscious bodily gratifications. Naturally, this displacement was provoked by, and represented, a crisis in the transference relationship, and the analytical task thus became that of finding the area into which the libido had been displaced to mobilize it so that it could become available again for productive work. That meant that the analyst had to watch carefully for signs, especially in the patient's behavior in the analytical situation, that would tell him in which particular area the analytical process had stirred up some unconscious conflict, which attracted the libido away from the analytical work. This resulted in an increased cathexis that brought the drive representations near consciousness, but in the last moment the repression forced a compromise, and a hitherto dormant or latent habit became more prominent. The particular habit was determined by (1) the crisis in the transference; (2) the original drive representation; and (3) the repressive forces.

The analyst's active intervention could then take two forms. He could propose that the patient cease to indulge in this particular habit, that is, give up the concealed satisfaction of his repressed wishes; or, on the contrary, he could encourage the patient to enjoy it openly and freely. It was hoped that a successful intervention by the analyst would cause a considerable increase of tension in the patient and that this, in turn, would produce two results: a breakthrough into consciousness of a hitherto repressed instinctual urge or drive, changing an unpleasurable symptom into a pleasurable satisfaction, thereby strengthening and extending the rule of the patient's ego; and further, by removing resistances, it would start the patient's dried-up or stagnant associations flowing again.

Evidently, this procedure is a legitimate extension of the observations described in "Transitory Symptom-Constructions." There the analyst was a passive observer, watching the emergence and then the disappearance of the transitory symptoms, though admittedly contributing to their disappearance by his interpretations; here the analyst changed into an experimenter who had his share both in producing, or at any rate exacerbating, a symptom and then in helping the patient to master it by integrating the underlying drive component into his ego.

It is important to note that these interventions could be considered as an extension of Freud's famous principle that the analytic treatment ought to be carried out in abstinence, or even in privation. It was this apparent conforming with his rule of abstinence that enabled Freud to support these experiments. From his side, Ferenczi, in virtually all of his papers on active technique, was at pains to emphasize that the suggestion for these experiments came from Freud and that they were only a legitimate extension of the principle of abstinence or privation.

In the early papers on active technique the habits and symptoms subjected to these experiments were those having a predominantly genital structure, and they could be understood, in the first instance, as displaced masturbations or as masturbatory equivalents. It was only in his paper "Psychoanalysis of Sexual Habits" (1925) that he described in detail the extension of these experiments to the field of pregenital activities and character traits. This paper is perhaps the most important publication dealing with "active technique." Apart from the extension just mentioned, it contains important theoretical, and especially metapsychological, considerations, which cannot be discussed here, as well as the clarification of two crucial issues. One is about the relative role of analyst and patient with regard to activity; it was only here that Ferenczi stated explicitly and clearly that the term "active technique" meant that the patient should do or refrain from doing something, that is, that the patient should be active, whereas the analyst's activity should be restricted to suggesting to the patient what he should do and then encouraging him to do it. The second clarification—one could even call it qualification or modification—was about the form of the analyst's intervention. In the earlier papers this was described as a command, rule, prohibition, or forbidding—all indicating a rather forceful role. Ferenczi mentioned here for the first time—true, only in a footnote—that the intervention should take the form of friendly advice or of a suggestion. Although this footnote is somewhat in contrast to the body of the paper and certainly to the previous papers, this new formulation in it heralded important changes to come.

If the active intervention happened, as Ferenczi recommended, toward the end of the treatment, the breakthrough achieved by it had sufficient momentum, in quite a few cases, to last till the termination and thus helped considerably to finish the treatment successfully. Unfortunately, in a great number of cases the momentum died out and the patients relapsed. In other cases, when a date for termination was fixed by the analyst, the patient's state was such that the treatment could not be finished at that date, or if it could, the patient returned after a few months in a poor state, asking for more help. It must be stated that Freud foresaw this possibility, and when his experiences convinced him that successs was elusive and unpredictable he abandoned the idea of activity, and this topic is not mentioned in his writings after 1919.

Ferenczi had the same mixed experiences with his active technique, and he reported about his failures in his successive papers, though in a rather ambivalent way at first. On the one hand he admitted their existence; on the other, he tried to reassure himself that they were only odd cases, that there was no systematic error in his idea of active technique. This is largely the picture emerging from his paper "Contra-Indications to the 'Active' Psycho-Analytical Technique" (1926). Behind this self-consoling façade some fore-runners of the coming new period can already be discerned: Activity is recognized as a serious disturbance of the patient's developing transference, and in consequence it is suggested that it should not be applied before the firm establishment of a transference relationship; the aim of any activity is described as a repetition of a frustrating situation in infancy under more favorable conditions, which have to be maintained by the analysts; and, lastly, Ferenczi mentions his idea that, in some cases, instead of raising the tension by some active intervention, it might be advisable to reduce it by suggesting to the patient that he relax his tensed-up muscles, among them the anxiously overcontrolled sphincter muscles.

This was the end of the period of "active technique," an unhappy experiment that brought a great deal of criticism in Ferenczi and contributed considerably to the estrangement between him and the Berlin analysts, foremost among them Sachs, Abraham, and Alexander, to whom must be added Jones in London. True, there was another disagreement, which was perhaps still more important than the problem of "active technique," and that was about the book written jointly by Rank and Ferenczi, published in 1924. This is a most curious book with an interesting history. At the Berlin Congress in 1922 Freud announced a prize essay with the topic "The Relationship between Analytical Technique and Analytical Theory." In particular, the task was "to examine how far the technique has influenced the theory and how far the two help or hinder each other at the present stage." Both Rank and Ferenczi started to work on this problem independently, but when they learned about each other's attempt they decided to collaborate on a joint book instead. Incidentally, there was no entry for the prize essay. The book itself has two titles, one on the frontpiece: *The Developmental Aims of Psychoanalysis,* with the subtitle "On the Interaction of Theory and Praxis," whereas on the page headings the title is "Developmental Ways of Psychoanalysis."

The book (especially the chapters by Rank) is written in a somewhat heavy German style, which makes it rather difficult to read. Unfortunately, the only English translation in existence is so poor that it makes this shortcoming practically unbearable. The book contains a courageous but much-too-harsh criticism of the then prevailing analytical techniques, which unnecessarily offended a number of analysts. Owing to emotional turmoil, which was caused by the tone of the book, the fact that it also contained two very important new ideas was completely overlooked. One idea was that everything that happens in the analytical situation should be considered, first and foremost, as a phenomenon of transference, a combination between repeating something from the past and reacting to something in the actual situation; the other, that in the understanding of the phenomena of transference much more attention should be directed to the very primitive forms of relationships such as that between a mother and her child.

Pointers to Future Developments

This period started about 1927 and lasted until Ferenczi's death in 1933. It, too, was preceded by a lull in Ferenczi's writing, indicating a crisis. In 1925 he published only two papers; 1926 was almost a normal year. This was followed in 1927 by no papers at all. The first paper belonging to this period was published in 1928, "The Adaptation of the Family to the Child." The whole pattern of Ferenczi's publications changed from then on, though it is true that this change was already foreshadowed in the later years of the previous period. Very few papers were published in any one year—in some only one or two—but each of them denoted a major advance in Ferenczi's ideas. The short clinical papers, in which Ferenczi described in a delightfully concise form one or the other of his striking observations in the analytical situation, disappeared completely, the last of them being published in 1923.

In all, he published only seven major papers during these years, but a number of highly important notes and fragments were found in his handwriting among his papers originating in the years 1930 to 1933, which prove that Ferenczi remained the same exquisite observer and clinician as before. But he decided not to publish his observations as he had done in earlier years, possibly because he was not certain of how these would be received by the analytical world. Another important sign of the uneasy estrangement between Ferenczi and his colleagues is that a number of his major papers belonging to this period were not translated at that time into English and were published in English only in 1955 in his "Final Contributions," more than twenty years after his death.

It is no wonder, then, that this period, during which perhaps the most important of Ferenczi's technical experiments took place, is the least known, especially by English readers.

As we have seen in the previous section, Ferenczi gave up the active technique rather reluctantly. The reason for his reluctance was that it yielded a wealth of revealing clinical material that led to most promising theoretical inferences and, last but not least, also to a number of undeniable therapeutic successes. Equally undeniable, however, were a number of failures, and these presented an irresistible challenge to Ferenczi, whose axiom was that as long as a patient was willing to continue his treatment the analyst must find techniques to help him, no matter how difficult this task might be. Ferenczi gradually realized that raising the tension in the patient intentionally by some active intervention did not always lead to an increase in the intensity of frustration or privation; although apparently suffering under the increase of tension, some patients accepted it with equanimity and even asked for more. This led to an impasse in the therapy and presented a puzzling problem for Ferenczi.

As mentioned, Freud had the same experience and apparently decided to give up experimenting in this direction. Ferenczi, however, was so impressed by the primitive nature of his patients' reactions in this phase that he decided on further experimentations. He knew from his previous experiences, especially when trying to understand the formal elements of the patient's behavior in the analytical situation, that any event in this situation must be understood as an interplay between the patient's transference, that is, his compulsion to repeat, and the analyst's countertransference, that is, his technique. As the former had to be accepted as a constant, almost unalterable, factor (at any rate for the time being), if he wanted to get out of the impasse, he had to accept the task of changing the other factor, his technique. He first attempted to mitigate the force of his active intervention so that, instead of command or prohibition, it became advice or suggestion. The next step was to abandon even the gentlest form of active intervention, concentrate his attention on what the patient might expect from his analyst, and make his technique elastic enough so as not to frustrate the patient's expectations unnecessarily. This marks the beginning of his critical examination of the technical principle of abstinence and privation. He reached this point in 1927–1928 and published his results in three papers, which are, in addition to "The Adaptation of the Family to the Child," already mentioned, "The Problem of the Termination of the Analysis" and "The Elasticity of Psycho-Analytical Technique."

The next question Ferenczi had to face was how far this elasticity should go. He was familiar with two models from previous experiences. One was the classical technique with its sympathetic objective passivity and with its apparently imperturbable and unlimited patience; the other was the active technique with its correctly aimed interventions based on painstaking observations and empathy. By now he had an idea why the active technique failed him. True, it led to a re-enactment in the analytic situation of some traumatic experiences from childhood, but in some cases this re-enactment was not followed by a resolution of the repetition compulsion because the prevailing conditions in the analytic situation were apparently not favorable enough. The active intervention, which led to the re-enactment, in far too many cases seemed to increase the tension in the analytic situation to a pitch that was inimical to a resolution and instead produced a repetition of the original trauma. If this train of thought were correct, the logical next step would be to experiment with the only variable over which the analyst had some control, that is, the prevailing tension in the analytical situation. As mentioned, this line of thought was already foreshadowed in his paper, "Contra-Indications to the 'Active' Psycho-Analytical Technique," in which he advocated the use of relaxation in certain cases. This relaxation, reducing the actual tension under which the patient had to work, included as a matter of course both the mental and the bodily aspects of the personality. The need for relaxation demanded a further modification of Ferenczi's technique. His guiding principle, which was command and prohibition at the height of the active technique, and was first changed to advice and suggestion and then to elasticity, was again changed to forbearance and even to indulgence. The technique of this period and the results achieved by it were published in three papers, "The Unwelcome Child and His Death-Instinct" (1929), "The Principles of Relaxation and Neocatharsis" (1930), and "Child-Analysis in the Analysis of Adults" (1931). As the title of this last paper shows, he set the limits of his forbearance and indulgence with his patients roughly at what a child might expect from an adult who is fond of him.

I cannot discuss, within the limits of this chapter, all the theoretical implications or the many problems raised by this last change of technique. All I can do is to indicate some of the centers around which these problems are clustered. These are "repetition," "regression," and "acting out"; for the rest, I refer the reader to the original publications. However, I wish to single out one particularly important result. Using this technique, Ferenczi discovered that infantile pathogenic traumas, when reactivated by analytic treatment, appear to have a biphasic structure. In the first phase the infant, or the child, appears to have been subject to a traumatic over- or understimulation by his environment, which means one or the other of his most important adult objects. When, in the second phase, the child tried to obtain reparation, comfort, or even mere understanding from the same adults, they —under the pressure of their own conscious or unconscious guilt feelings—

had to deny any participation in the previous phase and had to show, by their words and behavior, that they really did not know what all the fuss was about—or, to use our terminology, though they were most sympathetic and objective, they clearly showed that they were not involved. On many occasions Ferenczi had to admit to his patients that bringing back to consciousness the traumatic events to the extent of their repetition, and then, watching them with the traditional sympathetic detachment, was very similar in its structure to the original trauma. Ferenczi came to the conclusion that even the classical analytic technique, insofar as it caused the patient to remember or to repeat the original trauma while the analyst maintained his objective sympathetic passivity, in some cases might create similar conditions.

What can be done to avoid this undesirable outcome? Ferenczi had no doubt that, since regression, especially in severely ill patients, cannot be avoided, the first task of the analyst was to help, or at any rate not to hinder, his patient's regression, that is, the patient's repetition of the traumatic events in the analytic situation. The analyst must bear with this process and watch most carefully to discover the maximum tension that his patient will be able to bear and work with, and he must see to it that the tension shall at no time go beyond this level. This, he thought, could be achieved by the analyst's positive response to the regressed patient's longings, cravings, or needs. This was a definite departure from Freud's rule of abstinence, and I shall return to a discussion of its consequences.

Another important factor that may inordinately increase the tension in the analytic situation is the analyst's insincerity, which repeats the insincerity of the adults around the traumatized child. The recognition of this danger led to Ferenczi's last published paper, an address to the Wiesbaden Congress in 1932, "Confusion of Tongues between Adults and the Child," with the subtitle "The Language of Tenderness and of Passion." To show Ferenczi's state of mind, it should be mentioned that the original title of this paper, as announced in the program, was "The Passions of Adults and Their Influence on the Sexual and Character Development of Children." Among the many interesting problems raised in it, I wish to single out one because of its technical importance. This is what Ferenczi called the analyst's "professional hypocrisy," which, so to speak, repeats the professional hypocrisy of the educators, that is, of parents and other adults in the child's environment. To cite an instance: The analyst on a particular day may be somewhat tired and truly in need of rest; still, he may not feel justified in canceling his next patient, and he receives him in the usual manner. The patient unavoidably feels that something is wrong with his analyst, but the analyst's impeccable behavior prevents him from becoming aware of this and even if the analyst tries, halfheartedly, to get hold of his feelings, it is very likely that his attempts will be interpreted as criticism, projection, that is, something pertaining to himself. Is this the right technique, or should the analyst admit his weariness? If he starts with this admission, that is, an interpretation of his countertransference, an endless spiral may develop leading to the sterile analysis of the analyst.

A considered answer to these and similar problems is difficult enough if one takes into account the conscious implications only. However, as Ferenczi correctly pointed out, the dependent child, and the dependent patient, stir up all sorts of emotional reactions in an adult over which his conscious control is only patchy and partial. Some of these emotions may be intense enough to qualify for being described as passions. Ferenczi was first among the analysts to recognize the crucial importance of these interactions, not only for the field of education, but also for analytical technique. He went even one step further when he pointed out that consistent and conscientious conformity with the classical role of analytical passivity may on occasion be merely a thin cover for stirred-up passions, foremost among them, cruelty.

His last paper on "Confusion of Tongues" and his "Notes and Fragments" from the years 1930 to 1932 give an eloquent testimony of how important the problem of the analyst's emotions became to Ferenczi in his last years. Everyone will agree in principle with his answer that the analyst's reactions must be absolutely sincere and honest and must be expressed in such an unsophisticated, simple way that the patient could not have any doubts about their meaning. Very grave problems arise, however, when we try to translate this principle into practice. Let us suppose the patient is in a highly disturbed state under the pressure of intense emotions or that he is deeply regressed, having little ego power at his disposal. Which words of the conventional adult language will then retain their agreed conventional meaning, so that they could be used with confidence to convey the analyst's sincerity to the patient? Or, is it more advisable to use simple gestures in such cases, for instance, to hold the patient's hand? When is the use of countertransference interpretations legitimate, and when does it amount to an irresponsible burdening of a defenseless patient with the analyst's subjective problems? Every analyst will, I think, agree that there is an optimal tension, more or less characteristic of every individual patient, that is, that one gets the impression that the treatment proceeds best when this tension is maintained in the analytical situation. The question is what sort of technical means we have to control the prevailing tension in the analytical situation. Should it be done exclusively by interpretations, or are other means permissible if we apparently cannot achieve by interpretations a reliable re-establishment of the optimal tension?

On the basis of his experiments Ferenczi arrived, in his last period, at the conclusion that an honest use of sincere affection and kindness was permissible in cases in which his interpretations had proved ineffective and useless. He was fully aware of the great dangers to which he exposed both himself and his patients when embarking on this line of experiments, but he thought that it was perhaps safe to allow things to go about as far as a child might expect them to go from an adult who was fond of him. How far this was a legitimate experiment and how far it was only a symptom of the immense desire in Ferenczi for love and affection is impossible to decide, since he died before his experiments could be concluded. Knowing his character, the most likely answer will be that it was both, and had he lived longer, it is virtually certain that he would have had to write a paper under some such title as "Contraindications to the Analytical Techniques of Relaxation and Indulgence." Whatever the case may be, it is true that the problems discovered by him in the late 1920's and early 1930's are still in the center of psychoanalytical research.

Postscript

In 1926, in the same year as "Contra-Indications to the 'Active' Psycho-Analytical Technique," Ferenczi published a paper, of which the correct title in English would be "The Problem of the Acceptance of Unpleasure," with the subtitle "Advances in the Recognition of the Sense of Reality." Unfortunately, this paper was translated in the transitional period, after it had been recognized that a standard English psychoanalytic terminology must be created, but before this task could be completed. In consequence, the reader is misled time and again to accept a phrase in its present standard meaning, although in fact it represents only an unsuccessful struggle with the difficult German text. This is the more deplorable because this is a highly important paper, written at a critical point in Ferenczi's development at the time when he was about to give up his experiments with "active technique" and to start on his last experiments.

The actual stimulus for this paper was an article by Freud, on "Negation," which appeared in 1925, barely a year earlier. In this Freud introduced a new concept, negation, as an in-between phase between repressing and accepting an unpleasant or painful part of reality. When repression cannot be maintained any longer, the existence of frustrating objects, that is, unpleasure, is admitted to consciousness in principle, but its actual existence is negated. Ferenczi, in his paper, asks the question of how it is possible for the individual, or for his ego, to make the next step, which means to accept and live with pain and unpleasure instead of flying away from it or repressing it. Evidently intellectual understanding of the whole situation may help considerably in this task, but in severe cases of unpleasure its power is insufficient.

The problem how to accept unpleasure is, of course, the cardinal problem of adaptation, to which Ferenczi returned time and again in his writings. In addition to being a cardinal problem for any theory of adaptation it also has a central position for the theory of education and for the theory of analytical technique.[1]

Here again, I must omit the many interesting theoretical and meta-psychological implications and limit my discussion to the technical problem, which asks what is the explanation of why some people can achieve this task on their own, some with the help of analytical treatment, and yet others either have very great difficulty even with excellent analytical help or may prove unable to perform it.

In "The Problem of Acceptance of Unpleasure" Ferenczi gives only a general answer to this problem. He states that in the analytical situation it is transference love that enables the patient to accept painful facts, and by the end of the treatment, the patient must be able to renounce his trans-ference love, which will be possible only if the analysis has enabled him to find compensation in his relationships with objects of reality. Further, we know that two more factors play an important part in the tolerance of unpleasure. One is an innate ability of the individual to tolerate tension and pain, which is modified by the other factor, his individual development that determines the structure of his ego and with it the amount of pain and unpleasure that he can tolerate without major trouble. Both factors show a very high variability from one individual to the next. The great problem that occupied Ferenczi practically throughout his professional life was in which way the analyst should modify his technique so as to enable his patient to develop the right sort and the right amount of transference love, which would help him in achieving the necessary adaptation during his analytical treatment. Ferenczi belonged among those people for whom the level of skills that they master is merely an acceptable base line and who

---

[1] Ferenczi's principal papers dealing with this problem are: "Introjection and Transference" (1909); "Stages in the Development of the Sense of Reality" (1913); "Stages in the Development of the Erotic Sense of Reality," Chapter 3 of *Thalassa* (1924).

cannot help feeling any problem that demands still greater skill from them to be an irresistible obligation. The technical experiments reported in this short review bear witness to what this obligation meant to Ferenczi.

In the first period, which I called his "Contributions to the Classical Technique," his answer lay in demanding from himself a considerable extension of his field of observation, more precise observations, and more understanding and better knowledge of the human unconscious. In the second period, that of "active technique," he demanded from himself still more precise observations and still more knowledge so that he could improve his understanding of his patients and develop a secure empathy, enabling him to intervene in the treatment at the right time and in the right way. When he realized that this method did not reliably produce the results that he aimed at, his answer was again demanding still more precise observations leading to better-founded knowledge. This safer foundation was to include, in addition to everything that Ferenczi had learned in the previous periods, his new insights gained while he was caring for his patients with the object of insuring that the tension and unpleasure in the analytical situation would never go beyond the level that the patient—with his actual ego structure, with all his neurotic conflicts and traumatic scars—could tolerate safely. He thought he would be able to achieve it by a special kind of forbearance, kindness, or even indulgence. In his last published paper he described two of the many factors determining his special kind of forbearance and indulgence as absolute honesty and sincerity; some of the others are hinted at rather cryptically in his posthumous "Notes and Fragments."

Although more than thirty years have elapsed since Ferenczi died of pernicious anemia before completing his last period of experiments, the technical problems raised by him are still not finally answered. For some years it looked as if psychoanalysis had definitely rejected his ideas. However, in the last ten years or so, the problems raised by him have attracted more and more interest. The final judgment rests with the future.

REFERENCES

All the papers by Ferenczi mentioned in this chapter have been reprinted— in addition to their original publication in various periodicals—in the following three volumes:

I. *First Contributions to Psychoanalysis* (second edition, London: Hogarth Press, 1952). (Also published as *Sex in Psychoanalysis,* Basic Books, New York, 1952.)

II. *Further Contributions to the Theory and Technique of Psychoanalysis* (second edition, London: Hogarth Press, 1950). (Also published by Basic Books, New York 1950.)

III. *Final Contributions to the Problems and Methods of Psychoanalysis* (second edition, London: Hogarth Press, 1955). (Also published by Basic Books, New York, 1955.)

1909 Introjection and transference. I.35.

1911 On obscene words. I.132.

1912 Dirigible dreams. III.313.
Transitory symptom-construction during the analysis. I.193.

1913 To whom does one relate one's dreams? II.349.
Stages in the development of the sense of reality. I.213.
A transitory symptom: the position during treatment. II.242.

1914 Sensations of giddiness at the end of the psycho-analytic session. II.239.
On falling asleep during the analysis. II.249.
Embarrassed hands. II.315.

1915 Psychogenic anomalies of voice production. II.105.
Talkativeness. II.252.

1917 Dreams of the unsuspecting. II.346.

1919 Technical difficulties in the analysis of a case of hysteria. II.189.
On the technique of psycho-analysis. II.177.

1921 The further development of an active therapy in psycho-analysis. II.198.

1923 Ptyalism in an oral-erotic. II.315.
The Dream of the "Clever Baby." II.349.
Washing-compulsion and masturbation. II.311.

1924 On forced fantasies. II.
With Otto Rank: *The development of psychoanalysis* (New York: Nervous and Mental Diseases Publication Co.).
Thalassa; theory of genitality. (New York, *Psychoanalytic Quarterly;* several later impressions.)

1925 Psycho-analysis of sexual habits. II.259.

1926 Contra-indications to the "active" psycho-analytical technique. II.217.
The problem of acceptance of unpleasant ideas. II.366.

1927 The problem of the termination of the analysis. III.77.

1928 The adaptation of the family to the child. III.61.
The elasticity of psycho-analytic technique. III.87.

1929 The unwelcome child and his death-instinct. III.102.

1930 The principles of relaxation and neocatharsis. III.108.

1931 Child-analysis in the analysis of adults. III.126.

1933 Confusion of tongues between adults and the child. III.156.

Posthumous: Notes and fragments. III.216.

I wish to warn the reader that the first two volumes were translated before a standard English analytical terminology had been agreed on; in consequence, the English text does not always correspond exactly to the original German.

6

MELANIE KLEIN'S TECHNIQUE

Hanna Segal

The Rationale

The Kleinian technique is psychoanalytical and strictly based on Freudian psychoanalytic concepts. The formal setting is the same as in classical Freudian analysis; the patient is offered five or six fifty-minute sessions a week; a couch is provided for him to recline on, with the analyst sitting behind him; he is invited to free-associate, and the analyst interprets his associations. Not only is this formal setting the same as that in classical technique, but in all essentials the psychoanalytical principles as laid down by Freud are adhered to. The role of the analyst is confined to interpreting the patient's material, and all criticism, advice, encouragement, reassurance, and the like, is rigorously avoided. The interpretations are centered on the transference situation, impartially taking up manifestations of positive and negative transference as they appear. By transference I mean here not only the "here-and-now" relation to the analyst, but the relation to the analyst including reference to past relationships as transferred onto the analyst, and current problems and relationships in their interrelationship to the transference. Special attention is paid to the transference onto the analyst of internal figures from the patient's inner world. The level at which the interpretations are given, again as indicated by Freud, is determined by the level of the patient's maximum unconscious anxiety. In these respects, the Kleinian analyst may be considered to be following the classical Freudian technique with the greatest exactitude, more so indeed than most other Freudian analysts, who find that they have to alter their analytical technique in some of its essential aspects when dealing with prepsychotic, psychotic, or psychopathic patients. Analysts using the Kleinian approach (Rosenfeld, 1965; Segal, 1950, 1956; Bion, 1956, 1957, 1958, 1959) find it both possible and useful to retain the strictly psychoanalytical technique even with these patients.

Could it be said, therefore, that there is no room for the term "Kleinian technique"? It seems to me that it is legitimate to speak of a technique as developed by Melanie Klein in that the nature of the interpretations given to the patient and the changes of emphasis in the analytical process show, in fact, a departure, or, as Melanie Klein saw it, an evolution from the classical technique. She saw aspects of material not seen before, and interpreting those aspects, she revealed further material that might not have been reached otherwise and that, in turn, dictated new interpretations, seldom, if ever, used in the classical technique.

To understand the rationale of the Kleinian approach and to appreciate the way in which the technique grew, it is best to place it in its historical setting. When Melanie Klein, in the 1920's, started her work with children, she assumed that Freud's method could be applied to children with only such modifications as would not alter the essence of the psychoanalytical relationship and the interpretative process. Since children do not verbalize easily, and since play is one of their major means of expression, she provided each child patient with a drawer of small, simple toys and play material, and she interpreted their play, behavior, and verbal communications in the way in which she would have interpreted an adult's free associations. She observed that children develop a transference, both positive and negative, very rapidly and often intensely. She found that the children's communications, through various activities in the session, revealed their unconscious conflicts with the same, and often indeed greater, clarity as the adults' free associations. The analysis of children fully confirmed Freud's deductions about childhood derived from work with adults, but, as might be expected, certain new facts emerged. The Oedipus complex and the superego seemed both to be in evidence at an earlier age than one would have expected and to have pregenital, as well as genital, forms. Indeed, the roots of the Oedipal situation seemed to lie as far back as the second oral phase. The superego of the small child was equally well in evidence, possessed of savage and primitive oral, anal, and urethral characteristics. She was impressed by the prevalence and power of the mechanisms of projection and introjection; the introjections leading to the building of a complex inner world and the projections coloring most of the child's perceptions of reality. Splitting was very active as an early mechanism preceding repression, and the child's development appeared to be a constant struggle toward integration and the overcoming of powerful splitting mechanisms. Once seen in the child, those more primitive levels of experience could be understood and detected in the material of adult patients.

The Concept of Phantasy

Working at the primitive level of the child's world led Melanie Klein to broaden the concept of unconscious phantasy.

> As the work of psychoanalysis, in particular the analysis of young children, has gone on and our knowledge of early mental life has developed, the relationships which we have come to discern between the earliest mental processes and the later more specialized types of mental functioning commonly called "phantasies" have led many of us to extend the connotation of the term "phantasy" in the sense which is now to be developed. (A tendency to widen the significance of the term is already apparent in many of Freud's own writings, including a discussion of unconscious phantasy.) (Susan Isaacs, 1952.)

Unconscious phantasy springs directly from the instincts and their polarity and from the conflicts between them. Susan Isaacs defined it as "the mental correlate of the instincts" or "the psychic equivalent of the instincts." In the infant's omnipotent world instincts express themselves as the phantasy of their fulfillment. "To the desire to love and eat corresponds the phantasy of an ideal love-, life- and food-giving breast; to the desire to destroy, equally vivid phantasies of an object shattered, destroyed and attacking" (Segal, 1964). Phantasy in the Kleinian view is primitive, dynamic, and constantly active, coloring external reality and constantly interplaying with it. "Reality experience interacting with unconscious phantasy gradually alters the character of phantasies, and memory traces of reality experiences are incorporated into phantasy life. I have stressed earlier that the original phantasies are of a crude and primitive nature, directly concerned with the satisfaction of instincts, experienced in a somatic as well as a mental way, and, since our instincts are always active, so a primitive layer of primary phantasies are active in all of us. From the core, later phantasies evolve. They become altered by contact with reality, by conflict, by maturational growth. As instincts develop instinct derivatives, so the early primitive phantasies develop later derivatives and they can be displaced, symbolized and elaborated and can even penetrate into consciousness as daydreams, imagination, etc." (Segal, 1964). This broader concept of phantasy provides a link between the concept of instinct and that of ego mechanisms.

What Freud picturesquely calls here "the language of the oral impulse," he elsewhere calls "the mental expression" of an instinct, i.e. the phantasies which are the psychic representatives of a bodily aim. In this actual example,[1] Freud is showing us the phantasy that is the mental equivalent of an *instinct*. But he is at one and the same time formulating the subjective aspect of the *mechanism* of introjection (or projection). Thus *phantasy is the link between the id impulse and the ego mechanism*, the means by which the one is transmuted into the other. "I want to eat that and therefore I have eaten it" is a phantasy which represents the id impulse in the psychic life; it is at the same time the subjective experiencing of the mechanism or function of the introjection (Isaacs, 1952).

This applies to all mental mechanisms, even when they are specifically used as defenses.

We are all familiar with phantasying as a defensive function. It is a flight from reality and a defence against frustration. This seems contradictory to the concept of phantasy as an expression of instinct. The contradiction, however, is more apparent than real; since phantasy aims at fulfilling instinctual striving in the absence of reality satisfaction, that function in itself is a defence against reality. But, as mental life becomes more complicated, phantasy is called upon as a defence in various situations of stress. For instance, manic phantasies act as a defence against the underlying depression. The question arises of the relation between the defensive function of phantasy and mechanisms of defence. It is Isaacs' contention that what we call mechanisms of defence is an abstract description from an observer's point of view of what is in fact the functioning of unconscious phantasy. That is, for instance, when we speak of repression, the patient may be hav-

---

[1] The example of introjection is from Freud's paper on "Negation."

ing a detailed phantasy, say, of dams built inside his body holding back floods, floods being the way he may represent in phantasy his instincts. When we speak of denial, we may find a phantasy in which the denied objects are actually annihilated, and so on. The mechanisms of introjection and projection, which long precede repression and exist from the beginning of mental life, are related to phantasies of incorporation and ejection; phantasies which are, to begin with, of a very concrete somatic nature. Clinically, if the analysis is to be an alive experience to the patient, we do not interpret to him mechanisms, we interpret and help him to relive the phantasies contained in the mechanisms (Segal, 1964).

The understanding of Melanie Klein's use of the concept of phantasy is necessary for the understanding of her technical approach to resistance, if we take resistance to be synonymous with defenses against insight. The criticism has been advanced that the Kleinian analyst interprets the content of unconscious phantasies and neglects the analysis of defenses. This criticism is, I think, based on a misunderstanding of our way of handling defenses. We attach great importance to analyzing the unconscious anxiety that is defended against in conjunction with the analysis of the defenses against it, so that the emergence of the defended material into consciousness is facilitated not only by the analysis of the defenses but also by the lessening of the unconscious anxiety. This is particularly important when one reaches into the deep psychotic layers of the personality, as otherwise the ego may be flooded by psychotic anxieties. In the early days of psychoanalysis it was considered dangerous to analyze prepsychotics because it was believed that analysis of defenses could expose the weak ego to a psychotic breakdown. This anxiety was fully justified. It is far safer to analyze prepsychotics now, when we do not analyze predominantly resistance or defenses, leaving the ego defenseless but have some understanding of the psychotic phantasies and anxieties that necessitate these defenses and can modify these anxieties by interpretations, which are directed at the content as well as at the defenses against it. The concept of mental mechanisms as one facet of phantasy life implies also that there is less division between interpretations of defense and those of content, and interpretation can deal more readily with the patient's total experience.

The same applies to the interpretations of structure. Susan Isaacs established the connection between the concepts of instinct, mental mechanism, and phantasy. I have extended it further, connecting phantasy with ego and superego structure, a connection that is implied in Susan Isaacs' paper, but not explicitly stated.

If one views the mechanisms of projection and introjection as being based on primitive phantasies of incorporation and ejection, the connection between phantasy and mental structure becomes immediately apparent. The phantasies of objects which are being introjected into the ego, as well as the loss of the ego by phantasies of projective identification, affect the structure of personality. When Freud described the super ego as an internal object in active relationship with the id and the ego, he was accused by academic psychologists of being "anthropomorphic," but what was he in fact describing? This structure within the ego is the end result of complex phantasies. The child in phantasy projects some of his own aggression into a parental figure; he then in phantasy incorporates this figure and, again in phantasy, attributes to this figure various attitudes and functions. Melanie Klein has shown that other objects, earlier than the superego described by Freud, are similarly introjected, and a complex internal world is built in phantasy and structuralized. The fact that structure is partly determined by unconscious phantasy is of paramount importance from the therapeutic point of view, since we have access to these phantasies in the analytic situation and, through mobilizing them and helping the patient to relive and remodel them in the process of analytical treatment, we can affect the structure of the patient's personality (Segal, 1963).

The First Session

This view of phantasy affects the technique, in that the patient's material is looked at differently than in the classical technique. All the patient's communications in the session are viewed as containing an element of unconscious phantasy, though they may seem concerned with incontrovertible external facts. For instance, a patient may open a session by complaining that it is cold and raining. The analyst will keep an open mind about a possible phantasy content. Is the patient complaining of the analyst's unfriendliness? Is he complaining about the interval between sessions, and if so, did he feel like a baby left crying in the cold or like a baby left with a wet nappy? Did he feel that his omnipotent urination has led to a flood? No interpretation will be given, of course, until further material provides the meaning, but the analyst is alerted to the fact of coldness and wetness as a communication about something in the patient's inner world as well as in the weather.

In the phantasy world of the analysand, the most important figure is the person of the analyst. To say that all communications are seen as communications about the patient's phantasy as well as current external life is equivalent to saying that all communications contain something relevant to the transference situation. In Kleinian technique the interpretation of the transference is often more central than in the classical technique.

Our understanding of the central role played by unconscious phantasy and transference affects the course of the analysis from the very first session. The question is often asked by students, should transference be interpreted in the first session? If we follow the principle that the interpretation should be given at the level of the greatest unconscious anxiety and that what we want to establish contact with is the patient's unconscious phantasy, then it is obvious that, in the vast majority of cases, a transference interpretation will impose itself. In my own experience I have not had a case in which I did not have to interpret the transference from the start. A patient undertaking a psychoanalysis is bound to come to his first session full of hopes and fears and is sure to have formed phantasies about the analyst as soon as he came in contact with him, or even before—as soon as he knew he was going to meet him. These hopes and fears, and the resistance against them, are often more clearly presented in the first session than in later ones. Interpreting them has the effect of both lessening the unconscious anxiety and, from the start, focusing the patient's attention on the central role of the analyst in his unconscious. These interpretations have, of course, to be formulated in a way that is acceptable and understandable to a patient as yet unfamiliar with the analytic technique. To give a not uncommon example, an obviously frigid and "shut-in" woman patient, in her first session, is first silent, then expresses some anxiety about how to behave, what to say, and so forth. The analyst may interpret her fear of his getting in touch with her mind. Then the patient proceeds to describe her father as a violent man, often drunk, who used to terrify her. The analyst can interpret that she hopes he will get in touch with her and understand her, but is also frightened that his interpretations will be violent and terrifying and that he will penetrate her mind and damage it. In this situation the fear of being physically raped, which may already be clear to the analyst, need not be interpreted, but its mental equivalent is near enough to the patient's anxieties to be brought into consciousness. A correct interpretation of this anxiety is necessary to enable the patient to "open out."

Another question, often asked in relation to the first session, concerns the level of interpretation. Should interpretations be deep or superficial? This again is dictated by the principle of interpreting at the level at which anxiety is active. It is by no means true that the patient presents first genital, then anal, and finally oral material. He presents material at the level at which, at that moment, anxiety is centered. For instance, to establish contact with a schizophrenic, it is usually necessary from the start to interpret the most primitive forms of projective identification if one is to get in touch with him at all. Thus, I interpreted, in the first session, to a schizophrenic adolescent, that she felt she had put all her "sickness" (the word she used) into me the moment she entered the room, and, as a result, felt me to be a sick and frightening person. A little later in the session I interpreted that she was afraid that my talking would put the "sickness" back into her. These interpretations, in my view, lessened her immediate paranoid reactions and enabled her to stay in the room and communicate with me.

Even in the relatively healthy individual, however, oral or anal anxieties may be clearly presented in the transference situation in the first session. Thus, a candidate started the session by declaring his determination to be qualified in the minimum time and to get in all the analysis he could in the shortest possible time. Later in the session he spoke of his digestive troubles and, in another context, of cows, presenting a picture of his phantasy about the relation to the analyst so clearly as to enable me to make the interpretation that I was the cow, like the mother who breast-fed him, and that he felt that he was going to empty me greedily, as fast as possible, of all my analysis —milk; this interpretation which immediately brought out material about his guilt in relation to exhausting and exploiting his mother.

I have described the approach to the first session in order to emphasize that, from the start, we try to get in touch with the patient's unconscious phantasy, as manifested in the transference. This does not mean, however, that analysis is concerned with the description of phantasies in the void. A full interpretation of an unconscious phantasy involves all its aspects. It has to be traced to its original instinctual source, so that the impulses underlying the phantasy are laid bare. At the same time, the defensive aspects of the phantasy have to be taken into account, and the relation has to be traced between phantasy and external reality in the past and the present.

It is the contention of Melanie Klein and her co-workers that the application of these principles in the analysis of children, adults and, in more recent years, psychotic patients as well, has enabled us to reach deeper layers of the unconscious. These deeper layers must be taken into consideration if we are to understand the analysand's anxieties and the structure of his internal world, the basis of which is laid in early infancy. This accounts for the fact that interpretations at an oral or anal level and of introjective or projective mechanisms play a much larger part than in the classical technique.

The Paranoid-Schizoid Position

In the development of psychoanalysis, as in most sciences, there is an interrelation between technical innovations and theoretical concepts, changes in technique revealing new material, leading to new theoretical formulations, and the theoretical concepts in turn leading to new techniques. It is impossible to speak of Melanie Klein's technique without bringing in some aspects of theory. As is probably well known by now, Melanie Klein describes two stages in the oral phase, corresponding roughly to Abraham's preambivalent and ambivalent stages. She calls them the paranoid-schizoid and the depressive positions and describes two different types of ego and object-relation organization belonging to these two stages. In the paranoid-schizoid position, the infant has no concept of a whole person. He is related to part objects, primarily the breast. He also experiences no ambivalence. His object is split into an ideal and a persecutory one, and the prevalent anxiety at that stage is of a persecutory nature, the fear that the persecutors may invade and destroy the self and the ideal object. The aim of the infant is to acquire, possess, and identify with the ideal object and to project and keep at bay both the bad objects and his own destructive impulses. Splitting, introjection, and projection are very active as mechanisms of defense. The analysis of these persecutory anxieties and of the defenses against them plays an important part in Kleinian technique. For instance, if the analyst is very idealized, he will be particularly watchful for the appearance of bad figures in the patient's extra-analytical life and take every opportunity of interpreting them as split-off bad aspects of himself. He will also be watchful for the projection of the patient's own destructive impulses into these bad figures.

An important mechanism evolved in the paranoid-schizoid position is that of projective identification. In projective identification, a part of the patient's ego is in phantasy projected into the object controlling it, using it and projecting into it his own characteristics. Projective identification illustrates perhaps most clearly the connection between instincts, phantasy, and mechanisms of defense. It is a phantasy that is usually very elaborate and detailed; it is an expression of instincts that both libidinal and aggressive desires are felt to be omnipotently satisfied by the phantasy; it is, however, also a mechanism of defense in the same way in which projection is; it rids the self of unwanted parts. It may also be used as a defense, for instance, against separation anxiety. Here is an example of the difference between interpreting only projection and interpreting projective identification. A student reported a case in which his woman patient, preceding a holiday break, was describing how her children bickered and were jealous of one another in relation to her. The student interpreted that the children represented herself, jealous about him in relation to the holiday break, an interpretation that she accepted without being much moved. He did not interpret that she felt that she had put a jealous and angry part of herself into the children and that that part of her was changing and controlling them. The second interpretation, for which there was plenty of material in preceding and subsequent sessions, was of very great importance, in that it could be shown to the patient how, by subtle manipulations, she was in fact forcing the children to carry those parts of herself. Often a transference situation can only be understood in terms of projective identification, a situation, for instance, in which the patient is silent and withdrawn, inducing in the analyst a feeling of helplessness, rejection, and lack of understanding, because the patient has projected into the analyst the child part of himself with all its feelings.

A schizophrenic patient, whose analysis I supervised, at the beginning of his analysis used to stand with his back to the analyst, a huge table separating them. This patient had been separated from his mother and sent overseas when he was a small child. The analyst interpreted mainly that the table represented the ocean that separated him from his mother and how he used it to "turn the tables on her." In turning his back to her, he was the rejecting mother, and he was putting into the analyst the desperate child part of himself. Following certain indications, such as the patient's change of posture, and using her countertransference feelings, she could interpret in great detail the kind of feelings he felt he was projecting into her. The patient reacted to this interpretation sometimes as a persecution, which would then be interpreted as his feeling that she was forcibly and perhaps vengefully pushing these feelings back into him. Gradually the feelings of persecution lessened, the patient gave up his posture behind the table and felt able to communicate with the analyst by speech. Such a situation can also be seen as reversal, a well-known mechanism described by Freud. It is not, however, sufficient to interpret to the patient that he is reversing the situation of separation. One has to interpret in detail his introjective identification with the rejecting mother and the projective identification of the rejected child part of himself, identifying and describing its feelings and interpreting the detail of the phantasy how this part is projected. For instance, the feces and the flatus may contain the parts that the patient wishes to project. Hence, turning his back to the analyst could have not only a symbolic meaning but could also relate to phantasies connected with his wish to defecate into the analyst.

States of mind in which projective identification predominates may leave the patient feeling depleted, since part of himself is missing, persecuted by the analyst filled with his projections, and confused with the analyst. This is particularly noticeable in the case of the schizophrenic, who immediately forms a violent psychotic transference, whose anxiety and confusion can only be relieved by interpretations of identification (Rosenfeld, 1965; Segal, 1964).

It is to be emphasized, however, that the analysis of the paranoid-schizoid object relationships and defenses is not confined to the analysis of the psychotic and the prepsychotic only; in that the schizoid defenses, though originating in the earliest stages of development, are repeatedly regressed to and revived as a defense against feelings aroused in the depressive position.

The Depressive Position

The depressive position starts when the infant begins to recognize his mother. Throughout the paranoid-schizoid position, normal processes of maturation are helped by, and help in turn, the psychological drive to integration, and eventually, sufficient integration is achieved for the infant to recognize his mother as a whole object. The concept of the whole object contrasts both with that of the part object and that of the object split into good and bad. The infant begins to recognize his mother not as a collection of anatomical parts, breasts that feed him, hands that tend him, eyes that smile or frighten, but as a whole person with an independent existence of her own, who is the source of both his good and his bad experiences. This integration in his perception of his object goes *pari passu* with the integration in his own self. He gradually realizes that it is the same infant, himself, who both loves and hates the same person, his mother. He experiences ambivalence. This change in his object relations brings with it a change in the content of his anxieties. While he was previously afraid that he would be destroyed by his persecutors, now he dreads that his own aggression will destroy his ambivalently loved object. His anxiety has changed from a paranoid to a depressive one. Since at that stage the infant's phantasies are felt as omnipotent, he is exposed to the experience that his aggression has destroyed his mother, leaving in its wake feelings of guilt, irretrievable loss, and mourning. His mother's absence is often experienced as a death. As the depressive position starts in the oral stage of development, where the infant's love and hatred are linked with phantasies of incorporation, this ambivalence is felt also in relation to the mother as an internal object, and in states of depressive anxiety and mourning, the infant feels that he has lost not only his mother in the external world, but that his internal object is destroyed as well. Melanie Klein viewed these depressive anxieties as part of normal development and an unavoidable corollary to the process of integration. They become reawakened up to a point in any subsequent situation of loss. There is a difference here between the Kleinian view and the classical view. In the classical view, melancholic illness involves ambivalence in relation to an internal object and regression to an oral fixation (Freud, 1917; Abraham, 1912), but normal mourning involves only the loss of an external object. In the Kleinian view, ambivalence toward an internal object and the depressive anxieties associated with it are a normal stage of development and are reawakened in the normal mourning. It is often contended by classical Freudian analysts that when a patient is actually mourning it is usually an unproductive period in his analysis, Kleinian analysts, in contrast, find that analysis of mourning situations and tracing them to their early roots often helps the patient greatly in working through the mourning and coming out of it enriched by the experience.

I should like to describe here the dream of a patient soon after his mother's death. He dreamed that he was crawling on all fours around marshy ground, a kind of bog. He woke up with a sinking feeling, a mixture of depression and nausea. He described the nausea as a feeling as though the marshy ground were bubbling up inside his stomach. He associated first to crawling on all fours and connected it with an incident too long to report in detail, referring to his mother's pregnancy when he was a toddler, and the acute feelings of rage and loss he experienced in relation to his mother about the time of his sister's birth. Then he tried to describe the marshy ground, but found it very difficult, until he suddenly realized that it looked exactly like a microscope slide of a cancerous breast. His mother did not die of cancer of the breast, but he always thought this was the disease she would die of. He remembered hitting her in the breast and being terrified she would develop cancer. A further analysis of his dream led to a great deal of material about his early phantasies of attacking his mother's breast orally and anally and incorporating a destroyed breast as a focal point of his depression and the psychosomatic ailments in his childhood, reproduced in his nausea on the morning following his dream. The death of his mother reawakened all his earlier experiences of losing her, as at the birth of his sister and at weaning, and made him experience the loss as one of his internal mother as well, now experienced as the marshy bog in his internal world. This bog also represented the analytical breast identified with the original breast of his mother, and he expressed anxiety that his analysis might be "bogged down." Thus, his mourning situation could be analyzed both in relation to its early genetic roots and in the transference.

The Manic Defenses

The intensity of pain and anxiety in the depressive position mobilizes new and powerful defenses, namely the system of manic defenses. The manic defenses involve a regression to splitting, denial, idealization, and projection, basically schizoid mechanisms, but organized into a system to protect the ego from the experience of depressive anxiety. Since the depressive anxiety arises out of the infant's recognition of the mother as a whole object on whom he depends and in relation to whom he can experience ambivalence and the subsequent guilt and fear of loss, this whole relation has to be denied. Denial of the importance of his object and triumph over it, control, contempt, and devaluation take the place of depressive feelings.

A patient, following recognition of his oral attachment to the analyst, his greed for analysis, and his angry urinary attacks against her, had the following two dreams. In the first dream, he saw a house on fire and collapsing, but he drove past it, thinking it had little importance. In the second dream, he stole two buns from a bread shop, but he thought it did not matter very much, as they were such little buns. He defended himself against his depressive feelings about phantasies of stealing the analyst's breasts and destroying her body with his urine by denial and contempt. The anxiety and guilt about the fire is dealt with by denial—"it had little importance"—and the guilt about stealing by contempt, the analysis being represented by "such little buns." The fire associated among other things with the burning in his stomach (he had a gastric ulcer), and the collapsing house reminded him of his recurring anxieties about a depressive collapse, so that it could be clearly shown to him how those attacks were directed at the analyst and analysis in his internal world. He frequently dealt with his anxieties about his mental and physical health in typically manic ways illustrated in this dream.

The manic defenses lead to a vicious circle. The depression results from the original attack on the object; the manic defenses preclude the ego from the experience of depression, but they also preclude a working through of the depressive position and necessitate a further attack on the object by denial, triumph, and contempt, thereby increasing the underlying depression. It is well known that where manic phenomena are encountered one has to look for the underlying depression. It is less well known that where there is a presenting depressive illness, one has to look for unconscious manic defense systems, precluding the working through of the depressive feelings. In the Kleinian view, the triumph over the internal object, which Freud describes as a feature of melancholic illness, is part of manic defenses perpetuating a situation of depression.

The working through of the depressive position in normal development depends on the capacity to make reparation. When the infant feels that in his hatred he has destroyed his good external and internal object, he experiences not only an intense feeling of guilt and loss but also pining and a longing to restore the lost loved object externally and internally, and to re-create the lost harmony and well-being. He mobilizes all his love and creativity to that end. It is this reparative drive that, in the Kleinian view, is the most important source of mental growth and creativity. The dream of a patient illustrates this. She dreamed that she was putting together a jigsaw puzzle representing a house in a landscape. The associations led to many past situations, particularly in her parental home. The putting together of the jigsaw puzzle was the analytical process, felt by her as a restoration and re-creation inside her of what was felt by her as a very shattered internal world, but it also represented a book she was currently writing, her wish to write being stimulated by this need to produce a whole picture out of shattered fragments.

With the repeated experiences of loss and recovery of his object, a recovery that is felt by him to be also a re-creation, the infant acquires an increasing confidence in the strength of his good object and in his own love and creativity. It is in the depressive position also that reality sense gradually develops. The depressive anxiety about the object leads the infant to withdraw his projections and to allow his object a more independent and separate existence. In recognizing his own ambivalence and his phantasies, he becomes aware of his inner reality and begins to differentiate it from the external reality of his object. A successful working through of the depressive position is fundamental to mental health. In the process of working through, the ego becomes integrated, capable of reality-testing and sublimation, and it is enriched from the introjection and assimilation of good objects. This in turn lessens his omnipotence and therefore his guilt and fear of loss.

It will be clear from the foregoing that technically we attach the greatest importance to the analysis of the manic and schizoid defenses to enable the patient to experience depressive anxiety and to work it through by way of restoration of the internal objects and the self. The paranoid-schizoid and depressive positions are not only stages of development. They are two types of ego integration and organization, and the ego has a constant struggle to maintain a state of integration.

Throughout his lifetime an individual oscillates between a paranoid-schizoid and a depressive internal organization. These oscillations vary in force with each individual psychopathology. At one end of the spectrum there is the schizophrenic or autistic patient who may rarely reach a depressive integration. At the other end is the fully mature individual with the well-integrated inner world, a person who has largely overcome depressive anxiety, who has a trust in a well-established good internal object and his own creative potential, and who has the capacity to deal with such depressive anxiety as is unavoidably stirred in realistic and creative ways. The analysis of the Oedipus complex in the Kleinian, as in the Freudian, technique remains a central task, but the technique is affected by the considerations stated above, and the paranoid-schizoid and depressive components in the Oedipal situation are carefully taken up.

Oedipus Complex

A patient presented the following dream. He dreamed that he was in a strange place where the wash place was out in the open, so that he had to undress and wash naked. There were other naked people present. He suddenly noticed on a kind of platform a couple facing one another, each pointing at the other an identical lethal weapon. It was like a camera, but more bottle-shaped, and it was covered by something like a camera hood made out of tinfoil. If the tinfoil were lifted, a lethal ray or radiation would be released. He was absolutely sick with anxiety, knowing beforehand what would happen. One of them, probably the woman, lifted the hood, and he hoped for a moment that the other one would not retaliate, since it was so senseless, but of course he retaliated immediately, and the dreamer felt a sense of hopelessness, doom, and despair at the senselessness of the destruction. He also felt some anxiety about himself because he thought that he might have been in the field of the rays and that they might have got into him. His associations started with the fear of nuclear warfare, but then turned to memories of his sexual curiosity in childhood. The camera with the lethal ray associated in his mind with his fear of his mother's eyes, who, he felt, could control and attack his father and himself by looking. Sometimes he felt that her looks could kill. The association he found most upsetting was to the tinfoil. He knew precisely what it reminded him of. He had purchased two bottles of brandy as Christmas presents, one for his analyst (a woman) and one for his wife's analyst (a man). He was shocked at the thought that his gifts to this couple of analysts appeared in his dream as lethal weapons, with which they were supposed to annihilate one another. This dream is clearly concerned with the patient's Oedipal feelings, his sexual curiosity about his parents, and his hostility, which changed their intercourse into a lethal combat.

In the analysis of this dream, in addition to analyzing the patient's curiosity about the parents' sexual intercourse and his jealous feelings about it, both in the transference and in terms of his memories emerging from the repression, the following elements have been taken up: (1) The projective elements in his voyeurism. (2) Its effect on his perception of his parents in relation to himself (his fear of his mother's controlling eyes) and to one another (their intercourse becoming a mutual lethal attack). (3) The introjection of the situation, expressed in the dream by the patient's feeling that he is "in the field of the rays," that they "may have got into him" and the effect of this introjection on the patient's internal world, particularly his hypochondriacal anxiety, always fairly active in this patient and referred to by him in connection with anxiety about himself in the dream. (4) The depressive element, which is evidenced by his tremendous feeling of pity and loss; though the hostility is projected into the parents and they become dangerous to one another and to him, they are felt in the dream to be victims as much as persecutors, and obviously love and concern for them are retained in a large measure.[2]

I have stated before that Melanie Klein found in the analysis of very small children that the Oedipus complex has very early roots in the oral phase. When she developed later the concept of the depressive position, it became clear that the Oedipus complex begins at the same time. This indeed is implicit in the definition of the depressive position. If the infant becomes aware of his mother as a whole person, a whole separate person leading a life of her own, having other relationships of her own, he is immediately exposed to the experience of sexual jealousy. The fact that his world is still colored by his omnipotent projections increases his jealousy, for when he senses the emotional tie between his parents, he fantasies them as giving one another precisely those satisfactions he desires for himself. Thus he will experience his jealousy first of all in oral terms, but the triangular situation will

[2] The appearance of the phallic woman (she has the same weapon as the man) as related to the patient's projection into her of his own dangerous penis—the brandy bottle.

have the configuration and the intensity of the Oedipus complex described by Freud.

The child's experience of the Oedipal situation will be dictated by the stage of his own libidinal development and expresses itself to begin with in oral terms. Also, the earlier the stage of the Oedipus complex, the more it will be dominated by the infant's omnipotent projections. This is very important technically because, in analyzing the early roots of the Oedipal conflict, one liberates it from the dominance of omnipotent mechanisms and phantasies. Tracing the Oedipus complex to its early roots enables one also to analyze the complex interplay between the early relationship to the breast and the Oedipus complex; for instance, how anxieties experienced in relation to the breast make the infant turn to the penis or, conversely, how the Oedipal jealousy may affect the feeding relationship to the breast.

Here is an example of how Oedipal jealousy interferes with the introjection of a good breast. The patient had been for months, off and on, preoccupied with a situation in his office. There was a young couple, Mr. and Mrs. L., of whom he was constantly complaining. They were interfering with his work and his relationships and were in a collusive relationship with their boss, Mr. R., who was thoroughly hated by the patient. In the session preceding the one I am going to describe in more detail he told me that he had heard that Mrs. L. was on the point of a breakdown and might be leaving the office. He felt suddenly terribly sorry for the L.'s. He realized that for months he had been complaining what a nuisance they were to him and had never given a thought to their predicament and the pressure they were under from Mr. R., whose paranoia, intrigues, and incessant demands were preying upon them and poisoning them. He was near tears speaking about them. He said that Mr. R. was behaving mentally just the way he was physically. The patient had often referred in the past to Mr. R.'s tendency to diarrhea—"just shitting all over the place." Mr. R. often, in the analysis, played the role of the bad sexual father, who dirtied the mother, but also that of the patient's split-off "dirtying" self projected into the father. The next day the patient started the session by complaining of headache and diarrhea. He then said that he had had three short dreams. In the first dream he had spent twenty-four hours speaking to Mrs. M. (the wife of a psychoanalyst). In the second, he saw some beautiful mountains, round and white, like a woman's breast, with a most beautiful lake, but he knew that the lake was full of some infection or poison, so that he could neither drink nor bathe in it, and he had to go away. In the third dream, he was in a holiday resort. The mistress of the hotel was a kind of courtesan and he wanted to kiss her, but had some anxiety about her as a dirty prostitute. The first associations were to Mrs. M. A few days previously he had seen Dr. M. giving me a lift in a Rolls-Royce and felt very jealous. The mountain landscape made him think of the forthcoming analytic holiday. The poison in the water associated in his mind with a typhoid epidemic in Switzerland, which in turn reminded him of his own diarrhea. He had also the previous day read in a newspaper about an infection in tinned food, so that a couple of tins could poison a whole family. He was particularly impressed by the thought of secret poison or infection because the lake looked so beautiful and unspoilt.

The interpretation dealt in essence with the situation in which the patient's Oedipal jealousy, stirred by the holiday and by the sight of the rich Dr. M. driving his analyst off in a car, interrupts the idealized feeding situation represented in the first dream and leads to a secret anal attack by diarrhea against the analyst as the feeding mother, so that the lake connected with the beautiful white mountains (the breast) becomes poisonous to him, like a couple of tins of poisoned food. The interpretation also emphasized how secret these attacks were, since on the face of it his relation to the analyst was so good. This interpretation mobilized an admission of many hostile thoughts about the analysis and the analyst personally and suspicions that the analytical treatment would make him worse. His thoughts then returned to the couple at the office, expressing tremendous concern and anxiety about them, particularly Mrs. L., repeating, "This poor woman, will she ever recover?" He knew that his concern was for the analyst and the analysis, would it ever recover from his secret dirtying? As he went on speaking of the couple, it gradually sounded more and more as if he were speaking about himself, because the expressions he applied to them were increasingly reminiscent of things he said about himself when he was depressed—"How will they ever get out of this mess? They will never recover from it, they won't be able to cope," and one got an increasingly clear picture of his introjection of, and his identification with, a parental couple irrecoverably ruined and destroyed by the Mr. R. part of himself. In this patient's experience, one can also see a move from a paranoid to a more depressive experience of his Oedipus complex. He starts by being completely persecuted by the L.'s as a parental couple. In his dreams and the associations to it there is also a paranoid suspicion of the feeding breast, represented by the infected lake, and, in the transference, his suspicions of the analyst. Toward the end of the session, his feeling in relation to mother—"this poor woman"—and the parental couple is full of guilt and concern. He is particularly concerned with this destroyed couple in his internal world and with his identification with them.

Working Through

These oscillations between the parnoid-schizoid and the depressive feelings underlie, in my opinion, the process of working through. In the analytic situation, the patient relives his relation to his original objects. His attachment to them has to be lived through again and given up again. In Freud's view, no object can be given up without being introjected into the ego. In the Kleinian view, this introjection is part of the depressive process. No object can be given up successfully without a complete process of mourning, as in the depressive position, ending in the introjection of a good internal object, strengthening the ego. Any new insight of any importance necessitates this process. The pain of the mourning situation mobilizes new manic and schizoid defenses, but with each repeated experience the ego is strengthened, the good object is more securely established, and the need to have recourse to new defenses is lessened. The process of working through is completed when some aspect of the object has been given up in this way.

It is impossible to speak of the Kleinian technique of today without mentioning the special attention paid to the factor of envy. Since the publication of *Envy and Gratitude* (Klein, 1957), the analysis of envy has played an increasingly important role. The analysis of early oral anxieties led Melanie Klein to believe that envy has very early roots and plays a large part in the infant's relation to the breast. She distinguishes between it and greed and jealousy and considers it more primitive than jealousy. "Jealousy is based on love and aims at the possession of the loved object and the removal of the rival. It pertains to a triangular relationship and therefore to a time of life when objects are clearly recognized and differentiated from one another. Envy, on the other hand, is a two-part relation in which the subject envies the object for some possession or quality; no other live object need enter into it. Jealousy is necessarily a whole-object relationship, while envy is essentially experienced in terms of part-objects, though it persists into whole-object relationships.

Greed aims at the possession of all the goodness that can be extracted from the object, regardless of consequences; this may result in the destruction of the object and the spoiling of its goodness, but the destruction is incidental to the ruthless acquirement. Envy aims at being as good as the object, but, when this is felt as impossible, it aims at spoiling the goodness of the object, to remove the source of envious feelings. It is this spoiling aspect of envy that is so destructive to development, since the very source of goodness that the infant depends on is turned bad, and good introjections, therefore, cannot be achieved. Envy, though arising from primitive love and admiration, has a less strong libidinal component than greed and is suffused with the death instinct. As it attacks the source of life, it may be considered to be the earliest direct externalization of the death instinct. Envy stirs as soon as the infant becomes aware of the breast as a source of life and good experience; the real gratification which he experiences at the breast, reinforced by idealization, so powerful in early infancy, makes him feel that the breast is the source of all comforts, physical and mental, an inexhaustible reservoir of food and warmth, love, understanding and wisdom. The blissful experience of satisfaction which this wonderful object can give will increase his love and his desire to possess, preserve and protect it, but the same experience stirs in him also the wish to be himself the source of such perfection. He experiences painful feelings of envy which carry with them the desire to spoil the qualities of the object which can give him such painful feelings (Segal, 1964).

The importance of envy lies in the fact that it interferes with the normal operation of the schizoid mechanisms. Splitting into an ideal and a bad object cannot be established, since it is the ideal object that is the object of envy, and therefore hostility. Thus, the introjection of an ideal object, which could become the core of ego, is disturbed at its very roots. Defenses against envy may be equally detrimental to growth. The devaluation of the object and the projection of envy into it give rise to persecutory anxiety and lead to the formation of an envious superego, which interferes with the development of the ego. The analysis of patients suffering from an excessively severe superego often reveals that it is the envious aspect of the superego that is felt as most damaging, since it is directed not only against the aggressive wishes of the ego, but also, and often predominantly, against any positive or creative strivings of the ego. In the analytical situation, envy manifests itself often by negative therapeutic reactions. As soon as the analysis is felt as good, and the analyst is felt as the source of the good analysis, it has to be attacked and destroyed. Envy brings in its wake feelings of hopelessness. Bad experiences are bad, but good experiences also become bad, since they stir envy; therefore there seems to be no hope for a good experience. Since a good object cannot be introjected, the ego does not feel that it can grow and eventually bridge the gap between the self and the original object by introjection and assimilation, and this in turn increases envy, leading again to hopelessness. The analysis of envy, which has been split off, denied, and projected, is extremely painful and disturbing, but it reintroduces hope through the establishment of a good and enviable object. Latent appreciation can be mobilized and the battle can be fought again between love and gratitude and envy.

It is difficult to give a brief example here, since envy is usually heavily defended against and has to be tracked in painful detail, but I would like to describe the dream of one patient, showing some emergence of hope, when, for the first time, he could admit some envy in relation to the analyst. This patient, a borderline case, came to the first session carrying two bags of food, a Thermos bottle of coffee and one of tea, and throughout the session fed himself a number of drugs, such as dexidrine. He made it clear from the start who had possession and control of the feeding breast. In the early stages of his analysis, he developed the following pattern. He would frequently miss or come very late, but after the session he would spend hours in the lavatory, doing his "post analysis," that is, writing notes on his session, categorizing them, drawing conclusions, and so forth. He often said that this "post analysis" was of far more value to him than the analysis. Since the patient had a large number of anal perversions, it was not difficult to show him, with the help of his dreams, that in his phantasy he was feeding himself on his own feces, considered as far superior to the mother's food. His feeling of superiority was so absolute that an interpretation of envy would have been quite laughable to him, though the enormity of his envy of both men and women, particularly women, was blatantly obvious. One could, however, get at it by interpreting his projective identification. There was no doubt in his mind about the analyst's inferiority and her feelings of dependence on him, rejection by him, envy of his riches, and so forth. The analyst, in his mind, had the same characteristics as his extremely envious superego, by which he was controlled to such a degree that he was not allowed, for instance, to read a book or listen to the radio, because it wasted time. He felt equally controlled and nagged by his analyst. Accompanying this was a state of despair of such absoluteness that it had become painless. When finally he began to be aware of his own envy in relation to the analyst, primarily as a feeding breast, he had the following dream. He dreamed that under an enormous pile of dead leaves he found a single snowdrop, white as a drop of milk. His waking association was that at last, under a pile of feces, he had found a single drop of milk as a sign of hope.

The discovery of early envy and the way in which it operates has given great impetus to new work, particularly with psychotics (Bion, 1959) and other intractable cases, for instance, severe acting out and drug addiction (Rosenfeld, 1965). It is, however, impossible in this chapter to treat of it at length.

Termination of Analysis

Has the Kleinian outlook on analysis altered the criteria for the termination of an analysis and the therapeutic aim? In certain basic ways the criteria remain the same—the lifting of repression, insight, freeing the patient from early fixations and inhibitions, and enabling him to form full and satisfactory personal relationships.

The Kleinian analyst will be guided in his evaluation of the therapeutic progress mainly by his assessment of the patient's internal world; he will try to evaluate the state of integration in the patient's ego and his internal objects and his capacity to maintain the state of integration in situations of stress.

Melanie Klein (1950) wrote:

My criterion for the termination of an analysis is, therefore, as follows: have persecutory and depressive anxieties been sufficiently reduced in the course of the analysis, and has the patient's relation to the external world been sufficiently strengthened to enable him to deal satisfactorily with the situation of mourning arising at this point? By analysing as fully as possible both the negative and the positive transference, persecutory and depressive anxieties are diminished and the patient becomes increasingly able to synthesise the contrasting aspects of the primary objects, and the feelings towards them, thus establishing a more realistic and secure attitude to the internal and the external world. If these processes have been sufficiently experienced in the transference situation both the idealisation of the analyst and the feelings of being persecuted by him are diminished; the patient can then cope more successfully with the feelings of loss caused by the termination of the analysis and with that part of the work of mourning which he has to carry out by himself after the end of the analysis.

REFERENCES

BION, W. R. Development of schizophrenic thought. *International Journal of Psychoanalysis.* 1956, 37, 344–346.

BION, W. R. The differentiation of the psychotic from the non-psychotic personalities. *International Journal of Psychoanalysis,* 1957, 38, 266–275.

BION, W. R. On hallucination. *International Journal of Psychoanalysis,* 1958, 39, 341–349.

BION, W. R. Attacks on linking. *International Journal of Psychoanalysis,* 1959, 40, 308–315.

ISAACS, SUSAN. The nature and function of phantasy. (*Developments in psychoanalysis*, 1952.) *International Journal of Psychoanalysis*, 1948, 29, 73–97.

KLEIN, MELANIE. Psychoanalysis of children (*Contributions to Psychoanalysis*) (Trans. by Alix Strachey). New York: Norton, 1932.

KLEIN, MELANIE. On the criteria for the termination of an analysis. *International Journal of Psychoanalysis*, 1950, 31, 78–80, 204.

KLEIN, MELANIE. *Envy and gratitude*. New York: Basic Books, 1957.

ROSENFELD, HERBERT A. *Psychotic states: a psychoanalytical approach*. London: Hogarth Press, 1965.

SEGAL, HANNA. Some aspects of the analysis of a schizophrenic. *Internationa Journal of Psychoanalysis*, 1950, 31, 268–278.

SEGAL, HANNA. Depression in the schizophrenic. *International Journal of Psychoanalysis*, 1956, 37, 339–343.

SEGAL, HANNA. Curative factors in psychoanalysis. *International Journal of Psychoanalysis*, 1962, 43, 212–217.

SEGAL, HANNA. *Introduction to the work of Melanie Klein*. New York: Basic Books, 1964.

7

THE TECHNIQUES OF PSYCHOANALYSIS DEVELOPED BY FRANZ ALEXANDER AND THOMAS FRENCH

Sheldon T. Selesnick

When Alexander published his selected papers, which had appeared over a period of forty years, under the title of *The Scope of Psychoanalysis,* he chose Thomas French to write the introduction. This was not a mere exchange of professional courtesies, as revealed by a personal communication between the two men. On the flyleaf of a copy of French's work, *The Integration of Behavior,* presented by the author to Alexander, we find the inscription: "To Franz Alexander who has done so much to stimulate and encourage my interest in the therapeutic process." In the Introduction to *The Scope of Psychoanalysis* (1961) Alexander was characterized by French as

The author wishes to acknowledge the helpful suggestions with regard to this manuscript given to him by Drs. Thomas M. French, Judd Marmor, and Hedda Bolgar.

"an investigator who has been extremely fertile, both in ideas and in projects for testing them" (p. 5). Indeed, French and Alexander worked so closely together, cross-fertilizing each other's thinking, that it is often difficult to determine with any degree of certainty which of the two was the first to germinate a specific idea. In their collaboration, these men each originated basic formulations in the field of psychosomatic medicine. French integrated psychological principles, especially Gestalt theories, into psychoanalysis; Alexander's contributions to sociology, esthetics, forensic psychiatry, cultural history, and political science broadened the scope of psychoanalysis. All this has been summarized in Franz Alexander and Thomas M. French, *Psychoanalysis Integrated and Expanded* (Selesnick, 1964). What concerns us here are the reforms of classical psychoanalysis inaugurated by Alexander and French, which have had a lasting and profound effect upon psychoanalytic practice.

Psychoanalysis and Psychotherapy—A Continuum

Hanns Sachs, Alexander's teacher, had forewarned that ". . . it is simpler to think in contradictions than in precise gradations of thought" (Fliess, 1937). In all their studies Alexander and French continually demonstrated the futility of attempting solutions according to Aristotelian dichotomies. Indeed, Alexander felt the necessity of restating his position a month before his death (in March 1964), as can be seen from this statement, which was published posthumously: "One of the greatest weaknesses of the human mind consists in a kind of laziness, in the urge to find either/or solutions and to explain everything from one single principle, rather than to consider the multiplicity of factors in their interrelationships" (Alexander, 1964, p. 237).

Following Freud, who had compared psychoanalysis to pure gold and psychotherapy to a cheap alloy, it had become customary to regard psychoanalysis and psychotherapy as different and distinct procedures. Freud had not foreseen that psychotherapy could be founded on the same psychodynamic principles as psychoanalysis. Alexander, French, and their colleagues at the Chicago Psychoanalytic Institute advocated in their book *Psychoanalytic Therapy* (1946) that the rigid distinctions between psychoanalysis and psychotherapy be abandoned. Alexander remarked that "French was the first among us to state explicitly that there is no essential difference between the various procedures, that the difference lies merely in the extent to which the various therapeutic principles and techniques are utilized. We are working with the same theories [in psychotherapy and psychoanalysis]" (Alexander, 1964a, p. 7). He further explained that "what makes the procedure psychoanalytic is . . . that it is based on psychoanalytic knowledge. What makes it psychoanalytic is that the therapist knows what is going on in the patient and knows what he is doing in terms of existing psychodynamic knowledge" (Alexander, 1962). To consider treatment psychoanalytic merely because a patient reclines on a couch and is seen by an analyst a certain number of fifty-minute hours per week over many years means relying on formal and superficial criteria. Alexander and French predicted that, in opposition to standardized procedure, a new flexible orientation was on its way, "according to which the various forms of psychotherapy as well as the classical psychoanalytic procedure are considered as different applications of the universally valid principles of psychodynamics" (Alexander, 1950, p. 4).

When a clear-cut distinction between psychoanalysis and psychoanalytic psychotherapy fades, the question arises, when does a therapist utilize uncovering and when supportive techniques? This crucial decision is based on the relative strength of ego integration, a psychodiagnostic criterion. Alexander stressed that the assessment of ego functions, that is, the perception of internal and external realities, the integration of these perceptions, and the executive action mediated by motor modalities, aids in diagnosis. When the ego is stronger, it can withstand anxiety aroused by confrontations and genetic interpretations, but if the ego is relatively weak, supportive measures (reassurance, environmental manipulation, suggestion, abreaction, gratification of dependency needs) are required. Thus, psychoanalysis and supportive psychotherapy can be viewed as a continuum; at one extreme the ego is intact and more uncovering therapy is indicated; at the opposite end of the scale ego functioning is poor, and a more supportive approach is in order. However, most often the two procedures are combined in working with one patient.

We have come to realize that even in the strictest classical analysis there are powerful supportive aspects. During the initial phase of an analysis, decisions are postponed, which consequently relieve the patient of tensions. The mere presence of an interested person who speaks in reassuring tones is in itself supportive. How often it is said of analysts, or even of friends for that matter, that it is their demeanor and tone of voice that are most comforting. It is senseless to assume that supportive psychotherapeutic measures are superficial and beneath the dignity of an analyst. Supportive therapy is the older of the two and has prescientific roots. Supportive psychotherapy today is an important tool in the armamentarium of the psychoanalyst, just as digitalis is in the hands of the internist. To continue the analogy, digitalis is not considered superficial treatment today in spite of its prescientific origin and early use. There are now scientific indications for it (Carson and Selesnick, 1959).

To relegate supportive treatment solely to intuition means to return to a prescientific or pre-Freudian position; all psychotherapies should be based on a thorough appreciation of psychodynamics.

Alexander and French have repeatedly been criticized by fundamentalist psychoanalysts who think that the identity of the analyst would be threatened and the field opened to charlatans if no distinction were made between psychoanalysis and psychoanalytic psychotherapy. This is not a valid argument for conserving such a distinction, since this danger is not so great as that resulting from artificial differentiations. Developments in the field of psychotherapy have been and are still hampered by the fact that psychoanalytic institutes are slow to recognize the great significance of broadening the therapeutic applications of psychoanalytic knowledge, and continue to restrict their teaching almost exclusively to the practice of the standard psychoanalytic procedure. The "gold" of the standard procedure itself needs to be further purified from the nontherapeutic components preserved by custom and tradition. Some psychoanalytic institutes maintain a conservative viewpoint, even though over the years it has not been standard analytic procedure that has been enriched but solid psychodynamic knowledge, which has achieved broader therapeutic applications than originally envisioned by Freud (Alexander and Selesnick, 1966). Critics, and even some followers, inappropriately applied the label "neo-Freudian" to Alexander and French, as if they had founded a new school opposed to the Freudian school. This was not their intention. To modify, adapt, and make a more economical application of Freudian principles will do more to preserve the foundations of scientific psychoanalysis than inflexible adherence to outmoded concepts, intending to preserve a great tradition but ultimately leading to sterile codification.

Corrective Emotional Experience

There are certain essential psychodynamic principles on which all psychoanalytic treatment depends. These are: (1) The range of the conscious ego is enhanced when repressed material becomes conscious during treatment. Once the ego has become aware of hitherto unconscious impulses, it attempts to integrate them so that they become part of the voluntary behavior, avoiding internalized conflict. The difficulty is that the patient will resist becoming aware of unconscious ideation; to surmount this resistance becomes the key technical problem of the analysis. (2) The patient's recognition of unconscious material is achieved through the analyst's interpretation of free associations, slips of the tongue, and dreams. Further mobilization of unconscious material occurs through emotional experiences in the analytic situation. In the transference the patient repeats interpersonal attitudes that characterized his childish feelings about his parents or other significant people in his childhood. The process of transference is enhanced when the analyst encourages the patient to express himself freely (Alexander and Selesnick, 1966).

Historically, two main points have been emphasized in the technique of psychoanalysis. One stresses the importance of conscious insight into breaking up neurotic patterns; the other accentuates emotional experiences occurring during treatment. These techniques are not mutually exclusive, yet controversial discussions revolve about the relative importance of cognitive and experiential factors. The classical analysts following Freud considered that insight into repressed libidinal impulses was of primary therapeutic necessity. As early as the 1920's, however, Ferenczi and Rank (1925) had proposed that the renewed experience of outmoded patterns in the transference was the primary therapeutic vehicle. Alexander and French emphasize that both experience and insight operate in all dynamic psychotherapies. However, they believe that if insight is not accompanied by an emotional release, it has little value. They concurred with Otto Fenichel, who believed that purely cognitive interpretations supply "dynamically ineffective knowledge."

When Alexander speaks of emotional experience during treatment, he does not refer to reliving old patterns but to a new and "corrective emotional experience." This concept, as French pointed out, "is Alexander's outstanding contribution to understanding of the therapeutic process in psychoanalytic treatment" (French, 1961, p. 9). If the attitude of the analyst differs from that of the parent with whom the patient had formed a neurotic relationship, then there is a dramatic highlighting of the dissimilarity between the previous situation and the new one experienced in the transference. If the pathogenic attitude of the parent was overly permissive and the analyst has a firmer and less permissive attitude, the atmosphere of the transference is conducive to a corrective emotional experience. If the original infantile neurosis developed as the result of a strict, punitive parental attitude, the permissive and kindly position of the analyst would lead the patient to experience the difference in attitudes. It is paramount, according to Alexander, that the patient *experience through feeling* this difference between the therapist's attitude and that of the parent with whom he had formed a neurotic relationship. Alexander stressed that one of the ego's basic functions is to adjust to external reality. When a patient continues to act toward the therapist according to earlier patterns and the therapist's reaction is different from what the patient expected, he experiences the irrationality of his own emotional reactions. Gradually, the patient can correct old emotional patterns as his ego finds it necessary to adjust to the new situation. To quote Alexander, "As soon as the neurotic patterns are revived and brought into the realm of consciousness, the ego has the opportunity to adjust them to the changed conditions" (1965, p. 89). The corrective emotional experience, which is similar to emotional reconditioning, is derived from the fact that the analyst responds to the patient's emotional reactions in a way that counteracts or neutralizes the disturbing influence of the patient.

Everyone is familiar with stories of individuals whose lives were dramatically changed through a significant experience with a meaningful person. Alexander refers to Victor Hugo's *Les Misérables*, in which Jean Valjean had such an experience (Alexander and French, 1946). Valjean, an ex-convict, was perpetually victimized by persons in authority. He was overwhelmed when a bishop who mhe had tried to rob treated him with unexpected kindness. Valjean's conversion, indeed his metamorphosis, occurred when the bishop allowed him to keep the object he had stolen. The bishop, of course, reacted intuitively, recognizing somehow Valjean's need for this experience. Analysts and psychotherapists, and in fact all perceptive people, such as Aichhorn and Father Flanagan, have responded intuitively to those in need. Alexander, however, proposed that the analyst must not allow his reactions to depend on fortuitous circumstances nor on intuition. He suggested that the therapist play an active part in creating a proper atmosphere for the patient's development in therapy. A therapist has a whole range of emotional attitudes upon which he can call when dealing with a given individual. If he is aware of the patient's psychodynamics and the significant pathogenic attitudes of the parental figures, he is in a position to act with greater wisdom in correcting the patient's attitudes with respect to these figures. It should be emphasized, however, that the therapist's assumption of a calculated attitude is not to be misconstrued as one of play-acting or of adopting a spurious approach. If the situation calls for permissiveness and the therapist is not by nature a permissive person, obviously he cannot employ this attitude with the patient. Prolonged and even interminable analysis may be the result of the therapist's inability to relate genuinely in a corrective way with his patient. If analyst and patient, however, are able to create the climate of a corrective emotional experience, the patient should come to feel, after repeated corrective experiences, the irrationality of his transference attitude. The transference situation is always less intense than the original parent-child relationship; consequently, the adult ego is not completely overwhelmed and has a better chance to make a new adjustment. Alexander demonstrated that the revival of early memories frequently occurs after the patient has gone through a corrective experience, whereas previously it was believed that insight alone was the necessary stimulus to revive early recollections.

One of Alexander's patients, when asked what he felt was most helpful to him in his analysis, replied,

> Each time I would attempt a new venture, my father discouraged me. Once when I was to give a speech, my father said: "You are not a public speaker and you have no business on the podium." Dr. Alexander, on the other hand, encouraged me in my new projects, and gave me the feeling that I would be successful. Each time I had expected discouragement because I recalled incidents of my childhood when my father became frightened as I ventured into explorations.

Alexander declared that his behavior toward this patient was calculated to counteract this paternal reaction. He also claimed that this was an easy position for him to take inasmuch as he had confidence in the patient. It was also within his personality framework for Alexander to behave in this way inasmuch as he himself was an individual who exuded confidence and optimism.

Psychiatric nurses and the staff on psychiatric services are expected to assume certain attitudes based on psychodynamic considerations toward patients. Yet it is argued that analysts themselves should behave in a more neutral manner. Others besides Alexander have stressed that the classical model of the impassive analyst who behaves like a combination of robot and IBM machine, recording the data, then making interpretations of that data, is an absurd caricature. Marmor (1960) put the issue most succinctly: "The original theoretical dictum that the analyst must be a shadowy neutral, impersonal, and a value-free figure, is coming to be recognized not only as a practical impossibility, but even as being in some instances at least of questionable therapeutic value." In the case described above, it was precisely the fact that Alexander was evaluative—more positive than the patient's father —that led to the corrective experience. This judgmental attitude becomes more interesting when we realize that the patient, in this instance, was a training candidate in an analytic institute. A training analyst's judgment of a candidate has a direct bearing on when the latter will begin his dream seminars, take his first patient into analysis, and graduate from the institute.

Perhaps it is precisely because the therapist is involved with the patient that the corrective experience takes place.

When Alexander proposes that the therapist's attitude be "emotionally detached" (1953) and at the same time be "involved," he seems to be contradictory. In describing the manner in which he promoted a corrective experience in a patient, Alexander wrote, "My attitude was not simply objective and helpful, it was consistently tolerant and definitely encouraging, exactly the opposite of his father's attitude" (1950a). Alexander could not have been uninvolved in this patient's future. Anyone who cares is not indifferent. The important consideration is that the therapist's involvement is not of the same magnitude as that of the significant parent, and an even more decisive factor is its different *quality*. Perhaps this qualitative difference was in Alexander's mind when he began an analysis with a statement such as, "Let us understand each other. You and I are forming an alliance and through this friendship we will explore your thoughts, your feelings, and come to some recognition of your unconscious conflicts. Now, if we are to have a foe, it is not each other, but it is those unconscious demanding and self-punitive attitudes that you have toward yourself and which came about because of experiences in your childhood."

Such a therapeutic alliance is possible because the analyst functions in a noncondemnatory manner. He encourages what in the past has been unnecessarily discouraged by the parents and even rewards the patient for expressing feelings that were formerly forbidden. Alexander enjoyed talking about a cartoon in *The New Yorker* in which a therapist admonishes a patient, saying, "Naughty, naughty, today you again have had a few nice thoughts." To Alexander, this caricature is an overexaggeration of the therapist's attitude, which encourages not only expression of forbidden thoughts in general but even those directed toward the therapist. In commenting on this cartoon, Alexander remarked that the correct therapeutic attitude is not that of anger when a patient says, "Why, you are an ass"; indeed the therapist should welcome it by replying, "Bravo, that is what I want to hear" (Alexander, 1965, p. 87). In the past, the patient's ego had to repress such ego-alien thoughts, but as he repeatedly encounters the opposite attitude in his analyst, unconscious and hitherto repressed material has a chance to emerge into consciousness. This release from repression, together with the challenge forced upon the ego to find an appropriate readjustment to the new and unique relationship with the analyst, constitutes the essence of the corrective emotional experience.

The axis about which the corrective emotional experience revolves is still the transference. The intrapsychic conflict is displaced by means of projection onto the analyst. If the bond between them is strong enough, the patient's feeling toward the analyst can develop sufficient intensity to be meaningful. Maintaining the transference at optimum intensity is by no means an easy task. All too frequently the transference becomes charged to such a degree that excessive dependency yearnings result in transference resistance. Alexander pointed out that transference, like X-rays, can be given in overdoses (1956, p. 165). An overly strong emotional attachment to the analyst, French warns, overwhelms the integrative capacity of the ego and impairs its over-all functioning (1936). Where the transference neurosis has overripened, that is, has gone beyond an optimum intensity, protracted analysis is inevitable. Freud (1913) described this intensive, dependent transference situation as one in which the patient's wish to be cured has been exchanged for the wish to be treated. It has become axiomatic in some analytic circles to consider that a prolonged analysis indicates a better analysis. Alexander and French believed that this is a very poor generalization, and in their analytic work with neurotics they continuously attempted to counteract dependent gratifications or regressions. It is erroneous to indicate routinely to patients that the analysis will be a very long process or will go on indefinitely. This encourages from the onset regressive strivings that are already inherent in the analytic procedure.

Regression and the Real Life Situation

Alexander (1956) called attention to Freud's distinction between two forms of regression. One is a return to unresolved traumatic situations in order to master these unpleasant life experiences. As the patient recounts the incidents with affect, his abreactions as well as the analyst's interpretations of them are essential to working through and resolving the trauma. A second type of regression produces preoccupation with thoughts going back to a time when the patient was receiving a great deal of gratification. This preconflictual, pretraumatic period of the patient's life represents fixation points to which the patient returns in order to evade current problems. Both patient and analyst may receive a great deal of pleasure from discussing these thoughts, the patient by reliving the gratifying past and the analyst by looking into deep analytic material. But such a *regressive evasion* of later conflicts may result in extended plateaus and periods of stagnation in the patient's adaptive responses to his environment.

A twenty-seven-year-old man had overcome severe study and sexual inhibitions. During his analysis he married and maintained a good sexual adjustment. A short time after passing the bar examinations he returned to the analyst with acute symptoms of anxiety, anorexia, and insomnia. He immediately resumed discussion of his early relationship with his mother, his sexual attachment to his sister, and his rivalry with his father. After several weeks, he dreamed that he was lying on a soft, warm bed and that the analyst was pointing to the door. In the dream, the patient was paralyzed and could not leave the bed. His association was that outside the door were situations that could arouse tremendous anxiety. It soon became apparent that he would rather expound on areas already explored with the analyst because they were now safe in the comfortable environment of the analytic situation (the soft, warm bed) rather than discuss his anxieties with regard to his work obligations. He returned to his old pattern of procrastination and hoped to engage the analyst in a comforting relationship again. The analyst did not permit this evasion of present life-situations by a retreat into the past and brought the patient to focus on various alternatives in solving his realistic work situation.

The fact that Freud regarded the goals of genetic research and therapy to be identical frequently encouraged analysts to neglect present life-situations in favor of a preoccupation with the past. French specifically expressed the position of Alexander, Rado, and others who feel that all too often analysis is concentrated inappropriately only on the past: "We are interested in the past as a source of stereotyped behavior patterns, but our primary interest is in helping the patient find a solution for his present problems by correcting these unsuccessful patterns, by helping him to take account of the differences between present and past" (Alexander and French, 1946, p. 92). The patient is given "repeated opportunity for actual efforts at readjustment within the transference situation. Then when the patient attempts to put his new attitudes into practice in outside life, he will find they have become second nature" (Alexander and French, p. 95).

Many times we lose sight of the fact that the patient comes to treatment because of difficult present life-situations. The following is such an example:

Analytic colleagues treated a married couple separately. There were significant changes in their attitudes toward themselves and in their roles as parents. Nevertheless, the marital situation remained inharmonious. Both analysts did little to encourage discussions of their actual marital situation. Later the couple went to a marriage counselor who reported that they were confused as to their respective roles in the home. Their problems were as banal as the question of who was to take out the garbage, "Not the son of an aristocratic Spanish father," said one patient; the other patient was just as vehement, "Not the daughter of an aristocratic Hungarian." Neglecting the actual life-situation resulted in an accumulation of garbage in their lives!

The relevance of the patient's present problems, however, does not imply that the past can be ignored as irrelevant. Many so-called neo-Freudians went to this extreme and saw little advantage in uncovering the patient's past history. However, without such an uncovering the analyst can never understand the patient nor help him gain insight into the habitual patterns of neurotic adaptation that developed from early life experiences. Exploration of the past is essential but, of course, should not be an end in itself and must be avoided when it becomes a regressive evasion of current conflicts. Rado's *adaptational technique* is in accord with the position of Alexander and French, that the aim of therapy is not exploration of the past and must be subordinated to understanding current conflicts.

Principle of Flexibility

In order to induce optimal intensity in the transference as well as to discourage an overwhelmingly intense dependent transference, members of the Chicago Institute of Psychoanalysis recommended certain innovations in analytic technique. These modifications were employed for a short time at the Berlin Psychoanalytic Institute where they were called *Fractioned Analysis*. They are now associated with the principle of flexibility of Alexander and French. At propitious moments the analyst may manipulate the frequency of analytic interviews or recommend a temporary interruption of treatment. In some cases, as, for example, with acting-out patients, it may be necessary to increase the frequency of the interviews in order to develop a more intense transference relationship. This encourages a tendency toward identification with the analyst, who then has an opportunity to exert a restraining influence on the patient's impulses. Frequently, however, especially with those patients who use analysis as a substitute for life experiences, it is better to reduce the frequency of the interviews or to set a tentative termination date for the analysis. Owing to these experimental manipulations, dependency on the analytic situation becomes a focal issue. The patient may discover that he can manage quite well without the analyst, and soon a more permanent separation may be recommended. Preparatory interruptions were found to be an excellent means of gauging the proper time for terminating the treatment. Alexander, French, and some of their colleagues at the Chicago Psychoanalytic Institute learned that the emotional reaction to previous interruptions is a more important clue than such criteria as recollection of infantile memories or the depth of intellectual insight. In cases when, during interruptions or reductions in frequency, feelings of yearning for the analyst become more intense upon returning to the analysis or upon increasing the frequency of the interviews, the patient may be able now to verbalize those feelings and thus gain greater insight into the nature of his dependent strivings. It is insight based on emotional experience, especially with regard to the transference, that is the aim of these stratagems. Therefore, as Alexander stated, "One may question the effectiveness of such measures, but there is no reason to consider them as contradictory to the basic principles of psychoanalysis, namely, to impart insight based on emotional experience" (1956, p. 143).

Such maneuvers require that the analyst have the proper respect for the recuperative powers of the patient's ego. Patients in analysis naturally talk about their disturbances. Sometimes both analyst and patient lose sight of healthier areas of the patient's personality. They become convinced that the patient is so disturbed that analysis is indispensable and that it must be maintained continually. Psychoanalytic institutes that require frequent contacts for supervised analyses encourage the student to believe in the efficacy of closely spaced sessions. The analyst who has experimented with interruptions and less frequent interviews may find that his results are as good or better than with the standard procedure (Alexander, 1962, p. 175). Alexander summed up certain major drawbacks of the classical psychoanalytic technique: "I see the main shortcomings of the standard psychoanalytic procedure in the overestimation of cognitive insight versus learning from emotional experience and practice as well as in the underestimation of the natural integrative powers of the ego. This manifests itself in an overemphasis upon the therapist's uninterrupted activities, invoking the dangers of overtreatment." (1964a, p. 192).

Importance of the Therapist's Personality

We have noted that Alexander and French were also critical of the model of the classical analyst who, as an "uninvolved intellect," is a blank screen, as it were, on which the patient projects his feelings and attitudes. Yet, the analyst's attitudes toward the patient, whether conscious, unconscious, or even countertransference attitudes, may be crucial to the patient's recovery. An important factor in any psychotherapeutic procedure, Alexander believed, is the patient's feeling that the treatment will be successful.[1] If the analyst shares this belief, then the patient's confidence increases, and his motivation toward analytic work is enhanced. French, who meticulously described the process of psychological integration, stressed that whereas the integrative capacity of the ego collapses under excessive pressure, it tends to increase when there is confidence in attaining a goal. In other words, the integrative capacity is based on *hope* just as the integrative task arises out of needs (French, 1952, Vol. 1, p. 57). Expectation of success makes it possible to withstand painful frustration and pressure of other disturbing demands while concentrating the motor discharge in an effort to achieve the desired goal (p. 225). According to Alexander, the most certain indication that an analysis will be unsuccessful is when the therapist, and subsequently the patient, loses confidence in the treatment procedure. More important than the theoretical model used by the therapist is belief in himself and in his technique, with a consequent communication of these feelings to the patient.

French, however, conceives of the role of hope in therapy somewhat differently. He places much less importance on the patient's conscious confidence in the success of the therapy. Repudiation by the patient of his own preconscious hopes is an extremely common resistance; but therapy may be successful in spite of the patient's pessimism if this resistance is properly handled.

On the other hand, latent hopes of finding solutions for unconscious conflicts, as they emerge successively, are the essential ingredient of the therapeutic incentive that makes successful therapy possible. Such therapeutically significant hopes are based always in part on the realities of the therapeutic situation; but they are rarely, if ever, conscious. They are preconscious hopes, which the patient must struggle energetically to repudiate.

These hopes are based on present reality. Why, then, do they have to be repudiated? The reason is that these present reality-based hopes were too closely associated to other hopes, dating back to the patient's childhood, which had led to disastrous consequences. As a result of this fact, similar hopes, if reactivated during the therapy, would lead inevitably to mobiliza-

---

[1] French emphasizes, however, that patients frequently come to analysis with preconscious hopes, which they repudiate because they are associated with traumatic childhood memories. This need to repudiate hopes accounts for much of the resistance and pessimism in analysis. The analyst must encourage the patient's realistic hopes to emerge progressively, to become dissociated from the memory of earlier traumatic consequences, so that they can be lived through to fulfillment in the therapeutic situation (French and Wheeler, 1963).

tion of disturbing emotions arising out of the old traumatic memory. The patient's present hopes in the therapy had to be repudiated in order to prevent such reactivation of the associated traumatic memory.

In therapy, however, the analyst must encourage the patient's reality-based hopes to emerge progressively, as incentive for the therapeutic process. The analyst does this by giving explicit recognition to the present realities toward which the patient's new hope is oriented. The effect of encouraging the patient's new hope, however, will not be immediately beneficial. Instead of helping, reactivation of the new hope leads to some degree of reactivation of the associated traumatic memory pattern. When this occurs, the patient may then be preoccupied for weeks or months with disturbances resulting from this reactivation.

The therapist's interpretation is designed not for present but for future effect. Ultimately, he expects, the disturbing affects will be dissipated or discharged. Then hopes similar to those that were repudiated will begin to emerge again. When this occurs, he expects that his earlier interpretations will have had a latent effect. His previous explicit recognition of the patient's new hopes will have increased their integrative capacity, even though they have remained latent. Now these hopes will emerge more boldly and persist longer before they are repudiated. Ultimately, they may become dissociated from the memory of earlier traumatic consequences, so that they can be lived through to fulfillment in the therapeutic situation (French and Wheeler, 1963).

Every therapist has experienced conscious attitudes unrelated to figures in his own past, which therefore cannot be categorized as countertransference. When revealed to the patient, these attitudes have powerful therapeutic effects. These effects are especially beneficial when the therapist's attitude is different from that of the traumatogenic attitude of a parent. The analyst who enjoys being with a patient and looks forward to their sessions together may find that therapy is going better than the psychodiagnostics predicted. The therapist may have unconscious attitudes, some of which may be classified as countertransference, that may be harmful or helpful depending upon the patient's history. If such attitudes are not controlled they may be detrimental, but occasionally, provided the analyst is honest with the patient, there may be a dramatic breakthrough of material. The following is a good example:

> In the analysis of a female patient, the analyst had the opportunity to become aware of his own unconscious feelings toward the patient. She was a young, attractive woman and because of guilt feelings regarding her sexual

wishes toward her father had never been able to experience sexual pleasure. It became necessary one day to change her appointment from 11:00 A.M. to 1:00 P.M. The analyst handed her a note which read, "Next appointment, 1:00 A.M." She asked the analyst the meaning of this slip. The analyst replied spontaneously, "Because you are a good-looking woman I am sexually attracted to you as I would be to any attractive woman. I feel no guilt about this because I am in control of my feelings and it would be against my moral standards to act upon them."

The patient's mother had always shied away from sexual discussions. The young woman, now identifying with the analyst's guilt-free attitude, soon began discussing her sexual feelings toward her analyst. This led eventually to recollections concerning her sexual feelings toward her father. In less than one month she was for the first time experiencing orgasm with her husband.

Such admission of personal feelings is not recommended as a standard procedure. However, the better the analyst understands his own feelings about his patient, the more he will be able to appreciate the patient's transference reactions. This is a view held not only by Alexander and French but also by Frieda Fromm-Reichmann (1957), Therese Benedek (1953), Paula Heimann (1950), and others.

There is no question that an overly intensive involvement of the therapist with his patient may very well impair the analytic process. Hopefully, the training analysis prepares candidates to become sufficiently aware of their countertransference reactions. To control or utilize countertransference attitudes as methods of helping patients develop corrective emotional experiences requires keen clinical judgment as well as self-awareness.

Psychotherapeutic Process and Learning Theory

Painstaking experimental work will be required before the basic issues of the therapeutic process are fully understood. This is as true today as when the authors of *Psychoanalytic Therapy* first expressed it. "We believe and hope that our book is only a beginning and that it will encourage a free experimental spirit which will make use of all that detailed knowledge which has been accumulated in the last fifty years in this vital branch of science (Alexander and French, 1946, p. 341). During the last eight years of his life Alexander headed in Los Angeles an empirical study project designed to investigate the therapeutic process. Three analysts observed through a one-way mirror the progress of treatment, which was being recorded. One of them, Norman Levy (1961), pointed out that the therapist in action is unreliable as an observer because he cannot objectively see himself, nor is he ever completely aware of his feelings and attitudes. Furthermore, some of the important therapeutic transactions occur as nonverbal communications, which largely escape the therapist's full awareness. It will take several years before the exhaustive data collected in this project can be classified and processed. An important by-product of this study, however, lies in a revised teaching of psychoanalytic techniques. The student has the opportunity to hear recordings of an actual analytic session instead of listening to a lecture by a supervisor on how to conduct therapy.

While studying the material collected in this project, Alexander came to the conclusion that much of the psychoanalytic process can be understood in terms of learning theory. During the treatment the patient, through insight and through the interpersonal experience with the analyst, is able to unlearn old patterns and learn new modes of adaptation.

A decisive problem in psychoanalysis is the development of a meaningful relationship between the analyst and the patient. Initially, this relationship is distorted because the patient transfers feelings that belong to the past into the therapeutic situation. These old learned patterns, which were once adaptive, have become maladaptive, but insights gained during the analytic procedure enable the patient to apply a changed attitude to new situations. This process of relearning is complex but follows the principles of learning theory. In the therapeutic transaction there are elements of cognition as well as learning from experiences. Both contribute to emotional insight; in this context "emotional" refers to the interpersonal experience in the transference, and "insight" refers to the cognitive component (Alexander, 1963, p. 447). Every learning process, including psychoanalytic treatment, is an attempt to focus on this problem of emotional insight.

Judd Marmor stated that several research studies point to the fact that verbal reactions of the therapist act as either positive or negative reinforcing stimuli, thereby encouraging certain responses and discouraging others. These reactions on the part of the therapist serve as "reward-punishment cues," or conditioning stimuli. The analyst tacitly approves of mature reaction patterns, whereas his disapproval tends to inhibit less mature attitudes. According to Marmor, "this process requires frequent repetition before the previous, overlearned conditioned responses become extinguished and the new conditioned responses (habit patterns) become firmly established" (1964, p. 271). Marmor also refers to experimental studies that demonstrate that "intermittent and irregular reinforcements are more effective than frequent or regular ones in changing patterns of behavior or maintaining desired ones" (1964, p. 272). This, of course, has direct bearing on the value of vacations from treatment and changes in frequency of visits, as proposed by Alexander and French.

Every intellectual effort, even when it concerns entirely non-utilitarian preoccupations, such as playful puzzle-solving efforts, is motivated by an urge for mastery and is rewarded with some resolution of tensions. In psychotherapy the reward is a less conflictual interpersonal relationship. The patient achieves this first by favorably relating to the therapist, then to others in his environment, and finally to his "cherished image of himself" (Alexander, 1963, p. 448). An impasse may occur in therapy when the patient's symptoms become pleasurable ("secondary gains" from the neurosis). Learning theory suggests that the neurotic pattern originally had some adaptive value. However, the pattern tends to become overlearned, and neurotic symptoms, gaining "positive reinforcement," become more "resistant to extinction" (Marmor, 1964, p. 267). Alexander predicted that in the future proponents of learning theory and psychoanalysts would find some means of greater collaboration. In the past, experimental psychologists have felt professional distrust for the less precise concepts of psychoanalysis. However, this approach, Alexander points out, neglected to deal with the most vital problems of human behavior simply because they were not amenable to experimentation. It is unfortunate that most psychoanalytic institutes confine their activities to training psychiatrists for the practice of psychoanalysis, and not in psychoanalytic research. Only recently and in very exceptional circumstances have research psychologists and social scientists been accepted for work in analytic institutes.

Hedda Bolgar (1960), another member of Alexander's research team engaged in investigating the therapeutic process, predicts that a thorough appreciation of the relearning process, as utilized in psychoanalysis, hinges on a better understanding of the role played by the value system of the analyst. She points out that over half of the analyst's statements are evaluative, originating partly in the value system of psychoanalysis, but also reflecting his personal value system.

Theories of Dreams and Instincts

Since psychoanalysts are necessarily concerned with dreams—the royal road to the unconscious—the discussion of the psychoanalytic techniques of Alexander and French would be incomplete without mentioning their original contributions to the understanding of the dream process. In his writings on criminology, in describing the neurotic character, and in differentiating shame from guilt, Alexander has frequently commented about the problems of unconscious guilt (Selesnick, 1964). As early as 1925, after studying the phenomena described in "Dreams in Pairs or Series," Alexander came to the conclusion that a person who experiences self-punishment in a dream has thereby placated his conscience and consequently can couple this dream with another in which a forbidden impulse is gratified. In further analyzing the problem of guilt in "About Dreams with Unpleasant Content" (1930), Alexander made it clear that dreams are stimulated not only by forbidden id impulses seeking release of tension, as was formerly believed; the superego also makes demands on the ego for relief of tensions created by guilt feelings. The superego, an incorporation of external mores, has aspects of external reality, which French elucidated in his article, "Reality Testing in Dreams" (1937b). In French's model, ego functioning goes on continuously during sleep as well as during the waking state. The "integrative processes underlying rational behavior, neurotic behavior, and dreams have component elements that are common to all three" (French, 1952, Vol. I, p. 69). French deduced this continuous operation of the integrative function of the ego, following the uncovering of attempts at reality-testing and problem-solving in consecutive dreams. In his dreams a patient does not necessarily solve his problem as a whole. The "dream ego," by dealing separately with each aspect of the conflict situation, is able to come to grips with it in simpler, less conflictual terms and is thus, in a sense, more successful than the ego when awake (French, 1939). Viewed in this perspective the dream is similar to the trial-and error method of learning used by the individual who gropes to adjust to a strange or frightening situation (French, 1937a). The following is an example of a patient attempting to cope with an anxiety-arousing reality situation in a dream using the trial-and-error method:

A twenty-five-year-old woman was asked to consider the possibility of interrupting her analysis while on vacation. Upon her return she announced her decision to discontinue treatment. She had come into analysis because of vague feelings of discomfort and free-floating anxiety, which were revealed to be due to unconscious guilt over repressed sexual desires. Now feeling more comfortable, she relates the following dream: "I had asked my boy friend to forget our quarrel, and I took off my brassiere. Then, I felt tense just as when I came into analysis. I ran out of the room toward an elderly man who seemed so benevolent. His arms were extended as though he were going to comfort me. Then, suddenly he dropped his arms, smiled, and walked out of the room."

Her associations were: (1) The night before she had quarreled with her boy friend and had broken a date with him. She had realized that the only bond between them was sexual attraction. (2) She also wondered about the propriety of breast-feeding a baby in public as a friend had done on the previous day. She stated that the breast symbolized sexuality and that she could not look upon it as an organ of nurture.

The patient, anxious about her decision to discontinue treatment, was attempting to deal with this anxiety by trying it out in the dream. In the first sequence she ran away from the sexual implications, as she had done prior to her analysis, but as the dream continued she tested her feelings by seeing the benevolent therapist withdraw his support. In the dream, as in real life, she was preparing to face her anxiety about sexual matters without the analyst's support.

Crucial to the art of interpretation, according to French, is helping the patient to become aware of the "focal conflict" or "the center from which the patient's thoughts radiate" (1958, p. 100). The manifest content of the dream is scrutinized for evidence of the focal conflict instead of for evidence of past conflicts. In the dream just related, the patient's unacceptable wish (dependency on the analyst) conflicts with her pride, and thus she attempts to reject her dependency. The first trial in the dream is denial of dependency through the process of reversal: She gives herself sexually as she presents her bare breasts to her boy friend, also denying her own wish for nurture by this act. Anxiety over this solution leads her to attempt to gratify her dependent wishes by returning to the support of the analyst. This is in conflict with her pride, and she arranges for the analyst's departure. She is thus caught in the dilemma: "I cannot have sexual feelings in an adult way, yet I cannot be a dependent child." The analytic task in that session would be to make the patient aware of this conflict.

Even the waking life does not take a course based primarily on conscious reasoning, but is guided by the same practical grasp of a situation that a dream utilizes in struggling with a problem (French, 1958, p. 73). French (1939) thus considers it more appropriate to compare dreamwork to rational behavior than oppose it to rational *thinking,* as Freud does in the concept of the primary and secondary processes. French's dynamic point of view envisages not an opposition but a continuous gamut of goal-directed behavior and thought.

In the foregoing discussion we have tried to make clear why French and Alexander were so intensely occupied with the adaptive function of the ego and with the importance of object relations. As we have shown, their approach was not founded on libido theory. How, then, did Alexander and

French deal with instincts from the vantage point of ego psychology? They came to the conclusion that psychological processes can be considered from the perspective of integrative and disintegrative forces rather than as a contest between life instincts and death instincts. French arrived at this position while exploring the mechanisms of normal integrated goal behavior. Alexander's view is based on the phenomena of sex and play. According to him, there are three fundamental dynamic principles governing the mental apparatus and biological behavior in living organisms (1951). The first is the principle of homeostasis (stability) by which the ego maintains equilibrium through the "coordination of the biological needs with each other and with the existing and everchanging environmental conditions" (1958). The second fundamental dynamism Alexander labeled the "principle of economy" or inertia, by which the organism substitutes automatic and therefore effortless behavior for adjustments requiring effort. This economical mechanism releases energy with which the organism can meet new situations requiring expenditure of effort. Unfortunately, responses that worked in the past and became automatic may deter the individual from meeting new challenges. The repetition of effortless patterns may interfere with learning and lead the individual into stagnation. Homeostasis and stability nevertheless are necessary for initial adaptation and for the preservation of life.

In order to explain growth and propagation, Alexander (1958) introduced a third principle, the concept of "surplus energy," which is energy "not needed to maintain life." Surplus energy comes about when the accumulation of energy is greater than what is needed for growth or elimination. Excess energy disturbs homeostasis just as much as a lack of it, and demands discharge. Surplus energy is discharged in growth. When growth stops, surplus energy is discharged by propagation. Unicellular organisms divide; primates produce germ cells. The psychological parallel in human beings is that during growth the individual is interested only in its own development (infantile narcissism). The mature individual is able to find object love, or genitality. Surplus energy, however, does not manifest itself exclusively in object love. The young infant, satiated by maternal care, abounds with surplus energy, which finds expression in playful maneuvers. Initially, the child moves his limbs and searches with his eyes, not aiming at a utilitarian goal, but simply for pleasurable sensations. These playful movements belong in the category of Hartmann's autonomous functions of the ego. What Alexander emphasized was the association of these pleasurable sensations with pregenital eroticism; he reminds us that the Greek god, Eros, represented as a child, was a god of play and love. Pregenital sexuality discharges surplus excitation "regardless of the quality of the drive" (1948, p. 76). Clinical validation for this thesis may be found in adult perversions where any emotional content—whether hostility, voyeurism, sadism, masochism, or other—can serve for sexual gratification. Frequently, Alexander notes, sexual sadists are inhibited individuals who can express their pent-up aggression only through sexually sadistic acts. *Rather than stressing two different instincts (sexual and nonsexual), he proposes that the emphasis should be on the frame of reference. If an impulse serves the interest of the organism (subordinated to a goal structure), it is nonsexual. If the discharge occurs as a manifestation of surplus energy (a goal in itself) and is not subservient to the interest of the entire organism, the impulse is sexual.* Alexander stated that "Thomas French's lucid description of goal structures was of great help in formulating this view" (1961, p. 18). The child's playful excursions, which initially served no useful purpose, gradually become organized into goal structures. The child's play eventually enables him to master his body as well as his bodily functions.[2] Initially, the child flexes and extends his hand for mere pleasurable sensation, but he gradually learns to use his hand to seize objects. This becomes a component part of a goal structure that serves the interest of the entire organism.

As French noted, loss of hope or excessive frustration leads to disorganization of a goal structure. In this state of overexcitation, disintegration of behavior occurs, and once again impulses may be discharged sexually (that is, for no utilitarian purpose). For example, killing an animal for the pleasure of killing is a sexually sadistic act, releasing excess excitation; it is an aim in itself and is not subordinated to a utilitarian goal structure. Energy formerly expressed in motivated, goal-directed behavior becomes surplus energy again at the time of disorganization.

To enable us to appreciate the far-reaching implications of surplus energy Alexander reminds us that creativity and cultural advancement are sociological manifestations of surplus energy. While man was engaged in mere adaptation and organized his goals toward survival, his achievements were pedestrian: "Culture is the product of man's leisure and not the sweat of his brow; his productive abilities become liberated when he is relieved from the necessities of the struggle for survival" (Alexander, 1958, p. 188).

[2] Harlow (1961) demonstrated that monkeys raised with mother surrogates made of cloth would not mate if they had no opportunity for play with other infant monkeys.

Summary

It is true that Alexander and French were the first to study systematically the psychoanalytic process in order to shorten psychoanalytic treatment (Gilman, 1965). Other important contributions resulted from their individual and joint efforts to abandon rigid distinctions between dynamic psychotherapy and psychoanalysis, to emphasize the emotional experience in the analytic situation, to stress the importance of the corrective emotional experience, to encourage a flexible approach in therapy, to take into account present life conditions, to avoid unnecessary regressions, and to recognize the significance of the analyst's personality and attitudes. Equally stimulating were their formulations governing dream processes and instinct theory. All these endeavors inspired others to follow their challenging spirit of inquiry and to explore further the problems of psychoanalytic techniques.

REFERENCES

ALEXANDER, F. Dreams in pairs or series. *International Journal of Psychoanalysis,* 1925, 6, 446–452.

ALEXANDER, F. About dreams with unpleasant content. *Psychiatric Quarterly,* 1930, 4, 447–452.

ALEXANDER, F. *Fundamentals of psychoanalysis.* New York: Norton, 1948.

ALEXANDER, F. Analysis of the therapeutic factors in psychoanalytic treatment. *Psychoanalytic Quarterly,* 1950, 19, 482–500. (a)

ALEXANDER, F. Essentials in psychotherapy. *The Journal of the Michigan State Medical Society,* 1950, 49, 549–551, 567. (b)

ALEXANDER, F. Three fundamental dynamic principles of the mental apparatus and of behavior of living organisms. *Dialectica,* 1951, 5, 239–245.

ALEXANDER, F. Current views on psychotherapy. *Psychiatry,* 1953, 16, 113–122.

ALEXANDER, F. *Psychoanalysis and psychotherapy.* New York: Norton, 1956.

ALEXANDER, F. A contribution to the theory of play. *Psychoanalytic Quarterly,* 1958, 28, 175–193.

ALEXANDER, F. Current problems in dynamic psychotherapy in its relationship to psychoanalysis. *American Journal of Psychiatry,* 1959, 116, 322–325.

ALEXANDER, F. *The scope of psychoanalysis: 1921–1961.* New York: Basic Books, 1961.

ALEXANDER, F. *Psychoanalytic education for practice, science and psychoanalysis.* Vol. 5. New York: Grune and Stratton, 1962, pp. 176–177.

ALEXANDER, F. The dynamics of psychotherapy in the light of learning theory. *The American Journal of Psychiatry,* 1963, 120, 447.

ALEXANDER, F. *Evaluation of psychotherapy, evaluation of psychiatric treatment.* New York: Grune and Stratton, 1964. (a)

ALEXANDER, F. Social significance of psychoanalysis and psychotherapy. *Archives of General Psychiatry,* 1964, 11, 237. (b)

ALEXANDER, F. Psychoanalytic contributions to short-term psychotherapy. In L. R. Wolberg (Ed.), *Short-term psychotherapy.* New York: Grune and Stratton, 1965.

ALEXANDER, F., and FRENCH, T. M. *Psychoanalytic therapy.* New York: Ronald Press, 1946.

ALEXANDER, F., and SELESNICK, S. T. *History of psychiatry.* New York: Harper and Row, 1966.

BENEDEK, THERESA. Dynamics of the countertransference. *Bulletin of the Menninger Clinic,* 1953, 17, 201.

BOLGAR, HEDDA. Values in therapy, in psychoanalysis and human values. *Science and Psychoanalysis.* Vol. 3. New York: Grune and Stratton, 1960. Pp. 362–367.

CARSON, I. M., and SELESNICK, S. T. Ego strengthening aspects of supportive psychotherapy. *American Journal of Psychotherapy,* 1959, 13, 298–318.

FERENCZI, S., and RANK, O. *The development of psychoanalysis.* New York: Nervous and Mental Diseases Publications, 1925.

FLIESS, R. Review of Hanns Sachs, *Zur Menschenkenntniss. Psychoanalytic Quarterly,* 1937, 6, 119–121.

FRENCH, T. M. A clinical study of learning in the course of psychoanalytic treatment. *Psychoanalytic Quarterly,* 1936, 5, 148–194.

FRENCH, T. M. Reality and the unconscious. *Psychoanalytic Quarterly,* 1937, 6, 23–61. (a)

FRENCH, T. M. Reality testing in dreams. *Psychoanalytic Quarterly,* 1937, 6, 62–77. (b)

FRENCH, T. M. Insight and distortion in dreams. *International Journal of Psychoanalysis,* 1939, 20, 287–298.

FRENCH, T. M. *The integration of behavior,* Vol. 1. Chicago: Univ. of Chicago Press, 1952.

FRENCH, T. M. *The integration of behavior,* Vol. 3. Chicago: Univ. of Chicago Press, 1958.

FRENCH, T. M. Introduction in F. Alexander, *The scope of psychoanalysis, 1921–1961.* New York: Basic Books, 1961.

FRENCH, T. M., WHEELER, D. R., Hope and repudiation in psychoanalytic therapy. *International Journal of Psychoanalysis,* 1963, 44, 304–316.

FREUD, S. Further recommendations in the technique of psychoanalysis (1913), Standard Edition, Vol. 12, pp. 121–144.

FROMM-REICHMANN, FRIEDA. *Principles of intensive psychotherapy.* London: Allen and Unwin, 1957.

GILMAN, R. Brief psychotherapy: a psychoanalytic view. *American Journal of Psychiatry*, 1965, **22**, 602.

HARLOW, H. *Determinants of infant behavior.* New York: Wiley, 1961.

HEIMANN, PAULA. On countertransference. *International Journal of Psychoanalysis*, 1950, **31**, 81.

LEVY, N. Psychoanalysis and the social processes. *Science and Psychoanalysis*, 1961, **4**, 125–149.

MARMOR, J. The reintegration of psychoanalysis into psychiatric practice. *Archives of General Psychiatry*, 1960, **3**, 569–574.

MARMOR, J. Psychoanalytic therapy and theories of learning. In J. H. Masserman (Ed.), *Science and psychoanalysis*, Vol. 7. New York: Grune and Stratton, 1964.

SELESNICK, S., ALEXANDER, F., and FRENCH, T. M. Psychoanalysis integrated and expanded. *Science and Psychoanalysis*, Vol. 7. New York: Grune and Stratton, 1964.

8

DIRECT PSYCHOANALYTIC METHODS OF JOHN ROSEN

David Rubinstein

In the living room of a row house in a poor neighborhood in North Philadelphia, a group of doctors, psychologists, students, and social workers sat intent on the scene in front of them. John Rosen was treating a patient.

Big and powerful-looking, the patient was kneeling in front of Rosen, who was sitting on a couch. In tears, he was looking up at Rosen, saying in an anguished voice: "God, I am going to die! Please, God . . ." Rosen, in a loud, impressive voice, recited back: "I am God! You will not be killed!"

The patient held on to Rosen's hand in despair, shaking with fear: "Please . . . Oh, God . . ." Rosen embraced his head tenderly, reassuring him in a warm, confident voice: "I am God. You will live. You will be all right."

It was the first time many of those present had seen such a thing. Distasteful impressions from observing other therapists and patients were suddenly dispelled by the performance of this man who dared approach and talk to a psychotic patient with such self-assurance. I had other opportunities to observe Rosen and his techniques and learned more about his theory and his method, which I will discuss in this chapter.

The Department of Psychiatry at Temple University Medical School had invited Rosen to participate in a long-term research project. His patients were hospitalized in a nearby house, which had been converted into a residential unit. Rosen's method of treatment was observed and analyzed, and his case material and results were carefully scrutinized. This was probably one of the few occasions in the history of psychotherapy in which a therapist has allowed "public" exposure of his methods.

Rationale

THEORETICAL PRINCIPLES

One of Rosen's most important theoretical points is that there are not numerous "mental diseases"—paranoia, manic-depressive reactions, the various types of schizophrenia—but only one: psychosis, which includes the different diagnostic categories. Furthermore, and also contrary to the traditional view, Rosen states that the psychosis is a disorder differing mainly in *degree* from neurosis or from what is considered normal. And a psychotic individual can be observed to move from one phase to another. As a psychotic recovers, for example, he moves into a "neoneurosis" phase, which is in some respects similar to prepsychotic neurosis, but modified by the psychotic experience. The different phases are considered by Rosen to correspond to levels of regression, following Freud's theory of psychosexual development, from "late anal" (least psychotic) to "early oral" (most psychotic). None of the phases of psychosis are clear-cut, and any psychotic individual may manifest oral, anal, or even genital characteristics in any one phase (Sullivan, 1964).

The psychotic's purpose of regressing to earlier stages of psychosexual development is to "seek the mother he knew" (Rosen, 1963). Each of the phases can be conceived as a way the patient seeks to re-experience some aspect of the original infantile relationship with her. But mother is more than the physical flesh-and-blood being who gives birth to her child. Rosen includes in his concept of *mother* the entire environment that served as experience in the early infantile stage of life. The psychotic, according to this reasoning, tries to reproduce the original experience, the original maternal environment. All of his efforts are directed toward re-creating "mother" out of people, objects, or the thin air (Rosen, 1962).

The superego acquired by the psychotic from this early maternal environment has never been integrated with his ego satisfactorily. In Rosen's terms it is "harsh," impossible to satisfy, "indigestible." The superego as an internalized representation of "mother" is indispensable; yet, as a malevolent "mother," it is deadly (Sullivan, 1964).

The original relationship with mother becomes vivid and even more painful when the ego ultimately gives up its struggle with this malevolent superego and seeks relief in regression. The ego, however, cannot easily reverse the process of regression. It can only try out the various modes of action that Rosen distinguishes as the eight phases of psychosis (1962).

Not that in Rosen's concept the superego has a different genesis than in classical Freudian theory. Rosen describes the superego as the psychical embodiment of the early maternal environment, coming into existence soon after birth and acquiring its important characteristics during the child's first and second years (Sullivan, 1964).

The normal child gradually acquires a reasonable and comfortable superego through a process of imitation, incorporation, and identification. The child who will become neurotic or psychotic acquires an unreasonable or uncomfortable superego. The patient refers to this paradoxical mother-superego in terms of "poisoned milk" or "bad mother" or "black breast," or behaviorally by refusing to eat, overturning the breakfast table, vomiting his meals, and so forth (Rosen, 1953b).

A large part of the direct analyst's activity is devoted to the understanding of specific examples of psychotic behavior in terms of this general theoretical orientation. The analyst consistently relates the manifest content of the psychotic's behavior to the latent content of his current phase of regression, according to the basic proposition that the patient is re-experiencing his oral and anal relationships with his early maternal environment.

The governing principle of direct analysis is that the therapist accepts the parental role the psychotic or neurotic patient thrusts upon him, interacting according to cues supplied by the patient. With a psychotic, he must act like an idealized mother who must bring up the neoinfantile individual all over again (Rosen, 1953b). Resolution of psychosis means that the patient has successfully identified with the therapist in a maternal role.

Rosen considers that he then enters into a neoneurotic phase, a modified form of the prepsychotic stage. His contention is that the best way of handling the neoneurotic phase is to continue the foster-parent approach.

As in any neurosis, the essential problem in the neoneurotic phase is the Oedipus complex. Rosen maintains that now that the patient has identified successfully with mother, the individual must develop a satisfactory relationship with father: The boy must learn to identify with father; the girl must learn to imitate certain aspects of mother's attitude toward father. In neither case does the child actually wish to engage in sexual intercourse with the parent of the opposite sex (Rosen, 1962; Sullivan, 1964). Therefore, in the neoneurotic phase, the therapist takes the appropriate paternal role.

The therapist must function parentally to guide the patient toward maturity and independence, mindful that he is a person who has grown up physically without growing up psychically (Rosen, 1964a).

THE CONCEPT OF TRANSFERENCE

Rosen's concept of transference differs markedly from that of orthodox psychoanalysis. The conventional psychoanalytic position, as described by Hendrick (1958), is that the analyst discloses as little of his actual self as practical, since every detail of the real person that is known to the patient will distort the transference picture of the projected subjective situations. The analyst avoids directing the patient, morally or otherwise, to an adjustment that fits his own theory of what it should be like or how it should be lived. In contrast, Rosen feels that transference is not created or aroused by the psychoanalyst or by the psychoanalytic situation (Rosen, 1964b). Transference is an expression of the individual's need for his early maternal environment. Transference exists prior to engagement in the psychotherapeutic experience and is independent of the psychoanalytic relationship. The patient lives in a chronic state of transference; transference of libidinal attachments is a diffuse experience, always ongoing and never fulfilled. It is an expression of his insatiable need that brings the individual into such a relationship.

Rosen attempts to focus these diffuse libidinal attachments upon himself, to make himself the prime object of the individual's transferred feelings. In contrast to classical psychoanalysis, he attempts to direct the individual toward an adjustment. He feels this is a technical move of primary importance in the therapeutic process. Every effort is made to gain enough influence over the individual, to change him, and to alter his perceptions, expectations, and the demands of his parental introject, his superego. The direct analyst serves in this fashion the role of teacher and educator, whose aim is to *substitute* for the individual's parents.

Rosen believes that this *utilization* of the individual's transferred needs focused on the therapist is a major distinctive point in the therapeutic process of direct analysis. He believes that transference can be utilized therapeutically and that it does not produce the supposedly dire consequences of therapeutic intervention.

Compare Rosen's concept of transference with Menninger's (1958) definition of transference "as the unrealistic roles or identities unconsciously ascribed to a therapist by a patient in the regression of the psychoanalytic treatment and the patient's reactions to this representation derived from earlier experiences." This latter definition stresses the *roles or identities ascribed* (to the therapist) by the patient, whereas Rosen stresses the patient's *needs*. These two different frameworks for the definition of the concept explain the different uses made of the transference phenomenon. *Needs* are ever-present and everlasting in the patient, and they become all-encompassing as the individual functions closer to a primary-process level. Ascribed *roles* or *identities* are temporary, fleeting, and are functions of the immature ego.

The orthodox analyst's position stresses the *irrationality* of the roles ascribed to him and helps the patient to gain insight into the unconscious dynamics underlying this process in the hope that such insight will contribute to a healthier ego development. Rosen takes advantage of the patient's needs in order to turn himself into the central figure of the patient's life according to the governing principle of direct analysis. He assumes that becoming the focus for the patient's transferred feelings gives the therapist the strategic position necessary to direct and teach the patient a healthier adjustment to life.

The term "direct" for the method of analysis advocated by Rosen (1953b) was suggested by Federn, apparently referring to the way the therapist deals with the psychotic's unconscious in a direct manner. To some observers the term is better applied to the "honest directness in dealing with the patient" (English, 1961) and encompasses: (1) the forcefulness of the method; (2) the interpretation of the libido phase rather than the manifest content of the psychotic behavior; (3) the repetition of the therapist's interpretations over the patient's resistance; and (4) the guidance of the patient to accept rather than await insight. To other observers a more appropriate term is "directive" analysis, since it characterizes the therapist's attitude toward the patient (Kubie, 1964; Rubinstein, 1964).

Rosen's first contribution to psychiatric literature was "A method of Resolving Acute Catatonic Excitement" (1946). In succeeding writings he suggested that the same method be utilized in the treatment of hebephrenics and paranoids alike. He suggested further that psychotic behavior be viewed as the manifest content of a prolonged "dream," which can be interpreted in terms of Freud's "dream symbolism," and that the presentation of interpretations to the psychotic be used to bring about a rapid resolution of the psychosis.

In 1947 Rosen reported the results of treatment of 37 psychotics during his residency at Brooklyn State Hospital and, the New York Psychiatric Institute. According to his report, all 37 cases recovered from psychosis. Anyone claiming such results had to attract attention, from curiosity about either the method or the person who claimed the results. However, in a follow-up statement (1952), Rosen reported that 6 cases had relapsed into psychosis.

Rosen's claims aroused a heated controversy (Lipton, 1949; Redlich, 1952), which has lasted until the 1960's (Rogers, 1961). Some authors have limited themselves to commenting on Rosen's personal qualities and to suggesting ways of examining his affirmations (McKinnon, 1959; Kubie, 1961; Lewin, 1962). Members of the New York Psychiatric Institute went so far as to re-examine Rosen's original cases (Horwitz et al., 1958). They reported that they had been able to identify and recheck 19 of the original 37 cases. They disputed the original diagnosis on 7 of the patients and concluded that, in the 12 remaining cases, Rosen's treatment did not evidence any sustained therapeutic result.

It was in this setting that Rosen was invited to participate in the project sponsored by the Department of Psychiatry at Temple University Medical School. Some literature has already been produced by participants in the project (Brody, 1959; English et al., 1961; Scheflen, 1964). Final publication of the report by the school's Evaluation Committee will make a significant contribution to a long-term evaluation of Rosen's techniques.[1]

---

[1] Since this chapter went to press, the Evaluation Committee published a report concluding that the group of patients treated by Rosen at Temple University Medical School, after a follow-up of five years, did not show significantly better results than a random control group or a designated control group. (Bookhammer, Meyers, Schober, and Piotrowski, 1966).

Technique

Before describing the direct-analysis technique of John Rosen I will discuss the personality of the man, his use of assistant therapists, and the setting where treatment takes place—elements in the total therapeutic environment that are integral to the technique itself.

ROSEN: THE DIRECT ANALYST

As Scheflen (1961) has mentioned, all observers have been impressed with the way the personality of John Rosen dominates interaction in the treatment unit. Assertiveness, self-assurance, and colorful language, combined with an intensely masculine outlook, are some of the ingredients of Rosen's unique personality. His sentences are clear, uttered with deep conviction in a warm, loud voice. Rosen's sense of conviction in direct analysis runs deep: He calls other approaches futile, delaying, distracting, or even harmful. He communicates this conviction to his assistants and ultimately to his patients.

When Rosen demonstrates his method of treatment, he takes on his most characteristic role, that of healer and teacher, with characteristic authoritativeness. He allows no distractions of any kind, including telephone interruptions, whispering, and the like. In the profound and solemn silence imposed, Rosen demonstrates the rare ability to hold everyone's attention for prolonged periods. He likes to treat patients in the presence of others, explaining that it is a good way to teach his method. When colleagues visit, Rosen often introduces them to the patient with the remark that they have come to see how he cures a psychotic case. Rosen displays remarkable charm, friendliness, and warmth in treating a patient in the presence of a group. He is gentle with the most difficult and withdrawn patients, and he meets aggressive ones with kind and gentle understanding, many times with tricks aimed at controlling their aggressive behavior. Many of these tricks would be considered outrageous from the standpoint of normal doctor-patient relationships in our cultural setting, absolutely immoral from the standpoint of secondary-process rational thinking. But the direct analyst, by communicating with the patient at a primary-process level and dealing with him through his own unconscious, utilizes the patient's psychotic tricks to handle his behavior.

However, Rosen is capable of dramatic shifts of affect. He may become impatient, irritable, and extremely angry if something does not happen the way he expected. He may show lack of interest, after having been affectionately interested in a case, if the patient does not demonstrate the expected behavior and changes as programmed by Rosen. He may spend hours with a patient used to only a few minutes of attention, but may turn into minutes what used to be a few hours' session with the same patient. Many have observed that Rosen's primary passion is the acutely disturbed new patient and that when the patient has recovered from acute symptomatology he tends to devote less of his time to that patient. It is as if the patient's conforming to the demands of Rosen diminishes the therapist's motivation to conquer the psychosis.

The relationship between the personality of the therapist and his technique becomes especially noticeable while observing Dr. Rosen with a patient. Rosen's approach to the schizophrenic's problem is deeply intertwined with his own personality and approach to the management of human behavior. It is difficult to say if others could repeat his demonstrations without mimicking his personality features, attitudes, and approaches to the patient. Some of his principles and techniques have been utilized by others, but the approach has not maintained itself purely Rosenian: It has been imparted with the personal characteristics of the practitioner. True of any psychotherapeutic technique, this becomes especially true where techniques and theoretical framework have not been sufficiently structured. The fact that Rosen utilizes the intensity and impact of his unique personality, which is something more than just a series of technical principles, builds in the therapist's personality as a factor in treatment. Anyone utilizing such an intense and direct approach to the patient will have to throw in his own personality, which may not necessarily be Rosen's. To that extent it will make a difference between that person's technique and the one employed by Rosen. In a word, we may learn from Rosen, but can we truly repeat what he does?

ASSISTANT THERAPISTS

Rosen's use of assistant therapists is so much a part of his technique that a consideration of direct analysis cannot disregard it. Assistants are often recent college graduates interested in the social or psychological sciences, who have demonstrated interest in Rosen's theories and in the treatment of psychotic patients. Their motivation is evaluated through an interview with Rosen himself or one of his chief assistants.

Rosen has often claimed that a good method of evaluating a candidate's ability to work with schizophrenics is to appraise his ability to understand his own unconscious, at least in terms of accepting patients' needs as phenomena he has known in himself. Rosen has suggested that candidates be exposed to the method of free association as practiced in the technique of psychoanalysis. He claims that a series of about twenty sessions should be enough to make an appraisal of the candidate's qualities. If a candidate can face his own unconscious, he has a good chance of being able to deal with and understand the patient's unconscious. If a candidate is unable to grasp the dynamics of the unconscious in free-association sessions, then it is unlikely that he will ever work well with psychotic patients.

The assistants are both male and female. (However, it is obvious that Rosen considers the therapist's a man's job; I do not know of any woman who has been recognized by him as a good direct analyst.) The females act as mothers of the home unit wherein the patients live. The woman cooks and attends to various chores proper to females in our American culture; she also offers tenderness and care in moments of despair and extreme anxiety. She may or may not be married to the male assistant who shares the same unit.

Assistants provide around-the-clock coverage for the patients. They are instructed to protect the patient from self-inflicted injury or uncontrolled outbursts of aggression which may frighten him. Delusional and autistic withdrawal are continuously interrupted by active participation and interference of the assistants. The patient is not allowed to be alone at any moment. Various types of activities are encouraged—playing cards, ping-pong, watching television, walking, shopping, all in the company of one or more assistants. Assistants help in feeding the patient when necessary, as well as dressing and grooming him. An assistant may hold hands with a patient, hold him (at least his head) on his or her lap in moments of panic or extreme anxiety. No caressing, kissing, or erotic arousals are permitted. Acting out on the part of assistants is met with extreme disapproval by Rosen and leads to dismissal. In general, the assistants constitute a very cohesive group and are eager to carry out Rosen's instructions for the proper care of his patients. They provide continuous and relentless pressure against unacceptable behavior and give support to more mature expressions. They praise and encourage the patient to give up "craziness," and they endlessly repeat interpretations and comments initiated by Rosen in a treatment session. Discipline and demands by Rosen are reinforced at all times. Assistants are responsible for the creation of a definite atmosphere, which involves the prevention of undue distractions, the enhancement of the therapist's omnipotence, and absolute refusal to mediate or interfere in the one-to-one relationship between Rosen and his patient. At times the assistants may play the role of persecutor to the patient while Rosen becomes the benevolent, omnipotent protector.

As a rule, assistants sit in at every treatment session, except when Rosen decides otherwise. Their presence constitutes a cohesive, flexible, and contrasting group that Rosen utilizes as a background for his technique. An assistant may be exemplified as having been through the "craziness" and having been cured. He may be utilized to reinforce Rosen's interpretations, comments, or specific aims in treatment. Information about the patient's behavior, whether "crazy" or normal, is provided by the assistant. Frequently, the assistant becomes the target for split transference relationships from the ambivalent patient who prefers to become angry with the assistant while remaining loving toward Rosen.

Rosen uses physical restraint minimally. Since he does not agree with the use of tranquilizers, it becomes necessary for him to feel reassured of his own protection if the patient becomes assaultive or unusually aggressive. The presence of assistants at all sessions means he can feel free to evoke anger or violent response from the patient. Rosen's side remarks to the assistants are intended for the patient and seem to reach him on a deeper level when directed in this fashion. For example, he may ask an assistant, "How many of these Jesus Christ cases have we had this week?" To which the assistant may respond, "About 20 cases . . ." According to Rosen this ridicule may help to weaken the psychotic's belief in his delusions.

The assistant's presence is also regarded as a safeguard against accusations the patient may make. Unable to distinguish between wish and deed, fantasy and reality, the psychotic may accuse the therapist of spying, cruel treatment, sexual advances, and so forth. Assistants serve as witnesses of what actually transpires during the sessions.

Rosen's firm belief in himself as a crusader dedicated to conquering psychosis is communicated to his assistants. The assistant therapists empathize and identify with the man who is unequivocally the master, even when he is absent. They call him "Doc" among themselves. His name is constantly on their lips and on those of the patients. The assistant therapists assume his attitudes, predicate his philosophy of treatment, repeat his sentences, and adopt his very gestures. Rosen's arrival in a treatment unit is felt immediately. All other activity stops; everyone concentrates on his movements, words, and commands. It is no wonder that Scheflen (1961) describes Rosen's manner as paternal rather than maternal, a curious contrast to Rosen's formulation of the therapist as a substitute mother.

It is not difficult to realize that all kinds of group phenomena occur in this setting with Rosen as leader. Competition, scapegoating, jealousy, and so forth are commonplace. Acting out and other group mechanisms lead into emotionally loaded incidents, during which the patient occasionally becomes involved.

The assistant often encourages and reassures the therapist, giving him a feeling of support and empathy by manifesting that he, the assistant, has joined the cause of the "boss," namely, the treatment of the schizophrenic patient. In this process both are rewarded. The dedication to rescuing the patient from psychosis, the gratification of the need to feel important and to belong are well met in the relationship between Rosen and his assistants. It creates a common binding force, which helps to cement the group. All other therapeutic approaches are disregarded; some are even considered harmful. A feeling of exclusiveness creates a common bond, and the patient is invited to give up his "craziness" and join the group. However, ambivalent feelings are not discussed openly with Rosen. He expects full support, devotion, and relinquishing of personal needs for the benefit of the case. Hostility tends to be acted out in the group process among the assistants or toward the patient. The assistants expectantly await the defeat of the psychosis; signs of progress are hopefully anticipated. If they do not occur as expected, ambivalence toward the patient or the leader may appear. If the treatment appears to be successful (as evidenced by the disappearance of psychotic symptomatology), the group seems to enter a period of high morale, in which mutual support, optimism, and increased devotion are characteristic. On the other hand, a period of low morale and disorganized function of the group may be the result of a discouraging patient, with whom "Doc" Rosen has not been successful in demonstrating his skills.

THE SETTING

Another important aspect of direct analysis is the setting. As practiced by Rosen, treatment takes place in residential units where one or two patients live with the assistant therapists. These residential units are usually cottages scattered over a neighboring area. Visiting other units gives the patients and assistants some feeling of belonging to a large family. Some therapists have attempted to utilize Rosen's principles in a hospital setting, but obviously many modifications have to be introduced in the administration and personnel before this can be accomplished. A general hospital is not organized for the type of intensive and continuous care this technique demands. In the Temple University Medical School project Rosen attempted to apply his method in an urban setting. The results and process phenomena observed in that setting have been reported by Scheflen (1961). Rosen postulates that care of the psychotic individual must go on twenty-four hours a day, seven days a week, as with a newborn baby. Therefore, the treatment unit is tailored to the intense needs of the patient. Rosen feels that this is the most favorable setting in which to deal with the physical stresses and strains that underlie psychosis, to identify them for the psychotic, and to bring about his conscious understanding of them.

Treatment

THE FIRST THERAPEUTIC INTERVIEW

Rosen (1962) has indicated that one of the first aims of the therapist is to secure the psychotic's love and trust and that this is best accomplished by convincing the patient that he is being understood. From the first encounter with the patient, Rosen attempts to generate and maintain a conversation in which his understanding of the psychotic experiences can be developed and communicated to the patient. Rosen (1962) accepts that it is not the words of themselves that are therapeutic, as for example those used in the scene at the beginning of this chapter. He feels that therapy lies in the gradually developing relationship between the psychiatrist and the patient.

The first session with the patient starts as soon as possible after his arrival at the treatment unit. However, therapy may start at the place of admission or on the way to the treatment unit, since Rosen likes to get the patient directly from the admitting hospital. The content and length of the first session are largely determined by the condition of the psychotic and the mood of the therapist. Rosen avoids establishing a therapeutic dialogue with the patient who has been tranquilized, preferring to wait until the effects of the drug have worn off. While establishing a therapeutic dialogue with the patient, Rosen conveys to him in many different ways that the therapist protects him, that he is safe in the comfortable home with the new family. Importing this notion of safety from the perilous environment (the mother who is out) and the threatening impulses (the mother who is in) is a constant in this method of treatment. The patient is continuously made aware that he may trust the omnipotent therapist. Foregoing this trust means to continue under the influence of the "malevolent mother" and therefore to continue the "insanity." The patient is promised eternal care— if he accepts the therapist as his omnipotent benefactor and protector, giving up the "bad mother." At his first contact, Rosen tells the patient what he believes to be the cause of his "insanity." The role of the "bad mother" as the cause of the patient's distress is sometimes established after a few minutes in the initial interview, after Rosen has established some historical facts that support this view for the patient.

Frequently, some of these ideas are presented to the patient by the assistant therapists even before Rosen has met with the patient. They also announce the rules by which the patient will live in the unit. And they help to define everyone's roles and induce a feeling of hopefulness in the patient pending the arrival of "Doctor Rosen."

Rosen sums up the patient's situation in the first interview by establishing that the patient is insane, incompetent, and in need of help. Scheflen (1961) feels that Rosen, the direct analyst, instructs the patient in four main principles in his initial contact: (1) the therapist is in control; (2) the patient has an illness that is a result of his mother's failure to supply what he needed; (3) the direct analyst and his assistants fulfill the fantasy of the all-providing parent; and (4) the patient has a current precipitating problem, probably sexual in nature, which will eventually be looked into. There is no question that Rosen is extremely skillful in establishing rapport in a very few minutes with withdrawn and evasive patients. It is a most fascinating experience to watch, and it is one of his outstanding skills.

Rosen's role is that of benefactor, seeking to sever the patient's ties to infantile figures. He is the benevolent parent, insisting that the patient accept him as the loving new mother or as the master and disciplinarian, inducing the patient to obey commands and house rules. The idea is continuously enacted to the patient by Rosen himself and by his assistants in his absence: The patient ought to give up the psychosis and join the group by becoming *normal* while the promise is offered that as soon as the patient is cured he may become an assistant therapist and help in the cure of other patients. Dramatizations, exemplifications, and presentations of former patients who come to witness the treatment of a new patient are frequent resources in the performance of the therapist.

An important point in the technique of direct analysis is that Rosen does not always practice treatment under the special circumstances of the scheduled "treatment session." Impromptu therapeutic sessions take place whenever and wherever the psychiatrist is talking with the patient.

Sometimes the briefest meetings, or even telephone conversations, will be utilized for treatment. These interchanges may also occur while the therapist is having a meal with the patient and the assistants at the treatment unit, inspecting the patient's room, or while talking to the assistants within the hearing range of the patient with the intention of being overheard. When Rosen announces to the assistants or a patient, "Now let's have a treatment session," after having spent half an hour talking to the patient "informally" over a cup of coffee, he does not mean literally that whatever went on before his announcement was not treatment. On the contrary, the most meaningful interactions and most significant interpretations may take place when the patient is not programmed for a treatment session. After Rosen has established that the formal component of treatment is the scheduled session, he sits down face-to-face with the patient in the presence of assistants and guests. While the therapist pays close attention to the current manifest content, in order to find out what the patient is "dreaming about," he tries to arrive at some understanding of the latent meaning of the manifestations. The understanding gained is conveyed to the patient after the psychotic's attention has been captured and held. According to Rosen, the patient has "taken in" the psychiatrist in the process of imitation, incorporation, and identification. As the session proceeds, the therapist improvises much of what he says and does, to suit the individual he is treating and the particular occasion. Raising or lowering his voice, putting an arm around the patient's shoulder, and discussing or ignoring certain matters are some of the techniques used by Rosen.

"DIRECT INTERPRETATION"

It is Rosen's feeling that an effective encounter with the psychotic patient in the first treatment interview depends on the psychiatrist's understanding of the manifest content of the psychosis. Such manifestation may appear in anything the patient is saying or doing. Understanding of the manifest content and interpretation at the level of the latent content are primary aims in the first treatment session, in order to formulate a dynamic interpretation of the patient's illness and to determine the most effective strategic therapeutic planning. I must mention that there seems to be some contradiction between these statements and another one mentioned above—namely, that the most important factor is not "direct interpretation" as a translation of manifest content in "latent" terms, but rather as a means of establishing the therapist's understanding of the patient.

It has been mentioned that Rosen tries to define for the psychotic the therapist's assumptions regarding the unconscious dynamics of the patient's distress from the first moments of the therapeutic encounter. It is obvious that this is done in the framework of a hypothesis that tries to explain in a global way the psychodynamics and etiology of psychotic behavior. Many questions have been raised concerning the validity of such "understanding," considering that an a priori position is taken based on the information given by the patient, which seems to fit into the previously formulated hypothesis. It is true that Rosen has insisted that the "direct interpretation, i.e., interpreting directly to the patient the unconscious meaning of his manifestations, is not a key that magically resolves the psychotic behavior and puts everything in order again." He has repeatedly stated that its primary aim is to convey "understanding" to the patient that there is another person, the psychiatrist, who is interested enough to understand the meaning of the patient's behavior, and who is willing to take over the regulating and controlling of such behavior. Rosen does this impressively, with words that impose a dramatic effect on patient and observers alike. And he is successful, despite the impression of inner detachment that Rosen imparts to many people (English, 1961). Brody (1959) has noted that in the usual form of psychotherapy the physician makes intellectual comments about the affects of the patient; Rosen, instead, makes affective responses to the intellectual content of the patient.

Rosen has insisted that the patient's manifestations are equivalent to the manifest content of dream material, as viewed by psychoanalytic theory. One of his major assumptions, as a matter of fact, is that psychotic behavior in a patient is the equivalent of a long-lasting dream. It follows then that he would handle the psychotic material the same way he would utilize the dream material, that is, as symbolic clues to understand the dynamics of the patient's unconscious.

His techniques of utilizing these symbolic manifestations differ from the regular technique employed in psychoanalysis. As Rosen does not expect the psychotic patient to associate freely to his dream, no analytic work is done with this material except what the therapist *assumes* regarding the latent meanings of such symbolic behavior in the light of his own experiences and hypotheses. There are other differences from the conventional analytic approach worth mentioning. (1) Rosen's interpretation of symbols usually is related to an oral and/or anal level of psychosexual development. He believes that apparently genital symbols are in essence oral or anal if produced while the patient is regressed to a pregenital phase. (2) The patient is confronted with the therapist's interpretation as soon as possible; there is no working-through process by the patient. Rosen thinks that the psychotic, in contrast to the neurotic, patient is always prepared for an accurate interpretation and that inaccurate interpretations are harmless to the psychotic. By making patent the latent meaning of the psychotic behavior, as viewed by the therapist, he gives some relief to the patient from the tortures inflicted by the superego and encourages the patient to pay more attention to the therapist. (3) After such a confrontation, Rosen explains the reasoning behind the interpretation and its connection with the patient's manifestation, thereby facilitating incorporation of the therapist as a more palatable superego component and enhancing the therapist's teaching role. (4) Rosen's interpretation of symbolic behavior attributes a more universal value to symbols than does the conventional approach to dream symbolism. The direct analyst has fewer clues because of his a priori approach, and must rely more on his own intuition and phantasy. As a result, the interpretation of symbolic behavior from one patient to the next is more similar because the interpreter is the same.

DIRECT ANALYSIS AND RESISTANCE

What strikes the reader of direct-analysis literature is the scarcity of reference to the subject of resistance, which is found so frequently in the literature of other forms of psychotherapy. Rosen hardly refers to it in the course of his writings. There are only brief hints of the theme of resistance, in a very indirect way, in one of his first papers on "The Survival Function of Schizophrenia" (1953b). Seemingly, Rosen thinks that in schizophrenia there are no evidences of resistance, when he says that "the dream goes on and on . . . the unconscious material appears without interference from healthy resistances, exposing a variety of core conflicts which are only shabbily disguised." He explains that the continuous dream and consequent lack of resistance serve a survival function in the schizophrenic, whereby the psychotic experience is a psychologic response to something the individual conceives to be a death-threatening deprivation. Such a response involves an imaginative (hallucinatory, delusional) experience, which gains the force of reality to the patient.

Brody (1959) quotes Rosen as saying that psychotic delusions and hallucinations represent heroic attempts to live. The patient is most reluctant to relinquish his psychosis, a life-saving maneuver, for a more realistic way of life. The psychotic has turned away from people and does not want treatment. The direct analyst ignores this and imposes treatment on the patient. He is "awakened" from the dreamlike state and is compelled to look at reality, by being forced first to establish a one-to-one relationship with the therapist and then to face his problems and establish object relationships.

Sagredo (1964) argues that it is fallacious to say that the psychotic has no resistances, because actually he lives in the unconscious and resists

reality, whereas the neurotic individual resists the awareness of the unconscious. Because the psychotic is unwilling to give up his defenses against
the reality he knows as hostile and unacceptable, the therapist has to try
to create another reality more acceptable to the patient.

Rosen may overcome a patient's resistances by accusing him of lying
or by stating that he is stupid or "crazy" (English, 1961). He does not tell
the patient that he is resisting the interpretation or that he is avoiding
insight. Either the patient looks at reality as interpreted by the therapist or
he has to face losing the therapist's approval. The forcefulness of this
maneuver, group pressure from the assistants, plus confinement to the
treatment unit leave no escape from Rosen's disapproval. The patient cannot
ignore Rosen. He must face up to Rosen's assumption that the therapist
knows better.

THE WORKING-THROUGH PROCESS IN DIRECT ANALYSIS

Several attempts have been made to analyze the process of Rosen's
techniques (Brody, 1959; Scheflen, 1961; English *et al.*, 1961). What
appears to be a very unstructured interchange between Rosen and the
patient has been analyzed as having a program and definitely following a
pattern—this despite Rosen's affirmations that the direct analyst should not
stick to any routine of treatment, nor have a standard repertoire of techniques nor stereotyped set of remarks. On the other hand, Rosen (1962)
confirms that two main topics prevail in his interaction with the psychotic
patient—the malevolence of the psychotic's bad mother (the superego)
and the benevolence of the good mother (the psychiatrist). Most of the
strategies followed in this method are aimed at proving these topics.

In direct analysis the therapist pays much more attention to the *here-and-
now* situation and presenting manifestations of the patient than in conventional psychoanalysis, under the assumption that what the psychotic
is expressing is the result of the bare unconscious. The therapist selects from
the patient's day-to-day expressions whatever he feels is most important to
direct the patient's attention and prove his point. Any manifestation may
become the most important or most significant one depending on the
therapist's aim. Alarming symptomatology, from the viewpoint of another
observer, may be passed over without comment, and apparently insignificant
manifestations may attract the therapist's attention for the whole session.
Rosen (1962) maintains that it is impossible to predict how a particular
treatment session will progress, or what topics he will raise and how he will
deal with them. He leaves much to his own flexibility and imagination. De-

spite this flexibility, the technique does not seem to be markedly individualized to the patient, according to Scheflen (1961). The same general strategies are employed regardless of individual dynamics. This might be a result of the rather simplified and generalized body of theory utilized in direct analysis. A further recommendation stressed by Rosen (1962) is that all communication with the patient be in very simple, basic language. No scientific terminology or sophisticated technical terms are used. Assistants are also instructed to talk readily and warmly with the patient in simple English, since medical and psychoanalytic terminology would impede verbal communication.

A primary task in treatment is to make conscious to the patient what is unconscious. Rosen (1962) understands that what he attempts to do with the psychotic is similar to what Freud did in treating neurotic patients, that is, to make patent to him the latent meanings of his manifestations. This effort becomes the key activity of the therapist.

However, other observers have interpreted in somewhat different ways what Rosen does. Scheflen (1961) felt that Rosen used, with persistence and resourcefulness, a series of devices for persuasion and influence and that he carried out these maneuvers in an authoritarian relationship in which the patient evidenced overdependence, that is, wanted to be influenced. Some of the most common techniques of forceful persuasion used in direct analysis, as observed by Scheflen, were promising and rewarding, threatening and punishing, suggesting and instructing, rendering service, using group pressure, ridiculing, shaming and discrediting, and so forth.

For a faithful examination of these techniques the reader is referred to the study published by Scheflen (1961). Forceful persuasion can be utilized more easily when done in a group setting. We have already mentioned and described Rosen's utilization of the group of assistants. The cohesiveness of the whole group, with Rosen as the undisputed leader, causes the patient to feel as an outsider, and he is treated as one while he is "insane." The patient is forcibly put in the position of either joining the group or fighting it. Should the patient "give up the insanity" his welcome into the group is obvious; it becomes a celebration as everyone showers him with praise and gratifying remarks. The group's approval is further expressed by the invitation to become an assistant therapist for the next patient. Quite often this opportunity is actually offered to some patients, as a sign of confidence and as an initiation rite. The same author concluded that Rosen tended to pursue, with each patient, four successive goals: (1) to establish a particular type of authoritarian-dependent relationship; (2) to retrain the patient's thinking and behavior; (3) to manage drives toward maturation, particularly in handling sexual impulses; and (4) to terminate the relationship by contrasting the literal and metaphorical meaning of the relationship and preparing for discharge without causing retrogression. These goals are programmed with a certain order of application and priority. Structuring the authoritarian relationship and forcing the repudiation of psychotic behavior preceded management of sexual feelings and termination. Once the patient capitulates, or at least pretends to capitulate, to the direct analyst's definition of the authoritarian-dependent relationship, there is a marked decrease in overt psychotic behavior and a change in the patient's manner of relating from withdrawal and evasion to manifest dependency. This turning point introduces the initiation of management of sexual behavior and the termination process of treatment. Any indication of defiance of the direct analyst's rules for normal behavior brings about a restructuring of the authoritarian-dependent relationship by the therapist. The governing principle of direct analysis finds full application throughout the whole process of treatment.

Brody (1959) speculated along similar lines. He felt that Rosen makes every effort to disrupt previous identifications to induce the patient to identify with him. This forceful manner is based on the assumption that the therapist can modify the patient's superego and foster the introjection of Rosen's superego, or the group's superego. The therapist interprets the evidence of new identifications as a sign that the narcissistic defenses of the patient have been penetrated and that he is now capable of investing some libido in the therapist. Hence, the patient starts on the way to recovery (English, 1961; Bacon, 1961; Settlage, 1961).

According to Brody (1959) Rosen's remarks to the patient are primarily aimed at evoking guilt, not at giving insight. Labeling the patient's manifestations as shameful or stupid would seem to aim at having the patient repudiate his own symptoms. This maneuver of "distancing from the psychosis" finds further confirmation in Rosen's attempt to have the patient re-enact the psychosis. After the patient loses his psychotic symptoms, Rosen coaches him to re-enact those symptoms. If the patient during his psychosis spoke to imaginary voices, Rosen will insist that he again speak to these voices. The patient will usually resist, but should he comply Rosen treats the patient "as if insane."

A frequent approach is to convince the patient of the advantages of "having been insane," as it affords the experience of becoming acquainted with one's own unconscious. It is concluded from this that the best assistant therapists are those who have experienced a period of psychosis. Rosen also instructs the patient not to divulge that he has been psychotic, owing to the prejudices he may encounter in the period of rehabilitation.

English (1961) observed that Rosen tends to produce a psychological vacuum into which the patient is pulled by the very forces of his own needs. Once Rosen feels the patient is emotionally involved and has capitulated to the demands of identification, Rosen would subtly threaten to withdraw. It is his seduction by giving and then by threatening withdrawal that enhances his importance in the feelings of the patient. A rhythmic alternation of love and deprivation, closeness and distance, giving and taking away, is characteristic in Rosen's technique, and is a more prevailing practice than the governing principle of omnipotent love.

It follows from this whole theoretical assumption and Rosen's direct-analysis technique that dream interpretation is a completely different task when compared with more conventional practices.

If Rosen assumes that psychotic manifestations are equivalents of dream manifestations of the neurotic or the normal individual, it follows that his approach to dream material would not be too different from the way he handles psychotic manifestations. One major assumption is implied. The psychotic does not dream. According to Rosen, the patient is on the way to recovery when dream material does appear. As mentioned earlier, it is characteristic technique in this method that the therapist selects from the current content (dream or psychotic manifestation) whatever he feels intuitively is strategically important to lead the patient into understanding the meaning of this survival struggle.

TERMINATION OF TREATMENT AND CONCEPT OF CURE

Rosen utilizes a specific landmark to determine termination of the psychotic phase in the patient, namely the disappearance of certain psychotic symptoms (i.e., hallucinations and delusions). Resolution of the psychosis means not only the disappearance of these symptoms but also the incorporation of, and identification with, the therapist. It means that the patient has modified the old superego structure and has accepted the modifications introduced by the therapist. The resolution of the psychosis marks the beginning of his progression from the oral level of psychosexual development to the level appropriate to his physical development (Rosen, 1962). Accordingly, the procedures used during the termination phase of treatment are intended to encourage and aid the individual as a parent would his own child during psychosexual progression and development.

There are a number of maneuvers that herald the termination of treatment. The therapist announces dramatically that the insanity is nearly over or that the unit is no longer locked, or he may ask the patient to run errands for him. If the patient continues to be asymptomatic he is praised by Rosen and the assistants, and arrangements are made for the patient to visit home, to move out of the unit, or to return to his school or job.

The final return home is conditional. The patient continues to see the therapist on a more informal and irregular schedule, as determined according to Rosen's conceptions about the neoneurotic phase. A long-lasting bond of affection and interest is usually established between therapist and patient in those cases where actual resolution has taken place. Dependency needs are not fostered in this phase; on the contrary, Scheflen (1961) feels that Rosen very subtly loses interest in the patient after the major symptoms disappear.

Treatment during the neoneurotic phase becomes even more crucial than in the psychotic phase, and perhaps more difficult. Rosen no longer follows a conventional analytic procedure in this stage as he used to recommend initially in his work. He now feels that conventional analysis for some of these individuals could be useless or even harmful. He stresses that the neoneurotic is like a growing adolescent, that the treatment unit is like a foster home, and that the family situation is available to him at any time.

Treatment sessions in the neoneurotic stage are ordinarily held in private, and scheduled on a weekly or biweekly basis, or according to need. Outwardly they resemble the treatment sessions with psychotics in that there is a face-to-face encounter between therapist and patient. The verbal content of these sessions may include occasional direct interpretations but never a transference interpretation, since the transference is presumed to have subsided with the resolution of psychosis (Sullivan, 1964).

The subject matter of these sessions with the neoneurotic is usually circumscribed to current circumstantial issues, activities, or problems. No reference is made to conflicts. There is no resemblance to a conventional psychoanalytic session, or to any of the other reconstructive types of psychotherapy. It seems more like a supportive-reassuring type of session.

Resolution of the neoneurotic stage seems to be a gradual and subtle process. Any tendency to regression, or actual reappearance of psychotic manifestations, is dealt with as in the psychotic stage and with the same theoretical framework.

Rosen (1962) gives some hints about his awareness of the intricacies of the psychotic's dynamics and the role family relationships play in it when he warns that the individual's maturity meets its severest test when he returns to his family.

Despite his statement that the road back from psychosis appears to be the reverse of the road down (Rosen, 1962), and despite the continued assumption of the role of the early maternal environment in the determination of the patient's responses, it does not seem that in Rosen's method of treatment enough attention is paid to the family environment during the rehabilitation program of the psychotic patient. The assumption that the therapist's intervention in the patient's life and the modification of the superego structure are enough to modify the ongoing dynamics between the patient and his family does not seem to be true in many cases. The patient belongs to an intricate system of family relationships in which, more often than not, other members are equally disturbed.

Finally, resolution of the neoneurosis is brought about when the patient is able to resolve the Oedipus complex, that is, identification with mother and father. As mentioned earlier, in Rosen's terms the therapist ideally functions first as a mother in the psychotic phase, then as a father in the neoneurotic phase. The proper identification and incorporation of these roles brings about the resolution of the psychotic and neoneurotic phase of illness.

Some Final Comments

It is important to present a few additional comments and questions raised while observing Rosen and reviewing his writings.

Many observers have questioned his insistence on comparing his method with psychoanalysis and demonstrating his incorporation of and identification with Freudian theory. Rosen does not analyze the transference, which is a central aspect of psychoanalysis, and he subscribes to a different interpretation of what transference is and stands for. It is true that he employs Freudian terminology, but it is my understanding that the same words have a different meaning in each theory. In reference to psychosexual development, he modifies radically conceptions about the appearance and functions of the various stages as proposed in conventional psychoanalytic theory. He departs from the classical agreement about the genesis and functions of the superego and does not seem fully satisfied with the ascribed functions of the ego and id.

Rosen's insistence on using the term psychoanalysis for his method of treatment, even though it departs so much from the classical understanding of this term, has created a good deal of antagonism. Rosen has been courageous enough to depart from conventional methods of treatment and from orthodox thinking; why must he insist on his affiliation to and incorporation of psychoanalysis?

There is no question that Rosen has proven many times his unique capability of reaching the most regressed and chronically ill patients and introducing modifications in their behavior. We have referred to the qualities of his personality and the special characteristics of his technique that may be responsible for this resourceful aspect of his treatment. On the other hand, we have had the repeated experience that many psychotic patients are extremely flexible in the initial phase of their illness. A reversal of the psychotic's manifestations is not such a difficult task to accomplish; this can be done quite easily with various therapeutic approaches. The major problem arises in the long-term efficacy of prognosis and treatment of the chronically ill patient. I do not know if we possess, at the present time, statistical studies to demonstrate that one treatment method is superior to others or that one therapist is better than another. We do have indications that a patient may turn asymptomatic with a certain technique or treatment; but this in turn does not prove that the therapist's theoretical assumptions are correct.

At the present time it is difficult to ignore the work being done with families of psychotic patients (Zuk and Rubinstein, 1965). Theory has evolved from the simple, one-to-one relationship with the schizophrenogenic mother to consider the effects of pathogenic family systems that spring up around the psychotic family member. The mother-child relationship may be a too-simplified model to explain different aspects of current pathologic relationships encountered in the psychotic's life. Furthermore, the formula proposed by Rosen for the psychotic's persistence in his behavior (he seeks the mother he knew who is at the same time deadly but indispensable) may be ignoring such other dynamic aspects as mutual symbiotic relationships, transference relationships within the family system, ill-defined ego boundaries within the family on the pattern of Bowen's (1960) concept of the undifferentiated ego mass, and so forth. Such concepts belong to a higher level of abstraction than earlier hypotheses concerning the infant-mother relationship alone.

Direct interpretation cannot be understood out of its context; it is not an isolated phenomenon. Scheflen (1965), for example, has described some of the nonverbal phenomena occurring in the context of verbal communication. If we consider all the variables occurring in the context of the spoken language, we have to accept that a more complicated message does get through to the patient rather than the simple verbal one. A therapist interpreting directly to a patient in the presence of a group of people, demonstrating his technique, creates a situation that is of a higher hierarchical level compared to the same therapist uttering the same words to the same patient in the quiet of his office.

Psychotherapy as a set of rules and techniques cannot be isolated from the person who implements it. Technique and instrument become highly intertwined and inseparable. Technique, style, and personality are variants and different aspects of the highly complex instrumentality we call the therapist.

Rosen has been able to arouse tremendous interest and simultaneous anger and hostility. Some of these reactions are explained by the fact that we still feel lost and hopeless in the presence of a deeply regressed psychotic. A man, or a method, claiming as much as Rosen is bound to attract attention. He is like the magician in the park, and we are so often like children wishing to see the rabbit come out of the hat. Then too, how many times are we secretly wishing, with curious ambivalence, that the magician will be fooled and not be able to perform the miracle?

REFERENCES

[NOTE: I wish to acknowledge my gratitude to Dr. O. Spurgeon English for reading my manuscript and offering suggestions.]

BACON, C. L. The Rosen treatment of the psychoses from the viewpoint of identity. In O. S. English *et al., Direct analysis and schizophrenia.* New York: Grune and Stratton, 1961.

BOOKHAMMER, R. S., MEYERS, R. W., SCHOBER, C. C., and PIOTROWSKI, Z. A. A five-year follow-up study of schizophrenics treated by Rosen's "direct analysis" compared with controls. *American Journal of Psychiatry,* 1966, 123, 602–604.

BOWEN, M. A family concept of schizophrenics. In D. D. Jackson (Ed.), *The etiology of schizophrenia.* New York: Basic Books, 1960.

BRADY, M. W. *Observations on direct analysis, the therapeutic technique of Dr. John N. Rosen.* New York: Vantage Press, 1959.

ENGLISH, O. S. Clinical observations on direct analysis. In O. S. English, W. W. Hampe, C. L. Bacon and C. F. Settlage, *Direct analysis and schizophrenia.* New York: Grune and Stratton, 1961.

FEDERN, P. *Ego-psychology and the psychosis.* New York: Basic Books, 1952.

HENDRICK, IVES. *Facts and theories of psychoanalysis.* New York: Knopf, 1958.

HORWITZ, W. A., POLATIN, P., KOLB, L. C., and HOCH, P. H. A study of cases of schizophrenia treated by direct analysis. *American Journal of Psychiatry,* 1958, 114, 780–783.

KUBIE, L. S. In S. Scarizza (Ed.), *Proceedings of the first international congress of direct psychoanalysis,* Rome, 1964. Doylestown, Pa.: The Doylestown Foundation.

KUBIE, L. S. Preface. In A. E. Scheflen, *A psychotherapy of schizophrenia: direct analysis.* Springfield, Ill.: Charles C Thomas, 1961.

LEWIN, B. D. Review of A. E. Scheflen, *A psychotherapy of schizophrenia: direct analysis. Journal of Nervous and Mental Diseases,* 1962, 134, 578–581.

LIPTON, S. D. Some comparisons of psychotherapeutic methods in schizophrenia. *Psychiatric Quarterly,* 1949, 23, 705–711.

McKINNON, K. M. A clinical evaluation of the method of direct analysis in the treatment of psychosis. *Journal of Clinical Psychology,* 1959, 15, 80–96.

MENNINGER, K. *Theory of psychoanalytic technique.* New York: Basic Books, 1958.

REDLICH, F. C. The concept of schizophrenia and its implications for therapy. In E. B. Brady and F. C. Redlich (Eds.), *Psychotherapy with schizophrenics.* New York: International Universities Press, 1952.

ROGERS, C. R. A theory of psychotherapy with schizophrenics and a proposal for its empirical investigation. In J. G. Dawson *et al.* (Eds.), *Psychotherapy with schizophrenics.* Baton Rouge: Louisiana State Univ. Press, 1961.

ROSEN, J. N. A method of resolving acute catatonic excitement. *Psychiatric Quarterly,* 1946, 20, 183–189.

ROSEN, J. N. The treatment of schizophrenic psychosis by direct analytic therapy. *Psychiatric Quarterly,* 1947, 21, 117–131.

ROSEN, J. N. Note, 1952. In *Direct analysis, selected papers.* New York: Grune and Stratton, 1953. Pp. 95–96. (a)

ROSEN, J. N. *Direct analysis: selected papers.* New York: Grune and Stratton, 1953. (b)

ROSEN, J. N. Transference: a concept of its origin, its purpose, and its fate. *International Journal of Psychotherapy, Psychosomatic, Special Education,* 1954, 2, 300.

ROSEN, J. N. *Direct psychoanalytic psychiatry.* New York: Grune and Stratton, 1962.

ROSEN, J. N. *The concept of early maternal environment in direct psychoanalysis.* Doylestown, Pa.: The Doylestown Foundation, 1963.

ROSEN, J. N. *Psychoanalysis direct and indirect.* Doylestown, Pa.: The Doylestown Foundation, 1964. (a)

ROSEN, J. N. Direct psychoanalysis. In J. H. Masserman (Ed.), *Current psychiatric therapies.* Vol. IV. New York: Grune and Stratton, 1964. (b)

RUBINSTEIN, D. In S. Scarizza (Ed.), *Proceedings of the first international congress of direct psychoanalysis,* Rome, 1964. Doylestown, Pa.: The Doylestown Foundation, 1964.

SAGREDO, O. In S. Scarizza (Ed.), *Proceedings of the first international congress of direct psychoanalysis,* Rome, 1964. Doylestown, Pa.: The Doylestown Foundation, 1964.

SCHEFLEN, A. E. *A psychotherapy of schizophrenia.* Springfield, Ill.: Charles C Thomas, 1961.

SCHEFLEN, A. E. *Stream and structure of communicational behavior.* Philadelphia: Eastern Pa. Psychiatric Institute, 1965.

SEARLES, H. Review of J. N. Rosen, *Direct psychoanalytic psychiatry. International Journal of Psychoanalysis,* 1964, **45**, 597–602.

SETTLAGE, C. F. On the psychodynamics of direct analysis. In O. S. English *et al., Direct analysis and schizophrenia.* New York: Grune and Stratton, 1961.

SULLIVAN, C. I. Recent developments in direct psychoanalysis. *Psychoanalytic Review,* 1964, **51**, 382–400.

ZUK, G., and RUBINSTEIN, D. A. Review of concepts in the study and treatment of families of schizophrenics. In I. Boszormenyi-Nagy and J. L. Framo (Eds.), *Intensive family therapy.* New York: Harper & Row, 1965.

9

INTERACTIONAL PSYCHOANALYSIS

Benjamin B. Wolman

Freud's clinical papers do not offer a consistent picture of how the psychoanalytic technique should be applied. Freud himself modified his technique on several occasions, but these changes were not always made explicit. Freud never gave a complete and comprehensive picture of the psychoanalytic method of treatment.

The technique of treatment evolved gradually over a long period of time. Major changes were made in the course of the development of psychoanalytic technique, notably in the transition from the cathartic method to psychoanalysis proper. Several significant changes have been made irrespective of the major theoretical issues. These modifications in technique were not necessarily accidental or erratic. A close study of Freud's clinical work discloses a definite and quite consistent pattern. It was not the analyst who changed his attitude. Distinct categories of patients developed certain attitudes toward the analyst, and the analyst, in turn, had to modify his therapeutic technique. The reactions of the analyst were determined by the patients' behavior.

241

The patient's attitude toward the analyst is a transference phenomenon, but at the same time it is a "here-and-now" relationship. Apparently, from the inception of Freud's work, the analyst's reaction to the patient was the ever important clue (Freud, 1891).

In 1890, Freud became aware of the unconscious forces that prevented recall of the past. These forces are called resistance (Freud, 1894), and they are a continuation of the process of repression. In 1892, Freud discovered the phenomenon of transference. Gradually, transference became the crucial issue in psychoanalytic treatment. Love and hate became interlaced into the fabric of transference feelings that the patient wove around the person of the analyst. Overcoming of resistance, reconstruction of the infantile conflict, and insight into its re-experience in the transference situation became the bedrock of psychoanalytic procedure.

During the years 1912 to 1915 Freud wrote several papers dealing with the technique, stressing transference resistance. The crucial statement on this issue declares that every conflict "is played out in the phenomenon of the transference" (1912a, p. 108).

Treatment of Hysterics

The basic elements of Freud's technique, namely the passive-receptive, nonparticipant, nonactive listening to the patient's free associations, was developed in his work with hysterics. Originally, Freud, under the influence of Charcot, used hypnotic suggestion, gradually substituting it with the cathartic method (Breuer and Freud, 1895). Eventually, hypnosis was given up, but the suggestive pressure of concentration continued. In Freud's treatment of Mrs. Emmy, in 1889, the free-association technique was applied for the first time.

Certainly the reclining position, the apparently passive attitude of the analyst, and the avoidance of reality stimuli facilitated both the process of regression and a substantial reduction of the ego's defenses. In this regressive state of mind repressed elements are likely to appear, and transference is facilitated.

Freud never insisted on a uniform psychoanalytic procedure. In his severe criticism of the so-called wild psychoanalysis in 1910, he wrote: "My impression was that the lady in question was suffering from anxiety-hysteria, and the whole value of such nosographical distinctions, one which quite justifies them, lies in the fact that they indicate a different etiology and a different therapy" (Freud, 1910b).

The main tenets of psychoanalytic technique, developed in the work with hysterics, were based on the expectancy of ambivalent feelings on the part of the patient who oscillated between positive and negative attitudes toward the analyst. Both attitudes reflected libidinal and destructive cathexes, largely encouraged by the passive-receptive attitude of the analyst. Thus, the patient re-experienced in a nutshell his neurotic conflict. The gradual resolution of resistances and the interpretation of the unconscious conflict was the choice method. The irrationality of the ambivalence toward the analyst was open to interpretation.

Limitations of the Technique

The limits of the psychoanalytic treatment of hysterics were not determined by the type or quality of this neurosis, but by the degree of topographic regression. Freud wrote in 1904 that the patient "must be capable of a psychically normal condition; during periods of confusion or melancholic depression nothing can be accomplished even in cases of hysteria" (Freud, 1904, p. 254).

In other words, whenever a hysteric regresses into a severe depressive state, the usual technique was not applicable. Abraham, in his paper on treatment of manic-depressive disorders (1911), suggested starting analysis in the periods comparatively free from depression. Thirteen years later, Abraham again mentioned Freud's advice to start psychoanalysis of "melancholiac" at a time "when they are just coming out of a depressive state and entering upon a free interval" (Abraham, 1924, p. 476).

In the "Future Prospects of Psycho-Analytic Therapy" (1910a) presented to the Nuremberg Congress, Freud advocated the support of the denial mechanisms in the hypomanic states. Obviously, Freud and his early associates were aware of the fact that not all patients act in the same way. Some of them require substantial modifications of the technique, and Freud found some of them unsuitable for psychoanalytic treatment. Freud wrote about these cases in the *Introductory Lectures on Psycho-Analysis* (1916–1917) as follows:

Many attempts at treatment made in the beginning of psychoanalysis were failures because they were undertaken with cases altogether unsuited to the procedure, which nowadays we should exclude by following certain indications. These indications, however, could only be discovered by trying. In the beginning we did not know that paranoia and dementia praecox, when fully developed, are not amenable to analysis; we were still justified in trying the method on all kinds of disorders (p. 399).

Obsessions and Phobias

Although this method worked well with hysterics and with manic-depressives in remission (Abraham, 1911, 1924), it apparently did not work so well with obsessive-compulsives or phobics (so-called anxiety hysterics), failed with schizophrenics, and did not work at all with psychopaths. Apparently the necessary modifications were determined (1) by the *level* of regression within a certain type of disorder; and (2) by the *type* of disorder. Let us start with the second.

Freud was aware of the need to modify the technique in the treatment of obsessive-compulsives. As early as 1894, Freud observed the tendency of obsessive-compulsives to use free associations as a method of resistance.

In the most important paper "The Future Prospects of Psycho-Analytic Therapy" (1910a) Freud stated clearly:

We are also now coming to the opinion that the analytic technique must undergo certain modifications according to the nature of the disease and the dominating instinctual trends in the patient. Our therapy was, in fact, first designed for conversion-hysteria; in anxiety-hysteria (phobias) we must alter our procedure to some extent. The fact is that these patients cannot bring out the material necessary for resolving the phobia so long as they feel protected by retaining their phobic condition. One cannot, of course, induce them to give up their protective measures and work under the influence of anxiety from the beginning of the treatment. One must therefore help them by interpreting their unconscious to them until they can make up their minds to do without the protection of their phobia and expose themselves to a now comparatively moderate degree of anxiety. Only when they have done so does the material necessary for achieving solution of the phobia become accessible. Other modifications of technique which seem to me not yet ready for discussion will be required in the treatment of obsessional neurosis. In this connection very important questions arise, which are not yet elucidated: how far the instincts involved in the conflict in the patient are to be allowed some gratification during the treatment, and what difference it then makes whether these impulses are active (sadistic) or passive (masochistic) in nature.

Freud was even more outspoken in his address on "Lines of Advance in Psychoanalytic Therapy" read before the Fifth International Psychoanalytic Congress in 1918 in Budapest (published in 1919). He wrote:

Lastly, another quite different kind of activity is necessitated by the gradually growing appreciation that the various forms of disease treated by us cannot all be dealt with by the same technique. It would be premature to discuss this in detail, but I can give two examples of the way in which a new kind of activity comes into question. Our technique grew up in the treatment of hysteria and is still directed principally to the cure of this affection. But the phobias have already made it necessary for us to go beyond our former limits. One can hardly ever master a phobia if one waits till the patient lets the analysis influence him to give it up. He will never in that case bring for the analysis the material indispensable for a convincing solution of the phobia. One must proceed differently. Take the example of agoraphobia; there are two classes of it, one slight and the other severe. Patients belonging to the first indeed suffer from anxiety when they go about alone, but they have not yet given up going out alone on that account; the others protect themselves from the anxiety by altogether giving up going about alone. With these last, one succeeds only when one can induce them through the influence of the analysis to behave like the first class, that is, to go about alone and to struggle with their anxiety while they make the attempt. One first achieves, therefore, a considerable moderation of the phobia, and it is only when this has been attained by the physician's recommendation that the association and memories come into the patient's mind enabling the phobia to be solved.

In severe cases of obsessive acts a passive waiting attitude seems even less well adapted: indeed in general these cases incline to favor an asymptomatic process of cure, an interminable protraction of the treatment; in their analysis there is always the danger of a great deal coming to light without its effecting any change in them. I think there is little doubt that here the correct technique can only be to wait until the treatment itself has become a compulsion, and then with this counter-compulsion, forcibly to suppress the compulsion of the disease.

Freud faced unsurmountable difficulties in the treatment of schizophrenics. Schizophrenics reacted to the reclining position and to the analyst's silence with an apparent and far-reaching regression. Freud believed that schizophrenia was a nontransference neurosis. Furthermore, "If the patient's ego is to be a useful ally in our common work," wrote Freud in the *Outline* (1938, p. 63), it must, however hard it may be pressed by the hostile powers, have retained a certain degree of coherence, a fragment at least of understanding for the demands of reality. But this is not to be expected from the ego of a psychotic; it cannot carry out a pact of this sort, indeed it can scarcely engage in it. It will very soon toss us away and the help we offer it, to join the portions of the external world that no longer mean anything to it. Thus we learn that we must renounce the idea of trying our plan of cure upon psychotics—renounce it forever, perhaps, or only for the moment, until we have discovered some other plan better suited for that purpose.

Apparently, the classic technique had its limitations. Freud did not elaborate a way out. He had, however, given numerous hints about how these problems could be handled, and on several occasions he did show specific ways out.

Freud's Three Types

In 1931 Freud published a short paper on "Libidinal Types." In this paper he distinguished three libidinal types, namely the *erotic, obsessive,* and *narcissistic.*

The *erotic* type is easily characterized. Erotics are persons whose main interest—the relatively largest amount of their libido—is focused on love. Loving, but above all being loved, is for them the most important thing in life. They are governed by the dread of loss of love, and this makes them peculiarly dependent on those who may withhold their love from them. Even in its pure form this type is a very common one. Variations occur according as it is blended with another type and as the element of aggression in it is strong or weak. From the social and cultural standpoint this type represents the elementary instinctual claims of the id, to which the other psychical agencies have become docile.

The second type is that which I have termed the *obsessional*—a name which may at first seem rather strange; its distinctive characteristic is the supremacy exercised by the super-ego, which is segregated from the ego with great accompanying tension. Persons of this type are governed by anxiety of conscience instead of by the dread of losing love; they exhibit, we might say, an inner instead of an outer dependence; they develop a high degree of self-reliance, and from the social standpoint they are the true upholders of civilization, for the most part in a conservative spirit.

The characteristics of the third type, justly called the *narcissistic,* are in the main negatively described. There is no tension between ego and superego—indeed, starting from this type one would hardly have arrived at the notion of a super-ego; there is no preponderance of erotic needs; the main interest is focused on self-preservation; the type is independent and not easily overawed. The ego has a considerable amount of aggression available, one manifestation of this being a proneness to activity; where love is in question, loving is preferred to being loved. People of this type impress others as being "personalities"; it is on them that their fellow-men are specially likely to lean; they readily assume the role of the leader, give a fresh stimulus to cultural development or break down existing conditions (1931, pp. 248–249).

Interindividual Cathexis

Freud's paper on "Libidinal Types" was the starting point in my own thinking. I felt, however, that a theory of personality types required certain additional concepts. Whenever Freud was talking about object relations, he applied the concept of *cathexis*. Cathexis, a term borrowed from static electricity, means charge or investment of some amount of energy. Freud, always being faithful to the principles of monism (cf. Wolman, 1965a), assumed that mental energy is a derivative and continuation of the bio-chemical energy of the living organisms, which is, in turn, part and parcel of the universal energy of electric particles. Mental energy is either a creative libido, activated by Eros, the instinctual drive of life, or destructive energy (often called destrudo), activated by Thanatos, the instinctual drive of death.

My modifications in the framework of psychoanalytic theory include the concept of *interindividual cathexis* and the idea of *Ares,* the instinctual drive of hostility (Wolman, 1960, Chap. 15; 1966a, 1966b). To the idea of Ares I am devoting the monograph *Eros and Ares* (in press).

The concept of interindividual cathexis describes what happens with mental energy. When individual A loves B, his libido is cathected into B. Accordingly, little of his libido is left for his own self-cathexis. Hence, Federn (1952) and Wolman (1957) assume that in schizophrenia (to be discussed later) a lavish object cathexis inevitably leads to an impoverishment in self-cathexis.

Following some of Freud's hints in the above-mentioned essay on the libidinal types and adding the concept of interindividual cathexis, I proposed (1965b, 1966c) a complete system of classification of mental disorders, based on a somewhat modified psychoanalytic concept combined with sociopsychological categories.

One may classify objects in many different ways. One may classify animals and plants according to their color or their size. People can be classified as strong or weak, tall or short, male or female, and so on. No classification system as such is better than, or superior to, another. For a real estate broker, mankind is divided into those who buy and those who take up his time without buying. A music teacher may divide people into nonplayers, beginners, good players, and virtuosos.

Classification leads to the formation of general and abstract concepts. Whenever objects or events are grouped into classes or categories on the basis of at least one common denominator, statements pertaining to the entire class can be made. Since all sciences have general rules, classification is an important step forward.

Two rules must be followed in classification, namely *economy* and *usefulness*. A classification is economical when no object within a given system of classification belongs to more than one class and when every single object is included in a certain class. For instance, if one classifies people according to their height, and marks those below five feet as short and those above six feet as tall, he omits those between five and six feet; should one classify six feet as short and above five feet as tall, those between five and six feet will belong to two classes, and the classification will be uneconomical.

Classification of mental disorders that deals only with symptomatology can hardly be economical. For instance, depressions are related to a great many mental disorders. Hallucinations, anxieties, phobias, homosexual impulses, psychosomatic disorders, addictions, and antisocial acts can be found in more than one type of mental disorder.

Apparently, mental disorders can be classified in more than one way (Zilboorg and Henry, 1941), but a classification becomes scientifically useful only when it can be used to *explain* present behavior (symptoms) by invoking past causes and when, given past causes, one can *predict* their future outcome. Scientific classification must be based on etiologic factors.

Mental disorders can be produced by either organic or nonorganic factors. Organic or somatogenic disorders can be either genosomatogenic if inherited, or ecosomatogenic if acquired through interaction with physicochemical factors such as germs, poisons, physical injuries, and so on.

All mental disorders exclusive of the inherited ones are a product of interaction between the organism and the environment. If this interaction is physical or chemical, the disorder is called ecosomatogenic. If it is neither physical nor chemical, it should be called *sociogenic*. Thus, all mental disorders fall into one of the three classes: genosomatogenic, ecosomatogenic, or sociogenic. The so-called psychogenic mental disorders are a product of interaction with the social environment. They are caused either by *cathexes* or by *conditioning*. In either case, the sociogenic mental disorders are produced by harmful influences of environmental factors.

These environmental factors affect the intraindividual balance of cathexes. The infant is prone to go through the oral, anal, urethral, and phallic stages. The very fact of the developmental stages is biologically determined. However, the *way* the individual infant will go through them is determined by sociocultural factors. The level and severity of fixations and regressions largely depends upon the *interaction* between the infant and his home environment. The parent-child interaction may facilitate or prevent growth, may encourage object relations or foster secondary narcissism, and may block or speed up discharges of libido and destrudo. The formation of ego and superego is largely a product of interaction between the individual and his environment.

Pathogenesis of mutual disorders is, to a great extent, the story of parent-child relationships and their impact on child development and personality formation. There is no doubt that the same pathogenic patterns are reflected in transference. The family drama is re-enacted by the patients, who ascribe to the analyst the actions, motives, and personality traits of their parents. This re-enacted drama is the vehicle for cure.

Three Socio-Psychological Patterns

The way the neurosis was formed is re-enacted in the analytic sessions and, in many cases, also outside of the sessions. A neurotic interacts in a neurotic fashion not only with his analyst, but only the analyst can offer insight and resolution of the neurotic conflict.

This interaction is always a discharge of libido and destrudo cathexes. Since interaction is also an overt sociopsychological process, I have tried to develop observational behavioral categories. These categories have easily been ordered to the psychoanalytic conceptual system.

I have distinguished three interactional patterns depending upon whether the main purpose of the interaction is the satisfaction of the individual's own needs (*instrumental*), or his partner's needs (*vectorial*), or both (*mutual* or *mutual acceptance*).

When people enter a social relationship in order to have their own needs satisfied—when their purpose is to take and not to give—*instrumental* relationship is formed. Each individual regards the other as tools or instruments to be used for his well-being. The life of an infant starts as a parasitic process; the infant must receive all that is necessary for his survival. The relation of an infant toward his mother is the prototype of instrumentalism.

Mutual or mutual-acceptance relationships develop gradually through maturation and learning. In the nursery school or playground, the child is already presented with the opposition of other children to his instrumentalism. Gradually the child learns to share, to take turns, to trade toys, and to accept give and take as a basis for interaction.

Mutuality achieves its peak in friendship and marriage. Each partner desires to make his partner happy and expects that the same is his partner's feeling. Successful marriage is based on mutuality; each marital partner is determined to do his best for the well-being of his or her partner and expects the same from the other party.

Parenthood is the prototype of *vectorialism*. Parents give life, protect and care for it, irrespective of their child's looks, health, I.Q., disposition, or success. The more the infant needs their help, the more sympathy he elicits.

Children could not make good parents; they demand love to be given to them; they are instrumental. Childish adults are also instrumental, and they cannot be adequate parents. To be an adequate parent one needs to feel strong, friendly, and willing to give, and one must be ready to care without asking anything in return. To give without asking or expecting anything in return is the highest degree of love and is the essence of vectorialism.

A normal or well-adjusted individual is balanced in social interaction. He is instrumental in the struggle for survival, mutual in relationships with friends and in marriage, and vectorial in regard to children and to those who need help. He is reasonably selfish, reasonably mutual, and reasonably vectorial.

Mentally disturbed individuals cannot preserve this balance. They are *hyperinstrumental,* displaying infantile selfishness and parasitism; they neglect themselves and worry constantly about others in a morbid *hypervectorialism;* or they exaggerate in giving and in taking, in shifting moods of *paramutualism.*

Needless to say, these three types correspond to three types of libido balances. In *hyperinstrumental* types the libido is self-hypercathected and object-hypocathected, and destrudo is loosely object-cathected. The psychopaths belong to this category. In *hypervectorial* types the libido is self-hypocathected and object-hypercathected. The destrudo is kept under rigid control, but breaks through in psychotic deterioration. Obsessions, phobias, neurasthenias, and schizophrenic psychoses belong to this category. In *paramutual* types, libido and destrudo easily shift back and forth from self-cathexis to object-cathexis. Conversion hysterics, dissociative reactions, and manic-depressive disorders fall into this category. The hyperinstrumental type comes close to Freud's narcissistic type; the hypervectorial resembles the obsessive type; the paramutual corresponds to Freud's erotic type.

The Hyperinstrumental Type

In the essay "A Seventeenth Century Demonological Neurosis" (1923), Freud stressed the enormous difficulty in treating patients who derive a substantial secondary gain from their neurosis. In these cases neurosis serves as a protective shield that masks the desire to achieve gratification at the expense of others. (Cf. Cleckley, 1950.)

In the hyperinstrumental type of neurosis, symptom formation is determined by secondary gain. The main motivation is to get something without giving anything in return. Hyperinstrumentals demand consideration, love, and affection, but they have none of these feelings for anyone except themselves. They are exploitative, selfish, and brutal to others and sentimental toward themselves. They never blame themselves, but always blame others for whatever misfortunes they experience. The hyperinstrumental looks at the world with the eyes of a hungry, weak, and greedy infant and believes that he is surrounded by selfish, unfair, and powerful enemies (Wolman, 1966c).

The *hyperinstrumentals* are usually called psychopaths or sociopaths. They are overtly selfish, dishonest, and disloyal, yet believe in their own good will and innocence. Hyperinstrumentals are prone to pity themselves and cry over their own sufferings and deprivations but to have neither empathy nor sympathy for anyone else. They have no moral restraints, no consideration, and no compassion for anyone except themselves. They may or may not become criminals, depending on whether they fear retaliation. The hyperinstrumental symptom formation offers a great deal of secondary gain, for it helps to win privileges from the environment. The "sick role" is played out at its best.

The personality structure of the hyperinstrumental or psychopathic type can be described in psychoanalytic terms as follows. Their libido is self-hypercathected, for the hyperinstrumental type has never outgrown his primary narcissism. The self-hypercathexis makes him oversensitive to pain and hypochondriac. The hyperinstrumental has no true object love, but he

CLASSIFICATION OF
SOCIOGENIC MENTAL DISORDERS

Types	Hyperinstrumentalism	Paramutualism	Hypervectorialism
Levels	I	M	V
Neurosis	HYPERINSTRU-MENTAL NEUROSIS (Certain anxiety and depressive reactions)	PARAMUTUAL NEUROSIS (Dissociative and conversion reactions)	HYPERVECTORIAL NEUROSIS (Obsessional, phobic, and neurasthenic reactions)
Character Neurosis	HYPERINSTRU-MENTAL CHARACTER NEUROSIS (Sociopathic or psychopathic personality)	PARAMUTUAL CHARACTER NEUROSIS (Cyclothymic and passive-aggressive personality)	HYPERVECTORIAL CHARACTER NEUROSIS (Schizoid and compulsive personality)
Latent Psychosis	LATENT HYPERINSTRU-MENTAL PSYCHOSIS (Psychopathic reactions bordering on psychosis)	LATENT PARAMUTUAL PSYCHOSIS (Borderline manic-depressive psychosis)	LATENT VECTORIASIS PRAECOX (Borderline and latent schizophrenia)
Manifest Psychosis	HYPERINSTRU-MENTAL PSYCHOSIS (Psychotic psychopathy and moral insanity)	PARAMUTUAL PSYCHOSIS (Manifest manic-depressive psychosis)	VECTORIASIS PRAECOX (Manifest schizophrenia)
Dementia	Collapse of Personality Structure		

may identify with the underdog and cry when watching sentimental movies. Whatever object relations he has are on an exploitative, primitive-instrumental, or oral-cannibalistic level. He uses people and is inclined to destroy them whenever they refuse to be used. The hyperinstrumental type views others as enemies bound to devour him unless he devours them. His object relations are permeated with hostility, and his destrudo is object-directed. Whoever he perceives as weak, he treats the way the Nazis treated the Jews; he sees himself as an innocent, poor, hungry creature who has to defend himself against his enemies. He feels sorry for himself, but has no pity for his victims. He is a coward and is brutal toward those who fear him, but he is obedient and subservient to those he fears.

The hyperinstrumental has no superego, no guilt feelings, no moral principles, and no ethical standards. He has to satisfy needs, of course, but they are his own needs only. If he has a superego, it always sides with the id. "*Ich muss es haben*" is his motto. His gods are commercialized, and he can bribe them; or they are mercenaries who should help him to conquer his *Lebensraum*. His ego may be weak, but it, too, always sides with the id.

From the structural point of view, the id is the ruling force in the personality of a psychopath. The weak or practically nonexisting superego has little if anything to say.

Every one of these three types can be divided into five *levels* of deterioration, largely related to the strength of the ego. As long as the ego exercises some degree of control over the id, using a variety of defense mechanisms, the personality remains on the *neurotic* level. As soon as the ego accepts the defenses and uses them as a *protective shield, character neurosis* results. When the ego fails but still retains some vestige of control, the hyperinstrumental *latent psychosis* is produced. When the ego has lost its grip on reality, the result is a manifest hyperinstrumental psychosis, so well described as *moral insanity*. When the total personality structure collapses, a dementive stage begins. (See the table on page 252.)

The Hypervectorial Type

Hypervectorials are the extreme opposite of hyperinstrumentals, for they act in a vectorial manner even in situations in which normal behavior is usually instrumental. In their childhood they were not allowed to be instrumental as most other children were, but they were forced by their parents to assume too early and too severe commitments. They were "overdemanded," held responsible, and forced to worry prematurely. As adults they are overanxious to please others. Unless they are badly deteriorated, they seem to believe that life is a duty to be honored or a ritual to be followed. They display a variety of obsessive and phobic symptoms aimed at warding off the fear of their own hostility. They have sympathy for everyone except themselves. When they are in love, they are either shallow or deeply involved and are often domineering and despotic in their overprotectiveness. When their exaggerated self-controls fail, they regress into autistic seclusion.

In psychoanalytic terms the hypervectorials have an overgrown, severe, and overdemanding superego. Their libido is object-hypercathected and self-hypocathected. The destrudo is usually self-directed, and symptom formation is geared to primary gain, mainly to alleviation of guilt feelings.

The hypervectorial disorder is represented on the neurotic level by three distinct syndromes, namely the phobic, the neurosthenic, and the obsessive. In some cases the neurotic symptoms "take over" and become a sort of "armor": Thus an obsessive, schizoid, or hypervectorial (I use the three terms synonymously) character neurosis develops. When the defenses fail, latent schizophrenia begins, which may lead to a manifest and, in some neglected cases, to a dementive stage.

K. Abraham erroneously linked obsessions to manic-depressive disorders, but in 1911 Bleuler (1950, pp. 449 ff.) and later on the mainstream of psychoanalytic thought recognized the connection between obsession and schizophrenia (Fenichel, 1945, pp. 424 ff.). Freud's analysis of the obsessive neurosis (also called psychasthenia) pointed to the typical relationship between the ego and the superego. In this neurosis the superego "is very exacting, but the ego rebels against the guilt feeling imposed by the superego" (Freud, 1920). This "rebellion" is, I believe, nothing else but the dependence-independence syndrome of schizophrenia reflecting the internalized maternal demands, the child's hostile rebellion against them, and the child's fear that his hostile rebellion may kill his mother. Hence, ritualistic compulsions develop to ward off the threat of doing something wrong. Practically every obsessive-compulsive neurotic, in striking similarity to schizophrenics, is tormented by recurring thoughts that he may hurt his relatives, or commit a sacrilege, or eliminate in public, or practice incest or homosexuality. There is there the invariable feeling of "being pushed to do something wrong and pulled back from doing it." "Do" and "don't" are indispensable elements of this neurosis. The impulses "consist of something terrifying such as temptations to commit serious crimes, so that the patient not only repudiates them as alien but flees from them in horror and guards himself by prohibitions, precautions, and restrictions against the possibility of carrying them out" (Freud, 1915–1917, p. 229).

The main defense mechanisms in the obsessive neurosis are repression, displacement, undoing, and reaction formation. The individual feels compelled to perform certain activities that cannot be rationally justified. Many obsessive-compulsive patients keep washing and scrubbing their hands, although they know that there is no real need for such continual washing. Obsessive actions "are mostly repetitions and ceremonial elaborations of ordinary everyday performances, making these common necessary actions—

going to bed, washing, dressing for walks, etc.—into highly laborious tasks of almost insuperable difficulty" (Freud, 1915–1917, pp. 229–230).

Phobias are probably as frequent in this neurosis as compulsions. Phobias apply the mechanism of displacement (A. Freud, 1946). Fear of becoming a rapist was displaced in one patient of mine and transformed into a fear of going out and of being in the open, called agoraphobia. A man who feared hurting his father developed a fear of cutting bread; a female patient displaced her fear of a penis into a fear of roosters.

Phobias can change into compulsive actions, and obsessive thoughts can turn into phobias. Psychoanalytic theory offers an ample explanation of these phenomena. The obsessive-compulsive neurotic who is

> threatened by the rebellion of his (regressively distorted) sensual and hostile demands feels protected as long as he behaves in an "orderly" manner. . . . The unconscious anal-sadistic drives, however, usually sabotage orderliness. . . . Any disturbance of "routine" unconsciously means murder and incest. . . . Compulsion ensures against the menace of dangerous spontaneity. . . . The compulsion neurotic is aware that he has instinct nevertheless. He can never achieve the satisfying feeling that he is actually following the rules, that enough rules are provided to govern all possibilities, and that he knows all the rules sufficiently (Fenichel, 1945, pp. 284–285).

When schizophrenics improve, they frequently go back to a neurotic stage of the hypervectorial type. This phenomena has been observed by J. N. Rosen:

> We have observed that without exception every psychotic patient we have had has passed through a phase of his illness which was characterized by a preponderance of paranoid ideas. Many patients remain at this stage which the colleagues agree to call paranoid; some go on for one reason or another to levels of deeper regression, namely hebephrenia and catatonia, and others even improve back to a severe form of neurosis, particularly of the obsessive-compulsive type (Rosen, 1953, p. 97).

Compulsions and Schizophrenia

E. Bleuler (1950, pp. 449 ff.) as early as 1911 underscored the connection between catatonic automatisms, hallucinations, and obsessive ideas and compulsive acts. He wrote: "When compulsive ideas occur in conjunction with schizophrenia, the symptoms of the latter disease become manifest very early in the course of the illness and . . . assume a prominent position" (p. 451). Bleuler quoted a case of a man who sexually desired one of his relatives; after some time, voices accused him of a sex crime; then they whispered that he was going to cause a disaster. When after eleven years the compulsive ideas became converted into commanding voices, the patient committed a murderous attack. Bleuler's case was apparently a case of an obsessive-compulsive neurotic who turned into a latent and later into a manifest schizophrenic. The basic conflict in schizophrenia, the struggle against one's own impulses that threaten the hypercathected love object, is always present in the obsessive neurosis.

As early as 1894 Freud explained that repressed ideas lead to obsessive-compulsive symptoms. In some cases, however, "the ego rejects the unbearable idea together with its associated affect and behaves as if the idea never occurred to the person at all. But, as soon as this process has been successfully carried through, the person in question will have developed a psychosis, and his state can only be described as one of 'hallucinatory confusion'" (Freud, 1894, Vol. 3, p. 52).

My interpretation of the transition of an obsession into a hallucination is somewhat different; it is the victory of the repressed desire that breaks through the defense mechanisms. Hallucinations bear witness to a defeat of the ego that has lost its contact with reality (Wolman, 1966a, Chap. 4).

Preschizophrenia or hypervectorial neurosis has a rich symptomatology; the so-called obsessive-compulsive neurosis is, probably, not a clinical entity but a cluster of observable symptoms; obsessive neurosis is one of the syndromes of the hypervectorial neurosis.

Once we understand the economy processes, that is, the balance of cathexes of libido and destrudo, the topography, that is, the relative position of conscious, preconscious, and unconscious processes, and the structure, that is, the interaction of the id, ego, and superego, the variety of symptoms ceases to be an unpredictable aggregate. It becomes instead a clear though complex fabric of interrelated factors, which points to the basic hypervectorial personality distortion that is typical of both the hypervectorial neurosis and the hypervectorial psychosis (schizophrenia).

Obsessive-compulsive neurotics were criticized in their childhood for not being good enough, for hurting their poor mothers, and for being ungrateful and unfair. Irate mothers may say to a naughty child, "I will kill you." Mothers of children who develop anyone of the hypervectorial disorders tell their children, "You are killing your mother." Whether mothers punish or not, they always put the blame on their children. The hypervectorial child has no way to win, no way to prove or to expiate; mother holds the grudge for an unlimited time and makes the child feel responsible for her troubles.

Obsessive-compulsive neurotics are "overdemanded," criticized, blamed, and held responsible for their mother's true or imaginary hardships. Their inadequate and not-too-parental parents blame their children and involve them emotionally. All hypervectorials were forced into a precocious object hypercathexis with their parents; and all of them became their parents' protectors and parents.

There has been somewhat less confusion about sex roles in the families of obsessive-compulsives as compared to manifest schizophrenics; there has been less irrationality in interaction and little violence between the parents. The resulting disorder was less severe, yet the basic schizogenic family patterns were present in all obsessive-compulsive neurotics (Wolman, 1966a).

An obsessive-compulsive neurotic always worries about his parents. One patient always asked in his childhood where his parents were going and when they would be back; during the day he would wait at the corner before the house. When they went to a show or to the movies, he had to know the row and the numbers of their seats. He would lie in bed with his eyes wide open and wait till they came back, worrying about his "poor" parents.

Obsessive-compulsive neurosis starts, as do all other hypervectorial disorders or the group of schizophrenias, as an object hypercathexis. Mothers of the hypervectorials were demanding, instrumental, and "imperialistic" in regard to their husbands; fathers were instrumental and insisted on being the only child of their own wives. Both parents were instrumental in regard to their children, the mother in a subtle-symbiotic, the father in a competitive or seductive way. More research is needed to find more precisely to what extent the moderation in the schizogenic family patterns leads to less serious hypervectorial disorders in offspring.

On the neurotic level of the hypervectorial disorder, compulsive and phobic symptoms can be grouped into clusters or syndromes. In the typical hypervectorial struggle of the ego against the pressure of the superego, compulsions and phobias play an outstanding and easily observable role. The ego frequently protects itself against the onslaught of the superego by using displacements and repressions. When the ego fails, compulsions may turn into catatonic automatism and phobias may become delusions. For instance, the fear of bacteria may turn into delusions of being destroyed by them.

The Paramutual Type

The paramutuals (hysterics, manic-depressives, etc.) are masters of inconsistency. The paramutuals may overdo their love for others as hypervectorials do, or they may feel no love whatsoever for others and be as narcissistic as the hyperinstrumentals. The paramutuals are very demanding and expect their love objects to reciprocate generously and repay their love with a high interest rate. When a paramutual is in love he usually becomes hyperaffectionate, showering his love objects with protectiveness and tenderness, and he exaggerates and overdoes his readiness for self-sacrifice. Should, however, the love object not reciprocate, the love of the paramutual easily turns into a vehement hatred. His assumedly giving, undemanding, and unselfish love may turn into a selfish, malicious, and even brutal hostility. Not only is his object love easily transformed into hate, but the same process takes place in his intraindividual cathexes. The hysterics or manic-depressives usually love themselves very much, but when they are rejected by others, their self-directed love can be momentarily turned into hate and can lead to suicide attempts. The shifting cyclic moods reflect their libido and destrudo disbalance. Their mood is elated when they feel loved, and then they believe themselves to be great, strong, and wonderful.

When a paramutual feels rejected, he believes he is weak, unworthy, and destitute. He then becomes hostile, and his mood is depressed. These fluctuations in mood give rise to the name manic-depressive. Actually, they are fluctuations of exaggerated feelings of love and hate toward the self and others. In a loving mood the paramutuals are Dr. Jekyll; in a hating mood they are Mr. Hyde. Since none of these moods are lasting, they often give the impression of being insincere and often even dishonest. Actually, they swing from extreme honesty to dishonesty, from love to hate, from heroism to cowardice, from self-sacrifice to extreme selfishness.

The paramutual or the cyclothymic type is a "love addict" who feels hate whenever he feels rejected. His libido swings back and forth from object cathexis to self-cathexis and from libido to destrudo, depending on whether or not he feels loved.

I do not adhere to Abraham's timetable of fixations, but undoubtedly there are oral-aggressive elements in this group of disorders. When hysterics or manic-depressives receive libido cathexis from without, they love themselves and love those who love them, and they express their feeling in a verbose, exultant, and inconsistent manner. The paramutual believes himself to be ready for any self-sacrifice, though he loves only those who love him and is actually in love only with himself. His "giving" attitude is immediately discontinued if not met with abundant love, praise, and other rewards. A rejected paramutual hates himself and others: The loving Dr. Jekyll turns into the hating Mr. Hyde. On a neurotic level (hysteria and related conditions) the paramutual sounds theatrical and melodramatic, as a soap-opera actor who seems to believe himself to be a hero, unaware of the fact that he is just overplaying his role. Charcot's patients dramatically acted out this syndrome of swinging moods, dramatization, imaginary illnesses, and a variety of psychosomatic symptoms. Paramutuals are rarely if ever conscious liars, but they are easily carried away by their swinging emotions and do and say things that are not true; in calmer moods they may admit that they have been carried away in their *pseudologia fantastica* and have overdramatized their feelings. On a psychotic level, in manic-depressive psychosis, they lose contact with reality and are driven by the blind forces of libido and destrudo (Wolman, 1966d).

As long as the ego of the paramutual controls, to some extent, the swinging libido and destrudo cathexes, a neurosis is maintained. On latent and manifest psychotic levels the ego surrenders to the inconsistent superego. Depression ensues whenever the ego is viciously attacked by the superego; the danger of suicide is quite great in these cases. Whenever the ego surrenders to the superego and merges with it, a blissful state of elation and exulted mania develops. The manic-depressive patient experiences in a manic state the feelings of an infant or those of a neonate who craves becoming one with his mother's body. In elation the superego embraces the ego; in such a euphoric, blissful mood the paramutual psychotic experiences oceanic love for himself and for the entire universe. Obviously, secondary gain or the winning of social approval, and primary gain from thwarting the unbearable depression are the objectives of symptom formation in paramutual disorders.

Neurosis-Psychosis

In a paper on "Neurosis and Psychosis" published in 1924, Freud stated the following: "Neurosis is a result of a conflict between the ego and its id, whereas psychosis is the analogous outcome of a similar disturbance in relation between the ego and its environment [outer world]." In the same paper, Freud also distinguished "narcissistic neurosis," where the conflict took place between the ego and the superego. In the *Outline of Psychoanalysis*, written in 1938, he wrote that "the precipitating cause of the outbreak of psychosis is either that reality has become intolerably painful or that the instincts have become extraordinarily intensified," which caused the withdrawal of the ego from reality (Freud, 1938, p. 114).

The difference between neurosis and psychosis depends on the strength of the ego. Neurosis persists as long as the ego preserves its contact with the external world and controls the id. A break with reality and a victory of the impulses of the id signalize a full, manifest psychosis. Psychosis is most often a neurosis that failed.

As mentioned before, not all psychotics were neurotic prior to becoming psychotics, although many of them certainly were. Psychosis may start in childhood with a failing ego that never was strong enough to develop a neurosis. In some cases the development toward schizophrenia was temporarily or entirely stopped with the help of neurotic defense mechanisms that have produced ego-protective symptoms.

The analyst must be keenly aware of not only what *type* of disorder he treats but also of what the *level* of the disorder is. The type is largely determined by the economy of cathexes. The level depends mainly on topographic and structural factors. In neurosis and character neurosis the unconscious is repressed; in latent psychosis the unconscious is just about to break through; in manifest psychosis the breakthrough is a *fait accompli;* in dementive psychosis very little of the conscious is left.

In neurosis the ego struggles with the help of defense mechanisms. Of course, in the hyperinstrumental type the neurosis is characterized by a mild warding off of the id impulses with no superego intervention. In hypervectorial neuroses (phobias, neurasthenias, and obsessions) there is a desperate struggle against the id and mainly superego. In hysterics and other paramutual neuroses the ego swings from a struggle against the superego to a merger with it. In all types of character neuroses the neurotic symptoms become an intrinsic part of the ego or "blended into personality" (Fenichel, 1945, p. 463 ff.).

On the neurotic and character-neurotic levels the main methods of classic psychoanalysis are applicable. I shall, however, suggest below certain modifications of the technique according to the three types. On the character-neurosis level one has to consider W. Reich's ideas, as exposed in the early edition of his work (1933). On the latent and manifest psychotic *levels* far-reaching modifications are necessary (cf. Federn, 1952; Wolman, 1959, 1966a). The framework of a collective volume does not permit a detailed description; I shall, however, outline the main modifications related to the three *types,* limiting my presentation to the neurotic level.

Transference as Interaction

The management of transference and resistance is the core of psycho-analytic treatment. Transference is a process of *interindividual cathexis* in which one cathects his love or hate in people who remind him of significant figures of his past. I am inclined to see in transference an application of the principle of "repetition compulsion." Transference also occurs outside the psychoanalytic relationship. When a man falls in love with a girl because she reminds him of his mother, he is repeating a past situation and his present interindividual libido cathexis is based on past experiences. Human preferences for music, resort places, fashions, and colors are often a result of past cathexes re-experienced in a transference situation.

Resistance is a process of *intraindividual cathexis.* The same inhibitory forces of ego or superego that acted as anticathexes and repressants are reactivated as resistances in the psychoanalytic process. Present resistance is a continuation of past repressions.

Both transference and resistance are parts of here-and-now behavior. The patient relates to the analyst partly on the basis of past experiences, but he partly reacts to the real situation. His demands for instinctual gratifica-tion are mainly transference, they represent a reactivation of his past infantile wishes. But an adult patient is not an infant. He is an adult who pays for therapeutic services, and his demands, rational or irrational, are a part of the here-and-now situation.

In the process of treatment the analyst is never truly passive. His very presence, his age, sex, looks, manner of speech, and certainly his sparse comments are interactional phenomena. They are powerful factors in shaping the patient's feelings, thoughts, and actions, partially in trans-ference and certainly in the realistic part of the patient's attitudes.

Thus, whatever goes on between the analyst and his patient is a process of interaction. It is always an *exchange of cathexes,* perceived correctly or misinterpreted by the patient and sometimes also by the analyst. The silent analyst may be perceived by his patients as a taciturn or unfriendly indi-vidual, who is, or pretends to be, or tries to give the impression of being, an omnipotent figure. If the analyst really tries to impress, it is his counter-transference blunder. But whatever he tries to do, and whatever he says or does, there is always interaction.

Therefore, I venture to say that *transference is always manipulated by the analyst.* Not only do I agree with F. Alexander and T. French (1946) that transference *should be* regulated, but I would say that *it is always, wittingly or unwittingly, regulated* by the analyst.

Every psychoanalytic treatment is, as Fenichel put it, "based on the analyst's influence on the patient" (1945, p. 447). I suggest that this influence be made explicit in the theory of psychoanalytic treatment and that the analyst become more *aware* of the nature of their influence, for no matter what the analyst's point of view is, he anyway and always *regulates transference*. He regulates it by imposing the "basic rule," by suggesting the reclining position, by saying or not saying, "How are you?" by smiling or not smiling, and so on.

Several years ago I observed interindividual processes on a closed ward. Although my policy was one of a strict nonparticipant observation, my very presence on the ward influenced the behavior of the patients (Wolman, 1964). In the one-to-one relationship everything pertaining to the analyst *must* affect the patient and influence the transference irrespective of the analyst's intentions.

Marmor criticized the classic approach. He wrote that "The original theoretical dictum that the analyst must be a shadowy, neutral, impersonal, and a value-free figure is coming to be recognized not only as a practical impossibility, but even as being in some instances at least of questionable therapeutic value" (Marmor, 1960). My contention is that since no analyst is really "shadowy, neutral, etc.," he must *be aware of what he is and what he is doing.* I prefer the explicit to the implicit attitude. Instead of influencing by default, I prefer influencing in a rational and planned manner. Instead of a purely intuitive approach, I suggest a carefully chosen therapeutic strategy related to the clinical types and levels of deterioration.

Freud's difficulty with schizophrenics as compared with Federn's success with them is a case in point. The insistence on a reclining position facilitated topographic regression; this regression was promoted even more by the "basic rule" of free association; and finally, the analyst's remoteness and silence contributed to the schizophrenic tension and withdrawal. No wonder Freud believed that schizophrenia is a nontransference disorder (Freud, 1915–1917; Fenichel, 1945, Chap. 18). But Federn, who admitted schizophrenics to his home, witnessed most profound transference (1952). In my own work with schizophrenics described in a recently published monograph (Wolman, 1966a), I have advocated the rule of *getting involved* with the patient's cause *without getting involved* with the patient in a personal way (avoidance of countertransference).

The analyst's role in shaping the patient's transference is only a part of the truth. Transference, as a repetition of past cathexes, greatly depends on the past interindividual experiences. In transference, the patient re-enacts the pathogenesis of neurosis. Freud was aware of the differences in the types of transference. I have been trying to make this awareness more explicit and to explain it in terms of the above-mentioned three sociopsychological types of overt behavior. The concept of the three types is isomorphic to the Freudian balance of inter- and intraindividual cathexes. The hyperinstrumental type represents self-hypercathexis and object hypocathexis of libido; the hypervectorial type is based on self-hypocathexis and object hypercathexis of libido; the paramutual swings from one extreme to the other.

Treatment of the Paramutual Type

Freud's description of transference given in 1920 in *Beyond the Pleasure Principle* fits the paramutual type of neurosis (conversion hysteria, etc.).

> Loss of love and failure leave behind them a permanent injury to self-assurance in the form of a narcissistic scar, which . . . contributes more than anything to the "sense of inferiority." The tie of affection, which binds the child as a rule to the parent of the opposite sex, succumbs to disappointment. . . .
>
> Patients repeat all of these invented situations and painful emotions in the transference and revive them with the greatest ingenuity. They seek to bring about the interruption of the treatment while it is still incomplete; they contrive once more to feel themselves scorned. . . . None of these things can have produced pleasure in the past. . . . But no lesson has been learned from the old experience of these activities having led instead only to unpleasure (Freud, 1920, pp. 22–23).

This repetition compulsion is undoubtedly a universal phenomenon, but not all neurotics repeat the same behavioral patterns. The above description of rejected love is typical for *paramutuals* only.

It seems that noninvolvement is the best way to handle this type of transference. The paramutual neurotic quickly develops positive transference. He or she falls in love with the allegedly omnipotent and benevolent parental figure. The analyst's attentive attitude is perceived as a keen interest in the patient, who, in turn, responds with glowing love to the meager signs of approval. The analyst represents the benevolent superego that does not criticize the patient no matter what the patient says. The true parents, and especially the mother of the hysteric, were highly critical of the patient. Only on those occasions when the patient was very ill or in great danger did the parents show any affection. The paramutual dreams of the "lost paradise," when he was one with his mother, and he tries to recapture it by self-defeat. As long as the paramutual believes that he is loved, he re-enacts in transference the oral love for himself, the analyst, and everyone else.

The paramutuals easily swing from positive to negative transference. As long as they imagine that the analyst loves them, they are in a blissful euphoria. Most symptoms disappear, and the analytic hours become, as one of my patients put it, "the happiest hours in one's life."

But this imaginary love does not suffice for a long time. Pretty soon they begin to demand more attention, more love, and more tangential proof of the analyst's alleged love for them. A male hysteric who developed a homosexual crush in transference demanded an increased number of sessions and the right to call me several times a day. He planned to take an apartment nearby. A young woman complained: "You are nice to all your patients. But I am not just a patient. I love you. Why can't you make me happy?" A male patient said: "I know that you are a homosexual. Why can't we?" A learned female patient assured me that "active" psychoanalysts slept with their patients.

The paramutuals protest the iron rule of frustrating the instinctual demands of patients. Their love turns easily into hate, object hate of the analyst and self-hate of themselves. Libido recedes and destrudo takes over. Paramutual patients either hate the analyst (interindividual cathexes of destrudo) or hate themselves (intraindividual cathexis of destrudo), or both. "I know you hate me, you detest me, you cannot stand me," said a charming twenty-eight-year-old female hysteric. "You are right. I hate myself too. I know I do not deserve to be loved."

In the transference process, the paramutual patient goes through the love-hate swings of his past experience, shifting from positive to negative transference back and forth.

Woe to the analyst who lets himself be drawn into the treadmill of the emotional ups and downs of a paramutual patient! The detached, objective, matter-of-fact treatment of transference combined with an incisive interpretation of resistance and transference used as a resistance is the choice method. Let us remember that the treatment of paramutuals has been the bedrock of the classic psychoanalysis.

Treatment of the Hypervectorials

I do not plan to give here a detailed description of the interactional technique; I intend to prepare in the future a separate monograph with several typical case illustrations. In the framework of the present collective volume I intend to dwell mainly on the *rationale* of the interactional technique, keeping descriptive material at a minimum. My main purpose is to show that my modifications in the classic technique were derived from Freud's clinical writings.

The peculiar difficulty in working with cases of hypervectorial neurosis lies in their excessive resistance. One of the motives of resistance is a strong need for punishment, associated with masochistic wishes. This unconscious need for punishment corresponds "to a piece of aggressiveness which has been internalized and taken over by the superego."

"We are in doubt whether we ought to suppose that all aggressiveness that has turned back from the external world is bound by the superego, and so used against the ego, or whether a part of it carries on its silent sinister activity as a free destructive instinct in the ego and the id. Probably there is a division of this kind but we know nothing further about it. When first the superego is set up, there is no doubt that the function is endowed with that part of the child's aggressiveness against its parents for which it can find no discharge outward on account of its love fixation and external difficulties; and for this reason, the severity of the superego need not correspond to the severity of its upbringing" (Freud, 1933, p. 150).

And further on Freud wrote:

> People in whom this unconscious guilt feeling is dominant, distinguish themselves under analytic treatment of exhibiting . . . a negative therapeutic reaction. In the normal course of events, if one gives a patient the solution of a symptom, at least the temporary disappearance of the symptom should result, with these patients, on the contrary, the effect is a momentary intensification of the symptom and the suffering that accompanies it. It often needs only a word of praise of their behavior during the cure, the utterance of a few words of hope as to the progress of analysis, to bring about an unmistakable aggravation of their condition. . . . Their behavior will appear as an expression of an unconscious sense of guilt, which favors illness with its attendant suffering and handicaps (1933, pp. 150–151).

The analyst's passive attitude and nonparticipant listening to free association certainly is not the choice method of dealing with hypervectorial neurotics. Such an attitude produces too much anxiety and may therefore foster topographic regression.

The analyst's silent and passive listening may be perceived by hypervectorial neurotics (obsessives, phobics, and neurasthenics) as a rejection. They do not protest against rejection; they tend to accept it as a well-deserved punishment. One cannot cure a masochist by rejecting him.

Freud (as quoted above in the section on Obsessions and Phobias) recommended active interpretation and direct influence. As soon as transference is established, the analyst must induce the phobic patient to mollify his phobic overt behavior prior to the resolution of the underlying unconscious motives.

Negative transference can turn into resistance. The hypervectorial neurotic is *afraid* to give up his defenses, especially the compulsions and phobias. Compulsions and phobias serve as protection against the patient's own hostile feelings toward his parents, re-enacted in transference. "I am afraid I may hurt you," said a twenty-eight-year-old patient. "I feel like doing something very bad."

This hostility requires a thorough interpretation; otherwise, the patient may repress it and turn it inward. Expression of hostility must be encouraged; but interpretation and working through of hostility is necessary not only with hypervectorials.

Without resolving it, the fear of the patient's own hostility will result in prolonged periods of arid silence, resembling the stuporous attitude of catatonics who fear to say and do the wrong thing.

In the process of psychoanalytic treatment of hypervectorials, a passive, detached attitude on the part of the analyst will unduly prolong the treatment and, perhaps, make analysis interminable. The analyst must be vectorial, that is, genuinely friendly. He must not, however, transgress his professional role, nor violate the ethical and professional rules of frustrating the patient's instinctual demands. He must never fall into the trap of counter-transference and become a copy of the incestuous and seductive or seducible parent. A moderate, aim-inhibited interest in the patient's well-being is necessary. Such an attitude of friendliness and respect for the patient will help to increase the patient's self-esteem and improve the intraindividual balance of libido cathexes. (Cf. Wolman, 1966a, Ch. 6.)

The dictatorial, overdemanding, irrational superego of hypervectorials must be reshaped. Its irrationality must be exposed and the ensuing severe guilt feelings interpreted and worked through. The analyst must time his interpretations, but he cannot wait forever. The armor of resistances must be taken apart before any significant progress can be accomplished.

The best method of handling the exaggerated accusations of the superego is to support the ego. Ego therapy is the necessary last phase of analysis with all types, but in the treatment of hypervectorials it plays a significant role in the resolution of transference. The hypervectorial patients tend to ascribe to the analyst the role their parents played and their superego continues to play, and the analyst may soon discover that the patient ascribes to him dictatorial and punitive tendencies. A continuous check and recheck and testing of reality is necessary to support the ego and to counteract the deep-rooted tendencies for rationalization, projection, and displacement.

The profound transference of hypervectorials may make analysis interminable. Many neurasthenic, phobic, and obsession patients (the hypervectorials) may feel kind of an obligation toward the analyst as if he were their "poor" mommy or daddy. They may fear that he will die if abandoned by them.

It seems advisable to *prevent* too deep a transference in all hypervectorials, especially in the more severe cases. The more outspoken the analyst is, the smaller are the chances for a deep transference. When a hysteric showers the analyst with personal questions, the analyst either does not respond or analyzes the patient's curiosity. But when a frightened obsessive neurotic or latent schizophrenic poses the same question, a frank and honest answer seems to be advisable. The patient's questions, "Are you married; do you have children?" and so on, should be answered by the analyst in a matter-of-fact fashion. There is no reason to surrender to countertransference and confide in the patient, but a clear-cut answer keeps him close to reality and reduces the danger of too vehement a transference.

Treatment of Hyperinstrumentals

Suffering is the main motive that forces people to seek professional help. Small wonder that the hyperinstrumentals (psychopaths) rarely seek psychoanalysis. They have little reason to seek help, for they rarely suffer severe inner conflicts; as a rule they make others suffer. Being highly self-cathected, they may occasionally suffer from hypochondrial fears, anxiety states caused by the erupting id impulses, or inferiority feelings stemming from defeat or frustration. They may also seek secondary gain by assuming the sick role or wearing the mask of being innocent victims of misfortunes. When they come for help, they seek immediate results and are prone to break off the analysis as soon as they feel better.

In some Veterans' Administration hospitals hyperinstrumentals become hard-core cases who resist any therapy. They prefer staying in the hospital and continuing a parasitic life. One of my psychopathic patients used to hospitalize himself frequently with a variety of imaginary physical illnesses. Whenever he faced difficulties in business or in marital life, he escaped into illness. He came to me for treatment to "get something out of it" and to "get the right guidance." Of course, he bragged to whomever he knew that he had serious mental problems and was undergoing psychoanalysis.

The psychopaths, on all five levels, are not inclined to invest their libido in anyone; and their transference, if any, stays shallow. Whereas I have urged the prevention of a too-deep transference in hypervectorials, the crucial task with hyperinstrumentals is to foster as deep a transference as possible and mollify their negative transference. Needless to say, hyperinstrumentals hate whoever frustrates their wishes for immediate gratification.

Manipulation of transference in these cases is not an easy task. The hyperinstrumentals have learned in their childhood to defend themselves against unfair and rejecting parents or absentee or overindulgent parents. In either case, the pre-hyperinstrumental has never had the opportunity to identify with any of his parents. Most of the hyperinstrumentals are polymorphous perverts. Although they are very aggressive, they perceive themselves as defenseless, innocent children. This attitude colors their oral-aggressive transference.

One patient spent hour after hour directing against me most malicious accusations. Whatever wrong was done to her by her parents (truly or in her imagination) was ascribed to me. She expected retaliation on my part, which, of course, never came. Her amazement at the lack of hostility was, as Alexander would put it, "a therapeutic corrective experience."

Another patient was describing his fantastically ingenious deceits and frauds. "Everybody does it, don't they?" he asked. His father and mother were exceedingly permissive, but the outer world was less permissive; he was caught and punished. He believed the world was hostile to him and developed paranoid fears.

The analyst who treats psychopaths cannot stay neutral. Normality includes social adjustment and a reasonable balance of inter- and intra-individual cathexes; it includes a balanced love for oneself and others and a balance of criticism of oneself and others. A rational superego is an indispensable part of a healthy personality.

Thus the analyst faces a complex task. His silent permissiveness may be misinterpreted as siding with the id. An expression of disapproval by the analyst is not good either, for this may lead to the inclusion of the analyst in the paranoid picture of world conspiracy against the poor, innocent patient. The analyst must take a stand and help in developing the patient's superego, but he must wait till the transference is sufficiently strong. Interpretation must wait until the patient is ready to accept it, and even then firmness must be combined with caution. An exclusively passive or a too-early and too-active intervention may lead to a breaking off of the treatment.

Remarks on Treatment of Psychotics

A detailed description of work with schizophrenia has been given elsewhere (Wolman, 1966a), and a description of treatment of manic-depressive psychotics is forthcoming. Therapy of psychotics must necessarily differ from the classic analysis (Bychowski, 1952; Eissler, 1954; Brody and Redlich, 1952; Mendelson, 1960; and others). Some authors prefer to avoid the name psychoanalysis in such cases, but a clear-cut distinction between psychoanalysis proper and psychoanalytic psychotherapy seems rather impossible. Whatever the term used, psychoanalysis or psychoanalytic therapy, the modifications in the technique must be far-reaching when one works with psychotics.

The main modifications are dictated by the comparative weakness of the ego. Every analytic treatment is interaction, classic or modified, and, as such, must be geared to the specific needs of the patient. I did not discuss those aspects of technique that apply to all three *types* of patients, such as dream interpretation and working through. The differences are related to the five *levels*. In working with overt psychotics dream interpretation is superfluous; with latent psychotics it may be dangerous. The removal of defense mechanisms is necessary in the treatment of neurotics; it is the main task in working with character neurotics; with psychotics one may have to support the neurotic defenses (I have called them ego-protective symptoms, 1966a) against the danger of a total collapse of the ego.

In his "Recommendations to Physicians Practicing Psychoanalysis" (1912b) Freud cautioned analysts against being overambitious and recommended "tolerance for the patients' weakness." This advice must be strongly recommended in regard to psychotics. The final stage of psychoanalysis is, as Glover put it (1955, p. 139), dedicated to *transference weaning* and *ego readaptation*. Treatment of psychotics is from the beginning to the end a readaptation of the ego. Supportive therapy is necessary for all three types, but it must be applied differently for each type. Testing reality, manipulating of the superego, and even a directive approach may be necessary at the initial phase of treatment of the psychotic.

Instead of a Summary

I hope I have drawn the implications and inferences from Freud's teaching and continued his work in the direction that could be logically derived from the general course of his thought. I am profoundly indebted to Anna Freud, H. Hartmann, E. Kris, and R. Loewenstein for the new ideas on ego therapy, and I have been mostly influenced by P. Federn's work with psychotics and F. Alexander's and T. French's modification in the technique.

I do not suggest radical changes in technique. What I propose is mainly to *look into* what is actually going on in the psychoanalytic situation and to call a spade a spade. I try to make the interactional process explicit.

Freud said in 1907: "The patient is compelled to give up his resistance to please us. Our cures are cures of love. . . . To the extent that transference exists—to that extent can we bring about cures . . ." (Nunberg and Federn, 1962, Vol. 1, p. 101). I suggested taking a close look at the types of transference, revising accordingly the classification of mental disorders, and adjusting, whenever necessary, the technique to the three clinical types and the five levels.

At this point I do substantially deviate from Freud in the theory and classification of mental disorders. I believe Freud was unnecessarily loyal to Kraepelin's system. I venture to say that my system of classification into hypovectorials, paramutuals, and hyperinstrumentals makes better use of Freud's concepts of cathexis than Freud's three types and is certainly better than the system Freud borrowed from Kraepelin. These and other modifications in the psychoanalytical conceptual framework and technique are, I believe, in harmony with Freud's basic concepts and in better agreement with clinical data.

REFERENCES

[Note: S.E. refers to *The Standard Edition of the complete psychological works of Sigmund Freud* (London: Hogarth Press).]

ABRAHAM, K. Notes on the psychoanalytic investigation and treatment of manic-depressive insanity and allied conditions (1911). *Selected papers.*

London: Hogarth, 1927. Pp. 137–156. (Also published by Basic Books, New York, 1953.)

ABRAHAM, K. A short study of the development of the libido, viewed in the light of mental disorders (1924). *Ibid.,* pp. 418–479.

ALEXANDER, F., and FRENCH, T. M. *Psychoanalytic therapy.* New York: Ronald Press, 1946.

BLEULER, E. *Dementia praecox or the group of schizophrenias* (1911). New York: International Universities Press, 1950.

BOUDY, E. B., and REDLICH, F. C. (Eds.) *Psychotherapy with schizophrenics: a symposium.* New York: International Universities Press, 1952.

BREUER, J., and FREUD, S. Studies on hysteria (1895) S.E., Vol. 2. (Also published by Basic Books, New York, 1957.)

BYCHOWSKI, G. *Psychotherapy of psychosis.* New York: Grune and Stratton, 1952.

CLECKLEY, H. *The mask of sanity* (2nd ed.). St. Louis: Mosby, 1950.

EISSLER, K. R. Notes upon defects of ego structure in schizophrenia. *International Journal of Psychoanalysis,* 1954, **35,** 141–146.

FEDERN, P. *Ego psychology and the psychoses.* New York: Basic Books, 1952.

FENICHEL, O. *The psychoanalytic theory of neurosis.* New York: Norton, 1945.

FREUD, ANNA. *The ego and the mechanisms of defense.* New York: International Universities Press, 1946.

FREUD, S. *On aphasia, a critical study* (1891). New York: International Universities Press, 1953.

FREUD, S. The neuro-psychoses of defence (1894). S.E., Vol. 3, pp. 45–61.

FREUD, S. Freud's psycho-analytic procedure (1904). S.E., Vol. 7, pp. 249–256.

FREUD, S. The future prospects of psycho-analytic theory (1910). S.E., Vol. 11, pp. 139–152. (a)

FREUD, S. "Wild" psychoanalysis (1910). S.E., Vol. 2, pp. 219–230. (b)

FREUD, S. The dynamics of transference (1912). S.E., Vol. 12, pp. 97–108. (a)

FREUD, S. Recommendations to physicians practicing psychoanalysis (1912). S.E., Vol. 12, pp. 109–120. (b)

FREUD, S. The unconscious (1915). S.E., Vol. 14, pp. 166–215.

FREUD, S. *Introductory lectures on psycho-analysis* (1915–1917). S.E., Vols. 15 and 16.

FREUD, S. Lines of advance in psychoanalytic therapy (1919). S.E., Vol. 17, pp. 157–168.

FREUD, S. *Beyond the pleasure principle* (1920). S.E., Vol. 18, pp. 1–64.

FREUD, S. A seventeenth century demonological neurosis (1923). S.E., Vol. 19, pp. 72–105.

FREUD, S. Neurosis and psychosis. (1924). S.E., Vol. 19, pp. 149–153.

FREUD, S. Libidinal types (1931). S.E., Vol. 21, pp. 217–220.

FREUD, S. *New introductory lectures on psychoanalysis* (1933). S.E., Vol. 22.

FREUD, S. *An outline of psychoanalysis* (1938). S.E., Vol. 23.

GLOVER, E. *The technique of psychoanalysis.* New York: International Universities Press, 1955.

MARMOR, J. The reintegration of psychoanalysis into psychiatric practice. *Archives of General Psychiatry,* 1960, **3,** 569–574.

MENDELSON, M. *Psychoanalytic concept of depression.* Springfield, Ill.: Charles C Thomas, 1960.

NUNBERG, H., and FEDERN, E. (Eds.) *Minutes of the Vienna Psychoanalytic Society.* New York: International Universities Press, 1962.

PANEL: Validation of psychoanalytic techniques. *Journal of the American Psychoanalytic Association,* 1955, 496–505.

REICH, W. *Character analysis* (1933). (3rd ed.) New York: Orgone Press, 1949.

ROSEN, J. N. *Direct analysis.* New York: Grune and Stratton, 1953.

WOLMAN, B. B. Explorations in latent schizophrenia. *American Journal of Psychotherapy,* 1957, **11,** 560–588.

WOLMAN, B. B. Psychotherapy with latent schizophrenics. *American Journal of Psychotherapy,* 1959, **13,** 343–359.

WOLMAN, B. B. *Contemporary theories and system in psychology.* New York: Harper and Row, 1960.

WOLMAN, B. B. Non-participant observation on a closed ward. *Acta Psychotherapeutica,* 1964, **12,** 61–71.

WOLMAN, B. B. Principles of monistic transitionism. In B. B. Wolman and E. Nagel (Eds.), *Scientific psychology: principles and approaches.* New York: Basic Books, 1965. Pp. 563–585. (a)

WOLMAN, B. B. Mental health and mental disorders. In *Handbook of clinical psychology.* New York: McGraw-Hill, 1965. Pp. 1119–1141. (b)

WOLMAN, B. B. *Vectoriasis praecox or the group of schizophrenias.* Springfield, Ill.: Charles C Thomas, 1966. (a)

WOLMAN, B. B. Transference and countertransference as interindividual cathexis. *Psychoanalytic Review,* 1966, **53,** 255–265. (b)

WOLMAN, B. B. Classification of mental disorders. *Acta Psychotherapeutica,* 1966, **14,** 50–65. (c)

WOLMAN, B. B. Dr. Jekyll and Mr. Hyde: a new theory of the manic-depressive disorder. *Transactions of the New York Academy of Science,* 1966, **28,** 1020–1932. (d)

ZILBOORG, G., and HENRY, G. W. *A history of medical psychology.* New York: Norton, 1941.

10

TECHNIQUES FOR
THE RESOLUTION OF
THE NARCISSISTIC
DEFENSE

Hyman Spotnitz

The clinical phenomena analyzed in the present chapter inspired half a century ago Freud's reference to the "stone wall which cannot be surmounted.... In the narcissistic neuroses the resistance is insuperable; at the most we can satisfy our curiosity by craning our necks for a glimpse or two at what is going on over the wall" (1935, p. 336). Subsequent explorations substantially modified the bleakness of Freud's impression and emphasized the conclusion he drew from it: His own therapeutic method would "have to be replaced by other methods" to deal effectively with the narcissistic defense. Such a method can be, nevertheless, formulated and conducted within the basic framework of Freudian psychoanalysis.

The method I have described here has been employed for many years by analytically trained psychotherapists in the treatment of adults, adolescents and children, with appropriate modifications, in private practice and psychiatric clinics. An application of the method in a short-term therapy program for six hospitalized patients is reported by Davis (1965–1966). Although the majority of patients have been schizophrenic or borderline cases, this approach has been applied also in other conditions marked by regression to preverbal levels of functioning, notably severe depression, hypochondriasis, and psychosomatic disorders. A gross inability of the patient to manage the release of aggressive impulses in healthful and socially appropriate ways has been viewed as an indication for the use of the method.

Effective application of the method is contingent on recognition of hostile impulses in the patient and the effects they induce in the practitioner (Winnicott, 1958), and the ability of the patient to control the release of potentially explosive forces without damage to himself, the analyst, and the treatment situation. Goal-oriented functioning, emotional resiliency, and self-command are required. Characteristic countertransference problems and the use of the realistically induced emotions as a source of therapeutic leverage are discussed in earlier publications (Spotnitz, 1961b, 1963–1964).

Rationale of the Method

The candidate for psychoanalytic therapy is an individual who has used faulty patterns of self-expression in adjusting to his environment and the exigencies of life. The treatment is designed to reactivate these pathological patterns of adjustment, to help the patient outgrow any need to use them compulsively or involuntarily, and to provide the highly specific defense-freeing and psychological-growth experiences that will facilitate his emotional evolution.

The pathological narcissistic defense is attributed to the disorganizing influence of unconscious aggressive impulses. The defense is understood to be a primitive mental structure, set up in the undifferentiated stage of emotional development, which interfered with the completion of maturational sequences. The structure appears to be in part innate, in part environmentally conditioned. A high potential for aggressive impulsivity may be a genetic or constitutional predisposition. There may have been disequilibrium between the mother's early emotional training and the child's impulsivity.

It is reasonable to assume that the aggressive impulsivity was mobilized by frustration. Even in those cases where the frustrating experience appears to have been relatively inconsequential, frustration-aggression presents itself as the central problem because of the pattern that was set up early in life to deal with impulsivity.

Many failures reported in the early psychoanalytic treatment of extremely narcissistic people may be attributed, to some extent, to the fact that the narcissistic defense conveys the impression that its nuclear force is self-love. Clinical experience does not support this notion. The patient appears to be wholly wrapped up in himself, but self-love cloaks self-hatred, which is the core problem. Hatred was turned back upon the ego, and the object field of the mind was obliterated to protect the external object against the discharge of destructive impulsivity (Bloch, 1965; Clevans, 1957). Running away psychologically from hostile impulses into nonfeeling states and self-preoccupations eventually becomes a compulsive operation. The polarity that figures significantly in the narcissistic defense is self-hatred and object love. The treatment is based on this working hypothesis, which was formulated more extensively in other publications. (Spotnitz and Nagelberg, 1960; Spotnitz, 1961b, 1967.)

In the sense that the bottling up of destructive impulsives drains off energy from vital mental processes, the narcissistic defense is dealt with as a specific maladaptation that interfered with maturation of the personality and blocked its further growth. The patient is approached as an individual whose spontaneous emotional evolution was impeded in his earliest interchanges with natural objects and who requires a corrective series of interchanges with a therapeutic object.

In that role, the analyst helps the patient to maintain the narcissistic defense and gradually develop more healthy defenses. To enable him to reach as quickly as possible the goal of the treatment—personality maturation—the analyst addresses himself to the resolution of the forces that block maturation.

The analyst operates indirectly as a maturational agent. His communications are *not* designed to appease the patient's maturational needs. Nor are they designed to transform unconscious into conscious material, to help him experience catharsis, to gain an understanding of himself, or to acquire new insights. Catharsis per se is not regarded as significant, but it is experienced by the patient as he is trained to articulate whatever he feels, thinks, and remembers without engaging in the analytic sessions in any other motor activity. Insight and the other just-mentioned phenomena may emerge as by-products of the relationship, but they are of secondary value. The crucial task is to nullify the effects of the forces that interfered with the patient's growth and to catalyze maturation.

All personality deviations are dealt with under the operational formula of investigating transference-resistance phenomena and intervening only for the sake of their resolution. Symptoms are not analyzed per se and are dealt with only to the extent to which they interfere with analytic progress. The analyst's reaction to symptoms must not either encourage or discourage the patient from revealing psychotic material.

The treatment is conceptualized as a therapeutic process of resistance analysis. All obstacles to meaningful verbal communication fall under the heading of resistance; thus they must be resolved and not overcome. Resistance to the verbalization of negative feelings requires attention from the beginning of the treatment. Resistance is dealt with on a priority basis throughout each case, the five classic types of resistance being observed in each category.

Transference is evoked in a nonstimulating way, and the patient's need to experience it in a state of mild tension is respected. Negative-transference manifestations are dealt with first. Transference, which develops first on a narcissistic basis and is superseded by object transference, is dealt with as resistance when it interferes with progress, and fully resolved.

The treatment is structured to prevent regression too severe to be dealt with in the course of the session. To avoid the danger of precipitating an acute psychotic episode, a distinction is made between a purposeful engaging in a retrograde process and running away involuntarily from the treatment situation into the past to prevent the release of frustration-aggression. Regressive tendencies are dealt with as resistance until the patient is capable of appropriately expressing his reactions to the frustrations experienced in the relationship. The patient is trained to stay in the present and simply remember the past.

Initial Interview

The opening of a case may be preceded by a series of maneuvers reflecting the need of a highly narcissistic individual to defend himself against the stresses of the analytic situation. Letters or telephone calls are often received from relatives or friends inquiring about the availability of the practitioner's services, or these may be repeatedly solicited by the prospective patient himself before he mobilizes himself to make a definite appointment and come to the office. The patient is motivated to do so primarily by a strong desire to be relieved of his misery, and his arrival may signify no more than that he has decided to investigate the possibility of finding such relief.

The initial interview is devoted to formulating a tentative diagnosis and establishing the treatment contract. A brief family history is also taken. Names of parents, siblings, and grandparents, occupations, divorces, and causes of death, for example, often contain clues to family patterns of emotional illness as well as the nature of the candidate's own childhood experience. The identity of the person referring him may also be of some significance, and this information or the reason for the referral is also discussed if he wishes to do so.

A brief history of the onset of the illness and development of symptoms is desirable but not indispensable. The candidate is placed under no pressure to give information that he has withheld; the diagnostic impression is based on his voluntary disclosures. One of the few questions I usually ask a prospective patient is why he wants treatment. Whatever answer he gives clears the way for an exploration of his attitude about it and for an evaluation of his willingness and ability to cooperate under mutually agreeable arrangements.

The patient's questions are usually countered with the analyst's questions. A full and straightforward explanation of pathology is undesirable because it may be experienced as a narcissistic injury, an attack on his ego by someone who does not like him, understand him, or speak his language.

It is equally undesirable for the practitioner to reveal information about himself. Even if it is solicited, the disclosures made by the analyst might be interpreted as a sign of weakness, lack of self-confidence, or professional insecurity.

It is preferable not to volunteer information on the treatment under consideration, especially with respect to its length, difficulties, and the results anticipated. Promises, explicit or implicit, of a successful outcome are out of order. Such assurances are rarely helpful. In a negatively suggestible person, for example, they may unconsciously stimulate a strong resolve to defeat the analyst. When a question regarding outcome is raised by a person who indicates a specific need for an answer, it is advisable to investigate the unconscious meaning of the question before formulating a response.

In my experience, uncertainty and ignorance "anesthetize" the pre-Oedipal patient against the discomforts and stresses of the therapeutic undertaking that lies ahead. The less he knows about either its tribulations or potential benefits and the less aware he is of what is actually going on in the relationship prior to its final stage, the more capable he will be of concentrating his energy on the crucial task of verbal communication. Moreover, if the emotional tone of the practitioner's statements throughout the interview is one of genuine interest without warmth or urgency, the counterforce operating in a person who is apprehensive about committing himself to the undertaking is minimized. A trial period of about six weeks is usually suggested. The analyst attributes the discontinuance to his own incapacity if the relationship is terminated at that time.

The establishment of a relationship in which analytic work can go on systematically is one of the early goals of treatment, but the ability to function accordingly is not a prerequisite for it. The practitioner shoulders virtually all responsibility for developing an effectual alliance when the case opens. As it proceeds, the patient becomes more and more cooperative; as termination approaches, he usually is fully cooperative.

The minimum demands consistent with the treatment of his condition on an ambulatory basis are that the patient lie on the couch and talk. He is not instructed to free-associate. As the opening move in educating him to do so, he may be asked to tell his "life story" or simply to talk of his experiences; a severely disturbed individual may begin by recounting how he traveled to the office, what he ate for breakfast, and the like.

Time and fee are fixed during the first interview, but no formal declaration is volunteered on other contractual matters. Arrangements and rules are flexibly formulated as dynamic tools of therapy. The patient is told that talking is the only activity that is "cooperative" during his sessions and is gradually educated to the idea that he is expected to verbalize his impulses, thoughts, feelings, and memories. It is also impressed on him, in due time, that regularity and promptness in attendance and payment of fees are expected of him. Early in treatment, resistance tends to cluster around these areas and, in some cases, the couch position.

I prefer to start a patient on one session a week and investigate the maximum intensity of treatment desirable for the case during its first stage. He may be seen more often if he is capable of digesting psychological nourishment at a faster tempo. Under exceptional circumstances he may respond to five or even six weekly sessions; however, from one to three sessions usually provide as much emotional feeding as can be healthfully assimilated.

The patient is assisted to continue for two years, the minimum period necessary for significant change to occur. At the end of that period, he is usually given the option to discontinue and return later if he wishes to make further progress. A minimum of five years is required for personality maturation for an individual who enters treatment to resolve the narcissistic defense. The case may go on much longer, its ultimate duration depending on the willingness of both parties to work together and the mutual recognition that worth-while progress is being made and is likely to continue. Otherwise, termination is recommended.

Transference

By functioning as an ego-syntonic object, the analyst facilitates the development of transference on a narcissistic basis as well as its eventual transformation into object transference.

As the patient re-experiences the emotional charge of his early object relations, the pathological patterns he set up for blocking the release of negative feelings come into play. These blockages are systematically studied from the beginning of the treatment, but the analyst reveals no interest in them until his present and more powerful influence makes them reducible.

To permit the narcissistic transference to develop fully, interventions are cued to the patient's *verbal* attempts to solicit some information about his characteristic preoccupations, to satisfy his personal interest in the practitioner, or to convert silence or monologue into dialogue through a casual question. In previous reports, such behavior has been referred to as "contact functioning," and its use as a timer and operational guide to goal-oriented communication has been discussed (Spotnitz, Nagelberg and Feldman, 1956; Spotnitz, 1961b). The contact functioning helps the analyst to provide frustration and gratification in the precise balance needed to prevent the aggressive impulses from shattering the narcissistic defense.

To facilitate the release of such impulsivity on what is, in effect, a self-demand basis, the analyst reflects the verbal attempts to establish contact without giving the information requested. Instead, he investigates why the patient wants it. At times, contact functioning helps him engage in meaningful communication, but generally it operates as resistance. In joining or psychologically reflecting the pattern, the analyst is usually oriented toward the following objectives:

The attitude expressed by the patient is met with unspoken acceptance. He is not contradicted; no attempt is made to modify his thoughts and feelings. The analyst refrains from asserting himself as a personality. He does not explain, for instance, why the patient relates to him as an extension of himself rather than as a separate and different person. The possibility of serving as a narcissistic-transference object is foreclosed if the analyst corrects the misperceptions and distortions of reality. The "feeding back" of his own attitudes gives the patient feelings of being understood; more than that, he tends to move away from the original position.

When the occasion presents itself, the patient's attention is directed to external objects. What motivated him to set up the narcissistic defense has to be determined. Usually the attitudes he experienced from his earliest objects had something to do with its establishment.

As much as possible, pressure is taken off the ego and shifted to the object. When, for example, the patient is bogged down with worry over his deviant tendencies, it may be indicated to him there is nothing seriously amiss aside from the fact that he was not trained properly. Undoubtedly, he can be retrained; the only question is whether the analyst is capable of doing it.

When the transference is established, the patient may talk about what he imagines is going on in the analyst's mind. The patient may feel that the analyst does not want him to relax his defenses, especially in expressing hostility. Instead of attributing it to the frustration inherent in the treatment situation, he says, in effect, "I am making myself miserable." The "I" may be the object rather than the ego. On the other hand, the "you" he talks about may actually be the ego. In other words, some of the feelings transferred reflect attitudes of significant objects that were incorporated in the infantile ego. Unless such feelings are sorted out from those which the patient originally experienced himself, it is impossible to reconstruct his earliest object relations.

It has been pointed out that the analyst begins to deal with this mélange of ego-object attitudes when he has become more emotionally significant to the patient than his original objects. Narcissistic-transference manifestations that interfere with communication are then joined or psychologically reflected.

Negative transference is dealt with first. To facilitate the discharge of frustration-aggression, the analyst presents himself as a willing target for verbal abuse. As an essential safeguard against explosive behavior, the patient's own resistance to *acting* on his destructive impulses is consistently joined and even reinforced if necessary. Moreover, another line is drawn between therapeutically desirable utterances and those which yield sadistic gratification.

By identifying with the patient in feelings and thoughts, the analyst helps the patient to identify with him in behavior. The patient also becomes more and more aware of positive feelings for his transference object. As he oscillates between states of negative and positive transference, what was at first little more than an ego percept becomes a real object.

After the compulsive grip of the narcissistic defense has been relaxed and new modes of behavior have been established with the aid of the ego-syntonic object, the patient feels secure enough to relate to a different object.

He becomes aware of strong cravings for a livelier one. The development of object transference is facilitated by demonstrations of how the patient should handle himself, especially in those interpersonal situations in which he tends to resort to the narcissistic defense (Nelson, 1962; Spotnitz, 1961b). In a state of object transference, he explores the differences between himself and his object. Having acquired the ability to experience and give expression to his feelings, he is in a position to defy, comply, or cooperate, depending on his own preference. By that time he has passed the emotional age of two and is much less narcissistic.

Resistance

A counterforce is mobilized when the patient is directed to talk at the beginning of the treatment. As this counterforce waxes and wanes in the case, it gives rise to countless manifestations, which the analyst recognizes and deals with as resistance. Attempts to overcome the resistance of an extremely narcissistic patient serve to intensify the counterforce. In order to diminish it, the pressure for progress is carefully controlled.

Although the counterforce must be weakened, it must also be preserved because it represents the totality of the patient's experience in the perceptual field. He is therefore permitted to maintain the old field until he can function with integrity in the new perceptual field that is created in the analytic relationship. Until he feels secure about his behavior, can release his psychological energy healthfully and constructively, and relates appropriately to an object that is regarded as cooperative and reliable, the patient needs the freedom to return to the old experiences. Some failures in treatment occur because the old perceptual field is not re-created with sufficient intensity or preserved long enough for the patient to make an unequivocal choice between the two fields.

To help him make this choice, his undifferentiated ego-object percepts are permitted to become highly charged with emotion before they are dealt with in the context of resistance. Coincidentally, freedom from undue pressure to commit himself to the new perceptual field diminishes the counterforce. What motivates him ultimately to give up the narcissistic defense is difficult to determine. However, when the counterforce to progress is approached in the manner just suggested, one observes that the patient outgrows his immature attitudes. He begins to feel that anything is preferable to the old mode of functioning.

The analyst also operates on the premise that resistance performs a communication function. Inadequate, incomplete, and indirect forms of communication are characteristic of a person at the pre-Oedipal level and are accepted as such rather than being regarded as the absence of communication. His nonverbal messages and primitive modes of behavior as he resists the instruction to talk out his feelings, thoughts, and memories usually provide some information about him that is grist for analysis. He is educated, not forced, to communicate consistently in adult language.

It is also recognized that many resistance patterns of a severely regressed patient are the "holding" operations he unconsciously resorts to in other interpersonal situations, in the interests of self-preservation and object protection. Their survival function is respected. The analyst does not attempt to resolve them until they can be given up without detriment to the patient's psychic economy.

The analyst intervenes promptly to nullify the influence of any pattern of behavior that, if permitted to continue, would break off the treatment (Brody, 1964). Whereas the chronic and stable defenses are preserved, new symptoms, sudden exacerbations of old ones, and mounting evidence of the stiffening of the narcissistic defense are focused on, if only to deactivate those forms of resistance that could destroy the therapeutic relationship. At any time when the corrosive effects of destructive impulsivity become manifest and the patient's characteristic defense against explosive behavior is strongly activated, it is a matter of extreme urgency to provide some communication that will help him verbalize his hostility as forcefully as possible.

Also included in the category of treatment-destructive resistance—patterns connected with accumulated frustration-aggression blocked from verbal discharge or being discharged indirectly through aberrant behavior—is extreme tardiness or absence without notice of a person who has previously been punctual and faithful in attendance. These and similar problems— unwillingness to leave promptly at the end of the session or impulsive behavior such as jumping off the couch—are repeatedly discussed. The analyst does not wait for the patient to bring them up.

The storing up of frustration-aggression in a pattern that is conducive to personality fragmentation is one of the two special forms of resistance to which the narcissistic defense gives rise. The other form is directly connected with the tendency of a severely disturbed patient to communicate primarily through nonverbal behavior. If these resistances to appropriate verbal communications are beyond the comprehension of the practitioner, they may put a great strain on the relationship. Neither of these special forms of resistance responds to interpretation until the patient is capable of communicating consistently in adult language.

Whether or not a resistance to talking will disrupt the treatment depends on the meaning of the silence. An important clue is the anxiety level in the immediate situation. As long as the patient remains comfortable and relaxed, he is permitted to maintain silence, especially in the early stage of treatment, but if he is suffering or in a state of conflict, it is desirable to find out why he cannot talk and remove the obstacles to verbal communication. What he says is of no immediate consequence; any utterance is preferable to prolonged silence in those circumstances. If it cannot be interrupted by asking questions, the analyst may have to talk for a while, preferably about impersonal matters, which often stimulates the patient to follow suit. Recognition that the analyst is not particularly eager for him to talk about himself temporarily diminishes the resistance. In other words, the counterforce is worked on by controlling the display of eagerness.

The analyst is in a position to deal with other resistances when the treatment-destructive patterns do not operate. Accorded second priority are the patterns that communicate inertia and disinterest in change—status quo resistance. These attempts to "stay put" in treatment are usually observed after the patient begins to feel relatively comfortable in his sessions, and they may continue for protracted periods. The resistant attitudes convey the impression that the need for ameliorative change is minimal. Problems are concealed, and the general picture presented is that of the "good" patient.

The third category of resistance shifts from the clinging to the current situation toward apprehension concerning the effects of new experiences. The patient resists learning how to make progress; he may ask for rules and directions and resist meaningful communication. He may demonstrate unwillingness to move ahead into a new territory or to say what he really thinks and feels, with or without regard for the consequences.

Fourth priority is given to the resistance to cooperating with the analyst. The patient may prefer to remain self-preoccupied rather than to discuss or share the responsibility for problems that develop in the relationship. He tends to follow instructions literally and to react negatively to the idea that he has reached the point where it is incumbent on him to contribute more broadly to the solution of his emotional problems. The patient has reached an important milestone when these resistances are resolved. In a cooperative frame of mind he can voluntarily check the expression of his feelings of hostility in nondamaging ways. Analytic progress along the standard lines then becomes possible.

The treatment-destructive resistances disappear when the forces preventing the release of frustration-aggression in feelings and language are permanently resolved. To the extent to which the other categories of resistance mentioned above also operate to check such release, their resolution is secured in the same way. However, these three forms of resistance are maintained in part by the paucity or defective nature of the patient's identification patterns. The use of paradigmatic techniques (Nelson, 1962) and analytic group psychotherapy (Ormont, 1964; Spotnitz, 1957, 1961a) are recommended procedures for dealing with that aspect of the problem, especially for a person whose life provides few opportunities to form wholesome identifications.

Interpretation of Unconscious

The excessively narcissistic patient tends to react negatively to explanations of what is going on in his mind. Information may traumatize the relationship by provoking resentment and mortification, which he is unable to verbalize at the time; thus his withdrawal tendencies may become even stronger. Interpretations must be withheld until the patient is able to communicate in adult language unless they will improve his immediate functioning.

The analyst must keep in mind the unconscious significance of the patient's feelings, thoughts, and memories and nonverbal activity in the session. Emotional communications are provided to help the patient verbalize his own insights. When the patient's questions are psychologically reflected and repeatedly countered with questions, he usually answers them himself. The analyst limits himself to placing the stamp of approval on correct self-interpretations when the opportunity presents itself. He does not reveal interest in investigating disturbing feelings or thoughts, especially in psychotic material, nor does he give any information about them.

Dreams are responded to in the same manner. The patient's tendencies to flood the analyst with dreams whenever he is eager to please him and to withhold such disclosures when he is inclined to displease are thus discouraged. Dreams are studied as part of the total production of the session rather than as a special form of communication, and the analyst does not work actively to secure associations to them. Whatever is reported is usually included in the summary of unconscious problems. Occasionally a few questions are asked about a dream, primarily to clarify it. This approach, as Freud pointed out (1923), minimizes the danger that the patient will be influenced by the analyst's attitude to provide one or another kind of material.

As the case proceeds, understanding is communicated at the rate at which it can be healthfully assimilated. Interpretation of unconscious mechanisms usually begins during the second year of treatment.

When the patient is permitted to emerge from his misconceptions and distortions of reality while being weaned away from his defective identifications, he gradually emerges from that state with the sharpening of the distinctions between himself and others. When his new perceptual field is established with the aid of appropriate emotional communications, cravings for self-understanding and contact with reality begin to develop. After manifesting interest in finding out what the analyst thinks and feels, he becomes aware of similar strivings in relation to other people on his own horizon and, eventually, genuine concern with the world-at-large, or with a specific activity or area of knowledge.

In the final stage of treatment, Oedipal problems are dealt with, and object-transference resistance is resolved. Interpretations may be provided, but as much as possible the explanations of unconscious mechanisms are sought for in the relationship. Insight into the pathological tendencies mastered earlier in the case often develops in the course of discussions of resistance patterns. Explanations of how they were permanently resolved may also be given to a patient who is keenly interested in understanding the therapeutic maneuvers. Interpretations and self-interpretations of the narcissistic defense on a retrospective basis often dominate the last months of treatment.

Working Through

Working through of the narcissistic defense is a process of repeating the same emotional communication over and over again until the patient is sufficiently impressed to give up resistant behavior. Instead of working through an interpretation, the analyst, in essence, works through *to* the interpretation.

When he recognizes a resistance pattern that commands his attention on the basis of the priority system already mentioned, he analyzes it and devises some strategy for dealing with it. In one session he may use one joining procedure consistently or two or more alternatively. As the analyst observes the patient's response to the emotional communication, he may develop various hypotheses about the resistant behavior, which he is joining in one way or another through these procedures. The theory that leads to the permanent resolution of the resistance pattern is assumed to be the correct interpretation.

It is also assumed that repeated explanations of a preverbal pattern will be ineffectual, other than to resolve it temporarily, as long as it yields some needed gratification. The psychological need that is being appeased is called to the patient's attention when the pattern operates, and the analyst applies himself to drain it of gratification—provided that he can respond with genuine feeling at the moment (Spotnitz, 1963–1964).

To secure the release of the emotional charge motivating a preverbal pattern, the analyst often reflects its configuration in his own communication. When the patient's pathological pattern of bottling up frustration-aggression comes into operation, he resists talking in a meaningful way about himself, and his expressions of low regard for himself are echoed by the analyst to reverse the flow of mobilized aggression from the ego to the object. After the patient has acquired some feeling for the therapist as an external object, the procedure of "low rating" the object is employed to help the patient discharge the hostility with which he is attacking his own ego (Nagelberg and Spotnitz, 1958). The procedure of "outcrazying the patient," that is, exaggerating to the point of absurdity an imaginary exploit or invention the patient talks about, is also effective in securing the release of aggressive impulses in the form of emotionally crystallized and verbally discharged energy.

As the narcissistic defense is gradually mastered and outgrown, interpretation becomes an increasingly important aspect of the working-through process. The task of resolving resistance permanently approaches a successful conclusion when the patient is capable of cooperating actively without developing undesirable states of tension. Thereafter, the analyst shifts from emotional communication to interpretation as his judgment dictates.

In the course of the case, resistance is dealt with at all levels, and each component of a pattern is examined. Working through is not compartmentalized or approached as a discrete operation. It is conceptualized as an aspect of the progress of understanding the origin and history of each resistance pattern and of recognizing why it operates in the current situation.

The Final Stage

There is relatively little evidence of the narcissistic defense in the final stage. The patient demonstrates the ability to verbalize spontaneously both negative and positive feelings. But the progress made earlier in the case has to be stabilized. The patient must be educated to use voluntarily and intentionally the normal defense mechanisms, in contradistinction to the old involuntary and compulsive defenses he has outgrown. Exercises in "defense maneuverability" are provided. Otherwise, treatment at this stage is not basically different from that of the Oedipal patient.

The analyst broaches the subject of termination as soon as it appears feasible because it meets with prolonged opposition. The patient tends to revert to the old narcissistic behavior and complains of new problems cropping up. Resistance to termination includes both patterns.

Although the old ones have been drained of their compulsive force, they are still at his disposal. Tendencies to reactivate them are especially difficult to deal with if his current life experience is not conducive to emotional reactiveness. In the process of learning how to behave appropriately without shutting out feelings, the patient may communicate that he feels like an actor trying out several roles in succession in order to determine which is most appealing, or he may equate undisciplined behavior with being "genuine." However, the old resistance patterns can be resolved with relative ease by applying the procedures that were effective early in the treatment.

It is desirable to test out the patient's inclination to return to the old modes of functioning. The feelings the patient has induced in the analyst are therefore "fed back" to him in graduated doses until any tendencies to "clam up" or react explosively are resolved. The use of this procedure, which I refer to as the toxoid response (1963–1964), has served its purpose when the patient verbalizes his insights and indicates that he has had enough of the "old stuff."

The patient displays intense interest in understanding his personal history and in exploring every aspect of his current behavior. Formal interpretations are provided when he demonstrates the ability to talk of himself with some detachment. However, the artful use of "why," which gives him the opportunity to formulate his own explanations, is often preferable.

The patient talks spontaneously, in an animated voice, and appears thoroughly at ease during the last six months of treatment. He lies on his back, arms and legs uncrossed; on occasion he may sit up on the couch by prearrangement, but he feels no need to behave impulsively during the session. He reports his current activities and tries to relate them to his memories of events in the remote past. Dreams are also reported regularly, and he participates actively in their analysis. The free associations of each session include references to his sex life, and he talks freely of his thoughts and feelings about the analyst. He remains within the normal range of variability in attendance and payment of fees.

The Concept of Cure

The communications of a highly narcissistic individual in the early months of treatment often remind me of an old-fashioned music box playing the same thin tune over and over again. The narcissistic patient appears to be bogged down in the basic and essentially gross feelings of childhood. Effective treatment slowly enriches his personality with more feeling tones, and eventually the communications become fully "orchestrated." The hierarchy of feelings that characterize emotional evolution appear to develop in the patient. This is one aspect of the emergence of the mature personality, which is equated with successful outcome of the case.

Effective treatment also equips the patient with an abundance of action patterns that facilitate the discharge of feelings, so that he no longer has to go out of contact with reality to prevent himself from behaving destructively. He is able to feel and express appropriately, and also to accept both love and hate and the derivatives of both emotions. The give-and-take is important and often changes his whole orientation to life. The patient can relate comfortably to people even while experiencing rage and faces up to painful realities without the support of the old narcissistic defense. It is virtually impossible to secure an evidence of the resolved pathological patterns except through careful diagnostic testing or skillful interviewing.

But their resolution does not mean that he has solved all of his emotional problems, nor is it a guarantee that he won't encounter new ones in the future. Cure is not cure-all, but it encompasses a notable increase in the patient's capacity for self-fulfillment and happiness, the ability to behave appropriately in all normal situations and to meet the impact of abnormally traumatic ones with considerable resiliency. He has sufficient understanding of himself to deal independently with conflicts of ordinary magnitude.

The recovered patient is a much more sociocentric human being than when he entered treatment. His family and associates are impressed with the improvements in his functioning at home, at work, and in social situations. He is more understanding of other people and finds it easier to get along with them regardless of differences in perspectives and attitudes. He discovers that it is possible to live among them with a sense of emotional integrity and self-respect instead of living alone behind the stone wall of narcissism.

REFERENCES

[Note: S.E. refers to *The Standard Edition of the complete psychological works of Sigmund Freud* (London: Hogarth Press).]

BLOCH, DOROTHY. Feelings that kill; the effect of the wish for infanticide in neurotic depression. *Psychoanalytic Review*, 1965, **52**, 51–66.

BRODY, S. Syndrome of the treatment rejecting patient. *Psychoanalytic Review*, 1964, **51**, 243–252.

CLEVANS, ETHEL. The fear of a schizophrenic man. *Psychoanalysis*, 1957, **5** (No. 4), 58–67.

DAVIS, H. L. Short-term psychoanalytic therapy with hospitalized schizophrenics. *Psychoanalytic Review*, 1965–1966, **52**, 421–448.

FREUD, S. *A general introduction to psychoanalysis*. New York: Liveright, 1935. 26th lecture.

FREUD, S. Remarks on the theory and practice of dream interpretation (1923). S.E., Vol. 19, pp. 109–121.

NAGELBERG, L., and SPOTNITZ, H. Strengthening the ego through the release of frustration-aggression. *American Journal of Orthopsychiatry*, 1958, **28**, 794–801.

NELSON, MARIE C. Effect of paradigmatic techniques on the psychic economy of borderline patients. *Psychiatry*, 1962, **25** (No. 2), 119–134.

ORMONT, L. R. The resolution of resistances by conjoint psychoanalysis. *Psychoanalytic Review*, 1964, **51**, 425–437.

SPOTNITZ, H. The borderline schizophrenic in group psychotherapy. *International Journal of Group Psychotherapy*, 1957, **7**, 155–174.

SPOTNITZ, H. *The couch and the circle*. New York: Knopf, 1961. (a)

SPOTNITZ, H. The narcissistic defense in schizophrenia. *Psychoanalysis and the Psychoanalytic Review*, 1961, **48** (No. 4), 24–42. Also Monograph Report No. 1, New York: Stuyvesant Polyclinic, Psychology Dept., 1961. (b)

SPOTNITZ, H. The toxoid response. *Psychoanalytic Review*, 1963–1964, **50**, 611–624. Also in *Insulation and immunization in schizophrenia*. New York: Stuyvesant Polyclinic, Psychology Dept., Monograph Report No. 3, 1963. Pp. 26–39.

SPOTNITZ, H. *Modern psychoanalysis of the schizophrenic patient; theory of the technique*. New York: Grune and Stratton, 1967.

SPOTNITZ, H., and NAGELBERG, L. A preanalytic technique for resolving the narcissistic defense. *Psychiatry*, 1960, **23** (No. 2), 193–197.

SPOTNITZ, H., NAGELBERG, L., and FELDMAN, YONATA. Ego reinforcement in the schizophrenic child. *American Journal of Orthopsychiatry*, 1956, **26**, 146–164.

WINNICOTT, D. W. Hate in the countertransference. *Collected papers*. New York: Basic Books, 1958. Pp. 194–203.

11

RESPONSIVE
ACTION IN
PSYCHOANALYSIS

Martin Grotjahn

Definition

"Responsive action" is a term used to characterize the therapist's reaction to the patient's unconscious needs. It is important to realize the difference between unconscious needs to which the therapist has to respond and conscious wishes or desires, which are a very different matter and which the therapist has, as a rule, not to fulfill. The therapist responds to the therapeutic situation with understanding, insight, interpretation, emotion, and he may eventually state his opinion or initiate action. He will always leave to the patient the freedom to agree or to oppose. In any case, the therapist will hope that the patient will deal with the analyst's response.

The therapist's responsive action should be genuine and spontaneous. His technical skill should be expressed only in the degree to which it shows his responsiveness, but not in its emotional nature, which should always be spontaneous and genuine. His response may vary between the giving of subliminal cues, the asking of well-timed questions, and the show of a clearly active response.

In the development of psychoanalytic technique the emphasis has shifted from the transference neurosis to the study of countertransference and presently is directed toward a deeper understanding of interaction between therapist and patient. Experimental interaction should under no circumstances detract from the importance of transference and countertransference or a genetic approach. An emotional analytic experience of relatedness should never replace insight, but add to it. Responsive action integrates all three essential aspects of the analytic process.

Dynamics

Responsive action is based upon dynamic and genetic understanding. An accurate, constant, and consistent awareness of the transference-countertransference situation and of the unconscious needs of the patient is fundamental.

Many a gifted therapist may be able to base his spontaneous reaction toward the patient and toward the therapeutic situation upon empathy, intuition, and his natural sense of tact and timing. Without analytic insight and integration of this knowledge the average analyst may endanger the health of his patients by getting into countertransference difficulties. He may also endanger his own (or his family's) health by constantly activating his own unconscious and allowing it to break through repression without being fully aware of it.

There is an additional reason why only the analyzed therapist is capable of using the technical tool of responsive action with full responsibility. Through his analysis he avoids the danger of becoming patterned in his responsiveness. At least theoretically he should become, through analysis, more open-minded and tolerant of a manifold, multileveled and multi-channeled communication in human interaction. He should consider responsive action as a form of communication. Such communication can never be understood on the level of present time alone. It must include the always present past.

It is possible that group psychotherapy, and most important family therapy, owes its efficiency to the wealth and many-sidedness, the intensity and truth of its inherent, spontaneous, responsive action. This became evident to me when I instituted this kind of therapy to patients in the terminal phase of psychoanalysis. It seems to me that many patients, in spite of the skill and training of their analysts in the interpretation of resistance and transference, do learn how to deal with their therapists in a one-to-one relationship. The patients are faced with a more difficult onslaught of responsive interaction in the group or family situation. This challenge, if properly handled, may lead the analyzed person to carry his insight into action.

Indication

Responsive action is always indicated, as it is always present. If it were otherwise, then the patient's tape recorder could talk to the analyst's tape recorder, and the two could be synchronized by computers in mechanized togetherness.

As always in the field of psychotherapy and psychoanalysis the application of responsive action is a question of degree and of doing it right. Responsive action can be overdone, as it can be perverted and abused. Potential dangers, however, can never be reasons for abandoning a technique that is efficient and probably essential when used properly.

If the mother-child relationship is taken as a model situation of psychotherapy and as a model for understanding the essential therapeutic process, then we see that the unresponsive, mechanized mother may develop a physically healthy but schizophrenic child, which behaves like one of Harlow's monkeys.

Responsive action is particularly indicated in crisis or impulsive situations. It is often effective with certain character types who need more emotional responses from the therapist in order to overcome their feelings of alienation from the world of reality, which they have turned from in disgust, hostile frustration, or bitterness.

Technique

Responsive action may be mistaken for transference gratification, corrective emotional experience, or role-taking. It differs from all of these techniques by virtue of its emphasis on the therapist's response to the patient's emotional and factual situation as different from the transference situation. The therapist retains his identity: He is helping the patient to gain insight and to indicate necessary behavioral changes. Role-taking, implicit in responsive action, is of secondary significance. Responsive action is reality-directed but grows out of the transference-countertransference situation. The emphasis is on response and in this way is only indirectly on interpretation.

The function of the analyst has been compared with the reflective function of the mirror, which reflects mostly the phenomena of the transference neurosis. The responsive analyst could be compared with a talking mirror, as in the fairy tales. The responsive mirror does not only reflect in-sight but explains in many ways: "Look what you do to people, as for instance right now to me, your analyst." (Or to your spouse in family therapy, or other patients in the therapeutic group.) In this way the therapist's response is insight-giving and can be considered as a different form of interpretation. The corrective emotional experience would be placed on a more experiential plane.

Ideally speaking, responsiveness is not directiveness. Its function is communicative, not directive or advisory. Advice is patient-directed, whereas stating one's opinion is therapist-directed. It is like the difference between feeding and eating. Giving advice is like feeding; listening to the therapist's opinion is an invitation to eat. The one technique binds; the other is supposed to free the individual. It also becomes more and more obvious that the giving of advice is ineffective; people know what to do, they must learn in therapy why they are unable to do what they have to do. Freedom is the ability to do what has to be done.

The asking of questions is a standard method of analytic etiquette. The technique of questioning ranges from the proverbial "Hm?" or similar prodding sounds, to pointed inquiries. Questions indicate the analyst's curiosity, interest, sympathy, or simply his attention. They may also be intended to prevent the patient from following his associations into the blue yonder and to stay here, to go into details, or to work on a resistance.

Questions will give the patients the first clues about his therapist; they are usually the first bits of verbal knowledge from which the patient builds his image of his therapist. Simultaneously, they give him the ways and methods of how to deal with his therapist. This can be done in the interest of the working alliance as well as in the service of resistance. To know about it, to become aware of the dynamics of asking questions, is of great therapeutic importance. The whole field of technique and dynamics of questioning could be started with the problem of responsive action, of which it is a special aspect.

The test of correctly applied responsive action is when it is followed by a new burst of therapeutic work in which the therapist may resume the more traditional, more distant, and more interpretative attitude of the model technique.

Summary and Conclusions

The term responsive action is presented and described here as a psychotherapeutic analytic technique. The term is of value as a unifying concept in contemporary attempts to understand the essentials of the therapeutic process. It relates to concepts as corrective emotional experience, role-taking, therapeutic alliance, and other terms and concepts that indicate the analytic development from the study of transference neurosis to the role of countertransference, to the recognition of interaction and human experience, and, finally, to the integration of all three.

Responsive action may be an essential part of every therapeutic process, including the analytic one. Intervention as well as nonintervention are different forms of responsive action: A silent or unresponsive mother may influence the child profoundly and lastingly. There is a long, gradual transition leading from an analyst who seeks to observe the transference neurosis with the least active participation on his part, limiting himself to interpretation. The line leads from him to the analytic therapist who is aware of his role as a responsive observer and who utilizes the transference in analysis and in the extra-analytic situation for interpretation and also for active response for the benefit of the therapy.

Psychoanalysis had to proceed the way it did for historical reasons. A study of the individual and his unconscious has been of paramount importance, and it is still so. However, sixty years after Freud's discoveries we must make the next step and must not feel bound in misunderstood loyalty to a historical necessity, which was valid in the past but can now be supplemented by insight into dynamics that take part in all human situations, especially in therapeutic interaction. Their knowledge and conscious use is a scientific demand and leads to greater therapeutic efficiency.

REFERENCES

CLINICAL ILLUSTRATIONS

ALGER, I. The clinical handling of the analyst's responses. Paper presented at New York Medical College Department of Psychiatry Symposium on Transference and Counter-Transference, October 24, 1964.

GROTJAHN, M. Clinical illustrations from psychoanalytic family therapy. In B. Green (Ed.), *Psychotherapy of marital disharmony.* New York: The Free Press, 1965. Ch. 10.

GROTJAHN, M. Specific indications for psychoanalytic family therapy. In S. Rosenbaum and I. Alger (Eds.), *ibid.,* Ch. 22.

NATTERSON, J., and GROTJAHN, M. Responsive action in psychotherapy. *The American Journal of Psychiatry,* 1965, 122.

OTHER REFERENCES

ALEXANDER, F. The principle of flexibility. In F. Alexander, and T. French (Eds.), *Psychoanalytic therapy.* New York: Ronald Press, 1946.

GREENACRE, PHYLLIS. The role of transference, practical considerations, in relation to psychoanalytic therapy. *Journal of the American Psychoanalytic Association,* 1954, 2, 671–684.

GREENSON, R. *The working alliance and the transference neurosis.* Paper presented before the Cleveland Psychoanalytic Society, May 1964. An earlier version was presented before the Los Angeles Psychoanalytic Society, May 1963.

GROTJAHN, M. About the "third ear" in psychoanalysis. A review and critical evaluation of Theodor Reik's book: Listening with the third ear; the inner experience of a psychoanalyst. *The Psychoanalytic Review,* 1950, 37, 56–65.

GROTJAHN, M. Open end technique in psychoanalysis. *Psychoanalytic Quarterly,* 1964, 33, 270–271.

GROTJAHN, M. Psychoanalysis twenty-five years after the death of Sigmund Freud. *Psychological Reports,* 1965, 16, 965–968.

SZASZ, T. S. The communication of distress between child and parent, *British Journal of Medical Psychology,* 1959, 32, 161–170.

Part **III**

THE
NON-FREUDIAN
TECHNIQUES

12

ADLER'S INDIVIDUAL PSYCHOLOGY

Kurt A. Adler

Alfred Adler's theory of personality and general philosophy of life constitute a complete and unified system, the system of "individual psychology." The specific theory of neuroses and psychoses, with all the methods and techniques of analysis and treatment, is derived from it.

One of the basic assumptions in this system is that *life is movement* and that it must endlessly strive for a better adaptation to its environment. Adler says: "This compulsion to accomplish a better adaptation can never end; in this lies the basis for our concept of '*striving for superiority*'" (1933, p. 259).

Any failure of adaptation is experienced as a *feeling of inferiority,* or feeling of inadequacy—an actual pain—and the body, the feelings, and the mind will go to all lengths to overcome it and to establish or re-establish a position or feeling of superiority, which is the compensatory ideal—the *final goal.*

299

This ideal of superiority is always fictitious in nature, created by the individual as the imagined, complete, and final overcoming of all obstacles in his attempt at adaptation. It is the ideal of perfection, of being godlike and omnipotent. It is irrational in nature and tends to estrange the individual from reality because it suggests that he can overcome reality. It is a totally self-centered and self-conscious ideal, and as such it tends to bring a hostile and fighting attitude into our lives and tends to rob us of the simplicity and spontaneity of our feelings.

It is a moot question if individuals actually have such feelings of inferiority and goals of superiority. What a newborn infant actually feels can hardly be described in such terms; even later, the grown individual is at least partly unaware of such feelings, and at best he has only a dim presentiment of them. However, Adlerian theory maintains that the individual acts *as if* he had such a feeling of inferiority and *as if* he were striving with all the means at his command to overcome it. With such a hypothesis we are able to explain behavior more comprehensively and to test it in actual practice. Adler stated that

> The fictitious goal, vague and labile, not capable of being measured, constructed with very inadequate and ungifted powers (of the infant) has *no* real existence, and can therefore not fully be comprehended causally. It may, however, be understood as a teleological, artificial device (*Kunstgriff*) of the mind, which seeks orientation and which, in emergencies, is always constructed concretely (1930, p. 4).

In the unerring and single-minded pursuit of his goal, the individual will put all body functions, emotions, thoughts, perceptions, and the total pattern of his behavior into its service. The result is a unified striving, and as a consequence the personality will itself be a self-consistent, unified entity. Apparent ambivalences or contradictions found in a personality or in the individual's behavior are simply different methods used in the pursuit of a single goal.

For the understanding of a personality, we can therefore say: If we recognize the goal of a psychic expression or its life plan, we must expect that all partial expressions will be in harmony with it, and vice versa: correctly understood partial expressions must in their connections and totality add up to the picture of a unified life plan and its final goal.

Insofar as they all strive for perfection, for overcoming, for superiority, the final goal of all people is the same. However, each individual's conception in regard to the *meaning* of perfection, overcoming, superiority, is *unique.* Each individual has, after all, constructed his final goal as a compensation for *his* sense of inferiority regarding *his* body, *his* feeling in regard to the obstacles in *his* environment, and the experience of *his* advantages and disadvantages in *his* social relations. The personality is therefore a self-consistent, unified, and *unique* unit. An individual's mode of movement throughout life toward his goal is called his pattern or *style of life.*

Style of Life

From earliest infancy on, the child will test constantly, through trial and error, the most successful and most rewarding ways and means to pursue his goal. In his efforts of adaptation he rejects what he considers unsuccessful methods and repeats, improves, and intensively trains himself in successful ones. This creative self-training leads eventually (about the age of five) to a relatively fixed, unique style of life. To the objective observer, this style of life makes the individual recognizable and distinct; it differentiates him from any other personality in about the same way as a piece of music can be recognized by the unique style of the composer. This style of life will manifest itself in whatever a person does. It is the distinctive mark of the personality throughout his life. The individual himself is only vaguely aware of his own style and pattern of behavior. It has been constructed largely on a preverbal level, and it propels him toward his goal, without his awareness, mainly by its emotional impetus. Since it was for the most part never formulated in verbal concepts, it is, to a great extent, immune to verbal criticism; erroneous styles of life, which clash with the reality of social necessity, are modified little, if at all, by experience. The only way a style of life can change is by the realization of childhood errors made in its construction, and when these errors can be actively corrected by adopting a more social approach to life. Although such a change may occur in the course of life, owing to positive and constructive relationships and experiences, a grossly inadequate style of life, which conflicts sharply with reality —as we see in patients—can usually be changed only with the help of an analyst.

The system of Individual Psychology envisages behavior as determined by the individual's own thoughts, feelings, convictions, concepts, and ideas regarding his own person, his physical and social environment, and his relationship to that environment. It has therefore been called a "subjectivistic psychology" (Ansbacher, 1956, p. 286). It is an "ego psychology" par excellence. The human mind is seen as directed and governed by the individual's own self-created values, purposes, goals, and interests; his behavior therefore is, in the last analysis, the result of his striving toward these self-created goals.

The reality of his own nature (including his instincts or drives) as well as that of his natural and social environment and his relationship thereto, do *not*, of themselves, determine his behavior. It is his individual concepts and interpretations of all these, generated by his goal, which *do* determine his behavior. It is for this reason that Adler's personality theory has been called a "teleological psychology." Adler says: "We cannot think, feel, will or act without the perception of some goal" (1920, p. 2). And:

> More important for the understanding of a person than his heredity and his disposition, his objective experiences and his real environment,—is his subjective evaluation of these; an evaluation whose nature and form is dictated by his final goal, and which stands in a certain, though often strange relation to reality (1920, p. 4).

Again, Adler states:

> Psychological phenomena can never be understood or explained by energies, causes, instincts, impulses,—but only by knowing a person's goal. Experiences, traumata, sexual development mechanisms, etc., can never yield, by themselves, an explanation for anything; only the perspective in which these experiences, traumata, etc. are *seen* by the individual,—his individual way of seeing them (which is subordinate to his final goal) will yield an explanation. (Quoted by Ansbacher, 1956, p. 92.)

The reality of the individual's nature, his body, his heredity, his natural and social environment, and his experiences are, for Adler, only the material the individual uses to construct his personality. These factors, then, are not causes or reasons for the development of either his traits or characteristics or of his attitudes and behavior. Rather, they are incentives, hints, or lures, but not compelling necessities, for developing in a certain direction. They can therefore be used only as an indication of the existence of a certain statistical probability for predicting the development of a personality or behavior. The final determinant for what an individual will make of these realities remains with the individual himself, and is determined by the final goal he has set for himself.

Adler simplified this psychological-teleological axiom by stating that it mattered less where a person comes from than where he goes or intends to go. He also called his theory a psychology of "use," not of "possession."

An individual's use of his potentials matters more than his mere possession of them.

Social Interest

Individual Psychology is, in all its aspects, a *social* psychology. Adler was totally imbued with the conviction that human life is, first and foremost, social life. He repudiated psychologies that attempt to study or explain human behavior in isolation from its social environment. "No psychologist," Adler states, "is able to determine the meaning of any experience, if he fails to consider it in its social relation to society" (1939, p. 155). Long before the various schools of interpersonal relations developed, Adler had already propounded that consciousness itself is a social product, generated by the child's interrelation with his mother and family members. Social solidarity, the feeling of being at one with other human beings is, for Adler, the necessary condition for mental health. He believed that social embeddedness anchors the individual firmly in reality (because reality is in the main social reality) and thus counteracts the tendency of the fictitious, irrational goal, which estranges him from it. In this way, attitudes of co-operation and empathy, love and good will—all subsumed by Adler under the term "social feeling" or "social interest"—are far from moral concepts or preachings, but the *only* way man can achieve mental health, happiness, and lasting satisfaction.

Social feeling is the necessary factor for social adaptation. Without it an individual's thinking, feeling, willing, and acting would be left to the stimulus of his irrational goal of self-enhancement and self-aggrandizement, and thus become totally asocial or antisocial. A child learns the necessity for social adaptation in the environment of his family and society in general; he also learns that his own self-interest is best served by such an adaptation. Adler recognized the many factors in our society that work against the development of social interest, such as competition, class differences, and power struggle; but he maintained that since nothing can be created by anyone without direct or indirect help from, or cooperation with, others, the importance of social feelings is generally recognized and accepted, at least tacitly, even by those who offend against them, if only by their guilt feelings or the excuses they make. The prime issue in human life, then, is *to bring private interest into agreement with general human interest.*

At this point it is important to clarify the concept of *unconsciousness* in Adlerian psychology. "The unconscious," Adler states, "is nothing other than that which we have been unable to formulate in clear concepts. These concepts are not hiding away in some unconscious or subconscious recess of our minds, but are those parts of our conscious, the significance of which we have not fully understood" (1935a, p. 10). And further, "We cannot oppose 'consciousness' to 'unconsciousness' as if they were two antagonistic halves of an individual's existence. The conscious life becomes unconscious as soon as we fail to understand it; and as soon as we understand an unconscious tendency, it has already become conscious" (1964, p. 163).

As a rule, Adler preferred to speak of the "not understood" instead of the "unconscious." In general, the content of a person's fictitious goal and his life style remain largely withdrawn from his full understanding, and thus they remain unconscious. Particularly in neurosis, thinking, feeling, and acting, in the context of their motivation, have to remain unconscious or not understood in order to enable the neurotic to perpetuate his neurotic style of life undisturbed. The nonneurotic, also, will sift experiences, perceptions, and concept formations; he will order them according to his style of life and manage to remain largely unaware of such concepts, perceptions, and conclusions that threaten or contradict his style of life. A *biased perception* is the inevitable result; it can only be mitigated to some degree by his becoming aware of this fact and by consciously trying to counteract it.

The conflict between "instinct theory" and "ego psychology" started early between Freud and Adler. It was the inevitable result of Adler's concept of human *goal directedness* as the final activator of all human thinking, feeling, willing, acting, and perceiving. To start with, Adler considered instincts in human beings to be relatively weak, as compared with animals. In addition, he felt that social relations and the resulting social consciousness further weakened, altered, and modified the instincts to a point where they became unrecognizable, certainly unreconstructable in their original form. Whereas Freud insisted that the individual, ruled by his instincts, is striving backward toward an ego ideal consisting of his lost, absolute, primary narcissism—Adler insisted that the individual, ruled by his goal, modified by his social consciousness, is relentlessly pressing forward toward a self-created goal of becoming and overcoming, of mastery and superiority. (We may note here the rather striking similarity of Allport's views.)

Freud and Adler agreed that civilization and culture, art and science, are generated by social conditions imposed upon the instincts of man. Freud, however, believed that the necessary restrictions, laws, conventions, obligations, including language, love of neighbor, cooperation, mores, and so forth, are sublimations and chains on the freedom of the instincts, on the libido, and therefore on man. Adler, on the other hand, insisted that all these social impositions are necessary means for the achievement of greater freedom and scope for man, since our poor earth crust will not yield to a mere wish. He considered animals not free, but the slave of their instincts. Where Freud saw only the alternatives of anarchic freedom or repression, Adler envisaged increasing freedom and scope for mankind without repression, but with a rational, socially directed evaluation of man's needs, desires, and interests; their life style increasingly corresponding to high social values, to attitudes in which the progress of mankind is expressed in the highest possible degree, limited only by the realities of the society they live in. "Individual Psychology does not demand the repression of either justified or unjustified wishes. It teaches, however, that unjustified wishes must be recognized as being opposed to social feeling, and that they can be made to disappear, not by repression, but by some addition of *social interest*" (1939, p. 290). ". . . our cultural life, at every step, successfully forces the replacement and transformation of 'natural' forms of expression (instincts) in favor of 'social' ones" (1930, p. 74).

Although other social psychologies (Fromm, Horney, and Sullivan) admit of a social component in the psyche in addition to the instincts, Adler's position is that consciousness (a product of modified instincts) is the resultant of social relations forming and modifying the naturally existing psychic potentialities (instincts) of man. *Consciousness is generated by the socialization of the psyche.*

The main problems of life, the questions an individual has to answer in life and the tests he has to undergo, are social problems, social questions, and social tests. They all involve the problem of social relations; first with members of the family, later with those outside the family—in school, in friendship, in work, and in love.

Those individuals who have not developed in their childhood a sufficient amount of social feeling are dismally unprepared to solve or even face life's problems. They feel and know that they are unprepared and dread inevitable failure. They have experienced failure, and they dread its repetition. This threatening failure, this menacing defeat, raises an individual's feeling of inadequacy to unbearable heights. It is the anticipated blow to his self-image that makes the suffering so acute when failure is expected or experienced in an area in which his ego ideal demands that he be eminently successful. Failure in such an area is equivalent to an actual shock experience, with mobilization of endocrine output raised to a high pitch. Mind and emotions will race at breakneck speed in search of a solution to this dilemma. The individual is forced to construct *safeguarding devices* that will erase, avoid or deny defeat, diminish or abolish feelings of inadequacy, substitute an apparent or spurious victory for defeat, conceal or camouflage disaster to his ego ideal, or shift responsibility for failure. These are the functions the individual hopes the safeguarding devices will fulfill. These safeguarding devices are the symptoms of neuroses and psychoses. "Neuroses and psychoses," says Adler, "have the ultimate purpose of safe-guarding a person from a clash with reality, and by this avoidance (so he hopes) sparing him the danger of having the dark secret of his inadequacy revealed (to himself and others). What appears as different disease entities are only different safeguarding devices (symptoms), which indicate how one or the other individual believes he can dream (or fancy) himself into life, without losing the all-important feeling of his personal value, his significance and his idealized self-image" (1912, p. 219).

With this statement about the purposeful, though largely unconscious, construction and maintenance of the symptoms of neuroses and psychoses, the unity of *all* psychological, mental-emotional illness, disturbances, and deviations is established in Adlerian theory. It should be noted that these "safe-guarding devices" are not identical with what Freud later called "defense mechanisms," since the latter are supposed to defend against instinctual drives and impulses, whereas the former safeguard the ego from an imagined or threatened loss of self-esteem and prestige in its clash with social reality.

It is only natural that in this frantic search for means and ways of rescuing the ego from imminently anticipated disaster, old, tested, and well-trained methods that had been found successful in threats to the ego in childhood should be revived and resorted to in such an emergency. Of these methods, the asocial ones are already precursors to later neurotic and psychotic symptoms.

The Role of Childhood

All children, in their attempts to cope with life's difficulties, have tried out and tested all sort of methods to gain or regain their sense of security, mastery, and superiority, such as: expressions of fear to get support and affection (anxiety); displays of crying or pouting to force others to do their bidding and to feel sorry for them (depression); attempts at hurting themselves in order to blame, attack, or accuse others (suicide); construction of magical thought patterns or magical orders to undo feelings of impotence or insecurity and to avoid having to deal with the real problem (compulsion); denial of the reality of an occurrence and its unbearable feelings (schizoid); accusations of others to escape responsibility (paranoid); flight into fantasy to attempt life in a better, private world instead of the real one that is too difficult (psychoses); and many others.

The most successful and rewarding of these methods will have been used most frequently and trained in most intensively in childhood; and it is these methods that will be resorted to first and held on to with the greatest tenacity, in any case of emergency. Only if the preferred method should fail to provide the desired relief from unbearable tension, insecurity, feeling of inadequacy, if it should fail to re-establish for the ego at least the necessary semblance of a restored ego ideal, that is, if the person feels checkmated despite the intensive use of his chosen symptom, then—after a shorter or longer period of confusion—one or the other less intensively trained-in method is resorted to. This can be seen most clearly in cases where a neurotic has a psychotic breakdown.

This reaching back to childhood methods as an answer to, or warding off of, present (adult) difficulties is often referred to as "regression." Here again the fundamental difference between Freudian instinct theory and Adlerian goal-directed ego psychology can be seen clearly. Whereas for Freud there occurs a "flooding back" of the libido when it encounters an obstacle, for Adler, a relentless pressing forward toward the attainment of a goal, with the utilization of all psychic potentialities, is the crux of the matter. As far as the "reaching back" to childhood methods is concerned, Adler says: "Since every development in each phase mirrors the present and the future, we can never speak of a regression in the Freudian sense. Otherwise *every* psychic act would be a regression, since it always draws on experiences from the past" (1930, p. 73).

The experience of a shock, however, in an individual who is confronted with a demand for which the amount of his social feeling is insufficient, does not, in itself, create a neurosis. For a neurosis or psychosis to arise, it is necessary for the individual to perpetuate the effects of the shock symptoms within himself, while utilizing them for avoiding future clashes with reality, which, he feels, would spell certain disaster if he did not prevent them.

One often hears of a sudden onset of a neurosis or psychosis. But if one digs carefully into the childhood history of the neurotic, one can invariably find the childhood precursor of that symptom, which is now heightened to such an extent that it becomes a definite neurosis. A qualitative change, not simply an intensification of the symptom, occurs. Favorable circumstances, which abolish the demand for the solution of the threatening problem, will make the development of a neurosis from a shock experience unnecessary. The individual will then be able to carry on as he did before the shock. However, the neurotic life style, developed since childhood, remains, and when the individual is again confronted with the threatening problem, the neurotic symptom will re-emerge unless he has, in the meantime, increased his social feeling and his ability to cooperate to a degree where he dares to risk failure, having some confidence now of being able to cope with the situation.

An exogenous factor, the *one* life problem the individual lacks the courage to face, is present at the onset of every neurosis and psychosis. In the course of treatment this should be searched for and identified in every case. In many cases the patient, in the very first session, will mention quite blandly the problem for which he is obviously unprepared; but he cannot and will not make the connection between his problem and the symptom he developed. In other cases where social demands have been increasing only gradually, and the individual feels a similarly gradual increasing inability to cope with them, the shock experiences are minor, but repeated frequently. The exogenous factor then becomes more vaguely defined, spread over a wider area, encompassing a whole constellation of life problems. In this situation it will then be more difficult to pin-point the problem that generated the neurosis.

In connection with child guidance, Individual Psychology, perhaps more than any other school of psychology, has investigated the question of the prevention of neurosis. The question was: Which children fail to develop a sufficient amount of social feeling, sense of belonging, and ability to cooperate, and therefore suffer a more intense feeling of inadequacy, a lack of self-confidence and courage; and what induces them to develop in such a deficient manner? Adler pointed to three categories of children who are more prone to develop neuroses and psychoses:

1. Children who are born with organic deficiencies; those with motor, digestive, respiratory weaknesses, with visual or auditory handicaps, clumsy, weak or sickly children, etc. For any small adaptation to life, for the smallest satisfaction, they have to make such strenuous and concentrated efforts that their attention, constantly on themselves and their effort for adaptation and survival, have little left for concentration of their interest on others. (When you are drowning in a lake, you are not able to appreciate the beautiful scenery around you.) Others are of interest to them only for whatever help they can get from them in their frantic efforts. Dependent and exploitative relations are frequently the result, unless a very good and secure relationship has nevertheless enabled them to develop sufficient interest in other people.

2. Children who develop what Adler called a "pampered style of life." The choice of the word "pampered" may perhaps be unfortunate; first,

because it denotes coddling and loving, which are generally necessary in the upbringing of children; and second, because it may imply that there was a stupid or evil parent who committed the "great sin" of pampering the child. Such, however, was not Adler's meaning when he used this term. He was, rather, referring to those children who, because of a variety of circumstances, interpreted life to mean that they are, by right, entitled to everything with little or no effort or contribution on their part; that others exist only to serve them and support them, and that mastery and superiority means to be able to exploit others, lean heavily on them; and though they depend on them, they feel entitled to dictate to them the way their dependency needs must be fulfilled. They look for easy triumphs, praise, and admiration; they never trust their own powers to achieve a desired victory, are highly envious of others and prone to depreciate them, including those on whom they depend for help. As children they already show the precursors of such neurotic reactions as anxiety, depression, compulsion, etc.; they have various asocial habits and are always a burden instead of a help in the family. Actual overprotection and pampering may be a strong incentive for a child to make such interpretations and to develop a pampered style of life. The youngest child, for instance, the baby in the family, may easily develop such ideas about life when parents and other children do everything for him. (Sometimes, however, a child, in reaction, may rebel against such pampering.) In the first category mentioned, the physically handicapped children may be additionally endangered by a quite understandable overprotection given them by the parents. Also, the existence of impressively stronger siblings and their outstanding successes may easily impress a child with the impossibility of ever equalling them, and thus lead them to the pursuit of devious ways in competition with them, such as: seductiveness, pleas for sympathy by stressing their weakness, arousing guilt in others, or constructing alibis and excuses for their failure, and shifting the responsibility for it onto others. There are, in fact, innumerable situations and constellations that may induce a child to the conviction that feelings for others and cooperation with them are detrimental and dangerous to his goal and that exploitation and domination of others are the only successful means.

3. Children who have been neglected, rejected, or hated—the unwanted children. They, too, are prone to believe very early in life that the only ideal to strive for is to get support and service from others; but having been devoid of any experience with love, friendship, and cooperation, they not only do not know how to use these methods of social relations, but are, in fact, highly suspicious of them.

It is one task of prevention and guidance to make the child aware of his mistaken interpretations and to show him the benefits he would derive from more social behavior. It is also desirable to lead the parents to a more social and cooperative attitude for the child's benefit as well as their own. An upbringing in a family marked by strife, competition, and rivalry may induce a child to become convinced that winning *against* rather than winning in cooperation *with* someone is the only way to succeed or even to survive. As far as his family is concerned, a child may even be right in his conclusion; but later in life, in his personal relations in friendship, love, and in his work life, such an attitude can only lead to defeat. Such children, as well as many of those who have been neglected, may well develop a relatively great degree of activity in their fighting attitude against people, all of whom they consider as enemies they have to subdue; they do not plead for support, they take what they want; they do not dominate in devious ways, they dictate openly to their victims—they are the delinquent children, the sociopaths, and the criminals.

Neuroses and psychoses, on the other hand, are usually characterized by a lower degree of activity than would be expected in a normally functioning nonneurotic or nonpsychotic. All the symptoms are actually so designed as to reduce or exclude some or more, sometimes even all spheres of social activity. Anxiety symptoms make social activity impossible in one area or another; depression diminishes motor and other activities; obsessive-compulsive symptoms narrow the sphere of activity to ridiculous minutiae and thus exclude or diminish the tackling of real-life problems; fugues replace the real situation with one where little or nothing is demanded, and schizoid withdrawal and schizophrenic delusions and hallucinations obviously substitute for all battlefronts of real life. Adler says

> ... the neurotic has been a child to whom leaning on other people offered a possibility of success. Such a child experienced, developed and secured for himself during several years of his life an enriched and elevated position by obtaining everything easily, with the help of others. Thus he came to a standstill in the development of his social interest and acquired a picture of the world that promised him an easy and quick fulfillment of his wishes. In such a case, the development of great activity is not very urgent (1935b, p. 9).

Sexuality

Adlerian psychology, with its holistic attitude in regard to the personality, sees the role of sex quite clearly circumscribed. The sexual function, like any of the other functions, develops in accordance with the person's goal and style of life. Like other functions such as eating, drinking, talking, excreting, and so on, sex develops at first in a self-centered way, concerned with and determined only by one's own bodily needs. However, in the course of the necessary social adaptation, every function becomes socialized. The baby eats, drinks, talks, and eliminates in any way, at any time and at any place as his body needs dictate, without regard to other people or things around him. But in the course of his social development he will learn, for his own satisfaction as well as for the fulfillment of social demands, to do these things only in certain places, at certain times, in certain ways, having regard for the needs of others. In this way he integrates his functions with his social way of life.

Of all human functions, the sexual one achieves full development later than all the others, in prepuberty and puberty. It will therefore be guided in its social adaptation by an already existing, fixed style of life. In the beginning it is exercised in a self-centered way (pollution, masturbation) as are all other functions; but this self-centeredness is already mitigated to a great degree by social awareness of the needs of others (privacy, hiding) and by well-developed social concepts about the sexual function (men-women relationships).

In our society, the function of sex in mature relationships always implies a cooperative task for two people of the opposite sex. All failures in love, marriage, and in sex are the result of a lack of cooperation between them. Competition, striving for predominance, depreciation of the other, resentment, and hostility—these are the main factors that interfere with the development of a mature and integrated relationship. Such factors, however, pre-exist the development of the full sexual function and determine its use accordingly. In no way can the sexual function, or for that matter the sexual drive, be considered autonomous. The total personality uses *all* functions in line with the person's unique style of life.

Infantile precursors of the developing sexual function, such as tickling sensations and tumescence, can be termed sexual only on the basis of a theory that considers *all* pleasurable feelings to be sexual (Freud's libido theory). Adler considered the extreme extension of the meaning of sex by Freud, whereby it includes friendship, love between parents and children, and all friendly feelings between people, as a mere terminological neologism, without any value for greater understanding and cognition. Friendship, love of parents or children, and so forth are relationships necessary for the individual's goal of security, mastery, and overcoming, and are expressions of social feeling. The sexual function will become a part of such relationships only if the individual feels it enhances the achievement of his goal. This brings up the question of Adler's position in regard to the Oedipus complex, one of the pillars of the libido theory. According to Adler, the pampered child who wants to monopolize his mother and expects from her the fulfillment of *all* his wishes—having failed to extend his social interest to other people—will necessarily strive with every means to exclude *all* others from contact with his mother in order to possess her alone. The father, for him, is most frequently the chief competitor for the mother, although siblings also figure as competitors. If he is an only child the father is the only competitor; his aim then will be to exclude the father and possess the mother exclusively. For such a constellation the Oedipus saga is a very telling and colorful metaphor. This metaphor says that the child acts *as if* he wanted to marry his mother and kill the father. It is the mark of schizoids (schizo-types, Rado) to take symbolic language and metaphors literally.

The fact that boys and mothers, and girls and fathers, are usually more attached to each other, is easily understandable by the fact that mothers and fathers, by their own conditioning in our society, are prepared for a more tender, friendly, and giving attitude toward the other sex, and in their preparations for their future life, boys and girls, in imitation, assume a similar attitude toward the parent of the opposite sex. Sexuality cannot be held responsible for this preference. It is a socially induced phenomenon. Adler said: "We could, probably, induce an Oedipus complex in any child. All we should need is for the mother to spoil him and refuse to spread his interest to other people, and for his father to be comparatively indifferent and cold" (1931, p. 54).

Accordingly, there are in Adlerian psychology no developmental phases in the psychosexual development as proposed by Freud. From the rudimentary infantile and childhood precursors of the sexual function, the masturbatory phase develops, which, if a sufficient amount of social feelings is present, leads to the heterosexual phase. Lacking sufficient social interest and ability to cooperate, *all* sexual activities are considered, in essence, masturbatory in nature, be they homosexual or heterosexual, fetishistic or sadomasochistic. Only the integration of the sexual function with the highest form of social interest and feelings, that is, true love, leads to mature heterosexuality.

Temporary adolescent homosexual activities in our society are due to the much greater risk in and punishment for heterosexual relations; or to the usually justified feeling of being unprepared and inadequate, therefore anticipating rejection by the other sex; or to the need to prove one's manliness to other boys.

Homosexuality in adolescence that leads into adult homosexuality, however, is already a symptom of a neurosis, psychosis, or personality disorder. Such a development may occur in an individual who from childhood on has been discouraged, confused, and who has denied his natural gender role and trained himself for the opposite one. For homosexuality to become fixed, it is necessary that this denial and this training continue into the maturation period and become integrated with the use of the sexual function. If he does not do this, because of more favorable circumstances and greater encouragement—and this happens quite frequently—he will not become a homosexual; but his mannerism and expressive movements may nevertheless show quite clearly the early training for the opposite role; he may be said to have overcome or aborted the earlier homosexual development.

Each child who develops a homosexual way of life has his own unique reasons for doing so. It may be his own estimate of his body which he considers incapable of fulfilling his natural gender role—a judgment he usually derives from his experiences in the family—or from other experiences he interprets as convincing evidence that to be a man (or woman) would surely lead to a devastating loss of prestige and personal value. It is the anticipated social role in life, not sexuality, which leads to the early denial of one's normal gender role. Confirmation of this fact recently came from R. J. Stoller (1965, pp. 207–218), a Freudian, who investigated two boys born without penises. He found that they had developed a sense of maleness before the ages of three to five (the phallic stage), having had no social reasons to doubt or deny it.

The facts of life are that human beings are endowed with sexual organs and sexual functions, among the many other organs and functions they possess, and that it depends to the largest extent on their goals and their style of life as to how they will use their sexual and other organs and functions. This means that people's thoughts and feelings about themselves, about other people, and about their relationships with other people will determine the use of their organs and functions, including the sexual ones.

This fact is seen by every analyst in his daily practice. He observes in his patients, heterosexual and homosexual, that they use their sexual organs and functions for domination, humiliation, revenge, for making money, evading responsibilities, for a sense of victory, and so on. It is then always our task as analysts to help the patient change or modify his thoughts and feelings about himself, others and relationships with others, generally *and* sexually, in such a way that friendship rather than hostility, cooperation rather than competition, trust rather than suspicion, equality rather than domination and exploitation, closeness rather than distance, become more prominent in his thinking, feeling, and acting. It is not a question of the patient repressing asocial or antisocial wishes or drives, but a question of developing more social feelings and realizing emotionally and intellectually that his private interest is most effectively served when it is integrated with and goes parallel to common human social interest.

No one, therefore, "is" homosexual. Long and intensive training is needed to develop homosexuality. It is mainly done unconsciously (as is a good deal of self-training). However, the very reality of one's sexual organs makes it difficult to deny one's sex; therefore a majority of homosexuals find it already in childhood necessary to deny volition for their training and posture for the opposite role, and substitute compulsion for it. Such substitution is elevated to a general method and trained from childhood in all other areas as well, and thus we find an inordinate number of rather severe obsessive-compulsive neuroses in this group.

The logic of life in our society, however, demands, as a necessary condition for individual and social health, that we bring self-interest in this area (sexual gratification)—as in all other areas—into agreement with common human interests (the heterosexuality of our society). That this maxim is also the basis for all true morality is probably no accident.

All movements and all expressions of an individual operate in the service of his style of life, in the direction toward his self-created fictitious goal. One type of psychic movement and expression is expressed in fantasy, daydreams, and dreams during sleep.

One of the main characteristics of fantasy, daydreams, and especially dreams during sleep is that reality with its social demands and relations, its logic and common sense, is partly set aside, thus allowing free range to the fictitious goal. In sleep, particularly, the stimuli from external reality and the connection with social reality are reduced to a minimum, although such connections never entirely abolished. The style of life then, unfettered by logic and common sense, can pursue its fictitious goal and find fantastic solutions to its problems. Thus it can assuage the gnawing feelings of inferiority generated in waking life, the sense of being unable to solve problems, and the fear of failure if one should attempt to tackle them.

Dreams

The subject of a dream is always a problem, the solution of which the individual, in his waking life, is not sufficiently prepared for, is hesitant about, and does not know how to solve with logic and common sense in accordance with the demands of the community. He therefore cannot solve it in his dream either, except by the abolition of logic and common sense and the neglect of social demands and necessity. Every dream, then, poses one or more alternative solutions that are devoid of social feeling, logic, and common sense. They are, therefore, *asocial* solutions; they indicate the style of life of the individual as well as the particular life problems he fears. This holds for all dreams of patients; it is equally true for the dreams of most other individuals. Adler said that a rare person may have such a high degree of social feeling and be so integrated that in the dream he may continue his *social* search for a solution and even come up with a *social* answer; this, however, is rare.

What remains of the dream, if it is remembered—and even more so if it is forgotten—on waking, are the feelings and emotions it aroused. Mobilization of emotions in the service of the goal in the direction of a particular mode of solving a problem is one of the main purposes of the dream.

The purpose of the use of symbols and metaphors in the dream is to conceal the real meaning of the dream from the dreamer. Were he to understand that the solution of his problem, so easily accomplished in the dream and thereby erasing his feeling of inadequacy is, in actuality, a self-deception, then the purpose of the dream would be nullified.

Dreams cannot be fully understood and explained outside the context of the total personality. Any attempt to lay down rigid rules for the interpretation of dreams and their symbols is bound to fail, since it depends on the conception the dreamer has of these symbols, not on the therapist's. Only insofar as some symbols have a common meaning for most, but not for all people, can certain assumptions be entertained—but these assumptions must be verified in each case.

With this proviso firmly kept in mind, the following may be said about the meaning of certain common dream elements: Dreams of falling usually indicate a fear of loss of prestige or position and a warning to oneself not to climb too high. Dreams of flying indicate an active, ambitious person and an attitude that difficulties can easily be overcome. Dreams of paralysis indicate that he considers the problem to be insoluble. Dreams of taking examinations, if accompanied by anxiety, mean that he feels unprepared for the task ahead; if without anxiety, it may mean self-encouragement: "I did it before—I can do it again." Dreams of dead people often mean that he hasn't buried his dead yet and still remains under their influence; occasionally they may indicate thoughts of joining the dead, and thus imply suicidal tendencies. Dreams of missing a train or bus indicate a preparation for escape from a dreaded defeat by means of coming too late, leaving insufficient time to prepare, etc. Dreams about being improperly clothed indicate fear of being found out in an imperfection which one believes one has to hide. If a dreamer pictures himself as a mere spectator in his dream, it is safe to assume that he will be satisfied with an onlooker's role in waking life too. Sexual dreams may have many different meanings depending on their content, context and feelings in them. Some may indicate unpreparedness for sexual relations and a warning against them, others may be a training for them. Dreams of sex with others than one's partner will indicate hostility toward the partner. Homosexual dreams may be a training against relationships with the other sex or a self-reassurance that one can do without the other sex. Dreams of cruelty in which one takes part indicate rage and craving for revenge; the same is true for dreams of soiling, only they indicate a more passive-aggressive personality. Short dreams may indicate that he is seeking shortcuts to his problem. Long, complicated dreams show a search for excessive security, a hesitating attitude in his approach to his problem, or that he considers a variety of solutions. Recurrent dreams and dreams that are long remembered express the style of life most clearly and pinpoint the patient's goal of superiority. Forgotten dreams indicate that the emotional tone of the dream was strong, but the social conscience is also strong and prevents the thought material from forming; in analysis it may also indicate sabotage and non-cooperation. We may find absence of dreams (which means that the person doesn't even remember *that* he had a dream) in cases where an individual has reached a plateau, a resting point in his neurosis and in his treatment, and doesn't want to change any more.

As far as the value of dream interpretation for the patient is concerned, Adler states the following: "Dream interpretation, as we use it, has the purpose to demonstrate to the patient his preparations and nocturnal training, which usually discloses him to be the one who arranged for his suffering, and to show him how he, with the use of metaphors and tendentiously selected episodes, tries to view the presenting problem in such a way that it will permit him to continue to strive toward the goal he had long ago set for himself. We can always observe a corruption of logic and common sense, and occasionally spurious arguments" (1930, p. 146).

Adler referred to the undoing in dreams of insights begun or gained during analysis as the "Penelope Complex," in analogy to Penelope, the wife of Odysseus who, while waiting for him to return from the Trojan War, unraveled each night what she had knitted during the day; she did this, as you may recall, so that she would not have to marry one of her suitors as soon as the task was finished, as she had promised to do. In a similar way, by their use of the emotions aroused in the dream, which counteract logic and social sense, patients will often undo whatever understanding they may have gained in treatment.

Early Recollections

Adler considered the analysis of early childhood recollections, and their use in the understanding and treatment of patients, one of his most important innovations in the technique of individual psychology. The importance of this method is based on the fact that people's perceptions are biased in favor of their life style and that they will retain in memory only what is in accord with it and the goal they are driving at. As a rule, patients are quite unselfconscious about relating any early childhood memory; they are convinced that these are merely memories of actual trivial happenings, and they are completely unaware that childhood memories reveal, in reality, their present attitude toward life and toward themselves. A memory of the birth of a sibling, for instance, will reveal not only the patient's feeling of neglect by the mother, as well as his sibling rivalry and what his feelings were in regard to possible victory in this rivalry, but also, and mainly, his present feelings of neglect, rejection, and defeat by others. (In addition, the use of the sense and motor organs involved in these memories—visual, auditory, or motor—can give valuable hints for vocational guidance because they show the predilection, training, and even heredity gifts in these areas.) Early recollections, correctly understood in relation to the rest of the personality, will always point to the central interest of the individual. "Rightly understood, these conscious memories give us glimpses of depths just as profound as do those which are more or less suddenly recalled during treatment" (1937, p. 283).

It is of little consequence if the recollection is really the earliest, or if it is completely at odds with the facts as they occurred, or if it is pure invention, because the individual cannot even invent anything that is not in accord with his goal (strivings) and his style of life. (The same, by the way, holds true for invented dreams.) "There are no 'chance memories,'" Adler says,

out of the incalculable number of impressions which meet an individual, he chooses to remember only those which he feels, however darkly, to have a bearing on his situation. Thus his memories represent his "Story of My Life"; a story he repeats to himself to warn him or comfort him, to keep him concentrated on his goal, to prepare him, by means of past experiences, to meet the future with an already tested style of action (1931, p. 73).

To understand a patient through the use of his early recollections requires careful attention to the most minute details, and on eliciting the patient's feelings to them: Does he use "we" or "I" in his story? Is mother mentioned? Are accidents, dangers, punishments a part of his recollection? This might indicate his exaggerated tendency to stress the hostile side of life. Is the birth of a sibling mentioned? This might reveal excessive rivalry, competitiveness or fear of newcomers. A separation from the mother, such as the first school day, might reveal a greater dependency on the mother, or fear of new situations. Recollections of death or sickness often indicate great fear of these dangers and/or a preparation to fight them. (Interestingly, a majority of doctors and nurses give such stories as their first memories.) Absence of mother in many early recollections may indicate great resentment against mother's neglect or absence. Recollections of humiliating experiences may point to extreme caution toward people and dependency on their opinions. A recollection that tells of observing and watching rather than doing will indicate a visual type of person who prefers to let others do the work.

The crucial question an analyst must ask himself in his exploration of early memories is: What thought, what picture, what feelings does this patient keep constantly and vividly in his mind by this selective use of his memory, and what goal does he pursue by doing so?

Birth Order Position

Nowhere does the social and interpersonal character of Adler's psychology appear as clear and direct as in his use of the "birth order position" for the investigation and clarification of a person's goal and style of life.

Each child is in a unique position, owing to the existence or nonexistence of siblings about him; he will be decisively influenced by his position in the family. Although generalizations and vulgarizations of this concept have led to misuse and misunderstandings, a correct use of this method can be of enormous aid in arriving quickly at a thumbnail sketch of the individual's personality.

An only child, for instance, is in a very different situation than a child who has siblings. He does not have to share things, or the love of his parents, or the center of attention with any other child. There are no siblings to compete with. He may feel that the only competitor for his mother's love and attention is his father. To be deprived of the unique and exalted position in the family by the birth of another child may easily seem to the child a great injustice and catastrophe: He becomes the older child instead of the only one. His main efforts may then more readily be centered upon regaining his former special position. If his parents, particularly his mother, spoiled him—and it is difficult, as we know, for parents *not* to spoil an only child—this in itself often slows his development of interest in others. When he is *dethroned* by a newcomer he will redouble his efforts for favoritism in relation to his parents, especially his mother. If a second child comes three or more years later the older will respond to the newcomer with his already, at least partly, established style of life. If a newcomer comes before then, it may play a decisive part in the forming of his life style.

It is true that children in a constellation other than this may experience the shock of dethronement when the next child is born. However, they have already had the mitigating experience of sharing with one or more other children, which the oldest obviously could not have had. The latter is therefore more apt to be profoundly shocked by the arrival of a second child. We will more often find the oldest striving more frantically to regain the love and attention of the mother by crying, tempers, renewed bed-wetting, playing the baby, or, failing in these attempts, he may turn completely to the father—an attachment that may last all his life. If, however, he also fails to capture the interest of his father, he may develop the conviction that he is unlovable and of no interest to anyone; he may then become isolated, suspicious, and dream of the past when he was once the first and only one in his kingdom. Thus we find that oldest children are more frequently conservative, interested in the past, believing in rules and in the power structure; they are more apt to be pessimistic about the future, concerned with position and prestige, and generally suspicious and envious of strangers and newcomers.

A favorable development of an oldest child may occur where the child is well prepared for a new arrival and is included by the parents in the care of the baby. Such children are apt to develop paternal or maternal attitudes toward the younger ones, imitate the parents, and feel very responsible for the welfare of the other siblings. They often develop a great talent for organization and tend to be the custodians of order.

A special situation arises for an oldest boy when the second child is a girl. Girls develop somewhat faster than boys up to the seventeenth year, and the danger of the boy's being overtaken by the girl becomes especially great and often humiliating if she is a bright and well-developed girl. Her marked success in her studies fulfills all the expectations the parents had for the boy, and soon their attitude may be that "it is a shame the girl was not the boy, and the boy the girl." Various neurotic developments may arise from such pressures, among which total loss of self-confidence and homosexuality (if other factors favor it) are the most prominent.

The position of the second child is an entirely different one. From the beginning of his life he has had a "pacemaker." If the older child is not hostile to him, he is in a specially favorable situation. He will, as a rule, learn more rapidly, and develop faster. He is generally characterized by an attitude of being, as it were, in a race, and having to "catch up." Even as an adult he will often train himself after another pacemaker and try to catch up with him. Even in his dreams we often find that he is running and hurrying, as if he were in a race. "Oldest children, on the other hand, more often have dreams of falling. They are on top, but they are not sure they can keep their superiority" (1931, p. 149).

It is difficult for a second child to bend to authority. He does not believe in "eternal" laws or leadership and tends to be revolutionary, not necessarily in a social sense. Even when he cannot overtake the first child, he does not give up easily, but tries by devious means to be superior. "The mood of the second born is comparable to the envy of the dispossessed with the prevailing feeling of having been slighted" (1912, p. 379).

It should be stressed that it is *not* the numerical order of birth that makes the difference in the development of the style of life, but the position the child *feels* he has in his relations with his siblings and his parents. Thus, for instance, a second child may assume the position of the oldest child, especially if the latter is weak or sick, or for other reasons has early and irrevocably lost out to him.

The youngest child is also in a unique position. Of all the children he is, of course, never dethroned from his position; he remains always the baby. He may have many and varied types of pacemakers, but he has no followers who "breathe down his neck." He is constantly stimulated by the others, but as a rule he is not much pressured. Rather he pressures himself to overcome, to overtake, to become the first because he has been the last. (This has evidently been so since time immemorial with youngest children; we find in the fairy tales of many nations, and in the Bible, that it is so often the youngest who succeeds where the older ones fail.) The youngest child is often the only successful one in a family and sometimes supports all the others. Nevertheless, the youngest one is, as a rule, quite spoiled and frequently has exaggerated ambitions. When he fails in his ambition, spoiled as he is, he may not have the courage and self-confidence to try again, and will often experience a breakdown. This happens especially when he does not have the support of the rest of the family, or if some other situation causes him the loss of the privileged position he previously held.

Statistically, it may well be that the oldest and the youngest are more prone to develop neuroses and psychoses than other children.

The position of an only boy among girls, or an only girl among boys, is also a unique one, and must be evaluated. Both may tend to develop very masculine or very feminine traits. Both may feel isolated. Homosexuality is a decided possibility if early denial of their gender role fosters it.

Many other constellations are possible and have to be considered with regard to the specific influences in the development of the child's characteristics. R. Dreikurs (1963, p. 40) suggests that in each case we should find out which of the siblings the patient considered most unlike himself in character, temperament, and interests; thus we may find out his main competitor among the siblings.

Although the birth order position of the child can give the analyst a most important clue to the self-concept of the patient, the full implication this has on the patient can be understood only if the total family atmosphere and the surrounding circumstances are fully recognized.

Treatment: The Initial Phase

At the first encounter with the patient, the analyst may observe certain significant details about him. His posture, gait, the way he looks at the analyst, his hesitation or force of approach, his handshake, his introduction—these already tell the analyst much about the patient's personality, his mode of relating to people, and often about his problems and symptomatology.

It is usually advisable to maintain a casual, easy, and friendly atmosphere in the office and to avoid, as much as possible, any demand for formal conditions regarding the patient's behavior. He should be permitted to behave as he wants; the analyst should show his interest without making any demands in any way, even in regard to whether or not he sits, lies down, or talks. The explanation of what is expected from the patient during analysis and how the analysis is conducted should not be stressed at the beginning, because many meaningful expressions of the patient may be inhibited if formal rules of conduct are set down.

The analyst should approach each individual in a different way, just as he would nonpatients. Rigid rules of conduct for the analyst—"because this is an analytic situation"—only hinder the development of a trusting patient-analyst relationship. This is to say simply that the analyst should be un-selfconscious in his meeting with the patient, showing his sympathetic interest and his dedication to the patient and his problems, and generally treating him as a fellow human being. Tension should be kept at a minimum; if the patient is made to feel safe and relaxed, he will relate more easily and will reveal more.

It is important, of course, to obtain the details of the patient's personal history (including his marital status, household situation, type of work and his attitude toward it, etc.). Without full knowledge of the patient's social surroundings and his attitude toward them, the analyst will remain in the dark for a long time in regard to the meaning of the patient's expressions and the symptoms he complains of. It is essential to know under what social circumstances the symptoms arose.

Sometimes it is not possible to get these personal data at the beginning, either because the patient talks incessantly about his complaints, or because he has difficulties in talking at all. In these cases it is advisable to ascertain all the details about the complaints and symptoms and tactfully lead into their connections with the patient's living conditions and surroundings. It is advisable, wherever possible, to let the patient take the lead. The description of the symptoms can be advantageously used to establish the time when the symptoms started, whether they are constant or intermittent; what makes them vanish, what brings them on; what he has tried to counteract them (drugs or other remedies); what other physicians said about them, and his reactions to what they said; and whether he had similar symptoms, perhaps in a milder form, even before the onset he described.

In nearly all cases I take extensive notes of whatever the patient says about the symptoms and personal data. Patients usually do not object to this; on the contrary, they take it as a sign of interest on my part. It also serves to refresh the analyst's memory of data he may forget. This alone may make it more difficult for a patient to accuse the analyst of lack of interest, as he may be wont to do, in any case.

There is no reason for hesitating to interrupt a patient's story with questions that are designed to clarify, deepen, or widen an understanding of the exact nature of the symptoms or circumstances the patient describes. It gives the patient the feeling not only that the analyst is truly interested and is following his story but also that he is being understood.

From the very beginning, it is important to assure the patient that whatever he reveals or might reveal will be kept in strictest confidence. When a patient says he has a special revelation to make of something he has always kept secret and has never revealed to anyone, or fears he would be ruined if anyone knew, it is a good idea for the analyst to make it obvious (by some gesture) that he is no longer taking notes at this point. This would emphasize to the patient the analyst's assurance during and particularly after the session. On the other hand the analyst should never demand that the patient keep secret whatever transpires in the analysis.

It is also of advantage to allow more time than usual for the first session. Aside from gathering personal data, symptoms, and so forth, such things as the frequency and time of visits and the fee and method of payment have to be discussed. I usually try to leave an extra ten or fifteen minutes for these points and begin with the question as to when the patient would like to see me again. Either he, or I, then bring up the question of the frequency of visits, as well as the question of the fee in this connection.

At the beginning I find it advisable to see a patient frequently, about three or four times a week, and then to cut down to three or two times a week, depending on the case and the patient's circumstances. If he has any questions about this I explain that the work can also be done if visits are only once a week, but that it would take longer for him to feel any benefit, and I voice my concern that he might be discouraged if this takes too long, since I know that he is not very patient. It is quite safe to say this, since all neurotics are impatient, patience being the result of a feeling of security in the human community, which, obviously, a neurotic does not have. I also tell the patient how difficult it would be, especially in the beginning, to keep to the trend of thought and feeling we would be working on without losing continuity from one week to the next. All this is true, but the patient may understand it only if it has been somehow made clear to him that the work to be undertaken is largely his obligation and his responsibility.

On the other hand, patients who request to be seen every day, twice a day, or in double sessions usually want the analyst to do all their work, or want to escape from life by substituting analysis for it. It is important that these patients be told that analysis is not an end in itself and that its purpose is to help them in their life outside the analyst's office.

Sometimes a patient will ask: "Do you think you can cure me, Doctor?" I always say emphatically: "No." Then, after a short pause, during which the shock of this answer has had time to sink in, I add: "I can only try to teach you how to cure yourself." I give the same answer to the patient's parents and the husband or wife if they ask. I have found that this answer never deters a patient from coming for treatment, nor the relatives from agreeing to it. This answer also establishes, from the beginning, the patient's responsibility and the need for his cooperation. It also diminishes his resistance by depriving him of the opportunity to shift responsibility onto the analyst, or to blame him for being inept and incompetent.

When a patient is not sure about going into treatment, I suggest only *one* additional appointment, mainly for the purpose of discussing this question. If it happens that he has a list of several analysts to choose from, I encourage him to see the others and to make his own choice.

If a patient speaks of treatment he received from another therapist, one should be careful not to express disapproval either of the therapist or his methods; rather he should be asked what gains he made during the previous treatment. Disparaging remarks made about another therapist by a patient are usually to be viewed as being part either of his tendency toward depreciation in general, or as his attempt to ingratiate himself with the new analyst, or both.

During the first session, by obtaining some of the personal data, developmental history, symptoms, and complaints, and by observing the general attitude of the patient, the analyst should usually be able to obtain at least a rough thumbnail sketch of his personality, his goals, his conflict with the environment, his habitual modes of battling, and the life problem he fears to confront.

It is also important, at the very first session, to give the patient some encouragement for undertaking treatment. This is best given through the analyst's hopeful attitude and by his friendly noncritical interest. If possible, one should propose new ways of thinking about his condition. One can ask him, for instance, where he thinks his symptoms come from. As a rule, he will say he doesn't know. One may then ask: "They don't fall from heaven, do they?" The patient will usually agree. "And no one else could have possibly put them into you?" This, too, brings agreement. "Then you must produce these symptoms yourself?" The patient usually acknowledges that this must be the case. One can then say: "If *you* produce such symptoms, which are so painful and disturbing, you must have a powerful reason for doing so." At this point he is a bit confused or taken aback; nevertheless, it is quite likely that he may think about it in a new light until the next session.

Through such a confrontation a patient's responsibility for his symptoms and conduct is reaffirmed, and his interest is roused toward finding out the reasons for them; thus he is led to the beginning of the analytic work proper.

When he begins to examine the purpose of the symptoms and the possible gain he may derive from them, rather than merely complaining and using them as excuses for evading his life problems, he has seriously entered upon the work of the analysis.

Such a comparatively rapid beginning of an analysis can usually be accomplished in less serious cases. In severe neuroses, psychoses, and in schizoid and other severe personality disorders, the approach has to be, of necessity, much slower and much more cautious, inasmuch as the hostility against, and distrust of, the analyst is so great that almost everything the analyst states is interpreted as a judgment that offends and humiliates. Such patients will pick on and magnify the smallest detail and often will not even listen to the meaning of the analyst's words. In these cases, the analyst must first try to establish a trusting relationship, through unending sympathy, friendliness, and demonstrations of deep interest, which often has to be carried on more or less exclusively for a long period of time. Interpretation, confrontation, and insight have to be postponed or kept to a minimum until patients can tolerate them by developing greater social feeling and cooperation. Also, in the less severe neuroses, of course, great care must be taken not to offend, depreciate, judge, or humiliate patients.

It follows from the whole tenor of Individual Psychology that where an analyst cannot empathize with a patient, it is best to refer him to another therapist. A similar disposition is called for where he feels uneasy or insecure about the case (unless he is under supervision).

In line with the need to collaborate in analysis, the ideal situation is for patient and analyst to sit face-to-face, as equal fellow men. Almost all patients feel it to be a position of inferiority to lie on the couch while the analyst sits in lordlike fashion above him. Although transference is enhanced, the development of a genuine human relationship is made virtually impossible by such an unequal position. In psychotic cases, where patients are in desperate need to come to more friendly and accepting terms with reality, the crucial relationship with the analyst as friend and human being is the necessary bond. Lying on the couch does not help at all, but rather enhances unreality. If, however, a patient asks to be allowed to lie on the couch, he should, of course, be permitted to do so, after the reasons for this request are discussed. At the beginning of the analysis, a patient may request this because he is ashamed to reveal certain things while facing the analyst. Each patient of mine who has requested this has, after a short time, decided to sit and face me. In all cases the reasons for a face-to-face relationship have to be gone into.

Resistance and Transference

As a general rule, resistance has to be expected in every patient. In every case, each patient resists changing his style of life, his modes of operation, since he has constructed them precisely because they seemed to be the only methods by which he could ever hope to cope with life and avoid the total collapse of his prestige or self-image—a prospect that fills him with mortal fear. He is certain he can achieve significance only by the employment of his old, well-trained patterns and that he would be "nothing," irrevocably worthless, were he to give them up. He comes to analysis only because the price he pays for maintaining his symptoms, which have become a necessary part of his style of life, is too high, and he hopes that through analysis he will be able to reduce or abolish the agony he suffers without having to change. A change of his total attitude toward life is, in fact, furthest from his mind.

Any social activity a patient undertakes on his own, for which his social feeling and his faith in his ability to cooperate are not sufficiently developed, is bound to end in failure and thus will only increase his resistance, often to a point where analysis will come to a standstill. If, however, a patient proposes to undertake such a venture, the analyst should neither dissuade nor encourage him, but should simply state he is not sure the patient is ready for such an undertaking. If, nevertheless, the patient undertakes this venture and fails, as might have been expected, he will then come to the next session rather downcast, accusing himself of being worthless, and generally have a hopeless attitude regarding his progress in analysis. If the analyst had carefully prepared for such an outcome, it should be easy for him to make light of the failure, and again explain that the patient was simply not quite prepared, pointing to his insufficiently developed feeling for people and his exaggerated fear of failure. That the patient's purposeful (though unconscious) attempt to fail was a part of his resistance can often be proven to the patient, with considerable therapeutic effect. Also, it should be remembered that interpretations for which the patient is unprepared should be avoided, for they too can discourage him and increase his resistance.

During the entire course of analysis, a patient schemes, waking and sleeping, on how to maintain his neurotic system, despite overwhelming proof— to which the patient pays lip service—that he is creating his symptoms, and that they and his style of life are self-defeating, untenable, and not fulfilling the goal they were originally designed for.

A decrease in resistance can only be brought about when a patient develops contact with people on a more friendly and equal basis, enhancing greater confidence and self-esteem.

When a new patient shows no sign of resistance, he should be suspected of giving lip service only. By means of ingratiation, of compliance, and a show of cooperation, he is only scheming to win the analyst's high regard for him. Sooner or later this pretense will be discovered as being indeed a very powerful resistance; at this point the patient may then want to, or actually will, drop out of analysis.

As far as transference is concerned, it is obvious that a patient cannot possibly relate to the analyst in any way other than the way he relates, and has related, to everyone else in his life. He brings, after all, himself with all his attitudes also into the analyst's office. Depending on how he interprets or misinterprets the analyst's appearance, voice, attitude, and general demeanor, the patient will react to him out of his past experience. He has, after all, no other experiences to draw on.

It is characteristic of the neurotic's style of life, with his faulty self-image and erroneous view of relationships, to see himself either above or below everyone else, that is, to see relationships as unequal and competitive. When the patient meets the analyst, he will consider first and foremost: "Am I above or below him? Is he superior or inferior to me?" The patient has been plagued by this question in every one of his relationships. He never considers himself an equal to anyone. A relationship of two equals is something he cannot even imagine, and the idea of their cooperation is suspect to him. He knows only of bosses and underlings, masters and slaves, exploiters and exploited, oppressors and the oppressed. He wants to be the one on top; he is very guarded and suspicious of being dominated, dictated to, depreciated, or humiliated.

Analysis, however, is, par excellence, a relationship in which two people *have* to cooperate as equals in a common task. The analyst has to demonstrate, constantly and explicitly, throughout the analysis, that he considers the patient an equal, and that his cooperation is absolutely needed. The analyst himself has to be the veritable example of fellowship and cooperation. He must never be late for appointments, must always show the deepest interest, must never fight or compete with the patient, must never be offended, and at all times show concern for the patient's welfare. In a warm and friendly way he must always bring the fighting and competitive attitude of the patient back to the common task at hand.

This attitude of the analyst is, as a rule, incomprehensible to the patient. He will look for competitive and exploitative aspects, for depreciatory or humiliating nuances. There will be no lack of attempts to depreciate the analyst, to trap him in contradictions, or to prove his lack of interest. Patients who are dependent will often attempt to put the analyst on a pedestal (an honor he must always decline); subsequently, the patient will overthrow the man on the pedestal by proving that he was, after all, incapable of helping him.

Positive, negative, and libidinal transferences and transference love are all distortions of the patient, against which the analyst must confront him with a real relationship between two equals. Stress on equality and cooperation is paramount in counteracting the patient's distorted views. By persistently offering the patient a true relationship, the analyst promotes healthier attitudes, thoughts, and feelings. Once the patient has discarded his distorted view of the analyst for a much more real one, the analyst should encourage the patient to make similar changes in regard to other relationships. "Indeed, the task of the physician or psychologist," Adler says, "is to give the patient the experience of contact with a fellow-man, and then to enable him to transfer this awakened social feeling to others" (1964, p. 20).

What is called countertransference denotes only the analyst's style of life and his modes of relating to people, which he will also extend to his patients. It would be tragic, of course, for the analyst to misinterpret, in a grossly unrealistic way, his relationship with the patient. It might well indicate that the analyst's relationships in general are not cooperative, but rather competitive and exploitative. (Here the need for the re-education of the analyst is obvious.)

The sessions after the first one are devoted to the strengthening of the relationship with the analyst, the further enlistment of the patient's cooperation, and the more extensive exploration of the patient's life history and life style.

This is done by letting the patient take the analyst through his life history from childhood on, which the analyst broadens by inquiries into childhood habits, illnesses, and the patient's reactions to them; his early memories, relations with parents and siblings; his schooling, friendships, adolescence, sexual development; his choice of, and preparation for, work, marriage, and so forth. A composite picture emerges of the goals, the life style, self-image, the amount of social feelings present, and the problems the patient feels threatened by, all of which may modify or revise the picture the analyst originally formed of the patient.

The analyst, by ordering or combining attitudes, feelings, thoughts, and actions the patient reported, may lead the patient to consider new possibilities in regard to wishes, desires, and motivations. He may, at this point, offer tentative interpretations for the patient's consideration. With the material of dreams and their interpretations the patient may then be brought to a pass where he may feel that his self-image is no longer profitably served, and he may feel that he can no longer uphold it by continuing his style of life without some modification.

A powerful impact, with deep emotional insight, is brought about when a present symptom or pattern of the patient is correlated with symptoms (or their precursors) and patterns of his childhood. An example may illustrate this technique: A twenty-two-year-old girl, an only child, living with her widowed mother, came to the office with symptoms she had developed in the previous two months, of severe anxiety and fears that she would lose her mind. She was engaged and was expected to set the date for her marriage. Her earliest recollection was of her mother taking her to her first day in kindergarten; she cried and carried on so much when her mother wanted to leave that she was taken home and didn't have to go back. She said she cried so much because she was afraid that her mother would forget her and leave her there for good. She said she still had strong feelings of anxiety whenever she thought of it. When I said: "Oh, you were afraid your mother would forget you and leave you there for good? What do you think you are afraid of now?" A look of recognition came to her eyes and she whispered: "I am afraid of the same thing . . . if I get married."

This girl had maintained an appearance of being mature, adult, and independent, as her self-image demanded. She held a good job, was self-supporting, had "dates," and became engaged. But the prospect of getting married threatened her relationship with her mother, which was still the only relationship in which she felt secure. By mobilizing thoughts, feelings, and memories that produced fear and anxiety, and intensively concentrating on them, she created her present anxiety symptoms. These symptoms had the function of safeguarding her self-esteem and self-image: Now she could pretend to herself that it was her symptoms and not the lack of real independence that prevented her from leaving her mother. The strong emotion thus generated enabled her to avoid recognition of the relation between her action and her true motivation. But the parallel revealed to her of her fear in childhood and her present fear helped her to realize the motivation for mobilizing her present symptoms.

Another problem an analyst frequently has to deal with is a patient's inability to make decisions—his doubts and his wavering back and forth. This is, of course, a very common human tendency, but it is exaggerated in certain patients. It is sometimes called "fence-sitting" or ambivalence and sometimes parades under the name of "impartiality" or "eclecticism." It always indicates a lack of courage for taking responsibility for one's actions or convictions and stems essentially from fear of making a mistake that would expose one's inadequacy. I sometimes draw a roadfork for these patients and ask them how many decisions are open to them if they walk up that road and come to the fork. Some say "two," some say "three" (because you may also decide to turn back on the road you came on). No patient has ever told me "four." Then I make a big blot on the fork, and say: "Now you could also decide to stay put at that fork and not make up your mind; would that not also be a decision?" This puts responsibility upon the patient even for his *in*decision, behind which he may have been hiding, and which he may have used as an excuse for his failure to act more courageously, or not to act at all.

Guilt Feelings

In Adlerian psychology, the handling of guilt feelings differs from that of any other approach. I am not speaking now of cases where a person feels he has done wrong and is now determined to do better. I am speaking of neurotic guilt with its self-accusatory and self-depreciatory features. Guilt feelings, like all other feelings, are created and mobilized by the patient himself; they do not come from mystic realms, nor are they injected by any other person. And if he does create them in himself, he must have a powerful reason for doing so, since they are obviously nothing very pleasant to have. Guilt feelings are a form of dissociation. By setting himself up as the one who condemns the action he feels guilty about, the patient dissociates himself from the one who committed the act. The stronger the guilt feelings, the more he intoxicates himself with identifying himself with the critic, the judge of the culprit who committed the evil act or had the evil thought, and the more does he remove himself from being the actual person who had committed the act or had the thought. The self-image is thereby preserved and even enhanced, but only in an illusory way; it suffices for assuaging overwhelming feelings of inferiority by substituting a false nobility or even saintliness. In fact, some psychotics have used their guilt feelings to demonstrate that they are stricter with themselves about sin and therefore holier than even the priests who offered to absolve them from their sins. Nietzsche said: "Guilt feelings are mere wickedness."

The motive for creating guilt feelings has to be explained to the patient. He has to be impressed with the fact that with the development, however small, of social feeling that he put into practice, he would be more genuinely effective to himself and to others than by deceiving himself into only appearing so. There is a story of Adler that shows how guilt feelings can be handled in a light vein. He once said to a boy who came to him complaining of guilt feelings about masturbation: "You mean you masturbate *and* feel guilty? That is too much. One would be enough. Either masturbate *or* feel guilty." In this short statement is expressed the responsibility of the patient for creating guilt feelings, the choice he has, and how ridiculous it is to make a fuss about it. The real reason, as we learn from this case history, for creating guilt feelings was, of course, not masturbation, but something quite different. The boy was losing out in competition with his brother in school and needed some area where he could feel superior to him. Knowing that his brother also masturbated and feeling that this was sinful or evil, he chose this area to prove himself superior by developing these guilt feelings, and so presenting a more "noble mind," at least to himself and, hopefully, to others.

Obsessive-Compulsive Neurosis

It is a common human trend to create what Adler called "side-shows" in order to avoid dealing with the main problems people are faced with. This, of course, is exaggerated in neurotics and psychotics. The whole concentration is then on the side show, which is magnified to a ridiculous degree, so that the main question is thereby avoided. A girl was asked by a friend how she had managed to become pregnant, since she said she didn't like the man at all. She answered: "He had a bad cold, so I had to push him away here," making a gesture of pushing away his face. Here we see an example of how the whole structure of the obsessive-compulsive neurosis is, in the main, based on the construction of such side shows. They are often elevated to ridiculous importance, involving a furious and ostentatious battle to overcome them; this is supposed to make it obvious to the patient himself, as well as to others, that he has no time for, nor can he possibly concentrate on other —actually the real—problems that face him. The patient admits that the side issue is spurious, therefore he cannot admit volition for his actions and substitutes compulsion for it. Words and ideas are stressed and action is avoided, except for the repetitive actions in side issues. Time is the notorious enemy of the obsessive-compulsive neurotics, because it always seems to them to make demands on them for a social solution of life's problems, for which they feel unprepared and in which they anticipate failure. A great number of compulsions are therefore designed in such a way that much time is wasted with them.

Some compulsions, even those of long standing, can be greatly improved and even cured by inducing the patient to perform these very acts volitionally instead of shadow-fighting against his compulsion to do them. But this method will only be effective after the patient has realized his own construction of the compulsion, the purpose for which he created it, his fear in approaching his real problems without the safeguard of his compulsive mechanism, and after he has developed more social feeling for other people.

The compulsive patient indulges in a spurious method, trained since childhood, of heightening the sense of his own significance by painting tiny obstacles as mountainous difficulties, and then triumphing in overcoming them. He does the same with obsessive ideas, when, for instance, he succeeds in *not* jumping out of the window or *not* killing his children. The sense of his superiority is thus always stressed by it, and the test of his ability to cope with life's real problems avoided. Thus, compulsions and obsessions are designed to relieve the patient of the responsibility for dealing with the main problems and, at the same time, assuaging his feelings of inadequacy.

Depression

In Adlerian psychology the symptom of depression is understood and treated in a unique way. A special characteristic of depression, differing from most other neuroses, is the fact that the patient carefully hides his goal of superiority behind an avalanche of self-depreciation, self-accusation, and other expressions of inferiority. On closer scrutiny, however, these are revealed to be powerful methods for exploiting others, for dominating them, and for forcing them into his service. Others worry about him constantly, he is the center of attention, and thus his importance is assured. In addition, he is relieved of all social obligations and responsibilities. He cannot acknowledge, of course, that his purpose is to gain ascendance and domination over others by use of his symptoms. He therefore creates and expresses guilt feelings about being a burden to others. This again makes him feel superior as far as his sentiments are concerned (though not his actions).

Like all symptoms, depression has its precursors in childhood: excessive crying, pouting, whining, refusing to talk, eat, and so forth. Adler says: "The discouraged child who finds that he can tyrannize best by tears will be a cry-baby; and a direct line of development leads from the cry-baby to the adult depressed patient" (1956, p. 288). The patient tries "to approximate the well-tested picture of a helpless, weak, needy child, for he discovered from personal experience that it possesses a great and most compelling force" (1920, p. 243).

The battle of the depressed is, as a rule, directed against one main opponent: it may be the mother or father, the wife or husband, or someone else in the patient's immediate environment. He accuses his opponent, overtly or secretly, for his depression; he exacts tribute and takes revenge, and at the same time frustrates all effort to help him. In treatment he can easily substitute the analyst for his main opponent. He will characteristically say, "Now it's too late," and he will reject the very thing he complained had been denied him and which, he said, was the reason for his depression. One is reminded of the child who, after much fussing and crying, is finally offered what he wants, but says: "Now I don't want it."

By frustrating all people who want to help him, he depreciates them and thus feels superior to them. He maintains his depression by centering his attention on pessimistic anticipations on which he ruminates and then acts as if they had already occurred. Eventually, the analyst will have to show the patient the purpose for which he concentrates on pessimistic predictions and why he avoids optimistic perspectives—he would have to give up domination of others and he would have to start cooperating with them—a prospect he fears would only lead to his deepest humiliation.

Before this can be done, the rage, the anger, and the fury of the patient have to be uncovered and brought home. This would have the effect of denying the patient the possibility of hiding behind noble motives and sentiments. Then the guilt feelings are to be exposed and demolished for the sham they are.

It is most important that a patient's suicidal ideas be dealt with in connection with his rage and fury. Suicidal threats are usually designed to whip the opponent into line, especially when the latter attempts to escape the tyrannical domination of the patient. If the threats fail, attempts of suicide may follow. Whether preceded by threats or not, suicide attempts, successful or not, are always furious acts of revenge. The patient expects the opponent to be shattered by his act and to suffer lifelong guilt for not having acceded to his wishes. By removing himself from the scene of the battle with a grand gesture, he also intends to point up the worthlessness of others, and to absolve himself of all criticisms. In his mind he emerges as the victor. In childhood, the prototype of the potential suicide is the one who says, in essence, "Serves my mother right if I break my leg." There is always the implication that "Then she will suffer and be sorry." Similarly, the adult says, "See what you have driven me to do. Now you will suffer the rest of your life, and you will realize what a rare and sensitive person you've lost."

Since the threat of suicide must be considered an emergency situation, the treatment has to be immediate, forceful, and direct. Suicide or its intention has to be uncovered as a definitely insidious and vengeful device, filled with rage. I explain to my patients that the devious motive of this act has been recognized for ages by most people, so that many religions do not even allow suicides to be buried beside other people; that people try to forget suicides quickly and shy away from talking about them; and that no one will feel guilty on account of his action. To a patient who tested me with the question as to how I would feel if I were to read a notice of his suicide in the newspaper I answered that it is possible that some reporter, lacking any more important news, would pick up such a report from a police blotter. But the next day, the paper would already be old and only a dog, perhaps, might honor his suicide notice by lifting a leg over it in some corner. Such and similar attitudes toward suicide have an enormous effect on the patient. They make it very difficult for him to commit or even attempt suicide because it is deprived of its prestige value, its *beau geste:* His self-image is no longer safeguarded by it.

In psychotic depressions one may have to be more careful and slower in one's approach. The underlying rage, and perhaps the guilt feelings, can usually be dealt with immediately. The more total identification of the patient with his pessimistic predictions and anticipations, his devaluation of reality, and his denial of common logic, must be dealt with as in schizophrenia only after the patient's trust has been gained to an appreciable degree.

In the manic-depressive psychoses, the manic phase is characterized by a frantic effort of the patient to force a success in the service of his goal of superiority with which he has so much intoxicated himself that he appears to take literally the "all" in the "all-or-nothing" proposition, so often found in psychotics. It is not unlike alcoholic intoxication, which, by the way, is also often resorted to in order to overcome depression. The prototype of the manic-depressive is the child who begins everything with great enthusiasm, only to give it up just as quickly if immediate and brilliant success is not forthcoming. The intensity with which the goal is pursued is then replaced by crying, withdrawal, and accusations of others. Mania and depression are two different methods used alternatively in the pursuit of the same single goal. As soon as one method appears to fail, the other is resorted to. Both the manic and the depressed negate reality by the use of a delusion about their prophetic gift; one, by foreseeing that he will succeed in everything; the other, by foreseeing that everything will end in failure and disaster.

The fact that they always have an alternative, well-trained method available to them, both asocial, makes it difficult for them to adopt a social method of dealing with life. All patients first try a number of asocial methods before they are ready to give them up in desperation and dare to try a social way; but manic-depressives, when one alternative has failed, always try the other alternative "once more"; this is what makes their treatment so difficult. The unity of their two methods in the pursuit of a single goal must be demonstrated to them, constantly and repeatedly, their unrealistically exaggerated goal of superiority unmasked, and their social interest increased in the relationship with the therapist. By predicting the other phase of the cycle and preparing the patient for it, the analyst, through the interpretation of the patient's life style, can often lessen its intensity and this preparation can eventually lead to the patient's readiness to give up both phases altogether.

Schizophrenia

In the treatment of schizophrenics we have to keep particularly in mind that these patients have grown up with a much greater feeling of inferiority than other patients and that they have experienced much greater difficulties in adapting to life and to their social surroundings. With such great feelings of inferiority, the goal of superiority and the idealized self-image are, in compensation, exaggerated to a high degree. They are easily discouraged of ever achieving the exaggerated goal or of maintaining their idealized image. Certainly, any concrete goals, normally achievable in our society, will not suffice to make them feel that they are even on the way toward achieving their goal. All concrete goals, therefore, have to be discarded, and the schizophrenic is left alone with his fictional goal. This he then tends to take literally, and he tends to dogmatize it. The fantasy life increases as his actual social life decreases; his self-centeredness becomes extreme as his social feelings lag far behind. Real relationships never have a chance to develop; reality is increasingly denied, and the fantasy of his unreality is substituted for it. Logic and common sense are denied, and private logic is substituted. This private logic is often developed to a very high degree, and we often see schizophrenics using thought and language with astounding facility and seeming cleverness. On closer examination, however, the method or pattern of their highly biased private logic can be discerned.

The patient's aggrandized self-image does not permit the admission of his inability to solve problems. People around him are used for the personifications of his difficulties, and they are accused of preventing him from achieving his grandiose goals. This establishes the paranoid trend in the schizophrenic. Projecting himself headlong into the role he assumes, he creates voices and visions within himself, which warn or command him to do things or to avoid doing them, without his taking any responsibility for them. This is an exaggerated and more unreal form of substituting compulsion for volition, as we have seen in the obsessive-compulsive neuroses. These hallucinations may or may not be intelligible to the patient. He may be totally committed to their apparent objectivity—they appear quite foreign to him. Hopelessness is extreme and denotes the despair of ever being able to be of any significance in the real world. Adler considered hopelessness so characteristic of the schizophrenic that he once said, "We could probably, by systematic discouragement, make any child into a person who behaves like a schizoid" (1931, p. 46).

Before such a patient, as well as many other patients, can realize the nature and meaning of his behavior, a genuine relationship with the analyst, perhaps the first he has ever had, must be established. The confidence and hopefulness of the analyst may influence the patient to adopt a similar attitude. The respect and esteem shown the patient may increase his own self-esteem and self-respect, until he may eventually become convinced that cooperation, with at least one other human being, is both feasible and fruitful. He may then also believe that some concrete goals can be achieved by him, without humiliation, and that he can feel himself as a human being among his fellow-men.

To accomplish this, "the therapist," in the words of Adler, "must lose all thought of himself and all sensitivity about his own ascendance, and he must never expect anything of the patient. Since he is the belated assumption of maternal functions he must work with a corresponding devotion to the patient's needs" (1929, p. 124).

REFERENCES

ADLER, A. Über den nervösen Charakter. Munich: Bergmann. (English: The individual psychology of Alfred Adler. New York: Basic Books, 1956.)

ADLER, A. Praxis und Theorie der Individualpsychologie. Munich and Wiesbaden: Bergmann, 1920. (English: Practice and theory of individual psychology. New York: Humanities Press, 1951.)

ADLER, A. Das Problem der Homosexualität. Leipzig: S. Hirzel, 1930.

ADLER, A. What life should mean to you. New York: Little, Brown, 1931.

ADLER, A. Über den Ursprung des Strebens nach Überlegenheit und des Gemeinschaftegefühles. Internationale Zeitschrift für Individual Psychologie, 1933, 11. No. 4.

ADLER, A. The structure of neurosis. International Journal of Individual Psychology, 1935, 1, 2, 3. No. 2. (a)

ADLER, A. Prevention of neurosis. *International Journal of Individual Psychology,* 1935, **1** (4), 3–12. (b)

ADLER, A. Significance of early recollections. *International Journal of Individual Psychology,* 1937, **3** (4), 283–287.

ADLER, A. *Social interest.* New York: Putnam, 1939.

ADLER, A. *Problems of neurosis.* New York: Harper Torchbooks, 1964.

ANSBACHER, H. L., and ANSBACHER, ROWENA R. *The individual psychology of Alfred Adler.* New York: Basic Books, 1956.

DREIKURS, R. *Psychodynamics, psychotherapy and counselling.* Oregon: Univ. of Oregon Press, 1963.

STOLLER, R. J. *The Psychoanalytic Quarterly,* 1965, **34**, 207–218.

13

METHODS
OF TREATMENT
IN ANALYTICAL
PSYCHOLOGY

Gerhard Adler

General Remarks: The Rationale of Treatment

If I am to contribute a chapter on the methods of treatment in analytical psychology, I must from the start point out two problems that will complicate my task. The first is that the specific technique of analytical psychology does not exclude the use of more generalized analytical techniques; the second is that the technique of analytical psychology has, like that of every other analytical school, undergone, and is continually undergoing, considerable changes.

Regarding the first point I have only to quote Jung's own point of view (Jung, 1929, pp. 55 ff.), according to which he distinguishes four different

338

stages of analysis, each requiring a special technical approach: the first stage of "confession" (or the cathartic method); the second stage of "elucidation" or "interpretation" (in particular the interpretation of the transference, thus being very near to the "Freudian" approach); the third stage of "education" (the adaptation to social demands and needs, thus most nearly expressing the standpoint of Alfred Adler); and finally what he calls the stage of "transformation" (or "individuation"), in which the patient discovers and develops his unique individual pattern, the stage of "Jungian" analysis proper.

These stages are not meant to represent either consecutive or mutually exclusive stages of treatment, but different aspects of it, which interpenetrate and vary according to the needs of the particular patient and the therapeutic situation. Thus, treatment has to be undogmatic, flexible, and adjusted to the needs of the individual patient, and this specification is one of the main tenets of analytical psychology. In any case, it has to be understood that what Jung has termed "reductive" analysis in contradistinction to "synthetic" or "constructive" analysis (Jung, 1926–1943, pp. 81 ff.) plays a considerable role in the theory and technique of analytical psychology. So, in writing about the technique of analytical psychology, I shall take this to mean the *specific* technical approach and shall accordingly limit myself to that. But it has to be clearly understood that with such a limitation I am bound to give a rather incomplete picture of the technique of analytical psychology.

This brings me to the second point, the constant change in technique taking place in analytical psychology. It would be a sad reflection on any analytical school were it to become fixed in a static and dogmatic approach with regard to both theory and practice—a point, I am sure, with which psychoanalysts will agree. Just as Jung, writing, formulating, and re-formulating over a period of almost sixty years persistently developed and modified his ideas, thus perplexing readers who do not fully understand the phenomena of creative thought, so technique has undergone considerable changes during the six decades of Jung's psychotherapeutic activity, and is continuously undergoing changes and modifications in the light of new experience and theory among his pupils.

Such a process invariably leads to certain divergencies among followers of any school and to the development of certain trends that are frequently connected with geographical distribution. Thus, among analytical psychologists there are nowadays various points that are given different emphasis and that create a kind of continuum from an "orthodox" to an "unorthodox" approach; this statement also applies to technique. I do not consider it my task to go into these divergencies *in extenso*. To give the shortest possible indication of them, the "orthodox" approach tends to keep Jung's concepts "pure" and virtually unchanged, with the accent of its practical work on archetypal interpretation (the "synthetic-constructive" method); on the other side would be what might perhaps be called the "neo-Jungians," modifying Jung's concepts to a sometimes very considerable extent by a moderately well-integrated admixture of psychoanalytical concepts (various as those of Erik Erikson in the United States and Melanie Klein in England) and with the accent of their practical work on "reductive" interpretation. Finally, there would be a solid center group firmly linked to Jung's teachings, but accepting modifications in the light of further experience and using in their work a combination of reductive and constructive interpretation. I shall try to write this contribution from the angle of this center group.

For the reader interested in these particular problems I would like to mention first the publications of the C. G. Jung Institute in Zürich (*Studien aus dem C. G. Jung Institut*), to date seventeen volumes, which follow on the whole a more conservative line; second, the *Journal of Analytical Psychology,* published by the Society of Analytical Psychology, London, with the emphasis on a "neo-Jungian" point of view. In this short survey I shall not go into the variations of these approaches nor into their pros and cons, but shall try to concentrate on everything that expresses the specific additions and modifications that analytical psychology has made to the body of analytical technique. A full spectrum of the approach of analytical psychology can be found in the proceedings of the Congresses of the International Association for Analytical Psychology, of which two volumes have so far appeared, the first under the title *Current Trends in Analytical Psychology* (Adler, 1961b), the second under the title *The Archetype* (Guggenbühl-Craig, 1964).

Whereas it has thus to be understood that analytical psychology is only part of a general body of depth psychology, its starting point and aim are decidedly different from those of other schools (although even here recent developments on either side, analytical psychology and psychoanalysis, seem to have narrowed the gap). The starting point is that of the concept of the psyche as a self-regulating system by virtue of a compensatory relationship between conscious and unconscious (cf. Jung, 1928a, pp. 177 ff.; 1933, p. 153). Jung has described the theory of compensation as "a basic law of psychic behaviour" (cf. Jung, 1933, p. 153). In the particular framework of this book it seems unnecessary to point out that the psyche is not identical with consciousness and that the totality of the psyche can be understood only as an energic system of conscious and unconscious. In this "relatively closed" system (Jung, 1928a, p. 7) anything psychic that comes into association with the ego will take on the quality of consciousness (Jung, 1926, p. 323); otherwise it remains unconscious.

This concept of the psyche as a self-regulating system is the corollary of Jung's concept of individuation (Jung, 1923, pp. 561 ff.), that is, of a constantly progressing integration of the unconscious contents that leads to a continuously growing synthesis between the conscious mind (with the ego as its center) and the unconscious. This again presupposes a potentially constructive function of the unconscious manifesting itself mainly in dreams (which is thus far removed from the theory of dream as wish fulfillment). Only in passing can it be pointed out how closely this concept of the constructive-compensatory function of the unconscious is linked with Jung's theory of the collective unconscious and its archetypal images as the impersonal (or transpersonal) substratum of the psyche. (The knowledge of Jung's concepts of the archetype, the archetypal image, the collective unconscious and related basic concepts of analytical psychology must here be taken for granted.) These archetypal images act as unconscious "regulators" or "dominants" or typical forms of behavior (Jung, 1954, p. 204) (just as instincts are typical forms of action; cf. Jung, 1919, p. 135). These regulators spring into action whenever there is a psychic imbalance: The unconscious contains all those elements that are necessary for the self-regulation of the psyche (Jung, 1928a, pp. 177 ff.). Only from this angle can Jung's well-known theory of types (Jung, 1923) be properly understood; these types are not static positions but a dynamic interaction of polaristic psychic patterns of behavior and adjustment, in which any one-sidedness is complemented by its opposite, thus forming the starting point for further assimilations of unconscious contents.

This concept of a self-regulating psyche explains the central role of dream interpretation (cf. below) in the practice of analytical psychology, since it is here that the archetypal images manifest themselves in the form of symbols (Jacobi, 1959, p. 74). Here Jung's specific concept of the symbol has to be mentioned (Jung, 1923, pp. 601 ff.). To him a symbol is not the irreducible fixed translation of a dream element into an image, but expresses a novel and complex fact, which on account of just this novelty and complexity transcends conscious formulation. The symbol acts as a psychological transformer of energy; it is the means by which the mere instinctual flow of energy "can be utilized for effective work" (Jung, 1928a, pp. 42 ff.).

The psyche as a self-regulating system, the constructive relationship between conscious and unconscious, the collective unconscious as the layer of the psyche-providing regulators, the symbol as transformer of energy—all these are combined in Jung's concept of individuation, a process in which the individual achieves his unique pattern of personality through the progressive integration of unconscious contents. It is on these concepts that the treatment of analytical psychology rests and on the basis of which its specific technique has been developed. But here again it has to be remembered that this process of individuation can truly come into its own only when infantile fixations and complexes have been worked through and that, for this part of treatment, methods of a more general "psychoanalytic" character have to be applied. The aim in view, however, the goal of treatment in its ideal sense and in a suitable case, is certainly that of individuation—of the integration of the personality—leading to a different orientation toward life and to a different center of gravity: the "self" as the "totality of the conscious and the unconscious psyche" (Jung, 1955–1956, p. 110)—in contradistinction to the "ego" as "the central reference-point of consciousness"—and in which the opposing forces in the psyche have achieved their synthesis.

The First Interview

The importance of the first interview lies in the fact that it establishes the pattern of the future analytical work and relationship. There seem to be two main ways in which this will be achieved. The first is to make it quite clear to the patient why he is there and what is involved in analysis. The second concerns the attitude of the analyst, which produces a certain transference pattern right from the beginning. Whereas we may find ourselves on common ground with other schools regarding the first point, the second may reveal differences in method.

Regarding the first point, the patient should be left in no doubt why he is there, that is, he should be made aware of the fact that he has come to find out about himself by relating to the unconscious process. He has to realize that his symptoms are due to a conflict between conscious and unconscious and that such a conflict cannot be resolved by advice on the part of the analyst or by "good will" on the part of the patient, but only by the patient's trying to understand what is happening in his unconscious.

In this connection, the need for absolute frankness has to be made clear to him as well as the fact that, in spite of his wish to cooperate, he will find that resistances will constantly try to interfere and that he will have to try to be aware of all attempts on his part to repress or exclude, by whatever means, material that appears incompatible to him. In other words, the basic rule of psychoanalysis applies just as much to analytical psychology. In particular, the patient's attention will have to be drawn to the fact that strict obedience to the basic rule implies the sacrifice of many attitudes that are usually given a high place in the hierarchy of conscious values: loyalty, discretion, "decency," self-control, and so on.

The practical aspects will have to be discussed in an unequivocal way: questions of money, such as method of payment, payment for holidays or missed interviews, the need for strict regularity of interviews, holiday periods of analyst and patient. The problem of advice will have to be presented in more detail: that the patient has not come to get it and the analyst is not there to give it. Here the question of transference may be brought in: that asking for advice is in fact treating the analyst as a parent figure.

Here, then, we are at the beginning of the transference problem. Although strictly speaking this does not belong to our discussion of the first interview, I want to mention a particular problem, that of "couch versus armchair." Obviously, every analyst (and analytical school) will aim at establishing the kind of pattern of interview that corresponds to the concept of analysis and of the analytical relationship underlying the analyst's attitude. It is in this connection that the question of couch or armchair seems important because, although not necessarily arising in the first interview, it may do so, and in any case has a "first interview" content. Clearly, couch and armchair are highly significant for the particular transference and countertransference pattern, and this question will therefore have to be discussed in more detail in the section on transference. At this point, I want to mention it only briefly and with regard to the initial situation, since here the specific approach of analytical psychology finds its expression in a specific point of method.

The pros and cons of couch and chair have often been discussed and are, therefore, well known. They have almost become symbols of attitude for analysts. The couch, with the analyst sitting behind the patient, clearly aims at establishing as far as possible (I don't believe it *is* very far in actual fact) an "impersonal," "objective" analyst figure. That it also forms one of the defense mechanisms used by analysts for self-protection is evident, as is its importance for the countertransference. The reasons *for* the couch are well-enough-known to be mentioned only in passing: the freedom of the patient to use the analyst for his transference fantasies, the creation of a "dependent" position facilitating the emergence of infantile material, assisting relaxation and an attitude conducive to free association, and so forth. The couch may also allow the patient to develop a kind of intellectual detachment from his unconscious material; but all these special considerations, which in any case will vary with the type of patient, are secondary to the basic principle underlying the use of couch or armchair. This is that the chair gives expression to a greater flexibility in the analytical situation and, most important, to the "dialectical relationship" between patient and analyst, and thus to the dialectical process of analysis (Jung, 1935, p. 3). The analyst is exposed, and exposes himself deliberately, to the observing and scrutinizing view of the patient. Thus he is immediately on the same plane with the patient and therefore, symbolically and practically, much more part and partner of a mutual relationship. (More will be said about this whole problem when discussing transference and countertransference.)

On the other hand, it has to be acknowledged that the armchair may have its disadvantages in certain situations, for example, when a patient is particularly tense and needs the support of the couch for loosening up, or when transference fantasies are too strongly inhibited by facing the analyst. This fact is only another aspect of the necessary flexibility in the analyst's approach; and naturally couch and chair may both be used with the same patient according to his particular situation during the analytical process.

I want to mention for the sake of completeness that some of my colleagues, in particular those influenced to a certain extent by Freudian or neo-Freudian concepts, make more frequent use of the couch, just as some psychoanalysts seem to have become more flexible with regard to the use of the armchair (cf. Fairbairn, 1937, pp. 378 f.). But the basic principle of the dialectical relationship is accepted by all analytical psychologists as a crucial point of their method of treatment.

Transference and Countertransference

To return to the twin problems of transference and countertransference in more detail, it has to be said first of all that, generally speaking, here again analytical psychology agrees with the great importance of transference as a means of therapy. Jung has stated in one of his later works "that almost all cases requiring lengthy treatment gravitate round the phenomenon of transference, and that the success or failure of the treatment appears to be bound up with it in a very fundamental way" (1946, p. 164). It is through the transference that unresolved infantile conflicts, unconscious emotions, relational problems, and so on are activated, released, and made conscious. That the analysis of the transference in its positive and negative aspects forms a crucial part of every analysis should go without saying. The analytical psychologist's attitude to and interpretation of transference phenomena, such as ambivalence, resistance, acting out, improvements, or aggravations due to transference are in all likelihood largely identical with those of the psychoanalyst as far as such phenomena are referred back to the parental images.

The difference in outlook, and in the method following from it, seems to center on three main points: (1) a wider view of transference (particularly with regard to archetypal transference contents); (2) the attitude to countertransference; and (3) the relative importance given to transference in comparison with other methods of treatment.

(1) A wider view of transference in analytical psychology is taken in the sense that it is not conceived exclusively as the reproduction of "repressed infantile instinctual conflicts," which "find their representation in the feeling relations towards the analyst" (Fenichel, 1945, p. 559), but as a phenomenon by which the patient becomes aware of psychic functions in general that have been lacking in his conscious life. It may be a mechanism for calling into consciousness repressed contents (which then may represent repressed infantile material or in a wider sense other repressed material); but, more specifically, transference aims at calling into consciousness subliminal contents of a potentially constructive and prospective nature. The latter are not repressed but represent unlived and unrealized potentialities in the unconscious. Generally speaking, transference is not only a mechanism for the re-experience of repressed infantile sexual impulses, but a tool with the help of which the patient can integrate so far unrealized psychic faculties. In this way the transference can help the patient become aware of unconscious contents, which are needed for future development, that is, for the process of individuation.

Among such prospective unconscious material the primordial archetypal images are of particular significance, and it is on this that the specific approach of analytical psychology is focused. Applied to the interpretation of transference phenomena this means that underneath what appears as a merely personal transference relationship, archetypal, transpersonal images are active. Every intense experience of a personal nature will also actualize the corresponding archetypal image. In other words, every actual experience of, say, father or mother consists of a complex blend of two components: the parents as such and the archetypal image projected onto them. The personal experience acts as the evoking factor for the archetypal image (Neumann, 1961, p. 40), and the two together in their interpenetration form the imago. The archetypal aspect must never be overlooked in interpreting unconscious processes in general (cf. Adler, 1961a, pp. 13 ff.) and in the transference relationship in particular.

Thus the transference, as well as dealing with repressed infantile conflicts, also aims at raising into consciousness the archetypal, transpersonal substratum of personal experience. To interpret the transference literally and reductively as infantile sexual fantasy leads as often as not away from its real significance, which is to be sought not in its historical antecedents but in its purpose (Jung, 1916a, p. 74)—the setting in motion of the individuation process. This applies equally to positive and negative transference, which in their ambivalence refer to the essential inherent bipolarity of the archetypal image and to the bipolar pattern of life in general.

(2) Regarding the attitude to countertransference we come to a fundamental point in the theory and practice of analytical psychology. Here I must make it quite clear from the start that I shall use the term "countertransference" in a positive sense, as indicating the analyst's constructive subjective reaction arising from his own unconscious activated in the analytical relationship (which would perhaps be better described as the "analytical field"). As such it is an inevitable, necessary, and indeed desirable instrument of treatment. This constructive countertransference has, of course, to be most decisively distinguished from such undesirable countertransference manifestations as unconscious identifications and projections due to the analyst's unanalyzed neurotic complexes and leading to harmful unconscious involvements—in which case further analysis of the analyst is clearly indicated. (In another context I have designated these harmful countertransference manifestations as "counterprojections" in order to distinguish them from the constructive countertransference; cf. Adler, 1961a, p. 217.)

What I have in mind is the analyst's subjective reactions arising from his healthy, individual psychological pattern, which results in his individual way of work. Jung has emphasized time and again that analysis is a dialectical process occurring between two people and that the analyst "is equally a part of the psychic process of treatment and, therefore, equally exposed to the transforming influences" (Jung, 1929, p. 72). This "reciprocal reaction of two psychic systems" (Jung, 1935, p. 4) represents a constant challenge to the analyst, which has to be met on the level of the patient. It means the acceptance of "a dialectical procedure consisting in a comparison of our (the patient's and the analyst's) mutual findings" (1935, p. 5). This leads to an approach to the patient that is highly individual, since it is impossible to be dogmatic about individual facts or to assume superior a priori knowledge vis-à-vis the patient as a unique individual organism.

From this it follows that every analyst, whatever his school or theory or general approach, is challenged as an individual, and that up to a point his work will be individual in contrast to that of other, equally individually conditioned analysts. Jung has defined this individual pattern as the "personal equation" (Jung, 1923, p. 16). It is bound to lead to different emphases in observation and interpretation of which the "observer," that is, in this particular case the analyst has to be aware as much as possible but which will in any case lead to an individualized approach. Jung had originally linked this personal equation with his theory of types, Thus, he said that "typology represents an important means for determing the personal equation of the practising psychologist, who, through an exact knowledge of his differentiated and his inferior functions, can avoid serious mistakes in judging his patients" (Jung, 1936a, p. 600). But this personal equation clearly has its wider roots in every possible field of experience and mode of integration. It is obvious that the personal equation does away with the "impersonal" image of the analyst and with the sometimes naïvely expressed idea that it does not matter with which analyst a particular patient undergoes analysis since all that counts is that the analyst is adequately analyzed and has learned his technique. Unquestionable as the need for these two conditions is, the question of the individuality of the analyst remains, and it explains certain successes or failures in certain individual constellations of the analytical relationship. This is quite apart from the related question of the choice of a male or female analyst for certain patients (about which more will be said further on). The personal equation is part and parcel of what has been said above of the necessary individual approach to each patient and of the limitations of the generalized dogmatic approach.

I would like to give two brief examples of what I mean by this sort of dialectical relationship and constructive countertransference. A patient of mine, a married woman of forty-three, obsessional and with great difficulties of relating to other people (including her husband) and to reality had had a very bad relationship to her mother. (Among other things she had been left at the age of six months in the care of a nanny when her mother left India for a long stay in England.) One of her characteristic remarks was:

"How can one have contact with other people? Contact is so humiliating—I can only meet other people as an injured child. I cannot think of contact as something positive, only as a scolded child." She had no trust in the continuity of any relationship and had expressed her distrust in the words: "I could never believe that *b* would follow *a;* nothing seems ever certain." To my reply, "You were never sure if mother would still love you," she just said: "That sank in, I could feel it in my belly." It was during this latter exchange that I noticed the countertransference reaction I want to mention here. My patient's loneliness had moved me, and I felt warmly related to her in the wish to make her feel accepted. I had been smoking a pipe, which I just had to put down because something in me had said, "Mother does not smoke a pipe." When I put the pipe away—by no means an unusual action though always before for ordinary reasons—my patient suddenly stared at me as if in a moment of recognition that I was there after all, that she was not alone and unloved. Then she said, "I'd better look at you"; then, after a long silence, "But what shall I do next—what does one *do* with that feeling." This was followed by an important step toward a positive realization of her problem, which I need not go into here. What had apparently happened was that my conscious acceptance of my feeling function and identification with the mother figure had got across to the patient as the realization of the possibility of human relatedness. The effect was clearly reciprocal—my release of feeling activated in her a release of trust.

One more related example. It refers to a woman patient, again in her early forties. She also had had a very bad relationship to her mother, and analysis had released intense incestuous fantasies about her father. One particular interview had started with her asking me, with good enough objective reasons, for a change of appointment. Her anxiety in asking was evident, and I had hooked on to this. She feared that her request would be too much of an annoyance to me, that I would get cross, that I did not want to be bothered, and that I would reject her. In this connection she said, "I could never come to my mother with anything, I felt as if it was not due to me. I cannot remember that my need for love and security was ever connected with my mother. If I could only remember a broken relationship instead of a nonexistent one; there were not even hard words between us—even hard words need a relationship." While she was talking I had a strange physical fantasy—it was the sensation of having an open womb. It was into that that I could feel her words and emotions enter in an almost physical sense. It was at this point that my patient started disclosing intimate and disturbing details about her parents' relationship and her own involvement in it, which she had never been able to talk about before. Here again I would understand my countertransference reaction as the bridge over a so far unbridgeable gap in the patient's trust in any relationship.

These two instances show how emotions are released in the analyst through the patient's emotions and how, in their turn, they evoke the patient's constructive response. The first example also shows how a non-verbal, quasi-interpretative gesture conveys understanding to the patient. To the analyst, the conscious realization of his countertransference emotions acts as a source of information and as a tool for understanding the patient's unconscious process. In a way, in this situation analyst and patient are living something out together that has begun to happen between them on the unconscious plane and then becomes translated into conscious realization. In such a situation the analyst must be able to react and relate spontaneously through his relatedness to his own unconscious. In other words, "the analyst has a living relation to the unconscious at those points where the patient lacks it" (Fordham, 1957, p. 90). Needless to say, this is just as true of the negative countertransference, which releases "hate," the negative pole of relationship by which its ambivalent nature may become accessible to the patient without fear of retribution or rejection. It is evident what a challenge this represents to the analyst and that every deep analysis will affect him personally.

Here we have to refer back to our first point, the wider view of trans-ference applied by analytical psychologists and to Jung's view of the arche-typal substratum underlying what may appear as a merely personal trans-ference-countertransference relationship. In both the examples quoted above the mother figure who became constellated is more than the personal mother, more than a realization of her good potentialities: It is an activation of the mother archetype, of the Great Mother (cf. Neumann, 1955). This point will be elaborated further when discussing the general interpretation of the unconscious.

(3) Lastly, the relative importance of transference has to be discussed. Whereas for psychoanalysis transference is the main agent of analysis and of information about the patient's unconscious, to the analytical psychologist in general it will be only one of several instruments in his approach. Equally if not more important to him will be the interpretation of dreams (and to a lesser degree the more specialized method of active imagination).

This approach is based on Jung's concept of the psyche as a self-regulating system. This implies a compensatory relationship between conscious and unconscious. Since the unconscious expresses itself predominantly in dreams, it follows that for the self-regulating processes the understanding of dream material is of primary importance, and to this extent transference analysis has less prominence. (But compare what has been said above about similar self-regulating processes manifesting themselves in transference.) This point will be discussed again in more detail in the section dealing with the interpretation of the unconscious.

A few words have to be added about the choice of a male or female analyst. There are several points of view about this among analytical psychologists. The choice is closely bound up with the problem of multiple analysis, that is, analysis with more than one analyst, especially for purposes of training. Generally speaking, the reason for recommending more than one analyst, that is, analysts of different sex, either simultaneously or consecutively, is that in an analysis with either a man or a woman analyst different unconscious contents are constellated, or at least are constellated to a different degree. As far as training goes it is also felt desirable by some to have a more comprehensive experience of analysis and the transference relationship. On the other hand, other analytical psychologists feel that multiple analysis may produce a leakage in the transference relationship and do not find it desirable. This latter point of view is, for instance, held by the majority of the London Group and is implemented in its training program. On the other hand, the C. G. Jung Institute in Zürich uses multiple analysis in its training, and analysts trained in this tradition frequently find it desirable to send their patients for longer or shorter periods, and sometimes simultaneously, to analysts of the other sex. Equally, the training program of the New York Institute states: "The Board may request that a candidate have part of his analysis with a male and part with a female training analyst in order to provide him with a broad basis of experience." (There has been some vivid discussion of this problem mainly between some analysts in London and Zürich; cf. Plaut, Newton, Fordham, Edinger, 1961; Hillman, Plaut, Fordham 1962; Plaut, Bash, 1962.)

To my knowledge other groups hold similarly divergent views, and the final decision lies with the judgment of the individual analyst. I myself have occasionally made use of multiple analysis in the sense that I have either sent patients for a short intermediate period to a woman analyst or transferred them for good after analysis with me, and I have on the whole seen good results from this method. I do not use *simultaneous* analysis with a woman analyst, which, on the whole, seems too confusing for the patient and opens up too many possibilities for transference leakages and resistances. (For further material on transference and countertransference cf. Fordham,

1957; Frey-Wehrlin, 1962; Kraemer, 1958; Meier, 1959; Moody, 1955; Plaut, 1956; Prince, 1959; Whitmont, 1961.)

Resistance

Here again I shall try to present the aspects in which the analytical psychologist's attitude to resistance differs from other schools by starting from the almost superfluous observation that there is bound to be a great deal of common ground between the various schools. To all dynamic psychologists, it goes without saying that the active exclusion from consciousness of repressed contents forms one of the major problems of analytical treatment. Equally, all of us probably agree that every patient tries to cloak his resistance as effectively as possible and that there is virtually nothing under the sun that cannot or will not be used for this purpose: from minor obvious symptomatic actions like being late for appointments or missing them, seemingly valid but spurious arguments and intellectualizations, silences or compulsive talking, forgetting dreams or swamping the analyst with them, to the attitude of the "good" patient who conforms to what he assumes to be the analyst's expectations whether in "reasonableness" or dream content, and so on. In other words, we do know the enormous strength of resistance that manifests itself in these and other attitudes, and we all know that it may be just these resistances that provide the most helpful access to the patient's repressed unconscious material and that the absence of resistance may be a highly negative indication of psychic disturbance.

We may also all agree that resistance tries to maintain the status quo and to prevent new but feared possibilities and attitudes from emerging. But once all this is said, more or less subtle differences in both theoretical concepts and practical handling of the resistance have to be mentioned. They are naturally rooted in the different basic dynamic patterns of the various schools.

So far as the theoretical concepts are concerned, analytical psychology takes a wider view of the area of repressions than of the sphere of intolerable infantile sexual conflicts. Important as these early areas of conflict are to him, and necessary as their exploration is, there are other and later resistances of a very different kind at work, which form the starting point for his *specific* approach. Most important among them is any actual conflict situation that need not be based on infantile antecedents. Jung put this idea forward as early as 1913 (Jung, 1913, p. 181) when he stated that neurosis can be regarded "as a reaction to an actual conflict which naturally is found just as often among normal people but is solved by them without too much difficulty. The neurotic, however, remains in the grip of the conflict, and his neurosis seems to be more or less the consequence of his having got stuck" (1913, p. 181). Every such conflict can, of course, be regarded as having its cause in the past, but there are many specific situations where it proves much more fruitful to try to understand and interpret the pathogenic conflict as expressing the present.

A frequent problem of this kind is presented by the clash between collective and individual loyalties; another by the need to give up adjustments and attitudes, which have once been necessary and useful but have now become antiquated and prohibited. More often than not, these two aspects of resistance are closely connected. If, for example, a man has for most of his life worked for his social adjustment and has climbed to the top of the ladder after considerable effort, it will produce a violent resistance if he sees himself forced to abandon this pattern. I may need a neurotic symptom, very often in the form of a psychosomatic illness, to make him revise his attitude. It would, of course, be possible to look for infantile conflicts as the cause of his overestimation of social success (which, under certain conditions, may represent a completely "normal" and socially desirable use of his resources). But it seems more constructive to start from the actual conflict situation and to look into the actual but repressed need of the moment. Then we may find that a strongly extraverted person has come to the point where the need for a more complete understanding of, and approach to, life forces him to abandon his too one-sided extraverted adaptation in favor of a more introverted attitude aiming at understanding and insight instead of at success and social position. It is evident that this new need may entail sacrifices of considerable emotional significance and may, therefore, produce intense resistances of which, say, a psychosomatic illness with its escape avenue into physical symptomatology is an indication.

There are innumerable such situations of actual conflict at every possible age level, and they present a typical picture and produce specific resistances (cf. Jung's case in Jung, 1926, pp. 98 ff.). They are frequently characterized by identification with a certain point of view, whose sacrifice would demand a thorough overhaul of the life pattern. It may be just as much the rationalistic scientist whose resistance to an emerging artistic or religious need drives him into neurosis and resistance as the conventional religious person whose need for individual and perhaps unconventional experience proves too much for his personality structure or pattern of adjustment and has to be resolved by analytical treatment. In each case, the resistance has to be analyzed not so much as arising from infantile conflicts as against the background of the need of the moment.

Another important divergence in the practice of analytical psychology lies in the analyst's attitude to the phenomenon of resistance as such. This springs again directly from Jung's concept of the total psyche as a self-regulating system. This implies that besides repressed and incompatible material the unconscious also contains constructive and prospective elements, which in progressive acts of self-regulation, are aiming at the integration of psychic contents in the process of individuation. So far as treatment is concerned, this demands a continuous and careful check on the part of the analyst regarding the nature of unconscious material, whether it belongs to the area of repressed material or to that of prospective-constructive material (of which contents of the collective unconscious would form the predominant part).

This necessary differentiation will apply most frequently and importantly to dream interpretation. If dreams are understood as expressing mainly or exclusively repressed infantile sexual wishes or fears that have so far evaded the needs of the reality principle, they will produce intense resistances, which will make themselves felt vis-à-vis the interpretation of the analyst. If, on the other hand, dreams produce prospective-constructive material, the reaction of the patient, his yes or no, has to be taken much more directly as not necessarily arising from resistances at all. This does not mean that such dreams may not also produce resistances, but they would come from the sphere of the ego defending its limited adaptation against the demands of the nonego, which aim at new developments and an enlargement of the personality. Resistances in such cases are not directed against emergence of frustrations and fears associated with infantile sexual conflicts but against the emergence of a challenge from a prospective and thus more "knowledgeable" layer of the psyche. And, where such resistances against maturation and integration no longer exist, the analyst has to take the positive or negative reactions of the patient absolutely seriously without denying their validity by interpreting them as neurotic resistance.

Moreover it can happen, and happens in fact quite frequently, that dreams, by expressing the compensatory function of the unconscious, react to an inadequate interpretation of a previous dream (or other material) by formulating a criticism of it. To interpret such a dream or dream element as resistance would violate the individuality of the patient and seriously interfere with the progress of analysis. One of the main problems of every analytical psychologist is to learn how to distinguish between resistances that have to be analyzed and genuine statements of the unconscious that have to be accepted at their face value. Frequently the patient will not be aware of the meaning of such a dream himself, and whenever a dream may contain an objective criticism of the analyst or his interpretation, he has to be careful to watch his own resistance.

In other words, we have to accept the possibility that a patient's resistance may be directed against a faulty attitude of the analyst. If the analyst insists on his wrong or inadequate point of view, the patient's unconscious may react with all the well-known mechanisms of resistance, such as stopping dreaming, being late, canceling and forgetting appointments, to the extreme step of terminating the treatment. All this has certainly to be interpreted as a resistance, not against the emergence of incompatible material, but against the violation of the patient's integrity by the inadequacy of the analyst. Such situations are, naturally, precarious and open to misinterpretation, and here again an analyst has to have the necessary subtle touch. What has to be remembered is that resistances are a constant challenge to the awareness and consciousness of the analyst as well as of the patient. When the patient's resistance is justified, the situation can be resolved only by the analyst analyzing himself or working it through with a colleague.

It is most convincing and gratifying to see how the admission by the analyst of a mistake breaks the ice and how processes begin to flow again. Such an attitude is part of his acceptance of the countertransference as a positive factor and of his respect of the individuality of the patient. It frequently pays to watch one's own dreams in critical analytical situations for a correction or elucidation of one's own attitude. Jung reports such a case of "resistance" on the part of a patient to whom he had an unconscious negative countertransference. It was resolved by a compensatory dream of his and by a frank discussion with the patient: "I myself once happened to put too low a value on a patient, both intellectually and morally. In a dream I saw a castle perched on a high cliff, on the topmost tower was a balcony, and there sat my patient. I did not hesitate to tell her this dream at once, naturally with the best results" (Jung, 1928b, p. 177; 1926–1943, pp. 110 f.).

One last point about resistances that have to be taken as an indication of fact and not of repression. There are borderline cases and latent psychoses where too close a confrontation with the unconscious could be fatal. Here again we may find symptoms of resistance, whether in dreams or in the analytical situation, which in such cases we have to scrutinize carefully in order to find out if the limit of assimilative capacity has been reached and further confrontation with the unconscious is counterindicated. A patient of mine dreamed at the beginning of treatment of a steam engine under full steam, which was raised high above ground level on a platform just large enough to hold it. He was a highly intellectual type, with marked resistance against the unconscious; he had come to "consult" me for "slight" obsessional symptoms. I stopped analysis in the proper sense of the word (which had hardly begun), taking this dream as an indication that any further move would lead to a crash. All one can do with this type of resistance is advise against analysis and try to cover up what has emerged and, where possible, to use supportive psychotherapy for alleviating conflicts and facilitating every possible adjustment.

The Interpretation of the Unconscious

Here again there are large areas of common approach, and for this reason I shall concentrate on what appears to be the specific approach of analytical psychology. So far as common avenues of exploration and interpretation of the unconscious are concerned, free associations, dreams, emotional reactions and behavior patterns, resistances and slips, together with transference phenomena, all provide the material for interpretation. Of all these two need particular mention, since they represent the area where the approach of analytical psychology differs from that of other schools: transference and dreams. Here again it has to be understood that it is not so much the phenomena themselves as their interpretation and relative evaluation that define the differences in method. Special account will have to be given of the method of active imagination developed by Jung and used by most analytical psychologists, since this method is highly specific to analytical psychology.

As regards transference, it has been mentioned above that a great deal of its interpretation will necessarily be identical with that of other schools. This is due to the fundamental fact that the transference situation inevitably constellates the parental figures, and from that it follows that the past that has come to life in the transference will have to be analyzed.

As has been pointed out, the analysis of transference will, for the analytical psychologist, go hand-in-hand with the analysis of the actual conflict and of dreams. I hope it has been made clear to what extent the analysis of transference is identical with much of the work done by psychoanalysts and at what points analytical psychology takes a different, or wider, view of both transference and countertransference and of the interpretation of the unconscious in general.

Here a word seems to be indicated about the relative view of the interpretation of transference and dreams made by different analytical psychologists. As I said earlier, we can distinguish three main trends inside analytical psychology, and one of their most distinct features is the relative evaluation of transference and dreams (and active imagination). Orthodox analytical psychologists work almost exclusively with dreams, and where transference is interpreted it will be done in a specifically "Jungian" way, and the focus will be mainly on its archetypal aspect (more about this later). "Neo-Jungians" on the whole tend to give the transference a central place in their interpretative work and look at dreams largely from the angle of their transference significance. (A good description of their approach can be found in Fordham, 1957; cf. also Fordham, 1965.) They join, however, with the first group when, after lengthy analysis of childhood and general neurotic material, the individuation process proper can be analyzed, that is, when the "dependent transference" (Fordham, 1957, p. 81) has been dissolved and the "objective transference" has taken over, revealing the archetypal quality of the unconscious and frequently leading to active imagination. This last stage has been well designated as that of "symbolic friendship, a relationship not quite like any other since it has come into being as the product of the transference relationship but is no longer transference" (Henderson, 1955, p. 83). This last statement seems to me to express very well the approach of the center group, which tries to combine transference interpretation and dream interpretation without, however, regarding the latter mainly from the point of view of transference.

Returning to our main theme, the difference in methods of analytical psychology and other schools, I would first like to discuss the approach to dreams and to proceed from there to the equally, if not even more specific, method of active imagination and, lastly, to the archetypal interpretation of the transference.

It is evident that analytical psychology's different evaluation and interpretation of dreams spring from its different concept of the unconscious and of the psyche as a self-regulating system. This does not mean that dreams will not *also* be considered from the point of view of their transference significance. Equally, *possible* wish-fulfillment contents or the defensive use of dreams—whether by evading other burning issues or by complying with the alleged expectation of the analyst—will be taken into account.

These, as it were, negative considerations of dream content seem to us, however, not to do justice to the value of dreams as such. Dreams are not so much meant to conceal as to compensate; in other words, it is less a question of finding the latent dream thoughts behind the façade of the manifest dream content, in the sense of discovering the *repressed* meaning of the dream, than of unraveling their message couched in symbolic language. Jung has stated that he prefers "to keep as close to the dream statement as possible, and to try to formulate it in accordance with its manifest meaning. If it proves impossible to relate the meaning to the conscious situation of the dreamer then I frankly admit that I do not understand the dream . . ." (Jung, 1952a, p. 504 n.).

For this reason free associations, as psychoanalysis understands them, are only rarely used by analytical psychologists. Free associations, as Jung pointed out, can reveal the meaning of dream *components* and of the unconscious complexes, but they will not lead to the understanding of the dream as such. Instead, analytical psychology makes use of a method of amplification, a kind of "circular association," a circular movement around the various components of a dream (Adler, 1967, p. 45). This is a means "of elaborating the fantasy (contained in the dream) by observing the further fantasy material that adds itself to the fragment in a natural manner" (Jung, 1936–1937, p. 49). By making use of all possible analogous material, the *symbolic* meaning of the dream can be elucidated. Whereas the questions behind the method of free association are "What is the dream caused by?" and "What is it a symptom of?" the method of circular association and amplification is concerned with the questions, "What is the meaning of the dream as such?" and "What is it a symbol of?" The difference in approach is formulated in different statements of Freud and Jung. Freud has remarked that ". . . the dream is a pathological product, the first member of the series which includes the hysterical symptom, the obsession and the delusion among its members" (Freud, 1933, p. 26). Jung, on the other hand, says that "the dream describes the inner situation of the dreamer" (1933, p. 142), that it is a "spontaneous self-portrayal in symbolical form of the actual situation in the unconscious" (Jung, 1916b, p. 263). This again leads to the need to discover what one-sided and therefore inadequate conscious attitude to life is being compensated by the dream. Jung has defined the two methods of dream interpretation as the "causal-reductive" and the "synthetic-constructive" methods (Jung, 1926–1943, pp. 81 ff.).

In such short survey it is unfortunately impossible to give examples of the amplificatory method, which always produces a considerable amount of material. For examples the interested reader must be asked to consult the many publications from analytical psychologists. (To mention only a few: Adler, 1961a, Baynes, 1940; Harding, 1965; Jung, 1944, 1936b; Perry, 1953; Wickes, 1938.) In any case, every analyst knows how precarious it is to take single dreams out of the context of their series, since only the sequence of the dream process yields the necessary meaning and corrections. If, nevertheless, I venture to give two short and more or less schematic examples, this limitation has to be understood. The two dreams are meant to serve only as paradigms and their context has to be taken for granted.

The first concerns the case mentioned above of the man who has begun analysis because of physical symptoms—violent attacks of giddiness coupled with great anxiety whenever he traveled, whether by airplane or train, travels that his important position made inevitable. He was fifty-one when he had the following dream (cf. Adler, 1967, p. 48): "It is harvest time; I am sitting on a large waggon laden with hay which I am driving back to the barn, but the load of hay is so high that the lintel of the door into the barn knocks me on the head, so that I fall off my seat and wake up terrified in the act of falling." If we approach this dream from a reductive angle, we may take the barn as a symbol of the womb into which the dreamer tries to enter (incest); he is knocked down (castrated) as punishment for this incestuous longing. (It may be mentioned that, from the point of view of Alfred Adler's individual psychology, the dream could be interpreted as showing an exaggerated will to power, compensating for an inferiority complex.) Such a reductive interpretation is undoubtedly justified when the problem of the patient is still one of unresolved infantile fixations or infantile complexes. With a man of fifty-one, well adjusted to life, we could almost say too well adjusted, the problem is different and one to which only a constructive (prospective) interpretation can do justice. If we interpret the dream from this angle, we shall understand it as pointing to an "overloading" of the patient's "capacity," leading to a one-sided attitude, which needs compensation. The dream says: "You have done enough, even too much. You have brought your harvest in, now realize that your unconscious psyche protests against the 'too much'; look at other possibilities in your life, look out for activities that would round it off." Accordingly the ideal goal of analysis would be to help the patient to establish a harmonious relation between the need for success in the external world and the inner need: Outer and inner reality have to be reconciled. Only in passing I want to point out here a wider archetypal meaning of the dream: The overloaded, overemphasized ego attitude prevents the dreamer from returning to the archetypal Great Mother as the source of life and from entering into the place of the transforming mystery (cf. Jung, 1952b, II, Chap. 7; 1944, pp. 396 f.).

At this point a short interpolation seems necessary, regarding the question of the age limit for treatment. The patient was fifty-one, an age many psychoanalysts would regard as beyond the limits of deep analysis. But Jung's concept of the psyche as a self-regulating system, of the compensatory function of the unconscious, of the prospective-synthetic value of dreams, and last but not least of the individuation process as the proper concern of the second half of life, explains why analytical psychologists regard these later years not only as a legitimate but as a highly suitable setting for analytical treatment (cf. in particular Adler, 1961a, describing in great detail the case of a woman starting an analysis lasting for over five years in her forty-ninth year). Strictly speaking there is no upper age limit as long as the patient has the full mental capacity to cooperate. At this stage of life, say from sixty onward (obviously, individual variations are considerable) it can evidently no longer be a question of analyzing and releasing infantile repressions but of following the symbolic process and the unfolding and fulfillment of so far overlooked potentialities. Again, it goes without saying that in later years it is not, and cannot be, any longer a question of instinctual adjustment in the narrow sense of the word but of an adjustment to an a priori image of "wholeness," of the "total personality." In this context belongs Jung's concepts of the self as the totality of the conscious and unconscious psyche and of the mandala as symbolizing wholeness. Since Jung's own writings and those of other analytical psychologists contain innumerable elaborations on this theme, I cannot do better than refer the reader to the vast literature (cf. in particular Adler, 1961a; Baynes, 1940; Fordham, 1958; Harding, 1956, 1965; Jung, 1928b, 1944, 1951, 1955–1956; Martin, 1955; Neumann, 1954; Wickes, 1938).

I myself have analyzed patients right up to the age of seventy-five and know that they have had deeply meaningful and constructive experiences of the unconscious which led them to a new and highly satisfactory orientation, and many of my colleagues have had similar experiences. The integrative process is fully at work right to the end of life and can produce remarkably profound experiences that add to the fulfillment of the individual life pattern. Naturally, the higher the age the more the numinous fact of death has to be faced and adjusted to, and the unconscious is full of archetypal activity producing highly significant symbols that have to be understood and integrated for the sake of individuation.

To return to the question of dream interpretation, I want to discuss another aspect of it essential to analytical psychologists. The dream of the hay wagon has shown how the dream images have been taken as referring in part to objective outer reality (overloading = exaggerated emphasis on external achievement) and in part to inner subjective reality (the need for inner reorientation). Frequently these subjective and objective factors in dreams have to be distinguished clearly and lead to a significant flexibility in interpretation. Jung has distinguished between interpretation on the objective level ("every interpretation which equates the dream images with real objects") and interpretation on the subjective level (an interpretation that regards dream images "as tendencies or components of the subject"; Jung, 1926–1943, p. 83). If we add to this the transference content of the dream, we have three aspects that may have to be considered together or, according to the individual situation of the dreamer, one of which must be given preference. Once again I give a short schematic example:

A man, aged forty-five, dreamed: "I am riding in a car which is driven by a woman (unspecified). The woman leaves the car which immediately begins to run backwards. It is very nearly smashed by colliding with a wall." (For our present purpose of demonstrating the several possible aspects of interpretation, we can omit the dreamer's associations.) There would be first the transference significance. Apparently the analyst is at this point carrying the projection of the mother image, and the dreamer is frightened of being abandoned by mother. Then we would have to consider the interpretation on the objective level: The dreamer is not driving the car himself, but relies on a woman to do so. He is still too dependent on the initiative and guidance of another real person (mother, wife, or analyst). This leads to a regression with its inherent possibilities of catastrophe. Finally, the interpretation on the subjective level. Here the dream figures would be understood as symbolizing *inner* factors. The actual situation has to be taken into account: The dreamer is forty-five, well adjusted to reality, not excessively dependent on other people, but suffering from a feeling of frustration as if he has somehow missed important aspects of his life. This would make it most likely that the feminine figure represents an endopsychic feminine compensation of the masculine ego. The dream would thus emphasize the importance of his feminine nonego. Without the assistance of the *inner* woman, the "anima" figure (corresponding to the "animus" figure in female psychology; cf. Jung, 1928a, Chap. 2.), his existence would be menaced. In other words, he has to understand the meaning and importance of his unconscious, symbolized by the anima figure, for the necessary reorientation and widening of his outlook.

Since this is not the place for definitions and explanations of the basic concepts of analytical psychology, I must limit myself to the oversimplified statement that the anima can be roughly equated with the eros principle, and the animus with the logos principle, the integration of which is necessary if the (always approximate) wholeness of the personality is to be achieved in the process of individuation. It is then that the archetypal images become constellated, anima and animus being regular instances of this, and that archetypal symbols will appear of which the "mandala" mentioned further down is a frequent manifestation. Other such archetypal images are the "shadow" and, most important, the "self." (For this and other details of the concept of the archetypes the reader must be referred to the writings of Jung and his followers mentioned in the text.)

It is evident that the objective and subjective interpretations of the car dream point in opposite directions: in the one, the woman symbolizes infantile dependence, in the other, the prospective possibilities and needs. Which of the two has to be applied depends on the ego situation of the dreamer and on the conscious context (the actual situation) in which he finds himself. The age of the dreamer has to be taken into account. A younger patient is more likely to be in need of adaptation to external reality, whereas the problem of adaptation to, and integration of, the inner reality is mainly a problem of the second half of life—but these are generalizations to be modified in the light of experience and according to circumstances. Strictly speaking, it is the material as such that decides; frequently the situation may be quite ambivalent, and the analyst will point out both possibilities of interpretation and wait for the patient's reaction. Frequently the reaction emerges in the sequence of dreams, for which reason it is imperative not to interpret single dreams but to interpret the dream series, which alone provides the objective criteria for assessing the dream content. A related problem is the fact that one and the same dream changes its meaning; a dream interpreted at the beginning of analysis may be referred to again much later on either by dreamer or analyst and may then have to be understood differently. Dreams are never "finally" interpreted but are living facts that show constantly new aspects and meanings with the changing attitude and added experiences of the dreamer, as indeed does *any* meaningful datum of life. It can thus be seen that the apparently contradictory or even mutually exclusive interpretations on the objective and subjective level are in fact complementary and form part of the total pattern of development.

The further the process of individuation progresses, the more archetypal symbols will emerge and the more the archetypal layer of the psyche will have to be taken into consideration in the interpretation of unconscious material. The dream of a man approaching his fortieth year may serve as an illustration (cf. Adler, 1967, p. 140):

I watched two ritual acts which followed each other, something like a sacrificial act or dance. The first ritual proceeded as a circle sub-divided into four parts and some sort of sacrifice took place in the centre. The circle originated either through a dance movement in which people approached the centre from all sides, or it was a pattern traced on the ground. For some reason this first act was only preliminary or needed another one as its completion or redemption. This second act proceeded in a kind of circular movement which was sub-divided into six parts.

I do not want to go into the interpretation of this dream, which is concerned with the sacrifice of the ego attitude and the invocation of the self. But it is evident that it is full of archetypal motifs. The dreamer was deeply impressed by the importance of the dream and felt he had to draw it in order to do full justice to its significance. (The drawing, which belongs to the "mandala" type, is reproduced in Adler, 1967.) How such drawing can produce amplificatory material can be seen in the dreamer's description: "When I did the drawing the interaction of the two circles—the inner one in six parts and the outer one in four parts—developed immediately, with the 'altar' as centre. The altar reminded me also of a crystal. As I went on drawing there developed different layers: night- and day-sky, a water zone, two earth-layers and a fire zone."

Another brief example of an archetypal dream may conclude the discussion of this particular aspect of interpretation. It concerns the dream of a woman in her early forties, suffering from severe agoraphobia. The dream was dreamed approximately three years after the start of treatment. In the dream

she is lying in bed, nobody else is in the room but then, quite unexpectedly, something incredibly strong, like an electric current or a whirlwind completely penetrates and seizes her whole being, rapes her but without any negative connotation of the word: it is like an invasion by something superhuman to which resistance would be both impossible and senseless. In the dream she said the words: "Now it can happen."

The experience was so intense that she shook uncontrollably. (This dream is discussed in the context of other dreams of the patient in Adler, 1961c, p. 157.)

The archetypal significance of the dream is decisive. It is, of course, possible to interpret the overwhelming experience of "rape" as either an incestuous fantasy or as referring to the transference situation, and undoubtedly both aspects have their share in the imagery of the dream. But more important, and absolutely necessary for the understanding of the integrative function and effect of the dream, is the significance of being "invaded," "penetrated" by "something superhuman"—by a realization of an archetypal, fertilizing, "electrifying" power of a spiritual nature (wind = *pneuma*).

The transference significance of the dream has, as I say, to be taken into account. Generally speaking, one would understand it as the transference of the father imago to the analyst. But such an interpretation in terms of a purely personal relationship would be incomplete without the realization that the transference significance transcends the personal relationship to the analyst-father and refers to an archetypal, "transpersonal" power. It is an archetypal image of tremendous numinosity that, although constellated by the analyst, is transpersonal in the sense that it refers to him as an archetypal partner in the analytical relationship, to the archetypal image of the male creative principle. Equally, the incestuous aspect has to be understood in these transpersonal terms as referring to the archetypal father image, the partner in the "*coniunctio*." (As is well-known, it was the symbolic interpretation of incest that Jung first put forward in *Wandlungen und Symbole der Libido* [Jung, 1912] that led to the break between Freud and Jung.) For this the anonymous-numinous nature of the experience is characteristic. In mythology this experience is expressed by the great number of encounters with fertility gods, of which here only Donae, to whom Zeus appeared as golden rain (cf. the electric current in the dream) need be mentioned (cf. Neumann, 1953, pp. 16 ff.).

The encounter with these powerful archetypal images has its specific dangers for the analytical process, and they have to be carefully kept in mind and where necessary analyzed. They can be defined as the triple danger of becoming isolated by or inflated through or identified with the contents of these images (Henderson, 1955, p. 88). Isolation would manifest itself in a withdrawal into a fantasy world divorced from concrete reality. Although such a withdrawal may be unavoidable for short periods, the patient must always understand that the ultimate meaning of such images is to serve actual life and that the accession of energy derived from contact with them has finally to flow back into life and lead to a more complete understanding of it and adjustment to it. Equally, the numinous impact of these images can lead to an inflation in which the patient loses the awareness that they are not of his own making and becomes inflated with *his* importance instead of relating through his ego to *their* importance. This state is very similar to that of identification. In it the patient may identify with a "god-like" figure in a fantasy, a state Jung has described as "identification with the archetype of the mana personality" (Jung, 1928b, p. 233). Here again the patient may attribute to himself powers that derive, not from his ego, but from the collective unconscious and have to be related to the ego, their transpersonal numen being clearly distinguished from their significance for the enlargement of consciousness. (For this problem cf. James, 1902, who, in his special context and terminology gave three criteria for the legitimate constructive content of what we would call numinous, archetypal encounters: "Immediate luminousness, philosophical reasonableness, moral helpfulness." This last criterion seems to refer to the contribution such experiences have to make to actual life.)

The last example has, I hope, shown what is meant in analytical psychology by the concept of archetypal transference (for further case material cf. Adler, 1955, 1961a; see also Henderson, 1955). It takes place whenever transpersonal, archetypal contents are constellated inside the analytical situation. In such a situation the analyst will carry the projection of the masculine creative counterpart within the feminine psyche (and vice versa in the case of a male patient; the sex of the analyst is only of relative importance, since as a partner in the analytical relationship, he or she can carry projections, both personal and transpersonal, of the greatest variety). The analyst thus "incarnates" (Plaut, 1956, p. 17) the necessary partner in the process of integration leading to a "union of opposites" (a very important concept in analytical psychology: cf. Jung, 1928b, p. 80), or "*coniunctio*" (an equally crucial concept; cf. Jung, 1946, 1955–1956). The personal significance of the analyst is then transcended in an inner transpersonal archetypal experience in which the patient comes face to face with the nonego in him (or her) or, to use a term of Rudolf Otto's (1925), the "Wholly Other," which is always distinguished by its numinous, "divine" character.

It is essential to understand that such realization can take place only when the infantile and personal contents of the personal unconscious have been sufficiently integrated. In this process of integrating the personal contents, the analyst at first constellates and carries the projections of a personal nature, predominantly the parental images. By progressive integration of these contents a progressive realization of the meaning of the unconscious becomes possible until finally a spontaneous relationship to these archetypal contents can take place. Strictly speaking, there is always a transpersonal, archetypal aspect present in every transference phenomenon, but the interpretation has again to take account of the patient's state of consciousness and individual need of the moment.

The discussion of archetypal transference phenomena leads directly to the method of active imagination (Adler, 1967, pp. 56 ff., pp. 82 ff.; 1961a, pp. 49 ff., pp. 299 ff.; Fordham, 1958, p. 67 ff.; Jung, 1916a, pp. 76 ff.; 1944; 1950, pp. 290 ff.; 1955–1956; Henderson, 1955; Seifert, 1965; Weaver, 1964; Züblin, 1955, pp. 309 ff.; 1961, pp. 118 ff.). It is a method by which the patient can get in touch with his unconscious, thus narrowing the gap between conscious and unconscious. In this way constructive contents of the latter can flow over into the former, resulting in a high degree of coordination and cooperation between them. Jung originally called this method the "transcendent function" (Jung, 1916a), because it makes possible the transition from an attitude in which the unconscious is largely suppressed to another in which "the counter-position of the unconscious" (p. 87) becomes established. In this way the ego can come to terms with the unconscious, which results in a new, enlarged attitude of consciousness.

The method consists in a deliberate "dimming down" of consciousness, a passive concentration on the unconscious background. This makes it possible for new unconscious contents to emerge from the dark background, an act often accompanied by intense emotion. It is essential that active imagination should be conducted without any conscious expectation or program and that the unconscious should be given as far as possible a completely unprejudiced opportunity for self-expression. Although consciousness is voluntarily restricted to observing these new contents, it "puts its media of expression at the disposal of the unconscious contents" (Jung, 1916a, p. 85), so that one could well speak of a state of "active passivity." This means that although one remains passive and receptive, one focuses one's attention actively on what is going to emerge. This attitude could perhaps be compared with watching a film or listening to music: In either case one sits back and "takes in" something that is not of one's making.

In this way the unconscious contents can gain substance, mostly in the form of images, or perhaps words or dramatic processes. They can then be expressed in various ways: in verbal form, for example, as in stories or dialogues, or in paintings, clay, and so forth; dancing and music are rarer but not unique formulations of active imagination. Unfortunately, for technical reasons it is impossible to include examples of patients' drawings, but numerous examples can be found in almost all the literature quoted. Once the active imagination is formulated, the conscious mind takes over again by analyzing the content that has emerged, thus creating the possibility of integrating it into consciousness. (This belongs to the phase of "working through," about which more will be said in the next section.)

An essential feature of this technique is active participation in the emergent material (Jung, 1928b, pp. 213 ff.; 1955–1956, pp. 496 ff., pp. 529 f.). One can concentrate on a certain dream or fantasy image and imagine its possible development, or enter into a discussion with a fantasy or dream figure. But again, it is important that in such a discussion the answer arise spontaneously. This may seem a rather deliberate way of dealing with unconscious material, and it may appear open to self-deception and arbitrary interference. Although such interference does take place, one can learn to remain in the right "passive-active" attitude. The products of genuine active imagination carry an inner conviction that is clearly distinguishable from self-deception and definitely different from daydreams. In any case an experienced analyst will have the necessary criteria for assessing the value of the material. The effect of genuine active imagination has been well expressed by an analysand who underwent, apparently for research purposes, a Freudian and a Jungian analysis, each of nine months' duration, when he says that in active imagination "there is a positive feeling of coming to grips with reality" (Makhdum 1952, pp. 73 f., quoted from Dry, 1961, p. 147).

The method of active imagination can be applied at all stages of analysis. Jung, for instance, points out that one may start from a bad mood or any dream or fantasy image whose development is found to be necessary. In this way contents of the personal unconscious can be brought to the surface and integrated. Here active imagination serves not so much to establish the unconscious counterposition as to integrate suppressed or otherwise unknown ego contents. This is, strictly speaking, not the area of the transcendent function, which is characterized rather by the emergence of the nonego. This first kind of imagination can be understood as one aspect of the general "imaginative activity" (Jung, 1923, def. "fantasy"), which "is identical with the progress of the psychic energic process" (Jung, 1923, p. 581; cf. also Fordham, 1957, pp. 75 f.).

To give an example: A patient in his thirties had a recurrent fantasy in which he felt threatened by a completely veiled dark figure. He had never been able to discover its identity. I asked him to try to concentrate on this figure instead of suppressing it. He did so and in the end could imagine how he took off veil after veil until he discovered that it was a feminine figure. He had to summon up all his courage to undo the last veil covering her face and found with a tremendous shock that the face was that of his mother. It is just the courage needed to proceed with the unveiling and the final shock of discovery that testify to the genuineness of the fantasy and to having contacted a psychic reality. Another way of dealing with the recurrent fantasy might have been to ask the figure for its name (cf. Adler, 1967,

p. 60), or possibly to enter into conversation with it (cf. Adler, 1961a, pp. 143, 255, 373).

As seen, however, the area of active imagination proper is that in which a sufficiently well-established ego relates to the contents of the collective unconscious. For this reason the process of active imagination belongs as a rule to the later stages of analysis. I would like to give one last example of a woman patient in her forty-ninth year (cf. Adler, 1961a, pp. 205 ff.). This patient had started her analysis on account of a severe claustrophobia. For many months she had been engaged in a phase of analysis that had taxed her emotional resources to the limit. In particular, the encounter with what she called her "dark" side, the realization of the "shadow" (the primitive inferior side of the personality) had shaken her badly, and she felt "as if she was engaged in an all-in wrestling match," a fight so vivid to her that she "felt physically ill and shaken." At the same time she "no longer knew what she was struggling with or for what purpose." To overcome this painful impasse she decided to use active imagination (which she had learned to apply before) to face her "opponent," in other words to personify the conflict.

Such a personification of inner trends, impulses, and complexes plays an important part in active imagination. She succeeded with a tremendous effort of concentration. She could feel how a huge figure was looming over her. Then there "formed in my mind" (these were her actual words, showing the passive receptiveness with which she approached the process) a definite image of a male winged figure, an "angel," with tremendously powerful eyes. She drew this figure (Adler, 1961a, picture 15), and in the drawing the angel held in one hand a flash of lightning while with his other hand he forced the head of the woman back so as to expose her heart to the stroke of the lightning. The feeling aroused by this fantasy was most intense, but even more so was that aroused by the drawing. She described it as "unbearably strong," so that "she could not look it it for long at a time." This reaction shows both the genuineness of the experience and that it had opened up the deeper layers of the unconscious containing the numinous archetypal images. This is borne out by the figure of the angel and by the lightning, which she felt to be "a terrifically strong non-personal force," "an immense accession of energy." This latter point is of particular importance for the whole therapeutic process.

The active imagination continued with great intensity, but I have to limit myself here to barest outlines. In a further meditation she forced herself "to let what the picture represented happen to her." Then she experienced how the lightning struck her repeatedly, "as if a series of violent electric discharges ran through me and as if the structures through which it passed were broken down and reformed themselves in a different pattern." She was fully aware of the sexual significance of the experience: she compared the effect of the flashes of lightning passing through her body to the sexual climax. But for her this sexual description covered only a relatively superficial layer of the experience, and she knew that it was quite distinct from sex in the ordinary sense, for which reason she called it "mythological sex." The similarity of this experience to that of the dream of my agoraphobic patient is evident, and again the "angel" could be misunderstood as representing exclusively a personal transference experience. But here is the crux of the matter: Although this aspect is certainly present, it is only of relative importance. The crucial experience is of a transpersonal, archetypal nature and represents another example of what is meant by "archetypal transference." It is the experience of an inner power the numinous quality of which lies precisely in the irruption of the nonego into the sphere of the ego.

Finally, the experience was completed by the vision of a "mandala," which originated in a further active imagination: She looked into the angel's eyes and could see "a night-sky with stars; but not the sky as we see it above us, but the sky as you would see it if you were in the midst of it." It was to her "an extraordinary and ecstatic experience," which she expressed in an abstract painting (cf. Adler, 1961a, picture 16).

I should like to conclude this chapter with a brief remark on the use of amplification with regard to archetypal dreams. It has been shown above how in dream interpretation generally amplification of a dream image leads to an enrichment of this image and to the establishment of the general context of a dream. The same method is used in the interpretation of archetypal dreams; but some modification may occur here in that the analyst is—and has to be—frequently more active than with personal material. Archetypal dreams are full of mythological imagery, and therefore parallels from mythology, folklore, and religious symbology are very helpful and even necessary if the patient is to understand such dreams. Needless to say, the analyst must not bring in irrelevant associative material or try to impose his own point of view. Mythological material must be used only as far as it enriches the actual dream symbol and as far as it is therapeutically relevant to the psychological need and situation of the dreamer. In order to be able to use amplification for archetypal dreams the analyst has to have a sound and comprehensive knowledge of the sources, a need which, although it is an additional burden on the resources of the analyst, is highly rewarding both from the standpoint of his own development and of the contribution it makes to that of the patient.

Working Through

I treated the subject of interpretation of the unconscious extensively because its material seems to me particularly suited to present the specific approach of analytical psychology. I feel I can be very much briefer in treating working through, since here we tread on largely common ground with other schools. Every flash of insight, whether of a personal or a transpersonal nature, has to be followed up, scrutinized, looked at from every possible angle. In short, every bit of unconscious material that has emerged has to be firmly related to the ego and integrated into consciousness. In the initial stages of analysis this will in most cases, particularly with younger patients, mean a growing strengthening of the ego through constant interpretation of infantile complexes, resistances, projections, transference content, and so forth. It is so generally known how resistances tend to cloak and rationalize all these phenomena, and how they appear and reappear in ever new forms and configurations, that I do not feel the need to go into details.

Perhaps one essential difference lies in the constant use of dreams for the purpose of working through. This is where the importance of the dream series as against single dreams is again apparent, since in a dream series a continuous reformulation of the unresolved problems occurs. Dreams, in their compensatory function, tend to draw the attention of the dreamer to any self-deception with regard to unresolved problems. In particular, they have a convincing way of destroying illusions or inflationary reactions concerning "insights," which either are not genuine or have not truly broken through resistances and have therefore remained unintegrated.

In working through a patients' material particular attention should be paid to his projections as they manifest themselves both in the transference situation and in his relationships outside analysis. In such projections to other people, unconscious unresolved complexes give themselves away most easily, since they appear to the patient as "objective judgments" and thus as sufficiently justified, so that the need to conceal them is bypassed. Inside an analysis such projections are, of course, always transference phenomena; outside it they fulfill a parallel function in that it is largely through them that a patient's unconscious images become constellated and hence accessible to interpretation. They will have to be worked through again and again until the ego has genuinely taken possession of them and is accordingly enlarged and its boundaries more clearly defined and strengthened.

In earlier stages, it is the "shadow" projection in particular that will need constant attention and working through. Here the inferior, rejected contents of the unconscious manifest themselves and become formulated. As analysis progresses the anima-animus projection will increasingly have to be worked through: a male patient's primitive, undifferentiated contents (predominantly belonging to the side of feeling and eros), and a woman patient's masculine psychological contents (most likely expressing her undifferentiated logos side), will become recognizable in their individual manifestations. Particularly in the early stages, they will be mixed up with the parental images, whether by identification, thus keeping the logos-eros side infantile, or by a rejection leading to a similar result. In working through, a continuous differentiation can take place and anima-animus projections will gradually reveal their constructive aspects, that is, they will progressively be freed from their infantile components. The wife will cease to be the carrier of all feeling, expressing either a symbiotic relationship by which the husband has so far been exempted from the need to develop his own feeling, or else a negative projection of his own inferior feeling side, living evidence of the "stupidity of emotionality." Similarly, the husband will cease to be the perfect representative of logic and reason who exempts her from the need to develop her thinking side, living evidence of the "cold and destructive intellect." Instead, they will show each other the side that needs development if the personality is to be enlarged.

The same is true of the archetypal content of these images: Through the analytical relationship and in the process of life in general, this too will attain higher differentiation and show its creative potentialities. (For example, Jung has defined four stages of anima development in the symbolic figures of Eve, Helen of Troy, the Virgin Mary, and finally Sophia, each signifying a progressive stage of the eros side in man [Jung, 1946, p. 174].)

This working through also applies to the later stages of analysis with its increasingly archetypal material. Here the figures of anima and animus will appear more and more freed from projections and become increasingly internalized. Whatever projective or infantile material there still is in these archetypal images will need constant attention and reductive analysis. When, for instance, my patient had the realization of "mythological sex," such a flash of genuine insight had to be finally related to the ego and to consciousness by working through all possible remnants of unresolved complexes and personal transference contents, a task that, at this stage of analysis, one would expect to have been largely achieved but that one should never assume to be finally accomplished. To this stage would belong the working through of all elements of isolation, inflation, or identification (cf. Jung, 1946, p. 51).

Ultimately, the significance of the archetypal material as such and its amplifications have to be worked through. This brings us to the question of meaning: the meaning of the life of the individual patient and of his place in the collective situation of which he is part, and to which he has to find his answers if he aims at being a fully integrated personality. It is one of the characteristics of analytical psychology that it regards the question of meaning as part of analysis in general (Adler, 1964), and the answer, as far as the individual can formulate it for his individual life, as the aim of the analytical process. Here the working through, which started from the need to develop an adequate ego and to guarantee its constructive functioning, has reached a stage that leads out of analysis into the normal problems of life, which everybody has to face and solve in order to become an individual in his own right. So far as one can still speak here of "working through," this term has now to be understood in a very different and enlarged sense, which is devoid of any reference to neurotic resistances and complexes. Strictly speaking, the patient has stopped being a patient in the proper sense of the word. This situation clearly belongs to the final stage of analysis.

The Final Stage

The final stage of analysis is characterized by the patient's growing independence of the analysis and the transference relationship. The foregoing remarks will have made it clear how at this stage the patient has transcended the patient-analyst relationship and has become a mature partner in the common search for his individual truth and the individual meaning of his life. In other words, the further analysis progresses, the less it is concerned with neurotic problems, and their place is taken by the exploration of the archetypal contents of the unconscious and their meaning, through which the genuine spiritual need of the patient is expressed. Perhaps it could be best characterized by saying that at the final stage analysis is concerned with the problem of transformation (cf. Jung, 1952b). For all these reasons, the tranference relationship has ceased to operate in any decisive way except for its archetypal aspect. This explains, why the final stage has been designated as "symbolic friendship" (Henderson, 1955, p. 83). It is a relationship whose "symbolic nature takes nothing away from the authentic feeling of friendship" and in which "the friendship does not wrongly personalize the symbol" (Henderson, 1955, p. 83). It is a stage where it is no longer the ego that is the center of reference, but the self. This latter, in Jung's terminology, is supraordinate to the ego and represents the center of the total personality comprising both conscious and unconscious.

The growing independence of the patient has its consequences also with regard to the external setting of analysis. Interviews will be steadily decreased until in the end, the patient may come one a week or at even longer intervals. Parallel with this there goes a growing confidence of the patient in his capacity to work on his own and to understand his unconscious material independently of the analyst. More and more emphasis may, for instance, be laid on his working through his own dreams or fantasy material, and active imagination may play an increasing role in this independent attitude. This capacity to deal with his own unconscious material in one way or another is a sign of the maturation achieved in the analytical process: The mature individual now has independent access to the creative manifestations of the unconscious and will want to keep in touch with them. (This attitude depends of course on the understanding of the constructive-compensatory relationship between conscious and unconscious.)

Here an important qualification has to be made. What I have just described represents an "ideal" state of affairs. Relatively few patients reach such a stage of maturity, and there may be various degrees of final achievement. The status of the analytical relationship will be revised in the light of actual circumstances. A relationship of symbolic friendship may be beyond the reach of many a patient, and many a patient will be only too glad to have his symptom cured and to be free of the yoke of the unconscious. But the basic principle is the same: to aim at a growing independence of the person and assistance of the analyst. Thus, even with patients who are not capable of such final state of integration, one would tend to reduce the frequency of the interviews and to give them at least some way of understanding their unconscious processes by themselves, should they find them coming to the surface. In any case, no analyst will regard an analysis as "finished" as long as the personal transference is not worked through and understood. This latter point will always be the criterion for the approaching end of analysis in the narrower sense and of the status of a patient as patient. What goes beyond it belongs to the stages of analysis described above, in which the patient has ceased to be a patient in the proper sense of the word.

The Concept of Cure

The distinction I have just made between one state of affairs, in which analysis ends in transformation and maturation, and another, in which it ends with the cure of the symptom, immediately raises the problem of what we mean by "cure." Do we apply the criterion of the healed symptom, or do we think in terms of maturation and integration? Is cure in one sense to be regarded as cure in the other, and is for instance the persistence of a symptom necessarily the negative answer to the question of the meaning of cure?

The disappearance of a symptom may give to many patients a clear enough answer to the problem of cure and to a satisfactory result of treatment. At least, this is so, as far as concerns the reaction and assessment of the patient himself, who, after all, came for treatment in the hope that the end of it would find him free of the symptom. This is particularly true when we have been faced with a massive symptom like a severe phobia, depression, compulsion, psychosomatic disorder, and so on. The question becomes more complex if the patient has come not with a clearly delineated symptom as the few just mentioned, but rather with a general feeling of malaise, discontentment, "boredom," or of the aimlessness of his life.

To begin with the manifestly least complicated situation, the permanent disappearance of a massive symptom, this can undoubtedly be regarded as a "cure" of at least some kind. If this has been accomplished and the patient is satisfied we can happily agree with him and his own definition of cure. But what about those cases, only too well known to all analysts, of people who are freed of a symptom and yet, in losing it, seem to have lost in depth, interest, initiative, individuality, or similar positive attitudes?

At the other end of the scale, we find cases where an analysis has touched the symptom only slightly or not at all and the patient nevertheless feels with absolute conviction that he has derived immense benefit from treatment. These cases where the patient feels that his life has been enriched beyond measure, that the whole lengthy, expensive, painful process has been worth every penny, though it has left his symptom virtually untouched, force us to revise our ideas about cure.

And then there are the cases I have mentioned who came without a definite symptom, never develop one, and still persist for years with a vague unspecified aim in mind that keeps them in analysis, and, if it is ever attained or even more nearly approached, completely satisfies their original expectations. We may well ask: *What* aim?

Most puzzling of all, perhaps, are those cases where a patient has gone through the mill utterly and completely, where one feels that he would have fully "deserved" the disappearance of a symptom and it still persists. Leaving aside the ever-present possibility of the analyst's incomplete understanding, I still feel that these are cases in which, were the impulse of analysis removed, some process might also come to an end prematurely.

These and related experiences have made me, as I know they have analysts of other schools, highly skeptical of the conventional conception of a cure. They have taught me to realize and accept the apparently paradoxical fact that treatment is not a cure in the conventional sense of the word at all and that the analytical process is not even aiming at such a cure. What then are we aiming at, and what is the unconventional analytical conception of cure, which we may regard specific to our approach?

I would say that cure in the conventional sense is never the aim of analysis even when it is achieved. Analysis more adequately described seems to me one of the strictest disciplines we know for doing away with antiquated attitudes, helping create new constructive ones, vitalizing and enlarging the area of consciousness and of the personality—symptom or no symptom. In other words, the true aim of analysis is the maturation of the individual. Much as the disappearance of a symptom may satisfy me, I cannot even be sure that I have not deprived the patient of a precious tool for achieving the aim of maturation. For many a symptom can be understood as the constant spur that keeps the patient alive to the need for growing up and maturing, and aware of the processes leading to this end. It reminds me of the fairy tale in which the two eldest sons of the king fall asleep when they try to catch the thief of the golden apple. But the youngest son puts a nettle under his head that stings him each time he surrenders to his wish for sleep—and, of course, it is he who succeeds in the task.

In my experience, maturation is always bound up with one particular question: the question of the meaning of life, of life in general, and of individual life. This question may, of course, be considered as no longer belonging to the realm of analytical treatment. But if we regard analysis as dealing with "mental health," with the psychic well-being of the individual, then this question of meaning is highly relevant. Only a person who can experience his life as meaningful can accept it fully, and only with this inner conviction of meaningfulness will he really feel adjusted to life (and, for that matter, to death, which is such an important question for older patients). To put it briefly: Cure in the specific sense of analysis is the discovery of meaning.

How can such an aim be achieved by analysis, how can such an answer be found on the psychological plane? I believe it is here that analytical psychology has its most individual and valuable contribution to make. It is in the realm of inner reality, the "reality of the psyche" to which Jung devoted so much of his efforts, that we find help toward this goal. This inner reality has to do with archetypal images of transpersonal nature, with a nonego, with contents that transcend the ego personality. As archetypal images, they have on the one hand the character of timelessness or "eternity," and on the other carry a numinosity deriving from their nonego character. In the encounter with these eternal, numinous, transpersonal contents, the ego experiences itself as "the object of an unknown and supraordinate subject" (Jung, 1928b, p. 240)—the self. It is "the new centre of personality" (Jung, 1955–1956, p. 494) and in the realization of this center, of this "wholeness," which is the ideal achievement of analysis, lies the specific aim of analytical psychology.

I hope I have succeeded in showing that this aim cannot be achieved without first working through the infantile, pathological fixations and complexes by the hard discipline of a reductive analysis. But there is immensely more to the psyche than this regressive material. There is its own irreducible reality as the carrier of eternal images and processes through whose realization man can experience the inherent meaning and creative pattern of his existence. This is where true cure lies.

REFERENCES

ADLER, G. On the archetypal content of transference. In *Acta Psychotherapeutica*. Basel: Karger, 1955. Pp. 285–291.

ADLER, G. *The living symbol. A case study in the process of individuation.* New York: Pantheon, 1961a.

ADLER, G. (Ed.) *Current trends in analytical psychology.* London: Tavistock Publications, 1961b.

ADLER, G. Ego integration and patterns of coniunctio. In G. Adler (Ed.), *Current trends in analytical psychology.* London: Tavistock Publications, 1961c. Pp. 160–168.

ADLER, G. Die Sinnfrage in der Psychotherapie. In *Psychotherapeutische Probleme* (Studien aus dem C. G. Jung Institut Zürich XVII), Zürich: Rascher, 1964.

ADLER, G. *Studies in analytical psychology.* 2nd ed., New York: Putnam, 1967. London: Hodder & Stoughton, 1966.

BAYNES, H. G. *Mythology of the soul.* London: Baillière, Tindall and Cox, 1940.

DRY, AVIS M. *The psychology of Jung.* New York: Wiley, 1961.

FAIRBAIRN, W. R. D. Arms and the child. *Liverpool Quarterly,* 1937, 5, No. 1.

FAIRBAIRN, W. R. D. On the nature and aims of psychoanalytical treatment. *International Journal of Psychoanalysis,* 1958, 39, 5.

FENICHEL, O. *The psychoanalytic theory of neurosis.* New York: Norton, 1945.

FORDHAM, M. *New developments in analytical psychology.* London: Routledge and Kegan Paul, 1957.

FORDHAM, M. *The objective psyche.* London: Routledge and Kegan Paul, 1958.

FORDHAM, M. The importance of analysing childhood for assimilation of the shadow. *The Journal of Analytical Psychology,* 1965, 10, 1.

FREUD, S. *New introductory lectures on psycho-analysis* (1933). *Standard Edition,* Vol. 22.

FREY-WEHRLIN, C. T. Problems of dream interpretation. *The Journal of Analytical Psychology,* 1962, 7, 2.

GUGGENBÜHL-CRAIG, A. (Ed.) *Der Archetyp. The archetype.* Basel, New York: Karger, 1964.

HARDING, M. ESTHER. *Journey into self.* New York: Longmans, 1956.

HARDING, M. ESTHER. *The parental image.* New York: Putnam, 1965.

HENDERSON, J. L. Resolution of the transference in the light of C. G. Jung's psychology. *Acta Psychotherapeutica,* 1955, 3, 75–91.

HILLMAN, J., PLAUT A., and FORDHAM, M. Symposium on training, Part Two. *The Journal of Analytical Psychology,* 1962, 7, 1.

JACOBI, JOLANDE. *Complex/archetype/symbol.* New York: Pantheon, 1959.

JAMES, W. *The varieties of religious experience.* London, New York, and Toronto: Longmans, Green, 1902.

JUNG, C. G. *Wandlungen und Symbole der Libido* (1921). Leipzig and Vienna: Deuticke, 1912.

JUNG, C. G. *Versuch einer Darstellung der psychoanalytischen Theorie* (1913). (Translation, *The theory of psychoanalysis. Collected Works,* Vol. 4.)

JUNG, C. G. Die transzendente Funktion (1916). (Translation, The transcendent function. *Ibid.,* Vol. 8.) (a)

JUNG, C. G. The psychology of dreams (1916). Now: General aspects of dream psychology. *Ibid.,* Vol. 8. (b)

JUNG, C. G. Instinct and the unconscious (1919). *Collected Works,* Vol. 8.

JUNG, C. G. *Psychologische Typen.* (Translation, *Psychological types.* London: Kegan Paul, 1923; to be republished as *Collected Works,* Vol. 6.)

JUNG, C. G. *Geist und Leben* (1926). (Translation, *Spirit and life. Collected Works,* Vol. 8.)

JUNG, C. G. *Über die Psychologie des Unbewussten* (1926–1943). (Translation, *The psychology of the unconscious.* Collected Works, Vol. 7.)

JUNG, C. G. *Über die Energetik der Seele* (1928). (Translation, *On psychic energy. Ibid.,* Vol. 8.) (a)

JUNG, C. G. *Die Beziehungen zwischen dem Ich und dem Unbewussten* (1928),

2nd ed. (Translation, *The relations between the ego and the unconscious. Ibid.,* Vol. 7.) (b)

JUNG, C. G. Die Probleme der modernen Psychotherapie (1929). (Translation, Problems of modern psychotherapy. *Ibid.,* Vol. 16.)

JUNG, C. G. Dream analysis in its practical application (1933). (Now: The practical use of dream analysis. *Ibid.*)

JUNG, C. G. Grundsätzliches zur praktischen Psychotherapie (1935). (Translation, Principles of practical psychotherapy. *Ibid.*)

JUNG, C. G. Psychologische Typologie (1936). To be published as *Psychological types, Collected Works,* Vol. 6. (a)

JUNG, C. G. Traumsymbole des Individuationsprozesses (1936). (Translation, Individual dream symbolism in relation to alchemy. *Collected Works,* Vol. 12.) (b)

JUNG, C. G. The concept of the collective unconscious (1936–1937). *Collected Works,* Vol. 9, 1.

JUNG, C. G. *Psychologie und Alchemie* (1944). (Translation, *Psychology and alchemy. Ibid.,* Vol. 12.)

JUNG, C. G. Die Psychologie der Übertragung (1946). (Translation, Psychology of the transference. *Ibid.,* Vol. 16.)

JUNG, C. G. Zur Empirie des Individuationsprozesses (1950). (Translation, A study in the process of individuation. *Ibid.,* Vol. 9.)

JUNG, C. G. *Aion* (1951). (Translation, *Aion. Ibid.,* Vol. 9, 2.)

JUNG, C. G. Synchronizität als ein Prinzip akausaler Zusammenhänge (1952). Translation, Synchronicity: an acausal connecting principle. *Ibid.,* Vol. 8.) (a)

JUNG, C. G. *Symbole der Wandlung,* (1952). (Translation, *Symbols of transformation. Ibid.,* Vol. 5.) (b)

JUNG, C. G. Theoretische Überlegungen zum Wesen der Psychischen (1954). (Translation, On the nature of the psyche. *Ibid.,* Vol. 8.)

JUNG, C. G. *Mysterium Coniunctionis* (1955–1956). (Translation, *Mysterium Coniunctionis. Ibid.,* Vol. 14.)

JUNG, C. G., and LOY, R. *Psychotherapeutische Zeitfragen* (1914). (Translation, Some crucial points in psychoanalysis: a correspondence between Dr. Jung and Dr. Loy. *Collected Works,* Vol. 4.)

KRAEMER, W. P. The dangers of unrecognized counter-transference. *The Journal of Analytical Psychology,* 1958, 3, 1.

MAKHDUM, M. A. *A comparative study of Freudian and Jungian methods of analysis.* Unpublished Ph.D. thesis. London, 1952.

MARTIN, P. W. *Experiment in depth.* London: Routledge and Kegan Paul, 1955.

MEIER, C. A. Projection, transference and the subject-object relation. *The Journal of Analytical Psychology,* 1959, 4, 1.

MOODY, R. On the function of counter-transference. *The Journal of Analytical Psychology,* 1955, 1, 1.

NEUMANN, E. (1953). *Zur Psychologie des Weiblichen.* Zürich: Rascher, 1953.

NEUMANN, E. *The origins and history of consciousness.* New York: Pantheon, 1954.

NEUMANN, E. *The great mother.* New York: Pantheon, 1955.

NEUMANN, E. The significance of the genetic aspect for analytical psychology. In G. Adler (Ed.), *Current trends in analytical psychology.* London: Tavistock Publications, 1961. Pp. 37–53.

OTTO, R. *The idea of the holy.* New York: 1925.

PERRY, J. W. *The self in psychotic process.* Berkely and Los Angeles: Univ. of California Press, 1953.

PLAUT, A. The transference in analytical psychology. *British Journal of Medical Psychology,* 1956, **39**, 1.

PLAUT, A., NEWTON, M., FORDHAM, M., and EDINGER, E. F. Symposium on training. *The Journal of Analytical Psychology,* 1961, **5**, 2.

PLAUT, A., and BASH, K. W. Symposium on training (continued). *The Journal of Analytical Psychology,* 1962, **7**, 2.

PRINCE, G. S. The therapeutic function of the homosexual transference. *The Journal of Analytical Psychology,* 1954, **4**, 2.

SEIFERT, F., and SEIFERT-HELWIG, R. *Bilder und Urbilder.* Munich: Reinhart, 1965.

WEAVER, RIX. *The old wise woman.* London: Vincent Stuart, 1964.

WHITMONT, E. C. The magical dimension in transference and countertransference. In G. Adler (Ed.), *Current trends in analytical psychology,* London: Tavistock Publications, 1961. Pp. 176–197.

WICKES, FRANCES G. (1938). *The inner world of man.* New York and Toronto: Farrar and Rinehart, 1938.

ZÜBLIN, W. Die aktive Imagination in der Kinder-Psychotherapie. In *Studien zur Analytischen Psychologie C. G. Jungs.* Vol. 1. Zürich: Rascher, 1955. Pp. 309–318.

ZÜBLIN, W. The mother figure in the fantasies of a boy suffering from early deprivation. In G. Adler (Ed.), *Current trends in analytical psychology,* London: Tavistock Publications, 1961. Pp. 118–127.

14

ON HORNEY'S PSYCHOANALYTIC TECHNIQUES: DEVELOPMENTS AND PERSPECTIVES

Harold Kelman
Joseph W. Vollmerhausen

Basic Anxiety

"The Technique of Psychoanalytic Therapy" (1917), Horney's first paper, revealed her interest in therapy and its technique, and indicated some future directions of her theory. "The analytical theories have grown out of observations and experiences which were made in applying the method. The theories, in turn, later exerted their influence on the practice." From this research orientation she never deviated. "Psychoanalysis can free

379

a human being who was tied hands and feet. It cannot give him new arms or legs. Psychoanalysis, however, has shown us that much that we have regarded as constitutional merely represents a blockage of growth, a blockage which can be lifted" (1917). Her growth-centered orientation was affirmed. The plastic potentialities of constitution were recognized. Her holistic concept of blockages was defined and her constructive philosophy of therapy delineated.

In the next thirty-five years followed papers, courses, and books of a theoretical, clinical, and technical nature. First came a series on feminine psychology (Horney, 1967), which confronted Freud's male-oriented psychology, both to be transcended by a whole-person philosophy. *The Neurotic Personality of Our Time* (1937), her first book, was Horney's response to America's cultural and ideological heritage. In it she elaborated her concepts of basic anxiety and the neurotic character structure, and emphasized the importance of the actual situation. *New Ways in Psychoanalysis* (1939) was a critique of Freudian theory, based on twenty-five years' experience of working with it, and a further development of her own views. In *Self-Analysis* (1942) she discussed the feasibility, desirability, types, and limitations of self-analysis and amplified her ideas on neurotic trends.

Neurotic conflicts, their sources, their consequences, and the defenses against them are defined in *Our Inner Conflicts* (1945). In *Are You Considering Psychoanalysis?* (1946), edited by Horney, questions prospective patients raise are dealt with. *Neurosis and Human Growth* (1950), her last book, opens with "A Morality of Evolution," which asserts that man's essential nature and his spontaneous morality are inextricably one, thereby defining sickness, health, therapy, and the meaning of existence.

The primacy of Horney's interest in therapy is indicated by her first paper, by *New Ways* (1939) opening with, "My desire to make a critical reevaluation of psychoanalytical theories had its origin in a dissatisfaction with therapeutic results," by the clinical aspects of her papers, by each book containing sections devoted to therapy, and in giving many courses on therapy and technique. She was conducting a course on "Psychoanalytic Therapy" when she died in 1952. Her synopsis read, "These lectures do not intend to teach psychoanalytic technique but rather to present and discuss viewpoints which may help those who desire to develop their own ways of conducting analysis." In one of the lectures she said, "When we know what does what, how, then I could write the book on technique that I have been trying to write for years."

Horney expressed her deep interest in therapy by devoting herself to knowing better "What does what, how." Other problems precluded a book on technique besides her feeling the time was "not yet ripe." Fenichel (1941) mentioned this issue plus others, accounting for the paucity of literature on technique compared to theory, even more marked with regard to the theory of technique. The most cogent was "the infinite multiplicity of situations arising in analysis does not permit the formulation of general rules about how the analyst should act in every situation, because each situation is essentially unique." The task becomes almost awesome when to the uniqueness of each situation is added the uniqueness of the person of the analyst, of the patient, and of both engaged in a uniquely human co-operative venture guided by a theory, constantly evolving, holistic, and open-ended (Kelman, 1959a). A synoptic presentation of her latest theory formulations is essential background for discussing her principles of technique and their application (Wolman, 1954).

Implicit in Horney's holistic concepts is the assumption that there is no life course in which every developmental experience has been traumatic nor one from which all deleterious influences have been absent. As a result of harmonious constructive experiences on one hand and the destructive traumatic experiences on the other, the personality of the child develops around two nuclei and forms two basic patterns. In the one there is a basic feeling of confidence that one's striving for love and belonging as well as autonomy may be more or less realized. In the other, there is a basic feeling of helplessness and isolation in a potentially hostile world, which feeling would undermine the striving for autonomy and belonging.

The pattern that is most deeply and extensively embedded determines how the energies, abilities, and resources of the individual will be used. These may serve predominantly to support and maintain the defensive systems, or largely the constructive resources. These patterns proceed in changing proportions and in an oscillating manner. Adverse environmental and internal factors propel the development of the defensive systems, restrict growing ones, extend and embed basic anxiety, which is inextricable with basic hostility (1937, Chaps. 3 and 4). Each book gave new context and meaning to the concept of basic anxiety (Martin, 1945; Kelman, 1956b; Portnoy, 1959).

In order to keep his basic anxiety at a minimum, the child's spontaneous moves *toward* closeness in affection, or *away* from to be by himself, or *against* to affirm a stand, turn into compulsive *compliance, aggression,* and *detachment* (1945, Chaps. 3, 4, 5). While spontaneous moves are freely oscillating, the compulsive ones have the attributes of rigidity, absoluteness, and indiscriminateness, which lead to the formation and intensification of conflict. Horney called them "basic conflicts" (1945, Chap. 2), being the consequence of opposing needs and attitudes in regard to others.

The earliest integration of personality tends toward giving full rein to one set of needs and attitudes and suppressing the other set. This predominating trend (Horney, 1937, 1939, 1942), with its system of needs, attitudes, inhibitions, fears, and values becomes more extensively embedded. Oscillations in general, and particularly foreground ones in the other directions, become constricted.

Idealized Image

Horney postulated the "Idealized Image" (1945, Chap. 6) as a further attempt at the integration of the personality. The more deeply embedded trend becomes idealized in all its aspects and serves as a basis for identity feelings and as a directive for living. Compulsive compliance, for example, with its concomitant needs for affection, submissiveness, suppressed aggression, fear of hostility, and hope for satisfaction through being loved, becomes the all-loving, totally eager to please, the most gentle and kind soul whose absolute goodness remains unappreciated. This idealization is the work of imagination. The individual, however, also needs to make it an actuality.

The shifting of his energies toward actualizing the idealized self is what Horney calls "The Search for Glory" (1950, Chap. 1). In its service are the need for perfection, neurotic ambition, and the drive toward a vindictive triumph. Although a person may speak of wanting, actually, in this search, he is driven. The compulsiveness of the search is revealed in its indiscriminateness and insatiability, in the person's utter disregard for himself and his best interests, and in his reactions when frustrated. Dictated by his imagination, he aims at the absolute and the ultimate. His major direction in life shifts from a search for constructive self-realization to an almost total involvement of his potentialities with proving that he is his idealized self.

To maintain the fiction that he has attained his idealized image—for he is existing on an *as if* basis in an *as if* world—the individual needs constant proof and affirmation from others. His claims are in the service of this proof (1950, Chap. 2). These are not simply an expression of his wants or needs. They are the most stringent demands for recognition of his very special self and, as such, he feels entitled to have them fulfilled. Reality and the needs of others take second place. His response to nonfulfillment is a mixture of anxiety and vindictive fury and a deepening of the feeling that the world is indeed a hostile place.

The individual's value system is oriented toward actualizing his idealized image. He tries to mold himself by a constellation of shoulds and should nots through "The Tyranny of the Should" (1950, Chap. 3), into the image of his own perfection. These imperatives operate with utter disregard for their feasibility or even desirability. They operate on the premise that nothing is or should be impossible for oneself.

With all his strenuous efforts toward perfection, a person, so driven, does not gain what he so desperately needs: self-confidence and self-respect. Instead he develops an unrealistic pride in himself, which is based on imagined merits. Because the "Neurotic Pride" (1950, Chap. 4) is based on false premises, it is very vulnerable. There are automatic defenses erected against pride being endangered, and there are automatic ways of restoring it when it is hurt. The defensive maneuvers consist largely of a system of avoidances and an attitude of rigid righteousness. The chief way of restoring hurt pride is a retaliatory vindictiveness with a need to triumph over the offender as an attempt at self-vindication.

"The glorified self becomes a *phantom* to be pursued; it also becomes a measuring rod with which to measure his actual being" (Horney, 1950, Chap. 5). The neurotic cannot but despise his actual being, which, like reality, keeps interfering with his search for glory. Self-hate has an integrative function in the service of self-glorification: together with shoulds, claims, and neurotic pride, it constitutes what Horney called *the pride system*. This system is for the most part unconscious. Hate for the actual self is more on the surface and concerns itself with the person's actual as well as imagined limitations. More buried, for a long time in therapy, is the hatred for the real self, which opposes the whole search for glory.

Self-hate, when directly experienced, appears as merciless self-accusations, relentless demands on self, self-contempt, self-frustration, self-tormenting or self-destructive acts. Any one or more of these modes of operation may be perceptible. More often the process of self-hate is externalized. This increases and alters basic anxiety. The neurotic now feels and becomes more helpless and incapable of defending himself.

For the sake of unification and integration, the individual identifies himself *in toto* with his glorified or despised self. He experiences himself as one or the other and may vacillate from one identity to the other. More likely, the attempt at solution will be a kind of streamlining in either the expansive or self-effacing direction. Whatever the direction, it is sustained and supported by auxiliary defenses. Although they tend to reduce tension and smooth over the disruptive conflicts from the many contradictory attempts at solution, they contribute to a person's unawareness of himself as well as to the intrinsic feelings of weakness.

Foremost among these auxiliary defenses is the process of *alienation* from self. It is both an outcome of the neurotic development as well as a defensive measure to relieve tension (Horney, 1950, Chap. 6). In its more extreme form it appears as depersonalization. All that is compulsive moves the individual away from his real self as well as from his actual or empirical self. His possessions and experiences are not felt as his. He becomes numb and remote, a stranger to himself. His relations to himself and others become increasingly impersonal and mechanical. He loses the capacity to feel his own feelings, made worse by his neurotic pride dictating what he should and should not feel. He has lost his inner self-directedness and has become other and outward directed.

Another of the "General Measures to Relieve Tension" (Horney, 1950, Chap. 7) and to diminish conflict is the *externalization* of inner experience. This is a more comprehensive phenomenon than projection, which is concerned with "the shifting of blame and responsibility to someone else for subjectively rejected trends or qualities" (Horney, 1945, p. 116). Any psychic process, including aspects of the pride system and the real self, can be externalized. A further measure for tension reduction and an outcome of the preceding measures is *psychic fragmentation* or *compartmentalization*. When and as these fail to do away with disruptive conflicts, *automatic self-control* sets in to check all impulses indiscriminately. This results in an increased rigidity and constriction of the personality. The last auxiliary measure is the belief in the *supremacy of the mind*. It functions as a spectator of the self, gleefully and sadistically finding fault with it. It also functions as a magic ruler with beliefs in omnipotence and omniscience.

All these measures are homeostatic. Something more goal-directed is still necessary for the individual. He needs something that will give form, direction, and meaning to his whole personality. The energies, drives, and values of the individual become organized and integrated around three further directions of development, which Horney calls the three major solutions to intrapsychic conflict.

They are centrifugally and centripetally oriented, focus on the individual and his environments, mutually influencing each other in constructive and destructive ways. Because Horney's approach is neither a purely intrapsychic psychology nor solely an interpersonal theory of human relations, it is referred to as holistic. It is concerned with individual and environment as a unitary process. Likewise, because she is concerned with the moves toward self-realization and self-actualization, Horney rigorously differentiates solution from resolution. The neurotic attempts to *solve,* that is to do away with, to deny his conflicts. Only by analyzing the conditions that brought these conflicts into being and are perpetuating them can they be *resolved,* so that the energy previously invested in them and their attempts at solution becomes available for productive living. As a consequence of neurotic conflict-resolving, the person's center of gravity, which had shifted to the outside, now moves back into the center of his being.

The first of these three major solutions is the expansive one, which has the appeal and goal of mastery (Horney, 1950, Chap. 8). Here the individual is identified with his pride or with his standards, which may be predominantly narcissistic, perfectionistic, or arrogantly vindictive. The second is the self-effacing solution in which the individual identifies with his subdued self (Chap. 9). He has the goals of love and surrender. The third is the solution of resignation in which the individual aims at freedom and noninvolvement (Chap. 11). He attempts to remain out of the conflict between his expansive and self-effacing drives by withdrawing from active participation in life. This solution may have the form of *persistent resignation, rebellious resignation,* and those deteriorated states Horney called *shallow living.*

Each solution represents a complex interplay of drives, inhibitions, fears, sensitivities, and values. It determines the kinds of satisfaction attainable, what is to be avoided, the hierarchy of values and how that person will experience and relate to himself and others, in work and leisure, in sex and marriage, and to life's bigger questions.

While Horney's theoretical formulations became more systematic, though open-ended, her ideas on technique remained loosely organized. What emerged, particularly in her later courses on technique, was an increasing emphasis on the person of the analyst as his most important instrument in therapy. For giving structure to this topic, a brief summary of the symbolizing process is essential.

The Symbolizing Process

A universal forming process is postulated in which the symbolizing process plays a significant role. In much of his thinking on form and process Kelman (1956b, 1962a) follows Whyte (1950). The moment there is awareness of being and any of its attributes they have emerged into form. They have taken form through the forming process. Form may become organized as a sequential hierarchy of forms, denotable, conatable, and connotable. The forms may be vague, inchoate, increasingly defined and variously named. No attribute of being can be captured in a single, even in a whole series or matrix of forms. This impossibility can stimulate the continuing attempt to do so, which could be creative. Paul Klee's genius was directed, not to static form, but to the forming process, as a means of communicating his intuitions of art and living.

The symbolizing process, an aspect of human integrating, may be described metaphorically as a spiral or as a sequence of interconnected levels starting from the ground of all forms, phenomena, and appearances, variously named through time as *chit* (Hinduism), *hsing* (in Chinese philosophy), *tathata* (Zen), *pure fact* (Northrop, 1948) and *dasein* (existentialism). At the bottom of the spiral is *pure fact,* from which all forms emerge and back into which they are resorbed.

The lowest levels of the spiral are prerationative, which means they are prior to and essential to intellection in a human sense. It is at these levels that human communing takes place of which the communing of mother and infant are a fact and prototype and "the basis of all communication, hence also of the communication that makes psychotherapy possible" (Goldstein, 1954). It is "the strifeless phase of awareness . . . the preconscious mode" of Burrow (1964, Chap. 2) similar to the "prototaxic mode" of Sullivan (Mullahy, 1948). "Basic to all else in the development of the mind is a current of physiological continuity of child and mother, person and world" (Burrow, 1964, p. ix).

The forms pointing at, and expressive of, this continuity have been called preverbal, subverbal, and subliminal. It is from the prerationative levels that the forms we name empathy, intuition, insight, hunch, flash-feelings, psi-phenomena, mystic participation, and satori emerge. These levels participate in thoughtless imagery, metaphors, fantasies, and dreams, namely, before intellection takes over to dualistically structure these emerging processes and logically order them. As this happens, the rationative levels of the spiral emerge contained in fantasies, dreams, and thought, to the highest order of abstraction.

We can see how vast is the realm of "Prelogical Experience" (Tauber and Greene, 1959). It is the world of the immediately experienceable, the ineffable, the indescribable, the impressionistic, the purely factual and empirical, the positivistic component that is the mystical factor in knowledge.

The emerging forms become images by a process of imagizing, of which perceiving and imagining are aspects, evolved into perceptual and conceptual symbols. Imagining differs from perceiving only in one regard. The images formed are nonperceivable: A person can form symbols of the past and future and what is not spatially or temporally present to the senses. Feelings as such cannot be had directly in imagination, nor can sensations, autonomic responses, or urges; but we can have perceptual images of aspects of them. The imagizing process is crucial to our notion of the person of the analyst as therapist, as are all prerationative levels to Horney's ideas on unconscious processes and on the actual situation.

In *New Ways* (1939, p. 18) Horney said, "I regard as fundamental and most significant of Freud's findings his doctrines that psychic processes are strictly determined, that actions and feelings may be determined by unconscious motivations and that the motivations driving us are emotional forces." As her theories evolved, determinism became more relative through the inclusion of human spontaneity. Her notion of unconscious motivation was expanded by the concept of the real self and her extended definition of sickness. Concomitantly the emotional forces functioning as motivations were enhanced through the enlarged meaning of unconscious processes.

Brief mention is made regarding Horney's position on other aspects of Freudian theory to give meaning and context for the additional concepts to be discussed. "The libido theory in all its contentions is unsubstantiated" (1939, p. 68) was Horney's reason for discarding it. Her growth-oriented, holistic, process-patterned system thinking is a rejection of the repetition compulsion, fixation, regression, the id and death instincts. "Freud's mechanistic evolutionistic thinking ... implies that present manifestations not only are conditioned by the past, but contain nothing but the past; nothing really new is created in the process of development; what we see today is only the old in a changed form" (1939, p. 42). What Freud regarded as secondary process thinking, namely, creativity through sublimation, Horney regarded as primary, and what Freud called primary process thinking, Horney saw as a secondary consequence of growth blockage and distortion. She discarded the notion of the Oedipus complex but retained "the highly constructive finding that early relationships *in their totality* mold the character to an extent which can be scarcely overestimated" (1939, p. 87) but warned against a "one-sided fascination" with childhood.

We see unconscious processes as not directly observable, but inferred, and recognize that while the patient does not know, on another level he "knows that he knows" (Freud). We do not make unconscious processes identical with the prerationative levels of our postulated symbolic spiral because of the way we defined them and because of the holistic theory into which they fit. We do feel that these levels are analogous with and a close approximation to unconscious processes. We also feel that the notion of the symbolic spiral, which participates in defining the actual situation, communing and communicating, and the doctor-patient relationship, gives a much more comprehensive basis for mutual contacting of therapist and patient through having wider and deeper access to each other.

The structure and content of the prerationative levels define the therapist's task as aiding and maintaining a creative tensional situation through "Freer Associating" (Kelman, 1962). This attitude will be communicated to the patient, so that there may be less fear of unconscious processes, usually regarded as chaotic, unpredictable, and destructive. This focus on the prelogical, on the so-called latent, is no de-emphasizing of the logical, the so-called manifest, but a proportionate enlarging of the basis for understanding and explaining the logical, the directly observable. Also, this may be reassuring, particularly to those patients who compulsively intellectualize.

Our discussion of unconscious processes gives background for Horney's meaning of the actual situation. "Emphasis is put on the actually existing conflicts and the neurotic's attempts to solve them, on his actually existing anxieties and the defenses he has built up against them" (Horney, 1937, p. vii). In "Culture and Neurosis" (1939, Chap. 10) she further elaborated on the actual situation and in each book enlarged on the actual character structure.

With her concept of the actual situation a multidimensional genetics emerged. There is a historical genetics expressed as the dialectics of the genetics of the life history (Kelman, 1963a). The meaning of development and the influence of hereditary and constitutional factors interacting with environmental influences are delineated in a language of process and character structure. Of these Horney's description of the evolution of morbid dependency (1950, Chap. 10) is a detailed illustration.

An ontogeny of being became evident in her concept of basic anxiety and in her phenomenologic analysis of the being of the therapist. Her ontogeny of being, in the actual situation, included all dimensions of the present, extending backward into the past and forward into the future. The latter is evident in the dynamics of the real self as having acted in the past, as acting in the present, and as pointing toward action in the future. The genetics of the future are implied in her immediate and ultimate goals for therapy.

Kelman developed some of Horney's suggested meanings of the actual situation and added his own (Kelman, 1955b, 1962a). What we start and end with, and are always in and of, is the actual, total, immediate, present situation. This means that "the only place we can be is here, the only time we can be is now, and the only" organismal-environmental happenings becoming manifest as "feelings, sensations, perceptions and thoughts, signs, gestures and sounds which we can be, not have, are here-now." These happenings may be clothed in symbols having the time form of past, present, or future, and the place form of here and there. These "forms will be emerging and being resorbed back into their source. . . . We have two modes of knowing these phenomena, inferentially through rationality, and directly through numinous awareness. . . . The sole aim of such knowing . . . is the widening and deepening of here-now experiencing of those symbol forms and what they point at, preformed. . . . This aim becomes more possible in and through the relating process during which more moments of communing are obtaining" (Kelman, 1966).

Those symbol forms having the time form of past and the place attribute of there can be read as information, about back there then, and as having later confirmed degrees of accuracy and/or distortion. They can be seen and experienced as a defense, such as an externalization, or as an aspect of more extensive blocking. They can be understood and felt as aspects of the doctor-patient relationship in which the analyst is seen and experienced in a distorted manner as if he were identical with or, which is radically different, similar to, like, reminiscent of, or equivalent to a person in that patient's life, past, present, or future, and/or experienced as he is in reality, which also might be reminiscent of someone other than the analyst in that patient's past, present, and anticipated future, also seen realistically. All of these symbol forms may be read as changing perceptions of persons and events, there and then, past and future, as well as of here-now. This means we can change our past as memory, as aftereffects, as perceptions of it, as we can our enduring present and our anticipated futures (Ivimey, 1950; Kelman, 1955c, 1966).

Content selects form and not form content. The symbol forms selected will have the attributes of appropriateness, adequacy, relevance, preciseness, conciseness, and economy in manifesting and communicating the structure of the actual situation. In this sense symbolizing is creating even while creating a miscreation. It is always attempting curing, whether it succeeds or fails, and it is always expressive of the urge toward self-realization, whether that person may be getting sicker or healthier, in the immediate and/or in the long range.

The symbol forms and arrangements of them, happening into awareness, will be pointing at what brought them into being, what is perpetuating, embedding and resolving them, defined as conflicts, anxieties, defenses, and constructive forces, namely, at what retards and what supports self-realizing. All of these symbol forms will be pointing: at what is formed, foreground, and in awareness; at what is vague, being formed, and at "life's growing edge"; and at what may be inferred, unconscious, and helped into awareness. The analysis is conducted so as to favor a shift of energy investments in the patterns of process in that four-dimensional moving matrix, the actual situation, so that the balance increasingly favors self-realizing and opposes self-actualizing.

As this is happening, new symbol forms in new arrangements will be constantly emerging, illuminating these shifts and their connections. Meaning is the experiencing of the connectedness, interrelationship, and coherence of patterns, of the awareness of the how and what, in the here and now. From such experiencing emerge feelings of understanding and of knowledge, the explanations for why, who participated, or will participate, where and when. This means we conduct the analysis of the ongoing and changing actual situation so that the patient is searching for and finding his own interpretations, his own meanings. This means we are helping him toward conducting his own analysis, for in the final analysis who knows his wilderness better than the patient? As guides we know terrains in general, and many in specific, but we do not know his, about which he must be telling us, and usually is, if we can but look and see, listen and hear.

The Analyst

The suggested model of the symbolizing process can also give structure to what could have come into the field of the analyst's "evenly-hovering attention" (Freud) during his personal analysis, course in training, and experience with patients. As forms, expressive of and pointing at aspects of his being, they are manifestations of reactions, responses, and resonations to his confronting (*Begegnung*), contacting (empathy, intuition, intersubjectivity), relating (transference, transaction, the interpersonal relationship, the doctor-patient relationship, being with), and being in communion with his patient (being, being there, being at his patient's core of being while concomitantly being at his own). These forms are indicators and pointers at what attributes of his being are telling and showing him, what he could see and hear as information, knowledge, and wisdom regarding the immediacies transpiring.

The more widely, deeply, and openly he is attuned to and experienced with his person as instrument, which comes with rigorous training and obtains within the limits of his endowment and talents for analysis and the art of living, he could attain toward "the method of no method," which Leopold Auer taught his pupils, so that they played brilliant violin with "effortless effort." Then he also might discover that "the most successful cases are those in which one proceeds, as it were, aimlessly, and allows oneself to be overtaken by surprises, always presenting to them an open mind, free from expectations" (Freud, 1933).

Toward these ends, becoming attuned to and experienced with these forms, pointing at operations of the analyst's sensory and autonomic systems, as well as his emotive, conative, and cognitive processes, is integral to his training. As he is alert, open, can contain and live with these emerging forms, through experiencing their connectedness in the actual situation, their meanings will emerge. They are more likely to appear, with freshness and vividness, in an initial interview. Often they are not sufficiently respected or relied on, an experience ruefully confirmed months and years later in rereading the original notes to a supervising analyst consulted for help.

We can give but a few instances of each of these categories, which may emerge as, or into, vague indefinable sensings, ungraspable feelings and thoughts, as images, tunes, metaphors and analogies, as flash-feelings, flash thoughts, or as a character in or a whole plot of a play or book, or as a panoramic vision of something now or anticipated. They may come in response to the first telephone call, letter, impression in the waiting room, or as the initial interview proceeds. It may be a response to the climate, the aura, the total gestalt of that person. The form may be in sensory categories, as aesthetic pleasures or revulsions or be felt as an emotional uplifting. People have a real and metaphorical smell about them, pleasant or as a "malodorous presence." Some taste bitter, others sweet. People can sound off with the endless variations of their voices, as well as with gestures and facial expressions.

An analyst's sensory response may be of being pressed in on, grated upon, and clawed at, or he might have the uncomfortable feeling of an insubstantial wraith, or an absence being present. Autonomic responses are most telling: goose pimples, inner shivers, face feeling warm and blushing, perspiring, changes in pulse rate, heart action, breathing patterns, sexual sensations, and intestinal tightening and relaxing. Then there are the feelings of warmth and well-being, with an urge to some expression of lightheartedness. As a combination of kinesthetic, joint, and stereognostic responses unite with autonomic ones, the analyst can have the experience of being unbalanced or of internal dizziness as a most telling awareness of his patient.

For total responding, there must be a wanting and being open to feel and to feeling with the greatest degree of awareness without prejudgment, condemnation, embellishment, or intellectualization. Such feeling makes the feelings real, leads to their carrying conviction, a greater depth of involvement and personhood. This leads to wisdom, to a greater discrimination of what is spontaneous and compulsive, of types of feelings and their nuances, and to their intensity and extensity of imbeddedness. What follows is greater owning, accepting, being one's feelings from which come feelings of liberation, self-acceptance (Wenkart, 1955), and a stronger feeling of self (Rubins, 1962). Thereby constructive forces are identified, supported, extended, and expanded. They develop their own momentum, becoming more effective in opposing all that obstructs straighter growing.

Having had such experiences, the therapist will be attuned to their happening and be that much more sensitive in his timing, helping to move the feeling process in his patient. He will be more alert to directing him to his feelings, their absence, vagueness, deadness, and dullness. He will be able to expose his patient's compulsive feeling by order of his mind, and draw his attention to this self-deception regarding the genuineness of his pseudo-feelings. He will be able to help him contact his feelings, stay with them, become attuned to their rhythmicity, ultimately be able to enter and rest in foreknown pain-provoking situations. He will be able to show him how, from such experiences, there will be an accrual of feelings of being able, of confidence, and of courage.

Only through having experienced, in his personal analysis, the discriminations in being open and opening, in being closed and closing, all in compulsive and spontaneous ways, will he be attuned to them in his patient, all of which will help him experience these feelings and processes, specifically as aspects of the process of working through. Only after similar personal experiences will he be able to help his patient discriminate compulsive willing, having to will, wanting, spontaneous willing, willing not to will, motivationless motivation, and the "will-power of desirelessness" (Groddeck). The possibility of these processes is premised on the urge toward self-realization, variously described throughout human history as to its forms, the methods for moving toward it and the nature of its practitioners (Kelman, 1966). All methods and practitioners went the way of paradoxes. We are urged to be spontaneous, open, choiceless and whole, which some can ultimately become, while we are compulsive, closed, driven in our desires, and divided.

In "A Theory of Personality Change" (1964), evolved from his *Experiencing and the Creation of Meaning* (1962), Gendlin gives a detailed phenomenology of the experiencing process. He describes the steps by which experiencing of this inward felt process is sharpened. Some he calls "focusing" that continues until "the self-propelled feeling process" comes into awareness and is contacted, deepened, and widened. He also delineates the sequences and nature of the inner shifts that follow therefrom and details how his questions and interpretations participate in this process.

In analysis, as patients contact their "direct referents" (Gendlin) expressive of "the self-propelled feeling process," they say, "I feel it arising in me," "I feel it comes from me," "It seems to or feels like it belongs to me," "I feel like it moves me. It carries me. Also I feel I want to go along with it." In contrast are feelings they had experienced as coming from outside, as imposed, alien, forbidding, and cold. "I wanted to get away from them." "I felt threatened and I felt frightened. I wanted to run away. I felt helpless and bewildered. I felt confused by them."

As they experienced these inner movements as "mine," patients variously described the inner feel of supporting these processes. This obtains whether these feelings were pleasant or unpleasant, such as anxiety, conflict, hostility, or self-hate. This has happened through the therapist's supporting their containing these feelings and not running away. They paradoxically become able to "rest in anxiety" and "rest in panic." Once experienced, patients describe its liberating effects. With containing and resting in, feelings of owning emerge. Patients report feeling more of themselves and feeling themselves as being more. They begin to enter, live in, and live through experiences of greater depth and intensity. This may happen after experiencing quite some intensities of central conflict. They say, "I never felt so good in my life and I never felt so awful." They feel liberated through their meaningfully responding to the therapist's interpretation. "You have never been able to feel so good and never been able to feel so awful because you have never been able to feel so much."

In time, a shift from a predominance of the painful aspects of emerging feelings takes place, and with it, a concern about the pain falls away. Patients recognize, retrospectively, how fear of and fighting against pain had made it worse and how, paradoxically, openness to and accepting pain had made it less, after the immediate intensity of pain had passed. Pain is not desired or sought but accepted or borne as part of the living, growing process. The self-propelled feeling process takes on an increasing momentum, which patients come to more quickly recognize, attempt to contact, open themselves to it, rely on and seek to be carried by it.

Patients struggle to describe the feel of the inner processes by which they attempt to move themselves to the side of this self-propelling feeling process. Facial changes, movements of the trunk, extremities, and other parts of the body, expressive of such inner efforts, can be observed. They say, "I feel an inner movement, a moving over, a moving toward, a moving to the side of. It's hard to locate but I feel it clearly and it feels like it is in the center of me, all through my insides. I know I can do something about moving over to that side. I have done it before and am getting more of the feel of doing it and how to do it. I'm clearer about it and know how not to press too hard and how far I can go. I have a good feeling when I can do it, when I'm able to, a feeling of well-being, of warmth inside me. It's hard work and I know I must rest and give it time."

As there is more experience with palpating, becoming in tune with, and supporting this self-propelling feeling process, there is concomitantly a clearer feel of the processes that oppose it and a learning of inner ways to oppose the opposing, dilute its impact, and even begin to push back its borders. As this is happening a patient is learning self-analysis during an analysis in preparation for continuing on his own.

An analyst would have had experience with his own and patients' cognitive processes, with the rationative levels of the symbolic spiral. They are about what has been experienced, namely, after the fact and on reflection, Cognitive processes participate in hypnogogic reverie, fantasy, dream, and logical thought, to the highest order of abstraction. The analyst's experiences, with his person as instrument, in working with dreams, fantasies, thought processes, and behaviors, should have acquainted him with his strengths. Some are better at interpreting thought, and others have a flair for dreams, as obtains with degrees of competence with and interest in the variety of psychiatric disorders. What is crucial is that the analyst know them.

The more experience an analyst has with the various categories of his being, the more they will function in unison, be immediately available and without reflection. His responding will be with inventiveness and ingenuity, with appropriateness and adequacy to the requirements of the moment-to-moment immediacies. Though all levels of the spiral participate, it is the prerationative ones that contribute to that comprehensive form of being which we call understanding (*verstehen*) as contrasted with explaining (*erklären*).

Horney regarded "Understanding the Patient as the Basis of All Techniques" (Horney and Metzgar, 1956). About this comprehensive understanding she said,

> Understanding is a social and specific human process, a moving with one aspect of our being toward the stand which another person maintains, but while so moving still maintaining our own stand. Therefore, we can never be completely where the other person stands. We stand *under* the person's stand: we understand his position, and it is this which enables us to compare his stand with ours. . . . Understanding is therefore a movement

of emotional and intellectual energies. . . . Real understanding is a whole-hearted and receptive observing and "feeling into" the other person with all of one's own self.

Horney detailed the process by which an analyst came to such under-standing, how he defended himself against it, and how gradually he let go of his defending with concomitant experiencing of anxiety, conflict, hate, and self-hate. As this happened his patient's associations and behavior gradually begin to fit into larger wholes. In this understanding process the analyst's feelings are crucial. With it comes experiencing feelings of change, in the patient and in the doctor-patient relationship.

The notion of awareness has been very perceptively discussed by Watts (1951) and Krishnamurti (1954). Briefly it is all that comes within the purview of "evenly-hovering attention" (Freud). Martin (1956) delineated the attributes of the holistic therapist in relation to his patient, hence when exercising this kind of attention. They are: (1) a *nonteleologic attitude* which focuses on what; (2) *unconventionality*—namely, not becoming involved with the manifest and the conventional; (3) *unobtrusiveness;* (4) *incorruptibility;* (5) *respectful vigilance;* (6) *being threshold con-scious;* to which we would add (7) Krishnamurti's (1954) *choiceless awareness.*

In speaking of awareness, we must not ascribe a directing, controlling role to it, as in the outmoded concept of consciousness. "Attention is only a transitory focusing of the extended system of processes which guide be-havior" (Whyte, 1950). Schachtel (1959) expands the meaning of the attending process in "The Development of Focal Attention and the Emergence of Reality." The attending process can be focused now inwardly and now outwardly, as it is moved to do so, by the emerging processes. In "The Quality of the Analyst's Attention" (Cantor, 1959) Horney lists as attributes "wholeheartedness, comprehensiveness, and productiveness." In "The Analyst's Personal Equation" (Azorin, 1957) she gives a picture of what favors and obstructs the qualities that should be present in the analyst's attention. Among the "Desirable Qualities of a Good Analyst" are: (1) "maturity, directness, discernment and objectivity"; (2) "a real interest in and for the patients, and for their practical as well as psychological problems; (3) a prevalent striving toward self-realization, an honest wish to help patients toward their self-realization; (4) a capacity for healthy emotional involvement with the patient; (5) a searching mind with an untiring curiosity about challenging problems."

What interferes with the quality of the analyst's attention are his residual neurotic problems. They will interfere with what is positively required. He may try to come to an understanding too rapidly or tend to avoid anxiety, conflict, and hostility in his patient or being in it himself. His egocentricity and preconceived notions will cause him to have a distorted picture.

Our view of the person of the analyst as his most important instrument in therapy organically determines how we see transference. "Of Freud's discoveries I value most highly . . . it is his finding that one can utilize for therapy the patient's emotional reactions to the analyst and to the analytical situation" (1939, p. 154). Horney adds,

> Disentangled from the theoretical bias of the repetition compulsion . . . my viewpoint concerning the phenomenon is this: . . . the analytical relationship is one special form of human relationships and existing disturbances are bound to appear here as they appear elsewhere. The particular conditions under which an analysis is conducted render it possible to study these disturbances here more accurately than elsewhere and to convince the patient of their existence and the role they play [p. 167]. . . . The principle that the analyst's emotional reactions should be understood as a "counter-transference" may be objected to on the same grounds as the concept of transference (p. 166).

Doctor-Patient Relationship

As Horney's ideas on theory and technique evolved, the concept of the doctor-patient relationship emerged (Kelman, 1955a). This meant the whole person of the therapist in relationship with the whole person of the patient. All that is neurotic and healthy in each participates. Diagnosing and prognosing (Kelman, 1955b) as well as growing and learning throughout each therapy are essential for both. The therapist's experience in utilizing his person as means and ends will make communing more possible and quicker realization of what is obtaining, with more effective utilization of the varieties of imagery and symbolizations.

The therapist, the more whole he is, will be able to better discriminate: when a patient sees him as a magician; when he is externalizing his own attributes in a glorified or despised way; when he is truly touching on some of the analyst's own neurotic residuals; and when he is seeing him more realistically. That the patient will see him *as if* he were all kinds of people in his past, present, and future will become evident in the relationship, in his behaviors, associations, and in his dreams. In the service of working through some of these *as if* persons, in response to patients' overt and implied assertions, as they come up in associations and dreams, the analyst may ask such questions as "Who do you have me being? Who do I feel like today? Who do I remind you of? What would you have me saying in answer to your question? What if you experience me in the dream as your father? What if your mother in the dream stands for me?"

We do not agree with the theoretical premises for the transference neurosis, its inevitability, and the requirement that it, as such, be worked through. The phenomena which these assumptions attempt to explain are directly observable. We have indicated, based on our model of the symbolizing process, that the symbols chosen and the arrangements of them will appropriately and adequately point at and communicate what that patient is experiencing here-now, though, unconsciously and in awareness, to varying degrees, he may feel the persons, relationships, and situations conveyed in symbol forms here-now, *as if* they were identical with those back there-then.

The emergence of such symbol forms and arrangements experienced in the ways indicated, and with increasing intensities, is an expression of an increasing degree of threat from and involvement with, and in, the analytic process and relationship. As the analysis has proceeded and more peripheral defenses have been relinquished, the patient is opening himself to experiencing threats to major defenses having greater subjective value, such as dependency to the point of masochism, and expansiveness with its arrogant-vindictive components. At such points, when conflict, basic and central, with intensities of self-hate and onslaughts of anxiety and hostility are being experienced and flight is not available as a solution, a resurgence of intensified dependency needs and/or with assaultiveness with reference to the analyst, often occur. We feel that what is crucial to working through such difficult periods is the depth and strength of the doctor-patient relationship.

Basic trust makes possible a patient's willingness to go along with the therapy, stick through trying and painful periods, and for the therapist to take chances. Basic trust must be built slowly and carefully and on the clearest kind of evidence, where at all possible. This cannot be done by giving "false reassurance." We realize when we are giving defense or "superficial reassurance," namely, going with the tide, and also that what moves the analysis forward is "basic reassurance" (Martin, 1949), which is good analysis. For basic trust to develop, openness to, experience with, and guidance by the prerational levels are prerequisite. This means it must happen at and through the levels of "communion of mother and child"

(Goldstein, 1954), of "the prototaxic mode" (Sullivan 1953), "of physiological continuity of child and mother, person and world" (Burrow 1964), of unconscious processes.

Communicating and Communing

Communing (Kelman, 1958) is essential to all communicating in a human sense: in infancy before awareness of otherness obtains, and thereafter, conscious and unconscious, at the prerationative, preverbal, and verbal levels. For communing to happen more often, we must go the way of relating, exhausting its experiential possibilities. To experience what communing is, we must have descriptions for comparison but are confronted by the paradox that such descriptions would be about communing because it can be obtaining only when there is silence and when there is no "I" standing outside and reflecting on the process. While communing is obtaining, the dualisms in thinking, feeling, and being disappear. There are only oneness feelings. More accurately, there is the feeling of secondlessness, without any reflection. Communing is ultimately being, not as in existential philosophies but as what was meant by the saying that "Atman is Brahman and Brahman is Atman." Communing is essential to and the essence of being human, to self-realizing, to realizing others, for openness to cosmos, and becoming the spiritual dimension.

In the first twenty months most communicating with the infant is prerationative, demonstrable, contactual, and behavioral, expressed bodily, autonomically and through the senses. In her communing through the subliminal, inchoate, allusive, figurative, and metaphorical, the mother is communicating through her unique idioms, her world and that of her infant. All who commune in the infant's environment express these worlds in their mothering, fathering, brothering, and sistering, as do the extended family of persons, personing across time.

Since maximal communing occurs from birth through the earliest months and, as there is sensitivity, respect and love for that being's "Critical Periods of Behavior Development" (Scott, 1962), what the communing ones communicated will be the most deeply and extensively embedded behavior patterns, remembered in those early learned idioms. It is the analyst's task to learn the idioms of the languages of those seeking help so that he can hear and understand them toward communicating to patients ways of learning to unlearn their familiar idioms and their consequences and learn to learn new ways of learning and new idioms appropriate to their uniqueness as changing, evolving human beings moving in the direction of straighter growing. The analyst must be alert to idioms pointing at his patient's assets, which he once knew and forgot, or has known distortedly, or for which he has no idioms because he has never known and experienced those assets in awareness.

In his communing and relating, as man evolved, some of the aspects of the knowing process (Kelman, 1966) that participated were informing, explaining, instructing, teaching, educating, responding, experiencing, understanding, learning, and remembering toward acquiring information, having knowledge and becoming wise. Their philological roots, from Sanskrit to modern English, imply a human process having immediacy, intensities of experiencing involving dread, awe, reverence, respect, faith, trust, hope, love. This philological evolution reveals a moving from a predominance of the subjectifying attitude to that of an objectifying one, from the emotive and the prerationative to the conceptual, from showing to telling, from wisdom, to knowledge, to information. These organically determined patterns, affected through continuing interaction with environments in evolving sequences, could and have led to predominantly harmonious and healthy human integrating except when diverted from life's natural evolution. A perversion of these straighter growing possibilities was the consequence. A constricting of the spontaneously organic, perceptual, and conceptual took place with an imbedding of increasingly rigid bodily attitudes, feeling sets, and compulsive thought processes.

This comprehensive knowing is evident in Horney's theory and technique.

> The road of analytic therapy is an old one, advocated time and again throughout human history. In the terms of Socrates and Hindu philosophy, among others, it is the *road to reorientation and self-knowledge*. What is new and specific about it is the method of gaining self-knowledge, which we owe to the genius of Freud. . . . [1950, p. 341]. The way toward this goal—*outgoing* . . . destructive forces in ourselves—is an ever increasing awareness and understanding of ourselves. Self-knowledge, then, is not an aim in itself, but a means of liberating the forces of spontaneous growth. In this sense, to work at ourselves becomes not only the prime moral obligation, but at the same time, in a very real sense, the prime moral *privilege* (p. 15).

And, referring to working through of neurotic processes she warns

> *Becoming aware of all these factors does not mean having information about them but having knowledge of them* [p. 341]. . . . Furthermore, his

knowledge of himself must not remain an intellectual knowledge though it may start this way, but must become an *emotional experience* (p. 342).

In *Therapeutic Communication,* Ruesch (1961) asserts that "At times this process is referred to as therapy; at other times as education; some call it counseling; others simply friendship." All of these are aspects of the doctor-patient relationship. The comprehensive knowing process includes educating and therapy, which Freud also considered as part of analysis, as well as aspects of counseling that come under "general human help" and "friendship."

> When I speak of general human help I mean the way the analyst helps the patient—not through his interpretations but through his attitude toward the patient. This includes his willingness to understand, his unflagging interest in the patient's growth, his faith in the patient's existing potentialities, his firmness that permits him to view the patient's suffering with concern without letting himself be crushed by them, to remain unswayed by the patient's admiration and undaunted by the patient's attacks. The value of such an attitude is underrated by some and overrated by others (Horney, 1946, p. 202).

"You may wonder . . . whether the relationship between patient and analyst is not a kind of friendship. In a sense, it is friendship at its very best . . . though it lacks the measure of spontaneity and mutuality essential to a friendship" (p. 203). Following MacMurray, who distinguishes functional and personal relationships, Horney adds, though "Your analyst and you may like and respect each other . . . the relationship is for a definite purpose . . . it essentially is a functional one" (p. 204).

Discovering His Real Self

In the light of all the foregoing what do we mean by technique? In the Western world, more marked in the United States, we overemphasize the practical, technological "know-how" and have an antitheoretical, antiphilosophical, antiintellectual bias. Science is identified with applied science, its technical aspects and uses. Technique means a doer doing something to another something who is done to, both objectified, isolated things. The operations of these doings should be as simple as possible, observable, and teachable with predictable, repeatable results. This describes but limited aspects even of the artisan's and the craftsman's work and leaves out their artistry and craftsmanship.

What is the psychoanalyst's most important tool, instrument, guide, means, and end in therapy? As he participates with the whole of his being, with his sensing, feeling, thinking, and behaving, with his reacting, responding, and resonating, the meaning of technique becomes considerably revised. It is the outcome of all that has gone before, "so well learned, experienced and embedded that it can be forgotten to be immediately available without reflection for appropriate application with originality and inventiveness, because each situation is unique." Kelman adds (1965),

> Known categories can be but near to remote approximations to the requirements of moment-to-moment emerging contexts. Technique is no longer seen as simply what to do but an attitude in and of a process which points at what and how to be, feel, think and act. It no longer is something on top and at the surface of, but that which arises from the totality of processes and is immediately relevant to what the situation is requiring.

Our viewpoints on technique are consonant with the holistic theory of human nature and the goals in therapy that follow from them. They are not symptom removal, syndrome alleviation, amelioration of disease entity, all of which do happen in the course of therapy, but helping the individual outgrow his neurotic difficulties while concomitantly assisting his development in the direction of self-realization. The notion "cure" is appropriate to the goal of relief of symptoms; "we cannot 'cure' the wrong course which the development of a person has taken," but we can "assist him in gradually outgrowing it" (Horney, 1950, p. 333). There can be no tearing down first and then building up. The very resolution of the neurotic process, namely, the identifying, undermining, and dissipating of these patterns is only possible as simultaneously there is an identifying, supporting, and extending of the growing possibilities of the real self-system (Horney, Cantor, 1967a). The real self is postulated as an integrating principle, an ongoing dynamism, not as an entity or a thing to be revealed. "The *real self*" is "that central inner force, common to all human beings and yet unique in each, which is the deep source of growth." By "growth is meant . . . free, healthy development in accordance with the potentials of one's generic and individual nature" (Horney, 1950, p. 17).

While at times the analyst may seemingly function like a mirror and a revealer of the patient's unconscious, much more is required of him. He and the patient are whole persons, not part functions, integrating in moving fields and in oscillating equilibrium, while mutually influencing each other. With what is required of the analyst, it is inevitable that his values will participate. The issue is not whether they do or should. The fact is they do and he cannot operate without them. "Since neurosis involves questions of human behavior and human motivations, social and traditional evaluations inadvertently determine the problems tackled and the goal aimed at. . . . My opinion is that an absence of value judgments belongs among those ideals we should try rather to overcome than to cultivate" (Horney, 1939, pp. 296–297).

Horney further elaborates her position on moral values.

> Man, by his very nature and of his own accord, strives toward self-realization, and his set of values evolves from his striving. Apparently, he cannot, for example, develop his full human potentialities unless he is truthful to himself; unless he is active and productive; unless he relates himself to others in the spirit of mutuality. Apparently he cannot grow if he indulges in a "dark idolatry of self" (Shelley) and consistently attributes all his shortcomings to the deficiencies of others. He can grow, in the true sense, only if he assumes responsibility for himself. We arrive thus at a *morality of evolution* in which the criterion for what we cultivate or reject in ourselves lies in the question: is a particular attitude or drive inducive or obstructive to my human growth?

Bally stated that the task of psychoanalysis is "to reveal, develop and structure through analytic communication an appropriate character able to live courageously in a changing world" (1964). He spelled out the morality required of the analyst to effect this objective.

> Patient and doctor are today faced with the task of establishing self-assurance which is independent of achievement, in order to provide the patient with the basic security in society, the "primordial trust," which carries him through the changing roles he will have to play. . . . He must experience the analyst not as authoritarian father-ideal, but as representa-
ive and spokesman for an ideal group, which will finally receive him and
ve him meaning and purpose (1966).

Whereas a neurosis could be said to be an individually created value system, it lacks the freedom of creative self-realization. A compulsive, egocentric pseudomorality, characterized by moralizing and being moralistic, and stems from the entire neurotic defensive system, must be distinguished from an authentic, a spontaneous morality, which is the ultimate in being human, whole, and healthy.

Horney's *morality of evolution* serves not only as a guide and a direction but also provides the possibility, while the urge toward self-realization gives the motive power for the formation of a new identity as the old (pride-invested) identity is relinquished. "Outgrowing his neurotic egocentricity, he will become more aware of the broader issues involved in his particular life and in the world at large. From having been in his own mind the uniquely significant exception he will gradually experience himself as part of a bigger whole. And he will be willing and able to assume his share of responsibility in it and contribute to it in whatever way he is best able" (Horney, 1950, p. 365).

From the moment the analysis begins, there will be impediments to moving toward those goals. The forces of spontaneous growth do not simply emerge and evolve as the analysis proceeds but are constantly blocked by and perverted into patterns opposing change and tending toward maintaining the status quo. It was Freud's great discovery that while the patient wants to get well, he is unconsciously determined to remain ill. As the analyst attempts to help him move toward self-realization, he is confronted by the patient's determination to perfect his neurotic patterns. This difficulty must be brought clearly and explicitly into his awareness.

Among the consequences of unresolved conflicts (Horney, 1945, Part II) are *the impoverishment of the personality* and the devastating *waste of human energies* brought about by *indecisiveness, ineffectualness,* and *inertia. Moral integrity* is impaired by the decrease in sincerity and the burgeoning egocentricity. What follows are innumerable *pretenses* of love, goodness, sympathy, interest, knowledge, honesty, fairness, and suffering. An emerging awareness of how his neurosis impairs and impoverishes his life becomes a powerful incentive toward confronting those forces that tend toward obstructing his growth.

Our position regarding "abstinence," "privation," and "suffering" differs from Freud's because we assume a momentum coming from the urge toward self-realization and the ongoing suffering from unresolved conflicts and their consequences. We feel that the patient is continually creating his own privation, abstinence, and suffering and the urge to resolve them. In some patients the pressure for an immediate relief from pain fills their consciousness and seems to be their only motivation for coming to therapy and for keeping them in it. Other patients, who may or may not be aware of suffering from deadness, numbness, and inertia, need a higher level of pain and tension, because for them it means aliveness until something genuine replaces the suffering. Also it may be the only motivation available to them for the time being. We must be alert to the pain becoming an anesthetic and paralytic, as well as a narcotizer and addictive narcotic, as happens with the so-called masochistic patients.

Our aim is to maintain the pain, anxiety, and tension at a level most conducive to the work while avoiding unnecessary pain, economizing time, and helping the relationship to develop as rapidly as possible in the direction of "basic trust." By ameliorating and mitigating pain the analysis can be set moving. Also, our helping to reduce the unnecessary pain will be appreciated by the patient. Such accruing experiences are essential whenever the pain associated with experiencing basic and central conflict, as well as the accessions of anxiety and self-hate connected with the inevitable *disillusioning process,* become intense. Also such deepening of basic trust will enable the patient to accept and seek the abstaining of the analyst and attempt to be on his own for longer periods, struggling with his problems, and probing his depths. Then the patient will be able to experience the meaning of dying to live and the ultimates possible, alone and in silence, on the couch, which is not possible in the vis-à-vis position (Kelman, 1954). He will also experience the meaning and the unity of communing and communicating (Kelman, 1958a). Such experiences are educating the patient in self-analysis and in life.

Awareness that the analyst's values are involved and that counseling and "friendship in the best sense" participate is no false sentimentality nor imposition of the analyst's values on his patient. Rather it requires the rigor and clarity of the scientific attitude and of the phenomenologic approach essential to Freud's "evenly-hovering attention," which attitude involves a most active process. It also asks that there be moral compassion and moral toughness, prerequisite to confronting human problems, humanly and with humility. Then there can be that unity and harmony of dispassionate subjectivity and passionate objectivity in the analyst's most productive use of his person as his most important instrument of therapy and as technique.

As he is, the analyst will be able to define the nature of his patient's pain, tensions, and anxieties (Kelman, 1966). He will be able to delineate the nuances of his attitude toward his pain and the proportions of his suffering, which are sick and healthy in their functions, sources, and in his attitudes toward them. The issue then becomes how to deal with his patient's suffering, so that its irrational proportions become diminished and the possibilities for experiencing suffering in more rational proportions increase.

The aim in dealing with the patient's pain is to recognize when he is compulsively demanding relief and when he is working toward release from it. The first goes with a drive to solve, to deny, to disown pain and to experience it as an alien and imposed factor which, when aided and abetted by the patient and his environment, leads to moral weakness, moral torpitude, and cowardice. A patient, seeking release, is working toward resolving and becoming more aware of and owning his pain. Then he will be experiencing it as "mine" and "coming from me." While working toward this end, he is seeking and accepting the help of his analyst in further identifying with and becoming his pain, with the result that he will become morally tougher, with increasing integrity and greater courage. For courage is "the measure of a creative person . . . to enter with freer choice more anxiety situations and to do so more frequently. Self-realizing of human creative potentialities is only possible through chancing, through daring to leap into the unknown, and to put at stake and to threaten what has subjective value, rational and irrational" (Kelman, 1956b).

Resistance and Blockage

"By resistance is meant the energy with which an individual protects repressed feelings or thoughts against their integration into conscious awareness" (Horney, 1939, p. 34). As her theory evolved, while the notion of energy investment in hindrances to analytic progress remained, the mechanistic implications of the concept resistance were replaced by the holistic-process concept of blockage, which does not lend itself to finding the onus in the patient nor to the analyst's acquisition of a halo of frustrated innocence. The comprehensive concept of blockage (Horney, Zimmerman, 1956c) contains what is subsumed under repression; it includes the various categories of resistance and the processes more directly related to Horney's concept of neurotic character development.

Blockages may be experienced and seen as actively blocking and/or being blocked by patient and analyst and as having an inward and outward reference. It requires an alertness for and a being attuned to the where, when, and why the blocking occurred, also to the what and how of it, not only after the fact but as it is beginning to happen and is building up, perferably forestalling it to keep it to a minimum. Horney's motto of "blockages first" becomes more understandable when connected with her focus on movement in the analytic process requiring an alertness to its rhythm, tempo, and direction. It demands of the analyst that he be constantly asking what is slowing, blocking, and stalling the process and why the feeling of being stuck is there in patient and/or analyst.

Horney saw blockages as very specifically related to the three major solutions for intrapsychic conflict—the expansive, the self-effacing, and the resigned. In these areas blockages function to maintain the most deeply embedded solution and their main subjective values of mastery, love, and freedom. In a more general way the "Auxiliary Approaches to Artificial Harmony" (Horney, 1945, Chap. 8) and the "General Measures to Relieve Tension" (Horney, 1950, Chap. 7) serve as blockages to the experiencing of unfulfilled shoulds, self-hate, anxiety, compulsiveness, and conflict. The greatest blockages are against the experiencing of constructive moves and assets, through the immediate glorification of what has just occurred in the analysis, or its denigration, or its being politely ignored and denied. Blockages are most active in the doctor-patient relationship.

The forms in which blockages are manifest are myriad. The patient may be argumentative, sarcastic, assaultive, take shelter behind a façade of polite compliance; be evasive, forget the subject; or drop it. He may start talking in theoretical terms or treat the whole matter as if it were something alien that didn't concern him. Special factors will operate in regard to the analyst, determining the climate of the relationship. If the patient's need is for love, mastery, or freedom, he will become hypersensitive to what he regards as rejection, domination, or coercion. In addition (Horney, 1950, p. 339), "because his pride is bound to be hurt in the process, he tends easily to feel humiliated. Because of his expectations and claims, he often feels frustrated and abused. The mobilization of his self-accusations and self-contempt makes him feel accused and despised . . . also patients regularly overrate the analyst's significance. . . . He is not simply a human being who may help him. . . . He is the magician who has the power to plunge them into hell or lift them into heaven."

Although blockages are definite obstructions to progress and growth, they also point to what needs to be worked on in analysis. They aid in the process of working through and act as a protection against the potential damage from premature interpretations. In the earlier phases of the work, it may be in the interests of the analysis to go along with the blockages. It gives analyst and patient the time and opportunity to get acquainted and to help build the relationship. This can be done by responding to a demand and need for relief, by going along with the patient's seeking help to "get rid of the bad parts of his neurosis while perfecting the good." Both of these are blockages that can be turned to constructive use in strengthening the relationship and in helping the analysis gather momentum. In the process of working through, patients will have a variety of reactions, for example to interpretations, the so-called negative therapeutic reaction, and what Horney called *repercussions,* all of which can become serious blockages.

When the analysis is well under way and after the patient has been "grappling with his conflicts" come those "constructive periods" that "are followed by *repercussions* in which the essential element is a renewed onrush of self-hate and self-contempt. These self-destructive feelings may be experienced as such or they may be externalized through becoming vindictive, feeling abused, or having sadistic or masochistic fantasies. Or the patient may but vaguely recognize his self-hate but sharply feel the anxiety with which he responds to the self-destructive impulses. Or finally not even the anxiety appears as such, but his customary defenses against it—such as drinking, sexual activities, a compulsive need for company, or being arrogant or grandiose—become active again" (Horney, 1950, pp. 357–358).

Working Through

We have discussed many aspects of working through; under the analyst coming to experience and know himself as his best instrument of therapy; in the discussion of doctor-patient relationship and the subject of blockages. Working through is more than seeing how a neurotic trend originated and how it functions in the patient, outside the analytic relationship and in it. It means not only becoming intellectually aware but also emotionally experiencing it as his own, with its full intensity. A trend can only be understood through experiencing it in many contexts and through approaching it from many angles.

An attitude of placating, for example, is originally seen as part and parcel of the neurotic need for affection. When a patient's idealized image is under scrutiny, placating will be pointed at as an expression of his notion that he is a saint. When detachment comes to the fore, the placating quite obviously served the need to avoid friction. The compulsive nature of the attitude will be highlighted when the patient's fear of others and his leaning over backward from his own sadistic impulses come into view.

In addition to becoming emotionally aware of the attitude in its overt and covert forms, and of its compulsiveness, the patient needs to see and experience its subjective values as well as the adverse consequences of the attitude. When a patient first becomes aware of a neurotic trend, he tends to look for a cause, usually in childhood. By turning to the cause, its historical origins, he hopes to remove it. He must be helped toward becoming more familiar with the trend—as an aspect of working through. He must get to know the specific ways in which it manifests itself, the means he uses to cover it up, and his own attitudes toward it.

As an illustration we will show how one aspect of the arrogant vindictive character structure is worked through.

If, for instance, the patient's dread of being compliant has become clear, he must see the extent to which he resents, dreads, and despises in himself any form of self-effacement. He must recognize the checks he has unconsciously instituted to the end of eliminating from his life all possibilities of compliance and everything involved in compliant tendencies. He will understand, then, how attitudes apparently divergent all serve this one purpose; how he has numbed his sensitivity to others to the point of being unaware of their feelings, desires, or reactions; how this has made him highly inconsiderate; how he has choked off any feeling of fondness for others as well as any desire to be liked by them; how he disparages tender feelings and goodness in others; how he tends automatically to refuse requests; how in personal relationships he feels entitled to be moody, critical, and demanding but denies the partner any of these prerogatives (Horney, 1945, pp. 230, 231).

Working through leads us to seeing more of the patient's predominating expansive solutions and, particularly, his arrogant-vindictive solution. "Most expressions of vindictiveness have been described by others, and by myself, as sadistic trends," said Horney (1950, p. 199).

The term "sadistic" focuses on the satisfaction to be gained from the power to subject others to pain or indignity. Satisfaction—excitement, thrill, glee—undoubtedly can be present in sexual and non-sexual situations, and for these the term "sadistic" [1945, Chap. 12] seems to be sufficiently meaningful. My suggestion to replace the term "sadistic" in its general use by "vindictive" is based on the contention that for so-called sadistic trends vindictive needs are the crucial motivating force.

The attendant pride in the arrogant vindictive solution with its great emphasis on strength, mastery, will power, domination, and invulnerability as well as the passion for vindictive triumph, must be understood in connection with the dread of compliance. In addition, his basic belief that it's a "dog-eat-dog world" must come to light. With the emergence of softer feelings—tendencies to be sympathetic, helpful, and so on—there will be a conflict with accompanying feelings of chaos and profound anxiety. The emergence of anxiety frequently leads the patient to feel he is getting worse. It may be he has touched on attitudes and feelings that endanger his main defensive system or that hurt his pride. However, it may also indicate that the patient now feels strong enough to take the risk of facing his problems more squarely.

"Both the need to justify his claims and his responses to their frustration work like vicious circles, supplying constant fuel to his vindictiveness. So pervasive a vindictiveness naturally enters into the analytic relationship, too, and shows itself in many ways. It is one part of the so-called negative therapeutic reaction, by which we mean an acute impairment of condition after a constructive move ahead." When the defense is "subjectively indispensable," failure to recognize its many forms "may not merely delay the analytic process but may wreck it altogether" (Horney, 1950, p. 201). Such wrecking is an exaggeration of the so-called negative therapeutic reaction and happens with so-called masochistic patients. With them the implicit or explicit accusation is "you have ruined me"; the arrogant-vindictive patient's battle cry is "I will ruin you," which is his attempt at vengeance and vindication.

A paradoxical reaction to the decrease of anxiety seems to occur in the markedly self-effacing individual; whereas the arrogant vindictive individual will tend to minimize anxiety, he will maximize it. It is frequently observable that most of the activities of the self-effacing person will be carried out in a state of high tension. Peaceful living seems almost unbearable, and the creation of crises is a regular occurrence. This may not be seen in the early phases of the therapy of a self-effacing individual but in time will emerge. The sudden lowering of tension impairs his contact with reality and his sense of identity diminishes. He then experiences feelings of emptiness, loneliness, dissolution, wild disruptive anxiety, and suicidal self-hate (Kelman, 1959b).

What needs to be worked through in the self-effacing person has been indicated in the description of the self-effacing solution, which is for Horney a more comprehensive term than masochism, characteristics of which are most obvious in morbid dependency. "Morbid dependency is one of the most complicated phenomena with which we have to deal," said Horney.

We cannot explain the total picture as manifold branches of sexual masochism. . . . Nor is it all the inverted sadism of a weak and hopeless person. Nor do we grasp its essentials when focusing on the parasitic or symbiotic aspects, or on the neurotic's drive to lose himself. Nor, finally, can we regard the whole condition as being merely an externalization of pride and self-hate. . . . All such explanations give too static a picture. . . . Morbid dependency is . . . a process in which all or most of these factors come into play . . . and . . . though relevant to the total picture, are, as it were, too negative to account for the passionate character of the involvement. . . . But there is no passion without the expectation of some vital fulfillment . . . this factor, which in its turn cannot be isolated but may be grasped only in the framework of the whole self-effacing structure, is the drive for total surrender and the longing to find unity through merging with the partner (1950, p. 258).

Characteristically, we discover in such patients extremes of irrational expansiveness to the point of not only encompassing but being the universe, with others as mere aspects of themselves; on the other hand, the opposite extreme of irrational contracting to self-extinction and submerging in the all, which, at the same time, they feel they are. Such fluctuating processes evoke considerable anxiety and, to hold them in check, require an oppositional dualism with another person. This other may be factual or imaginary. The manipulation and control of this other becomes their consuming passion. Foreground anxiety may be used by the self-effacing person to control others and force his will upon them. More in the background is anxiety used as a motor force to catapult the individual against the significant other.

Some of the difficulties that confront the analyst in working with so-called masochistic people are described by Kelman (1959b)

. . . pain, past, present and future, and relief and release from it almost totally fill these patients' mental and emotional horizons, and the analytic sessions. They are constantly demanding that the analyst do something about their suffering and berating him because he hasn't done enough to relieve their pain. Here we come upon several paradoxes. The very heightened state of tension becomes a numbing narcotic, which they need and unconsciously create. Quantity becomes quality. So more tension means more narcosis. This in turn means not only maintaining but exaggerating the masochistic processes. As the therapist helps in resolving these patterns, he is giving constructive help, but it leads to lessening of the tension and thereby increasing the pain. This is one of the crucial dilemmas in the therapy of such patients. They, who demand relief from pain, must be helped to tolerate transient, and even prolonged increases of pain from the ultimate resolution of their problems.

More aspects of working through emerge as patients who fear unconscious processes can let go (Martin, 1951) into them and allow them to emerge: as compulsive intellectualizers and feelers can allow the emergence of the more spontaneous conceptual and perceptual patients; as patients who are compulsively wording, ideaing, and talking and who fear silence can let go into and experience its constructive values. This is most possible when a patient is using the couch most effectively for working at his problems, for contemplating, meditating, and opening himself to his depths so that he can be with himself, by himself, himself. Then the liberating and liberated unconscious processes can be predominantly manifestations of spontaneous creativity (Kelman, 1963b, 1964) and insight (Martin, 1952).

The Initial Interview

We see the initial interview (Horney, Cantor, 1957a,b) as a therapeutic possibility. The first session is a critical period in a patient's life. How the session is conducted may crucially determine the future course of therapy. Whereas the ultimate of openness and sensitivity to the patient's needs may start therapy off most auspiciously, their lack may cause it to flounder and/or fail. In the first session a patient can be most open and revealing of himself, whether aware of it or not. Usually he reveals more about his sickness and less about his assets. Often a therapist is most open in his perceptions of his patient, which too frequently are not heeded. The first session is a unique opportunity for starting the relationship off in a constructive direction and creating an attitude of trust.

We do not use such opening comments as, "What are your complaints? What's troubling you? Tell me about yourself. Start anywhere." Also we do not wait very long for the patient to start talking. Such openings structure the situation into a bothering, complaining, telling, or a painfully lost or silent one. What we often start with is, "Can I help you? What can I do for you?" We also feel the vis-à-vis position is better for the early periods of the therapy. It gives an opportunity to get a clearer picture of each other and the therapist has more visible clues to guide him. We may keep a patient in the vis-à-vis position when it becomes obvious how elusive and evasive he is and/or how compulsive is his intellectualizing. For whenever we feel that the patient feels isolated, flounders or goes into a panic state, or escapes into fantasy, we may ask him to leave the couch. Because of such and other defenses we may use a patient's bodily gestures and automatic responses not only as indicators, but we forcibly draw his attention to them, connect him with his organicity, and thereby undercut the defenses he uses to keep himself away from his own body and feelings.

There is some flexibility among our colleagues regarding the usual instructions given in a first interview. Many do not mention the couch or the fundamental rule in the first session; many others mention the importance of dreams, the twenty-four-hour rule, and arrangements regarding hours, fees, and payment. Each, however, tries to use all of these instructions toward the same end, helping the analysis move in a constructive direction.

Kelman is more flexible in all these matters toward helping make possible the emergence of "Freer Associating" (1962; Horney, Sheiner, 1967), of fantasies and dreams (Kelman, 1965), toward the most effective use of lateness and missed sessions and delays in payment. His feeling is that much can be done toward helping patients become freer in their associating without explicit mentioning of it, and thus Kelman believes that even the most uninformed person has some knowledge of dreams; thus he waits for the emergence of dreams and fantasies in therapy. In this way the dreams have a given context, can be discussed in their immediacy, and the patient is being educated in working with dreams without being aware of what has happened. This does not preclude asking a patient if he dreams and, on a rare occasion when none has been forthcoming, if he has dreamed. Once dreaming has occurred, asking about dreams has a different meaning and will be done more often.

Many wait until the first absence has occurred; it may happen for a host of reasons including illness. The specific instance is analyzed and used as an opportunity to explain the rule regarding absences. Some prefer twenty-four and others forty-eight hours' notice. The explanation is kept as simple as possible, namely, that a contractual arrangement has been made with mutual responsibilities. Whenever and as soon as cancellations occur, there is an opportunity for immediacy in analysis. When they happen with increasing frequency, this circumstance is also analyzed, and the whole meaning of analysis is re-examined, with the mentioning of the possibility that should frequent absence continue the analytic work might be interrupted. Lateness is also analyzed as it occurs.

Not because "real analytic patients" are fewer and the range of patients being treated by analysts is so much broader, but because it is our feeling that a patient coming to analysis is so upset, as he is, we feel that he would be further disturbed and confused by a long list of instructions. To give instructions at the beginning would be taking away many valuable opportunities for forwarding the analysis. In keeping with this attitude of flexibility, the number and time of sessions, as well as the fee arrangements, may be left open. A therapy may proceed session by session until a patient can accept regularity. It may move from one to two and from two to three sessions weekly. Because the situation required it, some patients have been seen for double session five times a week. When appropriate and effective, patients are informed regarding the analyst's vacation schedule and asked to arrange theirs accordingly. The way patients respond and deal with this suggestion can be most productive for the analysis. Because of problems of money, patients may want to pay cash, at each session or at odd dates. Such arrangements will be accepted until the more usual arrangements can be agreed on. With some patients it is most valuable to ask them how they would like to pay and request their keeping the records of the sessions and the dates of payment, indicating to them that the analyst will also keep a record and that no bills will be sent. The problems such an arrangement may bring to the fore can be most fruitful sources of analytic material.

This same flexibility obtains regarding "The Use of the Analytic Couch" (Kelman, 1954). He feels the issue is "What position and what moving from one physical position to another is better at a particular time for a particular patient to help move analysis forward more effectively?" Kelman also asked how can a patient be helped to avail himself effectively of physical mobility in the analytic situation and also how can this physical mobility be used to support and encourage all dimensions of mobility in patients for helping them toward self-realization. Because we see the analytic situation as a single integral reality, the preference and aversion for the couch and the vis-à-vis position of patients as well as of therapists with particular problems must be explored.

Our hope is that all patients will ultimately avail themselves of the couch in ways that it can be optimally used, for which no other position can be a substitute. We look to freer associating; more effective utilization of dreams; fantasies, and slips; a regularity of the numbers and time of sessions, of arrangements for payment, and a diminution to disappearance of absences and latenesses. In such an atmosphere the patient feels more trusting and secure. He knows where he stands with himself and his analyst as to time, place, person, and function. He can then more and more wholeheartedly focus on the task at hand. As this state of affairs is reached he is approaching interruption of regular sessions. We feel there is no termination to analysis because "man can change and go on changing as long as he lives" (Horney, 1945, p. 19). The issue becomes how best to gradually taper off the regular work and with mutual agreement.

Such questions as we usually ask, if a patient isn't already talking, are often enough to help him begin. A nod, a smile, an "um huh," or a "yes" will keep him talking. "Can you say a little more about this or that?" or "I wasn't quite clear about what you said about your wife, boss, or partner?" Such remarks may be all that is necessary to maintain the flow of associations. When a session ends with a patient saying "I didn't know I could talk, talk so much, or the time went so fast," we can feel that the analysis has had an auspicious beginning. When a patient is blocked, sometimes he may say, "Will you ask me some questions?" Something specific and concrete such as "Where were you born? What kind of work do you do?" may start him going with further questions eliciting a life history but with the purpose of helping the patient start talking and unburdening himself. Depending on the needs of the situation we may get a shorter or slightly more extensive life history or leave it for later interviews. In the first sessions we may also make a diagnostic and prognostic evaluation not only in terms of psychiatric nosology but also from the viewpoint of assets and liabilities for self-realization. We try to evaluate the patient's incentive for analysis, healthy and neurotic, what brought him to analysis at this time, and what went into his choice of analyst.

Interpretation

We do not believe that dreams are the *via regia* to the unconscious but one of the better ways of contacting it. Dreams and fantasies are extremely helpful for moving a patient toward freer associating, toward greater openness to the prelogical. The patient is helped to metaphorically move down the symbolic spiral to pure fact, to his ground of being. Thereby a patient's acquired distortions can be more quickly and effectively resolved and creative processes freed. Through our focus on here-now experiencing the patient's needs to see a dream as a thing, as unconnected with him, as something that happened in another place and time, can be more quickly resolved, so that he begins to experience its meaning in the ongoing context, namely, in which it was dreamed, comes up, and is being worked with.

Kelman (1962) offers some suggestions for working with fantasies. The subject might be opened with "I was not clear, would you mind repeating what you just told me?" And, if it feels safe, to ask, "Was that an actual happening you were describing?" These open-ended questions may lead to the description of a fantasy, to the subject of fantasying, or to associations suggesting further questions regarding fantasying. Such opportunities may appear from the beginning of analysis, but the timing is crucial. People who, because of their severe alienation, cannot distinguish between dream, fantasy, living in imagination, and reality, who are dominated by magical thinking, must be asked such questions with extreme caution. A too early discussion of such discriminations can lead to panic, confusional states, states of depersonalization, and breaking off of therapy. On occasion a psychotic episode, transitional or of longer standing, may be precipitated.

Whyte's (1950) expression "The extended system of processes which guide behavior" could subsume the many inner- and outer-directed processes we have been describing. Being processes, meaning being active and acting, we feel the passivity-activity controversy has arisen out of a lack of rigor in definition. All processes in nature, hence in human nature, are active. Passivity as a defense can be most active and tenacious. The quality and quantity of activity, inwardly and outwardly directed, is the issue. A therapist can be most active, consciously and unconsciously, while being silent (Kelman, 1955a). Interpreting, meaning giving many explanations and equaling being active, is a misnomer and poor technique.

What do we mean by interpreting and an interpretation? We must distinguish between what an interpretation intends and how it is interpreted by the patient. Then there is all that the therapist communicates unconsciously and unintended, and how the patient responds, in awareness and unconsciously. Of the forms of intended interpretations by the analyst, there is silence, "um huh," and "yes," with an endless variety of intonations, a question, a comment, such as "I see," or an expletive, and then what usually are referred to as interpretations, namely, statements about the meaning of a behavior, sequence of associations, fantasy, or a dream. The latter assumes that interpretations are statements, which we rarely make because we feel that what is implicit, indirect, open-ended, and in the form of a question (Kelman, 1962a) is a better form of interpreting.

We are aware that patients respond to questions literally and with closure, although given figuratively and open-ended. They are used to responding to a question in the conventional manner of yes, no, or to give some information. We are aware that patients will experience a question as being questioned, doubted, criticized, examined, and put on the spot. What we are attempting is to help them open themselves to questing. Patients are driven toward telling and being told, and we are out for showing, so that the patient becomes open to being shown. We want him to look at "what" and thereby experience "what and how," and undercut the compulsion to ask and answer why? what does it mean? who did what to whom in order to place blame?

What we mean by our questions can be brought out more clearly through a discussion of dreaming (Kelman, 1965). The aim is to help the patient toward wider and deeper here-now experiencing so that he interprets his own dreams. Experiencing the many dimensions of the symbols in the so-called manifest content, brought out by questions, leads to experiencing the connectedness of the dream symbols and the associations to the dream that is its meaning, its interpretation at that time. No dream has a right interpretation, and no dream is finally interpreted.

The "why" and "who" questions are almost never asked but almost always the "what" question. Questions are not actions to cause reactions but stimuli to prompt responses, processes to move other processes. Questions may be asked to obtain information, but the intent of the "what" questions is to function as pointers, to indicate directions in which to look. What we want is to allow the patient's "self-propelled feeling process" to move him in the direction of what is being pointed at. The more implicit and open-ended the pointer, the more loosely the field remains organized, with that many more open spaces to be filled and with a wider spectrum of creative possibilities. It is attempting to be working in the realm of prelogical experience, at life's growing edge, where "paradox forming and paradox resolving is greatest," where tension-producing and tension-reducing are constantly happening, where logical associative connections are loosest and prelogical forms maximal. It is there "where living is most open-ended," where "life's greatest potentialities are most immanent and can be realized," and where unexpected illuminations are most possible. Then there is emotional experiencing with a unity of insight and outsight (Kelman, 1962).

Because of the crucial import of feelings (Horney, Sheiner, 1966), one of the first questions is, "What did you feel in the dream? When you woke? As you tell me the dream now?" We practically never ask, "What do you think about the dream?" or "What do you think the dream means?" Sooner or later we may ask, "What did you feel about this or that?" meaning a symbol, behavior, or other piece of content. Other questions are, "What comes to you about Mr. X in the dream? What else about saying no to your mother? Anything further you can say about feeling like a bystander? What was going on in you as you were telling off your boss?" Not only to get a clearer picture of the dream, because we cannot recall certain details, or because we feel some have been left out, or because we feel it will be valuable to hear it retold now that it has been worked on, we may ask, "Would you mind repeating the dream? I wasn't quite clear about this or that part or parts of it." And of course it will be a different dream, in a few to many ways, from the first telling, all of which can be quite illuminating. Also it will be coming up in a new and different context.

All our questions have the form of process, ask about processes, and are aimed at the stimulating of processes. "What is going on? What is coming up? What more about?" to urge the patient onward, toward deepening and widening his experiencing of the dream. The questions will be prompted by the analyst's responding at all levels of his symbolic spiral. This enhances the possibilities of patient and analyst being attuned to and more extensively in contact with the unconscious and prerationative processes of both.

What do the analyst's questions mean to a patient? That the analyst has listened and heard; that he is attentive, interested, and wants to know more; that what he is asking has value and is worth looking at, going into, and exploring; that he is going along with the patient, willing to help, to guide, and illuminate the way. All of these are stimuli to greater trust and productivity and for the analysis becoming that much more a cooperative venture.

The question form of interpretation does not preclude "I wonder what you feel about this?" referring to a possible meaning of a dream or sequence of associations. The analyst might say "This is a possibility," or "I am not sure what it might mean," or "Maybe if we look at the dreams you brought up—in this session, this week, this month—and compare them." On occasion we might conjecture that a problem is being evaded, defined, or struggled with, or that this is the first time this situation, solution, person has appeared; or conversely that there was an absence of anxiety where there would have been anxiety in a similar situation. These and many other ways are used to make comparisons, to indicate change, movement, and the direction of it, as well as to identify where there is less of destructiveness and more of constructiveness.

What we want to indicate is that in the usual sense of interpretation our activity is limited but from the viewpoint of interpreting by open-ended questions we are very active. Also, we have tried to indicate how intensive is the activity with reference to the analyst in attending to himself as instrument in response to himself and to his patient. "Evenly-hovering attention" can be a most active process. There is the therapist's interpreting to himself, what he interprets in the many ways intended, and the patient's interpretations of what he intended to be interpreted and how he does it. Our preference for activity by the methods of open-end and indirection, and the question form of interpretation does not preclude interpretation as statements, and very forceful interventions required by almost all patients, from a few occasions, for longer periods, to being almost constantly necessary with certain types.

Interpreting from the unity of all levels of the symbolic spiral is evident in Horney's (Slater, 1956a) statement, "When he [the analyst] tries to convey his understanding of some part of it to the patient, he is making an interpretation." With her emphasis on feelings and understanding, she points up the need to be aware that our knowledge is only tentative. Interpretations are stimulating and revealing, merging into one another, all aimed at activating a forward move. In interpreting, Horney indicates the importance of "striving toward a democratic spirit," toward "clarity and precision," toward becoming "more and more sensitive to what the patient feels at the time being." With her motto of "blockages first," the immediacy and need for their interpretation has primacy. Timing of an interpretation is determined by its possibility for resolving existing and impending blocking and moving forward whatever is already in process, of a constructive nature, within the patient's tolerance and possibilities, with an economy of time and the avoidance of unnecessary pain, with the knowledge of the patient's character structure in awareness, and with a depth and clarity of feeling for the strength of the analytic relationship. In short, they are directed toward "The Aims of Psychoanalytic Therapy" (Horney, Slater, 1956b).

Premature interpretations may cause unnecessary pain, upset the patient beyond his tolerance for effective working, disturb the relationship, slow up the process, waste time, and may even lead to an interruption of the analysis. It is fortunate for patients that most of them have built-in self-protective devices and ways of disregarding premature interpretations, as well as those wide of the mark. All of this protects the analyst, which is well for him to know but not to misuse. Delayed interpretations, because they come out of context, after the clarity and intensity of it is gone, usually have little effect or may be effective to a degree but after quite some time has been lost.

"The ideal response to an interpretation would consist of the following. The patient would take the interpretation seriously, think and feel about it, have a conviction it was right and test it. This would lead to change." The responses may be "anxiety, hostility, and an attack against the analyst" as well as "pseudo-acceptance," "temporary aroused interest," and a "reaction of relief." Although the form of these responses range from the apparently positive to the apparently negative, only further follow-up can determine whether the interpretation was productive of change and movement. After the responses of anxiety and hostility there may either be acceptance and often aroused interest with change or a pseudo-acceptance and relief without change.

"The Evaluation of Change" (Horney, Slater, 1960) also requires careful scrutiny and follow-up.

> The patient's own statements concerning the ways he has or has not changed are often unreliable. . . . The analyst's neurotic tendencies, to the degree that they persist, will warp his judgment and make it difficult or even impossible for him to estimate the extent and nature of the patient's change. . . . External changes may affect the patient, making it difficult for the

analyst to determine whether the person's improvement (or worsening) is due to them, or the analytic process, or to both in varying degree.

We may seek for evidence of "less of the neurotic" and "more evidence of healthy thinking, feeling, and acting" as well as changes, in "the evolving doctor-patient relationship." To effectively evaluate change, we do it with regularity, every three or six months, so that we have some more clearly defined bases for comparison by which to measure increments and directions of change.

Further aids for evaluating change are the evolving patterns of "Freer Associating" (Kelman, 1962). They are participants in working through and expressive of it. They reveal the results of our conduct of the analysis and of our interpretations in the immediate and in the long range.

Initially, associations are expressions of thoughts about twoness, separateness, difference, and conflict which gradually become manifestations of feelings of oneness, togetherness, similarity, and cooperation. This happens through sequences initially reflecting thoughts about struggle to ultimately evidence of experiencing struggling. As the analysis proceeds there will be more experiencing of struggling, of struggling against struggling, and of what the struggling was for, against, with and about. One crucial form of struggling is rejecting/accepting. What the patient initially found unacceptable takes the form of an entity, whether it be a process internal or external to himself. It functions like a foreign body with which he must struggle until it becomes acceptable and accepted. The struggling continues to exhaustion and despair. Then there is a letting go, a surrendering, submitting, giving way, giving in, and in time genuine giving.

Ultimately, there will be feelings of fullness for which feelings of emptiness are prerequisite. In its patternings, freer associating will reflect more of courage, which is choicefully entering foreknown painful situations with possible future gain; which is leaps into the unknown, into formlessness; which is spontaneity. The patient will no longer have to be asked to "let himself go" or "admonished" not to push "aside." He will be freer associating. Paradoxically, he will have become the unbiased approach, the "basic rule," without having chosen to let go. It will have happened to him and in him (Kelman, 1962).

Freud once said any treatment can be considered psychoanalysis that works by undoing resistances and interpreting transferences, that is, any method that makes the ego face its pathogenic conflicts in their full emotional value by undoing the opposing defensive forces effective as "resistances," through the interpretation of derivatives and especially derivatives expressed in transference. This alone is the criterion . . . a "non-classical procedure" when the classical one is not possible, remains psychoanalysis (Fenichel, 1945).

We feel that what we have presented as the theory, the principles of technique, with concrete instances of its application, fulfills the criteria set by this definition of the theory of treatment in psychoanalysis.

REFERENCES

[Note: S.E. refers to *The Standard Edition of the complete psychological works of Sigmund Freud* (London: Hogarth Press).]

BALLY, G. Psychoanalysis and social change. *American Journal of Psychoanalysis,* 1964, **24**, 145–152.

BAILEY, G. Sociological aspects of psychoanalysis. *Bulletin of the New York Academy of Medicine,* 1966, **42**, No. 5, 343–355.

BURROW, T. *Preconscious foundations of human experience.* William E. Galt, (Ed.). New York: Basic Books, 1964.

FENICHEL, O. Problems of psychoanalytic technique. *Psychoanalytic Quarterly,* 1941, **1**.

FENICHEL, O. *The psychoanalytic theory of neurosis.* New York: Norton, 1945. P. 573.

FREUD, S. Recommendations to physicians practicing psychoanalysis (1912). S.E., Vol. 12.

GENDLIN, E. *Experiencing and the creation of meaning.* New York: Free Press, 1962.

GENDLIN, E. A theory of personality change. In P. Worchel and D. Byrne (Eds.), *Personality change.* New York: Wiley, 1964. Chap. 4.

GOLDSTEIN, K. The concept of transference in the treatment of organic and functional disease. *Acta Psychotherepeutica: Psychosomatica et Orthopaedagogica.* Vol. 2. Fasc. 3/4, 1954, 334–353.

HORNEY, KAREN. Die technik der psycho-analytischen therapie. *Zeitschrift F. Sexualwissenschaft,* 1917, **4**, 185.

HORNEY, KAREN. *The neurotic personality of our time.* New York: Norton, 1937.

HORNEY, KAREN. *New ways in psychoanalysis.* New York: Norton, 1939. P. 7.

HORNEY, KAREN. *Self-analysis.* New York: Norton, 1942.

HORNEY, KAREN. *Our inner conflicts.* New York: Norton, 1945.

HORNEY, KAREN (Ed.). What does the analyst do? In *Are you considering psychoanalysis?* New York: Norton, 1946. Pp. 187–210.

HORNEY, KAREN. *Neurosis and human growth.* New York: Norton, 1950.

HORNEY, KAREN. On feeling abused. *American Journal of Psychoanalysis,* 1951, 11, 5–72.

HORNEY, KAREN. The paucity of inner experiences. *American Journal of Psychoanalysis,* 1952, 12, 3–9.

HORNEY, KAREN. *Feminine psychology,* papers on. (Ed.) Kelman, H. New York: Norton, 1967.

HORNEY, KAREN, and AZORIN, L. The analyst's personal equation. *American Journal of Psychoanalysis,* 1957, 17, 34–38.

HORNEY, KAREN, and CANTOR, M. B. The initial interview. Part I. *American Journal of Psychoanalysis,* 1957, 17, 39–44.(a)

HORNEY, KAREN, and CANTOR, M. B. The initial interview. Part II. *American Journal of Psychoanalysis,* 1957, 17, 121–126. (b)

HORNEY, KAREN, and CANTOR, M. B. The quality of the analyst's attention. *American Journal of Psychoanalysis,* 1959, 19, 28–32.

HORNEY, KAREN, and CANTOR, M. B. Eliciting and mobilizing constructive forces. *American Journal of Psychoanalysis,* 1967, 27, 187.

HORNEY, KAREN, and METZGAR, E. Understanding the patient as the basis of all technique. *American Journal of Psychoanalysis,* 1956, 16, 26–31.

HORNEY, KAREN, and SHEINER, S. The importance of emotional experiences in the analytic process. *American Journal of Psychoanalysis,* 1966, 16, 88.

HORNEY, KAREN, and SHEINER, S. Free association. *American Journal of Psychoanalysis,* 1967, 17, 192.

HORNEY, KAREN, and SLATER, R. Interpretation. *American Journal of Psychoanalysis,* 1956, 16, 118–124. (a)

HORNEY, KAREN, and SLATER, R. Aims of psychoanalytic therapy. *American Journal of Psychoanalysis,* 1956, 16, 24–25. (b)

HORNEY, KAREN, and SLATER, R. Evaluation of change. *American Journal of Psychoanalysis,* 1960, 20, 3–7.

HORNEY, KAREN, and ZIMMERMAN, J. Blockages in therapy. *American Journal of Psychoanalysis,* 1956, 16, 112–117. (c)

IVIMEY, M. Childhood memories in psychoanalysis. *American Journal of Psychoanalysis,* 1950, 10, 38–47.

KELMAN, H. The use of the analytic couch. *American Journal of Psychoanalysis,* 1954, 14, 65–82.

KELMAN, H. The doctor-patient relationship. *American Journal of Psychoanalysis,* 1955, 15, 16–19. (a)

KELMAN, H. Diagnosing and prognosing in psychoanalysis. *American Journal of Psychoanalysis,* 1955, 15, 49–70. (b)

KELMAN, H. Life history as therapy. Part I. Evaluation of the literature. *American Journal of Psychoanalysis.* 1955, 15, 49–70; (c) Part II. On being aware, *American Journal of Psychoanalysis,* 1956, 16, 67–78; Part III. The symbolizing process. *American Journal of Psychoanalysis,* 1956, 16, 145–169. (a)

KELMAN, H. A unitary theory of anxiety. *American Journal of Psychoanalysis,* 1956, 17, 127–152. (b)

KELMAN, H. Communing and relating. Part I. Past and current perspectives. *American Journal of Psychoanalysis,* 1958, 18, 77–98; Part II. The mind structure of the East and West. *American Journal of Psychoanalysis,* 1958, 18, 158–170; Part III. Examples: general and clinical; Part IV. Communing as therapy. *American Journal of Psychoanalysis,* 1959, 19, 73–105; Part V. Separateness and togetherness. *American Journal of Psychoanalysis,* 1959, 19, 188–215; Communing and relating. *American Journal of Psychotherapy,* 1960, 14, 70–96; Communing as witness consciousness (Communion et la conscience témoin). In S. Nacht (Ed.), *Roger Godel—De L'Humanisme à L'Humain.* Paris: Belles Lettres Association, Guillaume Bede, 1963, 205–225; Communing and relating (monograph-manuscript).

KELMAN, H. The holistic approach (Horney). In S. Arieti (Ed.), *American handbook of psychiatry.* Vol. 2. New York: Basic Books, 1959. Pp. 1434–1452. (a)

KELMAN, H. Masochism and self-realization. In J. H. Masserman (Ed.), *Science and psychoanalysis.* Vol. 2. *Individual and family dynamics.* New York: Grune and Stratton, 1959. Pp. 21–30. (b)

KELMAN, H. Freer associating: its phenomenology and inherent paradoxes. *American Journal of Psychoanalysis,* 1962. 22, 176–200.

KELMAN, H. Toward a definition of mind. In J. M. Scher (Ed.), *Theories of the mind.* New York: Free Press, 1962. Pp. 253–270. (a)

KELMAN, H. *The process in psychoanalysis.* New York: American Institute for Psychoanalysis, 1963. (a)

KELMAN, H. Creative talent and creative passion as therapy. *American Journal of Psychoanalysis,* 1963, 23, 133–141. (b) In the symposium: Psychoanalysis as creative process. *American Journal of Psychoanalysis,* 1963, No. 2 and 1964, No. 1. (c)

KELMAN, H. Techniques of dream interpretation. *American Journal of Psychoanalysis,* 1965, 25, 3–20.

KELMAN, H. The changing image of psychoanalysis. *American Journal of Psychoanalysis,* 1966, 16.

KELMAN, H. Psychoanalysis: some philosophical considerations. In J. Marmor (Ed.), *Frontiers of psychoanalysis.* New York: Basic Books, 1967. Chap. 4.

KRISHNAMURTI, J. *The first and last freedom.* New York: Harper, 1954. Chap. 12, pp. 172–176.

MARTIN, A. R. The body's participation in dilemma and anxiety phenomena. *American Journal of Psychoanalysis,* 1945, 5, 28–48.

MARTIN, A. R. Reassurance in therapy. *American Journal of Psychoanalysis,* 1949, 9, 17–29.

MARTIN, A. R. The fear of relaxation and leisure. *American Journal of Psychoanalysis,* 1951, 11, 42–50.

MARTIN, A. R. The dynamics of insight. *American Journal of Psychoanalysis,* 1952, **12**, 24–38.

MARTIN, A. R. The whole patient in therapy. In Frieda Fromm-Reichmann and J. L. Moreno (Eds.), *Progress in psychotherapy.* New York: Grune and Stratton, 1956. Pp. 170–179.

MULLAHY, P. *Oedipus, myth and complex.* New York: Hermitage Press, 1948. Pp. 286–291.

NORTHROP, F. S. C. *The logic of the sciences and the humanities.* New York: Macmillan, 1948. Pp. 36–40.

PORTNOY, I. Anxiety states. In S. Arieti (Ed.), *American handbook of psychiatry.* Vol. 1. New York: Basic Books, 1959. Pp. 307–323.

RUBINS, J. L. On the early development of the self: its role in neurosis. *American Journal of Psychoanalysis,* 1962, **22**, 122–137.

RUESCH, J. *Therapeutic communication.* New York: Norton, 1961. P. 31.

SCHACHTEL, E. G. *Metamorphosis.* New York: Basic Books, 1959. Chap. 2.

SCOTT, J. P. Critical periods in behavioral development. *Science,* **138** (November 30), 1962, 949–958; Scott, J. P., and Fuller, J. L. (Eds.), *Genetics and the social behavior of the dog.* Chicago: Univ. of Chicago Press, 1965.

SULLIVAN, H. S. *The interpersonal theory of psychiatry.* New York: Norton, 1953.

TAUBER, E. S. and GREEN, M. R. *Prelogical experience. An inquiry into dreams and other creative processes.* New York: Basic Books, 1959.

WATTS, A. *The wisdom of insecurity.* New York: Pantheon, 1951. Chap. 5.

WENKART, A. Self-acceptance. *American Journal of Psychoanalysis,* 1955, **15**, 135–143.

WHYTE, L. I. *The next development in man.* New York: Mentor Book M5D, 1950; *Accent on form.* New York: Harper, 1954; *Aspects of form.* Bloomington, Indiana: Indiana Univ. Press. 1961, MB31.

WOLMAN, B. B. Psychoanalysis without libido. *American Journal of Psychotherapy,* 1954, **8**, 21–31.

15

THE INTERPERSONAL APPROACH TO TREATMENT WITH PARTICULAR EMPHASIS ON THE OBSESSIONAL

Earl G. Witenberg
Leopold Caligor

Rationale

Sullivan (1953a) defined psychiatry as "an expanding science concerned with the kinds of events and processes in which the psychiatrist participates while being an observant psychiatrist. . . . The actions or operations from which psychiatric information is derived are events in interpersonal fields which include the psychiatrist . . . events in which the

424

psychiatrist participates." The statement implies that mental illness is evidenced in interpersonal fields, stems from earlier interpersonal experiences, and can be cured by the social interaction between an expert and a patient. The primary function of the analyst is to understand how the patient has coped with anxiety stemming from the interpersonal events in his life that interfered with his development. He pays particular attention to how the patient has developed and has excluded from awareness salient aspects of himself because of the unfortunate attendance of anxiety. He is a participant-observer.

Treatment

Technique in the Sullivanian framework may be defined as the application of procedures, modes of relatedness, and modes of communication to help the patient become conscious of those parts of himself he has a stake in keeping out of awareness. The other methods used are education, focusing, clarification, reality-testing, and sometimes even intervention. The technical procedures applied depend upon the assumptions underlying the theory. Technique really is the "how to do," the "what to do," and the "when to do" and is based on a theory of therapy.

In the interpersonal framework there is a close relationship between therapy and theory. The basic underlying philosophical assumptions may be found in Sullivan's concept of therapy (Sullivan, 1952). First, the statement that "we are all more simply human than otherwise" means that there are possibilities for communication and collaboration in an interpersonal relationship between saint and devil, criminal and judge, mentally disordered and mentally ordered, in the absence of contempt and guilt. Second, all social situations are reciprocal, and they may be transformative. That is, in an interpersonal relationship the impact of one person on another may result in change. Third, knowledge and reality are safer and better to face than any fantasy construction or denial of reality. Fourth, destructiveness is always an interference in an interpersonal field. Fifth, one person in therapy does not have to accommodate to the special needs or handicaps of the other, outside of perhaps physical or organic needs.

Sullivan's approach is both operational and pragmatic. Theory and practice are interwoven by a group of hypotheses that are continuously tested and validated in the course of treatment. The goals in treatment are formulated as clearly as possible, if only tentatively, in the initial phase of treatment. Formulation of goals is accomplished by means of a careful and detailed history that enables one to evaluate the patient by focusing on specific events in the developmental epochs when things went askew for him. Predictions can also be made regarding the nature of the patient-doctor relationship, particularly transference phenomena. Hence, each treatment is a clinical inquiry into the patient's problems in living, which proceeds within a structured but flexible framework. Treatment is viewed as going on in a matrix of a patient-doctor relationship wherein all the aspects of the analyst's personality, his values, his attitudes, his previous life history including the significant people in his past, have to be considered, as well as all of these factors in the patient's life.

Another underlying assumption of the interpersonal approach is that specific interactions occurred between the child and his family constellation that resulted in *dissociation, substitution,* and *selective* inattention. These mechanisms are ways of coping with anxiety stemming from the relationships with significant persons; the data regarding the specific interactions are no longer available to the child. Dynamisms, *"the relatively enduring pattern of energy transformations which recurrently characterize the organism in its duration as a living organism"* (Sullivan, 1953a, p. 103), are patterned motivational systems which may be dissociated. For example, a child frightened in a particular context may react by displaying a bravado. Thereafter, the dissociated fear will continue and will come into awareness only under some particular circumstances, namely, analysis. Thus, significant parts of a person dissociated after a particular era are no longer available to him. This implies the need for a painstakingly detailed recapturing of specific events in the person's life. The assumption is that positive as well as negative aspects of the person were dissociated on the basis of anxiety between the child and the significant persons.

The particular ways in which the material has been dissociated will determine the type of mental disorder. Thus, the obsessional dynamism stems initially from a substitutive process in which the meaning of words was distorted in the development of the person. The schizophrenic person presumably experienced an overwhelming anxiety very early in life, which resulted in defective ways of coping with anxiety other than pathological identification. The manic-depressive disturbance, it is assumed, started later in life and involved attitudes of the significant people to the toddler, with problems of authority and particularly stereotyped attitudes, which resulted in a manic-depressive orientation. The hysteric was brought into a family where there was great disparity between the overt behavior and the covert attitudes of the parents; indeed, there was a great deal of insincerity.

These are the particular kinds of disorders to which the theory of therapy is applicable, but the unique technical use of Sullivan's approach is particularly pertinent to the schizophrenic, the paranoid, the manic-depressive, and the obsessional. This is based on his primary preoccupation in his thirty years of practice—twenty years with schizophrenics and ten years with obsessionals.

Therapeutic Flexibility

The operational framework extends into the appraisal of the patients. For example, the patient is not an angry person but someone who gets angry under conditions *x, y,* and *z.* The explication of these circumstances and the analysis of the anxiety engendered, which results in the patient becoming angry or hostile, are the painstaking detailed work that must be done in an operational framework.

The interpersonal approach permits the therapist flexibility in relatedness; the flexibility is not only in terms of the patient's uniqueness but also in terms of his diagnosis. An understanding of the nature of the difficulty in each of the diagnostic categories is essential. How much a therapist participates, the way in which he participates, and the techniques he uses in the therapy depend upon his evaluation of the patient's dynamics and diagnosis. Thus, a thorough history before beginning intensive treatment is basic.

The history starts with the present complaint: It is important to document the particular events that triggered the immediate reasons for the patient's coming at this time. The detailed anamnesis follows. It retraces the various developmental epochs starting with adolescence when the conflict among security needs, heterosexual needs, and the need for intimacy is evaluated; the preadolescent era with its need for relatedness to a member of the same sex and ways of coping with loneliness; the juvenile period with its problems in competition and peer-group relationships; childhood with its needs for cooperation with other people; and infancy with the need for tenderness. During the history-taking, one makes an effort to ascertain how well the person can associate; that is, how much motivation and understanding he has. For example, when the analyst asks the patient about the adolescent period, the patient's responses will enable the analyst to estimate the accuracy of the patient's perceptions and his sense of self at that period.

Much of what is ordinarily called unconscious is really unformulated. One draws the patient's attention, by one's questions, to various events in his life to which he has not attended but, yet, has not dissociated. The process is one of selective inattention in which the patient avoids things that cause moderate anxiety. But in the doctor-patient relationship questions about these events will evoke a direct response.

In the first phase of treatment the analyst asks the person questions about his formulations, questions that have to do with a search for additional data. He makes inquiries to see how aware the patient is of all the data with reference to a specific point. He evaluates how much the patient is interested in finding out about himself, how much he is troubled by the analyst's presentations of formulations, and how aware he is of limitations in his response. The analyst attempts to give the patient a "dose of medicine" and then watches the response to determine whether the dose is adequate or inadequate, or whether the patient has an allergic response to the formulation. Should there be an allergic response, he increases the dosage only gradually.

The analyst evaluates the patient's motivation—"Why is he coming?" He assesses the patient's psychological mindedness, his ability to associate to particular details and events of his life. He appraises the patient's integrative capacities, style of cognition, language, perceptiveness, reality-testing, and ways of coping with anxiety. He reflects upon the kind of interpersonal relationships that the patient has had. He listens with particular attention to the disturbances in communication caused by anxiety as seen in the avoidance of specific topics, the abrupt shifts in subject matter, and the changes in vocal tone. He notes changes in facial and body tonus. He makes a diagnosis and a formulation about the particular problems of the patient. He studies the parts of the personality that are available and not available to consciousness. Then the analyst makes a prognostic statement and finally a treatment plan, which includes information about the dissociated parts of the person, the mechanisms used—the phenomena of substitution, selective inattention, and dissociation.

Keeping in mind the diagnostic and prognostic data, he decides how to proceed. For example, if the patient predominantly uses the kind of dissociation typical of the hysteric, one has to deal primarily with material that comes from the relationship with the therapist and from dreams. That is, the emphasis is on dissociated data and parataxic distortion;[1] the goal is to

[1] Parataxic distortion was described by Sullivan (1954) as the patients' "substituting for the psychiatrist a person . . . strikingly different in most significant respects from the psychiatrist. The interviewee addresses his behavior toward this fictitious person who is temporarily in ascendancy over the reality of the psychiatrist and he interprets the psychiatrist's remarks and behavior on the basis of this same fictitious person."

make communications syntaxic.[2] The hysteric is unreliable in reporting the events in his current life-situation. He comes from a background in which dishonesty is a primary factor in relationship, and his need to manipulate is so great that the particular details of his life are best perceived in the parataxic distortions and the dream life. The treatment thus proceeds with an emphasis on regression and with little participation on the part of the therapist.

If the patient predominantly uses the substitutive devices of the obsessional, it is necessary to clarify the specific contexts from which the obsessions stem. Treatment proceeds on the basis of questions with continued repetition of experiences until the patient becomes aware of the anxiety that triggers off his obsessional mechanisms. His treatment cannot encourage regression. One does not make interpretations nor give him the kind of material that he can use in his obsessional system. The therapist is active, evocative, not overly challenging, and asks questions indirectly so that the obsessive can relate to them.

With the depressive, emphasis is initially on the communication disorder and the stereotypy in thinking. Regression is focused with special attention paid to the experiences of loss and secondary hostility. Parataxic distortions are noticed and examined within the treatment situation but only after being noted in external circumstances.

In the treatment of the character disorder, focus is initially on the transactions of the patient with others and the analyst, followed by a pin-pointing of the anxiety. Here too one does not encourage regression. Emphasis is on the parataxic distortion and the underlying anxiety in an attempt to make communication syntaxic.

With the schizophrenic one attempts to gain clarity about the triggering points of the anxieties that lead to the loss of adult referential processes and to the eruption of regressive states. The treatment, therefore, shuns the encouragement of regressive phenomena. The therapist remains real and lifelike and assiduously avoids increasing the patient's distortions.

The same is true for the psychopath as for the schizophrenic. Treatment proceeds in a focused way.

In the process of treatment it is assumed that all the representations of past experiences are present in the room for the patient. Also present are eidetic figures from the past for the analyst. Hopefully, these will not interfere, because of the analyst's self-awareness. The reason that treatment can proceed is that in every human transaction where contempt and hostility do

---

[2] Syntaxic refers to experience which is consensually validated.

not intervene there is the possibility for the patient's self-realization. The clarity of the analyst's statements, his empathy and understanding, his human qualities, are all basic to the therapy process. Included is the realization that there are definite limits to what one can achieve because of a lack of knowledge, the lack of capacity on the part of either human being, or the impact of irreversible traumatic experiences.

We have dealt with an overview of the assumptions and practice of interpersonal psychoanalysis. There have been many detailed explications of the treatment of schizophrenia and manic-depressive psychosis. The interested reader is referred to the references at the end of the chapter. The remainder of this chapter deals with obsessionalism and its treatment.

The Obsessional

Sullivan (1956) said, "A person can probably be called an obsessional neurotic if he cannot enter into any actual meaningful relations with a stranger without obtruding into an otherwise presumably informative, communicative situation the sort of thing which I think, perhaps, is best described as the stickiness which is caused by obsessional preoccupation." The obsessional is never completely successful in relieving anxiety. There is always a mild discomfort, a mild anxiety. The more anxious the obsessional gets, the more he resorts to magical verbal symbolic formation in lieu of simple, direct communication. These disturbances in magical verbal language are seen as the primary substitutive processes against anxiety. Sullivan was also impressed with their extreme vulnerability to anxiety. In addition he emphasized their helplessness and their really small-child fixation as well as their fear of their hostility and the need to protect themselves from it.

In evaluating a patient for treatment who suffers from the obsessional way of living, close attention must be paid to the kinds of interpersonal relationships the person has in his present-day living and also had in his past living. A primary concern is whether or not the obsessional can withstand regression, because the danger of precipitating a schizophrenic episode in an obsessional neurotic is real. This is to be differentiated from a certain phase of treatment where an almost psychotic-like rage develops in the obsessional as he gets in touch with the real hurt caused by the cruelty of the parents.

The problem in obsessionals is hypothesized as beginning in the era where speech first begins to develop. The use of language by the significant people to convey things other than what is felt and their use of stereotyped formulations give the child the feeling of unsureness and anxiety, that people essentially do not say what they mean, and that they substitute rather meaningless types of communication.

The problem with obsessionals to which Sullivan reacted strongly is that standard analytic procedures, and particularly free association, do not work. The obsessional associates away from, instead of to, the point. Thus, a different technical procedure has to be evolved. The procedure will essentially involve the client-expert relationship in which there is formality, acceptance, and challenging for data. The trend of questions is to narrow the context in which the obsession developed. Very often the obsessional will be left with a question or a tentative formulation at the end of a session in order to give continuity to the treatment. Questions are asked in a special kind of way; they are asked indirectly and sometimes in the third person. "Why" questions are avoided because they imply blame, which is an important area of sensitivity for the obsessional. The obsessional therefore does not feel cornered and is able to communicate at whatever level he is.

Regression is not encouraged with an obsessional, particularly in those obsessionals where there is the possibility of a schizophrenic break. When the patient repeats the same obsessional pattern without foresight or awareness that he is saying the same thing over and over again, the therapist may want to finish the story for him. And then when the patient says, "How did you know that?" the therapist points out that for thirty-six or more times the patient has told the same story and that it has always ended the same way and what is the reason for this. More than anyone else the obsessional is condemned to relive the past because he has forgotten the past.

The use of the couch is definitely not necessary, nor is it probably indicated with a truly obsessional person. Use of the couch tends to increase the depth of the patient's diminished self-esteem and to encourage regression, frequently a risky therapeutic procedure with an obsessional. Also, the silence evoked by the couch tends to encourage anxiety, and certainly these people have too much anxiety. Though silence and a hovering kind of attention is not enough for the obsessional, an attitude of friendliness or benevolence is equally inappropriate. Rather, a degree of formality, of distance, and of directness is indicated.

It is important to determine the amount and kind of contact the patient has had in the past and present in order to evaluate the risks inherent in regression during therapy. If the analyst finds gross evidence in taking the history that the patient had developed a good relationship with somebody in the past, who has been helpful and nourishing to the patient, then he does not have to be too concerned about the dangers inherent in the regression. For example, let us take a very obsessional patient who has an adoring husband who is very protective toward her and who really encourages her wish for self-assertion as well as offering her warmth and tenderness. Treatment in her case can go on in a rigorous way. In contrast, a patient who is involved in a malevolent relationship that is bound together by hostility, or where there is no ongoing relationship, would be seen as a decided risk with regression.

An illustration of this is a woman who had been in treatment for two years with a very gifted analyst. Therapy was terminated rather precipitously because the patient went into a demanding kind of panic, which resulted in hospitalization. There were two factors in the patient's life that immediately preceded her panic. One was the gradual realization of a lot of success on the part of her husband. This aroused her feelings of vindictiveness and envy. Because of his increased self-esteem he no longer responded in a hostile way to her belittling and devastating hostility, so that their hostile integration no longer worked. The second factor was her feeling that she could not compete with her analyst, a woman. She became increasingly anxious and depressed, and the demand for regression appeared at this point. She insisted that she needed to be taken care of, she needed medication, she wanted others to do everything for her. All these regressive phenomena appeared at this time.

After a week of hospitalization the hospital reported the following data: one, the patient formed a liaison with the sickest person on the ward; two, she believed that an atom bomb was going to destroy the whole world except the hospital; three, she had seen her husband drive up with a friend, and she had hallucinated him as her father and wondered where her mother was—why he was coming with this other person rather than with her mother. This seems to indicate that the regressive atmosphere of the hospital had precipitated an underlying schizophrenia, which was related to some disturbance in a very early developmental era, and which had been substantially defended against for many years. The question of how much and how one allows the obsessional to regress in the course of treatment is always to be most carefully evaluated.

One might describe Sullivan's approach as evocative rather than regressive; that is, the indirect way of asking questions, of not touching the person where he hurts most. The patient is evaluated not only on the basis of his history but on how he relates in the treatment process. One tries formulations, hypotheses about what is dissociated. Then, judging from the patient's reactions, one decides whether to be more direct or more indirect in dealing with the dissociated material, or whether to reinforce those parts of the self-system that have given the patient security in the past.

One aspect in treating the obsessional, stressed by Sullivan, is the need to clarify the context in which events of importance occur. It is most difficult to establish this consensual validation with an obsessional; he forever repeats that you do not quite understand, that you do not really have the facts just right. A constant clarification and a "bird-dogging" of the patient is required in order to insure that the feelings are recognized and the context in which the anxiety arises is brought into awareness. This constant clarification of feelings, anxiety, and the factual context is important and is frequently very frustrating to the analyst. This is illustrated in the following case. The patient, in the course of treatment, describes this vignette: He is lying on the bed with his two-year-old son, who starts crawling over him and accidentally kicks him in the groin. He is frightened and hurt a little, but he very gently lifts his son and puts him aside. Then the child starts crawling over him again and says, "I want to turn the radio on." The father again lifts him and puts him back and says, "I'll turn the radio on." And he turns the radio on. The son continues his effort to crawl across him and says, "I want to turn the radio on." And the father says, "It is on, I turned it on," at which point the wife who was an observer screams out irrationally, "That's your internal, eternal sadism." The patient said this made him feel an ice-cold rage, which he proceeded to relive on the couch with clenched fists and a harangue about how sick and tired he was of being humiliated by her rage and her wild analytic interpretations. The analyst listened to the rage and remained rather detached, knowing it stemmed from antecedent feelings. The analyst asked the patient if he could catch the feeling 15 seconds, 3 seconds, or 1 second before he experienced the rage. The patient had a lot of difficulty with this, at first saying that there was nothing before, that it was an instant rage, and finally stated that he had felt helpless. The analyst, trying to put himself in the patient's position, asked him if he had perhaps felt humiliated and pinned down. The patient responded with, "You know all those words that you're using to describe the experience give me a funny feeling in my back; make my back tense. And what comes to my mind is the feeling of being pinned down in wrestling. I didn't wrestle very much. I stayed away from it because I didn't like this kind of thing. But it is that feeling and that picture of somebody who is bigger sitting on my shoulders. What did you have in mind? Why did you bring up those particular feelings? What were you looking for? What are you after?" The analyst did not respond except to say, "I was looking for the feelings before you went into the rage," and that, "Identifying the feelings antecedent to a rage is important in clarifying the issues." The patient left at this point.

He came in the next session and asked, "Am I late?" which he was not; he stated that he was feeling better and that he had talked with his wife. He then began to express anger toward the analyst, complaining about some aspects of the way he practiced, which happened to be valid, but which the analyst felt were irrelevant to what was going on in the interview. Together, they explored the patient's feeling of being used as his chief complaint about all the significant people in his life. The patient allowed that this was so, and this led back to his feeling at the end of the last session, which he said had some validity. He then gave some spontaneous associations to his brother. He told about an unexpected visit by the brother—whom he now calls a "schnook"—and then related an early image of wrestling with the brother, being pinned down, and feeling humiliated and enraged. For the first thirteen years of his life he had let himself be used and humiliated by his brother, and only at the age of thirteen does he remember having been angry. The patient's affects during the hour ran the gamut of—I feel well— then displaying occasional anger, blandness at other times, then denying the significance of these feelings to him, yet was willing to admit that he objected to being used, and remarked: after all, doesn't everyone object? The analyst's focus during the hour was on the patient's avoidance of the intense emotional issue that had come up in the previous hours. But a step forward had been made in that the relationship of being humiliated was changed into an actual deep feeling of submission, and the need to submit to this older brother was evoked.

The closer one gets to the actual truth where the communication in the obsessive is truly syntaxic or is approaching syntaxic rather than being autistic or parataxic, the greater usually is the rage and hostility. At times these may approach psychotic-like proportions in that they seem to have no base in reality and are occupied with destruction. The intensity of the destructiveness makes for one of the most difficult and trying periods of treatment. It involves close watching and the ability to know what is going on. The therapist has to be particularly clear about his own hostilities and be able to accept them and to know that when in the presence of a person with psychotic-like rage one reacts almost naturally with a feeling of rage and anxiety; he must, therefore, be ready to cope with these reactions in himself. This implies that no obsessional can be fully treated unless he is seen a number of times a week, particularly in this important phase of the treatment, when the repressed or dissociated intense rage is brought into consciousness and must be tolerated, understood, and integrated.

One of the characteristics of the treatment process of an obsessional results from his ability to be a subtle manipulator. The obsessional is terribly alert not only to signs of anxiety in himself but in the other person. He is therefore able to know "where his analyst is weak," and at times he may divert the treatment from himself to an attack on the analyst and get the analyst to play the obsessional sticky game with him.

Of course, doubting is an important symptom of all obsessionals. Sullivan stressed that he was never able to get down to the roots of any doubts in a meaningful therapeutic way. Others prefer not to work with doubts and, in order to avoid getting involved in an obsessional game with the patient, they do not attempt to analyze them. Doubting probably serves a homeostatic function in keeping the obsessional system static, and its purpose is really to perpetuate the obsessional system. Doubting in therapy serves as a defense against clarification. One can never be certain that it is used for any other purpose.

On the other hand, there are other obsessional symptoms, such as tics, which are representative of dissociated material. The analysis of such symptoms must proceed along with the analysis of the whole person. That is, the meaning of a tic becomes clear only after there has been some real communication in other areas with the person and the nature of his interpersonal relationships and family struggle has been explored.

To believe one has resolved the obsessional neurosis when one has gained clarity about the happenings to the patient in his third or fourth year of life is naïve. It is necessary to explore earlier material that has been dissociated from the age when speech patterns were first being evolved and the relationships with people were beginning to be expressed in words and language. This is the source of the difficulty, and it occurs earlier than posited in the original Freudian formulation, which puts it in the Oedipal period.

In terms of implications for treatment goals, one never gets all the dissociated material in an obsessional. Nevertheless, it is important to clarify the issues, so that most of the communication of the person in his significant relationships is syntaxic rather than autistic. Clarity of communication can be achieved only with the recovery of dissociated material and particularly with a precise delineation of the specific issues that arose in the course of the patient's living and development. The *specific* is emphasized because obsessionals can all too easily misrepresent or leave things vague and indirect. Hopefully, as the patient achieves clarity and syntaxic communication with his analyst, there will be a transfer of effect to other people.

At termination of analysis the obsessional neurotic, in a way, still remains obsessional. For example, if he is stingy, suspicious, and cold, he will come out economical, careful, and reserved. Once the specific context within which his symptoms have developed has been examined and worked through, the obsessional neurotic can find himself relieved of these symptoms or able to cope very satisfactorily by using other devices.

The personality of the analyst as an active part of the therapy field must be constantly assessed. An analyst who tends to be sticky and cannot let people go would be the wrong choice for an obsessional. The analyst who needs to push, particularly where the patient is tender, is also wrong for the obsessional, who is terribly vulnerable to anxiety, and untoward reactions result from this kind of encounter. The expertise required is in being the participant-observer, in allowing the patient to go his own way, and in trying things out in a disinterested manner to see if the patient can make contact with the dissociated material.

The importance of the personality of the analyst and his self-understanding is apparent in the therapy transactions of a young analyst-in-training working with an obsessional patient. The patient is a man who suffers from Don Juanism and who also is troubled by homosexual fantasies. The young therapist had an opportunity to observe the actual happenings when the patient had been turned down by a girl with whom he had had a liaison for several years. The patient developed his homosexual fantasies at that point. The specific context was missed by the beginner, who failed to observe that the patient's homosexual fantasies were triggered by his anxiety about the rejection. This oversight was pointed out to the therapist by the supervisor, who suggested that the next time the patient reported the sequence, it should be noted aloud to him. In the supervisory session, the young analyst proceeded to reverse what the supervisor had said, stating that the anxiety around the homosexual fantasies triggered the rejection. The supervisor repeated the young analyst's statement and asked him if he thought that was what the supervisor had said, to which the young analyst replied, "Yes." The supervisor then repeated what he had said and advised the therapist to work this out with his own analyst.

The following week the patient came in tearful and self-pitying as a result of this rejection by the girl, but he had not been able to integrate any of the process. The supervisor listened to the young analyst respond to the patient with remarks containing valid data, but voiced in a contemptuous tone, following which he gave the patient a course in his dynamics actually aping what the supervisor had said in the previous interview. The supervisor let this go on and then pointed this out to the young analyst.

This young analyst coped with his anxieties, from whatever sources, in a typically obsessional way; namely, he put them into words that were less than syntaxic. The fact that the words were the reverse of what the supervisor had said is also typical of an obsessional defense against anxiety. His need to react to anxiety in another male may be an indication of his contempt for men who are in distress. His need to lecture is also a substitutive reaction to the anxiety evoked in him by the patient. In Freudian terminology, this therapist has a transference reaction to the patient. In other words, the patient's problems are real, they are deep, they are sincere. They are essentially the problems of a typical obsessional patient who may act out in the sexual as well as the verbal area. On the other hand, the young analyst's response is not that of an expert, but of someone who is using substitutive processes for his own anxieties in living. The therapeutic process is obscured 90 per cent by the therapist and 10 per cent by the patient. This is to be contrasted with countertransferential parataxic distortions on the part of the analyst who finds himself reacting with anxiety to the patient and is able to ask himself, "What is the patient doing that makes me anxious?" For example, if one is listening to an obsessional tell the story of a phone call and then change the subject just as the key line is about to be said, one experiences some discomfort and one says, "Well, what did you say?" This is a countertransferential response, in that one is kept dangling. Knowing exactly what is keeping the therapist dangling and responding to that is a therapeutic maneuver.

Harry Stack Sullivan (1956) said, "If the psychiatrist doesn't get in the patient's way, and doesn't prod the patient in some sensitive region, what is happening is that the context is being run again and again through the mill; and each time it is a little clearer than it was the time before. That is the way in which obsessional personalities seem to heal themselves." The obsessional person, because he has grown up in an environment in which directness has been avoided and in which communication has been used only for stereotyping or blaming, will tend to accept any criticism of himself as being valid. Because of this he, at times, becomes terribly self-pitying. Self-pity is the poor man's opiate. It is something to which an obsessional person can become addicted, and it can result in a grievous waste of time in the course of treatment. It is necessary to point out to the patient that one of the purposes of self-pity is to create a distance between himself and the other person so that there can be no meaningful communication and that it is truly a regression into a kind of autistic process. Feeling sorry for oneself becomes a way of life and of not assuming responsibility for the things that are going on. This kind of compulsive grief can arise in the course of treatment and is symbolized by a continuous repetition and a need to relive the same phenomena over and over again in the present.

An illustration of compulsive grieving is a patient who had a very pathological relationship with an older sister in a family from which the father was missing. This woman recovered a lot of material having to do with the symbiotic nature of her relatedness with her sister, which she kept on repeating and repeating in the course of telephone calls to the sister, who obviously was uninterested in her. She compulsively kept looking for permission from this sister to live. She grieved over the fact that she had such a relationship, but she did nothing to change it until it was pointed out to her that her interest seemed to be in reliving rather than changing. The meaning of this compulsive grief seemed to be a way of establishing a kind of priority on the approval of the mother, long since dead, who encouraged a relationship between the two girls.

Compulsive grief must be differentiated from true grief, a valid and useful process, which often appears in the course of treatment. At times, in the dyad, both patient and therapist are entitled to feel grief for what the patient had lost or for the damage that the patient had incurred in the past. Grief for any other period of life, such as the present in the patient, is out of place and is countertransferential, if not transferential, in nature.

In the course of psychoanalysis, very often the obsessional uncovers the kind of treatment that he experienced at the hands of a parent. Sullivan stressed the fact that the parents of obsessionals were cruel. It is probably more true that, owing to the developmental era within which the experience occurred, the patient experienced the frustrating activities of the parents, cloaked by conventional words, as cruelty, whereas they may or may not have been factually cruel.

In contrast to his activity in clarifying things, the therapist is sparing interpretation. The danger of premature interpretation in the obsessional is very great. The obsessional will take the interpretation and put it through his obsessional mill and just involve the therapist in a sticky kind of operation, particularly if the therapist has a stake in the interpretation. Interpretations to obsessionals should be few, sparse, and carried no further than the point at which they have become clear to the patient.

Sullivan advised rigorous treatment of any suicidal threat on the part of an obsessional patient. He felt that their suicidal threats in the course of treatment were a result of their feeling that the therapist had been too brutal with them. Sullivan took this as an invitation to some real brutality, and he would say to do it occasionally. There are differences of opinion about this. In any case, a simple and direct statement is indicated about the hostility implicit in the suicidal threat if this threat is directly related to the therapist.

In closing this discussion on obsessionalism and its treatment, it is appropriate to quote Sullivan (1956):

> In certain moods I would say that anything on earth can be relevant to the obsessional neurosis. Obsessionals have a genius for getting all sorts of things involved in their situations, but only for the purpose of befogging troublesomely inescapable insecurities. A good many of their satisfactions are pursued with almost blatantly simple directness. And quite often this simple directness is something which they cannot control, for that is all the development they ever had to make in that field. They are not as well socialized in the areas of certain of their needs for satisfaction as some of us are. Now and then they encounter somebody who points out what crude creatures they are in that area, and they cannot do anything about it. That is a real attack on the points where they are tender—on their prestige, their feeling of status. Under those circumstances, they will reach around for practically anything on earth and become harassed about it. It is just like the squid: a cloud of confusing details pours out in which everything becomes somewhat nebulous. That is much better, however, than the anxiety experienced at the threat to their rather feebly supported prestige. It is really too bad when the doctor collaborates in that and starts working diligently on a lot of stuff that is of as much real importance as the other side of the moon would be. I think that if one could really keep one's eye on the ball with these people, they would not necessarily be such remarkably slow therapeutic prospects. But it takes a high degree of alertness to sort out quickly what is relevant and what is merely convenient fog. I have invented, with very telling effect on my obsessional patients, a description of their way of life as the flypaper technique. That is, when the obsessional gets into an insecure situation with a significant person—where there is anger a difference of opinion or something of the sort—the other fellow has just about the same experience as a cat who has stepped on a sheet of flypaper. Every move made by this other fellow gets him stuck up somewhere else, so that finally all he can do is just glare. He may experience what the obsessional is doing as shifting the topic, misunderstanding everything, imputing the most astounding meanings and the lowest motives to him, and what not. All this simply means that in therapy you do not quarrel with an obsessional neurotic unless you want to have a lot of your time converted to as near nothing as the human being can convert time. What the obsessional is doing is a special instance of the befogging procedure that I mentioned before, except that now instead of picking up all sorts of irrelevant and immaterial extraneous details, he is picking up all the irrelevant and im-

material internal details, you might say, that he can find or suspect in the antagonist. As the antagonist, you realize that in a very remote and incredibly unrelated sense these accusations do, however, have some vague relevance; that's why they stick. So you rapidly become quite entangled; and that leads to such an increasingly foggy argument that within 15 minutes nobody knows what it was all about, but everybody is furious and frustrated. It is really not a great help to a therapist to have been involved in that special kind of entanglement.

Summary

In this chapter, we have discussed the interpersonal approach to treatment with particular emphasis on technique.

(1) Psychiatry and particularly the therapeutic encounter is defined in terms of the interpersonal field, which includes the psychiatrist.

(2) Mental disorder is seen as arising in an interpersonal field, evidenced in an interpersonal field, and capable of correction in an interpersonal field.

(3) Technique is defined as whatever the therapist does to modify and clarify the field of which he is a part.

(4) Emphasis is placed upon the following underlying assumptions of treatment: (a) We are more simply human than otherwise. (b) All interpersonal relationships are reciprocal and may be transformative. (c) Knowledge and reality are safer and better to face than any fantasy construction or denial of reality. (d) Destructiveness is always an interference in an interpersonal field. (e) No one person has to eventually accommodate to the special needs of the other.

(5) The necessity for taking a detailed history is emphasized. The importance of knowing the specific circumstances that make the patient come at the present time is stressed. The anamnesis by developmental eras is also discussed.

(6) A diagnosis is established from the history. A prognostic statement positing goals is made from the interchange in therapy and the evaluation of the history.

(7) A treatment plan is formulated utilizing the case history data, goals, and the technical approach applicable to the patient's diagnostic category. Technical approaches have been described for the hysteric, obsessional, depressive, character disorder, schizophrenic, and psychopath. Ways of reaching the dissociated aspects of the person when the mechanisms of selective inattention, dissociation, or substitution are involved are explicated.

The role of the analyst as participant-observer and the differences in the amount and kind of his participation are delineated. Discouragement or encouragement of regression and parataxic reactions are discussed.

(8) The possibilities and limitations of psychoanalysis are presented.

(9) The obsessional neurotic is defined. Special procedures to uncover and clarify the context within which the obsessions arise are enumerated. Ways of asking questions and of avoiding obsessional stickiness are suggested. Clinical examples are given, and how to avoid prolonging treatment is noted.

REFERENCES

HARRY STACK SULLIVAN

SULLIVAN, H. S. *Contributions of Harry Stack Sullivan.* P. Mullahy (Ed.). New York: Hermitage House, 1952. (Also cited in Will, O. A., Psychotherapy in reference to the schizophrenic reaction. In M. I. Stein [Ed.], *Contemporary Psychotherapies.* New York: Free Press, 1961.)

SULLIVAN, H. S. *The interpersonal theory of psychiatry.* Helen S. Perry and Mary L. Gawel (Eds.). New York: Norton, 1953a.

SULLIVAN, H. S. *Conceptions of modern psychiatry.* New York: Norton, 1953b.

SULLIVAN, H. S. *The psychiatric interview.* Helen S. Perry and Mary L. Gawel (Eds.). New York: Norton, 1954.

SULLIVAN, H. S. *Clinical studies in psychiatry.* Helen S. Perry, Mary L. Gawel, and Martha Gibbon (Eds.). New York: Norton, 1956.

SULLIVAN, H. S. *Schizophrenia as a human process.* New York: Norton, 1962.

MANIC-DEPRESSIVE PSYCHOSIS

COHEN, MABEL BLAKE *et al.* An intensive study of twelve cases of manic-depressive psychosis. *Psychiatry,* 1954, 17, 103–137.

FROMM-REICHMANN, FRIEDA. *Psychoanalysis and psychotherapy.* Chicago: Univ. of Chicago Press, 1959. Chaps. 17 and 18.

SULLIVAN, H. S. *Clinical studies in psychiatry.* New York: Norton, 1956. Chap. 13.

WEIGERT, EDITH. The psychotherapy of the affective psychoses. In *Psychotherapy of the psychoses.* New York: Basic Books, 1961. Chap. 14.

SCHIZOPHRENIA

BURNHAM, D. Autonomy and activity-passivity in the psychotherapy of a schizophrenic man. In *Psychotherapy of the psychoses.* New York: Basic Books, 1961. Chap. 8.

FROMM-REICHMANN, FRIEDA. *Psychoanalysis and psychotherapy*. Chicago: Univ. of Chicago Press, 1959. Chaps. 9 through 16.

SEARLES, H. F. The evolution of the mother transference in psychotherapy with the schizophrenic patient. In *Psychotherapy of the psychoses*. New York: Basic Books, 1961. Chap. 10.

STIERLIN, H. Individual therapy of schizophrenic patients and hospital structure. In *Psychotherapy of the psychoses*. New York: Basic Books, 1961. Chap. 13.

SULLIVAN, H. S. *Clinical studies in psychiatry*. New York: Norton, 1956. Chaps. 14 and 15.

SULLIVAN, H. S. *Schizophrenia as a human process*. New York: Norton, 1962.

WILL, O. A. Psychotherapy in reference to the schizophrenic reaction, and Comments on the psychotherapeutic intervention. In *Contemporary psychotherapies*. New York: Free Press, 1961a. Pp. 128–190.

WILL, O. A. Process, psychotherapy, and schizophrenia. In *Psychotherapy of the psychoses*. New York: Basic Books, 1961b. Chap. 1.

WILL, O. A. Schizophrenia and the psychotherapeutic field, and The schizophrenic patient, the psychotherapist and the consultant. *Contemporary psychoanalysis*, 1964–1965, 1, 1–29, 110–135.

16

EXISTENTIAL PSYCHOANALYSIS

Medard Boss
Gion Condrau

The term "existential psychoanalysis" is applied in psychiatry and psychotherapy to all those theoretical and practical deviations from the classical psychoanalysis of Sigmund Freud that replace the "libido theory" and the "psychic apparatus" by the immediately apprehensible human *existence*. Existential psychoanalysis bases its knowledge of the nature of man's being on the insights of existential philosophy, particularly on the work of the German philosopher Martin Heidegger, *Sein und Zeit* (which appeared in English under the title "Being and Time," New York, 1962) and his subsequent works.

The key term in the works of Heidegger and his followers is *Dasein,* popularly translated as "existence." In order to avoid confusion with other so-called existential-psychoanalytical schools, Medard Boss called his approach "daseinsanalytic." For this reason, then, in what follows the expression "existential psychoanalysis" is replaced by "Daseinsanalysis"—with the knowledge that, in so doing, we are employing a foreign word that is incapable of being adequately translated in a way that will be generally understood.

The present chapter is a presentation, partly word-for-word, partly in summary form, of the daseinsanalytic notions that have already been made known in several of the author's publications. Particular reference is made to the two works *Psychoanalysis and Daseinsanalysis* by Medard Boss (New York, Basic Books, 1963) and *Daseinsanalytische Psychotherapie* by Gion Condrau (Berne and Stuttgart, Hans Huber, 1963).

Rationale of the Method

Daseinsanalytic knowledge not only entails theoretical modifications in our comprehension of illness, but it is also most important for *psychotherapeutic practice*. Originally, it looked as if Daseinsanalysis was different from psychoanalysis only, or mainly, in its theoretical concept; but it then became evident that theory and practice are never to be separated entirely. Thus, the kind of theoretical comprehension of human nature which psychotherapy is based on is a matter of no small importance.

The psychotherapist who utilizes the insights of Daseinsanalysis makes fundamental discoveries that are important for his therapeutic behavior. First of all, he finds out that analysis of Dasein does not teach him, and cannot teach him, any particular new phrases or concepts that might serve to formulate his reflections on, or investigations of, psychopathology; nor does it teach him any terms to use when dealing with patients.

This knowledge limits the psychologist and psychotherapist to the description and investigation of all the immediately observable modes of human behavior and their equally perceptible underlying moods, and it limits him to speaking of them in everyday language.

The discovery that man is essentially one in whose meaning-disclosing relationships the phenomena of our world make their appearance develops, in the Daseinsanalytic therapist, a basic respect for the intrinsic value and essential content of everything that shines forth and comes into its being in the light of a Dasein. Because he has realized that the meaning and context of everything that comes his way shows itself directly to him, he has no need to destroy what he actually sees and hears from the analysand and to replace it with assumed forces supposedly underlying the patient's behavior and perception. Daseinsanalysis thus enables the practitioner to dispense with the tedious intellectual acrobatics required by psychoanalytic theory. He is free to discard the psychoanalytic libido theory as well as the labored psychoanalytic interpretations of symbols, both of them obstacles to an immediate understanding between physician and patient.

There is at least one great advantage in getting rid of the theoretical and speculative ballast of Freudian theory. The psychotherapist becomes less prejudiced. He can devote himself fully to the analysand in that "evenly-hovering attention" that Freud always demanded. He does not approach the patient from the point of view of a scientific theory; nor is his attention distracted by the observation of assumed anonymous forces within the patient. Instead, the analyst's behavior rests on the insight that, being human, he is called upon to disclose both things and men. This knowledge increases his sensitivity to all the obstacles which generally reduce the potential relationships of a patient to a few rigid and unauthentic modes of behavior.

Daseinsanalytic understanding of man imbues the analyst with a deep respect for everything he encounters. In the psychoanalytic situation, such respect means that the Daseinsanalyst can follow the basic rule of psychoanalysis even more consistently than the psychoanalyst, who is hampered by his theoretical prejudices. The analyst's respect for everything that he encounters makes it possible for him to take seriously and to regard without prejudice all behavior and all utterances the patient produces. He has no need to put in the patient's way new obstacles arising from his personal censorship based on theoretical prejudices. The Daseinsanalyst's conscience is clear when he consistently refrains from declaring that one kind of behavior (for instance, instinctual reactions) is more real or fundamental than another. Such impartiality is of great practical importance. It eliminates the danger of so-called unbreakable transference. This therapeutic difficulty often arises when the analyst attempts to reduce (by means of interpretation) a new mode of behavior, on the part of the patient to an earlier relationship in the patient's life, a relationship considered primary and causal *because* it took place earlier. If this budding possibility of relating is not permitted to unfold in its own fashion, it remains fixated on the embryonic level of the transference relationship. It is unlikely that this will happen if the patient's feelings are regarded as actually directed toward the analyst and thus accepted in their full reality, even though the patient's perception of the analyst is still distorted and restricted because of earlier experiences. The Daseinsanalyst's attitude toward patient feelings in the transference situation is characteristic of his attitude toward all happenings during the analytic treatment. What belongs to the creaturely realm, for example, is permitted to be just that. The realm of the divine is similarly recognized as possessing its own authenticity; it is not regarded as a product of sublimation of infantile, libidinous strivings, and thereby degraded to unreality.

Daseinsanalysis admits all phenomena on their own terms. Hence the therapist avoids a second danger, that of "curing" the patient's initial symptoms, then inducing a new neurosis best called "psychoanalytis." This syndrome (by no means rare) induces in its sufferers the habit of ritualistic thinking and talking in psychoanalytic terms and symbols. Cliques and sects are formed of similarly afflicted persons. While many such adherents may lose old symptoms, it is easy to detect the neurotic nature of their new conduct. Instead of staying close to the immediately observable appearances of the world, they disregard them and speculate about what is "behind" them, unaware that their observations do not support their deductions. Instead of dwelling in openness toward the things and people they encounter, they "interpret" these same phenomena, human and material. Generally such people cling rigidly to their theoretical convictions and take great pains to avoid people with different ideas. Their symptoms betray their inability to penetrate beyond the concepts and interpretations of psychoanalytic theory; they have failed to arrive at an open and immediate world relation. Their fear of being contaminated by other ideas betrays their neurotically restricted mode of living, where genuine freedom and openness is always experienced as a threat.

Transference

We have frequently mentioned the extent to which psychoanalytic therapy relies upon fundamental insights into human nature. These insights, although unexpressed in psychoanalytic theory, actually support psychoanalytic procedures. These insights have been explicitly developed since Freud's day in Heidegger's work. Therefore, it is no surprise that most of Freud's concrete suggestions concerning psychoanalytic technique remain unsurpassed in the eyes of the Daseinsanalyst. As a matter of fact, Daseinsanalysis gives psychotherapists a better understanding of the meaning of Freud's recommendations for psychoanalytic treatment than does Freud's own theory. It is by no means unusual to find Daseinsanalysts who adhere more strictly to most of Freud's practical suggestions than do those psychoanalysts whose theoretical orientation remains orthodox. There are only a few (though important) realms of therapy where Freud's secondary theories have negatively influenced therapeutic procedures. It is in these areas that the Daseinsanalyst approaches therapeutic problems differently from the orthodox analyst. Perhaps the most significant area in which Daseinsanalytic thinking differs from psychoanalytic thinking is in the conception of *transference*.

Freud believed that, in transference, the patient's buried and forgotten emotions of love or hate become actual and manifest. According to him, patients want to express in action—reproduce in the real-life relationship with the therapist—infantile feelings for their parents, which have been repressed. They want to "act them out," but they do not know what they are doing. Their acting out is an indication that they resist any consciousness of feelings they had for their parents early in life. These repressed feelings now hide behind the feelings for the analyst. The psychoanalytic treatment is designed to uncover this strategy of acting out. The patient is to be encouraged to remember feelings he had for infantile love objects, but to remember *only*. He is to "retain (them) within the mental sphere." In other words, the transference must be overcome. The implication is that only by frustrating the acting out can the patient be brought to remember infantile love objects and thus to detach himself gradually from the transference situation.

The Daseinsanalyst cannot agree with Freud's suggestions for the handling of transference and acting out. The reason is simple: He does not believe that the theoretical assumptions leading to Freud's suggestions are correct. Nowhere does Freud prove convincingly that the patient's feelings for the analyst do not arise from the present situation, that they are directed, not toward the analyst, but "really" toward the patient's father or mother. He even proves the contrary. First, he admits that "one has no right to dispute the genuine nature of the love which makes its appearance in the course of analytic treatment." Second, he confesses, in a different context, that a correct interpretation of an emotional attachment to the analyst as "transference" from somewhere else, or of acting out as "transference resistance," does not produce the results we expect from correct interpretations of neurotic behavior—namely, the cessation of it.

In contrast to Freud's view, the Daseinsanalyst knows beforehand that so-called transference does not "transfer" anything. He also knows that cures are not effected by months of "working through," during which the supposed meaning of the patient's relationship to the analyst and of his acting out are drilled into him. The Daseinsanalyst believes that "transference love or hate" is a genuine interpersonal relationship to the analyst as experienced by the analysand. The fact that the analysand behaves in an infantile manner and therefore misjudges the actual situation to a large extent (because of his emotional immaturity, which in turn is due to faulty training in his youth) does not detract from the genuineness of his present feelings. The analysand begins to love the analyst as soon as he becomes aware that he has found someone—possibly for the first time in his life—who really understands him and who accepts him even though he is stunted by his neurosis. He loves him all the more because the analyst permits him to unfold more fully his real and essential being within a safe, interpersonal relationship on the "playground of the transference." As we have said before, all genuine love of one person for another is based on the possibility that the loved one offers to the lover of more fully unfolding his own being-in-the-world with him. On the other hand, the patient will hate his analyst as long as he is still (because of his childhood experiences) open only to a child-father or child-mother relationship, which limits his perception of adults to frustrating experiences. He will hate him even more, and with good reason, if the analyst, because of his own so-called countertransference (i.e., his own neurotically restricted emotional attitude toward the patient) actually behaves like one of the former hated parents.

It is not surprising that anyone who carefully studies Freud's writings on the subject of transference will notice that he does not actually succeed, in spite of extreme efforts, in producing any evidence for the existence of such shiftable affects. The so-called positive transference is a case in point. Freud is not able to distinguish convincingly the nature of transference love from that of the genuine love of one partner for another in a normal love relationship. Eventually he is forced to admit that one has no right to dispute the genuine nature of the love that makes its appearance in the course of analytic treatment. Furthermore, every analyst can observe that transference love for the analyst appears at those moments of the treatment when the analyst has made his first insight-producing interpretations with their resulting emotional effects on the patient. It seems evident that the phenomenon of love appears when being together with a partner opens up an existence to hitherto unappropriated possibilities of relating to the world.

Transference is not a mere deception based on a faulty linking of affects and instincts to the wrong object, as Freud thought. Transference is always a genuine relationship between the analysand and the analyst. In each being-together, the partners disclose themselves to each other as human beings, that is to say, each as basically the same kind of being as the other. No secondary object cathexes, no "transfer of libido" from a "primarily narcissistic ego" to the "love object," no transfer of an affect from a former love object to a present-day partner are necessary for such disclosure, because it is of the primary nature of Dasein to disclose being, including human being. This means that no interpersonal relationship whatsoever necessitates a transfer of affect. Nor do we need the more modern concept of empathy to understand the immediate disclosure of one person to another. This, in turn, frees us of the obligation to explain yet another mysterious process, because the basic nature of empathy has never been elucidated.

To understand the specific phenomenon of so-called neurotic transference, we must realize that the primary openness of a human being for the discovery of encountered fellow human beings does not necessarily result in perceptions that do full justice to the one who is encountered. Man's basic nature as world-openness fundamentally and necessarily includes a closing in. The limitations of a neurotic's openness (in the sense of an understanding relationship with his world) are merely what psychology calls the neurotic distortions of his personality. He is—insofar as he is neurotic—limited to modes of disclosure and behavior similar to a child's. The great variety of mature, full, and free manners of relating are not available to him (as indeed they are not available to the healthy child, but for different reasons). This limitation enables us to understand the phenomena of transference in the narrow sense of the term, namely, the so-called neurotic distortion of transference. The following analogy may facilitate an understanding of what we mean.

A child plays with a burning candle. It closes its eyelids almost completely and it sees a starlike arrangement of narrow rays instead of a full-sized flame. Suppose that the child were to burn his eyelids while playing with the candle and that they became permanently sealed together. The child would then continue to perceive all candles in the same fashion for the rest of his life. But no one would maintain that this manner of perceiving the flame, as an adult, is due to a "transfer" of the experience he had, as a child, to a similar situation occurring in the present. The reason for the distortion of perceptions is the same in both childhood and adulthood: the closing of the eyelids. The situation of the adult neurotic is similar. His human condition is still so childlike and undeveloped that, to select an instance, he is open only to the perception of the father-like aspects of all the adult men he encounters. Thus, he behaves toward the analyst as if the latter were his father. Naturally, the limitation of possibilities for disclosing and relating persists in this neurotic, because of a father who inhibited the child's growth and was therefore partly disliked, even hated. Therefore, this neurotic will not even be open to all the possible father-son relationships. He will be able to exist only in a hate-ridden son-father relation. In the light of such reduced world openness, he can perceive only the hateful father aspects of any grown man he encounters, however spurious this aspect may actually be in any given person he meets.

Such patients as the neurotic in our example are often quite mature, insofar as their intellectual potentialities for relating are concerned. But this intellectual awareness does not as a rule have much influence in correcting the faulty relationship, precisely because it is only a peripheral maturity and not an encompassing one. This explains why the patient's intellectual realization that the analyst is not like his father has little, if any, influence on the patient's reaction to him. Viewing the situation in this fashion, it seems superfluous to assume that an earlier affect is displaced from an earlier object to the one in the transference situation. At the same time, we no longer need consider transference love an illusory phenomenon. On the contrary, Daseinsanalysis regards every analysand-analyst relationship as a genuine relationship *sui generis*. It is genuine despite the fact that the patient is carrying it out in a limited fashion, owing to his mental distortions. It could not be otherwise. The analysand-analyst relationship, like any other, is grounded in the primary being-with of one man and another, which is part of Dasein's primary world-disclosure. The patient's transference love is not, therefore, really love of someone else—the father, for instance. It is love of the analyst himself, no matter how immature and distorted it may appear because of the limitations of perception imposed on the patient by his earlier relationship to his real father. It would seem that many psychoanalysts classify the love and confidence patients show them as "transference phenomena" because they think such feelings do not befit a scientific attitude toward mankind. Fearing that they might be thought unscientific, they use this *terminus technicus* to assuage their uneasiness and to protect themselves against "real" love or hate.

Resistance

Daseinsanalysis enables the psychotherapist to carry out an "analysis of resistance," wherein the patient is tirelessly confronted with the limitations of his life and wherein these limitations are incessantly questioned, so that the possibility of a richer existence is implied. As a rule, neurotically reduced people regard their wretched interpersonal relations as the only ones possible. They do not know that greater freedom is available. If their restrictions are repeatedly questioned, previously nonadmitted possibilities of behavior regularly appear, along with perception of the things and fellow human beings who are part of these world-disclosing possibilities. The analyst practicing in this fashion will not try to persuade patients that much of what they feel and mean is only a cloak for opposite wishes and tendencies. He will thus avoid giving the impression of devaluating their experience, thereby confusing them and arousing unnecessary anxiety. However, the Daseinsanalyst's respect for phenomena should not be confused with an exclusive concern with those phenomena of which the patient is already fully aware. He knows that the patient's being, apart from overtly admitted and accepted modes of behavior includes a great many other modes of being, some of which the patient is trying hard not to become aware of, and many of which contrast with the overtly expressed modes. He also knows that these possibilities for relating have to be acknowledged by the patient as his own before he can get well. Nevertheless, all of the patient's modes of behavior—those openly carried out and those so far warded off—are considered autonomous by the therapist; he must treat all as valid. He must never try to deny the reality of a phenomenon.

Transference and resistance indisputably refer to actual phenomena of interhuman relationships, although in a veiled way. Observation repeatedly confirms how right Freud was when he stated that if the analyst allows the patient time, devotes serious interest to him, and acts with tact, a deep attachment of the patient to the analyst develops by itself. Nor can any analytical observer deny Freud's discovery that all patients in psychoanalytic treatment strongly resist total recognition of themselves. Every experienced analyst, therefore, will fully agree with Freud's observation that the pathological factor is not the patient's ignorance itself, but the root of this ignorance in his *inner resistances.*

Freud candidly admitted that it sounded improbable to suggest that the patient who seeks relief from his suffering in psychoanalysis would offer vigorous and tenacious resistance throughout the entire course of the treatment. And yet, he continued, this is exactly what happens. Nor is such resistance without analogies. Such behavior is comparable to that of a man who has rushed off to a dentist with a frightful toothache but who may very well fend the dentist off when he applies his forceps to the decayed tooth. Nor must resistances of this kind be narrowly condemned. They can turn out to be of the greatest assistance to the analysis, if a skillful technique is correctly employed to apply them most advantageously. Indeed, one may truthfully say that the overcoming of these resistances is the essential function of the analysis, that part of its function which alone assures us that we have achieved something for the patient.

Defense, nonadmittance, and the central importance of resistance in psychotherapy are phenomena that can readily be acknowledged without at the same time accepting Freud's assumption concerning them. We need not believe in instinctual representatives residing in a consciousness that is pictured as a reception room but that is yet capable of looking at things. Nor do we have to assume a psychic "doorkeeper" (the ego anthropomorphized) who locks up unwelcome ideas in the anteroom of the unconscious, nor accept speculations concerning changes of state and alterations of cathexis of undemonstrable instinctual representatives. If, without prejudice, we consider defenses as well as that which is defended against, resistance and the resisted, we begin to see that they have nothing whatever to do with Freud's hypotheses concerning the inner structure of the psyche or with any of the rest of his abstract speculations.

Interpretation of Unconscious

In psychoanalytic theory, the hypothesis of the unconscious as a constituent factor of the psychic apparatus is highly important. According to Freud's own testimony, his central aim was to demonstrate the thoroughgoing meaningfulness of all mental phenomena. The meaningfulness of a phenomenon was supposed to signify that the phenomenon has a definite position and value in the process of the unfolding and maturing of a person's existence. In his attempt to prove this, Freud found that he was forced to attack one of the unquestioned dogmas of most of the philosophers of his time, namely the doctrine that mind and consciousness are identical. Always endeavoring to prove the thoroughgoing meaningfulness of all mental phenomena, Freud arrived at the conception of a twofold "unconscious," a partner of consciousness but infinitely more powerful. Freud's "unconscious" soon became the most essential of all concepts introduced within the corpus of psychoanalytic theory. He went so far as to designate it as the "true psychical reality." The "quality of being conscious or not" always remained for him "the single ray of light that penetrates the obscurity of depth-psychology." The unconscious became so much the mark of psychoanalytic theory that psychoanalysis, and all doctrines derived from it, eventually became known as "depth" psychologies. "Depth" entered the picture because Freud, elaborating on Fechner's conception of "psychic localities," undertook to view mental phenomena in terms of a "topographic" approach, and to regard the unconscious as a "psychical locality," a "psychical system" "below" consciousness. Freud knew perfectly well that the assumption of an unconscious meant going beyond immediately observable phenomena. He underscored this awareness when he referred to the idea of psychic localities as "conjecture." Hence, he regarded his doctrine of the unconscious not as part of psychology but as part of metapsychology. Nevertheless, the starting point of his explorations beyond immediately observable phenomena was concrete observations. Among these, Freud cited the everyday occurrence that "an idea which is conscious now is no longer so a moment later. . . . What the idea was in the interval we do not know. We can say that it was latent." Freud also recalled Bernheim's experiments in which subjects were given suggestions during hypnosis, which they carried out after awakening, without knowing that the source of the suggestions was someone other than themselves. Freud also regarded as unexplainable phenomena parapraxes, neurotic symptoms, and dreams—all unexplainable, he thought, unless one assumed unconscious strivings and wishes behind them. However, as soon as he had dared to assume an unconscious, he found himself forced to introduce complicated distinctions between what is only "latently" unconscious (i.e., "preconscious") and what is unconscious in the narrow sense (i.e., phenomena inaccessible even to the preconscious). In later phases of his metapsychology, he even found it necessary to a large extent to replace the concepts of "conscious" and "unconscious" by those of "ego," "id," and "superego."

Fundamentally, the obscurity that veils the problem of the consciousness originates in the fact that it is impossible to understand "consciousness" as arising out of qualityless excitations and as a property of the surface of an apparatus. It is hardly worth mentioning that it is equally impossible to understand "consciousness" in connection with language in the way Freud tried to comprehend it. The phenomenon of human language cannot be reduced to residues and memories of sensory stimuli and auditory sensations; even the senseless gibberish of a parrot cannot be explained in this way. It remains unintelligible how consciousness can arise out of an enigmatic connection between "unconscious thought processes" and corresponding "auditory stimuli." Above all, it is simply not true that we perceive "auditory stimuli" when we hear a child cry, for instance, or a train whistle. Nor do we perceive only "visual stimuli" or "visual sensations" when we become aware of a tree standing over there in the garden. On the contrary, we primarily and directly hear *someone crying* or *something whistling;* we perceive a *tree* standing over there.

The phenomenon that the obscure concept of a consciousness conceals rather than elucidates is neither a mysterious property of an energy-laden psychic process that is qualityless as such nor is it a psychic locality within a subject or an apparatus. Such ideas make it forever impossible to understand my becoming aware of myself as well as of the table, the house, the people around me—aware of them, moreover, as what they actually are, that is, as *this* table, *that* house, *those* people. This "capacity" for becoming aware of something, hitherto thought of as a property or an act of a postulated, unclarified consciousness, is nothing of the kind, but simply evidence of man's primary openness and awareness, and this, in turn, is the very essence of his existence and never merely the property of an unknown X. The recognition that others have the same ability as I have to understand— or to become "conscious" of—something is not based on deduction or analogy (as are, according to Freud's own statements, his notions of a consciousness and an unconscious). This recognition is, rather, an integral part of man's fundamental openness for an immediate understanding and perceiving of a being as the being it is—of a human being, for instance, as a being that exists in the same way as the one who perceives.

The assumption of an unconscious is necessary only if one accepts Freud's underlying philosophy as obviously true. Then, of course, the hypothesis of a psychic container, a psychic locality, or a psychic system is unavoidable. All the manifold psychic transformation processes, which Freud assumed to be behind the immediately given phenomena, require such a psychic "black box," since admittedly they can never be seen.

One of the immeasurable advantages of the Daseinsanalytic understanding of man is the fact that it renders superfluous the assumption of an unconscious. Analysis of Dasein makes us realize that we have no basis for conjecturing the existence of subjective images that mirror an independent, external reality, nor for assuming processes (occurring in some intrapsychic locality) that fabricate ideas and thoughts corresponding more or less to this external reality. Instead, analysis of Dasein enables us to become aware that the things and fellow men an individual encounters appear to him— within the meaning-disclosing light of his Dasein—immediately (and without any subjective processes being involved). They appear as what they are, in accordance with the world-openness of his existence. Because it is the essence of Dasein to light up, illuminate, disclose, and perceive, we always find Dasein primordially *with* what it encounters, similar to so-called physical light. Light, too, is always "out there," shining *on* the things that appear within its luminous realm. Relating to the things in the way of being-with-them-primordially, of letting them shine forth and appear, Dasein spatializes itself into its relationships with what it encounters, in accordance with its close or distant concern for the encountered in any given case. This given man exists, consumes his time, and fulfills his

Dasein. Existing in this fashion, man depends on what he encounters as much as the encountered depends on the disclosing nature of man for its appearance.

Daseinsanalysis can grant an immediate and autonomous reality to all kinds of phenomena, which in Freud's view would be degraded from the outset to incorrect deceptions of the unconscious. Daseinsanalysis can grant this reality because it has not prejudged a whole host of phenomena according to an arbitrary decision about the nature of the world and reality. Daseinsanalysis makes it unnecessary to go beyond immediate experience. It can elucidate without difficulty, on the basis of immediate experience alone, all those psychic phenomena that compelled Freud to invent the unconscious.

The phenomenon that, above all others, made the assumption of an unconscious imperative to Freud was the dream. If one departs from the immediate experience of the dream and tries to explain dream phenomena with the help of abstract concepts elaborated in working with other types of subject matter, it is almost inevitable that one arrives at some such conclusion. This is what happened in the case of Freud.

He tells us so himself, in the following passage:

> We borrow the following thesis from the theory of hysteria: a normal train of thought is only submitted to abnormal psychical treatment . . . if an unconscious wish, derived from infancy and in a state of repression, has transferred on to it. In accordance with this thesis we have constructed our theory of dreams on the assumption that the dream-wish which provides the motive power invariably originates from the unconscious—an assumption which, as I myself am ready to admit, cannot be proved to hold generally, though neither can it be disproved.

Dream phenomena do not enable us to recognize infantile wishes as sources of dreams, nor to understand the transformation of a wish into a dream nor the dreamwork that supposedly accomplishes the transformation. It is not surprising, therefore, that all of these suppositions have to be placed in the unrecognizable darkness of a psychic interior, that is, the unconscious.

To demonstrate his theory of dreams as clearly as possible, Freud employed the following example at the end of *The Interpretation of Dreams*:

> A fourteen-year-old boy came to me for psychoanalytic treatment suffering from *tic convulsif,* hysterical vomiting, headaches, etc. I began the treatment by assuring him that if he shut his eyes he would see pictures or have ideas which he was then to communicate to me. He replied in pictures. His last

impression before coming to me was revived visually in his memory. He had been playing at draughts with his uncle and saw the board in front of him. He thought of various positions, favorable or unfavorable, and of the moves that one must not make. He then saw a dagger lying on the board—an object that belonged to his father but which his imagination placed on the board. Then there was a sickle lying on the board and next a scythe. And there now appeared a picture of an old peasant mowing the grass in front of the patient's distant home with a scythe. After a few days I discovered the meaning of this series of pictures. The boy had been upset by an unhappy family situation. He had a father who was a hard man, liable to fits of rage, who had been unhappily married to the patient's mother and whose educational method had consisted of threats. His father had been divorced by his mother, a tender and affectionate woman, had married again and had one day brought a young woman home with him who was to be the boy's new mother. It was during the first few days after this that the fourteen-year-old boy's illness had come on. His suppressed rage against his father was what had constructed this series of pictures with their understandable allusions. The material for them was provided by a recollection from mythology. The sickle was the one with which Zeus castrated his father; the scythe and the picture of the old peasant represented Kronos, the violent old man who devoured his children and on whom Zeus took such unfilial vengeance. His father's marriage gave the boy an opportunity of repaying the reproaches and threats which he had heard from his father long before because he had played with his genitals (cf. the playing of draughts; the forbidden moves; the dagger which could be used to kill). In this case long-repressed memories and derivatives from them which had remained unconscious slipped into consciousness by a roundabout path in the form of apparently meaningless pictures.

This example contains a great number of interpretive conclusions concerning affective and instinctual "derivatives" from the boy's unconscious. Apart from the fact that the essence of such "pictures" remains as usual completely unclarified, there is no proof whatsoever *in the dream phenomena themselves* for the intellectual deductions which Freud bases on them. These deductions were not made for the sake of the phenomenon of dreaming, but for the sake of the theory that dreams arise out of unconscious wishes. For this reason, this type of dream interpretation will never be able to defend itself against the accusation of utter arbitrariness. If, however, one does not accept the basis (admittedly unproved) for such deductions, the dagger and the scythe the boy perceives can be understood (without assuming either a consciousness or an unconscious) as things that correspond to the pitch to which he was attuned, most probably that of anxiety. People in the mood of anxiety are, in the main, open only to the perception of those features of the world that are a threat to them. So it was with this child. We would have to know a great deal more about the dagger and scythe of the boy's dreams—more than the references to mythology, which are Freud's and not the boy's—to be willing to label Freud's interpretations (that they derive from unconscious rage and death wishes) anything other than fantasies of the interpreter. It would be impossible to say, without precise knowledge of the mood and the meaningful content the peasant had for the boy, whether he sprang, on the contrary, from the boy's natural longing for the security of a home. One thing remains certain. In order to meaningfully understand this concluding example of *The Interpretation of Dreams,* we can dispense with a great deal of the preceding content of the book, but never with the very first sentence, a sentence that initiated a new epoch. To repeat: "Every dream reveals itself as a psychical structure which has a meaning and which can be inserted at an assignable point in the mental activities of his waking life." This sentence reflects the *élan* of the joy of discovery alive in a man who had just become aware of a new dimension— the thoroughgoing meaningfulness of all human phenomena—a man who had not, as yet, darkened this insight by theoretical regression into natural-scientific explanation.

Our necessary criticism of the assumption of an unconscious does not blind us to Freud's grasp of a realm fundamentally important to the Daseins-analytic understanding of man. In his untiring search for the unconscious, Freud was on the way to the concealed, to concealment as such. Without concealment and darkness, man would not be the world-disclosing being that he is. Light and darkness, concealment and disclosure, belong together inseparably; Freud must have sensed this. He said this, too, of the unconscious: that it contained the "indestructible" forces of the human mind, that it was the "true psychical reality." As a child of his power-hungry epoch, he felt the urge to make subjectivistic, psychologistic objects out of concealment in order to be able to drag it into the light of the technical intellect and make it usable. As it has always done, and will always do, the secret withstood such characteristically modern impertinence.

Working Through

Differences may be stated here as well. The most important one consists in the handling of "acting" as well as in the psychoanalytic question "why?" and the Daseinsanalytic question "why not?"

Freud has given us a masterful description of the way the resistances melt in the "fire of transference love" against the acquisition of hitherto-feared possibilities of living, but when the patient wants not only to think or talk about his relation to the analyst but wants also to experience his newly discovered possibilities in the language of his emotions and his body, Freud calls this the "acting-out of resistance." The Daseinsanalyst thinks otherwise. To him, the desire for emotional and physical acting out appears as much a part of the newly sprouting possibilities for relating as do the thoughts that go with these possibilities. Therefore, the Daseinsanalyst cannot regard such acting out as a repetition—in action—of repressed infantile emotions of love toward a parent, or even as resistance against becoming conscious of such old "love objects." He will carefully avoid transforming the so-called acting out into "psychic material," namely into remembering and verbal expression. On the contrary, he will let the acting out continue, to the greatest extent possible, without violating his own integrity, inner freedom, and selfless concern for the analysand. He will do this because he regards acting out as a *genuine* phenomenon, as, more often than not, the very opposite of an attempt to repress. Acting out may indicate that something is unfolding for the first time in the analysand's life. He dares to behave in a manner that has never before been permitted him (at least not sufficiently). Acting out in these cases can be neither a remembering nor a repetition. Thus the only therapeutically effective action by the therapist is *permission* to act out. With this permission it is possible for the patient to experience again and again, to practice, and eventually to acquire modes of behaving that had not been permitted in the relationship to his real parents and educators. It is harmful to attempt to "transform" acting out into remembering, especially if the therapist tries to accomplish this by calling the behavior of the analysand "infantile"; this has the derogatory implication that the patient should have overcome and abandoned such behavior long ago. But, on the contrary, the childlike modes of behavior that sprout for the first time in the analysand-analyst relationship should be valued as the precious starting points from which all future developments will arise. The analysand's being-himself will mature into ever more differentiated forms of relating, if the more primitive forms of relating are first permitted to unfold themselves fully. If this is allowed, maturer forms of behaving appear spontaneously. Thus the gradual detachment from the analytic situation happens *because* acting out is now permitted; it is not produced by a misinterpretation of acting out as renewal of childhood memories.

Actually Freud knew this, although, seduced by his theoretical assumptions, he did not mention it explicitly in his recommendations for the

practical handling of so-called transference. He contradicted his own definition of transference "as an erroneous linkage of an affect and an object"
when he stated that "one has no right to dispute the genuine nature of the
love which makes its appearance in the course of analytic treatment." Freud
the therapist, moreover, behaved, in actual treatment, as if he were cognizant of these Daseinsanalytic insights.

We have noted before that he admonished the analyst to "wait and let
things take their course," because in all patients capable of sublimation, the
process of healing usually "takes place from within as soon as their inhibitions have been removed by the analysis." These phrases imply that the
concept of "working through" is primarily a theoretical screen for permissiveness in regard to the trying out and practicing of newly admitted
ways of behaving in the analyst-analysand relationship. Incidentally, these
same remarks by Freud show how pointless it is for some critics of psychoanalysis to demand that "psychosynthesis" must follow psychoanalysis.
Obviously, what takes place of its own accord need not, in addition, be
accomplished by something else.

Of course, acting out—as any other phenomenon of psychoanalysis—*can*
be used for purposes of resistance and of hiding. Occasionally an analysand
uses, in analysis, ways of relating that he has practiced for some time and
taken over responsibly, in order to resist acceptance of still more feared ways
of living. If the patient does not make such behavior part of his relations
outside the analytic situation, if he persists in acting out *only* with the analyst, we may assume that his acting out serves to sabotage the responsible
acceptance of certain realms the patient still fears. It is easy to recognize
such acting out, for it has a counterfeit, playful, theatrical, and demonstra-
tive character. However, Freud's technique of analysis of resistance gives us
adequate means to surmount this difficulty.

It is important to remember that a neurotically inhibited person can
attempt to open himself in his relationship to the analyst only if the latter
meets him on a level that is genuinely his. With seriously ill people, this
is seldom the conceptual, intellectual-verbal level. Therefore, the analysand-
analyst relationship must often resemble that of an infant to his mother, if
the relationship is to be genuine and appropriate to the patient's condition.
At times this relationship can grow only if it is confined to the silent
language of gestures, sometimes even exclusively to silence, so that Dasein
may come to light and grow. Child analysis, by and large, has long since
renounced any attempt to transfer acting out into thoughts and memories.
But in the analysis of adults we have failed to recognize sufficiently that we
are dealing with people who have remained small children at the very core

of their existence and to whom we can genuinely relate only if we meet them on that same childlike level.

The analyst who urges his patients to regard all their acting out as a form of resistance against remembering their behavior toward former "love objects" wrongs his patients severely and endangers their chances of recovery. If the patients do what the therapist asks them to do, they demand either too much or too little of themselves. Either there is nothing to be remembered at all, because a patient is experiencing in his acting out toward the analyst a new way of interpersonal relating, a way that had never been open to him before; or a patient actually can realize that he is behaving toward his analyst in exactly the same distorted way as he remembers behaving in his youth toward his father or mother, in consequence of this or that excessive frustration or overpermissiveness on their part. But no actual, convincing evidence has ever been presented as to the effect of this kind of remembering as such. On the contrary, Freud's conviction that the mere remembering of the occasion when neurotic behavior was first produced and stamped on a child's existence will itself stop the compulsive repetition of such behavior is based on laws that can be applied satisfactorily only to physical objects. In the realm of physics, it is true, an effect will no longer be produced if its cause is eliminated; an electric motor, for instance, will come to a dead stop as soon as the current is turned off. Nothing that happens to a child, however, is capable of producing and maintaining any pattern of behavior in this causal sense. The experiences of childhood can only *limit* and *distort* the carrying out of innate possibilities of relating to the world. They cannot cause and produce the relationships themselves. Nor can such a pseudo-cause be rendered ineffectual by simply remembering it, by making it "conscious" and thus liberating a so-called fixated amount of libido. We cannot repeat often enough that no amount whatever of "blind" energies can ever produce and build a lucid human world consisting of meaning-disclosing relationships with what is encountered. Human existence is essentially not a physical process but primarily a historical event. This means that in every actual relation to something or somebody, Dasein's whole history is inherent and present, whether the historical unfolding of a certain kind of relationship is remembered explicitly or not.

What matters most, therapeutically, is not the recalling of the occasion when a neurotic pattern of relating to one's fellow men was acquired in childhood but finding the answer to two questions: Why has the patient remained, right up to the present time, caught within this same, restricted way of communicating? What is keeping him a prisoner of his neurotic behavior patterns right now? The general answer to these all-important questions is that neurotic patients usually cannot even imagine that another way of relating to people is possible. Some may know intellectually of a greater freedom, but they do not trust it sufficiently to try it out. Instead, they are most anxious to prove the contrary to themselves, by provoking their environment to continue the neurotically restricted way of communicating with them. For all neurotics, any change of the narrow perspective to which they are accustomed is terrifying, especially if it is a change toward greater freedom.

The last thing our analysands need is a theoretical reduction of their acting out to a transference phenomenon—or any other rational explanation of it. Nor do they need to account for it intellectually (with or without the corresponding "affects"), to reflect on it "consciously," to articulate it verbally, or to assume full responsibility for it. Their primary requirement is not some kind of conceptual recognition of their acting out, but rather the opportunity to live and to experience, over and over again, immediately and unreflectingly, their new ways of behavior within the safe relationship to the analyst.

Freud's advice that patients be urged to remember "consciously" and to articulate verbally as soon as possible what they are unreflectingly acting out seems to originate in his limited understanding of human language and "consciousness." Freud was of the opinion that nothing could become "conscious" (and thus be prevented from converting itself into a neurotic symptom) that was not connected with the memory traces of the sound of the name or word belonging to it. In unreflected-upon perception and action, however, there is as genuine an appropriation and unfolding of world-disclosing possibilities of behavior as takes place when we are moving within the realm of verbal utterances. For an unreflected-upon mode of spontaneous behavior also belongs to human language in its deepest sense. It too presupposes an awareness of the meaning and the references of the beings encountered. In fact, it precedes by far any conceptual reflection and knowledge of spoken words. The genuineness and priority of such an unreflected-upon, "merely" acted-out, appropriation of new ways of relating can easily be demonstrated. Every experienced analyst knows patients who recognized, and reflected upon, all their important "fixations" to earlier "love objects," who came to clothe these recognitions in proper and adequate words and concepts, and who even realized the full emotional content belonging to these relations—all without the slightest therapeutic effect. On the other hand, there are scores of patients who lost forever all their neurotic symptoms without any remembering of earlier "love objects," without any conceptualized or verbalized recognition of the hitherto warded-off possibilities of relating to their fellow human beings. They achieved this solely by acting out unreflectingly—and thereby appropriating and accepting—their immediately lived behavior toward the analyst.

The Daseinsanalyst often asks his patients "Why not?" thereby encouraging them to ever greater tests of daring. "Why is it that you don't dare to behave in such-and-such a manner during the analytic session?" is a question often asked in place of the usual analytic "Why?" If the "Why?" comes too early, before the analysand has had sufficient time for acting out, it puts excessive demands on him and may aggravate his condition rather than improve it. Most patients are caught in a mechanistic, causal-genetic interpretation of themselves. If we ask "Why?" prematurely, they will in most cases understand this to mean that they should look for the cause of their present behavior in an earlier period of their lives. At the same time, we may awaken false hopes in them. They may get the impression that simply finding the presumed cause of suffering (an event in early childhood, which "fixated libido" at a specific level of development) will remove the obstacles against getting well. But in the strict sense of the term, no event in the life history of a person can ever be the "cause" of neurotic symptoms. Personal experiences merely initiate inhibitions against fully carrying out all possible interpersonal relationships.

Any understanding and emotional experiencing of the parents' inadequate behavior, which stunted the growth of a patient in his youth, must be complemented, as we have already stated, by the tirelessly repeated question, "Why does he still, this very day, not dare to free himself of the restricting mentality of his childhood?" If this most important question is neglected, even in the later phases of therapy, the treatment may easily become sterile and result in the patient's eternal and stereotyped accusations against his parents.

It is true, of course, that many modern psychotherapists no longer understand the "Why?" of psychoanalysis as a question intended to elicit causes. Their questioning is actually meant to elicit illustrations from the life of the analysand, which will make the meaning—not the cause—of his symptoms clearer to him. Nevertheless, even such analysts often demand too much of the analysand. Their questioning implies a demand that the patient verbalize a "reasonable," cognitive explanation of his behavior. Such a demand ignores the immature and childlike constitution of a neurotic person; it overburdens him; it touches him only on the surface, by appealing to unauthentic (for him), learned, intellectual modes of relating. The following two illustrations from histories may serve to emphasize this point.

The psychotherapist once asked "Why?" in an attempt to enable a patient, a thirty-five-year-old woman, to arrive quickly at a rational understanding of her acting out. The question was asked at the wrong time; although the worst could eventually be avoided, the question probably added two years to the analysis. What happened was as follows: The patient, after tremendous inner resistance had been overcome, got off the couch and began to kneel on the floor, leaning against the couch. When the analyst asked her why she was doing this, she interpreted his question (as is only too often the case) as a prohibition. In reality, the analyst, faithful to Freud's advice, had intended to transform her acting out into a memory. The (supposed) meaning of this kneeling gesture was to be understood intellectually and expressed verbally. But the patient was not ready for such expression. Her condition was still comparable to that of a small child; she was still capable of expressing what she wanted to express only in the language of gestures appropriate to a small child.

Her kneeling was not an acting out of repressed memories at all. She had no memories of kneeling, repressed or otherwise, for the simple reason that her actual relationship to her parents had been of a kind that had never permitted either kneeling or *wanting* to kneel. Actually, her effort to kneel was her first attempt to make up for what she had never had, a groping plea to be permitted to be a trusting child—a child who is allowed to sit at her mother's knees and lean her head against them.

If a child kneels and leans against his mother's knees, he usually does not talk, much less explain what he is doing. The only adequate expression of the relationship is through gestures, possibly accompanied by inarticulate sounds of pleasure. Conceptually articulated thinking and talking about the experience must necessarily destroy the validity of the experience. If he asks this of a patient, the analyst drives him into artificial adulthood, where true maturation and recovery become impossible.

At this point in the course of the woman's analysis, everything depended on whether she would be permitted to experience an undisturbed, trusting mother-child relationship. Within the framework of such a relationship, the patient should have been given permission to kneel in the analyst's presence for some time to come. The therapist realized only much later how inadequate his questions were. He had interfered with, rather than abetted, her recovery. When he first noticed her intention to kneel, he should not have asked "Why?" If anything, he might have ventured to ask, "Why not?" thereby encouraging her. Only such encouragement on the part of the analyst would have induced the patient to follow Freud's basic rule to state everything that comes to mind. Her kneeling—a way of talking in the language she had mastered—would have constituted compliance with Freud's rule.

More than two years were required before the resistance aroused by the analyst's misplaced question was overcome and new trust established, creating the condition for the emergence of world relations, which the patient had defended herself against up until then. The main cause of this resistance was not fear of hitherto-rejected possibilities of living. Nor was it fear of greater freedom; she had no desire to adhere to familiar, although painful, behavior patterns. Nor were the two years of fruitless complaints by the patient due to a masochistic "repetition compulsion" arising from the unconscious. This resistance was strictly of the analyst's making. It had been released by his misunderstanding of the patient's infantile longing for trust. He had overstrained her. He had demanded that she understand her longing as an adult would (namely, on an intellectual level), while at this stage of her development only a silent gesture could genuinely demonstrate what she felt and what she was.

In another case, that of a male analysand, the therapist questioned even Freud's sacrosanct basic rule by asking, "Why not?" A compulsive patient, a physician, interpreted this rule—to tell all that comes to mind—as a confirmation of his conception of life as incessant slavery. Much too late (two years after the beginning of the analysis) the analyst asked the analysand (who was, as usual, pedantically and conscientiously torturing himself so as to be sure to say everything) why he did not permit himself for once *not* to say everything? Only then did the patient dare, little by little, to relax the laws within which his existence was encased. Eventually, he felt as comfortable in disobeying commands in the analytic situation as a child feels in his soft bed. This was the turning point in an analysis that had seemed hopeless until then.

Breaking the basic rule of psychoanalysis seems to imply exorbitant freedom. Nonetheless, this patient suffered the supreme frustration, in Freud's sense, although it was frustration of a specific kind. The question "Why not?" frustrated his persistence within his usual, compulsive behavior patterns. The patient himself stated that this frustrating permissiveness (or permissive frustration) had "shaken his world." It had pulled the rug out from under all the world relations he had hitherto known. Later, the same "Why not?" shook his world in another fashion. It became a healing factor. It gave him, for the first time, an opportunity to be a small child who did not have to be or do anything in particular. After he had overcome the fear of going insane, he was able to move into a freer relationship to the world and finally to achieve maturity as a free and candid self.

The Concept of Cure

Probably in no other field do we so easily and so frequently cherish pious, and impious, self-deceptions as in that of the psychoanalytic treatment. Our deceptions bear specifically on what we regard as therapeutically effective and curative. The reason for this is that our answers to the question: "What is effective in psychotherapy?" are really always provided in advance by our current theories on the nature of man and on the nature of the physician-patient relationship.

If, for instance, we believe that drives and a psychic energy feeding them, the libido, really exist, that the basis or fundamental stratum of man's being is even made up of such things, we can envisage the function of psycho-analysis as consisting solely in a relaxation of libidinous fixations. If we imagine the neurotic modes of behavior of a patient toward his analyst as involving "transference," that is, a transferring to the physician of feelings that really still apply to the parents and educators, we have to think of the successful treatment as being caused by an illuminative unmasking of these unconscious, intrapsychic manipulations, particularly by a raising into consciousness of corresponding unconscious Oedipal-infantile wishes. If we explain the neurotic condition as an unconscious obsession with archetypes from the collective unconscious, we are naturally bound to consider the effectiveness of an analysis as consisting in the conscious integration of these archetypal images or forces. The different evaluations of the so-called rational sphere of the human mind and its irrational, emotional side has finally divided modern psychoanalysts into two large camps. One group regards the real effectiveness of their method as consisting in that aspect of the physician-patient relationship which Franz Alexander called the "corrective emotional experience" in the treatment. The other group of psychoanalysts, rather, ascribes the main therapeutic function of the analysis to the conscious, conceptual-linguistic comprehension or elucidation of previously unconscious strivings.

In our efforts to get a clearer picture of what is really involved here, what strikes us as of primary importance is a psychotherapeutic intervention affecting psychoanalysts themselves; this would be a most beneficial, although painful, experience for us. This intervention would perforce lead to the insight that all the above-mentioned psychological concepts, such as drive, libido, archetypes, the unconscious, unconscious wishes, and also the having of affects and representations in a consciousness system in the mind, transference, and so on, are purely hypothetical, purely conceptual premises and conclusions. They can in principle be assumed to be behind the factually demonstrable phenomena, but their real existence can never be demonstrated.

If, in fact, we psychoanalysts, to an astonishing degree, move in a realm of dogmas and conceptual hypotheses and hypostatizations, surely what is urgently required is a retreat, as swift and complete a one as possible, to what immediately discloses itself in our dealings with our patients and is to be experienced there.

A brief consideration of a temporally and spatially unlimited fact may instil in us the required humility. There is no denying the fact that there is no kind of interpersonal behavior at all, which, under given circumstances, could not have the most striking therapeutic effect. Often the most amazing cures are brought about, for example, by grandmothers when they let snails crawl over the warts on their grandchildren's hands. Also, the so-called placebos dispensed in hospitals, in the form of inactive but harmless pills, produce the same effects. Autogenous training too sometimes has a permanent curative effect, as does consolation from pastors appealing to the Bible, even in cases where all psychoanalysis has failed. The shocks caused by heavy strokes of fortune are known to have dissipated neurotic symptoms forever. Interpretations in the manner of Freud, Jung, Adler, Szondi, and analysis of Dasein can have a curative effect—though this is far from implying that they must always have this effect.

What is immediately visible in the case of all these psychotherapeutically effected cures, even if in wholly differentiated form, consists always in what Sigmund Freud described as follows: "We make available to him [the patient in the psychoanalytic physician-patient relationship] the arena in which he is permitted to unfold in almost total freedom." This is an amazing statement from the theoretical determinist Freud, who, as a psychoanalytic practician, expressly designates as the *"principal means"* in therapy the disclosure to the patient, in our interpersonal relationship with him, of a *more free* openness. Only this, he maintains, can give him the courage to appropriate all his given, immediate possibilities of experiencing and behaving and to live them out in a responsible interpersonal relationship with others. Psychoanalysis, in other words, is effective, and is so only to the extent it allows the patient to gain his essential human freedom vis-à-vis himself and the world, and his freedom to place himself fully at the service of what he encounters.

If we are wholly in earnest about this "principal means" of Freudian psychoanalysis, we achieve by its agency a psychic transformation of the patient, changing his basic attunement of anxiety and mistrust to one characterized by a more trusting relationship to the world around him.

Any psychoanalytic cure is, in our view, based on such a transformation of an existence.

The finest thing about psychoanalysis is the fact that a psychic transformation attainable by psychoanalysis that is not dogmatically distorted is, as a rule, more lasting and more thoroughgoing than the changes in underlying conditions that can be effected by the other therapies. To borrow an expression from Freud once again, this is what makes it shine like gold beside the duller copper of less noble psychotherapeutic procedures.

Part IV

SPECIAL
TECHNIQUES
AND
ISSUES

17

PSYCHOANOLTYIC PSYCHOTHERAPY

Sidney Tarachow
Aaron Stein

Psychoanalytic psychotherapy, or, perhaps more accurately, psychoanalytically oriented psychotherapy, is a widely used and very effective form of psychotherapy. Despite this, it is not a clearly defined entity, and the term is applied to many different forms of psychotherapy. We shall attempt here the following: to define this form of psychotherapy; to indicate its relationship to other forms of psychotherapy, particularly to psychoanalysis; to formulate theoretical principles upon which it can be based; and to delineate the technical procedures for carrying out this form of treatment.

The Psychoanalytic Theory of Psychotherapy

Basic psychoanalytic theory with its "convenient working concepts of a dynamic-genetic-structural-economic nature of mental functioning and of the disturbances that result in neurotic and psychotic behavior" has been

471

described elsewhere (Fenichel, 1945) and will not be elaborated on. However, a few basic points might be reviewed, utilizing for this purpose the excellent and succinct summaries of Colby (1951) and Sterba (1959).

According to the psychoanalytic view, the mind is conceived of as "an apparatus which attempts to deal with entering volumes of excitation in order to preserve the equilibrium of a rest state," which is considered essentially to be "a flux of energy changes within a limited range" (Colby, 1951, p. 6). The rest state is constantly disturbed by stimuli—and as perceived by the mind, these mental stimuli may be either external or internal. The features of the surrounding environment as perceived by the organism are external stimuli. The internal stimuli, which result from the biochemical energy changes within the body, are experienced as impulses—sexual and aggressive wishes in psychoanalytic terminology. As these stimuli impinge on the mind, the rest state is disturbed by increasing tension, and

> the mind seeks to discharge or bind this tension. . . . The young and growing mind learns, in integrating its internal needs with its environment, through thousands of reward-punishment experiences, to curb, moderate, channelize, displace and postpone its wishes. . . . More specifically, a wish (internal tension-producing stimulus) may be totally gratified (tension discharged), totally denied (tension bound), or both gratified and denied (partially discharged, partially bound). The binding process is thought of in terms of defenses. In topographic form, wish-impulses from the id are regulated by the defenses of the ego and superego (Colby, 1951, p. 6).

Normally, the relationship between wishes and defenses is stabilized harmoniously "so that tensions are successfully managed with a satisfactory preservation of a relative rest state." When this tension is not successfully bound or discharged, a neurotic conflict or illness results. As Sterba (1959) put it, "Neurotic illness occurs when the equilibrium of the repressed instinctual impulse is disturbed in favor of the repressed impulse." The latter breaks into consciousness but is still denied direct gratification and makes its appearance in an altered form as the neurotic symptom. Usually there is more than one conflict in a given neurosis; since the neurotic conflicts are unconscious, they exert a great influence on the patient's mental life.

Based on the above, in theory, the goal of psychotherapy is

> to produce a favorable change in the disturbed balance of a conflictual wish-defense system, thus allowing a fuller gratification of the wish or at least a more suitable compromise. Since we cannot, to any great extent, influence by psychological means the origin of biological processes per se (wish-impulse), in therapy we manage a wish-defense conflict by modifying

the defense or ego component. Ideally we would like solely to attenuate or eradicate a pathogenic defense, but in actual practice, we probably annul some defenses while reinforcing others, the latter aiding binding rather than discharging functions. With the return of a relative equilibrium in a wish-defense conflict, tension diminishes and the symptoms decrease or vanish (Sterba, 1959).

Put in somewhat less theoretical terms, "the purposes of treatment are, first of all, to give the patient relief from suffering," and then to enable him to live "in stable equilibrium with himself, his immediate objects" and the world around him (Tarachow, 1963). The manner in which this is, hope-fully, accomplished will now be defined and described.

Some Definitions and a Classification

Although it may be stressing the obvious, perhaps a brief definition of psychotherapy per se would be in order. As defined in *A Psychiatric Glossary* (1964), psychotherapy is "the generic name for any type of treatment of psychiatric illness which is based primarily upon verbal and nonverbal communication with the patient. . . ." A somewhat more complete definition of psychotherapy from the psychoanalytic point of view would be as follows: Psychotherapy is the treatment, based primarily on verbal (and non-verbal) communication through the establishment of a relationship between the patient and therapist, of a person (with a certain constitution) whose illness (symptoms, or behavior causes difficulty, pain, or suffering) is the result of genetically or developmentally determined unconscious conflicts, so that he shows in his behavior and relationships and attitudes the effect of the presence of emotional constellations from the past. This definition includes the psychoanalytic theory of the causation of mental illness and stresses that the treatment in psychotherapy is based upon verbal communication, which is facilitated by a relationship between the patient and the therapist.

The essence of the psychoanalytic view is that the symptoms of mental illness stem from the operation of unconscious conflicts that began during the early development of the individual. Two other concepts that are important in psychotherapy are derived from this basic one. The first of these relates to repression: It is the concept that the early childhood conflicts have become unconscious as the result of repression; in order for these conflicts to become conscious, the effects of the repression must be overcome in the treatment; and the way in which the effects of this repression are manifested in the treatment is called resistance. The second concept concerns the effect of the transference on the psychotherapy. Transference may be briefly defined here as "the unconscious attachment to others in the present of feelings and attitudes which were originally associated with important figures in one's early life" (*A Psychiatric Glossary*, 1964). Transference is a universal phenomenon and enters into all relationships, but it is especially important in the psychotherapeutic relationship between the patient and the therapist.

Freud (1914) has stated "Any psychotherapy that deals primarily with . . . transference and defenses (or resistance) is psychoanalytic." Whereas this statement covers the essential elements, it is necessary to indicate more specifically the manner in which resistance and transference are handled in the various types of psychotherapy. From the psychoanalytic point of view, the way in which the transference and resistance are dealt with in any form of psychotherapy defines the psychotherapy.

These considerations emphasize the two fundamental elements—transference and defenses (resistance)—that need to be dealt with in psychotherapy. Using these basic concepts, it is possible to suggest a classification for the various types of psychotherapy. In line with classifications suggested by others (Knight, 1952; Alexander, 1954; Robbins, 1956), a simple but useful type of classification of the psychotherapies would be as follows: psychoanalysis, psychoanalytic psychotherapy, and supportive psychotherapy. In accordance with the concepts noted above, this classification—psychoanalysis, psychoanalytic psychotherapy (also called exploratory or expressive or insight psychotherapy), and supportive or suppressive psychotherapy —lists these psychotherapies in order of decreasing intensity; or, in order of decreasing uncovering and analyzing of the transference and resistance, and, therefore, of the underlying unconscious infantile conflicts.

In terms of the two important elements of transference and resistance, the difference between these three types of psychotherapy would be related to the way in which the transference and resistance are handled in each form of therapy. Accordingly, psychoanalysis would be that form of psychotherapy in which conditions are set up to focus the transference as freely as possible upon the analyst in order that the transference and, especially, the transference as a resistance, can be uncovered, that is, made conscious and analyzed. Again, in analysis the patient's resistances (including the transference as a resistance) would also be exposed, made conscious, and then analyzed to the fullest possible extent. In psychoanalytic psychotherapy, while the transference exists, it would be permitted to remain uninterpreted as a resistance, to a greater or lesser extent, and the uncovering and analysis of other types of resistance would be attempted only partially and in accordance with the needs of the patient in the treatment situation. In supportive psychotherapy, again while the transference exists and is utilized, it remains largely uninterpreted and it is not exposed and analyzed as a resistance. The same thing is true of the patient's resistances in supportive psychotherapy. They may be uncovered and analyzed to some degree, but they are left unanalyzed and uninterpreted to a great extent and, again according to the needs of the patient in the treatment situation, the defenses may be strengthened or bolstered.

In the classification given above, and in discussing how two fundamental elements in psychotherapy—transference and resistance—are handled, we have essentially defined the three forms of psychotherapy. However, to stress the important factors involved, partially in differentiating psychoanalysis and psychoanalytic psychotherapy, somewhat more complete definitions will be given.

Many attempts have been made to define psychoanalysis and psychoanalytic psychotherapy; it will suffice to cite a few of these. Rangell (1954) gives a comprehensive definition of psychoanalysis as follows:

> Psychoanalysis is a method of therapy *whereby* conditions are brought about favorable for the development of a transference neurosis, in which the past is restored in the present, *in order that,* through a systematic interpretative attack on the resistances which oppose it, there occurs a resolution of that neurosis (transference *and* infantile) *to the end* of bringing about structural changes in the mental apparatus of the patient to make the latter capable of optimum adaptation to *life.*

In this definition Rangell emphasizes the important point that the analyst set up conditions for the development of the tranference neurosis in order to expose, or, more accurately, to make available for analysis the infantile conflict. Thus, the analyst by means of *systematic interpretation* deals with the resistances (including those stemming from the transference) as well as other defenses so as to make the unconscious conflicts conscious and susceptible to the influence of the mature ego. Implicit within this definition is the concept that the analyst's activity is limited to interpretation.

Gill (1954) in his definition of psychoanalysis emphasizes specifically the point that Rangell indicated only implicitly. He states: "Psychoanalysis is that technique which, employed by a *neutral* analyst, results in the development of a regressive transference neurosis and the ultimate resolution of this neurosis *by techniques of interpretation alone.*" (The important points here have been italicized by the present writers.) By "a neutral analyst" Gill means a therapist who does or says nothing in the treatment situation that will lend any reality to the transference distortions of the patient; Gill (1954) elaborates on this at some length. The most important point is clearly stated and is to the effect that in analysis the analyst limits his interventions to interpretations—and interpretations alone. As will be noted below, this is the crucial point in distinguishing psychoanalysis from psychoanalytic psychotherapy.

These definitions stress the important elements. In psychoanalysis, conditions involved are set up so as to foster the focusing of the regressive transference drives of the patient upon the analyst. As a result of the analyst maintaining a neutral attitude and by limiting his interventions almost entirely to interpretations, the patient develops a transference neurosis.

> The material produced by and the behavior of the patient [in the analysis] are rigidly determined by his fantasies [as they are focused on the analyst] and are relatively free of external influences. (In this fashion, the drives connected with the unconscious infantile conflict are reactivated, displaced onto the analyst and exposed and faithfully reproduced in the manifestations of the transference neurosis.) This is what makes analysis of the transference possible. The analyst can be certain he is dealing with phenomena determined from within the patient. . . .

In other words, he can be reasonably certain that the phenomena of the transference neurosis stem from the patient's unconscious conflicts and not from any act of the therapist in the treatment situation.

Tarachow (1963) underlined these points when he delineated psychoanalysis and psychotherapy. "Psychoanalysis would be that treatment in which the transference, repression, other ego defenses and resistances, are all freely subjected to analysis and resolved as far as may be required by the task of dealing with the infantile intrapsychic conflicts and derivative symptoms. . . ." An even simpler definition would be: "Psychoanalysis is that treatment which takes into account the transference as a resistance . . ."; and, one could add, deals with it by interpretation alone and interprets it as completely as possible.

In contrast to this, "psychotherapy is a selective, limited treatment in which a rearrangement rather than a resolution of these elements is aimed at. The transference, repression, and resistances are dealt with in such a way that stability is preserved while trying at the same time to effect whatever therapeutic goals are desirable or possible" (Tarachow, 1963).

This definition of psychotherapy in contrast to psychoanalysis is a simplification and perhaps an oversimplification of the essential differences between these two forms of treatment. Many writers have struggled with the task of distinguishing between the two—Alexander (1954), Rangell (1954), Gill (1954), Bibring (1954), and Stone (1954) to name just a few, and a similar effort has been made by several Panels of The American Psychoanalytic Association (1953, 1954, 1955). Most authors agree that in psychotherapy the therapist is more active, that is, interacts more with the patient. In helping the latter deal with affects and conflicts, he selects certain areas upon which to focus the therapy; he leaves certain resistances and defenses undisturbed. The goal of psychotherapy is to help the patient stabilize his "wish-defense" equilibrium; accordingly, the therapist does not attempt to expose and analyze many aspects of the unconscious infantile conflicts. The transference in psychotherapy is handled so as to avoid excessively regressive manifestations of this. Most important of all, certain aspects of the transference—and particularly the transference as resistance—are left uninterpreted and thus can be considered by the patient as real.

The Psychoanalytic Theory of the Relationship in Psychoanalytic Psychotherapy

There are two main elements to be considered in describing, from the psychoanalytic point of view, the theory of the therapeutic relationship in psychoanalytic psychotherapy. The first of these is the well-known therapeutic alliance. This will be described only briefly; it has been more thoroughly described elsewhere, as cited by Greenson (1965) in his review of the literature.

The therapeutic alliance refers to the phenomenon of the split in the patient's ego, which occurs during the process of psychotherapy, particularly psychoanalytic psychotherapy, and especially in psychoanalysis. While one part of the patient's ego becomes involved in the affects and fantasies that are concerned with the transference that focuses infantile unconscious drives upon the figure of the therapist, another part of the patient's ego, the mature, reasoning, observing part, remains detached and, as an observer, judges and evaluates the data that are brought out in the psychotherapy. This mature, reasoning, observing part of the patient's ego enters into an alliance with the therapist—the analyst, in the case of psychoanalysis—in order to carry out the functions of evaluating, observing, reasoning, judging, reality-testing, and so on, of the data produced in the psychotherapeutic session. Obviously, the therapeutic alliance in any form of psychotherapy, and particularly in analysis, is an essential part of the therapeutic process, and psychotherapy cannot occur without it. It is one of the tasks of the therapist to foster the development of the therapeutic alliance and to indicate its necessity for the psychotherapeutic work to the patient, a point that Greenson (1965) has recently emphasized.

The second main concept to be considered in describing the therapeutic relationship in psychoanalytic psychotherapy has been elaborated by one of us (Tarachow, 1962) and has been designated as the therapeutic barrier. The theoretical considerations underlying the concept of the therapeutic barrier will be summarized below.

In any form of psychotherapy, both therapist and patient are confronted with a basic problem, the problem of object need. "The task of setting each other aside as a real object may be regarded as the central problem in the theory of the treatment process" (Tarachow, 1963).

This basic primary object need has been described and discussed by several writers (Stone, 1961; Greenacre, 1954; and Szurek, 1958; among others). It occurs under all circumstances and has no specific relationship to "any particular infantile projection or any specific neurotic structure. The need, in this sense, to take another person as object is neither transference nor countertransference" (Tarachow, 1963).

Every patient regards the therapist as real, regards all the manifestations of the treatment situation as real, and strives to regard the therapist as a real object. The therapist, vis-à-vis the patient, strives to do exactly the same. He, too, wants to regard the patient as real and to respond to the patient as a real object. Thus both patient and therapist have "a basic urge to mutual acting-out" in terms of this object need (Tarachow, 1963).

The basic urge in any relationship between two individuals is the temptation to regress in the character of object relationship, to dissolve ego boundaries and fuse, that is, to restore the symbiotic relationship that initially occurred with the mother. "Every new advance into reality is met by resistance and an effort to re-create the past as it had been before. . . . Object relations arose at that unhappy moment when the symbiotic bond with mother was disrupted" (Ferenczi, 1926) (and represent the first painful recognition and adjustment to reality). In a somewhat paradoxical fashion the

object relationship which we take as a mark of reality adjustment are really designed to circumvent the painful condition of reality. . . . There are two primary techniques aimed at the restoration of the pre-traumatic, blissful symbiotic fusion (with the mother): one is identification, the other is object relationship. One is repair from the inside and the other repair from the outside, and both are forced upon us as unwelcome necessities. At an early point in development there is not much difference between the two processes. . . . All these well-known observations are repeated here simply to underscore the generic problem of the constant temptation to move closer to objects, to have object relationships, to abandon mature ego, differentiation for narcissistic and anaclitic relationships, the temptation to identification, and finally and basically for fusion (Freud, 1923).

The therapist as well as the patient has to struggle constantly against this array of temptations to come closer together, with consequent blurring of the ego boundaries between patient and psychotherapist (Margolin, 1953; Tarachow, 1963).

This constant primary object need is, as has been noted previously, neither transference nor countertransference. Its presence in both patient and therapist complicates and interferes with the therapeutic relationship unless it is recognized and dealt with appropriately. Any successful therapeutic venture requires the intimate, real, and close working together of two minds—the therapeutic alliance. For this to develop, both the patient and the therapist must undertake, and be capable of, controlled ego splitting in the service of the treatment (Gill, 1954). Object relationships between the patient and the therapist would interfere with this. Consequently, it is necessary for the patient and the therapist to set up a barrier against the need for object relationship.

The matter is further complicated because certain aspects of the treatment relationship are real. This is true in any form of treatment, including psychoanalysis. The patient learns real things about the therapist both in and out of the office, and the therapist behaves in a real and human way toward the patient (Glover, 1955). The reality of certain aspects of the treatment relationship must be understood by the therapist, and if they are properly handled by the therapist, they constitute a necessary and useful part of the treatment (Greenacre, 1954; Stone, 1954; Gill, 1954). Among other things, it leads to identification with the reality aspects of the therapist, correcting transference distortions, and it supplies motivation for the necessary therapeutic work such as transference deprivation and the ego splitting of the therapeutic alliance (Tarachow, 1963). Finally, as has been pointed out by Menaker (1942) and Garner (1961), the situation on the treatment necessitates, even in analysis, the therapist making certain demands —talking, free association, and so on—to which the patient submits; the relationship that is established in this way is a sadomasochistic one.

How is a therapeutic situation created out of this real relationship between the two parties involved? It is created by an act of the therapist. The therapist imposes a barrier to reality. We shall term it the *therapeutic barrier*. The imposition of this barrier creates a therapeutic task for both therapist and patient. The real situation is transformed into an as-if situation demanding attention and comprehension. The act of the therapist which brings about this transformation is interpretation (Tarachow, 1963).

The degree of the barrier and the task imposed upon the patient may vary from patient to patient and from time to time, depending upon the clinical needs at the moment and the long-term goals of the treatment effort. At one end of the scale is the rigorous psychoanalytic technique, which puts the greatest demands on both. At the other end of the scale the entire relationship may be accepted as real, and the therapist may designedly enter all the phenomenology of the patient as a real object. This may be permitted to occur in some aspects of the treatment of psychoses, notably schizophrenia, and in the treatment of young and certain acting-out psychopaths.

Interpretation interferes with reality and with the acting out of the unconscious fantasy. This increases the pressure of the unconscious fantasy and brings it forward into free association, or at least into progressive conflict with the defensive forces that can be analyzed.

In psychoanalysis the same task is imposed on the therapist as on the patient. That is, to interpose a barrier to using each other as objects. In other forms of treatment the degree of deprivation for patient and therapist and the relinquishing of object need for each other vary. In some cases the therapist may permit the patient a high degree of reality in the latter's relation to the therapist. For the therapist, this might still only be a matter of technique and still it will retain the as-if character of the patient.

The therapeutic task for the therapist is his own struggle with his need for objects amidst a self-imposed therapeutic barrier. The problem of spontaneous and unplanned acts of the analyst arises from this consideration. The temptation to breach the barrier still assails the therapist at all times. If the patient pleads for help, the therapist wants to extend himself. If the patient is hostile, the therapist wants to fight; if the patient is unhappy the therapist wants to console him; if the patient is in need the therapist wants to give . . . the principal temptation is to play the role . . . for these reasons it is necessary for the therapist to observe himself constantly for any alteration in his behavior toward the patient (Glover, 1955).

When such alteration in behavior occurs the therapist is joined in collusion with the patient "in taking some aspect of the patient's behavior as real and has responded to it in some real, non-therapeutic way" (Tarachow, 1963).

These statements indicate certain aspects of the therapeutic barrier. Its operation in other aspects of treatment may be summarized here. By his interpretations, the therapist deprives the patient of the gratification of the object relationship in the treatment. This facilitates the treatment process, but imposes a real loss and disappointment on the patient. "The therapeutic task can be imposed only by means of a disappointment and by transformation of a real into an as-if relationship. We have thinking in place of reality (the reality of an object relationship); the uninterpreted relationship is real . . ." (Tarachow, 1963). As this process is repeated, especially in analysis, the patient works through his problems by reliving them in an as-if manner until they have been understood, integrated, and are no longer pathogenic (Kardos and Peto, 1956; Greenacre, 1959). In this way, the therapeutic barrier set up by the interpretations of the therapist requires the patient to relinquish infantile objects, but, by means of the therapeutic alliance, he is offered an adult real object in its place—the sympathetic therapist. Tarachow (1965) has commented on these paradoxical and antitheoretical aspects of the therapeutic process.

In psychoanalysis this barrier is strongest and the resultant frustration is most intense; the energy from this provides the dynamic force for the treatment. In analysis although the patient, from the beginning, sees the analyst as an object for gratification of unconscious infantile impulses, the analyst imposes a therapeutic barrier to this gratification, slowly but steadily denying this gratification to the patient and frustrating him in this fashion. The way in which the analyst accomplishes this is by treating all the transference manifestations in the analytic situation as unreal and by interpreting them accordingly.

In psychoanalytic psychotherapy this therapeutic barrier results in frustrations that are less stringent and less intense than in psychoanalysis. Those parts of the transference that are uninterpreted in psychoanalytic psychotherapy are seen by the patient as real and provide a certain amount of gratification—and thereby lessen the frustrations—in the therapeutic relationship. In supportive psychotherapy the transference is largely uninterpreted, and the various aspects of it that become manifest in the treatment situation are considered by the patient as real, with consequent gratification and a decrease in the degree of frustration in the therapeutic situation.

Indications for Psychoanalytic Psychotherapy

The indications for psychoanalysis are well known and need not be gone into in any great detail, since they have been thoroughly described by others (Fenichel, 1945; Gill, 1954; Stone, 1954). For our purpose the indications for psychoanalysis may be briefly summarized as follows: In patients with relatively intact personalities and ego strength in whom unconscious conflicts have led to the development of neurotic symptoms or mild to moderately severe characterological disturbances, psychoanalysis is indicated as the treatment of choice. In psychoanalysis, conditions are set up to focus upon the analyst transference manifestations as the object of an intense regressive transference neurosis so as to expose, that is, make conscious and thereby make available for analysis, the patient's underlying unconscious childhood conflicts. In order to be treated by analysis the patient's personality and ego strength must be sufficiently intact to permit the regressive changes leading to the transference neurosis and to permit the splitting of the ego that would make possible therapeutic alliance; his personality must be sufficiently intact so that he can withstand the stresses and strains of the regressive transference neurosis and the frustration imposed by the therapeutic barrier. These are the considerations that led Freud to indicate that only those patients who can develop transference in the sense of the transference neurosis (i.e., where the libidinal cathexes are flexible enough to be displaced or projected), and who are amenable to the analytic process or, as he calls it, "educatable," are suitable for analysis. Similarly, he indicated that only certain conditions based upon unconscious conflicts, namely, the "transference neuroses," are suitable for psychoanalysis. Where the nature of the underlying conflicts and the rigidity of the patient's personality tend too much toward the narcissistic side (i.e., the libidinal cathexes are too rigidly focused on the self), Freud felt that these patients with narcissistic neuroses, he called them, were not suitable for the ordinary type of psychoanalysis. More recently, work with patients who have narcissistic neuroses can be conducted along analytic lines, but modifications of the regular analytic technique are required (Stone, 1954; Anna Freud, 1954; Gill, 1954).

The indications for psychoanalytic psychotherapy, in contrast to those for psychoanalysis, can now be fairly clearly defined. Psychoanalytic psychotherapy would be utilized for patients whose underlying unconscious conflicts are of the nature that would tend toward the narcissistic side and whose ego strength and personality structure have undergone considerable deformation or weakening. Psychoanalytic psychotherapy would be used to uncover some of the underlying unconscious conflicts but without focusing the intense transference neurosis upon the therapist. Consequently, the patient would have to undergo less regressive change and would not be subjected to the same intense frustration of the patient in analysis. Obviously, the categories of patients that would fit into this group would be those with mixed psychiatric disorders: patients with neurotic symptoms together with some fairly severe characterological disturbance, and/or borderline conditions with increased narcissistic tendencies and considerable impairment of reality-testing. This includes a large number of the type of patients seen today, and there is general agreement (Gill, 1954; Stone, 1954; Robbins, 1956) that this kind of patient is best treated by exploratory or psychoanalytic psychotherapy.

In contrast to the above two groups of patients, patients who require supportive psychotherapy would be those whose ego strength and personality structure have been very considerably distorted and weakened and whose underlying unconscious conflicts tended toward the more primitive and narcissistic type. For this type of patient, intense regressive manifestations would be too threatening and too disturbing. While the transference is utilized, conditions are set up so as not to focus it in too regressive a fashion upon the therapist. The focus is on the strengthening of defenses and increased reality-testing, with little or no uncovering of unconscious childhood conflicts. The patients who fall into this group would be psychotics, particularly psychotics in remission, borderline cases with severe characterological disturbances and other severe symptoms, and patients with severe narcissistic tendencies (Wolman, 1966).

Structuring the Psychotherapeutic Relationship

Once the decision has been made, based upon the diagnostic evaluation of the patient and his problems, to use psychoanalytically oriented psychotherapy in the treatment, the way in which the arrangements of the treatment are set up are of considerable importance. They will have definite effects upon the transference, the way in which defenses are utilized and resistances manifested in the treatment, and in the way in which material is produced or not produced. Tarachow (1963), Stone (1954), and particularly Greenacre (1954) emphasize this.

The points involved can be summarized as follows. First, the most obvious point is to indicate clearly to the patient that he needs treatment and the particular type of treatment that is being recommended. This must be done carefully, and the patient must be given an opportunity to refuse to accept the treatment. At times the therapist will find it necessary to refuse to take a patient into treatment, and here again the way in which this is handled is important. Refusing to take a patient into treatment must be done in such a fashion so as not to further traumatize the patient or disturb any existing defenses.

In recommending psychoanalytic psychotherapy for a patient, it is important to indicate clearly to him the limitations of this form of treatment. At the present time, many patients have misconceptions about any kind of psychotherapy, all of which they call analysis, and they often have misconceptions about how the treatment works and what can be accomplished with it. The usual magic expectation held by the patient is that all he has to do is come and talk and soon, in some great blinding flash, complete insight will occur, and then all his difficulties will be resolved without any further effort being required of the patient. This is a very common misconception or fantasy concerning treatment. Accordingly, in explaining to the patient the need for this particular type of treatment, some statement should be made to indicate to him that it involves a discussion of his difficulties with a view to helping him understand some of the underlying factors involved and helping him help himself to overcome the symptoms and other difficulties involved. This at once defines the therapeutic nature of the treatment relationship and clarifies the roles of both the patient and the therapist. This also helps the patient to enter into the therapeutic alliance (Greenson, 1965).

Time and place arrangements are also important, if obvious, considerations. The frequency with which a patient is seen will depend upon the severity of the symptoms, and so on, but the danger of fostering a regressive relationship with the therapist must also be taken into account. This will determine how frequently a patient is seen; the less frequently a patient is seen the less danger there is of fostering a regressive dependent relationship. Greenacre (1954) has pointed out that the spacing of the interviews is also important. Interviews that are equally spaced apart supply support. Those which are arranged closer together provide the opportunity for more intensive work in the psychotherapy.

In regard to space arrangements, these again might seem obvious, but it is important at the beginning of the treatment to indicate clearly to the patient what the physical arrangements of the therapist's office are, including closets, bathrooms, waiting rooms, and so on. All of these, when clearly dealt with at the beginning of the treatment, provide reality factors in the treatment and help stabilize the patient's reactions to the treatment situation. The question of whether a patient should sit up facing the therapist or lie down on the couch is important here. Obviously, lying down on the couch has certain meanings to certain patients. Again, the decision will be based upon what is most useful to the patient, and a certain flexibility should be permitted to the patient, since with some patients, even those treated by psychoanalytic psychotherapy, it is easier for them to verbalize, particularly aggressive material, when they are not facing the therapist.

Another important series of considerations relate to what is said to the patient at the beginning of the treatment as regards the duration of the treatment and the outcome. Particularly with patients in whom the therapist recognizes the need to limit the treatment in various ways, it might be useful to indicate that the treatment will have a certain duration, six months or a year, or longer. This has its dangers, too, or may cause difficulties, but it does introduce a sometimes necessary thought into the patient's concept of the treatment, namely, that it will not go on indefinitely, that it will end at a certain time, and that it will be limited to certain objectives. All of this may cause certain reactions in the patient, and a statement to this effect may not be suitable for all patients but may be very useful and necessary with some. In contrast to psychoanalysis, a realistic indication that the treatment is limited and will end at a certain time is a useful and often very necessary factor in undertaking psychoanalytic psychotherapy.

The Principles of Psychoanalytic Psychotherapy

In accordance with the psychoanalytic theory, psychic malfunctioning or illness occurs when failure of the wish-defense system permits the operation of unconscious conflicts stemming from the childhood of the patient to produce tensions that interfere with present-day integration and functioning and lead to symptoms. By means of repression and the development of other defenses—"barriers to the disorderly expression of infantile and archaic wishes and drives"—the tensions stemming from these childhood conflicts are kept under control until the failure of the defenses results in symptoms. As already noted, a neurosis is a further attempt—a compromise between wish and defense—to control these primitive impulses.

We might also say that the total personality is a conglomeration of wish and defense. To speak in local, clinical terms, we might say that the obsessional neurosis is a barrier to and often a disguised gratification of archaic

anality or anal sadism; depression is a barrier to, and in fantasy, the gratification of cannibalistic love-murder; hysteria is the barrier to and also the
symbolic gratification of incestuous sexual wishes (Tarachow, 1963).

Because of the operation of the transference, during the course of any
type of psychotherapy, these unconscious infantile archaic wishes and drives
focus upon the therapist as an object for possible gratification. The characteristic defenses associated with these drives also become apparent in the
manifestations of the transference. The resistance the patient manifests in
the treatment results from the operation of these defenses and must be
overcome in order to expose the unconscious conflicts gradually.

A primary task in the psychotherapeutic endeavor is the existence of the
need for both the patient and therapist for each other as objects. "The task
of setting aside the other as the real object I would regard as the central
problem in the theory of the treatment process" (Tarachow, 1963). Putting this another way, it might be stated that in psychoanalytically oriented
psychotherapy, the major problem in dealing with the transference and
resistance to the treatment occurs in relationship to the need for both
therapist and patient for each other as real objects and that the kind of
therapy and its effectiveness will be related to the way in which the
therapist and the patient go about the task of setting aside each other as
real objects.

Just as the various types of psychotherapy can be defined in terms of
how the transference as a resistance and the resistance is exposed and dealt
with, a similar statement can be made to the effect that the various types of
psychotherapy are concerned with to what extent the therapist imposes,
upon himself and upon the patient, the task of setting each other aside as
real objects. Stated in this way, psychoanalysis, the most intensive form
of therapy, would constitute a type of treatment in which, at the very
beginning, the therapist's function is to help the patient gradually to give
up the hope of gratification from the therapist as an object, even while
helping the patient focus upon the analyst as a possible source of real object
gratification. In other types of psychotherapy, this deprivation and the
frustration of setting aside the therapist as a real object is imposed to a
less extreme degree.

In supportive psychotherapy, with psychotic or severely decompensated
patients, the least amount of frustration and deprivation of the patient in
terms of relinquishing the therapist as a source of real object gratification
is imposed upon the patient.

The principles and techniques employed in psychotherapy, as distinguished from psychoanalysis, have been described by many writers. The setting of limited goals in the sense of selecting a few dynamic issues upon which the psychotherapy is focused is emphasized (Stone, 1951, 1954; Knight, 1952; Gill, 1954; Bibring, 1954; etc.). Limiting the duration of the treatment is suggested by some (Coleman, 1949; Berliner, 1941; Stone, 1951; Alexander, 1954). It is repeatedly stated that the psychotherapy should focus upon "current material" and deal largely with the reality of daily events in the patient's life (Coleman, 1949; Stone, 1954; Knight, 1952).

One major principle upon which all authors agree is the manner in which defenses are handled in psychotherapy. Important and necessary defenses are left undisturbed; other defenses are strengthened in various ways. Resistance, therefore, is bypassed and not interpreted except in a limited fashion as necessitated by the psychotherapy (Stone, 1954; Gill, 1954; Rangell, 1954; Bibring, 1954; etc.).

Another major principle of psychotherapy in which most writers concur relates to the transference. They all stress that the conditions set up in the psychotherapy should be maintained in such a fashion as to avoid the development of excessively regressive transference manifestations. As has been noted previously, this prevents the development of a full-blown transference neurosis and is one of the major differences between psychotherapy and psychoanalysis (Rangell, 1954; Gill, 1954; Stone, 1954). Another important point in connection with the transference in psychotherapy is that many writers recommend some gratification of this in the sense of the therapist entering into the patient's life as a real person (Knight, 1952; Reider, 1955; Stone, 1954).

In addition to these principles of psychotherapy, specific techniques are suggested by many writers (Glover, 1931; Knight, 1952; Stone, 1951, 1954; Gill, 1951, 1954; Bibring, 1954; Reider, 1955; etc.). Glover (1931), for instance, lists: (1) facilitating repression by turning away from the problem; (2) the use of suggestion, which he characterizes as offering the patient transferred obsessional symptoms; and (3) partial truth and suggestion, and by supplying the patient with a benevolent phobia as a new symptom. Reider (1955) suggests helping the patient stabilize a set of projections, such as blaming the parents. Bibring (1954) distinguishes five different groups of basic therapeutic techniques: (1) suggestive, (2) abreactive, (3) manipulative, (4) clarifying, and (5) interpretive. The last is most characteristic of psychoanalysis and is used in a limited fashion in psychotherapy. Gill (1954) stresses the activity of the therapist in psychotherapy, in the sense of interaction with the patient, and the use of suggestion by the therapist in relation to the uninterpreted transference. Other psychotherapeutic techniques that are described are related to the efforts of the therapist in helping the patient establish controls, in strengthening the super ego where indicated, and in employing various measures to help strengthen ego functioning.

Despite the many and varied psychotherapeutic maneuvers indicated from this incomplete review of the literature, it is possible to suggest some psychoanalytic concepts underlying all of these. The theoretical considerations involved have been noted above, particularly those concerned with the therapeutic barrier.

The psychoanalytic concepts that are the basis for psychotherapy can be stated (Tarachow, 1963) as:

> three overriding principles of psychotherapy. Within these three principles any and all psychotherapeutic techniques should be comprehensible. . . . Any given technique may have the qualities of one or all of these three measures. . . . The following are the three measures:
> 1. Supply the infantile object in reality, i.e., the unanalyzed transference.
> 2. Supply displacements, i.e., new symptoms and/or resistances.
> 3. Supply stability, i.e., ego or superego building, or education or reality events.

Supplying the Infantile Object in Reality

This principle refers to "supplying an object in reality" for the patient and results largely from the unanalyzed (i.e., the uninterpreted) transference.

This principle of psychotherapy constitutes a major difference from psychoanalysis. This difference between psychoanalysis and psychotherapy in terms of object relationships and loneliness has been described previously (Tarachow, 1962, 1963). In psychoanalysis the analyst rejects the patient as an object and helps the patient to learn to reject the therapist as an object; the problems arising from object need are resolved by interpretation, and by interpretation alone (Tarachow, 1963; Stone, 1954; Rangell, 1954; Gill, 1954). In psychotherapy the patient and the therapist retain each other as objects in varying degrees because the therapist permits certain aspects of the transference to remain uninterpreted. Accordingly, patient and therapist have entered into each other's lives as real, serving as infantile, objects, to each other.

The same distinction between analysis and psychotherapy is made by Nunberg (1951) who states: "The psychoanalyst and the non-psychoanalyst differ in their treatment of this phenomenon (transference) in that the former treats the transference symptoms as illusions while the latter takes them at face value, i.e., as realities."

In psychotherapy, by his interacting with the patient (Gill, 1954) and allowing himself to be used by the patient as an object, the therapist actually intrudes into the life and personality of the patient and remains there. In effect, he offers himself for the creation of a new symptom. In psychoanalysis, the emphasis of the treatment is upon the analysis and the interpretation of the transference (which is also a new symptom) as a resistance. By contrast, in psychotherapy, the transference manifestations are regarded as a means by which the patient is helped toward better health, in the sense of maintaining his continued psychic functioning. The therapist lets the patient use him, via the transference manifestations, as a "building block in the ofttimes jerry-built structure of defenses the patient has erected. In analysis, this is (hopefully) resolved; in psychotherapy this is welcomed. What is resistance in analysis is a necessary stabilizing factor introduced into the patient's mental economy in psychotherapy" (Tarachow, 1963).

Another way of putting this follows: By leaving the transference uninterpreted and thereby supplying the patient's infantile needs by offering himself in varying degrees as an object, the therapist in psychoanalytic psychotherapy not only provides gratification (and thereby lessens the strain on the patient in the therapeutic processes by limiting the frustration), but he also permits the patient to use the uninterpreted transference reaction to the therapist as a stabilizing factor to rebuild defenses and strengthen ego functioning. This is in contrast to psychoanalysis; in analytic psychotherapy the therapist lets himself be used by the patient in various ways as a real object. This can range from offering sympathy and some degree of comfort by means of medication or some instruction or by imposing disciplinary controls as with hospitalized patients. The real object need of the patient can also be supplied in other ways as in making himself available at all times to the patient, in the frequency of the visits, by the therapist's interest and acceptance of reality events in the patient's life as real, by discussing with the patient how to deal with reality events, by educating him in terms of his understanding of his problems, and so on. The therapist in psychoanalytic psychotherapy is offering himself as a real object—a combination of doctor, parent, teacher—and thus supplying some of the patient's infantile needs for gratification from an object (Stone, 1954; Gill, 1954).

This has been done in a more direct way by various psychotherapists (Alexander, 1953; Rosen, 1947). If this is done in a controlled way in the therapeutic relationship with the therapist providing the gratifications as a therapist, rather than as a transference figure, and in the interests of the treatment, it can help the patient stabilize his mental functioning. Even when the therapist must act as a teacher or as an authority figure, or as someone who indicates to the patient the need for certain controls and disciplines, thereby taking a real place in the patient's life, this can have therapeutic usefulness in lessening tensions through partial discharge and in promoting strengthened ego functioning (Gill, 1954; Stone, 1951). More details about the specific techniques involved will be discussed later.

Supplying Displacements

Turning to the second of the principles of psychoanalytic psychotherapy, we shall consider what is meant by supplying displacements, that is, the development of new symptoms and/or resistance. Another way of expressing this as has been already indicated; the function of displacement in psychotherapy is to preserve or strengthen the defenses.

The concept of supplying displacements includes an entire array of manoeuvres in which the therapist selects the more ego-syntonic aspects of a problem and interprets only these, leaving undisturbed the more troublesome factors. In pathological menages, the heterosexual aspects might be dealt with. In pathological dependency relationships the libidinal aspects might be tolerable but not the hatred or murderous feelings. In working with dreams the manifest content or the immediate reality solving-problem aspects might be utilized. In passive-aggressive characters the aggressions might be worked with but the passivity may be gratified in the unanalyzed transference relationship (Tarachow, 1963).

An important aspect of this is for the therapist to understand that he has taken a limited approach. This may be done for a variety of reasons. The patient might not be able to tolerate his infantile or even his preconscious thoughts or feelings. Various factors in the treatment situation, the frequency of visits, and also the state of the patient's defenses and the danger of decompensation may also necessitate the therapist limiting his psychotherapeutic intervention to one aspect or one area. . . . It is correct psychotherapeutic technique to limit the scope of one's interpretation. The therapist should be aware that he is bypassing troublesome areas which might lead to symptoms or relapse later on; however, sometimes they do not (Gill, 1954; Stone, 1951).

Other ways of maintaining the patient's defenses and supplying displacement are concerned with the nature of interpretations used in psychotherapy. An important technique here is the use of "inexact" interpretation (Glover, 1931), in contrast to an incomplete one.

An inexact interpretation is offered as a definitive meaning of a certain arrangement of material, a meaning which, in the opinion of the therapist, actually falls short of the unconscious or infantile truth. The analyst has judged that the complete truth would be dangerous and intolerable to his patient. The patient seizes the inexact meaning eagerly because it helps him to continue to repress the truth; he can now turn his back on the truth with a newly-offered belief; in effect, he forms a new symptom. In a sense the patient has been offered a benevolent phobia and he grasps it eagerly. The real focus of the problem remains repressed and is displaced onto the given interpretation. This new symptom, in the displacement, is psychotherapeutic cure. . . . This type of psychotherapeutic intervention is on the side of defense (Tarachow, 1963).

More specifically, the use of displacements can be classified under four headings, as follows:

(1) *Displacement onto the transference; it is completely interpreted or not at all.* This has been discussed above in relation to supplying the infantile or reality object. As a result of this, and in addition, the uninterpreted transference enables the patient to displace onto the therapist the troublesome attitudes that belonged to figures in his early life. The therapist lets himself be used as a good parent or good teacher, and the gratifications thus received by the patient help him deal with his tensions and get better. This can be true even if negative transference attitudes are displaced onto the therapist; for example, the patient gets better to spite the therapist. Fenichel (1945) and Tarachow (1963) discuss this type of transference displacement and "cure" at some length.

(2) *Displacement in the benign phobic sense,* as described by Glover.

(3) *Displacement by projection.* Here the therapist accepts and goes along with the patient in blaming the environment and specific people in the environment, such as the parents. In this fashion, the intrapsychic conflicts that developed in relation to these outside factors is ignored or neglected. In effect, the patient is helped to establish a benign psychotherapeutic paranoia.

(4) *Displacement by introjection.* The therapist goes along with and helps

the patient blame something within his body. The patient is permitted to blame or attack his introjected objects, and the therapist goes along with the patient in regarding those somatic symptoms as real, and not as derivatives of his unconscious intrapsychic conflicts.

From the above, it can be seen that in supplying displacements, substitutes are offered for presenting symptoms. In the first one, an infantile object is supplied as a new symptom. In the second, a benign phobia is offered as another new symptom. In the third and fourth types of displacement, a benign delusion is offered in place of the presenting symptom. The cost of these displacements is the sacrifice of the knowledge of the truth; the reward is the restoration of functioning stability for the patient.

Supplying Stability

This third and last principle of psychotherapy—supplying stability—can be accomplished through the utilization of a number of factors. In general, like the other two principles of psychotherapy, supplying stability also operates in support of the defensive structures of the patient. As noted above, this is accomplished by ignoring certain aspects of unconscious conflicts, by leaving undisturbed various important defenses, and, in addition, by strengthening, aiding, and abetting certain other defenses.

Stability is also supplied by providing ego support. This can help the patient to validate the correctness of some of his perceptions and thinking, and, by encouraging these, providing narcissistic support for the patient. Participation by the therapist in a reality discussion of real events also provides ego support. Education and information also support and strengthen the patient's ego by enlarging its scope. Helping a weak ego in its struggle with a strong superego or against the strength of certain id impulse, also supplies stability.

Strengthening the superego in patients who are buffeted by strong impulses that lead to harmful behavior is another way in which the therapist can help the patient achieve stability in his psychic functioning. This must be done carefully and in the context of the therapy.

Finally, helping the patient become aware of reality and guiding him toward differentiating it from his inner distortions help to stabilize the psychic functioning of the patient. This type of "reality-testing" is done in a more or less limited way in psychotherapy as compared with psychoanalysis; carefully done, it can have very beneficial results, despite its limited nature.

The Techniques of Psychoanalytic Psychotherapy

In discussing the three principles of psychotherapy—supplying the infantile object, supplying displacements, supplying stability—some indications of the techniques used in accomplishing those aims were given. It may be useful to group these techniques under several headings and give a more detailed description of them.

The Attitude of the Therapist

Obviously, the attitude of the therapist is of basic importance in any form of psychotherapy. In psychoanalysis, the *neutral* attitude of the analyst is a basic dynamic factor in the treatment; it affects the transference and aids in the establishment of the necessary transference neurosis (Rangell, 1954; Gill, 1954; Stone, 1951, 1954; etc.).

In psychoanalytic psychotherapy the attitude of the therapist is more complicated because of the fact that he is more active than in psychoanalysis, that is, he interacts more with the patient, and, because of this and by virtue of the uninterpreted transference, he is more of a real figure. Also, since transference attitudes are not interpreted as completely as in analysis, the attitude of the therapist must be even more carefully maintained in psychotherapy than in psychoanalysis.

It is generally agreed that the most helpful attitude that needs to be maintained by the therapist in psychotherapy is one of calmness, continued interest, and sympathetic and understanding helpfulness. These necessary aspects of the therapist's attitude in psychotherapy are described by virtually every writer on the subject.

The calm, interested, helpful attitude of the therapist in psychotherapy differs from the neutral attitude of the analyst in psychoanalysis, a point emphasized by Gill (1954) and Stone (1951). It differs also from the manipulative and role-playing attitude advocated by certain workers, notably Alexander (1954). Paradoxically, it is present in the basic relationship in psychoanalysis, despite the neutral attitude of the analyst; this has been noted and commented upon by several authors, particularly Tarachow (1963).

This attitude—calm, interested, helpful—on the part of the therapist in psychotherapy has definite dynamic effects on the treatment and the transference. It provides support for the patient in dealing with his tensions. It often sustains the patient's contact with objects and with reality. It provides necessary gratification in the therapeutic relationship, as has been indicated previously. It provides the incentive and reward of a benign relationship in the therapy that enables the patient to undertake the tasks the treatment imposes upon him. It helps him somewhat to correct his infantile distorted views of object relationships, and it provides a model for identification with the therapist.

Conducting the Psychotherapy

Some aspects of the way in which psychoanalytic psychotherapy is conducted, in contrast to analytic sessions, have been mentioned in the section on structuring the psychotherapy. These related to having the patient sit up or lie down and to the frequency of visits.

At this point, it is important to mention that psychotherapeutic sessions are, in contrast to analysis, actively guided by the therapist. Most writers, and especially Stone (1951) and Tarachow (1963), emphasize this. It is necessary for the therapist to guide the patient in psychotherapeutic sessions so as to focus on certain kinds of material and to avoid others. Also, in this way the therapist helps the patient continue talking, since in psychotherapy resistance is often not interpreted. The therapist encourages the patient to speak as freely and as spontaneously as possible. In doing so, he may need to be fairly active—by asking questions, helping the patient find ways of expressing ideas and even affects.

The therapist may need to utilize various devices to relieve the patient's tensions, either in the therapeutic sessions or outside of them. Again, this is in direct contrast to psychoanalysis. He may provide minor gratifications, such as mild praise or encouragement. He may make himself available for telephone contact. He may help the patient deal with certain reality situations by counseling delay until the matter can be discussed further. In the sessions, he may let certain topics be dropped or bypassed to relieve increasing anxiety in the patient. He may tactfully need to set limits to, or in some way alter, regressive transference tendencies in the patient—undue familiarity, shaking hands unnecessarily, buying gifts, and the like—although at times he will go along with these.

Finally, to mention an obvious but important point, the chief aim of the therapist in psychotherapy is to have the patient talk as freely as possible about his feelings and ideas as they come up in connection with his difficulties. The dynamic effects of speech in treatment are well known. Speaking provides a controlled way of providing release for inner tensions. Verbalization—the need to convey affects and ideas into the spoken word—helps convert the primary process way of thinking about inner tensions into secondary process, so that these are available for evaluation and control by the ego.

Regression, Resistance, and Defenses

The way in which resistance and defenses are handled in psychotherapy in contrast to psychoanalysis has been discussed in some detail. A few comments may be in order at this point to emphasize certain technical points.

First, regressive manifestations may appear in psychotherapy as a result of a decompensation of the patient's defenses or as a result of the transference. Special emergency measures for dealing with a decompensating patient, such as hospitalization or medication, may be required and should be employed where indicated. In a patient in whom the decompensation of the defenses is not too aggravated, the therapist may need to tolerate the regressive tendencies in the therapy until such a time as he can confront the patient with them and then slowly and carefully thrust the therapeutic task of recognizing and dealing with them upon the patient. The task of tolerating the patient's regressive manifestations in the treatment places a heavy burden upon the therapist; Tarachow (1963) and Stone (1954) have commented upon this at length. If the therapist can tolerate this, he can observe and learn to know the characteristic style of the patient and the characteristic defenses he utilizes as they are manifested in the regressive attitudes of the patient.

Where the regressive attitudes of the patient stem from the transference, the therapist should check his own handling of this and often he will be able to see and correct his errors in handling the transference (Tarachow, 1963; Glover, 1955). This is possible but somewhat more difficult than in analysis because in psychotherapy the transference, particularly the transference as a resistance, is not interpreted as fully as in analysis. As noted before, the uninterpreted transference in psychotherapy leads to a real object relationship; this may be used by the therapist to encourage the patient to control and use some regressive manifestations.

Coming now to defenses, we have discussed above one of the principles involved in maintaining these. This is the supplying of displacements and the selective focusing on only a part of the patient's problems.

Some examples may be useful here. In the case of a patient with a powerful insoluble latent homosexual problem, any problems that arise in connection with women—with his wife if he is married, or with others if he is not—would be taken at face value, as heterosexual problems.

> Interpretations would be offered in a heterosexual context. Relationships to men would be dealt with not in terms of homosexual implications but preferably in terms of the aggressive and rivalrous facets. . . . The latent problem would remain untouched; the defenses would be permitted to remain intact by taking them at face value. . . . This means, of course, not tampering with any of the transference attitudes derived from the latent homosexuality (Tarachow, 1963).

Other examples may be cited to illustrate the necessity for dealing with only half the problem and leaving the defenses intact for the other half. In the case of the patient who is pathologically dependent upon another person—a parent or a marital partner—the therapist may help the patient work through the vicissitudes of the dependency without going into the destructive side of the relationship. A patient, a young man with a great deal of passivity, presents himself with a struggle against domination by a woman and offers many complaints about her cruelty. Here it would be important to understand that the patient's passivity is a defense against his own sadistic sexual aggressions against the woman. This defense must be dealt with carefully and preserved as much as necessary while the patient is carefully and slowly helped to face his own aggression. In the case of a borderline patient, a woman with almost delusional hypochondriacal concerns that helped control excessive sexual sadistic aggression, the defense of the hypochondriacal concerns was left relatively intact by helping her regard it as the necessary price she had to pay in order to carry out and achieve some success in her competitive theatrical and literary endeavors.

Again, the important point is that care needs to be exercised in selecting which aspect of a problem is to be dealt with in the psychotherapy. Defenses should be left intact or disturbed as little as possible. Ego-syntonic feelings should be buttressed even though they may be defenses against infantile wishes or conflicts.

Interpretations in Psychoanalytic Psychotherapy

As has been pointed out, the use of interpretation differs in psychotherapy as compared with psychoanalysis. In psychoanalysis, interpretation and interpretation alone is used in dealing with transference and resistance. In psychotherapy, greater or lesser areas of resistance remain uninterpreted or only partially interpreted.

Despite these limitations, interpretation of various kinds are an important, necessary part of the treatment in psychoanalytic psychotherapy. One important type of interpretation, the inexact interpretation of Glover (1931), was described above, and its usefulness in supplying displacement and maintaining necessary defenses was emphasized.

An interpretation is "the term applied to those explanations, given to the patient by the analyst, which add to their knowledge about themselves. Such knowledge is drawn by the analyst from ideas contained and expressed in the patient's own thoughts, feelings, words and behavior." This is Loewenstein's (1951) definition, and he states he purposely kept it quite general. Colby (1951) gives a similar definition and adds the other part of the function of an interpretation: "The therapeutic intent of the interpretation is to confront the patient with something in himself he has warded off and of which he is partially or totally unaware. Thus the unconscious is made conscious."

In any form of psychotherapy the process of interpretation is accomplished in a careful series of steps, each one of which prepares the patient for the next. Even prior to any interpretation the therapist uses what Colby calls interpositions—"questions, explanations, advisory suggestions, etc."—all of which help the patient to begin to understand something about the material he is producing. Colby goes on to give a useful classification of interpretations as follows: (1) Clarification interpretations— statements made by the therapist to crystallize the patient's thoughts and feelings around a particular subject, to focus his attention on something requiring further investigation and interpretation, or to summarize the understanding thus far achieved. (2) Comparison interpretations—here the therapist's statements are used to place two (or more) sets of events, thoughts, or feelings side by side for comparison, such as present or past, fantasy or reality, childhood and adulthood. (3) Wish-defense interpretations—here the therapist's statements point directly to the wish-defense components of a neurotic conflict. Bibring (1954) gives a similar progressive range of interpretations.

In giving interpretations, careful attention must be given to the way they are handled, including the language used, the timing and order in which they are given, and the dosage. All these factors are carefully described by Loewenstein (1951), Kris (1951), Hartmann (1951), and Colby (1951). Briefly, those considerations can be summarized as follows: Interpretations should be sparse and succinctly stated, using everyday language suitable for the patient and avoiding the use of technical and analytic terms. The best initial interpretations are simply restatements of the problem in somewhat more dynamic terms.

Interpretations should deal with the psychological realities of the individual, that is, the specific individual experiences of the patient in relation to a conflict, not the conflict itself. They should go from the surface to the depths, from what is known and occurs in the present to what exists in the past, which is less well known or unknown. The past is connected to the present gradually. Interpretations are given in a certain sequence: preparatory interventions or interpretations, interpreting resistances or defenses before id derivatives, and in analysis interpreting transference (again a resistance) before other material. An important neurotic symptom is not interpreted in the beginning, and mobile defenses are interpreted before rigid characterological defenses.

The dosage of interpretations is as important as the timing. Care must be taken that the patient is sufficiently distant from an anxiety-provoking emotional experience before an attempt at interpretation is made. In making wish-defense interpretations, not only should defenses have been carefully interpreted, but the therapist must try to gauge the patient's readiness to accept the interpretation and must word it carefully. At times this means interpreting a wish on less primitive terms or using milder terms to indicate an affect—interpretation upward, as it is called. At suitable times, interpretations are used to help the patient reconstruct important past experiences. Finally, in very sick patients with overt fantasies and pathological distortions of reality as symptoms, "interpretation back into reality" is used to help the patient become aware of "a genuine emotional experience" for which he has substituted the defensive symptom formation or the fantasy evasion (Stone, 1954).

Finally, as Tarachow (1963) and Loewenstein (1951) both have stressed, every interpretation results in a loss or deprivation for the patient; it frustrates the possibility of gratification and involves giving up an infantile object to some extent. In making interpretations the therapist must keep this in mind and make his comments as "tactfully" and considerately as possible. The paradox that the interpretation—the act of the therapist that deprives the patient of the infantile object—also provides him with an adult object in the form of the sympathetic therapist has been discussed by Tarachow (1963).

Loewenstein (1951) gives a beautifully simple and clear description of how interpretation is used. Although he is referring to analysis, what he says is largely applicable to psychotherapy also.

> It happens frequently in the beginning of analysis that a patient describes a number of events which strike the analyst as having similarities. The analyst's task is then to show the patient that all these events in his life have some elements in common. The next step is to point out that the patient behaved in a similar way in all these situations. The third step may be to demonstrate that this behavior was manifested in circumstances all of which involved competitive elements and where rivalry might have been expected. A further step, in a later stage of the analysis, would consist, for instance, in pointing out that in these situations rivalry does exist unconsciously, but is replaced by another kind of behavior, such as avoiding competition. In all these stages of analysis the interpretation of mechanisms, as opposed to content, is significant. In still a later stage of the analysis this behavior of the patient is shown to have originated in certain critical events of his life encompassing reactions and tendencies, as, for example, those we group under the heading of the Oedipus complex. The interpretation extends in installments throughout the analysis, and only in the last stages of treatment does an interpretation become complete, encompassing the origin of ego and id elements. . . . Thus, there is a gradual interpretation from a preparation to an interpretation.

This remarkably clear statement also indicates that almost all degrees of interpretation are possible in psychoanalytic psychotherapy except possibly the final complete one. The degree of insight possible by use of interpretation in this fashion in psychotherapy may conceivably be considerable and even of long duration as pointed out by Gill (1954), Stone (1954), and Myerson (1965).

Working Through in Psychotherapy

Working through is the process by means of which the patient relives his problems in an "as-if" manner in the treatment until they are understood, integrated, and no longer pathogenic. In psychoanalysis this occurs through the operations of the transference and particularly by means of the transference neurosis. Psychoanalytic working through is analogous to mastery through play—play indulged in by only part of the ego. Several writers make this point—Kardos and Peto (1956), Sterba (1959), and Greenacre (1959).

Working through is never so complete in psychotherapy as in psychoanalysis largely because of the realistic factor that not enough time is available. This is one of the limitations of psychotherapy as compared with psychoanalysis. However, a certain amount of working through is possible in psychotherapy. As noted above, there are periods in psychotherapy, particularly in the beginning, during which the patient displays characteristic defensive patterns, often of a regressive nature. The therapist's patient and understanding acceptance of these regressive defensive manifestations gives a patient a chance to "relive," in an "as-if" fashion, some of his problems in the safe atmosphere of the treatment.

Another factor that helps the patient work through some of his problems in psychotherapy is the therapist's selective focusing on limited sectors of his conflicts. If the therapist is accurate in his focusing upon the selected aspects of the conflict, and if he confronts the patient slowly and carefully with these limited aspects without burdening him too much, the patient usually works through this particular limited aspect of his conflict. Deutsch and Murphy (1955), Tarachow (1963), and Gill (1954) discuss this technique.

Reassurance and Support

Reassurance is frequently suggested as a psychotherapeutic measure. One should be aware of its complications and dangers. Reassurance is the assumption by the therapist of a real role in the patient's life. In one sense it fulfills the measure of supplying an object. However, the effects of this measure must be understood more completely. Reassurance sets up a new sadomasochistic relationship between the patient and therapist. It offers the patient a new and, on occasion, dangerous set of symptoms. The dangers are the risk of depression, masochistic fantasies, homosexual fantasies, or even paranoic ideas.

In connection with this, certain other considerations are important. Neurotic worry is a comfortable defensive masochistic flight from extreme sadistic preoccupations. When the therapist too quickly reassures the worrying patient, he offers the patient a new sadomasochistic object relationship but one in which the patient is now in the position of the helpless object. Obviously, then, a certain amount of worry in certain patients is a useful defense and should be accepted and not disturbed. Similarly, kindness should also be mentioned as an assault along with reassurance. A suggestion, too, would be an assault.

These considerations should be kept in mind in order to follow the principles of leaving defenses intact wherever necessary. The same thing would apply to an interpretation that is also an assault. Patients who have especially sensitive problems of passivity or latent homosexuality will become restless or angry or even refuse to listen to an interpretation. Therefore, an interpretation should rarely go as far as possible. It should be, by preference, short of its immediate intended goal. This gives the patient an opportunity to extend the interpretation; it gives him a greater share in the proceedings and will medicate to some extent the trauma of the assault of the interpretation.

The same considerations apply to support. Explicit verbal support has its dangers, as was discussed in connection with reassurance and kindness. The most effective support is permitting oneself to be real to the patient in some implied or indirect way. A comment about the weather is sufficient to notify the patient that you are in his world and have not withdrawn into the remote distances of the transference as-if. The patient then feels he is not alone. Such indirect joining in the realities of the patient has the fewest dangers. Of course, the greatest reassurance is provided by the attitude of the therapist, a calm, interested, accepting attitude, which does far more to reassure the patient than any explicit verbal comments.

Ego Support: I

Here we shall discuss techniques concerned with certain aspects of providing ego support for the patient in psychotherapy. These will be described under the following headings: (1) role of the therapist and role-playing; (2) object relations; and (3) gratification and deprivation. Some of the theoretical points involved have been noted previously; at this point we shall discuss the technical application of these.

(1) THE ROLE OF THE THERAPIST AND ROLE-PLAYING

In both psychotherapy and psychoanalysis the therapist undertakes the role of helping the patient. For effective treatment the patient should understand from the beginning that the therapist undertakes to help the patient to help himself by helping him understand the nature and causes of his difficulties and by helping him find effective ways of dealing with them. If this can be understood by the patient, he will be clear that the helpful role of the therapist is just that—as a therapist, and not as a parent, teacher, or priest. The patient should be helped to understand this with tact and consideration so that this reality basis for the treatment can be established and maintained in the face of the ensuing transference distortions. In analysis this is handled solely by interpretation; in psychotherapy it is handled partly by interpretation and partly by a consistent attitude on the part of the therapist.

The attitude of the therapist has been discussed previously; a calm, interested, helpful attitude on his part is the most natural and most useful one. Even during those necessary times in the analysis where the therapist interacts with the patient, for example, by providing medication, discussing reality events, supplying guidance—times when he takes the role of parent, teacher, and so on—maintenance of the calm, interested, and helpful attitude will indicate to the patient that those acts of the therapist are in the service of reality and of the treatment. The necessity of the therapist's scrutinizing carefully his responses to the patient and of his being aware of any departure from his usual therapeutic attitude has been discussed by Glover (1955) and Tarachow (1963).

Obviously, deliberate manipulations of the patient on the treatment and deliberate role-taking by the therapist are departures from the necessary therapeutic attitude and should be avoided. They may at times provide some momentary direct comfort and cause a temporary improvement, but they force the patient away from reality and impose a childlike masochistic dependence by the patient upon the therapist (Fenichel, 1945; Tarachow, 1963).

The calm and helpful attitude of the therapist who is consistently interested and listens is very meaningful to the patient and sustains him in maintaining his relations to reality and in facing the tasks of living and of treatment. It appeals to and strengthens the ego of the patient by providing an object in reality for it to reach out to and a realistically helpful relationship that enables the reality-oriented part of the patient's ego to enlarge its scope and try out its strength.

(2) GRATIFICATION AND DEPRIVATION

The theoretical issues involved here relate to object need on the part of both patient and therapist and have been discussed previously. For all patients, to some extent (even in analysis and certainly in "modified analysis"), the reality of the therapist and the treatment situation provides a real object to whom the patient can relate. This kind of gratification of object need on the treatment is essential for it to proceed.

In psychotherapy, it is also necessary to permit the patient certain other gratifications at times. Some patients require medication. It is necessary at times to encourage and even mildly praise certain patients. With others, discussion of reality events—at times an inquiry about how some physical condition is doing—and even some guidance is necessary. Accepting a gift, changing an appointment, noting a change in the patient's appearance or dress, all supply gratifications that should be offered to certain patients at certain times. Needless to say, care must be maintained to keep this within the therapeutic situation and to handle them with the proper attitude.

Deprivations in psychotherapy occur in relation to interpretation and to confronting the patient with the therapeutic task. The deprivations produced by interpretations relate to transference and the loss of gratification from an infantile object relationship in the treatment. The deprivation of the therapeutic task follows this. The patient is confronted with the pain of his warded-off affects and conflicts and is required to think and begin to deal with these. Instead of the comfort of an infantile object relationship, the patient is given the painful task of working in the treatment.

Ego Support: II

INFORMATION, EDUCATION, AND REALITY-TESTING

Here techniques related to helping the patient become more aware of reality are involved.

The patient may need to be informed of certain facts concerning the body or sex. In addition to these "facts of life" he may need to be instructed about the nature of certain reality relationships—an employee and an employer, a teacher and a student, and even a parent and a child. He may need to be helped to understand what people other than himself are like, what their needs or affects are, and so on. Needless to say, all such education— for such it is—expands and strengthens the ego. Education interferes with the access to the unconscious and blocks fantasies, but it contributes to stability not only by strengthening defenses but by enlarging the scope of the ego (Fenichel, 1945; Tarachow, 1963).

By helping the patient become more aware of reality, the therapist also helps the patient's ego to expand its scope and increase the effectiveness of its functioning. The therapist undertakes to help the patient understand reality, to understand other people, and to become aware of psychological functioning in general. The patient is helped to overcome denial or wishful thinking and to see the nature of his acts and behavior from the outside in terms of reality. For example, in a patient who lies or steals, the real nature of his acts can be made clear to him, and he can be helped to see the reality limits and the reality consequences involved. He can be helped to see the impact of his behavior on others and to understand the response and the affect of the other person. The distorted view of his own needs in relation to the demands of reality and the needs of others can be made clear to him. All of this involves helping the patient become aware of reality, reality-testing, a growth of the ego, and an expansion of its realistic functioning.

SUPEREGO SUPPORT

It is necessary at times to provide support for the patient's superego in order to help him deal with threatening id impulses or to aid him in developing controls against behavior that is destructive to himself or others. Here again the attitude of the therapist is important.

In psychotherapy, the therapist not only helps the patient to develop insight, but he also indicates to him certain moral standards and values. These are not expressed directly; they are implicit in the character and behavior of the therapist. This is true even in analysis, but it is even more important in psychotherapy. In psychotherapy, the therapist makes a sharper selection of which symptoms to pay attention to and which behavior to interpret. More attention is paid to current ego attitudes. This selection of elements is accepted by the patient as a value judgment on the part of the therapist. "The symptoms and actions subjected to interpretation are now treated as 'This is bad.' The symptoms and actions left undisturbed are accepted as, 'This is all right—this is good.'" Tarachow (1963) and Gill (1951) emphasize these points. As Gill puts it: "Egosyntonic attitudes are encouraged by praise, encouragement, and support; maladaptive behavior is discouraged subtly or directly."

Another aspect of this relates to helping the patient develop a superego that functions in a realistic and flexible fashion as a part of himself and as something that accepts him and his feelings. This involves a change in the overly strict infantile punitive superego that patients feel was imposed upon them by the parents, a superego that he fears but that he also values. Tarachow (1963) makes some valuable comments on this as follows: The patient comes into treatment with one set of values; he is helped to find another. In the treatment he learns that his feelings—his aggression and his love—are valued and he learns to value them; previously he has valued only his superego. In the infantile aspects of the patient's feeling, interpretations are either frustration or permission and are thought of as a command, a prohibition, or a value. In the treatment, the patient is helped to overcome such infantile valuations so that the therapist's remarks will be seen as rational and then can be accepted as one's own. This last rational step will be possible only if the emotional transference relationship is satisfactory, that is, if the patient values his therapist.

Special Clinical Problems

Briefly, certain technical applications of the therapeutic principles described above may be indicated for certain special clinical problems.

In a *borderline patient,* the symptoms all may be neurotic, but the patient is absorbed in himself and reality interests have been seriously sacrificed. This tendency of the patient to abandon reality is the key to the therapeutic management here. Accordingly, reality is stressed in three areas: (1) The reality of the transference—the therapist presents himself as a real person stresses the reality aspects of the relationship. (2) The reality orientation of the treatment—the patient's symptoms and his preoccupation with his body are avoided and the therapist's remarks and interventions are directed toward helping the patient develop a greater interest in real objects. (3) Education of the patient to understand the reality about him— his realistic perception of other people is validated, and he is helped to understand the reactions of other people.

The *obsessive-compulsive neurosis* is the most severe of all the psychoneuroses and is characterized by marked ambivalence, often extreme anal regression, and archaic and magical thinking. The principal defense is isolation of affect. In the treatment of these neuroses by psychotherapy, the archaic anality and sadism are not dealt with directly, and the main therapeutic effort is directed toward bridging the affective isolation—from the treatment situation, from the therapist, from memories, and from positive affects.

In certain forms of *acting out* and psychopathy, the principal defense mechanism is the magical oral denial. Here the transference is the vehicle of the treatment. The therapist maintains a constant and faithful attitude toward the real interests of the patient. Then, in due course, the patient can fall back on the reality of the relationship to the therapist and face the pain and depression of giving up his illusions.

The central issues in the management of the *depressed and suicidal patient* are the solutions of the problem of aggression and the presence or absence of object relations. These patients are deeply ambivalent. Their libidinal needs for love as well as their sadistic needs must be granted some gratification. When a patient is very deeply depressed, our authority helps to keep the aggressions in check. As they improve, or as a relationship to the therapist develops, the aggressions are permitted outlet. In either case the patient is saved from his overly strict superego.

PSYCHOTHERAPY AND "THE WIDENING SCOPE OF INDICATIONS FOR PSYCHOANALYSIS"

The widening scope of indications for psychoanalysis has been discussed by several writers—Anna Freud (1954), Gill (1954), and especially Leo Stone (1954, 1961). It is of some importance to mention this in relation to psychotherapy, since, as Stone (1954) puts it, "The scope of psychoanalytic therapy has widened from the transference psychoneurosis to include practically all psychogenic nosologic categories."

From this, it might seem that the indications for psychoanalysis are now the same as for psychotherapy. In the sense that "modified psychoanalysis" is used for the more severely ill and borderline cases, together with the use of temporary "parameters," this would seem to be so. However, the authors cited above and others all agree that parameters and other modifications of analytic technique must be temporary and eventually interpreted for the treatment to be truly considered psychoanalysis. As for the indications, Stone puts it as follows: "The transference neuroses and character disorders of equivalent degree of psycho-pathology remain the optimum general indications for the classical method" of psychoanalysis.

From the standpoint of the effectiveness of psychotherapy—exploratory or expressive or psychoanalytically oriented psychotherapy—all the authors cited above and Myerson (1965) point out despite the fact that the basic conflict or conflicts are not completely analyzed and despite the fact that certain aspects of the transference to the resistances are not worked through in psychotherapy, more than a superficial shift in defenses leading to better interpersonal adjustment and social adaptation can be accomplished. Gill (1954) states that intensive psychotherapy can lead to "intra-ego structural alterations" and that "the derivative conflicts develop a relative degree of autonomy and exist in a form which allows a relatively firm resolution." Stone (1954) describes one aspect of this as follows:

> ... in certain well-managed psychotherapeutic situations, where many of the ordinary emotional needs of the patient are met, within the limits of the physician-patient relationship, significant *pathological fragments* of the transference relationship . . . may separate from the integrated expression in this real professional relationship, and be utilized to great and genuine interpretative advantage by a skilful therapist.

Thus, properly applied, psychoanalytically oriented psychotherapy is an effective form of treatment for a large number of psychiatric conditions, and, properly used, it may help the patient not only to strengthen his defenses but also to alter significantly the nature of his psychic functioning in the direction of greater effectiveness.

REFERENCES

[Notes: S.E. refers to *The Standard Edition of the complete psychological works of Sigmund Freud* (London: Hogarth Press). Dr. Sidney Tarachow died on December 5, 1965. This chapter had been planned and worked out with Dr. Stein. The final form, together with any deficiencies or shortcomings, is the responsibility of Dr. Stein.]

ALEXANDER, F. Current views on psychotherapy, *Psychiatry,* 1953, 16, 113–122.

ALEXANDER, F. Psychoanalysis and psychotherapy. *Journal of the American Psychoanalytic Association,* 1954, 2, 722–733.

American Psychiatric Association. *A psychiatric glossary* (2nd ed.). Washington, D.C.: The Committee of Public Information, 1964.

BALINT, M. Changing therapeutical aims and techniques in psychoanalysis. *International Journal of Psychoanalysis,* 1950, 31, 117–124.

BENJAMIN, J. D. Psychoanalysis and nonanalytic psychotherapy. *Psychoanalytic Quarterly,* 1947, 16, 169–175.

BERLINER, B. Short psychoanalytic psychotherapy: its possibilities and its limitations. *Bulletin of the Menninger Clinic,* 1941, 5, 204–213.

BERLINER, B. On some psychodynamics of masochism. *Psychoanalytic Quarterly,* 1947, 16, 459–471.

BERMAN, L. Countertransference and attitudes of the analyst in the therapeutic process. Abstract in *Bulletin of the American Psychoanalytic Association,* 1949, 5, 46–48.

BIBRING, E. Psychoanalysis and dynamic psychotherapy, similarities and differences. *Journal of the American Psychoanalytic Association*, 1954, 2, 745–770.

BYCHOWSKI, G. The problem of latent psychosis. *Journal of the American Psychoanalytic Association*, 1953, 1, 484–503.

COLBY, K. M. *A primer for psychotherapists*. New York: Ronald Press, 1951.

COLEMAN, J. V. The initial phase of psychotherapy. *Bulletin of the Menninger Clinic*, 1949, 13, 189–197.

DEUTSCH, F., and MURPHY, W. F. *The clinical interview*, Vol. 1. *Diagnosis; a method of teaching associative exploration*. New York: International Universities Press, 1955.

EISSLER, K. R. The effect of the structure of the ego on psychoanalytic technique. *Journal of the American Psychoanalytic Association*, 1953, 1, 104–143.

EKSTEIN, R., and WALLERSTEIN, R. S. *The teaching and learning of psychotherapy*. New York: Basic Books, 1958.

FENICHEL, O. The psychoanalytic theory of neurosis. New York: Norton, 1945.

FERENCZI, S. The problem of acceptance of unpleasant ideas—advances in knowledge of the sense of reality (1926). In *Further contributions to the theory and technique of psychoanalysis*. London: Hogarth Press, 1950. Pp. 366–379.

FLEMING, J., and HAMBURG, D. Analysis of methods of teaching psychotherapy with description of a new approach. *American Medical Association Archives of Neurology and Psychiatry*, 1958, 79, 179–200.

FREUD, ANNA. The widening scope of indications for psychoanalysis. *Journal of the American Psychoanalytic Association*, 1954, 2, 607–620.

FREUD, S. *On the history of the psycho-analytic movement* (1914). S.E., Vol. 14.

FREUD, S. *The ego and the id* (1923). S.E., Vol. 19.

FREUD, S. Analysis terminable and interminable (1937). S.E., Vol. 23.

FROMM-REICHMANN, FRIEDA. *Principles of intensive psychotherapy*. Chicago: Univ. of Chicago Press, 1950.

FROMM-REICHMANN, FRIEDA. Psychoanalytic and general dynamic conceptions of theory and therapy. *Journal of the American Psychoanalytic Association*, 1954, 2, 711–721.

FROSCH, J. The psychotic character. Abstract in *Psychoanalytic Quarterly*, 1961, 30, 314–316.

GARNER, M. H. Passivity and activity in psychotherapy. *Archives of General Psychiatry*, 1961, 5, 411–417.

GILL, M. M. Ego psychology and psychotherapy. *Psychoanalytical Quarterly*, 1951, 20, 62–71.

GILL, M. M. Psychoanalysis and exploratory psychotherapy. *Journal of the American Psychoanalytic Association*, 1954, 2, 771–797.

GILLMAN, R. D. Brief psychotherapy: a psychoanalytic view. *American Journal of Psychiatry*, 1965, 122, 601–611.

GLOVER, E. The therapeutic effect of inexact interpretation: a contribution to the theory of suggestion. *International Journal of Psychoanalysis*, 1931, 12, 397–411.

GLOVER, E. *The technique of psychoanalysis.* New York: International Universities Press, 1955.

GLOVER, E. Psychoanalysis and psychotherapy. *British Journal of Medical Psychology*, 1930, 33, 73–82.

GREENACRE, PHYLLIS. The role of transference: practical considerations in relation to psychoanalytic therapy. *Journal of the American Psychoanalytic Association*, 1954, 2, 671–684.

GREENACRE, PHYLLIS. Certain technical problems in the transference relationship. *Journal of the American Psychoanalytic Association*, 1959, 7, 484–502.

GREENSON, R. R. The working alliance and the transference neurosis. *Psychoanalytic Quarterly*, 1965, 34, 155–181.

HARTMANN, H. Technical implications of ego psychology. *Psychoanalytic Quarterly*, 1951, 20, 31–43.

JOHNSON, A. M., and SZUREK, S. A. The genesis of anti-social acting out in children and adults. *Psychoanalytic Quarterly*, 1952, 21, 323–343.

KARDOS, E., and PETO, A. Contributions to the theory of play. *British Journal of Medical Psychology*, 1956, 29, 100–112.

KNIGHT, R. P. An evaluation of psychotherapeutic techniques. *Bulletin of the Menninger Clinic*, 1952, 16, 113–124.

KRIS, E. Ego psychology and interpretation in psychoanalytic therapy. *Psychoanalytic Quarterly*, 1951, 20, 15–30.

LOEWENSTEIN, R. M. The problem of interpretation. *Psychoanalytic Quarterly*, 1951, 20, 1–14.

MARGOLIN, S. Panel discussion. The essentials of psychotherapy as viewed by the psychoanalyst. *Journal of the American Psychoanalytic Association*, 1953, 1, 550–561.

MENAKER, E. The masochistic factor in the psychoanalytic situation. *Psychoanalytic Quarterly*, 1942, 11, 171–186.

MYERSON, P. G. Modes of insight. *Journal of the American Psychoanalytic Association*, 1965, 13, 771–783.

NUNBERG, H. Transference and reality. *International Journal of Psychoanalysis*, 1951, 32, 1–9.

NUNBERG, H. Panel discussion. Problems of identification. *Journal of the American Psychoanalytic Association*, 1953, 1, 547.

PANEL. The essentials of psychotherapy as viewed by the psychoanalyst. *Journal of the American Psychoanalytic Association*, 1953, 1, 550–561.

PANEL. Psychoanalysis and dynamic psychotherapy—similarities and differences. *Journal of the American Psychoanalytic Association*, 1954, 2, 152–166.

PANEL. Psychoanalysis and psychotherapy. *Journal of the American Psychoanalytic Association*, 1955, 3, 528–533.

RANGELL, L. Psychoanalysis and dynamic psychotherapy: similarities and differences. *Journal of the American Psychoanalytic Association*, 1954, 2, 734–744.

REIDER, N. Clinical notes on the defense structure in psychotherapy. *Samiksa*, 1952, 6, 70–118.

REIDER, N. A type of transference to institutions. *Journal of the Hillside Hospital*, 1953, 2, 23–29.

REIDER, N. Psychotherapy based on psychoanalytic principles. In J. L. McCary (Ed.), *Six approaches to psychotherapy*. New York: Dryden Press, 1955.

ROBBINS, L. L., and WALLERSTEIN, R. S. The psychotherapy project of the Menninger Foundation: IV concepts. *Bulletin of the Menninger Clinic*, 1956, 20, 239–262.

ROSEN, J. N. The treatment of schizophrenic psychosis by direct analytic therapy. *Psychiatric Quarterly*, 1947, 21, 3–37.

ROSEN, V. H. The initial psychiatric interview and the principles of psychotherapy; some recent contributions. *Journal of the American Psychoanalytic Association*, 1958, 6, 154–167.

SAUL, L. J. The psychoanalytic diagnostic interview. *Psychoanalytic Quarterly*, 1957, 26, 76–90.

STERBA, R. Psychoanalytic therapy. In M. Levitt (Ed.), *Readings in psychoanalytic psychology*. New York: Appleton-Century-Crofts, 1959. Pp. 273–286.

STONE, L. Psychoanalysis and brief psychotherapy. *Psychoanalytic Quarterly*, 1951, 20, 215–236.

STONE, L. The widening scope of psychoanalysis. *Journal of the American Psychoanalytic Association*, 1954, 2, 567–594.

STONE, L. *The psychoanalytic situation*. New York: International Universities Press, 1961.

SZUREK, S. A. *The roots of psychoanalysis and psychotherapy*. Springfield, Ill.: Charles C Thomas, 1958.

TARACHOW, S. Contribution to a symposium on the place of values in psychotherapy. *Journal of the Hillside Hospital*, 1954, 3, 19–24.

TARACHOW, S. Reality and interpretation in psychotherapy. *International Journal of Psychoanalysis*, 1962, 43, 377–387.

TARACHOW, S. *An introduction to psychotherapy*. New York: International Universities Press, 1963.

TARACHOW, S. Ambiguity and human imperfection. *Journal of the American Psychoanalytic Association*, 1965, 13, 85–102.

WALLERSTEIN, R. S. The goals of psychoanalysis: a survey of analytic viewpoints. *Journal of the American Psychoanalytic Association*, 1965, 13, 748–770.

18

PSYCHOANALYTICALLY ORIENTED GROUP PSYCHOTHERAPY

Max Day
Elvin V. Semrad

Participation of the psychoanalyst in a group psychotherapy provides opportunities to observe the repeated efforts of group members to establish equitable distances of affective operational relationships, to appreciate object anxiety (Freud, 1946, 1955) and the group members' experience with its management. He observes a member's struggles with object representations within himself and also with external objects, that is, with his fellow members. Familiarity with the perceptions, behavior, feelings, and attitudes manifest in group processes is necessary in moving from the concrete level to affective ways of thinking about the phenomena in their essence, in their application, and in their relevance to research (Semrad and Arsenian, 1952).

511

A psychotherapist trained and experienced in psychoanalysis uses psychoanalytic concepts to guide his practical actions in group therapy as he studies the dynamics of people working together in this way. He notes that the group situation modifies all processes and even introduces new factors. To say that there is psychoanalysis in a group is to be misleading. The term "group psychoanalysis" pays tribute to its common ground with psychoanalysis in its general, clinical, and theoretical orientation. Psychoanalysis remains the method of choice for the intimate, detailed working through of the infantile neurosis and of the personal transference neurosis under conditions of regression. The group situation is the best medium when the patient retains sufficient inner mobility to make control over present behavior possible, so that insight and adjustment can be achieved in the face of the present task and the present group.

Group psychotherapy must, as its main tasks, fulfill conditions of global communication of formulation, do justice to the individual members and their interactions, and allow the therapist to avail himself of the forces present in the situation. Psychoanalysis studies why and how people have become as they are. A major interest in group therapy is how people change; this is seen primarily in the here-and-now situation. The group provides a stage for action, reaction, and interaction within the therapeutic situation. The group gradually accepts responsibility for conducting its affairs and relies more and more upon its resources. The situation tends to reduce the severity of censorship within the individual, and id forces become more evident. The group, via its own authority, sets up its group boundaries. The boundaries of the individual egos between both the id and the superego are revised in favor of a more extensive and stronger ego structure. The working through of the transference situation in individual analysis has an equivalent in the group understanding, namely, the observation and interpretation of individual members' reactions toward each other, toward the group, and toward the leader.

Wolfe and Schwartz (1962) stress that psychoanalysis in a group is possible. The emphasis is on the individual in the group. For practical purposes group dynamics exist but have little bearing on the ongoing psychoanalysis.

Locke (1961) takes a similar position, maintaining that a patient can and is permitted to associate at length in a group setting. However, he cautions that a one-to-one relationship may be established between patient and therapist, which by definition automatically stops the group at that point and becomes an individual relationship with others listening. If the other patients are identified with the speaker, group processes continue in that they associate to the material he produces. Through the processes of empathy a fellow member can anticipate and even speak for the first, thus extending the original speaker's thought processes. If the subsequent speaker is projecting, the material produced is really his added to the associations of the first patient. Groups can be regarded as family, peers, social milieu, or as a cultural framework, depending upon the theoretical position of the therapist. These workers use the stimulation and potentialities of a multi-personal interactive setting to good effect and feel that therapy is more effective and intensive than is the treatment of the isolated individual.

Foulkes (1964) takes the position that differences in situation limit the preceding authors' constructs in testing and correcting premises, that is, differences in size of groups (up to ten, versus Foulkes' seven), preparation of patients by individual analysis, by their return to individual sessions if they become too anxious, by alternate sessions without the therapist, and so on. Foulkes believes that the gains claimed by Wolfe and Schwartz are heavily outweighed by the advantage of analyzing all conflicts in one single therapeutic situation at one and the same period of time, which minimizes the complexity of the transference situation and maximizes group dynamic aspects that build up into an "interconnected transactional network." Group analysis appears to take a different position both in practice and in theory by placing the group and the group situation decidedly in the center. According to Foulkes, the treatment of a patient within a group setting is so far removed from the psychoanalytic setup that it is misleading to call it psychoanalysis; it is psychotherapy with a psychoanalytic orientation. The interpersonal dynamics intensify and amplify the social interactional aspects of psychodynamics and introduce powerful new parameters. The analytic attitude of the therapist as the guiding principle of his interventions, developed from psychoanalytic experience, leads him to concern himself with the dynamic unconscious, the interpretation of resistances, defense reactions, transferences, and so on. Free association belongs to psychoanalysis and cannot be applied in a group. What happens in the group looks like an equivalent, group association; however, only occasionally does it occur in pure form (Semrad and Day, 1966).

Bion (1961) too stresses an approach that represents analysis of the group as a whole. He differs with Foulkes in the variety of his interpretations and in his view of their dynamic significance. He speaks of basic assumptions as the source of emotional drives toward aims far different from the overt task of the group or even from the task that would appear to be appropriate to Freud's view of the group as based on the family group. Approached from the point of view of psychotic anxiety, which is associated with fantasies of primitive object-part relationships, the basic assumption phenomena appear to have the characteristics of defensive reactions. It is necessary to work through both the stresses that pertain to family patterns as well as the more primitive anxieties of part-object relationships. There is no scientific justification for describing work of this kind as psychoanalysis. The therapeutic value to be attached to the procedure requires fully qualified psychoanalysts to carry on research, possibly with groups composed of individuals who themselves are having, or have had, psychoanalysis.

Wolman favors combined psychoanalytically oriented individual and group psychotherapy. His groups are composed according to a definite classificatory system (Wolman, 1966). All mental disorders are divided into three *types,* namely hyperinstrumentals whose libido is hyper self-cathected, hypervectorials whose libido is hyper object-cathected, and paramutuals whose libido swings from one extreme to another. Furthermore, Wolman distinguishes five *levels,* such as neurosis, character neurosis, latent psychosis, manifest psychosis, and dementive state. A therapeutic group is *horizontally* balanced when it is composed of all three types, and *vertically* balanced when it includes not too much dispersion of levels (Wolman, 1964).

Wolman finds in psychoanalytic group therapy transferences and increased reality testing, thus he recommends inclusion of psychotics in group treatment (Wolman, 1960 and 1967). According to his experience the group permits a good deal of corrective experiences by allowing the expression of hostility. The group often assumes the role of a collective ego and superego.

Each of these authorities, differing from the other, takes a strong position that distinguishes him from the other, sometimes on points that do not seem very consequential to the whole field. In redefining individual reaction within the group context in terms of knowledge of the individual and recognizing the interaction pattern or the interrelationship between people as a new phenomenon, it is axiomatic that everything happening in a group involves the group as a whole and presents an unending variety of configurations.

Group therapy is a clinical instrument of scientific investigation for the study of group dynamics, a new science in which education, psychology, and sociology meet. It may be the privilege of psychopathology, by means of analysis of disturbances in interpersonal relationships, the study of disturbances, disorganizations, and reorganizations of ego functions, to contribute significantly to the development of clinical tools, to illuminate and study the social life of man in all these dimensions.

Rationale as Applied to Training Groups

These same dynamics are at work in training groups (Day, 1966). Such groups run for an academic year, and their foreknowledge of this gives people a chance to measure and endure their revelations and protect themselves. They are given intellectual tasks, such as summarizing group phenomena and evaluating group trends as activities onto which they can project personal feelings, and so have the option to keep personal data concerning their private lives secret. In the course of this experience, the members have an opportunity to experience emotional participation in forming a therapeutic envelope. They have a chance to see themselves and others live through phases of testing-out and fusion before they can begin to individualize themselves and see others do so in the group. In the course of these forty meetings they develop a therapeutic alliance, a willingness to work together with the others, despite the frustrations, and for the sake of what they can learn; at the same time they have developed strong feelings of transference in relation to the leader and certain other members. This experience should increase their empathy for the suffering of their own patients in their own groups and may enable them to study groups. As yet we know of no correlation between such an emotional experience and the kind of therapist such a member becomes.

Groups with Psychotics

We and our associates have treated acute and chronic cases of schizophrenia and manic-depressive psychosis since 1946. We began by drawing on the example of Schilder (1936), who aimed for analytic group therapy in that he consistently demanded free association from the group, made consistent use of intuitive interpretation of the material presented by his patients, and maintained a passive, nonauthoritarian role as a therapist. Schilder believed the method's advantages lay in reducing resistances, and he often observed that material was produced in the group situation that did not appear during individual treatment. The fact that one patient brought material, which another very often hid, lessened the latter's resistance to both conscious and unconscious material. He considered transference phenomena not less outspoken than in the usual psychoanalytic treatment and made a serious attempt to encourage patients' insight into the transference situation. Discussions dealt with the individual's relation to other persons, to his own body and its functions, his attitude toward himself, his social relations, and his feelings about aggression and death. He reported no improvement in true psychotic depressions, but was "very much gratified" by the efficacy of group methods in schizophrenia.

Our group-therapy plan depends on the therapist's appreciation of the concepts of unconscious motivation, of infantile sexuality, of psychic conflict, of ego development, and of transference and resistance. A great impetus came from a better appreciation of the nature of "integrated personal functioning" (Whitehorn, 1944) and the self-induced difficulties involved therein, which emphasized the functioning of "a person as a person in response to his cathected person" and pointed to the utilization of such understanding in the strategy of treatment. Another cornerstone of our method is close scrutiny of the patient's interpersonal attitudes as these become manifest and modified during the development of the group situation. The role that allied personnel play in the therapeutic success of any plan cannot be underestimated; therefore, we include instruction of allied personnel (attendants, nurses, social workers, etc.) in techniques of the development and maintenance of a therapeutic hospital atmosphere, which must be experienced by *everyone* who comes in contact with the patient and which allows the patient recathexis of objects for more satisfying and rewarding interpersonal relationships.

Thus the basic dynamics have been viewed as operating in all three kinds of groups: neurotic, didactic, and psychotic.

Practical Considerations

Groups run from between five to sixteen members. Our training groups usually have between twelve and sixteen people. The material is richer, since more people are available to bring their talent and experience and to provide more intricate combinations of group phenomena. Our treatment groups run from six to ten and the material is more focused, simpler, and more easily comprehended by the therapist and members. At times a group of this size appears relatively frozen and rigid. Groups of psychotics run from ten to fifteen, again to supply a variety of talent for interactions.

Our groups are run in institutional settings, and therefore we make use of whatever physical setting is available. All irregularities, differences, and external discomforts come up for discussion and relate to the leader's benevolent or hostile attitude toward the group as seen by its members. Disparities in reality details are useful to the group. What is important is that the size of the group be consistent with the size of the meeting room. Too small a room raises intense feelings, and too large a room gives a disturbing feeling of being lost or unable to determine one's own destiny.

The setting is important for group therapy in the sense that the therapist has to have a milieu in which this form of treatment fits. Group therapy cannot be carried on very well *in vacuo,* especially by beginners. There must be an administration willing to lend its support to the program and to provide for the materials as well as for professional needs of the therapists. For the beginner, supervision and seminars for exchange of experience are necessary; for the advanced therapists, a chance to teach, do research, and publish are requirements. The administration must make it important, just as the therapist must make the work of his group important to the members.

Composition of the group bears on important considerations. When professionals are put into a group, they are allowed free choice to join or not to join these seminars. Occasionally some leave for reasons of their own. Though attempts are made to analyze their reasons, no outside efforts are made to keep them there beyond the unspoken pressures of the setting. This kind of split between therapist and administration is quite explicit with groups of psychotics and neurotics. There is a distinction in how this split is carried out; it should be arranged according to location, not diagnosis, that is, according to whether the group is an outpatient or inpatient group. Hospital patients have an administrator who prescribes group therapy and points the direction to the patient, who may then be in a state of resistance. If the patient lives at home there may be a separate administrator; otherwise the therapist must fill in this role by additional private meetings with the patient. The effects of the composition of a group become clear to us retrospectively; they are still a mystery, since they spring from the individual transferences that must unfold themselves in the group and that no one can predict. The final choice of the patient depends on the therapist's reaction to the patient. Therefore, decisions about composition often relate more to the personal interests of the therapist or to attempts to deal with massive aggression in particular patients than to specific theoretical reasoning.

The Initial Interview
with Training Groups and Neurotics

With groups of professionals and neurotics the opening interview sets the implicit tone for how the group is to function. Professionals are invited to give some personal background, beginning with where they were raised and what their training was, and also some idea of their expectations of this group experience. Neurotic patients have a well-prepared approach in detailing their personal problems. In either case, the leader makes it evident by his general permissiveness and active encouragement of group participation that the group will best gain self-understanding by enjoying the privilege of interacting spontaneously. In addition they are told that they have the concomitant responsibility to interact appropriately. The combined guiding principles of spontaneity and appropriateness provide the members with the comfort of possibilities for relief with a sense of control over their own destiny in the group situation. In fact, it mobilizes id and ego forces to struggle openly. This gives them the tools to work out procedures on each occasion as well as to formulate the mores or rules that each group seems to need.

The members feel out and sense at once that there will be no easy answers; thereupon begin the first efforts to get close while overwhelmed with the anxiety of unfamiliarity, helplessness, and fears of rejection. All and any of their efforts to get close are encouraged. The first meeting often ends on a note of overoptimism, as members realize with some relief that they have dealt successfully with the first meeting.

The other minimal requirements are detailed by the leader at some point, such as attendance, duration, and need for continuity. Some leaders may be more explicit in their approaches than others. We have found that certain simple guidelines in the contract or working agreement may be used implicitly to greater effect in making the leader's expectations known to the membership. In special circumstances these general principles can be used to work out the needs of a specific situation.

The Initial Interview with Psychotics

With psychotics the first meeting is opened by a brief orientation. Patients are reminded that they may be able to help each other. The group members are asked to express their opinions freely. The patients are assured that they may speak of anything they care to without restriction and that their opinions, feelings, and expressions may be helpful to others.

After the brief orientation, the physician essentially participates freely in casual conversation with the group on any subject the group may wish to bring up. He does not hold himself to a questioning role, but makes comments, listens, smiles, and does whatever seems appropriate to keep up a free-and-easy conversation, guided by the associated, expressive thoughts of the group as a whole. Thus through his reliability, considerateness, special acquaintance with human problems, and skill in recognizing them, he assists the group toward a more effective and gratifying orientation of attitudes, both in relation to a better understanding of personal issues and situations and to a more spontaneous participation in life. His lot is to do what other members of the group cannot do, that is, to be the figure in whom and on whom all the ambivalent feelings and fantasies will be enacted. He must be especially cautious not to permit the group to use any other member than himself as a scapegoat, and then only long enough to permit adequate study of the effect of displacements and their genesis.

Vicissitudes of Presence and Contact

This same general approach of giving members the opportunity for, and responsibility of, collaborating sets in motion powerful forces (Semrad *et al.*, 1963). The anger stimulated by the lack of immediate satisfaction and the extra stimulus provided by primitive anxieties force the membership to cope with dual problems of this anger and the need to make oneself at home enough to negotiate closeness. In the individual one can see psychological processes of suggestion, imitation, identification, contagion, and compulsion at work. In the group they appear in the form of cooperation, competition, and conformity.

Cooperation refers to the emotional activities inherent in the working of two or more persons to produce some common effect. Although most such activities facilitate collaboration and promote a feeling of common purpose and direction, some tend to be less helpful and more divisive in their effect (e.g., banding against the leader).

Competition focuses on the emotional aspects inherent in the striving of two or more persons for the same object. Competitive actions may have the dual effects of making the group more cohesive, yet rivalrous or divided into factions.

Conformity refers to behavior or attitudes that are regulated in group behavior through norms, prescribed roles, and consensus of the members. Manifestations of conformity range from defensive self-assertion tending toward disunity to unconscious compliance tending toward unity. Conformity in words, gesture and posture, attitude, and feelings often carries a quality of positive mutual feeling, usually reserved for libidinal expression. Viewed in the perspective of goal achievement, forces for conformity resist and channel competitive activities, transforming them into cooperation.

Cooperation, competition, and conformity as complex emotional activities vary at different levels and phases of group development. Each new group incident produces realignment in these interactions. Some have more impact than others. Some set the group back. The group repeatedly lives through threats of disintegration by trauma, frustration, jealousy, affection, anger, and loss. Mastery or simple endurance of the common experience tends toward cohesiveness and progress toward the goal.

The members participate in a deeper emotional experience in the presence of the leader and in contact with all other members. To some extent individuality is surrendered as members venture into new relationships with others. In some cases, individual ego capacities for relationships can be enriched or altered. Within the group, alteration of ego boundaries produces increased anxiety, which fosters both regressive dependency and counteractive aggression. Observation and acceptance of both dependent and counterdependent attitudes as natural under the circumstances makes it possible for all members to continue their participation with a feeling of comfort and security.

Under conditions of stress within the group's capacity to endure, growth and development occur. When stress exceeds the sum total of supports from individual personalities, group morale, environmental support, and effective leadership, the interactions and relationships take on a more disruptive, primitive, or disorganized character.

In our experience, groups seem to follow an endogenously unfolding program. The personality of the leader, personalities of the members, the group atmosphere, and interactions modulate the pace of developments. Loss and frustration especially stimulate reversion to withdrawal and group instability (Kaplan and Roman, 1961). The impact of a crisis varies depending upon when it occurs in the group's history. A later trial may find the group holding to more mature attitudes and behavior.

Phases in Training Groups

In the initial phase of testing out, members consciously feel out how to deal with the leader and one another and consciously negotiate closeness by seeing what is acceptable and what is not acceptable in the situation. Unconsciously, they test out the leader to ascertain that they have strength and are safe. They then move on to an artificial closeness, which is stifling in its pressure toward conformity and represents a combination of various personal primitive states of closeness derived from the backgrounds of the constituent members of the group. Gradually the members feel strong enough to challenge this conception of how the group is to work and move into greater individualization within the group. By then, members are less concerned with the loss of love for any particular characteristic they may be ashamed of and have the strength to show themselves as they are. This third phase of individualization, which takes about thirty meetings to achieve, appears to be the most fruitful time for free interaction and genuine self-study and mutual study. In training groups that run for about one year, this phase is usually interrupted prematurely by the demands of the academic situation and other training needs. The members are then hurried into looking at the final phase of termination. This can be a very useful period of evaluating what the emotional experience has meant to the individual. By then, each member is already in a state of transference extending in many directions and has a well-established therapeutic alliance with the group at large in the person of the leader. The sequelae of this premature termination for the future orientation of these trainees toward group therapy are important.

Phases in Neurotic Groups

The phases seen in training groups are similar to those seen in groups of neurotics, except that in the latter the members have an opportunity to reveal themselves as individuals for periods of time longer than one year. This allows for a richer exploration of the background of individual character attitudes and emotional problems as the multiple transferences of each member are revealed and investigated.

Most of these groups are probably also terminated prematurely in the sense that the therapist's needs in training settings so often dictate the duration of a group. Therefore many patients are forced to work out problems of termination sooner than would otherwise be necessary; for example, in privately run groups where this is not a factor. Even so, one-third to one-half of the patients can be helped sufficiently to work out within a year or two therapy problems that bring them to the group, so that they have relief in these areas, and they can then leave the group. This gives them an opportunity to work out termination within the group setting while the rest of the group may not be working on this issue. The remaining members then have a chance to work out losses within the group setting. This also allows for the continuous addition of new members to existing groups, so that members can look at the problems of birth, separation, and death at different times.

Phases in Psychotic Groups

During the introductory remarks of the therapist there is usually a quiet and attentive response from all the patients, including any who are excited and agitated. This is almost immediately broken by what we consider the first phase of the group-therapy process. At this time each individual seems to be testing in his own way the limits of tolerance of the group and of the therapist. This period is chiefly characterized by hostilities, shown in as many forms as the patients have at their command, and is usually directed toward the hospital and the special situation that is produced. Simultaneously with the overt testing of the situation, the less vocal members of the group occasionally show their accord with the expressed complaint by nodding or smiling or otherwise indicating approval. In this manner a feeling of identification is built up, whereby the group begins to become cohesive, and emotional release in one patient can be achieved via another patient's expression. This is an early sign of the second phase of group formation. Attempts are often made to form personal relationships without regard for the group activity. Full testing of the situation cannot be carried out by one or two patients, however, and most of the patients sooner or later become eager to be able to express themselves along with the aggressive members. In the early stages, when the dominating patient is testing the therapist, it is important that final rejection or silencing of this person be left to the other patients. If this silencing is done by the group rather than the therapist, it will strengthen the ties to the therapist because he will have demonstrated his ability to fulfill the role described above. It will permit the others to speak up without fear of being rebuked. Soon the patients begin to feel at home with each other and with the doctor. They can now recall each other's names, and they begin to relate to one another as more normal individuals would. On better acquaintance they can carry on conversation, often to the exclusion of the therapist. With the development of a feeling of unity and confidence and of the knowledge that their feelings will be respected, there is less anxiety about the present situation than there was formerly.

This permits the third stage of the group process to evolve. In this stage, the individual members participate more actively, the inner anxieties of each patient become manifest, and each begins to reveal the thoughts to which his strong feelings have been attached. During this stage bizarre delusions and hallucinations are revealed, and psychoneurotic complaints are aired. Some patients will greet such revelations by others with silence rather than openly express doubt, even though it is obvious by their downcast eyes that they question the normalcy of the experiences others express. Occasionally one of the patients will suggest a possible psychogenic explanation of such a confession, without insisting that it applies to the patient who has spoken. Disclosures of psychotic material eventually produce attempts to explain it. The most astute observations of this kind are likely to be made by other schizophrenic patients. In fact, they seem to understand their material well. By "appropriate comments," which show his understanding of present and past material, the therapist emphasizes material relevant to the dynamic processes in the etiology of psychotic illness. The material of this phase refers more and more to personal and interpersonal feelings. The first evidences of introspection usually appear during this phase. They are shown when one patient sees and criticizes in another patient these things that he himself has been feeling. Two patients may interpret a situation presented by one of their number quite differently. In other instances it is quite obvious that these criticisms apply to the critic himself.

Throughout the course of treatment the patients continue to ask the therapist for advice and opinions. This occurs whether the therapist feels obliged to answer their pleas or whether he avoids direct comment of his own and refers the question to other patients. He seems to be regarded as a protective yet authoritative figure, with all the qualities thus implied. Of course, the feelings of the therapist are conveyed through his verbal contributions as well as through his nonverbal activities. It has been noticed that a therapist of the opposite sex will inhibit the expression of sexual anxieties, which are more frequently and extensively discussed when the therapist is of the same sex. However, revelations of these anxieties are merely postponed with a therapist of the opposite sex and occur nevertheless.

Transference, Resistance, Interpretation of Unconscious Material, and Working Through

TRAINING GROUPS

Since training groups for professionals last about an academic year—thirty to forty meetings—not all that *can* happen in a therapy group actually does. The early phase of joining together is similar to that in groups of neurotics. Usually in a group of fifteen, one person will show a dramatic illustration of transference development; probably several others will feel similarly at the same time and not show it, since they wish to hide personal data in the setting. We encourage them to control the degree of exposure by helping them to divert their energies to an intellectual study of the group process in the form of weekly summaries and periodic summaries of series of several meetings. The affects that patients have about personal associations, fantasies, and other data are displaced in such groups onto their professional productions for their own protection, since they must work together every day during the life of the group and in the future as colleagues. Probably, if we questioned each member, we would find full-blown transference developments in every one of them, toward the end of the year.

GROUPS OF NEUROTICS

The web of relationships that holds a group together sparks interaction, so that inner conflicts can be externalized, acted out in the group, and analyzed; they spring from transferences that each member develops in a number of different directions. The leader encourages moving closer together for respectful cooperation, not out of fear, nor a need to please, but to have and give an opportunity for mutual study. Encouraging such intimacy and regression within the group therapy situation permits the mobilization of transferences. Closeness to others increases interpersonal conflicts, so that relationships are crystallized and the real and unreal elements can be disentangled. With a little encouragement the members are quick to learn to spot and analyze resistances. They need support to learn to withhold judgment and to study developing transference reactions over a period of time, so that they can see them as a unit.

Gradually, with leader and group support, members can begin to see how they repeat the past, where these patterns arose, and the necessity for them. Then they are freer to undo these patterns and experiment with other techniques of dealing with other people in the group and outside it. All this is similar to what happens in individual therapy.

The differences in technique in group and individual therapy stem from capacities for acting out conflicts within the view of witnesses and from the additional availability of the talents of the members to analyze resistances, conflicts, and transferences. The leader steps in only when members seem incapable of working with certain material. Furthermore, although there can be a certain amount of individual working through of transference origins of individual pathology, there is no possibility of free association as takes place in the psychoanalytic setting. Though the same material is tapped in a different way in a group, there cannot be the same kind of individual working out of nuclear fantasies.

There may be special versions of resistances acted out by the cooperation of two or more members with confluent pathology. The side which is satisfied in each member must be analyzed, as must the means by which the group contributes to this acting out.

Unconscious material is interpreted as it becomes preconsciously available. By then, members of the group can interpret much of what comes to the surface.

GROUPS OF PSYCHOTICS

The therapist often analyzes those situations that are manifest in interpersonal relationships with a patient or between patients. Often he finds that the most useful material for comment is the trivial situation of the moment, rather than the vital one. He learns about major situations from trivial ones and bases his comments on what the patient means rather than on what he actually says. Discussion proceeds until members of the group can verbalize the issues in similar language. The physician takes his cues for appropriate comments, which must be distinguished from interpretations, from the affects expressed in word and act. Through the respectful but candid interaction between the attitudes of the participants, knotty problems can be untangled with much greater effectiveness. The degree of subtlety necessary in appropriate comment seems proportional to the amount of anxiety a patient is experiencing, and should not be overdone.

Issues that need to be clarified vary in detail from personality to personality. Frequently the patient who shows predominant manic or depressive symptomatology is preoccupied with problems of self-respect and respect for others. These issues are frequently brought to a head by deprivations in real life or concealed equivalents of which the patient is unaware. The patients with schizophrenia are more concerned about affection.

If we focus in individual group sessions on the ways in which psychotic patients resist frank discussion and easy interaction in the group setting, as well as on the issues lying behind such resistances, we find ideas of physical danger, rejection, and feelings of being attracted to the therapist. Usually the patients have to deal with problems concerning their relationship with the therapist and the hospital before they feel free to discuss the prototypes of these problems in their prehospital and earlier lives.

Resistances are handled by clarifying their manifestations and investigating the issues underlying them. Each member of the group does not invariably maintain the progress of the group as a whole. Furthermore, there are times when upsetting factors apparently set the group back, and members revert to former attitudes. The absence of members, or the introduction of a new or strange member, provokes a return of the old complaints against the hospital. A change in the place of meeting or a radical change in the seating arrangement has the same effect. Sometimes an unusual event on the ward causes a slowing down of the group-therapy process. Usually these setbacks are of short duration.

Patients gradually begin to speak about their future plans and become more concerned about their situations outside the hospital, the people in that external situation, and the problems that the total situation of leaving the hospital and returning to the community presents. At the same time, the improved patient may appear somewhat aloof from the rest of the patients and does not so readily enter into group discussion. These observations constitute some of our most important clues to processes indicating the conclusion of a therapeutic group process.

The amount of time a given group will spend in any one stage is very difficult to predict. In a group one can observe that the more infantile in their reactions the members are, the less they can tolerate multiple group stimuli and can integrate them into appropriate responses. Motor responses are apt to take precedence over verbal responses. The ambivalence experienced in closeness is more dangerous in the more infantile person, fears of annihilation are more pronounced, and hence the defensive hostility is more overt. The intensity of the reaction works both ways, that is, working through of the hostility and finding that mutual warmth results, comes as a gratifying surprise and as a significant emotional experience, perhaps chiefly in the notion of the ability to use again latent ego-adaptive patterns or identifications abandoned during the psychosis.

THE THERAPIST

Since the focus of attention in group therapy is on the emotional inter-relationship between the patient and the therapist, as well as between patients, a few comments about the therapist are in order. It is fundamental that the therapist constantly seek better self-understanding as well as under-standing of his reactions to patients. A personal psychoanalysis or psycho-analytic training is most useful for this work. The therapist can also derive much support in doing group therapy, if given the opportunity, in group seminar discussions during which problems of countertransference as well as the patients' problems are discussed. It also strikes us that one of the principal differences between the highly skilled and the less skilled psychia-trist lies in the greater ability of the former to sense the nature of the personal issues with which the patient is preoccupied and the ability to utilize the patients' own words in clarifying these issues acceptably and conveying convincingly, yet with little verbalization, his interest in the patients' growth. It is our feeling that one of the chief obstacles to group psychotherapy lies in the therapists themselves (assuming that the patient, in his desire for health, constantly seeks our assistance, although in a manner evoking uneasiness in those who try to help him). We are like-wise impressed with the therapist's realization of his responsibility of not abandoning the treatment once the patient attempts to reject him. This may go on for days and weeks and seems to be related to the patient's desire to test the trustfulness of his doctor.

The Concept of Cure

The idea of cure in therapy poses many problems. In individual therapy the concept of cure implies that the patient is now able to deal with what-ever blocked him when he first had to come for help. In psychoanalysis, where we aim for a personality reconstruction of greater dimensions, we say that the original problem was solved and other energies released. We have also given the patient the technique to deal with new issues as they subsequently arise, but there is no feeling that all problems are solved, nor is there a protection against future illness. There is no such thing in any form of therapy.

THE IDEA OF CURE OR RESULTS IN TRAINING GROUPS

We give the professionals in a group an opportunity to watch a leader in action, to watch the formation of a group, to watch themselves, to watch other people, and to formulate this experience. We give them a model and a personally significant emotional experience. We do not know the exact meaning of this experience to each person for his future work as therapist or his use of what he may have learned about groups, whether in treatment situations or in administrative or other situations. We only know that gradually more people are turning to doing group therapy after having been in such groups, and they think it is related to the training experience.

CURE IN GROUPS OF NEUROTICS

Our general ideas (above) apply especially to results in group therapy with neurotics, in which we tend to tie results more closely to the original problem that brought patients to the group. In part this is pragmatic, since groups may terminate prematurely because of the therapist's training need. In long-term groups this is also true, since we want to help the patient deal with the life-situation that stymied him. To a certain extent he may have learned to manage new problems on his own, but not with the same detailed approach as in a psychoanalytic treatment. The biggest danger is to allow the patient to drift along endlessly in groups or to go from one group experience to another, so that being in a group becomes a way of life.

CURE IN GROUPS OF PSYCHOTIC PATIENTS

Evaluation of the results of therapy is one of the most difficult tasks we have to face. The literature does not provide a reliable frame of reference for comparison of results. Details of method, training of therapists, and degree of illness are very hard to assess. One of the best-designed experiments in this area, the Perry Point Experiment of Powdermaker and Frank (1953), fell short of success. The first year of the project was primarily a learning experience for the therapists and was not a test of the ultimate value of group therapy. At the end of the first year all but two of the doctors in charge of the groups left the hospital to continue training else-where. This repeats to some extent our own long-term experience. What-ever the answer to this problem is, the result is that our accumulation of knowledge of treatment of psychotics in groups, or otherwise, is slow.

Although therapeutic results must be reckoned on long-term changes, general benefits to the patient are fairly specific. The group situation pro-vides the patient with a safe, permissive tool for relating himself once more to others. It encourages the expression of suppressed hostility, mobilizes unconscious tensions, and permits their release. It further provides a setting in which the patient can learn more about how he operates as a person in his dealings with others and possibly acquire more effective ways of dealing with other people.

The self-imposed isolation of the patient may diminish as the opportunity to compare himself with others who also have severe conflicts over problems of everyday living is provided. He is given a setting in which he can acquire a perspective on his own problems and feelings.

Group therapy facilitates the task of caring for patients. Patients become more cooperative and less resistive with attendants, less abusive and as-saultive on the ward. Many of those who are incontinent show better control of excretory functions; others are less destructive of clothing and property, and the majority show greater neatness in dress and appearance.

In addition to these benefits to the patient, group therapy contributes to the general therapeutic atmosphere of a large state hospital in that it is possible to have more patients under treatment. This feeling that something is being done for the patients affects the allied personnel, who often show subtle but definite improvement in their attitudes toward the patient.

The therapist also shares in the benefits of group therapy. It contributes to his growth by affording the observation of patients in a new light. The group functions as a miniature of society in many ways and reveals much about new patients and how they handle themselves with others. In addition, the therapist is aware of the effect he has on the group as a person, while he also learns of his limitations. Certainly the therapist will become more keenly aware of the nonverbal cues through which human beings often convey their most intimate feelings to one another.

In 1947 a report on the present condition of 165 patients treated by this method was made. Those patients received from 35 to 40 group hours of treatment at the time. It was decided to keep these patients in group therapy as long as they remained in the hospital and to periodically evaluate benefit to these patients. These cases were both acute and chronic, with only 10 patients chosen from the disturbed wards. Of this number, 52 per cent were schizophrenic disorders, 28 per cent affective disorders, and the remainder of miscellaneous diagnoses. The age range of these patients was fourteen to eighty-four years. In 1947, 51 per cent of the acute patients had been released on trial visit, as compared to 27 per cent of the chronic patients. An additional 25 per cent of the acute patients showed noticeable improvement, that is, they showed remission in symptoms and improved behavior to the point at which they could be transferred to parole or to better wards in the hospital, compared to an additional 37 per cent of the chronic patients.

In 1950, 65 per cent of the acute patients were on visit, as compared to 34 per cent of the chronic patients. In 1951, 74 per cent of the acute patients, and 37 per cent of the chronic patients, were on visit. In other words, in the intervening four years, additional patients, both acute and chronic, were released on visit. The increase in patients on visit in this period was 23 per cent in the acute, and 10 per cent in the chronic, patients. The proportion of patients showing progressive improvement over the four-year period was slightly lower than the percentage of patients who had shown initial improvement in 1947.

About one-half of these patients had previously received, or were currently undergoing, other therapies, such as EST, in addition to group therapy. In the acute group the results with those receiving group therapy plus other therapies were about 3 per cent better in 1947 and 5 per cent better in 1950. In the chronic group, the results of those receiving group therapy plus other therapies were about 2 per cent better in 1947 and 11 per cent better in 1950.

Our plan of repeated follow-up ended in 1952 when the doctor in charge of this project became an analyst and decided to practice analysis in another part of the world. A study of interest is that Blau and Zilbach (1954), who treated eight patients on trial visit for one year in group psychotherapy. During this time none of the members was rehospitalized, and all were discharged, though many had had numerous previous admissions and had been unable to remain outside the hospital during the one-year trial visit period. Significant improvements in socialization, marital, and job adjustments were noted.

We feel that patients obtain from group therapy a social rehabilitation rather than a definite change in their personality trends. They sometimes develop the art of social intercourse during the group sessions, even without losing their delusional trends. Whether additional therapeutic gains can be achieved through this experience remains to be learned.

REFERENCES

[Note: S.E. refers to *The Standard Edition of the complete psychological works of Sigmund Freud* (London: Hogarth Press).]

BION, W. R. *Experience in groups.* New York: Basic Books, 1961.

BLAU, D., and ZILBACH, J. J. The use of group psychotherapy in posthospitalization treatment. A clinical report. *American Journal of Psychiatry,* 1954, 111, 244–247.

DAY, M. The natural history of training groups. Read at *Annual Conference of the American Group Psychotherapy Association,* Philadelphia, Jan. 28, 1966.

FOULKES, S. H. *Therapeutic group analysis.* New York: International Universities Press, 1964.

FREUD, ANNA. *The ego and the mechanisms of defense.* New York: International Universities Press, 1946.

FREUD, S. *Group psychology and the analysis of the ego* (1921). S.E., Vol. 21.

KAPLAN, S. R., and ROMAN, M. Characteristic responses in adult therapy groups to the introduction of new members: a reflection on group processes. *International Journal of Group Psychotherapy,* 1961, 11, 372–381.

LOCKE, N. *Group psychoanalysis, theory and technique.* New York: New York Univ. Press, 1961.

POWDERMAKER, FLORENCE, and FRANK, J. D. *Group psychotherapy.* Cambridge, Mass.: Harvard Univ. Press, 1953.

SCHILDER, P. The Analysis of ideologies as a psychotherapeutic method, especially in group therapy. *American Journal of Psychiatry,* 1936, 93, 601–617.

SEMRAD, E. V., and ARSENIAN, J. The use of group process in teaching group dynamics. *American Journal of Psychiatry,* 1952, 108, 358–363.

SEMRAD, E. V., and DAY, M., Group psychotherapy, *Journal of American Psychoanalytic Association.* Vol. 10, No. 3, July, 46, 591–618.

SEMRAD, E. V., KANTER S., SHAPIRO, D., and ARSENIAN, J. The field of group psychotherapy. *International Journal of Group Psychotherapy,* 1963, 13, 452–475.

WHITEHORN, J. Guide to interviewing technique. *Archives of Neurology and Psychiatry,* 1944, 52, 197–216.

WOLFE, A., and SCHWARTZ, E. K. *Psychoanalysis in groups.* New York: Grune and Stratton, 1962.

WOLMAN, B. B. Group psychotherapy with latent schizophrenics. *International Journal of Group Psychotherapy,* 1960, 10, 301–312.

WOLMAN, B. B. Hostility experiences in group psychotherapy. *International Journal of Social Psychiatry,* 1964, **10,** 55–61.

WOLMAN, B. B. Classification of mental disorders. *Acta Psychotherapeutica,* 1966, **14,** 50–65.

WOLMAN, B. B. Treatment of schizophrenics in groups. Paper read at the Annual Convention of the American Group Psychotherapy Association. New York, January, 1967.

19

HYPNOANALYSIS

Lewis R. Wolberg

Hypnoanalysis is an ambiguous term, which has, in its common usage, come to connote a diversity of technics employed during the course of psychoanalytic therapy. The semantic diffuseness of the word hypnoanalysis is unfortunate, since it now constitutes a kind of umbrella under which many forms of treatment find cover, some of which bear little resemblance to psychoanalysis. Strictly speaking, "hypnoanalysis" is not a technic in itself. It is an adjunctive device sometimes useful during the course of psychoanalytic treatment for the purpose of resolving resistances to the uncovering of repressed material. Incomplete in itself, it may be helpful at certain phases if applied diligently by analysts who are acquainted with the method and are able to reconcile it with their habitual procedures.

Not all psychoanalysts are, however, able to employ hypnoanalysis. Reasons for this are both historical and practical. The historical reasons date back to the man who more than any other person established hypnosis as an instrument with potentials that go beyond symptom removal (Freud, 1893–1895). The practical reasons relate to the stark fact that hypnosis introduces into the relationship a contaminant that not all therapists can handle. It brings out emotional undercurrents in patient and therapist that

533

may be disturbing to both and that call for special skills in management, particularly of transference and countertransference.

Psychoanalysis and Hypnosis

Psychoanalysis as a form of treatment is essentially concerned with the uncovering of unconscious conflict. Toward this end a number of organized procedures are implemented, the most important of which is the revivification in the relationship with the therapist (transference neurosis) of early pathogenic feelings and reactions with parental agencies (infantile neurosis), which form the core of the individual's present-day neurosis. The reliving of these destructive formative experiences in the more tolerant setting of the therapeutic relationship provides the patient with an opportunity for their gradual "working through" and resolution. The essential regression to early experiences is fostered by interpretation of the patient's resistances to unconscious aspects of his psyche. Such resistances spring up as the analyst uncovers manifestations of the unconscious through symbolic derivatives, employing technics originated by Freud, such as free association and dream interpretation.

Where indicated by virtue of the seriousness of the problem, where the patient is motivated and capable of change, and he can develop, endure, and work through a transference neurosis, psychoanalysis offers the individual the greatest opportunity for reconstructive change. This presupposes that the therapist is adequately trained and experienced in the technic of psychoanalysis and that he himself has resolved sufficient portions of his infantile neurosis to handle any countertransference reactions that may be mobilized in an intensive therapeutic relationship.

However, experienced as the analyst may be, and applying his skills appropriately to patients who possess adequate incentive and ego strength, obdurate resistances may still obstruct progress. Indeed, they may constitute insuperable blocks to the analytic process. Under such circumstances the interpolation of a hypnotic session or two may serve to put the patient back on the analytic track.

For example, a spontaneous dream, occurring after the first hypnotic session in a blocked patient who could not recall her dreams, revealed an important Oedipal conflict that permitted the analysis to proceed without further recourse to hypnosis:

I was asleep on a desk on a table in your office. I was lying on my side with my knees bent. You walked over to me. You were a shadowy figure that I could barely see through closed lids. I knew I should wake up, but I was curious to see what you would do and I lacked the will to awaken. You touched me. I had been covered, but you removed the cover and I remember thinking "I hope I have a pretty slip on." At first your touch was pleasant, sexual-like, and I felt rather guilty for not letting you know I was really awake. Gradually you began to turn into a sinister figure. You looked into my eyes with a light and said: "That's a lovely blue eye." I barely mumbled "It's green," feeling that if you didn't know the color of my eyes after all this time, it meant you didn't know me. I realized with a shock I didn't know the color of your eyes either. Brown, I thought, but I wasn't sure. Then you said to me: "What are the things I've told you?" I started to mumble: "Many things." You said: "No—I have told you nothing." I took this to mean that you are absolutely not responsible for anything I might do. These things made you seem sinister to me. You slowly began to change into another man who seemed to be a derelict, and I knew I *must* get up. I struggled to awaken myself and I finally succeeded. I ran to the door and ran out of the room, but there were a lot of people. In a mirror there I saw an utter ruin. I looked eighty years old and terribly ugly and, I believe, scarred. All the people were old and ugly. It was a village of discarded, use-less, and helpless people. A feeling of horror overcame me, and, as I stared at that face, I tried to comfort myself that it was only a nightmare and I would soon wake up, and I found it very difficult until I wasn't sure anymore if it was a nightmare or real. I finally woke up from the dream so frightened that I wanted to wake my husband, but I decided to try to calm down. I fell asleep again and had a second dream. I dreamed I had stayed up all night writing a paper you asked me to do. I started to bring it into the room you told me to. It was locked. I decided to have some coffee and come back. I did. This time your wife was in the room. She told me who she was. I said I knew. Then she told me she was your daughter's mother as though this made her a figure of great importance and dignity. This made me feel guilty and gave me the feeling that I could not see you anymore. She didn't want me to and in respect to her sacredness as a mother I couldn't.

The single hypnotic session apparently helped to resolve resistance to dream recall sufficiently to permit resumption of her analysis.

Questions that understandably concern the analyst who contemplates us-ing hypnosis are these: Will not hypnosis meddle with the noninterfering climate essential for undiluted transferential projections? Does not a technic that virtually puts the patient under the domination of the therapist tend to subjugate him and to mobilize undue dependency? What about the fear expressed in the literature of precipitating a psychosis, particularly in a schizoid patient? Is there not an undue concern with the unconscious during hypnosis to the neglect of the important conscious ego elements? Will not hypnosis merely succeed in liberating strangulated emotion in a cathartic outflow without, in any definitive way, altering the repressive forces? How can hypnoanalysis, which deals with the inner repudiated aspects of experience, succeed in effectuating the essential changes in character structure necessary for lasting change? How can hypnosis alter the severity of the superego when the hypnotist functions in the role of the commanding authority?

Traditionally accepted as propitious for the establishment of the appropriate climate for psychoanalysis are passivity, anonymity, and neutrality on the part of the analyst, and, for suitable technic, the rigid employment of the fundamental rule of free association. The "directiveness" and "activity" of hypnotic induction and trance utilization would seem to contradict these tactics. However, more and more there is a moving away from a too-literal interpretation of the orthodox canons of psychoanalysis. For example, Gitelson (1952) has emphasized that the analyst cannot be a mere screen. He is unable to conceal his true personality in the analytic situation. "He will appear as he is actually: in manner, speech and general spontaneity." The therapist will often take a stand on matters guided by his personal standards and the value orientation of his particular social group. Spitz (1956) has commented on the impossibility of observing the "fundamental rule" at all times. In this he agrees with Anna Freud (1946) who, remarking about free association, said that ". . . beginners in analysis have an idea that it is essential to succeed in inducing their patient really and invariably to give all their associations without modification or inhibition, i.e., to obey implicitly the fundamental rule of analysis. But even if this ideal were realized, it would not represent an advance. . . . Fortunately for analysis such docility in the patient is in practice impossible."

Insofar as the neutrality of the therapist is concerned, this is more apparent than real. The therapist is a human being with feelings, values, prejudices, and needs. He will reveal these to the patient sooner or later, if not verbally then nonverbally, both directly in his interpretations and indirectly in his silences, pauses, content of questions, and emphases. Although ideally the therapist should avoid prejudicial pronouncements and personal preferences, he should not deceive himself into feeling that he can always maintain an unbiased stand. Nor is this desirable. It may be quite suitable to apply value pressures where they are needed, and sometimes, as in acting-out proclivities, this is the only stratagem that makes sense. Though maintaining the philosophy that the patient has an inalienable right to his decisions, points of view, and behavioral twistings and turnings, the therapist does not need to accept the validity of such ideas and actions. There is then no such thing as complete "neutrality" in the therapist. Otherwise he would not care whether the patient remained sick or got well. The therapist has opinions and he has biases. He will display these in one way or another, if not one day then the next.

Activity in the course of psychoanalysis need not interrupt the spontaneous emergence of a transference neurosis. It may expedite it. This is the experience of many analysts who, frustrated by the shackles of passivity, finally emerge to express themselves more forcefully with their floundering patients. Hypnosis need not insert a controlling and directive influence, relegating the patient, as it is conventionally feared, to a regressive child-parent relationship. It may, on the contrary, break the infantile ties with the godlike image of the parent who, in the form of analyst, wields his mighty power with an Olympian silence. The basic problem is whether activity, such as the interpolation of hypnosis, is designed by the real needs of the situation or whether it is a manifestation of countertransference. In the latter case hypnosis can be considered a manipulative and interfering device that obstructs the analysis of the transference neurosis.

I have never been able to substantiate the suspicion so pervasive among professionals that hypnosis sponsors dependency. Dependency, where there is need for it, will precipitate with the most passive and detached therapists; it will not require encouragement through directive tactics. Nor do patients ever become addicted to and dependent on hypnosis. Such notions are aspects of the mythology that continues to invest hypnosis, promoted by those who have the least experience with the method.

Precipitation of psychosis by hypnosis is a manifestation of bad technic on the part of the therapists who, wielding hypnosis as a bludgeon, attempt to subdue their patients by invading the secret jungles of their unconscious. Patients with weak ego structures, such as borderline and psychotic individuals, interpret such maneuvers as a destructive attack, and their psychic reserves may, as a consequence, crumble. The culprit here is not hypnosis, but the destructive uses made of the hypnotic technic. Such violations are not restricted to hypnosis; they are manifest with "wild analysis" where the therapist, eager to open up reservoirs of inner conflict, applies himself to the explosion of resistance by aggressively delivering "deep" interpretations. The reports by some therapists of murderous and sexual assaults released in their patients through hypnosis are testimony, not of the potential dangers of hynosis, but of the technical insophistication of the practicing hypnotists, torturing an art to which they are not suited. I have worked hypnotically with virtually hundreds of borderline and psychotic patients, even paranoidal patients whose chief complaint was that they were being hypnotized by malevolent mesmerizers, with a reassuring effect and an actual restoration of their psychologic reserve. My technic here is, of course, supportive, aimed at relaxation and tension reduction. However, where I have felt rapport to be firm, I have been able to approach psychotic persons in considerable depth with not the slightest threat to their mental integrity.

The notion that hypnosis bypasses resistances to deal exclusively with the unconscious, only to have conscious barriers restored with awakening, is another of the legends about hypnosis. Any experienced hypnoanalyst is aware of the need to work with resistances rather than with repudiated drives and conflicts that evade the resistances. The uncovering of repressed material may come about with the hypnotic induction or the institution of certain hypnoanalytic technics. This is insufficient in itself. What is required is that the patient be challenged to understand why it is difficult for him to countenance or to acknowledge this material in the waking state. Pointed questions and injunctions to work on his resistances and to accept, reject, or modify the revealed material will ultimately register effects on the patient's ego. Changes will become manifest in the patient's dreams, as for instance, in less distorted symbolism, and in "spontaneous" insights that begin to emerge.

Thus, a patient, who had come to therapy for the correction of frigidity, brought in the following dream: "I dreamed I bought nuts and was eating them when I thought I should wash and drain them first. As I was washing and draining them, small cockroaches came out. And then there were trouser cuffs that I was washing and draining, and small cockroaches came out of the cuffs and seams. And as I was washing and draining, the cockroaches became more and more, and bigger and bigger."

The only associations the patient could offer were these: "Nuts mean when I'm downtown and miss lunch, a bag of nuts satisfies my appetite. We had some cockroaches in the kitchen—repulsive creatures, and I called in the exterminator." Under hypnosis, the patient, asked to associate to the dream, replied: "Nuts are testicles. I'm afraid of it. Why should women be made to do the dirty work? Men are free and wear trousers. The cockroaches are something big and overwhelming and frightening. They can hurt me." This opened the door to a discussion of the patient's fears of her masculine strivings, which she believed were blocking the assumption of a feminine role. Two weeks later the patient began to dream openly of possessing a penis, then to discuss her masculine impulses openly as she entered into competition with me in transference. Ultimately her frigidity resolved, and this was accompanied by an abandonment of her masculine dress and mannerisms.

A cathartic release of affect is often a dramatic by-product of hypnotic induction. No seasoned hypnoanalyst deceives himself about the virtues or permanence of this discharge, no matter how intensive are the stores of released energy that stream forth. The benefits of catharsis are largely diagnostic. The analyst gains an understanding of some of the conflicts burdening the patient, and he evolves strategies of working toward their sources. Whenever a patient responds to any of the hypnotic procedures with an emotional outburst, he may be directed toward an investigation of what is behind his distress.

Hypnosis by itself is quite insufficient in producing alterations in character structure. A working-through of the material liberated during the trance state is a *sine qua non* of reconstructive change. The technics essential for translation of insight into action are no different from those conventionally employed in psychoanalysis. However, hypnosis does provide the analyst with another tool for carving away obstructive resistances to change. Through hypnosis the patient may be helped to face fears that prevent utilizing what he has found out about himself. Many of my referrals are patients who possess a topical understanding of their problems, but yet are unable to take a leap into health. What they seem to need is both a greater awareness of their fears of change, and a helpful, mildly directive push over the brink of their resistance to change. This I have obligingly been able to provide for them, particularly through instructions in self-hypnosis. Insights gained in analysis have in this way become vitalized into more assertive dealings with life.

The hypnotist as the patient's superego is more an artifact than an actuality. When the patient's superego loses its severity, which it will do in successful hypnoanalysis, projections toward the hypnotist will change. He will become a benign or beneficent figure rather than a malevolent and commanding one. This presupposes that the hypnotist does not have a personal need to play God, and that he is capable of absorbing criticism that will sooner or later be leveled at him. Even with the most authoritarian hypnosis, the developing patient will eventually challenge the hypnotist's omniscient powers as part of his movement toward self-actualization.

Hypnosis and Psychoanalytically Oriented Therapy

Existing realities limit the application of formal psychoanalysis. First, most patients cannot afford four-to-five-times-a-week therapy over a three-to-five-year span. Second, there are relatively few trained psychoanalysts available to minister to patients who need, can afford, and can utilize psychoanalysis. Third, not all people have the incentive to enter into a prolonged and concentrated treatment effort, or possess the flexibility of defenses needed to evolve, face, and overcome a transference neurosis. Most of the failures in psychoanalytic treatment—and there are many—are due to the fact that psychoanalysis should not originally have been employed as the treatment method of choice, usually because of lack of motivation or fragility of the inherent defenses. Success would have been obtained more readily with less ambitious approaches.

The question follows, of course, as to whether technics other than formal psychoanalysis can have a reconstructive influence on the personality structure itself. The answer to this question is the pivot around which rotates much of the current controversy in the psychoanalytic field. In the main, we may say that formal psychoanalysis is not the only means toward extensive personality alterations. Reconstructive changes are occasionally possible in the medium of productive life experiences that do not repeat past traumatic happenings and that offer opportunities for corrective relearning. They are sometimes achievable in a therapeutic interpersonal relationship even though the relationship itself is not the focus for investigation. They are feasible in psychotherapy that deals with transference without its exaggerated eruption into a transference neurosis. The handling of resistance and transference, in a framework of greater directiveness than is employed in formal analysis, with a reduction of the number of weekly sessions, and a focusing on reality as well as the unconscious, is the province of "psychoanalytically oriented psychotherapy." Here the relationship of therapist to patient is somewhat different from that in formal psychoanalysis. It is less passive and detached, and more active and collaborative. In psychoanalytically oriented psychotherapy, hypnosis may play an important adjunctive role.

There are a number of ways in which hypnosis facilitates a program of psychoanalytically oriented psychotherapy (Wolberg, 1957). First, hypnosis may exert a positive influence on the relationship with the therapist by mobilizing the essential hope, faith, and trust that are parcels of every helping process and by cutting through resistances that delay the essential establishing of rapport. This is especially important in detached and fearful individuals who put up resistances to any kind of closeness and hence obstruct the evolvement of a working relationship. Second, hypnosis owing to its enhancement of suggestibility, will promote the absorption by the patient of positive pronouncements, verbal and nonverbal, which may alleviate, at least temporarily, symptoms that interfere with exploratory technics. Third, hypnosis often expedites emotional catharsis by opening up founts of bottled-up emotion, thereby promoting temporary relief and signaling some sources of residual conflict. Fourth, resistances to verbalization and free association are often readily lifted by even light hypnosis. Fifth, where motivation is lacking toward inquiry into sources of problems, hypnosis, through its tension-abating and symptom-relieving properties, may help convince the patient that he can derive benefits from treatment if he cooperates with its rules. Sixth, owing to its effect on resistances, hypnosis may help expedite such insight technics as dream recall and the release of forgotten memories. Seventh, hypnosis may light up transference, rapidly bringing fundamental problems to the surface. Eight, by dealing directly with resistances to change, hypnosis may expedite the working-through process, particularly the conversion of insight into action. Toward this end, teaching the patient self-hypnosis may be of value. Finally, hypnosis may sometimes be helpful in the termination of therapy, enabling the patient who has been taught self-relaxation and self-hypnosis to carry on analytic and synthetic processes by himself.

Hypnoanalytic Technics

A number of technics have been described (free association, dream induction, drawing, play therapy, dramatics, automatic writing, regression and revivification, crystal and mirror gazing, time distortion, hypnoplasty, and induction of experimental conflict) that, implemented during hypnosis, have as their purpose the uncovering and working through of unconscious processes (Wolberg, 1964). These embrace a variety of tactics to which different patients will respond with greater or lesser enthusiasm. However, in actual practice only a few need be consistently employed, namely free association under hypnosis and dream stimulation geared toward the analysis of resistance to understanding inner conflict and to the translation of insight into action. Though occasional patients, possessing special propensities, will respond dramatically to regression and revivification, mirror gazing, hypnodrama, and other stratagems; they will not be employed for the great majority of patients. The reason for this is that they require a very deep or somnambulistic trance, a state relatively few individuals can reach. Fortunately, patients may be approached through other devices that require only a light or medium trance, to which all persons, except those who willfully oppose, are susceptible.

Free association. Free association, the chief tool of psychoanalysis, may, owing to resistance, come to a stop. The usual interpretive activities may not succeed in releasing the patient from inhibitions that restrain his spontaneous verbalizations. Asking the patient to shut his eyes and to report any scenes or fantasies that flash before his mind may circumvent a temporary diversion. If this does not succeed, a light hypnotic state may suffice to eliminate the patient's resistance. Where pressure from inner drives and conflicts is great, the mere induction of hypnosis may bring forth a spontaneous outburst of violent emotion, which may or may not be accompanied by verbal content. Should such a sterile outburst occur, an attempt may be made to get the patient to report his associations through the employment of certain releasing technics, some of which have been described elsewhere (Wolberg, 1964). When free association is blocked by resistances impervious to the usual interpretive technics, hypnosis may be advantageously attempted.

A patient started her session by talking about baby and childhood pictures that she had found in an old album.

PT: When I look at baby pictures I begin to panic. (*Pause.*)

LRW: Tell me about this.

PT: (*Breathes heavily.*) I can't think. (*Long pause.*)

LRW: There's something about those baby pictures that frightened you.

PT: Yes. (*Pause.*)

LRW: Are they *your* baby pictures?

PT: Yes. I'm in all of them, although my father is in some of them, also my brother and mother are in some of them. I feel very detached from them. I keep looking at and staring at them. When I go through them, they just don't seem like me. I feel like I'm looking at somebody else. I feel very detached from it. I can't use them to bring back anything. (*Pause.*) The only thing I was able to do was to go back over diaries from high school on through to when I started analysis. I need to talk, but I am detached from all of it. I need to talk about high school, the length of time I was with Dr. . . . I can't remember any of it. I feel frightened of this because I don't know what it is. (*Long silence only unproductively interrupted by my questions. At this point I induce hypnosis to encourage her to associate freely in a trance state.*)

PT: All kinds of weird things that don't make any sense come into my mind.

These are the sorts of things that come all the time and don't make any sense, so I always block them out. (*Pause.*)

LRW: What things?

PT: That I am glad that my mother had cancer and had a breast removed. That I wish she was very fat. That at a certain point in my life it was very disgusting to me—and the picture of me with my father brings it back—that he had so much hair on his body. I never liked men with a lot of hair. This always nauseated me. Here my brother is so cute in the pictures. I'm getting dizzy. (*Pause.*) Feeling any hostile feelings makes me dizzy. It really upset me because my mother called me at school today saying that I had to come home this evening to sign a tax form or something, and I told her that I had been feeling so tired that I had figured that I hadn't been eating enough, and I started eating more. Then she said: "You'd better not get too fat," and I felt like killing her. (*Pause.*)

LRW: You felt like killing her for saying that?

PT: Yes. I've been extremely hostile toward my mother. I never feel that she accepts me the way I am. At school it is very frustrating because I want this Director to kind of be my mother and that just can't be. No wonder I feel so anxious every day when I leave. I have a separation anxiety. I didn't want to leave her when I went home. I want to be with her all the time. It's really a struggle to let out my feelings of hostility, but I'm letting them out and seeing that they are based on something, and that people understand them. (*Very heavy breathing.*) It's as if they both understand the teacher who I'm working with. She is over me. She understands that it is very difficult for me to work under her now, since originally I was the one running the group. I thought that she would be mad at me because I've been feeling so angry at her for coming in and taking over. Yet I took a chance and expressed this, and there was no retaliation of any sort. I told the Director that I had been doing things my way and even though they may prefer another way, I was just furious that somebody was coming in and that there was a lot of things which she did that I didn't like, and yet they were her way of doing them, and I really couldn't do anything about them since I wasn't running the group. I felt like screaming in there. Then she said, yes, that she understood this. (*Pause.*)

LRW: Don't you get disappointed when she doesn't act the part of your mother?

PT: Yes. I do, but I inhibit this so much. I've really been pushing this under. I've been saying that I can't. I haven't been in touch with my feelings, which is why I've been coming in and saying that I don't have anything to talk about. I would like to think that I've worked out this situation with the other teacher. I am very upset, but I've accepted the fact that she is in her position and I'm in mine and that I will learn from her. But I guess I still feel very resentful. (*Pause.*)

LRW: You still resent her very much.

PT: Yes. I guess I caught that at one point this afternoon and I was very upset at seeing it. (*Long silence.*)

LRW: See if an image comes to your mind. Tell me what you see.

PT: I keep seeing a leopard pacing up and down in his cage. He just walks back and forth and he can't get out. (*Pause.*) I just had a vision of feeding my brother to the leopard. I saw him as a little boy and I was going to throw him in the cage and he would be chewed up and then he wouldn't be around any longer. Then I would be loved.

LRW: You would have mommy and daddy all for yourself.

PT: Yes. . . . Thinking of it makes me very dizzy. That's what I feel, very guilty. I guess I hate him for getting married because I didn't want him to be happy. And I hate mother. I keep closing my door every night so that she won't come in and talk to me. I feel so anxious when she is around. But I guess I do need her to like me because I have been dependent on her so that I feel very panicky when I think she is sensing the fact that I don't want her to talk to me. Then she starts to avoid me. I've just been feeling so angry at everybody. I can't stop talking about myself to people. I feel completely isolated. (*Pause.*)

LRW: What set off this reaction?

PT: It was the history teacher I met. I kept writing in my diary how I loved him. It was the feeling like a child, seeing older men and liking them and feeling that I loved them, and feeling very anxious when they were around, very nervous. Wanting them to talk to me and yet being petrified lest they talk to me. I pretty much feel the same way with fellows now. I still feel like a little girl. I still feel that I don't want to get too close when I see somebody that I like. I want him to talk to me, but I would be terrified if he said anything—that I would stutter and I wouldn't be able to say anything. Because, who am I? It's as if any man that I like talks to me only as a big favor, or they are talking to me because I am a little girl. In a way I am so terrified that I would like to be rejected, sick, and I would like the men to know this, and that I am very disturbed and they had better not have anything to do with me. I wasn't really aware that I still feel this way until I broke up with this guy and started reading some of this. When I went folk dancing, I saw a guy who I had been seeing over and over again, and I started shaking because I wanted to talk to him. And yet I was terrified of saying anything to him and so I got very dizzy. I felt the same way then that I felt in high school with this history teacher. I like his looks, body, the way he moves, his smile, and his enthusiasm for dancing. He seemed to have a warmth about him. It kept going through my mind—he's a man and I'm a little girl. (*Pause.*)

LRW: Remind you of anything?

PT: I have no exact idea, but I would guess that it was probably not until I was fifteen. I have a memory of being physically close to father for a very long time. As a matter of fact, when I was going with George, if he would kiss me on the neck, my head started spinning, because my father used to do that. I panicked when he did that. I would say stop it over and over again. When he stopped, I felt all right. (*Pause.*)

LRW: Could you have had this same feeling toward your father? You've been denying the fact that you've had any deep, close feelings toward your father.

PT: Which would in turn mean that if I had this closeness with him for so long it would naturally make me furious at my mother for being around. As a matter of fact, I get a picture in my mind of his kissing her and of imagining that he hates it, and that he would much rather kiss me. This still goes through my mind now. She is horrible. How can he kiss her? She's old, like his mother. I always think of her as his mother. I always think of him as if he were my age. I think I feel that it would be perfectly natural that I should sleep with him. This sends me into a panic that I should think that way. (*Pause, during which the patient is visibly agitated.*)

LRW: What do you feel?

PT: I feel absolute disgust and nausea. But my feelings are still, if only he would let me love him, take care of him, and that his whole life has been ruined by my mother. Also that I would make him feel strong and masculine, and that she has emasculated him and made him into nothing. No wonder I was feeling so in a panic about going home this evening.

LRW: Do you think you may transfer any of these feelings toward other men?

PT: It becomes absolutely out of control. It becomes overpowering. It's really —though I was never conscious of it when I wrote in my diary—this is what was getting me with all these men that I used to see and liked. I just couldn't stand it. Yet I wasn't the least bit consciously aware until halfway through college of any sexual feelings. Never. I must have had it, but I never admitted it.

LRW: It may have been too dangerous for you to admit it.

PT: I guess I solved the problem of competing with mother by deciding that it would be safer to be a boy. The sexual feelings were too overpowering. I guess that's why I decided that I would never get married. I was aware of having trapped myself somehow. I decided that after folk dancing that night that I could never marry somebody who wasn't special to me, and yet I could never relate to such a person. I would be too terrified. I have a feeling that this is all connected with taking a passive role sexually. I keep having a tremendous feeling of wanting to be raped, of not doing anything, just wanting to be taken over.

LRW: Do you have fantasies about this?

PT: A vision keeps going through my mind. Such as the man in the folk-dance place. Just lying there and enjoying it. I don't know why. I think in that way I don't think I can be rejected. Because I won't really be involved in it. As a matter of fact, I think that this is most what I complained about with George. I didn't know why it bothered me so much that he is so shy and unaggressive. In that relationship with him, I played a very active role sexually. Now consciously this made me feel very good, but I wonder if I didn't feel very angry because of his lack of responsiveness. There is always a mixed fear, desire, and terror about being raped. It's equivalent to dying for me. Just losing any sense of self. And yet it still seems like the most pleasurable thing that could happen to me. I wonder if at some point I didn't have fantasies about sleeping with my father. Something just passed through my mind. Trying to go into my parents' room and finding it locked. I felt like tearing the house down; it made me so furious. I didn't know why.

LRW: Can you recapture what you might have been thinking?

PT: Yes. That they were sleeping together.

LRW: You knew that they were sleeping together?

PT: I didn't know it consciously. I would never admit any of these things.

LRW: Perhaps that you wanted to be in your mother's position?

PT: My God. I'm so dizzy.

LRW: That's how you felt when you were dancing with this man, dizzy.

PT: Yes. I now see the connection—when I was blocking out the fantasies that I was having about my father. Nausea and getting upset. I get that all the time now. I always get that around men that I like.

Mobilization of transference. It is to be expected that hypnosis will tend to mobilize transference, a contingency that can prove of help in repressed patients who deny their projections. How hypnosis may help bring transference feelings to the surface may be illustrated by a patient with anxiety hysteria who gradually had circumscribed her activities to avoid attacks of panic and uncomfortable physical symptoms, which focused on choking sensations and pains in the upper extremities and back. Free associations had come to a sudden pause, the patient professing a blankness in thinking at the same time that she experienced a recrudescence of her symptoms. Immediately prior to coming to my office for a few sessions she had experienced vague feelings of excitement and a frightening "lump in the throat." During the session she had little to say, other than to talk about her symptoms and to ramble about reality problems that were, she insisted, of important concern to her. Probings of her resistance yielded nothing. She remembered no dreams, and she vehemently denied any feelings about me other than that she trusted me and was sure of my concern for her. At the end of one session, I decided to attempt to break the deadlock by inducing hypnosis, giving her the suggestion that she would remember any important dreams and discuss them with me at the next hour. The suggestion was successful, as the following excerpt of the session illustrates:

PT: I was choking all Friday and I didn't know what it was, but I was working very hard and I didn't pay much attention to it. On Saturday it got much worse. The result was I withdrew Sunday quite a bit, and last night, in the middle of the night, I got up with such a nightmare, fright and screaming. What is it? I almost trusted a man. I almost trusted a man. It was a wild, wild nightmare. My shoulders and every part of my body was shaking. (*Pause.*) (*The patient apparently responded to my suggestion that she recall an important dream.*)

LRW: In other words, you had a nightmare in which you felt you trusted someone?

PT: Whether I wanted to trust him in sex or whether I was just trusting him, I don't know. But I had the feeling that I was just about to trust a man, and I was petrified. Can you imagine, after all this working, Dr. Wolberg. (*Pause.*) It was nice, fine, and good and wonderful, and I was just about to trust him and I started to go all to pieces. (*I got the impression at this moment that she was talking about her relationship with me, that she has begun to trust me, but that this threatens her defense against men that has up to this time served to protect her against hurt.*)

LRW: Anything precede the dream—the day before?

PT: Nothing except I had a date with this man. I have a problem with him even though I've had an affair with him two years before. As soon as I feel that his erection is good and strong, I must control from there on. In other words, as long as he is impotent, as long as he can't get an erection, I don't care and everything is all right. But the minute I feel that the erection is there, I panic. Now I think this is it. (*Apparently her need to control is essential; impotence in a man removes his threat to her.*)

LRW: Are you aware of the panic while it is happening?

PT: No.

LRW: This business of the old pattern of not permitting him penetration, how old is that?

PT: The funniest part is that when I am in control I allow it. Only when I feel that I'm in control. When I feel that he is not too erect. If he is really in there pitching, I turn to every other means to satisfy him and to do all sorts of things so as not to have him penetrate.

LRW: What about this business of control. What comes to your mind as far back as you can go? Shut your eyes, relax, breathe deeply, and tell me what comes to your mind. (*A suggestion such as this can induce a light hypnosis.*)

PT: (*Pause.*) Oh. I can't (*gasping*). It was a bus stop. I remember what I was wearing. I was wearing a little coat, hat, and little red scarf. The man had a stomach, and he was heavy and fat and sitting down on the bench of the bus stop. He must have had candy in his hand. He said: "Come here, little girl." And I did. Then he asked me to do that, to suck his penis. Then I did. I didn't understand what it was. Then all of a sudden something must have happened because I ran away into an empty lot. I ran screaming. All I can remember is my scarf flying in the air, and my books flying, and I ran home. I don't think that I ever told my parents. I never thought of it since.

LRW: It must have terrorized you.

PT: It must have done something. Evidently this is the big thing and all week I felt like choking. Just like now (*holds hands on throat*). Something about you (*gasping*). (*Transference feelings seem evident.*)

LRW: What do you feel with me?

PT: There was a time I felt in control.

LRW: But not now?

PT: No. Because when I got up in the nightmare, it could have been you. I don't know who it was. It was just men or a man. And yet I think that I associate this man with my father, because I remember saying once that my father was like this man. Therefore, I must have hated all men. (*The incident with the man at the bus stop may have been a cover memory for fantasies related to her father.*)

LRW: Do you feel that you trusted your father at all?

PT: Not really. Except when he was ill. When he was ill he had to rely on me even to go to the bathroom. So that this was the greatest thrill of my life. We have the story pretty much, but I can't seem to do anything about it. It makes me weak thinking of all this. This is most amazing. Why did I put this on today? (*Pointing to dress.*) I think I wanted to be choked. I had no business putting this on today. This is the highest-neck dress that I have. (*Masochism is a prominent aspect in this patient.*)

LRW: Why do you think that you want to be choked?

PT: Guilt feelings? I feel guilty. And yet it was guiltless.

LRW: Then what could you feel guilty about? Right now on the reality level?

PT: Nothing.

LRW: What could happen if you really let yourself go with a man? What is the worst thing that could happen in reality?

PT: Nothing. It is so hard to answer. I can feel it all the way down in my guts. How am I going to overcome this?

LRW: Perhaps if you talk about your feelings about me it will help.

PT: (*Pause.*) It's all there. I mean you, and father, and this man. I say to myself that it would be the grandest thing in the world to have that kind of relationship, a good relationship with you, because it is normal, natural, and yet . . . I tremble, get panicky. It is understandable. There I am and I have to work it out. At least one thing is good. We talk about it. There is nothing ever left unsaid now.

This session constituted a crucial breaking through of her resistance. The understanding that her associational block was produced by a fusion of images projected into transference enabled her to continue her analytic work. This was associated with a progressive bettering of her relationships with men, sexual and nonsexual, and with a consistent strengthening of other aspects of her personality.

Sometimes the hypnotic situation per se acts as the chief means for the working through of transference. A patient who easily entered into a deep hypnotic state became more and more recalcitrant to suggestions. He was submissive to his father (and to later male authority), and his rage was internalized with resulting depression and psychophysiological gastrointestinal symptoms. From his associations it was apparent that his acceding to my suggestion that we utilize hypnosis was to please me, as he had pleased his father by conforming to his male parent's whims. "For years I hated my father. He couldn't stand being contradicted. I remember needing to lose at cards deliberately so that father would not get upset by my winning. I never am able to be successful; it makes me too anxious." The resolution of his conflict with male authority was to a large extent worked through in transference. At first he fantasied, resisting hypnosis; then he deliberately resisted it, finally being unable to enter the hypnotic state on any level. Accompanying this were dreams of triumph and feelings of love for his father. "It's a healthier dream to feel love than hate. For the first time I realize I loved my father. I cried in my sleep. I felt father really loves me, but we had this wall between us. I awoke feeling I really loved him." This change in feeling was associated with a complete abatement of symptoms and was soon followed by a capacity to relate more cooperatively with men.

Dream induction. The stimulation of dream recall may be attempted through hypnotic suggestion. The quality of symbolism will depend on the depth of trance. In light hypnosis, the symbolic representations are like waking daydreams; in somnambulistic hypnosis, like night dreams. Where a patient shows resistance to remembering dreams, suggestions by the analyst during hypnosis, or by the patient himself during self-hypnosis, may facilitate recall. Dream content may be suggested with a selective focusing on special problems and conflicts.

For example, a man with a problem of impotence developed an ambivalent transference toward me. Because of his difficulty in remembering dreams, I induced hypnosis and suggested that he would dream regarding his feelings about his wife. That evening he dreamed:

Isabelle has injured her arm; actually it is her right hand. In fact we are in a hospital room. She is in bed. I am sitting in an easy chair waiting for her to become conscious. Actually her right hand had to be amputated. It was the result of an accident using a power tool while working on a piece of sculpture. She becomes conscious. She is unaware that her right hand has been amputated; the right forearm is heavily bandaged and she doesn't realize her hand is missing. (*The patient's wife has functioned with him as a mother figure. The patient during analysis has slowly been overcoming his submissive attitude toward her and has, to a better degree, been functioning sexually. This may be equated with his having castrated her in assuming a more dominant position.*)

At this point I awaken, and then fall asleep again. We are back in the same dream. My father and another elderly man enter to visit. I am surprised for one that he knows of the injury and that he has bothered to make this visit. We embrace in greeting each other. The other man reminds me of a friend, John Davis. I say that as long as they are visiting, I will go out and repark my car, which I do by driving it up from a Riverside Drive-like location right into a building somewhere.

I am back in the hospital room and ask my father, "Have you told her that her hand is missing?" He says, "Oh, no, not me, I haven't the courage. You'll have to tell her yourself." She is herself still unaware.

I think I awake again, but I am not sure. I may have dreamed this. The scene is uncertain, but a man who could be a French-Canadian guide with Indian blood and I are looking at a fragment of a canoe that is made out of metal. He points out that the quality of work tells him it came from the Old Town Canoe factory in Old Town, Maine. I am surprised. I know they only work in wood there, but somehow realize its been thirty-five years since I was there, so times could have changed.

We are now in your office waiting room, not here, but in a country village. I am talking with an unidentified person, perhaps a woman and the doctor with whom you share this office. This doctor is either a surgeon or some other highly technical practitioner of mechanistic medical skill. We are arguing about helping bums. I take the position that one who gives to a bum is really hostile to them, because the bum's pattern is to take and fail, and by offering giving-type help we keep him in that pattern. The doctor is derisive, contemptuous, and says this argument is really reaching too far and is either not intelligent or is overintelligent. But then, if I am there to see you, it is probably for some Freudian sort of reason (*said with great contempt!*), and that explains my unrealistic position. (*I am apparently fused here with his father.*)

In the midst of this argument my wife enters. She is wearing a blue and green plaid jumper, which she fills out appealingly. Her hip line is full, the bust is full and generous. She reminds me that we have to go somewhere and asks me to button the straps of her dress in the back. I button the straps and tell her to run along. I prefer to remain and continue the discussion. She is whole, there is no suggestion of the injury. In fact she looks wonderful and healthy. (*This is perhaps indicative of a better relationship with his wife.*)

We, the doctor and I, are in a driveway by a big white station wagon. We are waiting for the woman to come out of the house, another house nearby, so that we can drive somewhere and continue the discussion. He points out that I must have been in the office to see you and would I not now be missing that appointment. I say it is only 8 A.M. and my appointment is not until late afternoon and I awake.

The patient's associations brought out his ambivalent feelings toward me, which he recognized contained many of the attitudes he had toward his father.

Induction of Hypnosis

Perhaps the most suitable way to approach hypnotic induction is to assume that every patient, given the opportunity to shut his eyes and to relax, will, with repetitive suggestions, go into at least a light state of hypnosis. It is not necessary to strive for "deep" hypnosis except under special circumstances. In the great majority of cases, a light or medium hypnotic state will suffice. Technics, such as regression and revivification, the recovery of repressed memories, and the induction of experimental conflict, require a deep or somnambulistic trance. Since only 10 to 15 per cent of individuals are capable of achieving somnambulistic states, the use of these specialized hypnoanalytic procedures will be limited. Fortunately, such procedures are rarely necessary even where the patient is capable of entering a state of deep hypnosis. For all practical purposes, light hypnosis will be all that is required. Where deep hypnosis is desired for the more specialized hypnoanalytic procedures, instructions will be found elsewhere (Wolberg, 1964).

Because of the unfortunate association of hypnosis with charlatanry and magic, it is best to tell patients that they will be shown how to relax in order to help them associate more easily. The patient will then less readily enter into a contest with the analyst around the issue of whether he has been hypnotized or not. Should the patient inquire about the technic and ask if he has been hypnotized, the analyst may simply say that it is possible for all people to enter a mild hypnotic state as they relax. This is perfectly normal and may prove helpful.

The easiest way to induce hypnosis, in my experience, is through relaxation exercises involving the following four steps: (1) deep breathing; (2) progressive muscle relaxation; (3) visualization of a relaxed scene; and (4) counting slowly from 1 to 20. The pace of suggestions should be slow with occasional pauses between suggestions. The following is from a recording:

Now just settle back and shut your eyes. Breathe in deeply through your nostrils, right down into the pit of your stomach. D-e-e-p-l-y, d-e-e-p-l-y, d-e-e-p-l-y; but not so deeply that you are uncomfortable. Just deeply enough so that you feel the air soaking in. (*As the patient inspires, indicated by a heaving of the chest, the operator may say "in" and with expiration "out" for several breathing cycles.*) In . . . and out. D-e-e-p-l-y, d-e-e-p-l-y. In . . . and out. And as you feel the air soaking in, you begin to feel yourself getting t-i-r-e-d and r-e-l-a-x-e-d. Very r-e-l-a-x-e-d. Even d-r-o-w-s-y, d-r-o-w-s-y and relaxed. Drowsy and relaxed.

Now I want you to concentrate on the muscle groups that I point out to you. Loosen them, relax them while visualizing them. You will notice that you may be tense in certain areas and the idea is to relax yourself completely. Concentrate on your forehead. Loosen the muscles in your forehead. Now your eyes. Loosen the muscles around your eyes. Your eyelids relax. Now your face, your face relaxes. And your mouth . . . relax the muscles around your mouth, and even the inside of your mouth. Your chin; let it sag and feel heavy. And as you relax your muscles, your breathing continues r-e-g-u-l-a-r-l-y and d-e-e-p-l-y, deeply within yourself. Now your neck, your neck relaxes. Every muscle, every fiber in your neck relaxes. Your shoulders relax . . . your arms . . . your elbows . . . your forearms . . . your wrists . . . your hands . . . and your fingers relax. Your arms feel loose and limp; heavy and loose and limp. Your whole body begins to feel loose and limp. Your neck muscles relax; the front of your neck; the back muscles. Wiggle your head if necessary to get all the kinks out. Keep breathing deeply and relax. Now your chest. The front part of your chest relaxes . . . and the back part of your chest relaxes. Your abdomen . . . the pit of your stomach, that relaxes. The small of your back, loosen the muscles. Your hips . . . your thighs . . . your knees relax . . . even the muscles in your legs. Your ankles . . . your feet . . . and your toes. Your whole body feels loose and limp. And when I lift your arm, it will feel very relaxed. (*The left arm may be lifted slightly and released to see if it falls without assistance. If the patient controls it, the operator may say:* "*Make it loose and floppy; relax.*" *He may continue until the arm relaxes.*) And now as you feel the muscles relaxing, you will notice that you begin to feel heavy and relaxed and tired all over. Your body begins to feel v-e-r-y, v-e-r-y tired . . . and you are going to feel d-r-o-w-s-i-e-r, and d-r-o-w-s-i-e-r, from the top of your head right down to your toes. Every breath you take is going to soak in deeper and deeper and deeper, and you feel your body getting drowsier and drowsier.

And now, I want you to imagine, to visualize, the most relaxed and quiet and pleasant scene imaginable. Visualize a relaxed and pleasant, quiet scene. Any scene that is comfortable. It can be some scene in your past, of a scene you project in the future. It can be nothing more than being at the beach watching the water break on the shore. Or a lake with a sail-boat floating lazily by. Or merely looking at the blue sky with one or two billowy clouds moving slowly. Any scene that is quiet and pleasant and makes you feel drowsy. (*Some patients find it difficult to visualize a pleasant scene. Some begin to do so, but it is interrupted by unpleasant images. If the patient reports this at the end of the session, the operator may re-assure him that he will be able to do this more easily soon. In the meantime he may be told merely to visualize a blank wall or curtain, and, if any unpleasant obtrusions occur, to push these out of his mind.*) Drowsier and drowsier and drowsier. You are v-e-r-y weary, and every breath will send you in, deeper and deeper and deeper. (*The pace of suggestions must be slow, particularly with the count below.*)

As you visualize this quiet scene, I shall count from one to twenty, and when I reach the count of twenty, you will feel yourself in deep. One, deeper and deeper. Two, deeper and deeper and deeper. Three . . . drowsier and drowsier. Four, deeper and deeper. Five . . . drowsier and drowsier and drowsier. Six . . . seven, very tired, very relaxed. Eight, deeper and deeper. Nine . . . ten, drowsier and drowsier. Eleven, twelve, thirteen; deeper and deeper. D-r-o-w-s-i-e-r and d-r-o-w-s-i-e-r. Fourteen, drowsier and drowsier and drowsier. Fifteen . . . sixteen . . . seventeen; deeper and deeper. Eighteen . . . nineteen . . . and finally twenty.

I want you, for the next few minutes, to continue visualizing a quiet and wonderfully relaxed scene, and, as you do, you will get more and more and more relaxed. Your body will begin to get heavier and more relaxed, and you will get drowsier and drowsier. When I talk to you next, you'll be more deeply relaxed. (*Pause for a half-minute or so before proceeding.*)

The patient may then be instructed to say whatever comes to him as he customarily does in free association. He may also be asked to report any fantasies or images that appear before his mind.

A technique I have found valuable is that of suggesting that the patient imagine himself entering a theater and watching action on a stage. This permits him to project inner feelings and conflicts. The following instructions may be formulated:

I'm going to ask you to visualize yourself inside a theater. You are sitting in a seat in the second or third row. You are observing the stage. You notice that the curtains are drawn together. Raise your hand (or finger) when you visualize this. [When the patient raises his hand (or finger), suggestions continue: You are curious as to what is going on behind the curtain.] Then you notice a man (*or woman if the patient is a woman*) standing on the stage at the far end of the curtain. He has an expression of extreme fear and horror on his face as if he is observing behind the curtain the most frightening and horrible thing imaginable. You wonder what this may be, and you seem to absorb this man's fear. In a moment the curtain will open suddenly, and you will see what frightens this person. As soon as you do, tell me about it without waking up. As soon as you see action on the stage, tell me exactly what you see.

After the patient describes what he sees, he is told:

You continue to sit in the theater observing the stage. The curtain again is closed. You see the same man, but this time, instead of having a fearful expression on his face, he has a happy expression. It is as if he is filled with unbounded happiness and joy, and as you watch him you begin to participate in his happy feelings. You wonder what causes him to be so happy. In a moment the curtain will open suddenly, and you will see what makes him feel so happy. You will see the happiest and most delightful thing that can happen to a person. As soon as you see action on the stage, tell me exactly what you see.

Upon describing his fantasy, the patient is told:

What you have observed are fantasies. Fantasies are thought processes in a state of reverie. They are related to dreams. As a matter of fact, dreams are nothing more than fantasies in a state of sleep. Whenever in the future I ask you to dream while you are relaxed, it will be possible for you to let your mind wander and to have a series of thought processes similar to those I have just described. Or you may have an actual dream.

When I give you the suggestion to dream, just let yourself relax deeply enough so that a series of images comes to your mind. If you find it difficult to dream, imagine yourself in a theater, sitting in the second or third row, looking at the stage. As you watch the drawn curtain, it will suddenly open, and you will see action. For example, as you sit there now, I want you to go into a deep state and to have a dream, anything that happens to come to your mind. As soon as you have had this dream, tell me about it without waking up.

The fantasies that the patient has produced in reference to situations of fear and happiness may yield important clues to his conflicts. Later on, with this technic perfected, it may be possible to get the patient to dream about or to produce fantasies relating to any special topics, such as existing anxieties, resistance manifestations, and transference feelings toward the analyst.

To bring the patient out of hypnosis, a technic aimed at slow awakening is best. The following suggestions are offered:

Relax yourself completely. I am going to start bringing you out. I will count slowly from one to five, and, as I do, you will gradually become more and more awake. At the count of five, your eyes will open. You will have no headache, no dizziness, no confusion or any other uncomfortable symptoms. One, you are beginning to awaken now; two, slowly awaken; three, you feel more awake; four, you are getting wider and wider awake; five, your eyes begin to open gradually; wake up completely.

Some patients who can enter deep hypnosis, upon awakening, show untoward psychosomatic effects in the form of shivering, confusion, nausea, and headache. Where these sequelae are present, it is best to rehypnotize the person and to suggest that his symptoms will not be present when he awakens. These side reactions are most often present when the patient has been given a posthypnotic suggestion that he attempts to resist, either because it is opposed to his standards, or because he desires to maintain control of his actions without yielding to the commands of the operator. In such cases, rehypnosis and suggestion that symptoms will disappear are usually without avail. During rehypnosis the operator had best inform the patient that he will not have to follow the suggestions given to him. In some cases even this release will not neutralize the former suggestion, and psychosomatic symptoms will not disappear until the subject carries out the posthypnotic suggestion that has been made. At any rate all unusual symptoms following hypnosis disappear spontaneously in the course of several hours after the termination of the trance unless the patient is specially motivated to continue them. If so this will constitute a productive focus for analysis.

In some cases, the analyst may wish to secure the patient's cooperation by having him work on selected aspects of his problem by himself. Under such circumstances he may be instructed in the technic of self-hypnosis. Except for occasional borderline or psychotic patients, self-hypnosis poses no risks. It may actually be quite helpful where resistance is especially obdurate or when acting out interferes with the analytic process.

The technic of self-hypnosis is simple. It generally follows the method employed by the operator in his induction of hypnosis. Few of the deepening tactics will be required since the patient himself will, with practice, be able to achieve a level satisfactorily productive for analytic work. The method that is most easily applicable is that of hypnosis through relaxation described above. Toward the end of a hypnotic session, the patient may be given the suggestion that he will be able to put himself into a deeply relaxed state by practicing the relaxing exercises. The four phases: deep breathing, progressive muscle relaxation, visualization of a relaxed scene, and counting to oneself from one to twenty, are to be executed, followed by self-suggestions to explore a specific problem. To bring himself out of self-hypnosis, the patient is instructed to count slowly from one to five, at the end of which time he instructs himself to awaken. Many patients find it useful to use the word "you" instead of "I" in giving themselves instructions.

The patient will often improvise his own technics, once he masters the routine procedures. He will discover exploratory methods that work best for him. The most common complaints, which are actually resistances, are that he has no time to practice self-hypnosis or that he falls asleep with it. If the patient enters hypnosis too rapidly or too deeply, dozing off toward the end, he may be advised to begin his self-analytic work just before the point in his induction where he feels himself slipping in too profoundly. Patients do not get addicted to self-hypnosis. On the contrary, they have to be encouraged to continue with it, since they are apt to regard it as a chore.

Spontaneous trance experiences are often interesting and may reflect emotions, attitudes, and memories that are only lightly repressed. In the event the patient forgets these experiences, he may be encouraged to write them down after arousing himself. Untoward reactions during self-hypnosis are rare. Occasionally a borderline person may frighten himself. For example, one patient reported: "When I get into this fairly deep thing, I start getting frightened. I feel my arms get huge, one yard in diameter. My face and lips are going doughy and flabby. I feel I weigh two hundred pounds more than I do. I feel an awful grotesque bulk, like a prehistoric monster. I am ponderously huge. I feel I am slipping back into an atavistic, embryonic state. These don't feel like my own arms." Here analysis of his experience revealed a combination of impulses to return to the womb and to destroy and demolish the contents of his mother's body, as well as the world in general. The self-induced fantasy proved to be a great stimulant to his work in analysis. In most cases self-hypnosis is a pleasant experience.

In giving the patient specific directives, he may be told that he will be able to observe his thoughts, associations, and feelings and to remember important ones clearly. Many patients train themselves so that they can work out special problems as they arise. For example, when tension mounts, some patients may be able to arrive at the source through associating, fantasying, or dreaming in a self-induced hypnotic state, or, if they fail to do so immediately, to have a dream that evening that will contribute to their understanding of the problem.

Summary

Hypnosis may be valuable as an adjunctive aid both in formal psychoanalysis and psychoanalytically oriented psychotherapy. Its value lies chiefly in its capacity to resolve resistances to exploration, working through, and utilization of insight toward corrective personality change. Not all analysts are capable of employing hypnosis, and a period of experimentation will be necessary to determine what effect the interpolation of hypnosis has on one's technics. Example of how hypnoanalysis operates and a simple induction method are detailed.

REFERENCES

[Note: S.E. refers to *The Standard Edition of the complete psychological works of Sigmund Freud* (London: Hogarth Press).]

ANTEBI, R. N. Seven principles to overcome resistances in hypnoanalysis. *British Journal of Medical Psychology*, 1963, 36, 341–349.
BOWERS, M. K., and BRECHER, S. The emergence of multiple personalities in the course of hypnotic investigation. *International Journal of Clinical and Experimental Hypnosis*, 1955, 3, 188.

BRENMAN, M., and GILL, M. M. *Hypnotherapy.* Josiah Macy, Jr. Foundation. Review series, 1944, 2, No. 3.

BRENMAN, M., and GILL, M. M. *Hypnosis and related states.* New York: International Universities Press, 1959.

BRENMAN, M., GILL, M. M., and HACKER, F. J. Alterations in the state of the ego in hypnosis. *Bulletin of the Menninger Clinic,* 1947, 11, 60.

BRENMAN, M., GILL, M. M., and KNIGHT, R. P. Spontaneous fluctuations in depth hypnosis and their implications for ego-function. *International Journal of Psychoanalysis,* 1952, 33, Part 1.

BREUER, J., and FREUD, S. *Studies on hysteria* (1895). S.E., Vol. 2. (Also published by Basic Books, New York, 1957.)

CHERTOK, L. On the discovery of the cathartic method. *International Journal of Psychoanalysis,* 1961, 42, 284.

CONN, J. H. Hypnotic relaxation and analysis. In *Therapy through hypnosis.* New York: Citadel Press, 1952.

ERICKSON, M. H., and KUBIE, L. S. The permanent relief of an obsessional phobia by means of communications with an unsuspected dual personality. *Psychoanalytic Quarterly,* 1939, 8, 471.

FARBER, L. H., and FISHER, C. An experimental approach to dream psychology through the use of hypnosis. *Psychoanalytic Quarterly,* 1943, 12, 202.

FISHER, C. Studies on the nature of suggestion. Part 1: experimental induction of dreams by direct suggestion. *Journal of the American Psychoanalytic Association,* 1953, 1, 222.

FREUD, ANNA. *The ego and the mechanisms of defense.* New York: International Universities Press, 1946.

FREUD, S. Lines of advance in psychoanalytic therapy. (1919). S.E., Vol. 17, pp. 157–168.

FREUD, S. Freud's psychoanalytic procedure. (1904). S.E., Vol. 7, pp. 249–256.

FREYTAG, F. F. *The hypnoanalysis of an anxiety hysteria.* New York: Julian Press, 1959.

GILL, M., and MENNINGER, K. Techniques of hypnoanalysis illustrated in a case report. *Bulletin of the Menninger Clinic,* 1946, 10, 110–126.

GITELSON, M. The emotional position of the analyst in the psycho-analytic situation. *International Journal of Psychoanalysis,* 1952, 33, 1.

HADFIELD, J. A. Treatment by suggestion and hypnoanalysis. In E. Miller (Ed.), *Neuroses in war.* New York: Macmillan, 1940.

KLEMPERER, E. Hypnosis and hypnoanalysis. *Journal of the American Medical Association,* 1953, 8, 164.

KLEMPERER, E. Changes of the body image in hypnoanalysis. *International Journal of Clinical and Experimental Hypnosis,* 1954, 2, 157.

KLINE, M. V. Freud and hypnosis: a critical evaluation. *British Journal of Medical Hypnosis,* 1953, 4, 2.

KUBIE, L. S., and MARGOLIN, S. An apparatus for the use of breath sounds as a hypnogogic stimulus. *American Journal of Psychiatry,* 1944, 100, 610.

LINDNER, R. M. *Rebel without a cause. The hypnoanalysis of a criminal psychopath.* New York: Grune and Stratton, 1944.

LINDNER, R. M. Hypnoanalysis in a case of hysterical somnambulism. *Psychoanalytic Review,* 1945, 32, 325–339.

LINDNER, R. M. Hypnoanalysis as a psychotherapeutic technique. In Gustav Bychowsky and J. Louise Despert (Eds.), *Specialized techniques in psychotherapy.* New York: Basic Books, 1952. Pp. 25–39.

MAZER, M. An experimental study of the hypnotic dream. *Psychiatry.* 1951, 14, 265.

RAGINSKY, B. B. Sensory hypnoplasty with case illustrations. *International Journal of Clinical and Experimental Hypnosis,* 1962, 10, 205.

SCHNECK, J. M. Fragments of hypnoanalysis. *Diseases of the Nervous System,* 1951, 12, 369–372.

SCHNECK, J. M. Self-hypnotic dreams in hypnoanalysis. *International Journal of Clinical and Experimental Hypnosis,* 1953, 1, 44.

SPITZ, R. A. Transference: the analytic setting and its prototype. *International Journal of Psychoanalysis,* 1956, 37, 380.

STILLERMAN, B. The management in analytic hypnotherapy of the psychodynamic reaction to the induction of hypnosis. *International Journal of Clinical and Experimental Hypnosis,* 1957, 5, 3.

TAYLOR, W. S. A hypnoanalytic study of two cases of war neurosis. *Journal of Abnormal and Social Psychology,* 1922, 16, 344.

THIGPEN, C. H., and CLECKLEY, H. A case of multiple personality. *Journal of Abnormal and Social Psychology,* 1954, 49, 135.

WATKINS, J. G. *Hypnotherapy of war neuroses.* New York: Ronald Press, 1949.

WOLBERG, L. R. A mechanism of hysteria elucidated during hypnoanalysis. *Psychoanalytic Quarterly,* 1945, 14, No. 4.

WOLBERG, L. R. Hypnosis in psychoanalytic psychotherapy. In J. H. Masserman and J. L. Moreno (Eds.), *Progress in psychotherapy.* New York: Grune and Stratton, 1957.

WOLBERG, L. R. *Hypnoanalysis* (2nd ed.). New York: Grune and Stratton, 1964.

20

THE QUESTION OF RESEARCH IN PSYCHOANALYTIC TECHNIQUE

John E. Gedo
George H. Pollock

In discussing research in psychoanalytic technique, two considerations must be kept in mind: first, that the goal of the psychoanalytic procedure is therapy; second, the rationale for the existing technique—what its empirical roots are and what modifications have been introduced, by whom, when, and for what reason.

Research is undertaken when pressing unanswered questions have come to light or when a particular methodological or technical advance becomes necessary in order to obtain fresh observational data, either for hypothesis formulation or for hypothesis-testing. It follows from this that research in the area of psychoanalytic technique can be divided into two approximate

560

categories: on the one hand, studies of various aspects of current technique (and those of its modifications intended to broaden the range of applicability of psychoanalysis), and on the other hand, research into the theory of technique designed to produce a change in its basic paradigm. We are mindful of the arbitrariness of this dichotomy; however, in order to facilitate discussion we shall attempt to deal with each of these clusters separately. Limitations of space preclude consideration of a third major potential area for investigation of psychoanalytic technique, that of the study of the paramount tool of the psychoanalyst, interpretation. (For discussion of this problem, consult Devereux, 1951; Loewenstein, 1951; Schmidl, 1955.) Certain principles will be briefly outlined before we begin the more detailed consideration of these areas.

Basic Principles

The goal of any psychoanalytic procedure is that of therapy. The aim of gathering data for various types of studies can be met through associative anamnestic interviews arranged for this investigative purpose (e.g., Colby, 1960, 1961). When, however, a psychoanalytic procedure is employed, the motivation of the patient and that of the psychoanalyst must be of therapeutic benefit for the patient, lest, in the pursuit of another aim, the outcome of the treatment be jeopardized (Fox, 1958; Mahl and Karpe, 1953). In the process of every analysis, with the therapeutic procedure kept constant, data are gathered that can later be utilized in investigating a variety of problems. (See Bellak, 1961; Brenman, 1947; Ellis, 1949; Kubie, 1956; and Seeman, 1952.) Modifications of various components of the psychoanalytic procedure and technique may yield good therapeutic results, but if the limits of what constitutes "psychoanalysis" as a treatment technique are exceeded, the data can no longer be utilized directly to draw conclusions applicable to questions about psychoanalytic propositions.[1]

The basic model of psychoanalysis in current use has been defined with particular clarity by K. Eissler (1953). Two individuals, the patient and the analyst, agree to work together following certain ground rules. It is

[1] On the question of increasing the reliability of observational data by means of films and/or sound recordings, see Alexander, 1958; Brenman, 1947, 1948; Bronner, 1949; Kubie, 1952; Mahl, Dollard, and Redlich, 1954; Redlich, Dollard, and Newman, 1950; Renneker, 1960; and Sternberg, Chapman, and Shakow, 1958. For Freud's views about the feasibility of proving the reliability of analytic observations, see 1911–1915.

assumed that the analyst is competent, having mastered a body of theory and achieved skill in doing analytic work through experience. He must be in touch with his own inner psychological processes in order to be able to use them optimally in his work with patients. It is also assumed that the patient is well motivated for analytic treatment and that his neurosis is of a type which, in theory, can be treated by psychoanalysis successfully. The reality situation must be free of external obstacles to the analysis and even of readily available interferents that can be exploited by internal resistances. Finally, the patient's capacity to test reality must be strong enough to tolerate analytic "abstinence"—the short-term frustration of the procedure and the impact of confrontation with unconscious contents.

The analyst must have sufficient time to validate his observations and interpretations in the course of the numerous repetitions of the analysand's characteristic responses. Consistent and frequent contact also offers the patient emotional support. The many opportunities to differentiate between fantasies and reality permit the analysand to "learn" through insight and repetition.

For all these reasons the patient in analysis is seen frequently (four to five times per week), for interviews of standard duration (45 to 50 minutes), and over long periods of time. In order to minimize contamination of the externalizations transferred by the patient onto the analyst, the latter should be relatively unknown to the patient, and contact between them outside of the analysis should be avoided. The analysand's recumbent position, with the analyst present outside of the patient's field of vision, reduces the interference of external cues with the effort of self-observation.

In all research, one must be aware of the role of observation, imagination, intuition, and reason in the framing of the hypotheses that require testing. The canons of experimentation need not be reviewed here; we need note only the necessity for the careful planning and assessing of experiments designed to yield data that can confirm, refute, or elaborate the assumptions being examined.

The Evolution of Psychoanalytic Interview Procedure

Hartmann and Kris (1945) have long differentiated "the psychoanalytic interview," which they regard as an observational method, from "psychoanalytic therapy." It is indeed striking that, in contrast to the steady and continuing evolution of psychoanalytic technique (to be described in the next section), the nature of the psychoanalytic interview has remained constant for at least sixty-five years. Has this lack of innovation resulted from complete acceptance of the procedures evolved by Freud prior to 1900? Our search of the literature has uncovered no organized research on the effect of altering this variable; whenever the interview procedure changes, the treatment is regarded as psychotherapy (as distinct from "psychoanalytic therapy"), unless the change is a temporary one, unavoidably necessitated by clinical exigencies and ultimately subjected to resolution through analysis of its effects.

It is worth re-emphasizing that the fundamental arrangements of the psychoanalytic situation have remained unchanged since *before* the introduction of the "basic rule" of free association and its corollary, that the analyst's therapeutic task consists of interpretation. What he calls the "psycho-analytic set-up" or, "Freud's clinical setting" has been beautifully summarized by Winnicott (1954), who also stresses the difference between this and the technique of psychoanalysis and calls for more careful and detailed study of the influence of "the setting phenomena" in analysis. Stone (1961) has made a beginning of such studies; he has pointed out, in passing, that some of the features of the "classical analytic situation," which are now understood as dynamically powerful tools in the service of the therapeutic process, were originally devised for reasons of the analyst's convenience, which have been left far behind (p. 19).

Although organized research about the effects of variations in the setting phenomena has been lacking, most analysts have, of course, had experiences with such variations. The probing of such clinical data could illuminate the import of various elements of the psychoanalytic setup, provided that the difficult problem of the evaluation of the outcome of psychoanalytic therapy was properly handled. (The literature of outcome studies is quite extensive. As a sample, see Bronner, 1949; Cheney and Landis, 1935; Coriat, 1917; Deutch, H., 1959; Knight, 1941; Nunberg, 1954; Oberndorf, 1942, 1950; Oberndorf, Greenacre, and Kubie, 1948; Pfeffer, 1959, 1961; and Wallerstein, 1963; Wolman, 1964.) Szurek (1958) has discussed the difficulties (and the rewards) of such controlled investigative work in psychoanalysis, and Chassan (1956) has furnished us with the appropriate statistical tools. Clearly, outcome has to be evaluated on the basis of the entire metapsychological framework of psychoanalysis—not only in terms of criteria of adaptation or symptom removal; assessment can utilize double-blind techniques by employing judges who have had no share in the collection of the primary data. By these means it would be possible to study naturalistic analytic situations, that is, to avoid setting up artificial variations for experimental purposes. (It is generally agreed that such artificial situations may complicate and even vitiate the therapeutic task.) The fruitfulness of the Hampstead Clinic Index Project has amply demonstrated the feasibility of systematically collecting and ordering clinical data derived from psycho-analyses conducted for purely therapeutic purposes (see Sandler, 1962). The establishment of such "pools" of clinical material derived from many patients and many analysts, classified for ease of data retrieval, and available for the study of various questions, is probably the prerequisite for rigorous research in the area we are considering. It would permit investigation of the effect of variations in the frequency and duration of sessions, in the handling of fees, vacations, missed hours, outside financial support of the analysis, interruptions, changes of analysts, and so on. We cite these only as examples; the potential list of relevant parameters is inexhaustible.

In the absence of ongoing research into the "setting phenomena," we must turn our attention to the only instance of reasoned progress in their definition—Freud's reports of his technical procedures during his first decade of psychotherapeutic work (ca. 1889–1899). We shall here focus on the rationale of his choices about some aspects of the interview setting.

Many of the aspects of Freud's clinical setting were initially dictated by the tradition of medical patient care within which he began his psycho-therapeutic work, notably the inspiring example of Josef Breuer, his mentor and scientific collaborator. (See Schlessinger, Gedo, et al., 1967.) It was Breuer, a devoted and much sought-after "general practitioner" (as he somewhat thought of himself), who had devised the routine of daily ap-pointments of about one hour's duration. The frequency and length of sessions were determined empirically (one might even say titrated!) entirely in terms of the needs of his very sick patient, Anna O., whose clinical condition improved or deteriorated according to the degree to which her need for the "chimney sweeping" of the cathartic procedure had been met. Freud followed these procedures with most of the patients he described in Studies on Hysteria, at least some of whom were also very ill and, in the conceptual framework of today, needed the supportive relationship of daily contact with their therapist. The richness of the observations yielded by this intensity of contact awakened and nourished Freud's towering scientific curiosity. Demands on Freud's professional time were not par-ticularly great because of the hostility of the medical community toward him, so that he was under no pressure to divide his available energies among too many patients.

The use of a couch was originally necessitated by the requirement of applying hand pressure to the patient's head in the effort to overcome the resistance against recollection. This technique was utilized for a number of years after the abandonment of hypnosis. The analyst is still sitting (more or less) within arm's length of the patient's head. After Freud had abandoned the laying-on of hands (having found interpretation of resistance an easier and less demanding method of overcoming it than hectoring the patient had been), he continued to sit out of the patient's sight. Freud once expressed personal distaste for being looked at throughout the day as one reason for this choice, an explanation that Jones, for one, has found unconvincing.

Benedek (1953) has suggested that the analyst needs to be screened in order to have an opportunity to deal with his own emotions in relative privacy, that is, to recognize his countertransference and then to manage his feelings. The patient's recumbent position, on the other hand, is said to eliminate outside distractions; it also limits spontaneity of action (Fairbairn, 1952). In both ways, verbalization and focus on inner experience are facilitated.

Very little is known about the development of Freud's system of leasing his time on a retainer basis, but his technical recommendations in this regard are so explicit and forceful (Freud, 1911–1915) that one can only conclude that he arrived at this on the basis of trial and error. Freud was quite keenly aware of the fact that he was departing radically from the prevailing medical mores. He explained the necessity of dealing with money matters "with the same matter-of-course frankness to which he wishes to educate [patients] in things relating to sexual life," since "powerful sexual factors are involved in the value set upon [money]." To judge by the paucity of reports on the import of money in psychoanalysis, this recommendation has not been heeded too thoroughly. (See, however, Lorand and Console, 1958.)

In contrast to the lack of interest in the problem of the business aspects of psychoanalytic treatment, a great deal of attention has been paid to the matter of the analyst's emotional position. Jones (1955, Vol. 2, p. 230) has outlined the gradual evolution of Freud's analytic attitude, from the early days when patients had been invited to meals with the family, through an intermediate phase of familiarity as exemplified by the original record of the case of the Rat Man (Freud, 1909c) with whom he shared occasional refreshments during the analytic sessions. By 1912 (1911–1915, p. 128) Freud had concluded, "The doctor should be opaque to his patients and, like a mirror, should show them nothing but what is shown to him." In other words, the analyst should preserve his anonymity and "separate the patient's affectivity from his own" (Gitelson, 1952) in order to facilitate the systematic resolution of the transference. Recent contributions have emphasized that the analyst is unavoidably seen as a real object by the patient in addition to his role as the screen upon which transferences are displaced. It is quite clear, however, that Freud was forced to emphasize the need for analytic neutrality by the tendency of his early followers to exploit the transference by providing patients with novel experiences (e.g., Jung).

Some Principles of Research into the Theory of Psychoanalytic Technique: A Historical Review

Although Freud was never to write the systematic work on psychoanalytic technique he promised in 1910, he did produce a series of six *Papers on Technique* between 1911 and 1915. Strachey, in an "Introduction" to these (1958), notes that these communications ended a fifteen-year period of silence on the subject (except for what could be inferred from his major case histories of the period—Dora, Little Hans, and the Rat Man— and from the *Interpretation of Dreams*). This reluctance to codify his therapeutic procedures has deprived us of any systematic and explicit discussion by Freud of the theory of psychoanalytic technique. We do possess, however, a "full account" of his treatment procedures of 1895 in the last chapter of *Studies on Hysteria* (1895) which contains Freud's explanation of his evolving theoretical rationale.

From this description (and a number of expository works Freud was to write in later years, which gave a historical review of his psychoanalytic development, i.e., 1910, 1914, 1925) we can reconstruct the path of Freud's research. He had adopted the cathartic method evolved by Breuer and his talented patient, Anna O., in 1880–1882 after his disillusionment with the suggestion techniques he had learned from the Paris and Nancy pioneers. Difficulties in hypnotizing certain patients and the realization that hypnosis facilitated the development of transference love (cf. 1925, p. 27) led Freud to dispense with the hypnotic technique. He utilized his recollection that Bernheim's patients could be made to remember what had happened during the hypnosis if this were insisted on; thus Freud devised the "pressure technique" illustrated by the cases of Lucy R. and Elisabeth von R. in the *Studies*. This change in procedure produced a momentous discovery—that of the phenomenon of resistance. This clinical observation led to the theory of neuroses of defense and its corollary theory of treatment technique—the necessity of overcoming the resistance against recollecting the pathogenic traumata, that is, undoing repression, largely through "the personal influence of the physician" (Breuer and Freud, 1895, p. 283).

"A different view now had to be taken of the task of therapy. Its aim was no longer to 'abreact' an affect which had got on to the wrong lines but to uncover repressions and replace them by acts of judgment which might result either in the accepting or the condemning of what had formerly been repudiated. I showed my recognition of the new situation by no longer calling my method of investigation *catharsis* but psychoanalysis" (1925, p. 30).

The last five pages of the *Studies* take up the issue of transference as resistance and the overriding necessity of dispelling this obstacle by interpretation. Freud reports his discovery that the conflict could be worked through as it was repeated in the transference and the "illusion . . . melted away with the conclusion of the analysis" (1895, p. 304).

The change of paradigm in theory of technique described in the *Studies* is a representative example of the manner in which psychoanalytic research has operated in this area. The cardinal features can be summarized as follows: An earlier technique, serving as a method of data collection, yields a body of observations that necessitates an evolutionary change in theory. The new theory contains within it a necessary modification in the special theory of technique. New methods of clinical application are then devised to accomplish the goals called for by the new theory. These methods bring to light a new body of observational data, and the cycle can begin anew. In this sense, then, research in the theory of technique can only take place after a major conceptual advance in the psychoanalytic theory of behavior; each such advance necessitates applied research to fit a model technique into the newly formed model of the mind.

The next shift in method devised by Freud after the publication of the *Studies* was the substitution of the free-association techniques for that of pressure. This was apparently accomplished gradually and only came to its culmination with the analysis of the Rat Man in 1907. "The technique of analysis has changed to the extent that the psychoanalyst no longer seeks to elicit material in which he is interested, but permits the patient to follow his natural and spontaneous trains of thought" (Nunberg and Federn, 1962, p. 227).

In 1925, Freud was to describe this change so summarily that the laborious fifteen-year effort it represented was slurred over. Consequently, we have to reconstruct its history by inference. The treatment technique utilized in 1895 confronted Freud with his patients' dreams (e.g., S.E., **Vol.** 2, pp. 62, 74), and he reported some of his early efforts to arrive at their understanding by attempting to analyze his own. It was barely two months after the publication of the *Studies* that, as he was later to put it jocularly, "the Secret of Dreams was revealed to Dr. Sigmund Freud" (E. Freud, 1960). It is logical to assume that his success in producing associations that invariably proved to be relevant to the understanding of his own dreams without external pressure led Freud to apply the same methods in his work with patients. As Jones has pointed out (1955), ". . . for a long time . . . [Freud] continued to use the symptoms as starting points, and this habit was reinforced when it became a question of analyzing dreams. . . ."

This was the transitional technique recorded in the Dora case (Freud, 1905), a treatment carried out in the Fall of 1900. By 1904 Freud no longer asked his patients to close their eyes while associating (p. 250). It is not unlikely that the unfortunate outcome of his excessive focus on analyzing Dora's dreams alerted Freud to the pitfalls of controlling the flow of associations on the basis of the analyst's preconceptions (Freud, 1911–1915). At any rate, the technical innovation Freud announced to the Wednesday Evening Society in 1907 finally adjusted the technique of his treatment to the theory of the mind propounded by him in Chapter 7 of the *Interpretation of Dreams*. The end of this phase of applied research perfected a model of analytic technique in which Freud had sufficient confidence to enable him to plan a monograph on technique of which the 1911–1915 *Papers* were to be the concrete product. In most ways, these communications concentrate on discussing the application of the theory of psychoanalytic technique to the detailed procedures of an analytic treatment. However, "The Dynamics of Transference" (1912) takes up the crucial theoretical issue of "the most powerful resistance" in psychoanalytic therapy (namely the transference) and "Remembering, Repeating and Working Through" (1914) expands on the brief hint on this important technical theory with which *Studies on Hysteria* was concluded. These papers, then, formulate in theoretical terms the new discovery produced by the switch to the technique of free association—the realization that elucidating the resistance, that is, insight into the nature of the transference, is the prime vehicle of bringing out repressed content. "In this way the transference is changed from the strongest weapon of the resistance into the best instrument of the analytic treatment" (1925, p. 43). This insight concurrently clarified that, in the analysis of those patients whose psychopathology was amenable to psychoanalytic correction, the analyst's task consists of interpretation alone.

With the publication of Freud's *Papers on Technique,* the second major cycle of research in the theory of technique drew to its close. The next cycle was to last about twenty-five years and involved contributions from a number of investigators, although the role of Freud continued to be the pre-eminent one in the basic work of refining a general theory of the mind. In a brief historical note in his *Psychoanalytic Reader,* Robert Fliess has called attention to the publications that contained the clinical observations on which the theoretical advances of the next phase were to rest (p. 127). From his list, we wish to put stress on Freud's "Some Character-Types Met with in Psychoanalytic Work" (1916), his "Psychogenesis of a Case of Homosexuality in a Woman" (1920), and Abraham's "On a Particular Kind of Resistance against the Psychoanalytic Method" (1919), all of which describe, with particular clarity, constellations of unconscious resistances that render patients incapable of observing the basic rule of free association, even when confronted with being resistant.

The initial attempt to circumvent this obstacle was a technical suggestion by Ferenczi (1919) for overcoming an analytic impasse by actively prohibiting various behaviors that serve defensive purposes. Although Freud expressed some reservations, he voiced his qualified approval of this experiment (1919). In particular, he agreed that the analyst might have to insist on the symptom being relinquished in phobias and compulsions; indeed, it was Freud who had alerted Ferenczi to this possibility (Ferenczi, 1919, p. 201). The technical theory on which this recommendation is based is the "rule of abstinence," that is, that treatment must not permit the avoidance of conflict by various forms of acting-out behavior. It was on the manner of enforcing this rule that Ferenczi and Freud disagreed. Ferenczi carried out a series of experimental technical innovations from 1919 until his death in 1933. He introduced the renunciation of certain pleasurable activities by patients in stagnant analyses and considered provoking resistances by various active interventions (1920). Somewhat later he tried out the effects of voluntary alterations of muscle tonus during analytic sessions and reported the ill effects of commands and prohibitions of all kinds (1925). In collaboration with Otto Rank, Ferenczi proposed techniques stressing affectful repetition of the past rather than insight as the therapeutic tool (1923). However, he had poor results with duplicating Otto Rank's experiments with arbitrary time limits for termination. Still later, he tried techniques of gratification of frustrated infantile needs in certain intractable cases (1930 and 1931). In his last technical paper (1933) he discussed some of the difficulties of this approach.

In retrospect, the scientific fruits of Ferenczi's experiments in technique have turned out to be meager. In spite of a number of valuable and even brilliant observations buried among the chaff of negative results, no coherent and theoretically meaningful conclusions are discernible. Ferenczi's work in this area is saved from negligibility by his recurrent emphasis on a new observation he was enabled to make upon venturing away from the safety of Freud's by then "classical" procedure: the detection of the importance of the analyst's countertransference on the course of (stalemated) analyses. This observation was not fitted systematically into the matrix of psychoanalytic theory either; rather, it was reiterated in the manner of a psychoanalytic Cato, insisting on the iniquites of Carthage. Perhaps this was a hallmark of Ferenczi's scientific style—he did not refrain from expressing distaste for the alleged pedantry of better organized research. In its historical context, experimentation with analytic techniques was bound to fail in the era of Ferenczi's activity because the psychoanalytic theory of mental function on which it was based (that of the *Interpretation of Dreams* [1900], although amended in Freud's *Papers on Metapsychology* [1915]) was inadequate to explain the phenomena that were being studied. It had been formulated on the basis of observations made on hysterical and obsessional patients (the "transference neuroses") and could not be utilized for a full understanding of the character disorders, the therapy of which proved to be such a difficult task for the psychoanalytic technique of the time.

As is well known, it was Freud, once again, who perceived the need for a more generally applicable theoretical model and proceeded to develop one in the years 1920–1926. From the point of view of the theory of technique progress was again possible once the structural hypothesis had been formulated (Freud, 1923). The application of the new theory of mental function to the area of theory of technique was carried out principally at the Vienna Institute under the leadership of Wilhelm Reich. It is unfortunate that the failure of Ferenczi's innovations has been explained on an *ad hominem* basis, without due regard for the fundamental error in research strategy it involved. This same error has recurred several times since in the history of psychoanalysis, usually leading to sterile and doctrinaire controversies (see below).

Robert Fliess (1946) has described Reich's work on the theory of technique as the application of ego psychology to this problem. It will be recalled that the technical impasse noted in the analyses of character disorders came about as a result of unconscious resistances that did not yield when the patient was informed of what he was doing. Reich (1928) proposed substituting interpretation of the motive of the resistance for the previously used confrontation with its presence, and he pointed out that the characteristic form taken by the resistance is determined by infantile experience. The relation of these concepts to Freud's new theory of signal anxiety (Freud, 1926) is readily apparent. Moreover, Reich stressed that there is always a matrix of neurotic character behind the symptoms of the transference neuroses, too. The patient's attitudes and behavior now came under analytic scrutiny as components of the "character armor." Reich laid down the principle that interpretation of ego defenses must precede that of id strivings. By isolating certain ego-syntonic character traits as pathological, the analysis creates great anger, but Reich saw this as the prerequisite for overcoming the narcissistic defenses. He felt that resolution of character defenses gave direct access to the central infantile conflict. He elaborated his views in a series of papers (1929, 1930), but the magnitude of his contributions has tended to be minimized because of his separation from organized psychoanalysis in 1933 and his subsequent personal vicissitudes. The passage of thirty-five years has, of course, made Reich's papers look overly schematic and doctrinaire. (For a contemporary critique, see Fenichel, 1953.) In the context of 1930, however, they marked a decisive breakthrough in the theory of technique. Utilizing the principles he had outlined, analysts made extensive observations about the detailed mechanisms of the defensive operations of the ego and their patterning. These data and their theoretical implications were presented *in extenso* in Anna Freud's *The Ego and the Mechanisms of Defence* (1936), probably the outstanding single work in this wave of advance in psychoanalytic knowledge. It should be noted, however, that the mapping out of ego psychology is by no means complete even today, and much work in this area is still in progress.

With every gain in our understanding of ego functioning, the range of applicability of the classical technique of psychoanalysis has expanded. Simultaneously, psychoanalytic theory gained in explanatory power, so that it became possible to evolve the psychoanalytic theory of nonanalytic psychotherapeutic techniques. The pioneering work in this direction was Glover's 1933 classic, "The Therapeutic Results of Inexact Interpretation." The cardinal distinction that could now be made between analytic treatment on the one hand and all other therapies on the other was that psychoanalysis leads to a new solution of structural conflict (i.e., a conflict between ego and id), whereas other therapies do not alter the conflict but shift the balance of forces by altering the ego in some manner. Another area in the theory of technique that was opened up by the new findings of ego psychology concerned the psychoanalysis of children. This complex, and still controversial, subject deserves fuller discussion; for the sake of clarity of exposition it will therefore be taken up separately. At this point, the classical psychoanalytic technique of the mid-1930's has to be differentiated from its precursors. This task was initially accomplished in various passages of Anna Freud's book (1946). She pointed out that ego analysis "has to proceed by circuitous paths, it cannot follow out the ego activity directly . . . the only possibility is to reconstruct it from its influences on the patient's associations" (p. 14). Each piece of ego analysis permits the analysis of the id derivatives for the warding off of which it served as the defense. She also called attention to the phenomenon of transference of defenses (especially those which Reich had called "character defenses") and the possibility of reconstructing the history of the patient's development through their analysis. "Only the analysis of the ego's unconscious defensive operations can enable us to reconstruct the transformations which the instincts have undergone" (p. 21).

It seems fitting to assign the close of this third cycle of research in the theory of technique to the year 1937 when the octogenarian Freud produced his last two technical papers (1937a and 1937b), one on the theory of analytic interpretation by reconstruction, the other on the crucial problem of termination. His magisterial discussion of the limitations of psychoanalysis as a therapeutic tool carried the theory of technique to the limits then imposed by the theory of mental function worked out in the previous decade. This same year saw the initial (oral) presentation of Hartmann's *Ego Psychology and the Problem of Adaptation,* the work that has been the program of the subsequent evolution of psychoanalytic theory (see Rangell, 1965).

Over twenty-five years have now passed since the start of this new psychoanalytic epoch, and a great mass of data has been gathered by the new analytic methods (recently complemented by direct observations of childhood, etc.); but these observations have not resulted as yet in a definitive restatement of psychoanalytic theory. Many clarifications, amplifications, and modifications in the psychoanalytic theory of the mind have gained wide acceptance, but the closest thing to an integration of these into a comprehensive whole, Rappaport's *The Structure of Psychoanalytic Theory* (1960) was modestly and accurately subtitled "A Systematizing Attempt." In a discussion of "the present status of the system" of psychoanalytic theory, Rappaport points out that systematization is urgently needed but stresses his belief that we have not yet reached the stage where formalization and axiomatization would be fruitful (pp. 101–104).

In the absence of a general reformulation of theory, research in the theory of technique has run into the same problem that had defeated Ferenczi in the preceding phase of the development of psychoanalysis. The new ego psychology has begun to throw light on the psychopathology of the psychoses, borderline states, ego distortions, severe (narcissistic) pregenital character disorders, and so on, without as yet having produced the theoretical tools that would permit the reduction of the treatment techniques needed to deal with these conditions into a single theoretical framework. Eissler (1953) has designated the departures from the classical model of analytic technique necessary in these cases as "parameters." Note, however, that this extension of the theory of technique has merely broadened the scope of psychoanalysis (to allude to the title of a symposium on this subject); it has not thus far produced major advances applicable to psychoanalytic technique in general. About this, Hartmann (1964) has said, "Genuine technical discoveries we do not find in the latest phase of analysis; but the body of systematic psychological and psychopathological knowledge has been considerably increased."

There has been a great deal of work since 1937 that has attempted to utilize the adaptive point of view introduced into metapsychology by Hartmann (sometimes reductionistically, so that the resulting treatment techniques are no longer properly classifiable as psychoanalysis; e.g., Alexander, Rado). These efforts were stimulated in the milieu of American enthusiasm for psychotherapy after World War II, partly created by the admirable record of a military psychiatry widely influenced by psychoanalysis. The various proposals for a psychoanalytically oriented therapeutic technique lie outside the province of this review (see Schlessinger, Pollock, *et al.,* 1966; and Gedo, 1964). Hartmann himself (1964) has characterized the pull exerted by the emerging conceptualizations about the autonomous ego sphere on analytic technique as a shift, which, for the first time, makes it true that "we are dealing with a patient's total personality" (p. 145); and he has predicted that technical progress will develop on the basis of fuller study of intrasystemic functional units within the ego. The documentation of the accuracy of his prediction would take us into the details of recent contributions on technique without clarifying the evolution of theory. For the purposes of this review, it may suffice to state again that the fifteen intervening years since Hartmann's paper have failed to produce the "genuine technical discovery" that would constitute a change in paradigm in the theory of technique and that, in our opinion, such a discovery will not be made until the psychoanalytic theory of the mind is once again formalized on the basis of the new data that have been accumulating for over a quarter of a century. Recent work in the theory of technique has, by and large, concerned itself with deeper understanding of the psychoanalytic situation from the point of view of object relations. Much of this has been summarized, discussed, and amplified in Stone's excellent monograph, *The*

Psychoanalytic Situation (1961). (For the most recent contribution see Greenson, 1965.) The importance of these extensions of the theory of technique should not be minimized, but it must be recalled that their applicability is greatest in "borderline" cases where there are difficulties in establishing a workable therapeutic relationship, that is, once again we are discussing a broadening in scope, rather than a change in the technique of psychoanalysis (cf. Nunberg, 1951).

This relative lack of changes in technique in the analysis of adults has not been paralleled in the province of the analysis of children. This has always been a separate field of endeavor, and we shall now discuss its evolution separately.

The pioneering attempt to psychoanalyze a child took place early in 1908 when, under Freud's supervision, the infantile zoophobia of Little Hans was successfully resolved by analytic interventions. Freud attributed his success to the fact that the child's own father had carried out the treatment, and he failed to explore the possibilities of the procedure for other children. In his report of the case, Freud (1909a) did not discuss the theoretical rationale of the technique he had improvised to meet the child's inability to associate verbally. This technique had consisted of symbolic interpretation of the child's spontaneous play activity, that is, the equation of the child's play with an adult patient's free associations. (Note that this development succeeded the technical advance made in the case of the Rat Man in a matter of three or four months!)

Jones (1955, Vol. 2, p. 261) has stated that, "This feature was seized on later by Hermine von Hug-Hellmuth, and then far more profitably by Melanie Klein, as a cardinal device in the application of psychoanalysis with young children." Mrs. Klein has paid tribute to Ferenczi, Abraham, and Jones for stimulating and encouraging her interest in "play analysis" (1932, pp. 8–9). In the "Preface" to the third edition of her book (1948) she stressed the fact that her technique had not changed since its formulation: ". . . play technique—which I first evolved in 1922 and 1923 and which I presented in this book—still stands in all essentials . . ." (p. 13).

In 1932, when this work was published, Mrs. Klein wrote (p. 17), "Although several analysts, Dr. Hug-Hellmuth in especial, have since (1909) undertaken analyses of children, no fixed rules as regards its technique or application have been evolved." Her own technical recommendations did not alter the methods utilized in the Little Hans case to any significant extent, and her theory of technique assumed the essential identity of this procedure with the classical technique of adult analysis.

This assumption was questioned by Anna Freud (1927), whose writings on the subject utilized the psychoanalytic theory of mind proposed by Sigmund Freud in the 1920's and stressed the immaturity of the child's psychic apparatus and the child's actual dependence on external controls. This difference of opinion has never been resolved. Moreover, the reconstruction of the Kleinian child analysts has led to the well-known Kleinian theoretical formulations of mental development; and, inevitably, a special Kleinian technique of adult analysis has evolved as a consequence. This is not the place to engage in a critique of Kleinian psychoanalysis; our task consists in pinpointing the as yet unverified assumption on which it is based. It should be noted, however, that the lack of technical progress in Kleinian child analysis since 1922 (one might even say since the 1909 Little Hans case) may be indicative of a failure of scientific self-scrutiny.

In contrast, the views of Anna Freud and her child-analytic colleagues have undergone progressive evolution parallel with the intervening advances in general psychoanalytic theory. In 1945, Anna Freud stressed the importance of ego analysis in gaining the child's cooperation for the uncovering of the repressed content and laid special emphasis on the developmental aspects of childhood psychopathology. Indeed, Ernst Kris (1950) has claimed that child analysis could not develop until after the formulation of the structural hypothesis. Further, he has pointed out that ego psychology has "re-emphasized the character of psychoanalysis as a psychology of adaptation," so that Anna Freud's attention to a "detailed scrutiny of the child's concrete situation" (in contrast to the Kleinian neglect of environmental influences) is the technical counterpart of the advances in psychoanalytic theory since 1937.

The most recent statement of the theory of child analytic technique is contained in Anna Freud's book *Normality and Pathology in Childhood* (1965). She has carefully reviewed the similarities and differences between the analysis of adults and that of children (pp. 25–28) and their technical consequences. The absence of the capacity for free association is still the cardinal point in this regard (pp. 29–31), but Miss Freud has listed a series of additional handicaps that are imposed on child analysis as a result of the child's immature mental equipment. She has summarized these in the statement that, ". . . for long stretches of the analysis [the child analyst] has to manage without a therapeutic alliance with his patient." (Note the identity of technical preoccupations in the recent literature on adult analysis!)

In spite of these handicaps, Anna Freud now concedes that a "transference neurosis" may develop in the analysis of children. However, she has also described (pp. 38–39) the child's use of the relationship to the analyst as a "new experience," a feature that is present in the analyses of adults also. We believe this to be an important advance in the theory of technique, with particular relevance for the therapy of borderline and psychotic patients. (It also permits better understanding of Alexander's concept of "corrective emotional experience," Alexander and French, 1946.) It seems that psychoanalysis has hereby come to the threshold of being able to formulate a unified theory of its current therapeutic techniques with adults and children in all categories of psychopathology.

Conclusions

Our review of the history of the evolution of the psychoanalytic interview procedure and the parallel development of the theory of psychoanalytic technique has, we believe, demonstrated that advances in both areas have occurred in the absence of organized "research." Technical changes were proposed whenever the existing technique of psychoanalytic therapy proved to be deficient in dealing with certain types of patient. Modifications turned out to be fruitful when they were based on valid new theoretical models of mental functioning, that is, whenever they constituted the clinical application of psychoanalytic theory. We infer that current and future progress in this area must follow the elaboration of an even more satisfactory integration of available observational data into a valid and useful psychoanalytic psychology. If we have refrained from spelling out the most recent developments in technique (e.g., the analysis of intrasystemic conflicts within the ego), our decision is based on the fact that a consensus on the metapsychology on which these technical innovations have been based has not as yet been arrived at.

Unfortunately, innovations (both in setting phenomena and in the theory of technique) have sometimes been proposed in a hit-or-miss fashion. Genuine technical improvements must always be welcome; however, this self-evident desideratum does not justify change for its own sake or that arising from a variety of possible irrational motives. Only careful investigation and scientific study can reveal whether a particular proposal of technical changes has actual merit. We have discussed some of the prerequisites for organized research in this field in our section on interview procedure. We wish to re-emphasize the importance of follow-up studies and of outcome research in the assessment of various therapeutic techniques; explicit criteria of change and cure must be developed to make such studies possible. Psychoanalysis is still grappling with these issues; nor have the difficulties of gathering reliable raw data and reducing them so as to render them utilizable for the testing of hypotheses been definitively solved.

We have limited ourselves in this essay to some selected topics on the question of research in psychoanalytic technique. A great deal more needs to be said on the problems of research about discrete elements of technique (such as interpretation) as well as special therapeutic techniques (e.g., group psychoanalysis, etc.); however, consideration of such details lies beyond the scope of our purpose at present.

REFERENCES

[Note: S.E. refers to *The Standard Edition of the complete psychological works of Sigmund Freud* (London: Hogarth Press).]

ABRAHAM, K. On a particular kind of resistance against the psychoanalytic method (1919). *Selected papers.* Vol. 1. New York: Basic Books, 1953.

ALEXANDER, F. Psychoanalysis and psychotherapy. In *The scope of psychoanalysis.* New York: Basic Books, 1961.

ALEXANDER, F., and FRENCH, T. *Psychoanalytic therapy.* New York: Ronald Press, 1946.

ALEXANDER, F. Unexplored areas in psychoanalytic theory and treatment. *Behavioral Science*, 1958, 3, 293–316.

BELLAK, L. Research in psychoanalysis. *Psychoanalytic Quarterly*, 1961, 30, 519–548.

BENEDEK, T. Dynamics of the countertransference. *Bulletin of the Menninger Clinic*, 1953, 15, 332–337.

BRENMAN, M. Problems in clinical research. Round table (1946). *American Journal of Orthopsychiatry*, 1947, 17, 190–230.

BRENMAN, M. Research in psychotherapy. Round table (1947). *American Journal of Orthopsychiatry*, 1948, 18, 92–118.

BREUER, J., and FREUD, S. *Studies on hysteria* (1895). S.E., Vol. 2. (Also published by Basic Books, New York, 1957.)

BRONNER, A. F. The objective evaluation of psychotherapy. Round table (1948). *American Journal of Orthopsychiatry*, 1949, 19, 463–491.

CHASSAN, J. B. On probability theory and psychoanalytic research. *Psychiatry*, 1956, 19, 55–61.

CHENEY, C. O., and LANDIS, C. A program for the determination of the therapeutic effectiveness of the psychoanalytic method. *American Journal of Psychiatry*, 1935, 91, 1161–1165.

COLBY, J. M. On the greater amplifying power of causal-correlative over interrogative inputs in free association in an experimental psychoanalytic situation. *Journal of Nervous and Mental Diseases*, 1961, 133, 233–239.

COLBY, K. M. Experiment on the effects of an observer's presence on the imago system during psychoanalytic free-association. *Behavioral Science,* 1960, **5,** 216–232.

CORIAT, I. H. Some statistical results of the psychoanalytic treatment of the psychoneuroses. *Psychoanalytic Review,* 1917, **4,** 209–216.

DEUTSCH, H. Psychoanalytic therapy in the light of follow-up. *Journal of the American Psychoanalytic Association,* 1959, **7,** 445–458.

DEVEREUX, G. Some criteria for the timing of confrontations and interpretations. *International Journal of Psychoanalysis,* 1951, **32,** 19–24.

EISSLER, K. The effect of the structure of the ego on psychoanalytic technique. *Journal of the American Psychoanalytic Association,* 1953, **1,** 104–143.

ELLIS, A. E. Towards the improvement of psychoanalytic research. *Psychoanalytic Review,* 1949, **35,** 123–143.

FAIRBAIRN, W. R. D. Theoretical and experimental aspects of psycho-analysis. *British Journal of Medical Psychology,* 1952, **25,** 122–127.

FENICHEL, O. Concerning the theory of psychoanalytic technique (1935). In *The collected papers of Otto Fenichel.* New York: Norton, 1953.

FERENCZI, S. Technical difficulties in the analysis of a case of hysteria (1919). In *The theory and technique of psychoanalysis.* New York: Basic Books, 1952.

FERENCZI, S. The further development of an active therapy in psychoanalysis. *Ibid.,* 1920.

FERENCZI, S. Contraindications to the "active" psycho-analytical technique. *Ibid.,* 1925.

FERENCZI, S. (1930). The principles of relaxation and neocatharsis. In *Problems and methods of psychoanalysis.* New York: Basic Books, 1955.

FERENCZI, S. Child analysis in the analysis of adults. *Ibid.,* 1931.

FERENCZI, S. Confusion of tongues between adults and the child. *Ibid.,* 1933.

FERENCZI, S., and RANK, O. *The development of psychoanalysis* (1923). New York, Washington: Nervous and Mental Disease Publishing Co., 1925.

FLIESS, R. (Ed.). *The psychoanalytic reader.* New York: International Universities Press, 1946.

FOX, H. M. Effect of psychophysiological research on the transference. *Journal of the Psychoanalytic Association,* **6,** 413–432.

FREUD, ANNA. The theory of children's analysis (1927). In *The psychoanalytical treatment of children.* London: Imago, 1946.

FREUD, ANNA. *The ego and the mechanisms of defence* (1936). New York: International Universities Press, 1946.

FREUD, ANNA. Indications for child analysis (1945). In *The psychoanalytical treatment of children.* London: Imago, 1946.

FREUD, ANNA. *Normality and pathology in childhood.* New York: International Universities Press, 1965.

FREUD, E. (Ed.). *Letters of Sigmund Freud.* New York: Basic Books, 1960.

FREUD, S. Case histories (1895). S.E., Vol. 2, Pp. 19–182.

FREUD, S. *The interpretation of dreams* (1900). S.E., Vols. 4 and 5. (Also published by Basic Books, New York, 1955.)

FREUD, S. Freud's psycho-analytic procedure (1904). S.E., Vol. 7, pp. 249–256.

FREUD, S. Fragment of an analysis of a case of hysteria (1905). S.E., Vol 7, pp. 3–124.

FREUD, S. Analysis of a phobia in a five-year-old boy (1909). S.E., Vol. 10, pp. 5–149. (a)

FREUD, S. Notes upon a case of obsessional neurosis (1909). S.E., Vol. 10, pp. 153–220. (b)

FREUD, S. The original record of the case of the Rat-Man (1909). S.E., Vol. 10, pp. 253–318 (c)

FREUD, S. Five lectures on psychoanalysis (1910). S.E., Vol. 11, pp. 3–58. (a)

FREUD, S. The future prospects of psycho-analytic therapy (1910). S.E., Vol. 11, pp. 139–152. (b)

FREUD, S. *Papers on technique* (1911–1915). S.E., Vol. 12.

FREUD, S. The dynamics of transference (1912). S.E., Vol. 12, pp. 97–108.

FREUD, S. *On the history of the psycho-analytic movement* (1914). S.E., Vol. 14, pp. 7–66.

FREUD, S. *Papers on metapsychology* (1915). S.E., Vol. 14.

FREUD, S. Some character-types met with in psychoanalytic work (1916). S.E., Vol. 14, pp. 311–333.

FREUD, S. Lines of advance in psychoanalytic therapy (1919). S.E., Vol. 17, pp. 157–168.

FREUD, S. The psychogenesis of a case of homosexuality in a woman (1920). S.E., Vol. 18, pp. 145–172.

FREUD, S. *The ego and the id* (1923). Vol. 19, pp. 12–66.

FREUD, S. An autobiographical study (1925). S.E., Vol. 20, pp. 3–74.

FREUD, S. *Inhibitions, symptoms and anxiety* (1926). S.E., Vol. 20, pp. 87–174.

FREUD, S. Analysis, terminable and interminable (1937). S.E., Vol. 23. (a)

FREUD, S. Constructions in analysis (1937). S.E., Vol. 23, pp. 216–253. (b)

GEDO, J. Concepts for a classification of the psychotherapies. *International Journal of Psychoanalysis*, 1964, **45**, 530–539.

GITELSON, M. The emotional position of the analyst in the psychoanalytic situation. *International Journal of Psychoanalysis*, 1952, **33**, 1–10.

GLOVER, E. The therapeutic results of inexact interpretation. *International Journal of Psychoanalysis*, 1933, **12**, 397–411.

GREENSON, R. The working alliance and the transference neurosis, *Psychoanalytic Quarterly*, 1965, **34**, 155–181.

HARTMANN, H. *Ego psychology and the problem of adaptation* (1937). New York: International Universities Press, 1958.

HARTMANN, H. Technical implications of ego psychology (1951). In *Essays on ego psychology*. New York: International Universities Press, 1964.

HARTMANN, H., and KRIS, E. The genetic approach in psychoanalysis (1945).

In *Papers on psychoanalytic psychology*. Psychological Issues, Monograph 14, 1964.

JONES, E. *The life and work of Sigmund Freud* (Vols. 1 and 2). New York. Basic Books, 1953–1955.

KLEIN, MELANIE. *The psycho-analysis of children* (1932). London: Hogarth Press, 1959.

KNIGHT, R. The evaluation of the results of psychoanalytic therapy. *American Journal of Psychiatry*, 1941, 98, 434–446.

KRIS, E. Notes on the development and on some current problems of psychoanalytic child psychology. *Psychoanalytic Study of the Child*, 1950, 5, 24–46.

KUBIE, L. S. Problems and technique of psychoanalytic validation and progress. In E. Pumpian-Mindlin (Ed.), *Psychoanalysis as science*. Stanford: Stanford University Press, 1952.

KUBIE, L. S. The use of psychoanalysis as a research tool. *Psychiatric Research Reports*, 1956, 6, 112–150.

LOEWENSTEIN, R. M. The problem of interpretation. *Psychoanalytic Quarterly*, 1951, 20, 1–13.

LORAND, S., and CONSOLE, W. A. Therapeutic results in psycho-analytic treatment without fee. *International Journal of Psychoanalysis*, 1958, 39, 59–64.

MAHL, S. F., and KARPE, R. Emotions and HCL secretion during psychoanalytic hours. *Psychosomatic Medicine*, 1953, 15, 312–327.

MAHL, G. F., DOLLARD, J., and REDLICH, F. C. Facilities for the sound recording and observation of interviews. *Science*, 1954, 120, 135–139.

NUNBERG, H. Transference and reality, *International Journal of Psychoanalysis*, 1951, 32, 1–9.

NUNBERG, H. Evaluation of the results of psycho-analytic treatment. *International Journal of Psychoanalysis*, 1954, 35, 2–7.

NUNBERG, H., and FEDERN, E. (Eds.). *Minutes of the Vienna Psychoanalytic Society*. New York: International Universities Press, 1962.

OBERNDORF, C. P. Consideration of results with psychoanalytic psychotherapy. *American Journal of Psychiatry*, 1942, 99, 374–381.

OBERNDORF, C. P. Unsatisfactory results of psychoanalytic therapy. *Psychoanalytic Quarterly*, 1950, 19, 393–407.

OBERNDORF, C. P., GREENACRE, P., and KUBIE, L. Symposium on the evaluation of therapeutic results. *International Journal of Psychoanalysis*, 1948, 29, 7–33.

PFEFFER, A. Z. A procedure for evaluating the results of psychoanalysis: a preliminary report. *Journal of the American Psychoanalytic Association*, 1959, 7, 418–444.

PFEFFER, A. Z. Follow-up study of a satisfactory analysis. *Journal of the American Psychoanalytic Association*, 1961, 9, 698–718.

RANGELL, L. The scope of Heinz Hartmann. *International Journal of Psychoanalysis*, 1965, 46, 5–30.

RAPPAPORT, D. *The structure of psychoanalytic theory.* Psychological Issues, Monograph 6, 1960.

REDLICH, F. C., DOLLARD, J., and NEWMAN, R. High fidelity recording of psychotherapeutic interviews. *American Journal of Psychiatry,* 107, 42–48.

REICH, W. On the technique of character analysis (1928). In *Character analysis.* New York: Orgone Institute Press, 1949.

REICH, W. The genital character and the neurotic character (1929). *Ibid.*

REICH, W. Infantile phobia and character formation (1930). *Ibid.*

RENNEKER, R. E. Microscopic analysis of a sound tape: a method of studying preconscious communication in the therapeutic process. *Psychiatry,* 1960, 23, 347–355.

SANDLER, J. Research in psychoanalysis: the Hampstead Index as an instrument of psychoanalytic research. *International Journal of Psychoanalysis,* 1962, 43, 287–291.

SCHLESSINGER, N., POLLOCK, G., SABSHIN, M., SADOW, L., and GEDO, J. Psychoanalytic contributions to psychotherapy research. In L. A. Gottschalk and A. H. Auerbach (Eds.), *Methods of research in psychotherapy.* New York: Appleton-Century-Crofts, 1966.

SCHLESSINGER, N., GEDO, J., MILLER, J., POLLOCK, G., SABSHIN, M., and SADOW, L. The scientific styles of Breuer and Freud in the origins of psychoanalysis. *Journal of the American Psychoanalytic Association,* 1967, 15.

SCHMIDL, F. The problem of scientific validation in psychoanalytic interpretation. *International Journal of Psychoanalysis,* 1955, 36, 105–113.

SEEMAN, W. Psychoanalysis as a research technique. *Psychiatry,* 1952, 15, 81–89.

STERNBERG, R. S., CHAPMAN, J., and SHAKOW, D. Psychotherapy research and the problem of intrusions on privacy. *Psychiatry,* 1958, 21, 195–202.

STONE, L. *The psychoanalytic situation.* New York: International Universities Press, 1961.

STRACHEY, J. Introduction to Freud's *Papers on technique,* S.E. Vol. 12, 1958.

SZUREK, S. *Roots of psychoanalysis and psychotherapy.* Springfield, Ill.: Charles C Thomas, 1958.

WALLERSTEIN, R. S. The problem of assessment of change in psychotherapy. *International Journal of Psychoanalysis,* 1963, 44, 31–41.

WINNICOTT, D. Metapsychological and clinical aspects of regression within the psychoanalytical set-up. In *Collected papers.* New York: Basic Books, 1958.

WOLMAN, B. B. Evidence in psychoanalytic research. *Journal of the American Psychoanalytic Association,* 1964, 10, 55–61.

NAME INDEX

583

SUBJECT INDEX

abreaction, 24, 25, 29, 34, 102, 123, 193, 199, 487, 567

abstinence, principle of, 104, 115, 156–157, 160, 162, 403

acting in, 41, 45

acting out, 7, 41, 43–45, 103, 112, 115, 126, 129, 151, 161, 188, 345, 447, 458–463, 478, 480, 505–506

active imagination, 364–369

active technique, 20, 41, 47, 48, 148, 152, 154–159, 166, 264

actual neuroses, 38, 62, 75–76

adaptational technique, 201

addictions, 98, 99, 188, 248, 404

affect(s), 23–25, 28, 39, 41, 45, 79–80, 106, 448–450, 495, 505, 539, 567

aggression, 40, 52, 77, 79; dangerous, 107, 178; frustration-, 274–276, 282, 283, 286; liberated, 85; reaction formation against, 108; sadistic, 211, 496; vicissitudes of, 82

aggressive impulsivity, 110, 274–275, 279, 286

aggressiveness, 34, 35, 79, 81, 265, 268

aim inhibition, 41, 266

ambivalence, 176, 179–181, 243, 329, 345, 346, 349, 361, 505, 506, 526, 550–551

amnesia, 7; hypnosis and, 7, 17–18; hysterical, 17–18; infantile, 25, 32–34, 123

anaclitic attitude, 125, 127

anal characteristics, 28, 170, 174–175, 179, 188, 216, 217, 229, 249

analytic situation, 85, 86, 103, 116, 125, 148, 149, 156, 160, 161, 201, 321–322, 397

analytical psychology, methods of treatment in, 338–375; active imagination, 364–369; cure, concept of, 373–375; dream analysis, 341, 353–363, 368–369; final stage, 371–372; first interview, 342–344; rationale, 338–342; resistance and, 351–355; transference and countertransfer-ence, 344–351, 355; working through, 369–371

analyzability, 33–34, 133–136

anima-animus projection, 360, 370

anxiety, anal, 175; basic, 379–382; defenses against, 172, 176, 407, 430, 437; depressive, 178–182; ego and, 77; free-floating, 208; Freudian theory of, 5–6, 55, 70, 77, 82, 571; guilt and, 79; hypochondriacal, 183, 267, 496; obsessional, 430–437; oral, 175, 186; paranoid-schizoid, 176–178; repressed impulses and, 77; repressed instincts and, 70; separation, 176, 178

anxiety hysteria, 38, 242, 244

anxiety neurosis, 38, 70

archetypal images, 341, 345–346, 361–364, 370

attention, free-floating, 52; lapses of, 88; widening of, 19, 42

attention cathexis, 19–21, 24

awareness, choiceless, 395; ideational, 18; intellectual, 450; process, 35; reflective, 18–21, 24, 32, 33; somatic, 104

bed-wetting, 108, 110–111

Beyond the Pleasure Principle, 25, 53, 63, 263

birth order position, 318–321

bisexuality, 27, 80

blockage, 405–407

blocked affect, 23, 24

castration complex, 67–68, 74, 80–81, 123

catharsis, 45, 98, 275, 539, 541

cathartic method, 7, 16–19, 21, 23–24, 27, 31, 32, 45, 48, 61, 107, 242, 339

cathexis, attention, 19–21, 24; definition of, 247; interindividual, 10, 247–249, 261, 263, 264, 268; intraindividual, 10, 258, 261, 263, 264, 268; motivational 25; object, 65, 247, 250–252, 254, 258,

587

236; first interview, 226–228; interpretation, 228–230, 235; neoneurosis phase, 216–218, 235–236; rationale, 216–220; and resistance, 230–231; setting for, 225–226; termination, 234–236; theoretical principles, 216–218; transference, 218–220, 235–237; treatment, 226–236; working through, 231–234

disavowal, 65, 67, 69, 70, 73, 77, 79–80, 84, 85, 87–90

displacement, 110, 113, 156, 198–199, 254, 255, 257, 267, 450; in psychoanalytic psychotherapy, 476, 490–492

distortion, 33, 87, 328; parataxic, 428–429

doctor-patient relationship, 396–398, 428

Dora case, 14, 26–28, 30, 31, 35, 40, 52, 132, 566, 568

dream-analysis techniques, Adlerian, 314–317; of Alexander and French, 207–209; in analytical psychology, 341, 353–363, 368–369; Freudian, 5, 21–22, 27, 28, 31, 35–37, 39–40, 48, 55, 60–61, 66–67, 81, 82, 105, 455–457, 567–568; Kleinian, 179–184, 188; narcissistic, 284, 287; Rosen's, 229, 234

dual-instinct theory, 80–81, 89, 93

dynamic propositions, 22, 33, 35, 291

dynamic unconscious, 15, 18, 33

economy, principle of, 210

ego, adaptive function of, 209–210; alteration in, 22, 86; and anxiety, 77; autonomous functions of, 42, 95, 210; experiencing, 114; hyperinstrumental, 253; and id, conflict between, 9, 11, 68, 70, 259, 260; identification within, 57, 64; and insight, 124; masochistic, 79; mature, 96, 115, 479; metapsychological, 67; and neutralization, 22; normal, 86, 89–90, 101, 103, 105, 109; nucleus of, 56; observing, 114, 131; phantasy and, 172–173, 176; pleasure, 72–73; rational, 107; readaptation of, 269; and reality, 9, 69, 73, 85, 86, 88, 89, 193, 196, 253, 256, 259–260, 267; reintegration of, 110; and resistance, 53, 54, 63, 77–78, 86, 96, 105, 261; split in, 69, 70, 85, 88–90, 176, 180, 187, 479, 482; and superego, conflict between, 9, 11, 68, 85, 254, 257, 259, 260, 265; synthetic functions of, 21, 22; unconscious, 56, 63–64, 71, 86, 340–341, 365

Ego and the Id, The, 29, 63, 68

Ego and the Mechanisms of Defence, The, 94, 137, 571

ego defenses, 19–20, 130, 242, 253, 260, 353, 476

ego gifts, 36

ego ideal, 57, 64, 304, 305, 307

ego integration, 21, 24–25, 44–45, 182, 189, 193–195, 199, 202, 203, 208, 217, 371

ego interests, 41

ego-object percept, 280, 281

ego organization, 101, 182

ego psychology, 14, 15, 20, 22, 23, 35–36, 42, 48, 64, 71, 72, 126, 128, 209–210, 301, 304, 307, 570

ego strength, 9, 11, 62, 95–96, 100, 133, 134, 186, 193, 482–483, 488, 490

ego support, 501–504

ego-syntonic character traits, 571

ego-syntonic defenses, 490, 496

ego-syntonic object, 279–281

ego therapy, 9–10, 267, 270

ejection, 172, 173

emotional evolution, 274, 275, 288

emotional reconditioning, 196

empathy, 161, 166, 251, 291, 390, 449, 515

empiricism, 4, 6, 7, 28–30, 36, 46, 135

energy, accumulation of, 7, 210; biochemical, 247, 472; blind, 460; cathected, 77, 247, 250; destructive, 10, 243, 247, 249–252, 254, 256, 258, 259, 264; discharge of, 7, 210, 249, 286; emotionally crystallized, 286; libidinal, 10, 243, 247, 249–251, 256, 258, 259, 261, 264; mental, 5–7, 62, 247; nervous, 5; physical, 7; preservation of, universal law of, 7; psychological, 281; surplus, concept of, 210–211; verbally discharged, 286

envy, 186–188, 432

Envy and Gratitude, 186

epigenesis, 121–122

Eros and Ares, 247

eroticism, 81; pregenital, 210–211; urethral, 83, 110–111

evolutionism, 4, 6, 387

existential psychoanalysis, 24, 443–467; cure, concept of, 465–467; interpretation of unconscious, 452–457; rationale, 444–446; resistance, 450–452; transference, 446–450; working through, 457–465

false connections, resistance of, 23

fantasies, 16, 28, 30, 32, 46, 74–75, 81, 95, 104, 106–109, 111, 115, 118, 153, 314, 346, 348

father-child relationship, 196–197, 218, 448

female sexuality, 73–75, 89, 208–209

fetishism, 79–80, 88, 112, 312